WAR IN THE WILDERNESS

A symbiotic relationship: Chindit and mule – close companions under the forest canopy.
(Trustees of the Imperial War Museum)

THE CHINDITS' SONNET

As a small child, remembers the horror and fright,
Felt after a nightmare dreamed in the night;
So the feelings returned a hundred times worse,
Left him trembling and fearful – he uttered a curse.
A curse against Fate that had left him to dread,
Each waking hour with its now peaceful dead.
Here, none to comfort and soothe away fears,
Nor spoken, those soft words to banish all tears.
It was time for a grown man to gather his strength,
Must hurry, not worry, they will march the full length;
Span the breadth, reach the heights – together will ask,
Fear conquered, no flight, win and victory grasp?
My partners, my buddies, my best mates, my friends;
Together, forever; no beginnings, no ends.

Kathleen Ross
(Kathleen Ross' collection of poems, *Stars of Burma and Poems on the Theme of War*, was published in 2005.)

WAR IN THE WILDERNESS

The Chindits in Burma 1943–1944

TONY REDDING

To my father, John 'Jack' Redding – Chindit – and his brothers-in-arms.

To my wife, Philippa, and my grandchildren, Molly and Zach.

All royalties from the sale of this book are donated to Friends of the Chindits.

FRONT COVER The Queen's 21 Column Wireless Detachment cross the Kaukkwe Chaung at the end of three hard months in Burma with 16 Brigade. They are making for Broadway airstrip and evacuation to Assam. This photograph was taken by 21 Column's Intelligence Officer, Captain C.S. Phillips, on or around 1 May 1944, with Broadway just a couple of days away. In the foreground is NCO Signaller Tony Howard, leading the Detachment, followed by Muleteer Paddy Myers and 'Taxi', the mule laden with the Column's precious wireless and batteries. Taxi was playful and had a habit of deliberately leaning to one side while being loaded. Behind Myers are Wireless Operator Geordie Beaton, Muleteer Private Holmes with his mule, 'Dextrose' (carrying batteries), and, just entering the chaung, Wireless Operator George Hill. (Tony Howard)

First published 2011
This edition published 2015

By Spellmount, an imprint of
The History Press
The Mill, Brimscombe Port
Stroud, Gloucestershire, GL5 2QG
www.thehistorypress.co.uk

British Library Cataloguing in Publication Data.
A catalogue record for this book is available from the British Library.

ISBN 978 0 7509 6217 9

Typesetting and origination by The History Press
Printed and bound in Great Britain by TJ International Ltd

CONTENTS

FOREWORD

I remember, as a young girl, listening to my father tell stories about his father – Major-General Orde Wingate. Though Orde died two months before he was born, my father was inspired enough by his life and achievements, not only to pass on those tales, but also to dedicate much of his own life to the British Army. The stories that were recounted to me – of struggle, heroism and honour in almost unimaginable conditions – were often frightening but always amazing and enthralling. But I was young and, of course, having never had the opportunity to meet my grandfather myself, those stories were difficult for me to grasp and the experiences too remote from my own life to understand fully.

Over the years, my family and I have attended many gatherings and reunions of the Chindits at which we have had the chance to meet and chat with old comrades. They are a unique band of men who share an exceptional past. I have always been moved by the warmth of the welcome and the strength of the friendships that endure to this day, not just among the men but among their families too.

Tony Redding's book is a fascinating record of the Chindits' campaigns in Burma. Reading the recollections of people who lived through those experiences brings home the truth of the stories I used to hear. It is, for me, a moving, though often difficult, way to learn about my grandfather through the words and experiences of people who suffered and fought alongside him.

It is a privilege to be a Patron of the Friends of the Chindits and to be able to introduce these inspiring and dramatic stories. It is important that the endeavours of these men are remembered and that, through books such as this, the accounts of their lives and sacrifices are preserved.

Alice Wingate

Alice Wingate
Patron, Friends of the Chindits
Granddaughter of Major-General Orde Wingate

ACKNOWLEDGEMENTS

THIS BOOK was written with the active encouragement, support and participation of many people. Their generosity led to the achievement of my first objective: to tell the human story of the Chindits. I reviewed published work, personal papers, official documents, memoirs and unpublished accounts and combined this material with the memories of the veterans, the men who took part in the Chindit operations.

I have been fortunate. I found former Chindits to be patient and willing contributors. In many cases family members assisted, preparing material, sending photographs and dealing with correspondence. Many were eager to pay tribute to husbands and fathers. It is unnecessary to list the veterans here, as their personal accounts are to be found throughout the following narrative. I can only express my deep gratitude to all concerned.

That said, I must thank those who went to considerable trouble to read the chapters in draft. My 'readers' were: Frank Anderson, Larry Gaines, Denis Arnold, John Riggs, Ronald Swann, Bill Towill, Bill Smyly, Jack Hutchin, Ian Niven and John Knowles. Their comments have rescued this author from many potential embarrassments. I also remember my late father, Jack Redding. His example provided the spur, whenever the complexities of the Chindit war in Burma threatened to get the better of me!

I am grateful to Kathleen Ross, who was kind enough to accept my invitation to compose 'The Chindits' Sonnet'. I benefited from the professionalism of Ian Giles, who worked tirelessly to ready the photographic archive for publication. I also acknowledge the painstaking work of Julie Snook, who has produced a series of excellent maps from my rather inadequate sketches. Joy Kemp and Mandy Taylor provided constant support in the preparation of successive drafts and cheerfully tackled a host of research and related tasks. Their help was given over a long period and always in a willing manner. I must also pay tribute to my wife, Philippa, for her excellent proof-reading skills and, above all, her forbearance throughout the three years required to complete the book.

I owe much to Bill Smith and Corinne Simons, who inspired the book, took an active interest in its progress and, above all, provided essential material from the papers of the late Fred Gerrard, Paddy Dobney and Philip Graves-Morris, all of the York and Lancaster Battalion contributing two Columns to Operation *Thursday*. The substantial Dobney and Graves-Morris material, carefully typed and checked by Corinne, provided essential 'glue' holding together the narrative covering key periods during Operation *Thursday*. I have been fortunate in my relationship with the publisher, Shaun Barrington, who was an enthusiastic supporter of this project from the first.

Sadly, it is in the nature of such endeavours that a number of contributors died in the period leading to publication. In many cases, the families have continued to support the work and offer encouragement. I am pleased that the experiences of these brave men have been recorded.

PREFACE

MAJOR NEVILLE Hogan, MBE, Chairman of the Chindits Old Comrades' Association, is a straight-talking man. When I began work on this book and first approached him, he asked: 'Why now? Why talk to us now? After all, we are in our eighties. Some are in their nineties. In fact, most of us are dead!'

These initial comments were not encouraging. Happily, however, Neville Hogan's gruff exterior belies an extraordinarily generous heart. His help and support opened many doors. Some 50 veterans agreed to be interviewed. Family members were enthusiastic, providing documents, letters, photographs and several important unpublished accounts.

Hogan's question demands an answer. Why now? The reasons are personal, in part. My father, John 'Jack' Redding, was a Chindit with the 2nd Battalion, King's Own Royal Regiment. He took part in the Operation *Thursday* assault glider landings in the Burmese jungle clearing code-named 'Broadway'. In common with so many of his generation, he said little about his war. The family is left with half a dozen anecdotes, one or two of an exceedingly unpleasant character.

My father was overseas for four years and four months. He arrived back in England in March 1946. He assumed he had priority for demob but, to his surprise and fury, was told he would soon embark for further service abroad, this time to Palestine. This was too much. He argued his case and won, but the anger persisted for many years. He returned his medals and put the war behind him, beyond the occasional bout of recurrent malaria.

I never really talked to my father about his experience as a Chindit; I had the idea it would disturb him. In the late 1990s, my father entered his eighties and had a change of heart. He obtained a new set of medals, joined the Burma Star Association and marched past the Cenotaph later in the year. Indeed, he marched on three successive Novembers. On the final occasion we arrived early and visited the Garden of Remembrance in the grounds of Westminster Abbey. We reached the Chindits' plot. I asked if he wanted a cross, to remember someone. He asked for two, for farmer's boy Dave Davies, from Wiltshire and another close friend, 'Nobby' Evans. Both died in Burma; one was killed in action and the other succumbed to cerebral malaria. When I placed the crosses my father broke down. I realised, at that point, that my many questions would never be asked.

My father died in May 2005. Three years later, my wife and I, idle on a Sunday afternoon, visited the country's largest military 'Living History' event at the Kent County Showground. That day I met Bill Smith — 'Chindit Bill' — for the first time. It was an unforgettable encounter. Bill was dressed as a Chindit NCO, complete with his late father's bush hat, large pack and Thompson sub-machine gun. To my delight, his companions had two mules, equipped Chindit-fashion. Bill and I have much in common. Our fathers were Chindits. We wanted to find out more and we shared a deep admiration for those who took part in Wingate's two expeditions. My meeting with 'Chindit Bill' was the catalyst that prompted the preparation of this book.

War against a fanatical enemy, behind the lines in the North Burmese jungle, imposed physical and mental demands probably exceeding those experienced in any other form of combat. I make no apology for setting out the appalling nature of the Chindit experience, in often painful detail. How else would one measure the spirit and determination of those who endured?

This book is *not* an attempt to tell the story from the perspective of a military academic. I have no qualifications for such a project. Many books have considered Wingate's expeditions and the man himself. These works are of varying quality. Some were written by historians; others were produced by those who were there, notably Slim, Calvert, Fergusson and Masters.

This book is *not* the latest in a long series of attempts to tell Orde Charles Wingate's story. Wingate is an enigma, nearly 70 years after his death on a remote hillside in Assam. I have no wish to join the Wingate bandwagon. Books about him almost always set out to prove something: Wingate was a madman, who threw away the lives of too many good men for little real return; Wingate was a genius, far ahead of his time, who influenced Japanese strategic thinking and contributed significantly to the enemy's destruction in Burma. Towering far above the extremes is a simple fact: most of Wingate's Chindits idolised him. He won deep respect, affection and loyalty among most (but certainly not all) of his men.

To conclude, I have no wish to play the military academic. The purpose of this book is to document the Chindit operations through the memories of the veterans. It serves as a testament to their courage and extraordinary fortitude. It offers a human perspective for the children, grandchildren and those who come after. I have drawn on the extensive literature on Wingate and the Chindits so far as necessary to provide a context for personal accounts. I thank all those who so kindly gave their permission for quotations from those publications.

It was an honour and privilege to interview such a grand body of men. Most interviews were conducted in person. In many cases the memories shared were voiced for the first time. Openness came at a price. Some contributors felt the pain of events that occurred over six decades ago, still raw and vivid — as if they happened yesterday. A number of contributors were in failing health yet remained determined to contribute. One man, when asked if he could continue, remarked: 'I take each day as it comes, just as I did then!'

Naturally, there are limitations when recounting memories from over 60 years ago. There are many difficulties relating to chronology, locations, unresolved issues surrounding the complex Chindit operations and, of course, the interactions of personalities such as Wingate, Stilwell, Lentaigne, Fergusson, Calvert and Masters. That said, the author trusts that the operational narrative provides a robust spine for the personal commentaries — including those from the Mustang pilot flying top cover over Broadway clearing, the medical orderly who nursed Wingate after his suicide attempt, the man who took another's life to save him from possible torture and those who suffered the long trial of incarceration by the Japanese. Material from the interviews is presented for the most part in italics. Doubts over particular issues are mentioned in the text. That said, the responsibility for residual errors rests entirely with the author.

The contributors include Sergeant Major Bob Hobbs of Westgate, Kent. During our conversation I mentioned my father's Chindit service. Hobbs asked if he was still alive. When I said no, he paused, deep in thought, and then remarked: 'Your father may be gone, but he keeps very good company!' Hobbs' comment stayed with me throughout the preparation of this book. It was an inspiration. There is a large table in Valhalla, with a reserved seat for every Chindit.

Tony Redding
Ash, Canterbury, Kent

INTRODUCTION

ONE CAN only wonder at the physical and mental resilience of the Chindits. One factor stands out beyond all else: the alien character of the jungle environment for most who fought in North Burma. The author's father, for example, grew up in modest circumstances in one of the grimmer inner suburbs of South London, a different world indeed from the Burmese jungle.

George MacDonald Fraser (*Quartered Safe Out Here*) considers the jungle's impact on the individual:

> It is disconcerting to find yourself soldiering in an exotic oriental country which is medieval in outlook, against a barbarian enemy given to burying prisoners up to their neck or hanging them by the heels for bayonet practice ... where you could get your dinner off a tree, be eaten alive by mosquitoes and leeches ... wake in the morning to find your carelessly neglected mess tin occupied by a spider the size of a soup plate, watch your skin go white and puffy in ceaseless rain ... gape in wonder at huge, gilded pagodas silent in the wilderness and find yourself taken aback at the sight of a domestic water tap, because you haven't seen such a thing for months.

These pressures were compounded for the Chindits, operating behind enemy lines and as much the hunted as the hunters. Fraser added that service in Burma was 'with the possible exception of aircrew ... generally believed to be the worst ticket you could draw in the lottery of active service.'

The jungle offered psychological as well as physical challenges. There was immense mental pressure, with no prospect of relief. J.P. Cross (*Jungle Warfare*) comments: 'The very nature of primary jungle, its close-horizontal, all pervading, never-ending green of trees, vines, creepers and undergrowth prevents the eyes from seeing as far as the ears can hear, so voices have to be kept low and equipment so handled that it does not reverberate.'

Absolute silence, of course, was impossible in a Column of 400 men and their animals. Efforts to keep the noise down aggravated the tension. Bernard Fergusson (*Beyond the Chindwin*) described how this affected the nerves. During Operation *Longcloth* in 1943, when approaching Tonmakeng, Fergusson's Column met others on the track:

> I found that one Column had forbidden talking and was making all men converse in whispers. I was shocked to find this, for I am convinced it is bad psychology and leads to undue nervousness. Talking in a low voice is another thing altogether and can easily be acquired with training, but whispering is hard on the voice as well as the nerves and leads, moreover, to misunderstandings. It is a bad rule and this Column, I know, did away with it after a bit.

It is unfortunate that some lessons from Operation *Longcloth* were overlooked when Operation *Thursday* began the following year. Free conversation between men had a positive influence on morale. Rhodes James (*Chindit*) wrote of the central importance of comradeship: 'In the enforced intimacy of the Column, men became neighbours and bedfellows, sharing fires and pooling rations. Every man was found out for what he was and those who stood the test ... had good reason to be proud.' Cross described life in the jungle as

> ... a state of permanent dampness, rain or sweat, of stifling, mindless heat, of dirty clothes, of smelling bodies, of heavy loads, of cocked and loaded weapons, of tensed reflexes, of inaccurate maps, of constant vigilance, of tired limbs, of sore shoulders where equipment straps have bitten in, of a chafed crotch, of the craving for a cigarette and a cold beer for some and a cup of tea for others.

The enemy often became almost an aside in these appalling conditions. Cross added:

> The real fight was against the enervating climate, the demanding terrain, the corroding atmosphere of unrelieved tension, the fitfulness of sleep and lack of hot meals, of disease and of accident, of having to

carry everything everywhere as one side groped for the other like a grotesque game of blind man's bluff. All the while the soldier had to be ready for a split second contact, for a few minutes of hectic action when patrol bumped patrol or, after great effort, an attack was launched or an ambush sprung.

A Chindit Column Commander and his men had to be ready to face any eventuality. Two separate rendezvous positions (24 hours and subsequent) were agreed and communicated each day. Bill Towill (*A Chindit's Chronicle*) describes the significance of the RV:

> We were under constant threat of ambush or having to meet the enemy in a hard-fought action, in which some of our men might be scattered and not able to regroup immediately and it was therefore essential for everyone to know how they could link up with the main body again.

Each man marched with the equivalent of around half his bodyweight on his back. This was the very essence of Chindit soldiering. An iron will was required to bear such a load in tropical (and, later, Monsoon) conditions across some of the toughest country on Earth. Even in dry conditions the going was hard. Rhodes James:

> The continual plod through dust or mud, the back of the man in front, up, down, up, down, eyes fixed on his boots, inspecting each scrap of dust as it was shaken off his heel, the periodical shifting of his pack or changing of his arms, waiting for him to negotiate a difficult part of the track. Watching him impersonally, unconsciously, but cursing him for what he was, the maddening rhythm in our eyes. Mad? No, just very weary and inexpressibly bored, when each unusual move or faltering step becomes a major event.

The widespread belief that all Chindits were volunteers was a myth. Some officers and men did volunteer, for many different reasons. Some even volunteered twice, despite the sufferings of the first expedition. Yet most had no say in the matter. Some units consisted of unpromising material, though these Battalions blossomed as the unfit and unsuitable were weeded out in a gruelling training regime that removed every vestige of civilised life.

Observations on training — made by Cross — are probably as relevant today as they were in 1943 and 1944:

> Special training is necessary to accustom troops to the strange conditions of jungle life. This training

Adjusting a load: efforts to keep the noise down aggravated the tension. Lieutenant John Salazar took many photographs while inside Burma and these were circulated widely after the war. (John Riggs)

> ... must inculcate the ability to move quickly and silently, to find the way accurately and with confidence, to shoot to kill at disappearing targets from all positions on the ground, out of trees and from the hip, to carry out tactical operations in the jungle by means of battle drill without waiting for detailed orders. Above all, the highest pitch of physical toughness was, and still is, essential for everyone involved and the leadership of junior commanders must be confident, offensive and inspiring.

The men who experienced the strain of Chindit operations became extraordinarily close. They paired up. If safe to do so they made fires - one man would prepare two meals while his 'mucker' made cha. Pairs would shelter together and watch each other's backs at vulnerable moments, such as when answering calls of nature.

A lonely grave: Chindits bury a comrade, the grave marked by a simple bamboo cross. Later, efforts were made to recover remains for formal interment. (Trustees of the Imperial War Museum)

Companionship and food were the great influences on morale. The lengthy dependence on emergency K-rations did much to undermine Special Force's fighting capacity. Following Blackpool Block's fall and in the push towards Mogaung, Rhodes James wrote of a slow descent into starvation:

> For four months we had been existing on K-rations, which is, I think, a world record. These rations had been augmented to some extent but the K-ration remained the basis. Before going into operations we had been assured that the rations contained an ample reserve of calories and we believed it. The truth, we afterwards discovered, was something entirely different. The K-ration was only sufficient to keep up a man's strength for 10 days at fighting pitch.

The lack of bulk and sheer monotony of K-rations ground down the strongest:

> The exotic American flavours began to nauseate us ... the troops were weakened through unsuitable

rations and the process was accelerated by the fact that they could not make themselves eat all that was provided. Jaded appetites could be stirred by onions and we always welcomed them. Rice, which we obtained locally, was our greatest standby; it filled our bellies and left us deeply satisfied, while it could form the basis for all kinds of food. But there was not enough of it.

News from home was also important and occasionally available by air drop. This could have highly positive or disastrously negative effects on morale at the individual level. Some men receiving bad news from (or about) wives and girlfriends lost the will to live. Some men had low expectations. Major Denis Arnold, MC, commented dryly: 'I didn't expect any mail from home and received very little, although I did receive some herbal cigarettes from my mother!'

Disease was a part of daily life. Everyone appreciated the potentially fearful consequences of falling ill. Many felt it better to be killed than be seriously wounded or fall gravely ill. Disease brought many men very low, to the point of extreme indifference or even suicide. Denis

Arnold remembers two cases where men shot themselves – 'possibly in the deep depression that can result from a bout of scrub typhus.'

A report from the Medical Officer of the 4th Border Regiment (23 Brigade), following operations in the Naga Hills, reveals the extraordinary regime surrounding the treatment of the sick. Captain (later, Lieutenant Col.) H.W.W. Good's paper set out recommendations for tackling Chindit medical problems (Imperial War Museum, 87/37/1): 'Unless the Long Range Penetration Column becomes involved in a major action, the problem of sickness is far greater than that of battle casualties.' He added:

> It is obvious, from the very start, that a different attitude has to be taken towards sickness on LRP than is taken in any form of operations where one can either evacuate a sick man or hold him in a sick bay long enough to get him on his feet again.

Officers must set an example:

> If you are feeling groggy, go along and see the MO at one of the long halts and get some medicine and make yourself carry on, and you will find that the bulk of your men will do the same. You are also in a better moral position to drive on the unwilling.

Good went on to stress the value of a no-compromise regime during training: 'The maxim I used to lay down in lecturing troops was that as long as a man is conscious, is not in severe pain and has no impediment of locomotion, such as a severe injury to leg or foot, he will keep marching.' He had good things to say about the wide range of drugs and equipment made available to Column MOs: 'Practically every known complaint is catered for and the only thing impossible to prescribe is rest.'

On Mepacrine discipline, Good was emphatic on use of the malaria suppressant: 'Make sure to dispel the rumour that is always stated among the men that Mepacrine makes a man sterile. I can assure you such is not the case.'

Good's advice to Platoon Commanders on operations was, if possible, to look at all wounds: 'By this means you will become accustomed to seeing what may previously have seemed very frightening conditions and you will not get into a "flap" about them.' His advice extended to basic sanitation: 'Make it a drill that no man goes for a "rear" during a halt in the march, or in an area where a latrine is impracticable unless he brings a digging implement ... never permit a man to have a "rear" within 100 yards of a water point.'

Captain Good wrote with some authority. His Column operated with 23 Brigade from 10 April to 19 July 1944, in some of the most difficult mountain country in the world. His report notes, with understandable pride:

> We started some 400 strong and arrived at Imphal less two officers and 23 ORs. Of these, one officer and five ORs were killed and one officer and six ORs wounded. I think these figures speak for themselves, as the remaining 12 men were the only cases evacuated through illness.

As might be expected, many other Columns had a very different experience, with disease cutting great swathes in their ranks.

In every Chindit's mind was the fear of being left behind. This was the practice during the first expedition, although efforts might be made to lodge the sick or wounded in a friendly village, if any existed in the immediate area. During the second expedition, in 1944, the practice was to fly out the wounded and sick but, in practice, this was very difficult after the Monsoon broke in mid-May.

This book contains previously unpublished accounts from men unable to continue. They survived, against the odds, by their sheer determination to live. Philip Stibbe's prologue to *Return via Rangoon* sums up what it meant to be left behind:

> According to my watch it was 10am. I guess the day was 31 March 1943. I suddenly realised that I had been alone for 48 hours, alone in the Burmese jungle somewhere east of the Irrawaddy River and probably further east at that moment than any British soldier on active service. I had practically nothing to eat or drink and I was wounded in the chest ... I was not particularly cheerful but at no point during those 48 hours do I remember feeling despondent. I certainly spent some time praying to be given courage to face whatever lay ahead and this was an immense source of help.

Many Chindits refused to give in, even when their worst fears were realised. At the same time, of course, those left behind, with a spare water bottle and extra grenades, knew their chances of survival were virtually zero. Yet, in many cases they ordered their men – or simply told their mates – to leave them.

Fergusson (*The Wild Green Earth*) recalled the deep sense of deliverance felt by the 30 members of his dispersal party in 1943, having crossed the Chindwin to safety: 'For the last month we were all quite sure that, if only we got out, nothing on Earth would ever have the power to worry us again!'

Having had the honour to meet many Chindit veterans, over 60 years after these events in their young lives, the author found echoes of that self-assurance. Many men said, in so many words: 'We felt totally self-confident. We knew nothing we would face in life would ever be as bad as that'. Certainly, the author's father had that self-assurance. It remained with him for the rest of his life.

The following pages include some grim reading. Yet those seeking a reason for the resilience of the Chindits might find the answer in the wry humour of the men in the Columns. Captain Jeffrey of the Lancashire Fusiliers (*Sunbeams Like Swords*) wrote of his Batman's comments when they were in action at night. The men were in a ditch along a track:

Walker and I were making our usual pilgrimage from the rear of the Column to the front when we suddenly heard a voice from the ditch: 'Are there any Japs about, Walker?' Walker turned a grim face in the direction of the voice and said slowly: 'Yes. Thousands and thousands of them, Sir, and they're after you!'

RAF Officer W.A. Wilcox, with 23 Brigade's 76 Column (2nd Duke of Wellington's Regiment), wrote in a postscript to his book, *Chindit Column 76*: 'I apologise to the reader for the monotonous repetition of rain, pain and discomfort. In self defence, I can only assert that it was really so and leave it at that'. This author can muster a similar defence. These pages reflect the experiences and sufferings of brave men with sufficient goodwill and strength to share many painful memories.

1

AN EXCEPTIONAL MAN ...
AN EXTRAORDINARY PERSONALITY

'Wingate was a strange, excitable, moody creature, but he had fire in him. He could ignite other men.'

Field Marshal Viscount Slim

BRITISH COMMANDERS in the Far East had dismissed Japanese fighting qualities but then suffered humiliating defeats after the Pearl Harbor attack in December 1941. These crushing blows shifted opinion from one extreme to the other. J.P. Cross (*Jungle Warfare*) wrote that the prevailing view of the Japanese as 'second rate soldiers' changed rapidly. Now the enemy were regarded as

> ... supermen, experts in the jungle in a way never previously imagined, invincible, brave to a degree unsuspected and malignantly cruel in a manner few had ever contemplated modern man could be. They also despised the softness and lack of military endeavour in their enemies. They used the jungle as a conduit of movement; the Allies tried to fight the jungle and the enemy and, to start with, were unsuccessful against both.[1]

The Japanese soldier's aggression commanded respect:

> They fought with savage and, at times, hysterical fury. They were very brave. If 50 Japanese were holding a position, 45 of them would have to be killed before the rest would kill themselves and the position could be taken.[2]

Most Allied commanders – General (later, Field Marshal Viscount) Slim included – acknowledged this bravery. Slim commented:

> The strength of the Japanese Army lay not in its higher leadership, which, once its career of success had been checked, became confused, nor in its

special aptitude for jungle warfare, but in the spirit of the individual Japanese soldier. He fought and marched till he died.[3]

Yet the Japanese were not invincible. They were poorly organised and had a strange lack of discipline. Cross wrote: 'Fighting patrols, of about 20 men, were not very skilful. They liked to keep to paths and moved without precaution, often giving their presence away by soldiers talking.'[4]

Beyond fighting quality the Japanese drew strength from their recognition of the jungle as shelter and shield, rather than a second enemy. The Allies had no choice here: they had to adopt a similar attitude if they were to prevail. This change would take time. Certainly, it came too late to save Burma from conquest in 1942. It would take a truly exceptional man, with an extraordinary personality, to bring such change.

Orde Charles Wingate is by no means unique. Over the centuries many British military leaders of extraordinary quality have emerged to shape the course of events. It is not unusual for such reputations to be built on a combination of eccentricity and ability. Such men tend to make enemies among able yet more conventional men. From the very first, the entire enterprise – the strategic and tactical principles of Long Range Penetration and the fundamentals of what it meant to be a Chindit – belonged to Wingate alone. There were two Chindit expeditions: the Brigade-scale Operation *Longcloth* in 1943 and the much larger Operation *Thursday* in 1944. If a fundamental criticism can be levelled at Wingate, it is that LRP and the man became indivisible. He made himself virtually irreplaceable and, in doing so, exposed his force to much abuse after his untimely death in March 1944.

Eccentricity, ability and vision: Orde Charles Wingate, pictured in the final hours before his death in an air crash. (Trustees of the Imperial War Museum)

Wingate was born at Naini Tal, in the Himalayan foothills, on 26 February 1903. His parents were Plymouth Brethren, a strongly puritanical sect. Colonel Wingate, having returned to England with his family, led a spartan existence. Much of the family income was devoted to missionary causes. The Wingate children received their early education at home, away from other children.

Orde Wingate was a loner at Charterhouse School. He left in 1920 and entered the Royal Military Academy, Woolwich. He sought a commission in the Royal Artillery and joined 5 Medium Brigade. 'Cousin Rex' (Sir Reginald Wingate, a former Governor-General of the Sudan and High Commissioner of Egypt) watched over his progress. Presumably, Wingate took his advice; he enrolled at London's School of Oriental and African Studies.[5]

When posted to Egypt Wingate sent his luggage ahead, cycled across Europe and joined a ship at Genoa. In 1928 he was posted to the Sudan Defence Force. He was to spend six years in the Sudan. Wingate's appetite for exotic adventure led to an expedition with camels into the Libyan Desert in early 1933, ostensibly searching for the 'lost oasis' of Zerzura. He lived hard on dates, biscuits, cod liver oil and oranges. This foray allowed the 30-year-old Wingate to develop his qualities of leadership and self-discipline.[6]

Two life-changing events then occurred. During the voyage home from Egypt in March 1933 he met his future wife, Lorna Patterson, who was then just 16. They married on 24 January 1935. The second was his posting to Palestine, as an intelligence officer with 5th Infantry Division. The 1917 Balfour Declaration supported a Jewish National Home in Palestine, but no-one, at that time, could have foreseen the rise of Nazi Germany less than 20 years later and its pitiless persecution of the Jews. Jewish immigration in the wake of the Nuremburg Laws triggered more violence in Palestine. There was much British sympathy for the Arabs, but Wingate held a contrary view; he and Lorna became fervent Zionists.[7]

Wingate was self-opinionated, entirely free of self-doubt and a dogged advocate of the Jewish cause. As a young officer he cultivated powerful friends and worked hard – propelled by a genuine empathy – to overcome Jewish suspicions. Slowly, the doubters were converted and his friends included Jewish Agency leader Chaim Weizmann. By early 1937 Wingate was arguing that the Jews should be armed. He then went further, making a dangerous offer to assist in the organisation of an underground Jewish Defence Force.[7]

Wingate was out of his depth in the circles of high politics. He was a soldier with a sharp political edge to his tongue, yet his strong views radiated from a naive inner conviction, rather than political interest. Wingate was blind to politics at the sophisticated level. Consequently, many regarded him as extremely dangerous – a loose cannon.

The Peel Commission proposed the partition of Palestine into British, Jewish and Arab zones. Arab attacks on Jewish settlements intensified as General (later, Field Marshal Viscount) Wavell took command in Palestine. Wingate even engineered an opportunity to board Wavell's car, to have a face-to-face opportunity to present his ideas for Jewish night patrols to combat 'terrorists'.

Wavell's successor, General Haining, backed Wingate's 'Special Night Squads'; they began operating in June 1938. Each man was expected to be able to cover 15 miles of country by night. Each Squad had an Arabic speaker, to help win hearts and minds among local communities and make common cause against the 'terrorists'. These squads were an outstanding success, although Wingate himself was wounded in a skirmish. These exploits earned him a DSO.[8]

In late 1938 Wingate was in London, at Weizmann's request, pressing the Zionist case in the weeks leading up to the publication of another report, from the Woodhead Commission, but this had little effect. The report was negative towards Jewish interests and the Peel recommendation for partition was overturned. Wingate then came to Winston Churchill's attention at a dinner party in November, when he seized his chance to explain why the Special Night Squads had been so successful. His story fired Churchill's imagination; Wingate would be remembered. In contrast, Wingate's relationship with the Army establishment (other than with one or two prominent champions) continued to sour. Back in Jerusalem he found the Night Squads now had a new commander. On the other hand, he continued to gain trust in Jewish circles and became known as 'The Friend'.[9]

The first days of war saw Orde Wingate at his London flat, 49 Hill Street, unemployed but with powerful friends. They included Leo Amery (Secretary of State for India and Burma, May 1940–July 1945), who was to be instrumental in creating opportunities for Wingate in Abyssinia and, later, in the Far East. Yet Wingate's outspoken Zionist views continued to stir resentment and his personality displayed more than a touch of paranoia. On meeting David Ben-Gurion (later to become Israel's first Prime Minister) in London, he insisted they talk in a car, but not his car!

He was not alone in believing that he and the family were under surveillance. Writing in the early 1960s, Wingate's mother-in-law, Alice Ivy Hay, claimed:

> These apprehensions were not without foundation. In Jerusalem his telephone was tapped and many of his private letters were opened. He did not reject the possibility that recording machines might have been secreted in his apartment, or in his own car, and if ever he had anything important to say to anyone, he preferred to say it in the open – preferably in the middle of a field or open space. In London, his telephone was also tapped (and so was mine in Aberdeen).[10]

Thousands of men would be drawn to Orde Wingate's Chindit standard in a new World War. They included Bill Towill, born in 1920 and the elder of two brothers. His father had been wounded and gassed in the Great War, but had recovered sufficiently to run the family farm near Totnes, Devon.

Towill shared something with Wingate: his family environment was also shaped by strict religious belief. Towill's plans to become a solicitor were frustrated by war. Acting on conscientious grounds, he joined a local RAMC Territorial unit. The 11th Casualty Clearing Station was absorbed into the Regular Army within 72 hours of war being declared. They went to France as part of the British Expeditionary Force (BEF). The unit arrived at the little village of Pernois, near Amiens. The initial months of the 'Phoney War' passed quietly, yet there was a sobering reminder of reality nearby: a huge cemetery for thousands slaughtered in the mud of the Somme.

When the storm broke in May 1940, the German *Blitzkreig* sought to trap the BEF and the French northern armies against the coast. Towill's medical unit moved into Belgium but soon joined the general retreat towards the sea. Events pushed Bill Towill towards a crisis of conscience:

> *'It was the early morning of Friday, 31 May, exactly three weeks after the start of the Blitzkrieg, and we were at a little seaside resort called La Panne, just inside the Belgian border and some 11 miles along the beach from Dunkirk. Much of the BEF had already been evacuated. I came off night duty and found the rest of the unit formed up on the beach. We were told we were about to march off, but volunteers were wanted to stay with the wounded. So, the order was given: 'Volunteers, one step, forward march. Volunteers stand fast – remainder dismiss!' Too many men volunteered. The order was given a second time and still too many volunteered. Yet again the order was given and four of my colleagues and I were left. The rest moved off towards Dunkirk and we were joined by 20 volunteers from other medical units in the area. We were now under the command of Major J.L. Lovibond, one of our officers.'*

A large casino on the beach served as a hospital, but heavy shelling prompted a move to the underground shelter next door:

> *'The beach was under sporadic shellfire. This caused a lot of casualties among those still making their way past us, on to Dunkirk. We stretchered the wounded back to the shelter and gave what help we could. When night fell it became pitch black. We had no light to carry on, except from the flash of bursting shells. Chunks of shrapnel churned up the sand around us but, miraculously, we weren't hit.*
> *'At about 2am on Saturday, 1 June, a few of us accompanied the Major into the casino's huge ground floor room, which had been turned into a morgue. Around the walls, in orderly rows, were laid the bodies*

of scores of our dead. We had no chance of giving them proper burial. The Major did the best he could by reading the Burial Service over them. In the inky blackness, the only light was from the tiny flashlight the Major used to read from his prayer book. This reflected the light onto the lower half of his face. He came to a quite amazing passage, from Revelations 21: "And God shall wipe away all tears from their eyes; and there shall be no more death, neither sorrow, nor crying, neither shall there be any more pain: for the former things are passed away."

It would be difficult to over-state the impact of these words, in those circumstances, on a deeply religious 19-year-old lad. The sorrow, pain and death filling all our waking moments during the last three weeks seemed to have eaten into our souls. These great words of hope brought a special uplift to our failing spirits.'

Bill Towill's future as a Chindit during the second expedition, with 3rd/9th Gurkha Rifles, was determined by the luck of the draw:

'A couple of hours later the Major called us all together again. The last of our men had long since gone past us and we were quite alone. The Major said the Germans were just down the road and would soon be arriving. There was no need for all of us to be taken prisoner. He put 25 pieces of paper into his hat; each of us would draw one. Eight were numbered. If you drew a number, you stayed and were taken prisoner. If you drew a blank you had the chance to make your way to Dunkirk. Shakily, I put my hand into the hat and withdrew a piece of paper. This very simple act was one of the most important things I have ever done. The whole of the rest of my life depended upon it. Mercifully, I drew a blank.

Those of us free to go set off immediately. We soon reached the flimsy wire fence marking the boundary between Belgium and France; it had been trampled flat by the hordes who had passed over it. From time to time we tried, unsuccessfully, to relaunch boats stranded on the beach. Eventually Dunkirk came into view – it looked like a scene from Dante's Inferno.

A thick cloud of black smoke from burning oil tanks shrouded the whole area. The beach itself was under constant heavy shellfire, supplemented by bombing and strafing from the air. But what was most fearsome were the Stuka dive-bombers, with their unearthly screaming noise, attacking ships crowded with evacuees and often sinking them, leaving their occupants to almost certain death by drowning.'

Towill's small group joined the long queue still awaiting evacuation from the Eastern Mole, a timber jetty

on the outer side of the eastern breakwater. The back of the queue was at the end of the canal running into the harbour:

'As I looked down to the canal, on my left, I saw a number of British dead. They all had the same injury – the tops of their skulls had been taken off as if by a can-opener. They seemed to have been caught by an air-burst shell. This was not a healthy place to be.'

As dawn approached, the shelling and strafing intensified and Towill's group gave up queuing. Back on the beach Towill and the Major dug holes for themselves. At first light they dug themselves out three times when straddled by near misses. Late in the evening the attacks ceased and in that pause men clambered out of their holes in the sand, made their orderly way to the Mole and boarded a ship. It was Sunday, 2 June 1940, and the last day of the evacuation:

'I had had no sleep at all for three days and nights, so immediately I boarded I was out for the count. I have very few mementoes of the war but treasure a small

Return to the Far East: young Bill Smyly at Officer Training Unit, Mhou, on first commission with the 2nd Gurkhas. (Bill Smyly)

pewter hip flask with a slip of paper in the Major's hand which reads: 'Pte Towill. To commemorate some thirsty hours spent together on Dunkirk Beach, 1 and 2 June 1940. J.L. Lovibond, Major, RAMC.' That flask has never been filled.'

Shortly after Bill Towill's safe return he was recommended for a Commission. In the Autumn of 1941 he went to India as a Cadet.

Religious belief also played a central role in Bill Smyly's young life. He was born in 1922 in Peking. His father, a missionary Professor of Medicine, went to China in 1912 and stayed until the Communist takeover in 1949. He then pursued his work in Hong Kong and, subsequently, as a leprologist in Africa. Smyly was the eldest of three boys and the children were sent 'home' to school. They lived with their grandparents in County Down. His two brothers were too young for war service but Bill Smyly saw an opportunity to return to the Far East. He was just old enough to be accepted for training in India and he was to take part in both Chindit expeditions:

'I joined a draft for India in 1939. In China, my parents were interned by the Japanese, but put on the very last Exchange Ship bringing back diplomats. Mother and Dad were both doctors. Two doctors and the ship had no medical staff – perhaps that's why they were given passage.'

Neville Hogan, born in Rangoon in 1923, was the youngest of four children. His father was Irish and his mother a Karen. Hogan Senior was a shipping company administrator and his wife was a schoolteacher:

'Our life was comfortably middle class and very pleasant. We socialised with local people and the substantial English community then resident in Rangoon. I attended an English school in the city. Unlike so many other countries in the Far East at that time, racial issues had no significance in our lives. Marriage between couples of different ethnic background was commonplace.'

Hogan wanted to be a marine engineer but chickenpox affected his eyesight. He decided to study civil engineering at university. When war broke out in Europe, in September 1939, he joined the Territorials – the Burma Auxiliary Force:

'As I was just 16 I was told to try again when I had reached 18. I went back shortly afterwards, armed with my elder brother's birth certificate. I soon found myself

To be a Chindit: Neville Hogan used his brother's birth certificate to join the Burma Auxiliary Force. (Neville Hogan)

in the Machine Gun Section. We had some old, water-cooled Vickers guns.'

Hogan would command a Chindit Recce Platoon during Operation *Thursday* in 1944.

Howard 'Bob' Hobbs had a more modest start in life. He was born in North London in 1922. His father was wounded twice during the Great War, once in the hip and then in the stomach. Hobbs left school at 14 and went to work at electrical engineers Cox & Co. He repaired car magnetos and dynamos until his call-up in 1941, when he joined the RASC. Drafted overseas in 1942, Hobbs was posted to the Indian Army Clerical Corps. He soon became bored and this put him in the frame of mind to volunteer for Wingate's first expedition: 'I don't know why I volunteered. I suppose I wanted excitement. I certainly got it!'

Alec Gibson volunteered for military service. He was born in 1921 and lived in Surbiton, Surrey. As a young man Gibson sought a career in the aircraft

Posted to India: George Fulton went to the Far East after service with a Field Ambulance Unit in the Western Desert. (George Fulton)

year-old George worked for the Town Council and was courting his future wife, Jean. Two friends at the Council had joined the Territorials, attached to 15th Scottish General Hospital, but Fulton was loath to sacrifice two evenings a week. Nevertheless, he joined his friends in April 1939, his pay being 2/6 a night. He was called up on 1 September 1939, on the eve of war:

'I attempted to join the Royal Signals but they were full. I ended up at Southampton for basic training with the RAMC. My unit was part of 51st Highland Division. They put up a very stiff fight in France before going into captivity. Fortunately, our detachment was held back. We never went to France.'

Fulton had several close calls of this type. One half of his unit went to the Scottish east coast and the other to the west coast. Fulton went east, to take part in the ill-fated Norwegian campaign of 1940. Bergen fell as the voyage began and their ship turned back. Only a few weeks later the men were issued with topees, an obvious clue to a warm climate posting:

'We were about to go to North Africa and I asked to see the Colonel. I had got engaged on 1 September 1939 and had spent my £5 call-up money on an engagement ring. I now requested 24 hours' leave to get married. Permission granted! Jean and I were married in Aberdeen on 18 June 1940.'

One week later the 15th Scottish General Hospital – a dozen of Aberdeen's finest doctors, some 20 nurses and nearly 200 men – boarded the *Aquitania* at Liverpool. In the company of the *Queen Mary* and *Mauretania*, they sailed for Egypt. Fulton entered Tobruk fortress with 173rd Field Ambulance, having been transferred in with a small group of replacements: 'We lost 11 men at Tobruk, then moved to Syria, to join the Australian 11th Infantry Brigade in their fight against Vichy French forces.' Subsequently, Fulton was posted to India.

industry. When war began he was an apprentice design draughtsman with Hawker Aircraft at Kingston. The firm then scrapped its peacetime apprenticeships and Alec was offered a new job as a fitter. He was happy. He had been paid less than a pound a week as an apprentice and the new job boosted his money fivefold overnight. Nevertheless, he was discontented, as many of his friends had already joined up:

'Working in the aircraft industry was a "Reserved Occupation", but I went to the local Recruiting Office and volunteered for the Army. By that time I had moved to a local garage making small components for Hawker Aircraft. I got away with it. I mentioned "fitter" and "garage" but left out the Hawker name.'

Gibson's first taste of service life was as a Private with the East Surreys. He spent two years on aerodrome and coastal defence: 'Looking back, we were the first line of defence had the Germans invaded. In that event, we would have been wiped out on the beaches.'

George Fulton wanted to join the Territorials as war loomed but he had other things on his mind. He was born in 1919 and the family lived in Aberdeen, where his father was a porter in the busy fish market. Nineteen-

Orde Wingate's success in Palestine resulted in the award of a DSO. Allen (*Burma: The Longest War*) noted another consequence: 'transfer from an area where his pronounced pro-Zionist views were felt to be a political embarrassment, as well as somewhat peculiar in an Army Officer.'[11]

The march of events and powerful friends positioned Wingate for his next challenge. Italy entered the war in June 1940 and Wingate's flair for irregular warfare, together with his experience with the Sudan Defence Force, promised a significant role in ejecting the Italians from Abyssinia.

Leo Amery urged Wavell to employ Wingate, who had arrived in Cairo during October 1940. Wingate's mother-in-law later wrote: 'Next to leading a Jewish army, the idea of righting the injustice inflicted upon the Emperor of Abyssinia was at that time a project nearer to his heart than any other.'[12]

Haile Selassie was a rallying point and Wingate formed a close bond with him. He created 'Gideon Force', with around 2,000 Sudanese and Abyssinian Regulars, 1,000 Abyssinian guerrillas and a cadre of British officers and NCOs. Sound tactics, fighting prowess and bluff allowed Gideon Force to overcome 36,000 Italian troops with armoured cars, artillery and air support. The defeat of the Italians was achieved by much larger conventional forces; but Wingate had made his contribution and it was he who rode the Emperor's white horse (at Haile Selassie's insistence) during the victorious entry into Addis Ababa.[11]

With Haile Selassie restored, Orde Wingate returned to Cairo in June 1941. He was angry and greatly dissatisfied with his lot, despite his successes. The reasons are complex. Wingate had arrived in Egypt during the third quarter of 1940 with a plan to attack Libya. The concept included much original thinking and his ideas (including the use of remote bases and air supply) were applied later in a very different theatre of war. Wingate still smarted from GHQ's rejection of his Libyan proposals, his cold reception in Cairo after recent triumphs and his reduction in rank to Major. These negatives dominated his mood, rather than the satisfaction which should have been drawn from a highly positive outcome in Abyssinia and the earlier outstanding success in Palestine. Haile Selassie had entered Addis Ababa on 5 May 1941. Rooney (*Wingate and the Chindits*) wrote:

> In the Ethiopian campaign over 200,000 Italian troops were defeated by the five Commonwealth Divisions which operated from Eritrea and Kenya, but Wingate, with about two Battalions, grabbed the limelight for his brilliant work with Gideon Force.[13]

Wingate was to remain frustrated. The Army establishment disliked his methods, strident attitude and open commitment to Zionism. Wingate, for his part, was openly intolerant of opposition. He dwelt on the loss of the Special Night Squads, rejection of the Libyan plan and the break up of Gideon Force. Requests for an immediate return to active service were rejected. Wingate then overreached himself in a report peppered with intemperate language. This report, significantly, referred to his concept of 'Long Range Penetration', but

The Emperor restored: Haile Selassie and Orde Wingate formed a close bond. (Trustees of the Imperial War Museum)

one comment, in particular, caused grave offence. He wrote that the decision to disband Gideon Force was the mark of a 'military ape'.

Wingate's depression was aggravated by severe malaria and large, unsupervised doses of the suppressant Atabrin. This precursor to Mepacrine was known to amplify depression, potentially to the point of suicide. During the afternoon of 4 July 1941, Wingate had a temperature of 104°. He left his hotel in search of the local doctor. Finding the doctor absent, he returned to his room and attempted suicide. He took a revolver, put it to his head and pulled the trigger. It misfired. He then stabbed himself in the neck. Some accounts claim that an officer in the next room heard a noise and responded; others state that an hotel employee opened the door. In any event, Wingate was rushed to hospital.[14]

George Fulton kept a secret throughout his service with the Chindits over two years later, as a Medical Orderly with 14 Brigade. Fulton had been in Cairo on 4 July 1941. He was in his billet at the 15th Scottish General Hospital that afternoon. His Sergeant-Major opened the door and told him to prepare to nurse an officer who had attempted suicide:

'I was to report to the Officers' Ward at 6pm to begin "special nursing" – one patient, one Orderly. I did nearly three weeks of night duty, 6pm to 6am, looking after Orde Wingate, who was to be my Chindit chief in Burma.'

Entering the ward on that first evening, Fulton found Wingate unconscious following an operation. The patient's neck was heavily bandaged:

'When he came to, he found everyone was from Aberdeen, where his wife came from. We got on very well. One of the first things he asked for was some soda water. We had none but, later, I managed to get a few bottles for him. His dressings were changed during the day, but I gathered that the main wound was to the left side of the neck. He had missed the main artery. We chatted a lot as the days passed, although his mood was very quiet and sombre.

'At one point, when off duty, I went to the cinema and watched Haile Selassie restored as Emperor of Ethiopia on Movietone News. I mentioned this to Wingate and he replied: "That was lots of fun." He then said: "I want to show you something." He pulled three items out of his kit. I can remember two. There was a set of four interlocked gold rings, about 1¼ in. in diameter, presented to him by Haile Selassie. He then showed me another gift. It was the most beautiful gold watch. I remember it had Westminster Chimes. On the

back was an engraved representation of the Lion of Judah, wearing his crown, with diamonds, rubies and other precious stones. Throughout my service in India and Burma, I never told anyone I had nursed Wingate in Egypt. I had hoped to meet him again but never did.'

Over 20 years later, in 1963, Alice Hay wrote of her son-in-law:

I am convinced that Orde committed this act when he did not know what he was doing. If he had been fully conscious, he would not have bungled it so badly, for he was the most efficient man I ever knew at carrying through any job he undertook. I am equally certain that in no circumstances would he ever again have attempted to take his life.[15]

Wingate was fortunate. His psychologist understood the potentially catastrophic side-effects of Atabrin. On 22 July he declared him fit and ready to convalesce. Wingate sailed for England in September.

A Medical Board approved his regrading for active service after three months. With encouragement from his family, Wingate now rewrote his report on Abyssinia. Leo Amery and Cousin Rex helped him and the paper was circulated to people of influence. One copy reached Churchill. Lobbying activities tended to further inflame Wingate's detractors. Rooney wrote: 'His attempted suicide became a *cause célèbre* in Cairo and beyond ... the devotion of those who supported him was matched only by the viciousness of those who opposed him.'[14]

There were times when Orde Wingate's every action seemed to offend. He remains famous for his eccentricities and there are many stories of his odd behaviour. Some are true. The author's father talked of Wingate's passion for onions. When addressing troops he had the habit of drawing a raw onion from his pocket and munching it, praising its life-giving qualities. Many men have such memories. Sergeant Tony Aubrey of The King's (Liverpool) concluded that Wingate's faith in onions was well-placed:

While we were within reach of base, sacks of them used always to be available. A dixieful was continually simmering on the fire of my Platoon at night and, even if no-one else happened to feel onion-minded, I used to make a pretty good hole in the contents myself before going to sleep. Most of the men joined me after a day or two, though, and I can highly recommend a pound or two of boiled onions as a sleeping draught. We ate so many of them, raw and cooked, that sometimes I used to feel sorry for anyone who didn't care for them.[16]

Perhaps more disconcerting for the uninitiated was Wingate's habit of receiving officers and giving orders while naked. He tended to make his point in unforgettable ways. During training, apparently, Wingate came across a group of unarmed officers. Incensed at their defenceless condition, he drew his revolver, fired over their heads and told them to put their hands up. On another occasion, when a stream suddenly became a Monsoon torrent, Wingate swam to the group of officers expected at his Headquarters and promptly ordered them to swim back with him.[17]

Orde Wingate may have been declared fit after Cairo but his Army career required rescue at the highest level. Wavell intervened once again, encouraged by Amery. The outcome was a posting to the Far East. Wingate was far from grateful – he felt he was being sidelined and repeated the mistake of venting his feelings on paper. A vitriolic memorandum gave his growing body of enemies fresh ammunition.[14] The Far East, nonetheless, would provide fertile ground for Wingate's original mind and highly unorthodox approach to modern warfare.

Many regarded Wingate's Far East posting as a good solution all round, but his mother-in-law, Alice Hay (another passionate Zionist), shared his distaste. This was a digression from Wingate's *raison d'être*, the promotion of the Jewish cause. Summing up Wingate's own reaction, she commented: 'He felt it was a great waste of his experience to send him to a part of the world that he neither knew nor, indeed, particularly wanted to know. He was right. He should never have been sent to Burma at all; he should have been allowed to continue to operate in the Middle East.' Perhaps, however, the true measure of Orde Wingate's greatness is that he put aside deeply entrenched personal frustrations and set to work, developing his concept of Long Range Penetration and bringing it to its ultimate flowering in a Burmese setting.[18]

Yet there remained a heavy measure of discomfort in Wingate's relationships. Alice Hay painted a picture of a man with virtually every military and political hand set against him. On arriving in the Far East he expected opposition from every quarter and, in consequence, over-compensated – believing he had no choice if resistance was to be overcome.

The British had suffered a catastrophic defeat in Burma during 1942. The Japanese proved unstoppable and British forces were pushed across the Chindwin and into India. No-one felt the pain more than Neville Hogan; his country was swallowed by the Japanese. Hogan had been content with life before war came. Things tended to go his way and he had already achieved one ambition:

'I had always wanted to drive a Rolls-Royce. There were only five in Burma and one belonged to the Governor. The other four were Burma Auxiliary Force armoured cars, dating back to the early 1920s or even earlier. I soon got my wish, even if my Rolls-Royce had solid tyres and had seen better days.'

News of the Japanese attack on Pearl Harbor on 7 December 1941 came during Annual Camp:

'We were "embodied" immediately and despatched as a perimeter defence unit for Mingaladon, near Rangoon, the biggest of Burma's two main airfields. The Japanese bombed it on 24 December.'

Hogan watched, frozen in amazement, as a stick of bombs fell neatly between the detachment's four armoured cars and a huge dump of petrol cans. The only damage was a slight dent to one car, caused by shrapnel. A few weeks later they were ordered south to Moulmein. Information about the Japanese advance was scanty and they ran into an ambush nine miles north of their objective. The road was protected against Monsoon floods by high bunds. The enemy had selected a suitable bend and had blocked the road by felling a tree:

'I was driving the lead car when we rounded that bend. I saw four or five Japs firing at us. Our officer opened up with the Vickers. Each car had a crew of four but we had a passenger – a young British Gurkha officer who had been entrusted with a secret message, to be delivered in person. We weren't closed up for action and bullets went through our hatches and sprayed around inside the car. We were all hit, our passenger suffering a fatal wound. He was shot in the stomach and one look was quite enough to realise that there was no hope. I watched, mesmerised, as he put the sheet of paper bearing the message into his mouth and chewed it as he died.'

Neville Hogan received a bullet through his right leg and the others had various wounds. Fortunately, they avoided capture. Hogan was pleased to discover that the bullet had passed cleanly through his calf muscle, without hitting bone. Having evaded the Japanese at the roadblock they began the long trek from Southern Burma to Mandalay and then on towards the Chindwin. Hogan and his companions crossed this huge river and faced the final challenge – walking over the hills to the Tamu-Imphal area: 'I was more frightened of bumping into the Chinese than the Japs. The Chinese would kill you just to get their hands on a weapon.'

The Japanese completed their conquest of Burma by June 1942, stopping on the very borders of India. Hogan had escaped despite being wounded a second time while crossing the Sittang river. The Sittang Bridge was the scene of a major battle:

'We were on the east bank when the Japs came down the hill to attack us. This was my first experience of hand-to-hand fighting. The bridge was blown during the morning of 23 February and we were still on the east side. All we had between us were sidearms and around 20 rounds of .45 ammunition each.

'We scrounged some wood and began making rafts for the Gurkhas – all of whom couldn't swim – and some British non-swimmers. The river was up to 1,000 yards wide. I managed to swim across but many Gurkhas drowned; they refused to leave behind their rifles and steel helmets. During the crossing a mortar bomb exploded near me. Shrapnel hit me in the thigh, once again in the right leg. It felt as though I had been kicked.'

Hogan and his party made a rather exotic group:

'My four friends consisted of an Englishman, a Scot, a Jewish lad and 'Texas', a Persian crazy about America and cowboys. Our cowboy was always pretending to 'draw', like his heroes. Unfortunately, during his first action a bullet struck his weapon and took off the first digit of his trigger finger. He then began to practice drawing from the left. I warned him that, if he carried on, he'd probably get that trigger finger shot off, too.'

The five men were starving by the time they neared the Chindwin in May. During a halt under a tree, the Jewish soldier, 'Shamack', asked each of his comrades if they had anything to eat. Everyone said no. He then turned to Hogan again and asked for an aspirin. Hogan asked him if he had a headache. Shamack said no, adding: 'but I must have something to eat.' Despite their desperate condition they all dissolved into laughter: 'That remark kept us going. We used to say to each other: 'Has anyone got an aspirin for Shamack?'

Neville Hogan got out but many men succumbed when Burma was overrun in 1942. On reaching safety Hogan found he had exchanged one nightmare for another:

'No-one wanted to know us. We had no pay books and no papers to prove we were members of the Rangoon Battalion of the Burma Auxiliary Force. When we reached Calcutta we were out of money and ideas. We pleaded for recognition, adding that we

had all been wounded. Finally, someone listened. We were given clothes and rail warrants to Jhansi, where Burma Auxiliary Force survivors were concentrating. Subsequently, a new force was established, known as the Burma Intelligence Corps.'

Hogan's qualities won him rapid recognition. He was promoted to Captain and, later, Major, despite his tender years.

In the aftermath of the 1942 debacle General Wavell was receptive to new ideas. Orde Wingate was in his thoughts. He had supported Wingate following the Cairo suicide attempt. He was impressed by the successes of Gideon Force and Wingate's earlier achievements in Palestine. Given the virtual collapse of British Army morale in the Far East, Wavell had nothing to lose. He invited Wingate to present ideas for a reversal of fortunes.[11]

Unfortunately, Wingate was still dogged by a belief that he had been wronged. A diary entry for 19 February 1942 – just a few weeks before he arrived in the Far East – conveys his despondency and bitterness:

The Commander of the Patriot Forces in the most successful campaign we have had in this war is, for political reasons, reduced to Major from full Colonel at its close ... he writes a report considered important enough to be read by several members of the Cabinet, evolving a new theory of modern war and asking leave to apply it on some scale, however modest. His report, although in the hands of the War Office, is ignored by that establishment. He is not asked to see a solitary Staff Officer. Finally, immediately after his being noticed as still interesting himself in the affairs of Ethiopia, he is ordered away to a job derogatory to his military qualifications and seniority, in an artillery regiment ...[19]

Wingate's arrival, in March 1942, came too late to have any material effect on the Japanese advance through Burma. He had time, however, to develop ideas for countering enemy battle tactics. Wingate, now a full Colonel, saw how Japanese flanking and blocking tactics had disastrous consequences for all opponents relying on roads and conventional lines of communication. He then saw that air-dropped supplies could overcome this weakness. Allen wrote:

At one stroke this destroyed the soldier's dependence on a land line of communication. He could have everything, food, water, post, mules, jeeps, guns, ferried through the skies to wherever he happened to be. The only requisite was an efficient wireless system to signal dropping points with accuracy. With this advantage, Wingate saw that a force penetrating Japanese-held territory, to disrupt lines of communication, 'would achieve results out of all proportion to its size.'[20]

Orde Wingate's rapidly developing LRP ideas found a receptive mind in Major (later, Brigadier) Michael Calvert, then resident at Maymyo Bush Warfare School. They were kindred spirits. On returning to Delhi, Wingate then sought to persuade Wavell. He was a master at selling an idea. Slim wrote:

Wingate was a strange, excitable, moody creature, but he had fire in him. He could ignite other men. When he so fiercely advocated some project of his own, you might catch his enthusiasm or you might see palpable flaws in his arguments; you might be angry at his arrogance or outraged at so obvious a belief in the end, his end, justifying any means; but you could not be indifferent.[21]

The vulnerability of Japanese lines of communication in Burma was central to Wingate's plan. Future Chindit Column and Brigade Commander Bernard Fergusson said Wingate saw that a small force behind the lines 'could wreak havoc out of all proportion to its numbers'. If surprised it could disperse, evade pursuers and come together at an agreed rendezvous. Wingate appreciated the true significance of two innovations: air supply and wireless communications. He concluded that they had yet to be fully exploited. Fergusson added: 'His proposal was to cut the enemy's supply line, destroy his dumps, tie up troops unprofitably far behind the line, in the endeavour to protect these vulnerable areas, and generally help the Army proper on to its objectives.'[22]

A training centre for LRP troops was established near Gwalior, in the Central Provinces, during August 1942. Wingate would command this force, 77 Indian Infantry Brigade, and he would now have the chance to prove his theories. Michael Calvert (*Fighting Mad*) wrote:

Whatever anyone thought of Wingate and his methods, I don't think his sincerity was ever questioned. He was flat out to beat the Japs; that was the task in hand and everything was subservient to it.

He was not concerned if some of the things he did were unpopular: his only yardstick was whether they were necessary. This attitude was not everyone's cup of tea and perhaps it is not surprising that he made enemies. But I never blamed him for the way he acted, for I knew that at heart he

was the most understanding of men. He believed that the way to beat the Japs was to be tougher than they were and he drove himself relentlessly, as well as everyone else, to prove this. He could be very morose and depressed, but he would allow only his close friends to see his distress. I think these dark moods came from the strain that he built up inside himself; yet he would never relax his self-imposed disciplines. The tragedy is that he never lived to see the result of his personal sacrifices.[23]

Events in this theatre of war now offered the promise of a brighter future, following the dark days of 1942. Wingate's proposals were accepted. Furthermore, the first USAAF personnel had been in India for some months. Arriving in March 1942, these pioneers went on to establish Tenth Air Force, responsible for air supply flights over the Himalayas ('The Hump') and progressing an air campaign against the Japanese in Burma. US Army Engineers began constructing the Ledo Road out of India in December 1942. The aim was to link up with the Burma Road. The plan was to complete the 103 miles to Shingbwiyang by June 1943. The Ledo Road, however, had only reached the 83-mile marker by October 1943 – a measure of the Japanese Army's stubborn hold on Burma.[24]

The pieces fell into place for Wingate and his first expedition, Operation *Longcloth*. His future Chindits – with the exception of Calvert – had no inkling of what lay before them. Bill Smyly, meanwhile, had got his wish. He was back in the Far East, having been commissioned in the 2nd Gurkha Rifles. Jungle warfare was the very last thing on his mind:

'*I was thrilled with the whole thing, including Dehra Dun, in the Himalayan foothills. Most Saturdays I danced, or, rather, learned to dance, with the Colonel's daughter, Jean Fell, 14.*'

Having passed the obligatory language examination, Smyly was posted to the Regiment's 3rd Battalion, destined for Wingate's expedition. As a Brigade, the *Longcloth* force was rather small: two Battalions of infantry (one British and one Gurkha), a Battalion of The Burma Rifles (Burrifs) and specialised units, including the essential engineering expertise. The force was organised into eight Columns, each of around 400 men. Later, 6 Column was broken up during training, to bring the others up to strength as the unfit were weeded out. The Burrifs were distributed among the seven Columns. Bill Smyly:

'The Infantry Companies, the heart of each Column, were either British or Gurkha: 13th King's and 3rd/2nd Gurkhas, one Rifle Company to each Column. The transport Muleteers in all Columns were young Gurkhas, a special draft of 'Burma Gurkhas' from the 10th Gurkha Rifles.'

Wingate made a vivid first impression on virtually everyone he met. Smyly, who rapidly developed his own reputation as a highly effective Animal Transport Officer, was no exception:

'Wingate was inscrutable and didn't aim to charm! His tactic was to shock or impress but, that aside, it was clear he was on the ball. During training I remember going down the line, checking the mules. I had a habit of starting at the head and moving my hand down the neck to the withers. If there was a shiver on the withers he was tender and likely to gall. I was doing this when I felt there was someone standing behind me and looked round. It was Wingate: "How are they?" "A bit tender. No galls so far."

'As for LRP, we were told we were going to disrupt Jap communications in Burma, but it was not really clear what we were going to do. We would blow up bridges and cut railway lines but it all sounded a bit ad hoc. Any request for more detailed information was brushed aside on security grounds: 'It will all become clear once you are in.' It never was!'

Bill Towill had experienced the full horror and human loss of defeat in France but had a gentle introduction to service life in the Far East. Later, however, he took part in the vicious Arakan campaign and served with the Chindits. Towill arrived in Bombay in 1941 and attended the Indian Military Academy at Dehra Dun – the Indian Sandhurst:

'We were housed in beautifully appointed marquees, two to each marquee. The cadet sharing with me was Peter Whitehouse. He was a few years older than me and during his time at Oxford had won no less than four 'Blues', a quite remarkable record. Yet, though he was such an outstanding sportsman, he was quite unassuming and we got on famously. He was also a keen Christian, so on Sunday we decided to go to the cantonment church for the morning service. Afterwards we were greeted by two officers from the 9th Gurkha Rifles' regimental centre, just up the hill at a place called Birpur. We were also warmly welcomed by a lovely lady, Mrs Wise, who invited us to afternoon tea. This became a regular Sunday afternoon fixture for Peter and myself and another cadet, John Pearson, whom we had met at

the church. Mrs Wise had three daughters and the two eldest, Pamela and Patricia, were just about to go off to Simla for finishing school. Little did I know then that Pamela was to become my wife. We are still together after more than 60 years of marriage!'

Life was sweet at the Academy:

'We enjoyed wonderful food and well-appointed tables, with sparkling silverware and crisp napkins. This environment was entirely free of snobbery. I enjoyed it immensely, despite being pushed very hard. This was a condensed course of just four months, rather than the more usual 18 months. When we came to the end, Peter desperately wanted me to go with him to the Rajputana Rifles, a famous Indian regiment with which he had family connections; but I had fallen under the spell of the Gurkhas and opted for the 9th Gurkha Rifles. So Peter and I had a last wonderful holiday together in Kashmir, where we stayed on a houseboat on Dal Lake. At Rawalpindi we said goodbye to each other and I never saw him again. He was killed in action serving with the 1st Battalion of his regiment in Italy. What a terrible, terrible waste of what would almost certainly have been a marvellous life.'

In common with Neville Hogan, 2nd Lieutenant (later, Major) Towill saw some hard fighting before crossing Wingate's path:

'I did not follow the usual course for newly commissioned officers. I was not sent to the regimental centre, to be indoctrinated into the ways of the regiment, but went direct to the 3rd Battalion at a place called Jhikargacha Ghat. This was on the main railway line into Calcutta. We were brigaded with the 6th/11th Sikhs and 8th/8th Punjabis, to form the 4th Indian Infantry Brigade, part of 26th Division. It was easy to get into Calcutta for weekend leaves, so I took the earliest opportunity of calling at the address which Mrs Wise had given us, that to which she was shortly returning from Dehra Dun.

'I received a tremendous welcome from Mr and Mrs Wise and they wouldn't hear of me booking into a hotel but put up a bed for me on the veranda. It was a great delight to enjoy their hospitality on many occasions. Mr Wise was a Senior Director with Andrew Yule, a huge firm of managing agents, and, as such, managed all the affairs in India of an American oil company, Veedol Oil. The Wises were exceedingly hospitable, the dinner table was always laid for 12 and servicemen and women, regardless of rank, came in and filled the places, often without giving advance notice. There usually followed a *sing-song around the piano and a surprising amount of talent was displayed.'*

Bill Towill was sent on a driving and maintenance course in early 1943. On returning in March he found the Battalion, together with the rest of the Division, had gone into the Arakan. On reaching Brigade HQ he reported to his Colonel, Robbie Fawcett, who had bad news for Towill. Having achieved a course distinction, he had been ordered back as an instructor! Towill protested. Fawcett helped him to evade this unwanted posting but then sent him to Brigade HQ as Orderly Officer. He was also in charge of the HQ Defence Platoon:

'We were in the 'Tunnels' area and over the next couple of days moved south to contact the enemy. It was blisteringly hot. The sun drilled down on us from above and, with equal force, was reflected back from the whitish sand and stony ground over which we marched. I was to the rear of the Brigadier, in the recognised Gunga Din position – four paces right flank rear. He, Brigadier Hungerford, was a wonderful old gentleman but in his early forties and extremely ancient! As we were virtually grilled alive, I could see him gradually crumpling up.

'The Brigade had various brushes with the Japs, inflicting several casualties and receiving some ourselves, but it soon became clear that one of our problems, in urgent need of attention, was fire control. We had to avoid the temptation, when the Japs came screaming at our positions at night, just to loose off at them indiscriminately and in great volume, rather than firing only at a target actually seen.

'At one place I got the Defence Platoon in position for the night and warned them strictly about fire control. These orders were not easy to obey when unprotected by wire. In a dash of a very few yards, the enemy could be right in among us. But when the Japs came that night, screaming, shouting and firing, the volume of fire we loosed off in return was horrendous. There was, as I saw it, only one thing to do. Each offender I spotted received an enormous kick in the backside. My men came to fear me more than the Japs and, gradually, we got things under control. Looking back, I think I was extremely lucky not to have stopped a bullet.

'One of our officers, Major Frank Gerald "Jimmy" Blaker, won an outstanding MC in the Arakan. We were at a place called Taung Bazaar and a villager told Jimmy that there were about 50 Japs resting up in a nullah half a mile away. Taking two Platoons, Jimmy approached with extreme caution, took them by surprise, chased them for two miles, killed 16 and captured three, including an officer – the first to be captured in the Arakan – for the loss of two killed (one by a sword stroke) and a few lightly wounded. At that time there was so little good news from the front that Jimmy's exploit spread wide and proved a great morale booster.

'The real objective in the Arakan was to improve our supply lines by capturing Akyab, the only good port between Chittagong and Rangoon. In front of Akyab, however, the Japs had a line of very strong bunkered positions at Donbaik. When our Brigadier was evacuated sick, A.W. "Bill" Lowther took his place. He had commanded a Punjabi Battalion which had taken part in an attack on Donbaik. With great courage they had managed to get on top of one of the enemy strongpoints, only to be met by horrendous fire from adjoining positions. In less than half an hour Bill Lowther lost nearly half his Battalion. When he became our Brigadier he talked about this awful experience.

'In the Arakan we were forced back further than the line from which we had started and the Tunnels area, on the Maungdaw/Buthidaung road, with its splendid shelter, was converted by the Japs into a formidable defensive position, which was later to prove exceptionally difficult to recapture.'

❖

Alec Gibson had been recommended for a commission but OCTUs in Britain were over-subscribed. He and several others in his Battalion had the chance to attend OTU in India. Gibson went to the Far East and was commissioned into the Indian Army. In early January 1943 Indian Army units received a 'round-robin' calling for young officers surplus to requirements. No-one knew why they were wanted, but it had been realised that Wingate's *Longcloth* venture offered an ideal opportunity to train a relatively large number of junior officers as Platoon leaders. Typically, a Gurkha Company would be commanded by a Captain, assisted by one or more young British officers. The decision to draw in more junior officers for *Longcloth* was made at the last minute. One consequence was 2nd Lieutenant (later, Captain) Alec Gibson's immediate posting from 8th Gurkha Rifles Headquarters, Quetta, to Jhansi.

Gibson was accompanied by Harold James and Ian MacHorton (later to write a remarkable account of his survival, on being wounded and left behind during *Longcloth*). The three were posted to 3rd/2nd Gurkha Rifles. When they called on the Transport Officer at Jhansi, they were not encouraged by his off-hand comment: 'Oh! You're going to that lot in the jungle.' Alec Gibson became Cypher Officer with 3 Column during Operation *Longcloth*.

2nd Lieutenant MacHorton, meanwhile, was among those struck by Wingate's strange behaviour. During his jungle training he saw Wingate walking around holding a large, ticking alarm clock – presumably to remind everyone that there was no time to waste.[25]

Clearly, Wingate was a special man. The renowned explorer Wilfred Thesiger, who served with Wingate in Abyssinia, wrote with great perception and frankness about Wingate and his character. He described him as 'ruthlessly ambitious' and an 'idealist and a fanatic'. He also referred to Wingate's 'ungovernable temper'. Yet, on one occasion, Thesiger caught a glimpse of Wingate's true self:

> Personally, I was fortunate in my relationship with Wingate and he was never rude to me. Yet only once did I get past his self-imposed barrier. The two of us were sitting on a rock looking across a great sweep of mountain. Unexpectedly, he relaxed and began to talk. He told me of his stern, puritanical upbringing, his unhappy days at school, his unpopularity at Woolwich, his passion for fox-hunting and steeple-chasing and his dedication to Zionism. I asked him why he became a Zionist, not being a Jew. He answered that his interest in the Jews dated from his prep school, where he had been mercilessly bullied and the boys had organised what they called 'Wingate hunts'. He had been brought up on the Bible by devout parents and in those unhappy schooldays had found in the Old Testament a people who never gave in, though every man's hand was against them. He had accordingly identified them with himself. Perhaps in those early days Wingate's character had been permanently warped; yet, perhaps, it had been tempered too, and made resolute.[26]

Thesiger was in a good position to appreciate the meaning of Wingate's references to the bullying he had suffered. He referred to his own 'hurtful rejection' on arriving at prep school as a young boy, fresh from Abyssinia and entering 'an alien English world'.[27]

Notes

1. Cross, J.P. (1989), *Jungle Warfare*, 27–28
2. Ibid, 47
3. Slim, Field Marshal Viscount (1999), *Defeat into Victory*, 538
4. Cross, 80
5. Rooney, D. (2000), *Wingate and the Chindits: Redressing the Balance*, 13–21
6. Ibid, 22–26
7. Ibid, 27–35
8. Ibid, 36–40
9. Ibid, 43–46
10. Hay, Alice Ivy (1963), *There Was a Man of Genius: Letters to my Grandson, Orde Jonathan Wingate*, 90–91
11. Allen, L. (1986), *Burma: The Longest War 1941–45*, 118–119
12. Hay (1963), 95
13. Rooney (2000), 70
14. Ibid, 71–75
15. Hay (1963), 100
16. Halley, D. (1945), *With Wingate in Burma*, 26
17. Stibbe, P. (1995), *Return via Rangoon*, 20
18. Hay (1963), 101
19. Ibid, 97
20. Allen (1986), 120–121
21. Slim, 162
22. Fergusson, B. (1971), *Beyond the Chindwin*, 21
23. Calvert, M. (1996), *Fighting Mad*, 70
24. Larson, G.A. (2008), *Aerial Assault into Burma*, 107
25. MacHorton, I. (1958), *Safer Than a Known Way*, 68–69
26. Thesiger, W. (1988), *The Life of my Choice*, 333
27. Ibid, 432

2

OPERATION *LONGCLOTH*: AN EXPERIMENT IN CHINDIT WARFARE

Though they were to undertake an unprecedented operation, the men of 77 Indian Infantry Brigade were ordinary soldiers ... only the men of 142 Commando Company and the men of the Bush Warfare School in Burma could be called dedicated Special Forces.

William Fowler, We Gave Our Today

THE EVOLUTION of jungle fighting in Burma had a certain logic to it. Major Michael Calvert took a central role. He was a master of irregular warfare and extremely aggressive in his approach to combat in any environment. Earlier in the war he was a Demolitions Instructor at Lochailort Commando Training School, Scotland. He found a soulmate in Freddie Spencer Chapman, author of *The jungle is neutral,* who was in charge of fieldcraft training at Lochailort. Both were posted to Australia in October 1940 to join the newly established Infantry Training Centre at Wilson's Promontory, south of Melbourne.

Calvert later said that the fieldcraft skills shared by Chapman saved his life on several occasions in Burma. Rooney (*Mad Mike*) wrote:

He cited, in particular, training his eye to recognise a good spot for an ambush – whether to set one up or to avoid an enemy ambush – and, equally important, to listen and understand the noises of the jungle, especially the sign of danger when all animal noises fall silent.[1]

Calvert outlined the fundamentals set out by Freddie Spencer Chapman:

The first big lesson he taught me was always to be on the lookout for the likely ambush spot, such as the piece of rising ground ahead covered with rocks or trees or high undergrowth ... this had to be an automatic task, as the eyes took in the surroundings at any given moment. The second lesson ... which saved my life more than once, was that birds stopped singing, and most other wild animals also

became quiet and still, when human beings were near them.

A 1943 Indian Army Manual defined three types of jungle:

'Thin': jungle in which a man can move at a fair pace by picking his way.
'Thick': jungle a man can force his way through with the aid of a stick, without cutting.
'Dense': jungle so thick that cutting a way is essential.[2]

Jungle is often defined as 'primary' (vegetation in its original state) and 'secondary' (jungle cleared and regenerated). According to Cross, jungle combat

... is the nearest to night fighting that troops will get during daylight. In primary jungle visibility is usually limited to 20–30 yards. Foliage on the hilltops is relatively thin, compared to the extremely dense jungle in the valleys.[2]

Michael Calvert became an expert jungle fighter. In August 1941 he was posted as Chief Instructor at the Bush Warfare School, Maymyo, Burma. He was to train instructors for Chiang Kai-shek's Chinese. This ended with the Japanese invasion of Burma in January 1942. Rangoon fell on 8 March, Lashio on 29 April and Mandalay on 1 May. Myitkyina fell a week later.[3]

The Japanese were nearing Maymyo in late April. Calvert took a small force to hold the Gokteik Viaduct, a vital crossing on the Mandalay-Lashio road. Later, he sought permission to blow the viaduct but was refused. Subsequently, he was shocked when Lieutenant General

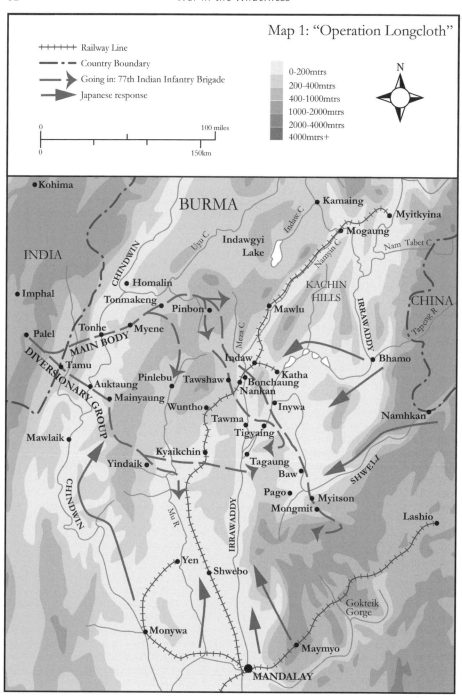

Map 1: "Operation Longcloth"

(later, Field Marshal, Lord) Alexander expressed disappointment at his 'failure' to destroy it. Calvert reminded him that he had been refused permission. Alexander replied that sensitivities had precluded official approval but he had thought it likely that Calvert, of all people, would disobey orders and blow it anyway!

Calvert participated in a deception allowing the Japanese to 'capture' secret documents in a staff car deliberately driven into enemy positions. The aim was to persuade the Japanese to make inappropriate troop deployments. The car was abandoned under fire. Calvert's group clashed with the Japanese and then dispersed. Calvert and two companions eventually reached the Chindwin. They were in a very poor state and received help from a party of Indian refugees. They reached safety disguised as women, dressed in saris.[4] During these adventures Calvert shrank from over 12 stone to less than eight stone.

Other exploits included a foray involving around 70 men from the Bush Warfare School. They commandeered a river steamer and set out to kill Japanese.[3] Such obvious eagerness to get to grips with the enemy attracted Orde Wingate's attention. After initial discussions at Maymyo, he summoned Calvert to Delhi to discuss a possible Long Range Penetration (LRP) operation in Burma during early 1943.

By August 1942 Calvert and Wingate were together at Gwalior, the newly established LRP training camp south of Delhi. They had much in common. Calvert's battle experience ranged from Shanghai to Norway. He also had the experience gained in Burma earlier in the year. Wingate's unpopularity was of no importance to Calvert and later, he would share in the consequences.[5]

Wavell and Wingate agreed that a Brigade-scale LRP expedition, Operation *Longcloth*, would attack Japanese lines of communication and attempt to force the enemy to withdraw units from the front.[6] Two British offensives were planned for 1943. The first was an attempt to seize the port of Akyab, in the Arakan, and ended in failure.[7] *Longcloth* was part of the second: an incursion into enemy territory coinciding with a push into Northern Burma by IV Corps from Imphal, Stilwell's Chinese from Ledo and Chinese forces from Yunnan. Wingate's 77 Indian Infantry Brigade would consist of the 13th King's Regiment (Liverpool) (The King's), the 3rd/2nd Gurkha Rifles (2 GR), 142 Commando and a unit of 2nd Burma Rifles (Burrifs), together with Signals, RAF detachments and HQ. The Brigade, totalling some 3,000 men, would penetrate the Japanese front, march some 200 miles towards Indaw and cut enemy lines of communication, attacking roads, railways, bridges and supply dumps.[8]

This Brigade was organised into eight Columns, broadly four British and four Gurkha. Each Column had three Infantry Platoons, a Support Platoon with mortars and Vickers machine guns and a Commando Platoon of sappers and infantry, for demolition tasks. There was also a Reconnaissance (Recce) Platoon of two officers and around 45 Burrifs. Fowler (*We Gave Our Today*) wrote: 'Though they were to undertake an unprecedented operation, the men of 77 Indian Infantry Brigade were ordinary soldiers ... only the men of 142 Commando Company and the men of the Bush Warfare School in Burma could be called dedicated Special Forces.'[9]

Each man now faced an extraordinary challenge. The harsh training reflected the many hardships and suffering ahead. Weaknesses were soon exposed. The King's had a higher than normal percentage of older men. Allen made a blunt comment:

> He (Wingate) was given a British Battalion which, on the surface, could hardly have been worse suited to the task he had in mind. This was the 13th King's (Liverpool). They had been on coastal defence duties in England before being drafted out to serve as garrisons in India. They were city-bred men, not only from Liverpool but from Glasgow and Manchester; most of them were married and many were over 30.[10]

The King's were at Secunderabad, on garrison duty, when the prospect of jungle fighting reared its head. Philip Stibbe, in *Return via Rangoon*, reflected wryly: 'Life there was enjoyable. All this would probably have gone on indefinitely had it not been for Brigadier Wingate.'[11]

The Brigadier relished a challenge. In his view any unit could be trained to meet the extraordinary LRP standards of fitness. Early on, this claim looked precarious. Large numbers of King's soldiers went sick. At one stage 70 per cent were absent from duty! Wingate's confidence seemed misplaced but as training continued the Battalion was transformed. The men became fit and hard. The Gurkhas, meanwhile, presented other challenges – especially a lack of enthusiasm for river crossings. The importance of this training became apparent in August 1942, when a Monsoon cloudburst flooded their jungle camp and the nearby river rose 30 ft. According to Rooney, Wingate and Calvert were among those who had to swim for it.[5]

The 'shake-out' of personnel was ruthless. At one point the King's strength fell from around 650 to 400 and 2 GR from 750 to 500. Inevitably, inexperienced men filled the gaps.[6]

Sickness rates soared in the incessant rain. Sick men leaving the King's were the envy of the others. Philip

Stibbe wrote: 'Colonel Robinson, who regarded the chance of going into Burma with Wingate as the most wonderful luck, was horrified and genuinely mystified by this attitude'. Robinson called a parade and gave everyone a piece of his mind. As far as he was concerned, the unfit were not 'lucky blighters' but 'poor devils'. Ironically, Wingate later decided Robinson was too old to go in.[12]

As for the high proportion of city men, Bernard Fergusson, who was to lead 5 Column, made a comment supporting Wingate's belief in the ability to train any unit for LRP: 'it is a fact that, in jungle warfare, the countryman has no advantage over the townsman after the first week of training'.[13]

Men responded differently to the jungle environment. Bob Hobbs did well, building on his reputation as a crack shot. He was made up to Sergeant before *Longcloth* began:

'I loved the jungle. I was my own boss. I could almost please myself. The rations were good – we had two large tins of bully each week. I also liked the biscuits, but they had to be soaked in tea, to soften them up.'

Hobbs shined and became a Sergeant-Major: 'I wanted to get on in the Army. I had an older brother who stayed a Private. Perhaps I wanted to show him'. His only setback was an attack of Dengue Fever: 'I think I caught this due to my habit of going for a cooling swim in the lake near our training area. Anyway, I soon recovered'.

Others had to work to settle into jungle life and the harsh LRP regime. Bill Smyly became Animal Transport Officer (ATO) with 5 Column:

'On one occasion during training I took a horse and rode back along the line of march to help the stragglers. One man grabbed a stirrup and another did the same on the other side. Others then hung onto their shoulders and, within a couple of minutes, I was towing a V-shaped formation of very tired men. The horse dragged them to the Column head and I went back for more. This worked splendidly in India but was no use in Burma. The tracks we used weren't wide enough. The Gurkhas thought the whole thing hilarious.'

Philip Stibbe described Smyly's arrival, in the company of his mules: 'He was a wonderful horseman and although being only nineteen – he was the youngest man in the Column – woe betide anyone, officer or other rank, who did not show due respect for his mules'.[14]

Smyly offers some interesting views on Fergusson, his own Column Commander, and 3 Column's Michael Calvert:

'Fergusson was a 'gent' – one of the old-fashioned aristocracy – but very different from Calvert (also a bit of a toff in his way). Fergusson lacked Calvert's overall grasp of Wingate's intentions. Calvert was a man among men, with a huge appetite for battle. His only interest was to get to grips with the Japanese. There was a nice story about Calvert in his Daily Telegraph obituary. During the retreat from Burma, he burst open the door of a village house he expected to be full of Gurkhas. Instead, he found Japanese officers at a staff meeting.'

There was a moment of silence and the Corporal standing alongside Calvert whispered, 'They're Japs!' Calvert then spoke: 'Excuse me, Gentlemen. Wrong door!' He closed the door behind them and heard a shout of laughter from the room as they fled.

'Fergusson was different. He had a very human temperament and a playful sense of humour. He knew every man's name and had an unusual sense of duty towards them. When Longcloth was over and Fergusson was back in Britain he wrote a letter to the families of every member of 5 Column. At that time I had been posted missing and he visited my parents, living in Dulwich.'

Fergusson and Calvert left compelling accounts of both Chindit campaigns. Fergusson's *Beyond the Chindwin* (Operation *Longcloth*) and *The Wild Green Earth* (Operation *Thursday*), are memorials to the courage and endurance of every Chindit. Calvert's *Prisoners of Hope* is definitive.

Orde Wingate's LRP Brigade consisted of seven Columns when *Longcloth* began; 6 Column's men plugged gaps left by the sick and those who couldn't cope with the training. The Columns formed two groups. The main force, 2 (Northern) Group (Lieutenant-Colonel S.A. 'Sam' Cooke), consisted of Calvert's 3 Column, Major Conron's 4 Column (Conron was later succeeded by Major Bromhead), Fergusson's 5 Column, Major Ken Gilkes' 7 Column and Major Walter Scott's 8 Column. 1 (Southern) Group, a diversionary force, was commanded by Lieutenant-Colonel Alexander and had two Columns: Major George Dunlop's 1 Column and Major Emmett's 2 Column. The 2nd Burma Rifles was commanded by Lieutenant-Colonel L.G. Wheeler. Wingate would lead the Brigade into Burma. Bill Smyly:

'We knew the Columns by their Commanders – Scott Column, Gilkes Column, Fergusson, Calvert and so on. We knew their names like we knew the Hollywood film stars. During training it was said that Major Gilkes, of

7 Column, wore out a new pair of boots in his efforts to wear them in!'

The first Brigade-scale exercise began in late September 1942. Many men must have questioned Wingate's parentage as the ruthless jungle training began to bite. During those early, exhausting marches, Philip Stibbe found he had an advantage:

> At school I had been made to learn by heart at least 12 lines of verse each day. 'Repetition' we called it and we thought it an archaic custom. Now, tramping through the Central Provinces of India, I passed the time recalling those lines and the miles seemed so much shorter.[15]

The men may have blamed Wingate for their lot yet they took him to their hearts at the same time. It is not easy to pinpoint exactly why Wingate so rapidly won such deep and long-lasting regard. Wavell's comment may touch the truth: 'No really great man is easy to serve and he was a stern taskmaster ... but all those worth their salt would rather attempt hard tasks under a great man than serve at ease under a lesser.'[16]

Men who could take such training took pride in their endurance. Beyond stuffy individuals who dislike any idiosyncrasy, most were amused by their Commander's eccentricities. Michael Calvert was already accustomed to Wingate's unusual behaviour, including his habit of dictating orders while naked and his preference for buffalo milk (he had four buffaloes stationed at Brigade HQ, to guarantee supply).

After its first large-scale exercise 77 Brigade marched north, reaching a remote camp near Malthone. Meanwhile, the search for a name for the new force, to replace the clumsy 'Long Range Penetration', produced results. According to Calvert, Wingate had talked with a holy man about a fabulous beast – described by some as half lion, half eagle. *Chinthé* statues guard the Burmese pagodas and Wingate saw a link between strength on the ground (the lion) and strength in the air (the eagle), reflecting his new concept for jungle warfare. It was a short step from '*Chinthe*' to 'Chindit', although the term did not take firm root until *Longcloth* was over.[17]

Sergeant Tony Aubrey of The King's set down his impressions of his first jungle training march. It began at 05.00 on 19 September 1942. He set out on this 52-mile trek only seven days after arriving in India. The first day was exhausting: 'The one and only vehicle attached to our long Column was an ambulance.'[18]

Aubrey saw several training accidents, including the death of a Commando instructing in the use of gelignite:

'An unusual sense of duty': Major (later, Brigadier) Bernard Fergusson commanded 5 Column during the 1943 expedition, Operation *Longcloth*, and 16 Brigade during the second, Operation *Thursday*, in 1944. Fergusson was always extremely well turned-out. This photograph was taken at the end of the 1944 operation, before he had the chance to clean up! (Trustees of the Imperial War Museum)

Carried away with zeal, he attempted the hazardous feat of tamping a stick home into its appointed hole with his bayonet. The gelignite resented such cavalier treatment. The demonstrator took no further interest in the expedition thereafter, being very dead, and one of the demonstratees had his leg blown off.[19]

When *Longcloth* began Aubrey was no novice. He had been a member of a small recce team which reached and crossed the Chindwin in December 1942. When he got back he found 6 Column had broken up and he moved to Scott's 8 Column.[20]

The 'signature' of Chindit warfare was the 'Everest' backpack. Bernard Fergusson regarded this as 'by no means a bad gadget but one has to have plenty of careful fitting before using it, or the weight is thrown on to the ball of the foot, with dire results...'[21]

The passage of the years has failed to soften recollections of that heavy pack. Fergusson wrote with disarming honesty:

As soon as I get a pack on my back I begin to develop a grievance. Woe betide anybody who talks to me as I march along, especially anybody who tries to be funny ... This goes on until I halt, when my pack comes off my back, the restriction on my blood vessels is eased and the milk of human kindness courses through me to such effect that I would offer the Devil himself a cup of tea.[22]

Skin problems developed after a few weeks of jungle living. Wet clothing and chaffing from packs and equipment aggravated them. In *Beyond the Chindwin*, Fergusson described the Chindit's burden:

The total weight on the man when we first set out was about 72 pounds – half the weight of the average man and more, in proportion to a man's weight, than the load carried by a mule. The Everest pack fitting alone weighed six pounds; seven days' rations 14 pounds ... Bren guns were carried on mules. The men also carried rifle and bayonet, dah or kukri, three grenades, groundsheet, spare shirt and trousers, four spare pairs of socks, jack-knife, rubber shoes, 'housewife', toggle-rope, canvas lifejacket, mess tin, ration bags, water bottle, chagul (water carrier) and many statutory odds and ends.[23]

The men grew tougher and stronger; but there were many late arrivals. They included Alec Gibson, joining 2 GR. He and Harold James were allocated to Calvert's 3 Column, Gibson becoming Cypher Officer. Captain Hastings, Adjutant at 2 Group, was unimpressed as he gazed at the new arrivals, dressed in their best uniforms. He asked dryly: 'Have you made your wills? We are going into Burma in three days.' Gibson was taken aback: 'They had been training for months but I had no jungle experience. In fact, I'd never been in the jungle! Furthermore, I spoke only a few words of Urdu and had no Gurkhali.' Fortunately, Gibson was extremely fit. He had risen through the ranks and long periods of infantry training had hardened him:

'The first day's march with full kit wasn't too bad, but the mules kept shedding their loads. I had the job of looking after those mules carrying wireless and other signals-related equipment. This was a new experience! I was very cautious around the animals and managed to avoid getting kicked. I soon discovered that mules are cunning. They expand their bellies as the girth is tightened, frustrating all efforts to stop loads slipping. The trick was to give them a kick at exactly the right moment. Our mules had not been debrayed and made plenty of noise.'

Section mules carrying weapons, wireless and other heavy gear were led by British Muleteers, one per animal. Gurkha Muleteers led the other mules, one per two animals. 5 Column ATO Bill Smyly had a fiery temperament and was an aggressive defender of animal welfare. Fergusson wrote: 'He was always, in consequence, in a state of feud with someone or other and I had my work cut out to keep the peace.'[24]

Men developed real affection for the mules. Michael Calvert had a soft spot for 'Mabel'. 'It is difficult to recall just how she differed from other mules, but there was that certain something about her.' Mule meat would help save many a Chindit *in extremis*, but 'no-one would have thought of eating Mabel'. This mule became Column mascot in Burma and returned safely to India.[17]

Fergusson's feelings for mules were entirely in character:

Of mules I should like to celebrate the virtues in a great epic poem. I love them from the tip of their Bolshie ears to the outer rim of their highly suspect hind hooves. The patient eyes and courageous hearts of the great family of mules move me with a real affection.[25]

Something about the extraordinary mental pressures of Chindit warfare appears to have worked on men's minds. Fergusson noted that some became passionately fond of their mules: 'I have seen men weeping at a mule's death who have not wept at a comrade's. I have seen men jeer at another Platoon whose mules were having to be helped to their feet, when their own had successfully negotiated whatever obstacle had proved too hard.' Fergusson recalled a Jock grabbing a mule's hairy ear, bringing it down to his mouth like a telephone receiver and speaking into it: 'Hallo, there!'[26]

Mules made a real contribution to Column morale. Bernard Fergusson:

The mules did more than their share in keeping us in a good temper and their fabled obstinacy, translated into terms of sticking to their job through thick and thin without urging, is a rare and fine quality. Their determination not to be left behind was pathetic and I shall always remember, as one of the saddest sights I have seen, the spectacle of a mule refusing to leave its half-Section, who was succumbing to a bullet wound. They were two animals who always refused to be separated and had to be worked together; they had come to us together and the men who brought them told us that they had never been apart. By the banks of the Irrawaddy one of them laid down and died; the other stood

Follow my leader: the 'Column Snake' crosses a river. This photograph was taken during the 1944 expedition. The Chindit in the left foreground is carrying a Sten gun. (Jim Unsworth)

and nuzzled it long after the breath had gone out of its body. At last it consented to come with us, but it was never any good again. It pined away to nothing, and, at last, we had to eat it.[26]

Flight Lieutenant Robert Thompson (later, Sir Robert Thompson, KBE, CMG, DSO, MC) joined Calvert's 3 Column. His first job was to train and fit out large mules to carry RAF wireless sets: 'The key with mules was to get their backs hardened and their saddles well fitted. This last required a lot of manipulating with long needles, to shift the stuffing into the right place.'[27]

New skills were acquired. Column Commanders and their officers learned how to select a track. Fergusson wrote: 'We learned never to despise a track that was only just off our line of advance. If it ran within 20 deg. of the right bearing, it was well worth using.'[28] The Columns' maps showed far fewer tracks than actually existed. Conflicts between map, compass and instinct were resolved by following the compass. Guides were of limited use, as their knowledge was highly localised. Security was paramount – guides were told the bare minimum and released only when they could do no harm if they talked.[29]

If the heavy pack was the signature of Chindit warfare, the Column Snake was its form. The advantages of a single file advance by 400 men and their animals outweighed the disadvantages, according to Fergusson (who should know, given that he marched into Burma twice). The Column Snake was difficult to control but also difficult to attack. Fergusson: 'If the leading Platoon gets involved, there is ample time for the rest of the Column to deploy and prepare for the engagement.' The main drawback is the fatigue of those towards the rear. Dozens of minor checks, lasting just a few seconds, increase in duration down the Column. Large gaps may appear, with those at the rear always struggling to catch up.[29]

An attempt would be made to solve this problem in 1944. Each Special Force Column eventually received six shoebox-sized walkie-talkies, to report gaps to the Column head.[30] This equipment was cumbersome and heavy; many walkie-talkies were 'lost' at the first opportunity.

Much depended on jungle density and the difficulty of the terrain. Gaps tended not to appear when the going was difficult, as progress, overall, was so slow. Bernard Fergusson: 'The irritating factor wasn't the

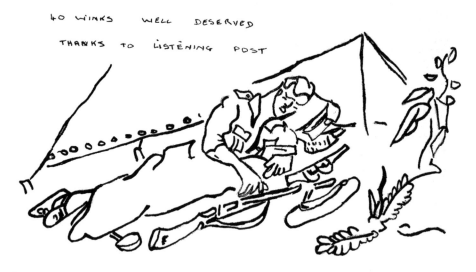

40 WINKS   WELL DESERVED

THANKS TO LISTENING POST

The ultimate luxury: pack off and stretched out full length! The artist responsible for this sketch and others in this book is unknown. The originals are in a sketchbook entitled 'Extracts from a Chindit's Diary'. Almost certainly, the artist was a Chindit serving with a 23 Brigade Column during the Imphal/Kohima fighting in 1944. (Tony Wailes)

constant galloping to catch up, but the standing about under a heavy load while the "slashers" in front completed the cutting of the track'.[30]

Even in relatively thin jungle slashers were required at the Column head, as laden mules needed a five-foot wide track.[31] Staggering up and down steep, jungle-covered slopes, very heavily laden, in tropical conditions, was exhausting and soul-destroying. Inevitably, men lost awareness of their surroundings. Fergusson explained:

> When you are carrying a heavy pack, with the best will in the world your eyes drop to the ground and stay there. Watch a Column on the move, standing five yards to the flank, and the odds are five to one that they will walk past you without spotting you, with heads bent and eyes downcast, like a Buddhist priest. It was necessary to detail a few men at a time to keep their eyes about them, relieving them every few minutes.[29]

Every man was severely tested, both mentally and physically. 5 Column's Commander confessed: 'After each hourly halt one swore one wouldn't look at one's watch until something like the hour was up, yet I always found that the first time I looked at it no more than 20 minutes out of the hour was gone.'[32] Fergusson enjoyed being wrapped up in 'a really good dream':

One that haunted me most, particularly towards evening, was the mere thought of lying stretched out full length. Such a posture seemed the ultimate luxury and it was hard to believe that, in an hour or two, this pleasure would actually be ours to enjoy for the whole long night.

He added: 'We marched until dusk, left the track, drew the secrecy of the jungle about us and bedded down with less fuss than the dog who walks three times round before he settles.' Yet security was always an issue. In dry country, with Japanese known to be in the area, the Column would bivouac away from water, for obvious reasons.[32]

Fergusson preserved the dignity of rank by selecting the 'Commander's Tree': 'Only I and my immediate staff may go near it and nobody else may settle down within 20 yards of it. It is my Command Post, my office, my dining room and my bed...' A whistle summoned the officers to 'Column Orders'.

Fergusson would confirm their position, declare the next rendezvous and give the time for moving off, very early the next morning. The relatively cool early hours were too precious to waste; he aimed to complete at least two hours' marching before breakfast. All fires were out an hour and a quarter after getting into night bivouac.[33]

The Column rendezvous was always forward, never back. The RV had to be easy to find, even without a

Taking a break: Major Walter Phipps, then a Company Commander with the 1st Bedfordshire and Hertfordshire, during training in India prior to Operation *Thursday* in 1944. Phipps went on to command 16 Column during the later stages. Note the canvas water bucket at his feet. (John Riggs)

map. They tended to be natural features (not subject to change) and a line rather than a point, much reducing the risk of overshooting. Typically, a stream running across the line of approach was selected. Two rendezvous points were given to the officers, but only the first could be passed on to NCOs.[34]

Column life was governed by routine. On reaching the night bivouac the animals were brought in, grouped by Platoon and unloaded at each side.

Each man was expected to check his kit. Regardless of items taken out for use in bivouac, all packs had to be shut and fastened.[35] Whenever possible, the animals were watered at the last stream before bivouac. Bernard Fergusson: 'The men were taught never to expect water at a bivouac. Except where there was a real water crisis, they were always expected to arrive in bivouac with full water bottles.'

If they came to a stream within half an hour of bivouac, the men were given the chance to fill their chaguls. If a stream was near the bivouac, the men would be allowed to drain their bottles and refill them (enemy permitting, of course).[33]

In hot conditions, the best defence against thirst was an uncomfortably long drink before starting out in the morning:

> If water was nearby, or if there was a reasonable prospect of a fill in the next hour or two of march-ing, all ranks were induced to drink as much as they were able, and far more than they wanted. Nobody wants to drink a whole water bottle before dawn, but it is a wise measure and the benefit to be derived from it lasts long into the day, even after the sun has been engaged for several hours on doing its worst.[36]

Columns averaged nine hours' sleep a night and, according to Fergusson, 'it wasn't a minute too much'.[37] Security was always on his mind. He had a strict rule: anyone coughing within 15 minutes of getting up in the morning had his cigarette ration docked.[36] The Column felt reasonably secure when obvious precau-tions were taken: moving off the track, into the jungle, and establishing sentry and listening posts. The track 'stops' were called in half an hour after dark unless the Japanese were thought to be near. Fergusson added: 'To be caught in bivouac you must either have been very unlucky or very careless: it was a thing that shouldn't happen'.[33]

In common with Sergeant-Major Hobbs, 5 Column's ATO found the first expedition's rations good. In fact, in some ways Bill Smyly preferred them to Operation *Thursday's* K-rations:

'Our rations for the first show were easier to carry. The K-rations (from Battle Creek, Michigan – home of Kellogg's Cornflakes) were marvellous but heavy. The best thing about the British rations in 1943 was the high concentrate biscuits dropped in cans. They looked a bit like large, square dog biscuits. They would swell up in tea and could be turned into a satisfying porridge. The biscuits filled you up and kept well as emergency rations. At one time we lasted 18 days on eight days' rations. You couldn't do that on K-rations. I was fond of these biscuits and, after the war, tried dog biscuits, but they are not the same!'

Most of Wingate's men would come dangerously close to starvation. Generally, rations were insufficient to sus-tain men struggling to cope with Operation *Longcloth's* extreme physical demands. Fergusson was scathing:

> The ration, at the best of times, was not too good. It was too meagre, at any rate, to try and make one day's last a day and a half without loss of stamina.

The dieticians were horrified at our using it at all, since it was originally designed for parachutists to live on for a maximum period of five days.

It consisted of 12 Shakapura biscuits, 2 oz. of cheese, some nuts and raisins, some dates, 20 ciga-rettes, tea, sugar and milk. In addition, there was supposed to be chocolate, but two packets out of three had acid drops instead. Such was one's frame of mind that, when one got acid drops instead of chocolate, one wanted to burst into tears and, such is my luck, I only got chocolate twice. I should add that there was also that extremely important item, a packet of salt.[38]

Bill Smyly is one of many who testify to Wingate's boundless enthusiasm for onions. He walked around with a pocketful, munching them like apples and praising their virtues to anyone within earshot. This might explain an unwelcome gift from the skies during *Longcloth*:

'A large bale was free-dropped to us. It was huge and you could smell it yards away. A solid block of dried onions, it must have weighed a quarter of a ton. Imagine being killed by a bale of onions falling from the sky! It was a problem. We couldn't eat it there and then and we couldn't take it with us. It smelt so strongly that your pack would remember it for a month. So we left it, but we all thought of it any time we happened to have bully beef.'

Wingate put his stamp on every aspect of training. His requirements were set out in written orders and leaf-lets. Philip Stibbe (*Return via Rangoon*) found these to be a strange mixture of good sense and the obscure: 'Saluting was to be cut down to a minimum. Everything was to be done at the double. Everyone must eat at least one raw onion per day. Only shorts would be worn when it was raining. Swearing must stop.' Wingate even decreed that all officers should have an 800-word vocabulary in both Urdu and Gurkhali. Failure to moni-tor progress on this front had the virtue of avoiding disappointment. Bill Smyly:

'The young Gurkhas, of course, did not speak English and I was supposed to speak Army Exam Urdu, which was not actually their native language. I wasn't very good but got by and the men were understanding and good fun. Obviously, they imitated me and had some cracks at 'Smyly Speak.'

The Column Commander usually marched at the Column head, just behind the 'slashers' and called out

Supplied from the skies: Chindit signal fires in a clearing, giving the direction of run for supply-dropping aircraft. (Trustees of the Imperial War Museum)

the route. He had to show real expertise in analysing the country ahead. Most Column maps were to the half-inch scale (covering around 35 miles square). The key to meaningful interpretation, according to Fergusson, was to understand the drainage (or 'tilt') of the country. The less developed the country, the more important this becomes: 'In a primitive and undeveloped land, man settles where there is water ... Where man settles, villages spring up. Between villages, tracks spring up. Villages become towns, tracks become roads and roads become railways...'

A close study of water systems will suggest the likely presence of villages: 'you can be sure that if villages are marked on the banks of a chaung, that chaung, at least, will have water throughout the year.'

Knowledge of the language would also allow deductions to be made from place-names. '*Kwin*', for example, means grassy clearing and might suggest a potential site for a supply drop. Nothing could be taken for granted, however, due to the Burmese habit of moving villages every 15–20 years. When a village moves, so do the tracks serving it.[39]

There was an art to planning a march. Fergusson would study the 'tilt' and watersheds. Tracks were the best routes as they indicated thinner jungle, but they are more risky. Column security could be compromised by gossip between local communities. Once again, an intelligent examination of the map would allow the Column Commander to make shrewd guesses about the extent to which terrain and water systems isolated communities and so contained information about their movements.[39]

No doubt, all Chindits would agree with Fergusson's observation: 'The most heart-breaking fate which can befall you is to find yourself travelling across the grain of the country.' A lengthy diversion was often better than repeated climbs and descents. Yet, no matter what the conditions, everyone hankered for a change in the going. It was a relief to leave thick jungle and walk along a chaung, until the soft sand created a yearning for solid going. Teak is the only form of jungle not requiring cutting teams at the Column head, but teak forests are dry and the Column Snake must put up with choking dust. Bamboo provides good cover from the air and the men can move beneath the clumps, with the branches forming an arch above them. Unfortunately, the arches are too low for mules and therefore must be cut, with the danger of noise alerting an enemy. Dead bamboo is worse, with no chance to pass underneath. Some bamboo is almost impenetrable: 'This is jungle so

FOOD FOLLOWED SUCCESSFUL AIR DROPS

Dining in 'bivvy': a Chindit cooking fire, with more rations descending from above. (Tony Wailes)

solid that it has to be cut out like the slice of a cake...' It was graded half-a-mile-an-hour jungle or 400 yards-an-hour jungle.[39]

In some circumstances cross-country travel was essential on security grounds. There were some basic principles to consider: the Column Commander might choose a track if he is in a hurry and believes the area free of Japanese. This decision might be clinched if there is no requirement to stay put at the destination. Equally, a cross-country route might be selected if there is no time pressure, the Column's presence is to be kept secret and the men are to stay put on arrival. Night marching was preferred for tracks and day marching for the far more difficult but more secure cross-country option.[39]

Many weeks of tough training ended in a Brigade-scale exercise in December 1942. This was observed by Wavell. Every aspect of LRP warfare was tested and preparations were complete by the early New Year. Fergusson told a close comrade that the chance of coming back was 'even money'. The odds in his Column turned out to be 3 to 1 against.[40]

Large-scale exercises, or 'schemes', highlighted the problem of crossing major obstacles – a road or valley floor with little or no cover. Column Commanders learned to take such problems in their stride. Bernard Fergusson:

> One is sometimes faced with the problem of crossing a valley two or three miles wide without a shred of cover. You see it on the map two or three days ahead of you and lose much sleep in wondering how you will do it. The answer lies in a moonlit night and I remember crossing such valleys three nights in succession, marching by moonlight ... and lying up each scorching day in friendly jungle.

Crossing a road in Column strength was always a challenge. It took 15 minutes or more for 400 men and around 65 animals to pass a given point. They learned from experience.

Fergusson's Column took to crossing a road or track in a single wave of small groups; all tell-tale signs were removed by brushing with leaves. If the Column was pursued it would break track, divide into small groups, march to an agreed compass bearing for a short period and then reform.[41] This manoeuvre was more difficult to achieve than to describe. In a number of cases, including that of 5 Column itself, the dispersed elements failed to come together again. Fergusson's own ATO, Bill Smyly, commented: 'The idea of breaking up into small groups and meeting up at some place 'ahead' would really be a good way of never seeing most of your Column again.'

In dry country the Japanese could be expected to patrol watercourses. During training, special precautions were taken when crossing streams, to disguise the crossing point, but this was much harder when faced with a wide, sandy chaung.[41]

Wingate's force held supply drop exercises during the 130–mile approach march from Dimapur. Aircraft from 31 Squadron, RAF, dropped to them. 'Firemen' built and tended signal fires and 'Pickers-up', complete with mules, brought in loads. 'Dumpmen' managed the collected stores. 'Recorders' watched from vantage points and, partnered by 'Markers', recorded the number of loads dropped on each run and the location of those falling outside the drop zone. A defensive screen protected the Column. Fergusson quickly picked up useful tips. He soon appreciated that the distribution of mail should be left to last, to avoid everyone taking time off to read the latest from home.[42]

Wingate's force marched forward at night, the road being reserved for IV Corps' vehicles during daylight. 5 Column's Philip Stibbe described a magnificent sunrise on the Manipur Road:

The vast mountain ranges flaunting themselves against the vivid morning sky, the silver sheen of the rivers gleaming below through the gaps in the mist, the long line of men and animals, each standing out in bold relief as the Column topped a rise in the road, all made an unforgettable impression.[43]

Reaching the Imphal Plain after nine nights, they camped five miles outside Imphal and made final preparations. Stibbe went forward to recce bivouac sites. He noticed that a Gurkha Battalion's mules seemed content munching bamboo leaves. He passed this on to Wingate, who ordered the practice to be adopted Brigade-wide. This much reduced their reliance on air-dropped fodder.[43]

Suddenly, however, *Longcloth* ran into trouble. At a conference in Delhi, opening on 1 February, Wavell learned that the Chinese Yunnan offensive was postponed.[17] *Longcloth* was not designed 'as a mere unsupported foray', but rather as part of the grand design for regaining Burma.[16]

This broader plan envisaged IV Corps advancing south from Imphal, towards the Chindwin, while General Stilwell's Chinese in the north would attack from Ledo towards Myitkyina. Furthermore, the Chinese would advance from Yunnan and there would be a push towards Akyab, in the Arakan.[8]

What would be the point of LRP attacks on Japanese lines of communication, in the absence of wider offensive action?

Wingate was told on 5 February. Wavell wrote: 'I flew up to Manipur and had a long discussion with Wingate, whether, in these circumstances, the raid should take place at all, since it now served no strategical purpose and the Japanese would be free to concentrate against it. He convinced me that the chances of getting the Brigade through and of extricating it again were good and that the experience to be gained would be invaluable and well worth the risk. There is no doubt too that cancellation would have been a bitter disappointment to troops keyed up to the pitch of action by months of training.'[16] Wingate was as persuasive as ever. His men began marching into Burma.

Fergusson was busy with his final preparations when told by Wavell that the wider offensives were cancelled. Fergusson later said of Wingate:

I know that doubt has been cast on his wisdom in pressing to be allowed to carry on independently and even – an intolerable impertinence, it has always seemed to me – in the wisdom of the Commander-in-Chief in allowing him to do so. I can only say that every Column Commander was in agreement; so would every officer, had they been consulted, and not one of us, even in the light of after-events, has ever regretted the decision.[44]

Philip Stibbe led No. 7 Platoon, one of 5 Column's three Rifle Platoons. When posted in, he found the men of 13th King's (Liverpool) 'difficult to understand and, at times, exasperating. Later, when I had become accustomed to their rather sardonic attitude to life, and stopped taking everything they said too seriously, we got along much better.'[45]

Wingate visited the Battalion. Stibbe provides an interesting sketch of this encounter:

It was impossible not to be impressed by Wingate; in appearance, in speech and in manner he was dynamic. Thick set and not very tall, he seemed endowed with immense physical energy, but it was his face which was so striking, particularly the deep set eyes glaring out from beneath his now famous sun helmet. He was inclined to stoop as he walked and, with his head and jaw thrust forward and his eyes half closed, as though in concentration, he looked what he was, a genius and a fanatical man of action.[45]

This encounter ended on a flat note:

After the parade had been dismissed, the Colonel took his six new officers to be introduced to the Brigadier. We stood uneasily outside the tent which was Brigade Headquarters. After a few minutes, Wingate stalked out, glared at us and then shook hands in silence. As he turned on his heel to withdraw, he growled, 'I hope you will all enjoy yourselves'. 'We hope so, too', one of us murmured as he disappeared.[45]

Wingate and his Brigade were soon on their way. Operation *Longcloth* had begun, against all odds. Wavell was present at their departure. Bill Smyly:

'Wavell was probably the one man in GHQ Delhi who supported Wingate and did not think him a crank. Their association went back years, to Palestine, and it was Wavell who decided the operation should go ahead. He came down personally to see us off and, of course, to say goodbye and good luck to Bernard Fergusson, who had been his ADC. On our parade, as we marched off, instead of us saluting him, he saluted us and wished us well.'

Notes

1. Rooney. D. (1997), *Mad Mike*, 24–25
2. Cross, J.P. (1989), *Jungle Warfare*, 12–13
3. Rooney. D. (1997), 27–34
4. Ibid, 35–40
5. Ibid, 42–45
6. Rooney, D. (2000), *Wingate and the Chindits: Redressing the Balance*, 77–78
7. Calvert, M. (1974), *Chindits: Long Range Penetration*, 9
8. Rooney. D. (1997), 44–46
9. Fowler, W. (2009), *We Gave Our Today: Burma 1941–1945*, 94
10. Allen, L. (1986), *Burma: The Longest War 1941–45*, 121
11. Stibbe, P. (1995), *Return via Rangoon*, 9–13
12. Ibid, 25–26
13. Fergusson, B. (1971), *Beyond the Chindwin*, 46
14. Stibbe, P. (1995), 36
15. Ibid, 39
16. Fergusson, B. (1971), Foreword
17. Calvert, M. (1996), *Fighting Mad*, 113–117
18. Halley, D. (1945), *With Wingate in Burma*, 19–22
19. Ibid, 29
20. Ibid, 35–51
21. Fergusson, B. (1971), 38
22. Ibid, 77–78
23. Ibid, 251–252
24. Ibid, 33
25. Fergusson, B. (1946), *The Wild Green Earth*, 238
26. Ibid, 240–241
27. Thompson, Sir Robert (1989), *Make for the Hills*, 19–20
28. Fergusson, B. (1946), 162
29. Ibid, 164–166
30. Ibid, 167–168
31. Ibid, 161
32. Ibid, 170–171
33. Ibid, 172–175
34. Ibid, 266–267
35. Ibid, 181–182
36. Ibid, 183–189
37. Ibid, 178
38. Fergusson, B. (1971), 101–102
39. Fergusson, B. (1946), 150–157
40. Fergusson, B. (1971), 47
41. Fergusson, B. (1946), 158–160
42. Ibid, 250
43. Stibbe, P. (1995) 53–55
44. Fergusson, B. (1971), 55
45. Stibbe, P. (1995) 15–19

3

BEHIND JAPANESE LINES

'Surrendering to some extent his own volition, every individual became absorbed into the Column consciousness or identity.'

Charles Carfrae, Chindit Column

Order of Battle: 77th Indian Infantry Brigade, Operation *Longcloth*

Commander   Brigadier Orde C. Wingate, DSO

No. 1 Group (Southern)
Lieutenant-Colonel Alexander, 3/2nd Gurkha Rifles (2 GR)

No. 1 Column	Major G. Dunlop, MC, Royal Scots
No. 2 Column	Major A. Emmett, 3/2nd Gurkha Rifles (2 GR)

No. 2 Group (Northern)
Lieutenant-Colonel S.A. Cooke, The Lincolnshire Regiment (attached, The King's (Liverpool) Regiment) (King's)

No. 3 Column	Major J.M. Calvert, Royal Engineers (RE)
No. 4 Column	Major Conron, 3/2nd Gurkha Rifles (2 GR)
	(later, Major R.B.G. Bromhead, Royal Berkshire Regiment)
No. 5 Column	Major B.E. Fergusson, The Black Watch (BW)
No. 7 Column	Major K.D. Gilkes, The King's (Liverpool) Regiment (King's)
No. 8 Column	Major W.P. Scott, The King's (Liverpool) Regiment (King's)

No. 6 Column was broken up during training, to bring other columns up to strength.

2nd Battalion The Burma Rifles
Lieutenant-Colonel L.G. Wheeler

Wingate's men soon discovered the difference between tough training and the even harsher reality of behind-the-lines warfare in the North Burmese jungle. The two Long Range Penetration groups set off on 8 February 1943. Southern Group's two Columns, led by Lieutenant-Colonel Alexander, were to cut the railway south of Wuntho and divert attention from the main body – Northern Group's five Columns. This larger group was to attack the railway and facilities around Nankan, in 'Railway Valley'. Southern Group would then rendezvous with the main body and, in favourable circumstances, the united force would cross the Irrawaddy and cut the Mandalay-Lashio railway.[1] Column Commanders had specific objectives: Bernard Fergusson's 5 Column had the Bonchaung Bridge and Gorge as targets.[2] Michael Calvert's 3 Column also had railway targets.

77 Brigade moved towards the Chindwin, the boundary separating British and Japanese forces. Fergusson found the night marches along the Manipur Road interminable: 'They were tolerable only because we were able to march in threes instead of single file, or Column Snake'.[3]

The Columns aimed to cover around 20 miles each night. Cypher Officer Alec Gibson was with Calvert's Column: 'The road spiralled round into mountainous country. It was pitch black most of the time but I wasn't too worried in this strange, new environment. I was too busy keeping up with everyone else'.

During those long, exhausting nights Column Commanders had plenty of time to think about their orders to leave behind wounded or sick who could no longer march. Fergusson wrote:

I gave the officers a talk the afternoon before we entrained. The thing that worried us all most was having to leave behind the wounded, but it was quite obvious that there was nothing else to be done for them and that to linger with them meant risking the success of the show. All had been taught the rudiments of First Aid, for what such rudiments are worth, all had been issued with morphia and told how to administer it, according to need, including a lethal dose. For the badly wounded, it might be possible to leave them in friendly villages and every officer had copies of a letter in Burmese, to be left with the villagers.[4]

Sergeant Tony Aubrey was with Scott's 8 Column. He saw many men dump unnecessary kit during the third day of the march to the Chindwin. He watched one officer jettison an unlikely catalogue of items: 'leather jerkins and camel hair coats, thigh boots and golfing shoes, and knives and torches and other gadgets in profusion. He was seen to offer a Private soldier a resplendent silver-plated shaving mirror, but the Tommy replied, with real regret, 'I'm sorry, Sir. I'm afraid I won't be wanting that now'.[5] Most men began growing beards. Shaving tackle weighed little, but every ounce of weight counted. In addition, a beard camouflaged the face and provided protection against mosquitoes.

Major Fergusson's Column reached Lokchau on 12 February and made for Tamu, to draw their *Longcloth* rations. Orde Wingate's *Order of the Day* of 14 February declared:

We have all had the opportunity of withdrawing and we are here because we have chosen to be here;

that is, we have chosen to bear the burden and heat of the day. Men who make this choice are above the average of courage. We need, therefore, have no fear for the staunchness and guts of our comrades. The motive which has led each and all of us to devote ourselves to what lies ahead cannot conceivably have been a bad motive. Comfort and security are not sacrificed voluntarily, for the sake of others, by ill-disposed people. Our motive, therefore, may be taken to be the desire to serve our day and generation in the way that seems nearest to our hand.

It concluded with words which resonate down the years:

Finally, knowing the vanity of man's effort and the confusion of his purpose, let us pray that God may accept our services and direct our endeavours so that, when we shall have done all, we may see the fruits of our labours and be satisfied.

————•—•————

Southern Group's two Columns opened their diversion by crossing the Chindwin at Auktaung. Wingate, however, did not expect to cross undetected despite the Auktaung feint. The main group was to cross at Tonhe, but the approaches became congested. Fergusson's Column crossed three miles upstream during the night of 15/16 February. Animal Transport Officer (ATO) Bill Smyly stared at the river, around 400 yards wide:

'I didn't really know how to get my mules across. We put canoes out in front, tied some mules together in a line and set out. It is impossible to drive mules across a river. They simply turn around and come back to the near bank. They have to be led across to the other side. We took them over in groups of 10. Bernard Fergusson didn't criticise me in his book, which was kind of him, but the canoes were his idea and he did more to get the mules over than I did.'

Calvert's 3 Column arrived at the Chindwin's west bank, moved into night bivouac and prepared to cross. The men were told to remove their boots and put on gym shoes, to keep the noise down. Cypher Officer Alec Gibson found the prospect unattractive:

'When I came up to the river, the Column's efforts to cross looked like a shambles. Confusion reigned in the darkness. There was a very strong current and even the best swimmers had so far failed to get a rope across to the opposite bank. This was essential, as none of our Gurkhas could swim. After a couple of failures with the rope, the attempt was abandoned for that night.

A good look at each other: a Chindit patrol surrounded by curious villagers. This photograph, taken during Operation *Thursday* in 1944, shows members of the Bedfordshire and Hertfordshire's 61 Column Recce Platoon. Villagers were eager to barter food for parachute cloth. The typical village house (just visible, right) is built on stilts – providing space underneath for livestock and giving good clearance from the Monsoon mud. (John Riggs)

Everyone returned to bivouac. I felt better inside. These men had been training for months, yet didn't seem to know how to cross a river. Perversely, as a complete novice I found this failure strangely comforting.'

Alec Gibson got his first real look at the river when dawn broke:

'It was quite formidable. The water was muddy and the current strong. There was a sandbank roughly in the middle.'

Gibson tied his kit and rifle into a waterproof groundsheet, having stripped for the swim:

'The widest stretch was around 200 yards, not too bad for a good swimmer. In fact, I went out and back three times that day. The rope connection with the far bank was secured during the morning. Boats were found to ferry across our non-swimmers and the packs and heavy equipment. The mules, however, were a nightmare. Some were reasonably happy to cross and others could be persuaded to follow them, but many proved unmanageable.'

Fergusson also found the crossing challenging:

The Chindwin was a good deal wider than anything we had previously tackled and, though we had had stronger currents to deal with, the combination of current and width proved formidable. The intention was to tow a light line over in one of the small rubber boats, make fast to the heavy line and, once the light line was across, to tow the heavy line over by hauling on the light. But the heavy rope kept being caught by the stream and whisked off to leeward and the light line parted every time. After strenuous efforts, we got the heavy line over, the far end coming ashore a long way down stream, and then we could not eliminate the sag. At last it became apparent that we had fouled the bottom. That began a weary cycle of twitching it, diving for it, dredging for it and then starting again. A fishing boat was put to work and rafts were built for those mules refusing to swim.[6]

He rated the Karens of The Burma Rifles as the best watermen: 'Their prowess in the water has to be seen to be believed. They would build boats from bamboo and groundsheets in a few minutes.'[7]

Fergusson's Column continued to march by night, resting up in the seclusion of deep jungle during daylight.[8] The Column Commander remained cautious: 'I never bivouacked within 500 yards of a track'.[9] His men met up with other Columns around Myene and they had their first good look at a Burmese village. It compared well with the 'squalor and poverty' of its Indian counterpart.[10]

ATO Bill Smyly watched over his 30 Muleteers, a full Platoon:

'They were all very young, 18 to 20 – the same age as me, actually, though I didn't think of this at the time. We were organised so that the Gurkhas – Transport Muleteers – led two mules each, while British Muleteers in the Rifle Company and special Sections (radio and so on) led a single mule. There was an enormous mule for the RAF Wireless Section, with its heavy equipment, called a 'Missouri', sired by a 'Maltese Jack' (whatever that is) out of a large American mare.

'Anyway, Gurkhas led two mules and we soon found it was best to let the follower follow free. Going over an obstacle, if the leading mule jumped and the follower resisted, the pair had to fall out of the line of march to have their harness adjusted. The Muleteers realised that the second mule, if unhitched, would tend to follow on naturally and, maybe, if it didn't the man behind could encourage it, or take over and lead.

'This worked well by day and was an advantage in rough country and at river crossings. On one dark night, however, the follower stopped to graze and a sleepy soldier behind him stopped too. The head of the Column went on into the night as the body of the Column queued up behind a grazing mule. I was near the back and could not understand the delay. The ATO is Column Marshal. It didn't seem particularly dark and I went forward to find out what was happening. On the way I found Bernard Fergusson stuck head down in a bush. Apparently, he was night blind, had fallen into the prickly bush and was now firmly pinned down by his very large rucksack. I pulled him out by his belt and he followed me with one hand on my shoulder. Obviously, he was more night blind than me. At the head we found the soldier, almost asleep, with his head on the mule's rump, and the major section of the whole Column queuing up behind this grazing animal.

'To give him credit, Fergusson didn't explode with anger, but he clearly felt that Smyly and his mules were out of control. He halted, summoned the officers forward, got onto the head of the Column by radio, telling them what had happened, and we all bedded down for the night where we were. As leading culprit I was given the worst watch of the night – a *punishment I deserved as much for laughing as for inefficiency. Later, I went to sleep and when I awoke I discovered I was night blind. I was supposed to patrol the Column, but couldn't see a thing. I smoked a horrible cheroot as a way of staying awake and then got up and tried to find my way up and down the Column Snake in the dark.'*

Passing the animals, Smyly spent part of the rest of the night leaning against a prone bullock, stroking its head, talking to it and trying to see in the dark:

'Later I mistook the sleeping Fergusson for another bullock. I began saying inappropriate things and he replied: 'Smyly? I'm glad you're back. Can you pull my groundsheet from under me and put it on top. I think it's going to rain.' It was 4 am and getting light.'

With the Chindwin behind them, Calvert's 3 Column marched on. Cypher Officer Alec Gibson, towards the rear, suffered the usual trials of those at the end of the Column Snake: frequent hold-ups and desperate attempts to close the gaps. It could be worse – the short straw was Rearguard. Men in this Section had to be relieved on a regular basis.

Despite all trials and discomforts, Gibson recalled the Column's positive atmosphere:

'Everyone got on well together, although communication was a problem. The front of the Column might send a message back in English. This would be translated into Gurkhali, then Burmese at some point and, finally, back into English. Not surprisingly, even the simplest message was often corrupted.'

It took 3 Column some days to settle into its routine. The heat sapped energy and sweat poured off the men as they struggled on. Alec Gibson:

'I don't remember taking salt tablets but I do recall that one of our Burmese officers always knew where to find rock salt. We took to sucking chunks of it as we marched.'

In the second half of February Fergusson's 5 Column made for Metkalet, but difficult country changed plans. They were ordered to Tonmakeng, close to the selected Brigade bivouac. Wingate had requested a big supply drop and he gave Fergusson's Column the job of receiving it. Meanwhile, the bulk of the force set out to attack Japanese-held Sinlamaung village, 20 miles to the south-east. The fighting group returned to the Brigade bivouac on 26 February, having found

Low pass: stores leave a Dakota over the DZ. (Jim Unsworth)

During the Tonmakeng supply drops 5 Column's Philip Stibbe discovered a sleeping sentry. Major Fergusson gave the man the choice of walking back to India alone or taking a flogging. Not surprisingly, he accepted the latter. CSM Cairns administered the punishment with a make-shift cat-o'-nine-tails fashioned from parachute cord.[14]

The problem of discipline within the Columns was much discussed before going in. Commenting on the dilemma posed by the sleeping sentry, Fergusson wrote:

> How do you punish a man for an offence like that, in circumstances like these? Shooting, thank good-ness, is no longer the recognised punishment; to hold a field general court martial and give him penal servitude hardly helps towards making him a useful soldier during the next few months; deten-tion, loss of pay, stoppage of leave, confinement to – Column? – none of these seem applicable.[15]

Bill Smyly, meanwhile, became increasingly restless. The ATO pressed his Column Commander for more militant employment and Fergusson began to oblige.

The jungle routine became firmly entrenched. Each Column had four or five groups for defence and com-mand purposes. The order of march changed daily, with the lead group moving to the rear the next day and the others moving up a slot. This spread the hardships at the Column tail.[16]

The men applied the fieldcraft skills picked up during training. The basics were set out some years later by J.P. Cross: never tread on what can be stepped over, never cut what can be broken naturally, never bend what can be moved, never move what can be passed without moving and never step on soft ground if a harder sur-face is available.

Cross wrote that the leader's ear should be attuned to normal jungle noises, to differentiate between natural and man-made sounds. He had to rely on his observation of broken twigs, branches and trampled undergrowth to detect the recent presence or proxim-ity of humans. 'He must readily recognise the danger of tracks converging at watering places, cultivations and habitations and to approach such areas with caution.'[17]

Many men had a deep loathing of the jungle's natu-ral hazards. Having crossed the Chindwin successfully, Alec Gibson did his level best to take the jungle insects in his stride:

'I couldn't avoid brushing against the undergrowth and red ants often dropped into my shirt. They sting like hell. Fortunately, there were very few malarial mosquitoes in our area, but we still took Mepacrine daily.'

Sinlamaung abandoned. They had destroyed the huts and Japanese stores. The Brigade-scale supply drop had been successful with aircraft dropping twice daily over a three-day period. The two Dakotas and a Hudson had a fighter escort. Fergusson's men were rewarded with two days' extra rations.[11] Major Calvert, typically, did not return empty-handed from Sinlamaung. He arrived with a Japanese officer's horse and an elephant, com-plete with Mahout.[12]

Sergeant Tony Aubrey, with 8 Column, watched the Brigade drop and was impressed:

Not even a single one of the sacks containing the corn for the mules burst. These were ingeniously packed, a 56 pound sack of corn being securely wrapped up in four hundredweight sacks stuffed with straw. When these ungainly bundles hit the ground, they bounced 10 ft into the air and anyone who had happened to be standing in their path wouldn't have lived to tell the tale.[13]

Every man pushed away his fears. Alec Gibson, still a jungle novice, was unprepared for the possibility of separation and the need to rely on his own wits to rejoin the Column:

'The Column Commander and perhaps four other officers had maps. Most of the time I hadn't a clue where we were. When in bivouac I was too busy with cyphers and mules to attend Calvert's conferences.'

Yet Calvert made a powerful impression on Gibson:

'He was a marvellous man – unsurpassed at map reading. At one stage we took an air drop and Calvert decided to cache some stores. Several days later he returned to that exact spot in the jungle and recovered the supplies. It was very impressive. He was a strong leader yet very approachable.'

If Gibson had concerns about becoming lost, he was in good company. No less a person than Bernard Fergusson wrote frankly about the occasion when his own jungle nightmare became a reality: 'I was that forlorn creature, a Column Commander who had lost his Column.' When he eventually rejoined the Column 'it felt like a miracle and I have never been more aware of God's mercy.'[18] The jungle was rich in hazards, from falling trees and rotten branches (which can be heard but not seen during the night) to an impressive array of stinging and biting creatures, from ants and flies to caterpillars, ticks, scorpions, centipedes and leeches. In common with Alec Gibson and everyone else, Fergusson detested the aggressive red ants of dry teak jungle,

> ... with the most vicious sting imaginable. They would stand on their heads and burrow into you as if with a pneumatic drill. If you were unlucky enough to brush a tree with your sleeve, you would spend the next 15 minutes in a torture, compared with which the martyrdom of Saint Sebastian was a holiday with pay.[19]

Leeches filled many British soldiers with disgust. Charles Carfrae wrote:

> One might observe numbers of leeches on the wet leaves of evergreen bushes bordering tracks, heads and bodies raised up in the shape of questionmarks as they made ready to attach themselves to any moving object brushing past. The creatures, looking like short lengths of bootlace when their stomachs remained empty, were adept at insinuating themselves between trouser and anklet – even through

lace-holes – and sometimes decided to attach themselves to our private parts, an impertinence providing welcome entertainment for all but the victim. More commonly, they fixed on legs or feet. Unless one happened to see patches of blood, or feel it oozing, their presence might remain undetected until the leeches had become fully gorged, blown up like miniature sausage balloons. A pinch of salt or lighted cigarette applied to their rear ends would make them drop off; it was when foolish or impatient soldiers tried to dislodge the things by force that their heads remained embedded, to cause nasty jungle sores or ulcers.[20]

The author's father, Private Jack Redding – who participated in the second Wingate operation – filled his young children with horror when describing his surprise at finding a large purple globe on his leg on waking one morning. It was impossible to stop his hand instinctively sweeping the offending object away, leaving the limb smeared heavily with blood.

The vegetation formed part of an unforgiving environment. Bernard Fergusson described prickly bamboo as Burma's biggest curse: 'the leaves and stalks tear your clothes and flesh to ribbons.' He also complained of Bizat bushes that shed dry particles which go down the neck and irritate the skin.[21] Many men found the jungle an eerie place. Fraser wrote:

> The chief irritant on stag (a two-hour watch by two men) was the 'up you bird' (I give the bowdlerised form of the name), familiar to all who have soldiered in the Far East. In fact, it is a large lizard ... It starts up at night and drives strong men mad, for its call is a harsh whirring sound culminating in a melodious 'Up you! Up you! Up you! Half an hour of this and you become convinced that there is a human being out there, chanting obscenely at you...[22]

Fergusson applied shrewd psychology when operating in dense jungle:

> In jungle country views are hard to come by and every one is precious. Submerged in jungle for days at a time, to reach the top of a range of hills and to see the view is as precious as the sight of the sea to the engineer of a fishing boat who, once in an hour, thrusts his head through the hatch, looks around him, and gulps a few lungfuls of salt sea air. Whenever possible on such an occasion, I used to halt the Column in the most advantageous place, where the most people could see, to give a chance to all officers to identify landmarks on their maps

9,000 FV + THE CLOUDS BELOW

LIKE COTTON WOOL SUSPENDED IN SPACE

'In jungle country views are hard to come by': every opportunity was taken to give Column officers a chance to orientate themselves. (Tony Wailes)

and point them out to their men. In days of long and weary marching, the more the men can be told, the better; they always took a great interest.[23]

NCOs of the finest quality watched over the Column Sections. Sergeant Major Bob Hobbs was the senior NCO responsible for a large group within his Column. Six Sergeants led the Sections:

'I spent my time at the back of this group, keeping everyone in line. They thought I was a right git. They all disliked me, but I had to be tough. Our march into Burma was very hard but I was extremely fit and never had any trouble with my feet. A chap in my group recommended soaking them in a solution of washing soda. I took his advice and never had problems with them.'

Following the Sinlamaung venture, Wingate held a conference and set out his intentions. The Brigade would move into the Mu Valley and begin negotiating the other valleys along the approach to the railway.

Calvert's 3 Column set out independently, but the other four Columns (4, 5, 7 and 8) left Tonmakeng together, using a so-called 'secret track'. The going was appalling. Philip Stibbe, in *Return via Rangoon*, wrote: 'all I know about that track was that it never remained on the level for more than a few yards ... Many rises were so steep that the only way the mules could climb them was at a run.'[24]

Wingate did nothing for morale by prohibiting tea before leaving bivouac in the morning, to save time and maintain security in the hour before dawn. From now on, the Columns would move off at first light, march for an hour, call a brief halt, march for another hour and then have breakfast. Later, the three-hour midday halt would give enough time for a meal, cleaning weapons and other jobs.[24]

The Columns entered the Mu Valley and turned south for Pinlebu. They would then head east, across the hills, to reach the Meza Valley and the road and railway. Wingate pressed his Column Commanders for more speed. During 5 Column's approach to the Pinlebu road, he gave Bernard Fergusson a personal demonstration of how to cut through dense jungle more efficiently. Rather than using two or three slashers in front, the Brigadier's method employed an entire Platoon. The leaders cut a narrow way, just wide enough for themselves, and the remaining slashers steadily widened it as they progressed, until it reached the 5 ft required to allow laden mules to pass.[25]

There were Japanese garrisons at Pinlebu and elsewhere in the area. 4 Column left the main body to attack Japanese-held Pinbon. Fergusson's 5 Column then took the lead, with 7 and 8 Columns and Brigade HQ following, in the advance on Pinlebu.[24] 8 Column attacked Pinlebu, calling in a heavy air strike on 4 March. They then found the Japanese had dispersed. Scott's Column withdrew and the enemy promptly counter-attacked an empty town.[26]

Pinlebu is 30 miles west of Nankan. 7 and 8 Columns, together with Brigade HQ, continued to use the road but 5 Column left it and entered the Nam Maw Valley. It was early March and they were trekking through an area free of Japanese. Rations were low and the men filled their spare socks with rice bought in the villages. An unwelcome item of wireless news caused some dismay. This broadcast reported attacks on a railway in Burma – a premature announcement, given that they were still two days away from their targets!

5 Column reached the top of a pass and began the approach to Bonchaung. Eighteen days had passed since the Chindwin crossing and they had yet to encounter a single Japanese soldier. Fergusson's Column was expected to cut the railway, then cross

the Irrawaddy and reach the Brigade rendezvous. The men had assumed they would attack the railway at night and cross the Irrawaddy at a remote location. Their Column Commander had very different ideas. They would blow the railway in daylight and cross at a major river town, using local boats. Fergusson chose the steamer station of Tigyaing and he hoped to cross on 10 March.[27]

By 5 March they were just three miles from Bonchaung Station. Fergusson briefed John Fraser's Burrif party to recce Tigyaing, some 35 miles distant. A fighting group then set out to attack Nankan, the next station south of Bonchaung. A third party, Philip Stibbe's Platoon and half the Commando Platoon, was sent to blow the gorge two miles south of Bonchaung Station. A fourth group – the remainder of the Column, led by Fergusson – would assault Bonchaung Station and members of the Commando Platoon would blow the three-span steel girder bridge. The parties set out on 6 March. All groups, bar Fraser's, were due to rendezvous by noon on 8 March on the Kunbaung Chaung. They would then join Fraser's group near Kwingi village, five miles from Tigyaing.

There was a brief skirmish with a small party of Japanese as the groups got under way. Stibbe's force pressed on: 'The next few miles lay through the worst country we had experienced. The jungle was incredibly thick and we had tremendous difficulty hacking a way through for our mules'.

Fergusson's party reached the railway and began preparing the bridge for demolition. So-called 'hasty' charges were set, to be blown should the demolition team be disturbed. Two miles away, at the gorge, Stibbe's party found the cutting had near vertical sides of solid rock. They heard the bridge blow at 9pm. It was then the turn of the gorge: 'The explosion was bigger and better than any of us had expected and it brought hundreds of tons of rock and earth crashing down onto the line'. They returned to the station, saw the wrecked bridge, crossed the river and bivouacked four miles away.[27]

Meanwhile, 3 Column was busy around Nankan. Having reached the operational area on 4 March, they had a two-day wait, so as to co-ordinate their activities with the Bonchaung attacks. 6 March was Calvert's 30th birthday and he celebrated by blowing up two large railway bridges (one with a 300 ft span). His men cut the line in over 70 other places. He also called in an air strike against Japanese positions at Wuntho, 10 miles south. Calvert expected a strong enemy reaction and set ambushes and booby-traps. They killed many Japanese yet avoided loss themselves. At around 13.15 two Japanese trucks carrying troops bumped Calvert's northern road block. A third truck then arrived. The

Gurkhas were hard-pressed, but were reinforced and drove off the enemy. Calvert was awarded the DSO.[28]

Elements of 5 Column had seen action in Kyaikin village that morning, before the bridge was blown. A Rifle Platoon skirmished with the enemy as Fergusson's main group closed with the station and bridge. A party entered Kyaikin village and ran into a truck full of Japanese infantry. The Gurkhas attacked with their kukris. They made a promising start, killing two of the enemy, but two men were then killed and five wounded when caught by machine gun fire after the initial action was over. Reinforcements arrived to deal with the remaining Japanese. Three wounded (including Platoon leader John Kerr) were taken a short distance into the now deserted village but the two others were too badly injured to be moved. Kerr was informed; all five men had to be left.

A further 16 Japanese died in the second round of fighting. Fergusson had a lucky escape. One of the Japanese 'dead' on the road suddenly sprang to life and aimed his weapon at the Column Commander. Fergusson's Batman, Peter Dorans, shot him before he could pull the trigger.[29] Six of Lieutenant Smyly's Gurkhas took part in the fighting:

'Gurkhas did not think that leading mules was what they had joined up to do, although they treated their animals well. As a compliment to my men, Fergusson offered to take six Gurkhas as a personal bodyguard. I asked for volunteers and they all volunteered. I told the Havildar (Sergeant) to sort it out and they drew lots. One Gurkha Naik (Corporal), Jhurimm Rai, killed five of the enemy. One of my Muleteers was also killed. They did well; the first Japanese soldier to jump out of the truck leapt out holding onto the tailboard with one hand and landed still holding onto the tailboard, with his back to Jhurimm Rai. As he landed he was in an almost perfect position for execution and Jhurimm Rai took his head off. The men returned proud of themselves but in a state of disbelief that a Gurkha could be killed in action.'

3 and 5 Columns then headed east, towards the Irrawaddy, having mauled the Mandalay-Myitkyina railway. The other Columns had mixed fortunes. Pinlebu had been attacked on 4 March, to draw the Japanese away from the main targets, Nankan and Bonchaung. As for the Southern Group, Major Dunlop's 1 Column had been the first to cut the railway, just north of Kyaikthin, carrying out demolitions on 3 March. Unfortunately, it had lost wireless contact with Brigade. During the preceding night 2 Column had fought an action near Kyaikthin and was dispersed. According to Rooney, this Column took the rash decision to march along

the railway and then bivouacked too near the line. When ambushed on leaving the bivouac, the Column Commander, Major Emmett, changed the agreed rendezvous during the action. His Column failed to come together again as a coherent fighting unit. Returning to the Northern Group, 4 Column, ordered to ambush the road north of Pinlebu, was itself ambushed. It broke up and lost cohesion. Consequently, Wingate had just four Columns under direction to continue *Longcloth*.[28]

3 Column was hard pressed as it made for the Irrawaddy. Calvert was told to wait a day or two for an airdrop, but the Japanese were hard on his heels. He welcomed an opportunity to enter elephant grass, but changed his mind when it became 12 ft tall with 2-in. thick stems. Suddenly, he realised he had a ready-made solution on four legs! The Column's elephant was brought to the front. At one point Calvert got too close to the beast and his men were delighted to see their Major hosed with urine.[30]

5 Column's jungle craft had been honed. They wasted little time entering and leaving bivouacs. When using a track, Fergusson and his Adjutant, Lieutenant Duncan Menzies, occasionally rode ahead for a few minutes to select a bivouac. More often than not, they halted where they were and then allocated positions to the Column elements as they came in. Sentry duty was by strict rotation, allowing men to have two out of every three nights free from interruption. The Column Commander declared the next rendezvous and set the time for moving off in the morning. Each Platoon was roused by sentries. There was no tea until the second halt, in line with Wingate's edict. A whistle announced 10 minutes to go before moving out. Mules were loaded and packs lifted. Another whistle signalled one minute and a final blast got the Column moving. During the midday halt the MO held sick parade, while Platoon Commanders inspected weapons and feet. Fergusson wrote:

> Signals would get Brigade on the air and the cypher people work away at their mysterious craft. Duncan would shove a marked map on to a convenient tree, where the men could study the 'day's run', as if they were aboard a luxury liner.[31]

Orde Wingate had to decide whether to cross the Irrawaddy or return to India. On 8 March he canvassed Calvert and Fergusson. Both backed an immediate crossing of the Irrawaddy. Subsequently, Southern Group's 1 Column made contact, having been out of touch for some three weeks. They had crossed the Irrawaddy at Tagaung, 40 miles to the south, during the night of 9/10 March.[26] Wingate made up his mind. Northern Group would cross during 10–13 March at the river town of

Tigyaing.[1] Calvert's 3 Column set out for Tigyaing but then heard from the Recce Platoon that, contrary to reports, it *was* occupied by Japanese. Another enemy force was based at Tawma, around eight miles west of the river. Following orders and ignoring his inclination to attack the Japanese beforehand, he began to cross just south of the enemy dispositions. Nevertheless, the Japanese challenged 3 Column's strong rearguard as the crossing progressed. A number of boats then put in a timely appearance and the crossing succeeded, at a cost of seven dead and six wounded. The latter reached the other side but had to be left with villagers.[12] According to Alec Gibson, one very badly wounded man was given a lethal dose of morphia. Calvert:

> I left a note for the Commander of the Japanese forces who would undoubtedly pick them up and said in it: 'These men have been fighting for their King and country, just as you have. They have fought gallantly and been wounded. I leave them confidently in your charge, knowing that with your well known traditions of Bushido, you will look after them as well as if they were your own.' I hoped that this might work and I learned long afterwards that it had done. The wounded men were treated reasonably.[12]

5 Column reached Tigyaing before 3 Column. Bernard Fergusson's account confirms Tigyaing as his preference:

> Instead of trying to slink across the Irrawaddy with our pitiful collection of rubber boats – an operation which would probably take several nights – I resolved to make for some town where boats were likely to be plentiful and to try to cross in one bold stroke. My choice fell on Tigyaing ... It was some 20 miles from Katha and still farther from Wuntho, the two garrisons most likely to come out and hunt us.[32]

Fergusson described his feelings on reaching Tigyaing:

> There, for the first time, I saw the Irrawaddy river. My first reaction was to thank my stars I had come to a ferry town, for getting across without the help of proper boats was obviously out of the question. It was fully a mile wide. Although much of the space was filled up with sandbanks, the actual channel was not less than half a mile.[33]

They crossed on 10 March. It began well and men came forward a Platoon at a time. They were issued with supplies, waded to the main sandbank and boarded the boats. Most were across when the Japanese came up from the south and clashed with the Column rear-guard. The last six men on the sandbank included Fergusson and Stibbe. Machine gun fire was heard as they boarded the last boat and their departure lacked dignity. The Column Commander was on all fours, with his behind exposed to enemy fire.[29] Wingate and 1,200 men reached Inywa village, some 10 miles north of Tigyaing, a few days later. They had crossed the river by 18 March.[34]

3 and 5 Columns continued south-east towards a new target, the Gokteik Gorge viaduct carrying the Mandalay/Lashio road and railway. Calvert could have destroyed this viaduct in 1942 but had orders to leave it intact. This fresh attempt would be difficult, as the viaduct was around 150 miles away. Calvert's Column would destroy the viaduct and Fergusson's men would guard the approach. Calvert was as aggressive as ever. His Column prepared three interlinked ambushes and sprung the trap on a Japanese Company. Calvert wrote: 'It was one of the most one-sided actions I have ever fought in. We simply shot them to pieces. About a hundred of the enemy were killed. We lost one man, a Gurkha NCO.'[12]

Wingate's decision to cross the Irrawaddy has been much criticised over the years. Yet Calvert and Fergusson firmly backed the crossing at the time. In taking this decision, Wingate must have taken into consideration inaccurate intelligence about the country east of the Irrawaddy. It turned out to be a waterless plain crossed by roads frequently patrolled by the Japanese. Furthermore, 77 Brigade's Columns would now go hungry. They had reached the maximum range of air supply with fighter protection.[35] Fergusson's ATO, Bill Smyly, recalls:

'We had dreams about food. We had been 28 days without supplies when Fergusson quoted Burns, saying that Heaven was oat cakes and honey – at which everyone groaned and laughed in a rather subdued, melancholy way. He sent a wireless message to Wingate, who thought bibles more efficient than codebooks. I think the message was Psalm 22:17 (I may tell all my bones. They look and stare upon me), to which Wingate replied with John 11:50 (Ye know nothing at all. It is expedient that one should die for the people).'

Wisely, Fergusson kept the Force Commander's response to himself, substituting something bland but more encouraging: (Be of good cheer: I will come unto you).[36]

Despite their extreme hunger, the men had meat on the hoof. Bill Smyly:

'Oddly, we still had a couple of bullocks with us. I don't know why we didn't slaughter one. I can't remember this being discussed at the time. Curiously, I don't think anyone thought about our animals as being 'food'.'

The men also went thirsty in the dry country east of the Irrawaddy. Smyly and many others eventually came to regard Wingate's decision as a mistake. His force was now confined within a triangular pocket formed by the Irrawaddy to the west, the Shweli to the east and a motorable track/road to the south. The Japanese pressure increased. In 3 Column, Cypher Officer Alec Gibson felt concern as they advanced ever deeper into Japanese-held Burma. His confidence began to wane when they crossed the Irrawaddy:

'Wireless traffic suggested that the entire Brigade had crossed successfully. I wasn't really worried until that point but, when we crossed the Irrawaddy, I remember thinking: 'We are certainly going a long way in'.'

It has been said that all Column Commanders supported the crossing of the Irrawaddy, but some probably harboured doubts. Indeed, 2 Group's Commander, Lieutenant-Colonel S.A. 'Sam' Cooke, confided to his diary:

It was obvious that we had already outmarched our strength and were no longer in a fit state to meet the Japanese in any strength. In spite of this, the Brigadier had made up his mind to cross the Irrawaddy and join the Columns which had already crossed over with success. My own opinion is that he was wrong in making this decision. Examination of a map of the area east of the Irrawaddy, into which we were to cross, showed that we were proposing to enter an area surrounded on three sides by quite formidable obstacles – to the east and north was the Shweli River and to the west would lie the Irrawaddy. Having moved into this area ... there was every possibility that we might be shut in by the Japanese. The knowledge we had of this area was scant and we had no information concerning water supplies.

Knowing that the present operations were not to be supported by any offensive on the part of British forces and that it would be physically impossible to endure the privations of the tropical Monsoon, he should, I consider, have been content with his present success and have kept his forces to the west of the Irrawaddy ... Lying in my blankets, physically exhausted, I found my brain pondering over all these problems and, in spite of the Brigadier's Order of the Day and its exhortations to greater efforts in the future, I felt we were entering upon what would prove to be a fruitless adventure, rather than a considered military operation.

3 Column's morale remained high, reflecting Calvert's superb leadership and aggression. The Column had disrupted rail communications around Nankan and repulsed all Japanese efforts to stop them. Yet hunger, exhaustion and disease, in the weeks to follow, took a heavy toll. Within all Columns the strain began to show as the men neared the Irrawaddy. Sergeant Tony Aubrey, with 8 Column, saw many animals put out of their misery. The Column's mood became subdued: 'There was little or no backchat to be heard in the ranks – always a bad sign, that – and everyone plodded doggedly on, the world reduced to a circumscribed vista of blistered heels, aching legs and close, foetid, menacing jungle.'[37]

On crossing the Irrawaddy the men continued to lose condition. They became lousy and many were deeply disturbed at their personal filth. Tony Aubrey:

> If you have never been in this charming condition, you can have no idea how maddening it is to know that your body is foul and to be able to do precisely nothing about it. At every halt, off came our shirts and fingers, knives and lighted matches were plied indefatigably, but all to no avail. Lousy we were and lousy we would remain until we returned to civilisation.[38]

8 Column, together with 7 Column, had fought a highly successful action and killed 219 Japanese for the loss of two dead and 17 wounded. During the fighting, on 23 March, Tony Aubrey was wounded, receiving a bullet in the right shoulder. 8 Column moved off to rendezvous with 5 Column. They joined up, overcame finer feelings about animal welfare and slaughtered some bullocks. The men rested for 48 hours, then received orders to return to India. The reaction was muted. Most men were lost in thought about the hundreds of miles of dense jungle and two major river crossings now separating them from the rest of their lives.[39]

Wingate accepted that he had no choice. Water was very scarce east of the river. Motorable roads would allow the Japanese to concentrate against them with ease. His men could no longer rely on air-dropped supplies and they would continue to weaken without adequate rations. Meanwhile, the Japanese began to block the routes back to India.

Some Columns were luckier than others with their air drops. On 18 March Calvert's Column received 10 tons – *Longcloth's* biggest supply drop.[40] 5 Column was far less fortunate. Bernard Fergusson wrote: 'The worst feature of the 1943 expedition, apart from having to abandon our wounded, was the lack of food. Only five aircraft could be spared us for our air supply and, of these, two were Hudsons, which proved useless for the purpose.' They were warned that the best they could hope for was a drop every seven days (and that seven days' rations might have to last 10 days).[41] The reality was much worse. They were in for 93 days and received just 20 days' rations.

This should convey the true value of the two-day ration 'bonus' awarded to 5 Column for receiving the Brigade drop. Fergusson's men left Tonmakeng with seven days' food, but had to wait *16 days* for another drop. Fortunately, they made the most of their opportunity to buy food at Tigyaing, when crossing the Irrawaddy. They then moved away from the river and rested the next day, 11 March, before making for Pegon and an air drop scheduled for 14 March. Everyone was extremely hungry at that point.[42] Fergusson noted how the Column's smokers suffered less from hunger pangs. He became convinced that the cigarette ration saved lives.[41] He added: 'I would say, without hesitation, that lack of food constitutes the biggest single assault upon morale. Apart from its purely chemical effects upon the body, it has woeful effects upon the mind.'

There was an unspoken dread that growing weakness might soon prove overwhelming, making it impossible to continue. Fergusson reflected: 'Of all the men whom I have had to leave, wounded, sick or starving, not one reproached me, or made the dreadful duty harder than it already was.'[43]

5 Column was just a few miles from Pegon and the promised air drop when it set out on 13 March, but the men soon found themselves in thick jungle riddled with deep defiles. Philip Stibbe's Platoon went ahead to prepare for the drop, scheduled for 10.00 the next day. Exhausted and desperate for water, they were lucky enough to find a well just outside Pegon and their good fortune continued with the purchase of chicken and rice for a rare and satisfying meal. Everything was ready by 09.00 on 14 March and the aircraft were on time, dropping five days' rations although everyone worried about how to make this last eight or nine days. The water situation remained serious. They took to digging out dry river beds, creating small pools of muddy water.[42]

On 17 March Bernard Fergusson briefed his Column. The men politely kept their feelings to themselves when told they were now operating further east than any other British troops.[42] They reached the Nam Mit chaung the next day and rested. Some took their first opportunity to wash since the Irrawaddy crossing a week earlier.

Fergusson was shocked by the deterioration in their physical condition. Philip Stibbe noted the mental deterioration. He suddenly became aware that many men were afraid of being alone in the jungle, even over distances of just a few hundred yards. From then on, his men always moved in pairs when on errands.[44] 5 Column ATO Bill Smyly provides a context for this fearful attitude:

'The reason for this was the fate of two men some days before we crossed the Irrawaddy. We were marching through open teak forest and stopped for the midday halt in an area where young teak trees and other vegetation offered delightful shade. The two men fell asleep and no-one wakened them when the whistles blew and the Column reformed to march off. They must have woken up to the nightmare of being alone. We sent out search parties and three days later we found their packs and rifles abandoned in a nullah, where they had been digging for water. We guessed they had abandoned their gear before hunting the Japanese to surrender. The effect on the rest of us was like a nightmare. What would we do in the jungle if we woke up and the Column had moved on? From that time each man was made responsible for two or three others, but we still had the nightmare because it had happened.'

While waiting for Wingate, Fergusson moved his bivouac for security reasons. He was worried about the obvious path created from the chaung to the bivouac and he was wise to move. A 50-strong Japanese patrol soon attacked the now empty bivouac. Another drop was scheduled for 23 March on the dry bed of the Nam Pan, 12 miles north. 5 Column set out slowly for this drop site, the men encouraged to take every opportunity to rest and husband their waning strength. The animals, however, began to drop out and die. They met up with 1 Column elements on reaching Nam Pan. These men had just taken a drop but warned that a Japanese unit had been tracking them.

The results of the 23 March drop were disappointing, yielding just three days' rations. 5 Column was ordered to make for Brigade HQ near Baw village, ready for another drop. On the way they heard mortar fire ahead and aircraft could be seen above the rendezvous. Fergusson and a Burrif party went ahead and failed to return by the appointed time, 04.00. The Column then made for the next rendezvous, north of Baw, and was soon reunited with Fergusson and his group. They made contact with Brigade and a new rendezvous was fixed. When they came together there was disappointment, as they received rations for just one day. The mood changed, however, with news that they were to return to India.[45]

Orde Wingate now had orders to return. Michael Calvert took the news badly – the Gokteik Viaduct would escape his attentions yet again. 3 Column Cypher Officer Alec Gibson was the first of Calvert's men to read the orders concerning the return. As he decoded the signal he was struck by a particular phrase: 'Strive to save all valuable personnel'. Gibson recalls thinking: 'Non-swimmers are probably not at a premium'. He took the message to his Column Commander:

'Calvert was upset at first. He wanted to continue to move forward. Yet it was clear there was no choice, due to the inability to drop supplies beyond the range of available fighter cover. With some sadness we prepared to split up for the return.'

Wingate ordered the Columns to divide into small dispersal groups, to increase the chances of reaching safety. True to form, Calvert wanted his Column to remain intact as a fighting unit, but eventually acquiesced. His command split into nine groups for the return. Their initial plan, to cross the Shweli and head north for Fort Hertz or China, was abandoned due to the growing Japanese presence. India became the goal. Calvert's dispersal conference was called during the afternoon of 30 March. Two or three officers were allocated to each dispersal group. Calvert advised on various routes and joined his officers in drinking a toast in rum. Each group took a different route, in the hope of avoiding detection.[46]

Alec Gibson and Lieutenant Ken Gourlay led one of two groups consisting of HQ personnel and Gurkhas. Alec Gibson:

'Navigation in the jungle is very difficult. It is absolutely critical to know exactly where you are when you start out. Naturally, it is impossible to follow an absolutely straight course in thick jungle and our maps were indifferent at best.'

Gibson calculated that it was about 120 miles to the Chindwin's east bank. Allowing for frequent diversions and ascents and descents in deep, narrow valleys, the actual distance would be closer to 180 miles:

'Before we left we ditched all heavy equipment. We had no wireless and no means of calling up supply drops. We would be living off the land. There was the obvious possibility of being killed or wounded but I didn't give that much thought. I just assumed I'd be OK. Yet we all knew we would be left behind if we were wounded or became too ill to march.'

Men took their chance to eat whenever they could. One party of Gurkhas led by Lieutenant Nick Neil shot a water buffalo in a pond, dragged it out of the water and dismembered it, quickly, fearful that the shot might have compromised them. Even so, they lit a fire, roasted strips of meat, then laid them on top of their packs, to dry in the sun as they marched on. It took them just 30 minutes to dispatch the animal, cook the meat and leave the scene.

Notes

1. Fowler, W. (2009), *We Gave Our Today: Burma 1941–1945*, 95–97
2. Fergusson, B. (1971), *Beyond the Chindwin*, 54
3. Ibid, 50–51
4. Ibid, 48
5. Halley, D. (1945), *With Wingate in Burma*, 54
6. Fergusson, B. (1971), 64–66
7. Ibid, 29–30
8. Ibid, 57
9. Ibid, 93
10. Stibbe, P. (1995), *Return via Rangoon*, 63
11. Ibid, 67–70
12. Calvert, M. (1996), *Fighting Mad*, 120–126
13. Halley, D. (1945), 69
14. Stibbe, P. (1995), 65–66
15. Fergusson, B. (1971), 72–73
16. Carfrae, C. (1985), *Chindit Column*, 146
17. Cross, J.P. (1989), *Jungle Warfare*, 19
18. Fergusson, B. (1971), 135–136
19. Ibid, 120–121
20. Carfrae, C. (1985), 154
21. Fergusson, B. (1971), 224
22. Fraser, G.M. (1995), *Quartered Safe Out Here*, 40
23. Fergusson, B. (1971), 89
24. Stibbe, P. (1995), 71–75
25. Fergusson, B. (1971), 85
26. Rooney, D. (2000), *Wingate and the Chindits: Redressing the Balance*, 84–87
27. Stibbe, P. (1995), 76–85
28. Rooney, D. (1997), *Mad Mike*, 50–53
29. Stibbe, P. (1995), 86–94
30. Calvert, M. (1996), 121–123
31. Fergusson, B. (1971), 115–116
32. Ibid, 91
33. Ibid, 105–106
34. Rooney, D. (2000), 88
35. Rooney, D. (1997), 54–57
36. Stibbe, P. (1995), 103
37. Halley, D. (1945), 75
38. Ibid, 82
39. Ibid, 86–95
40. Rooney, D. (2000), 90
41. Fergusson, B. (1946), *The Wild Green Earth*, 186–189
42. Stibbe, P. (1995), 95–102
43. Fergusson, B. (1946), 194–195
44. Stibbe, P. (1995), 104
45. Ibid, 105–111
46. Chinnery, P.D. (2002), *March or Die*, 69–70

4

GETTING OUT: THE STRUGGLE TO SURVIVE

'I was determined to get them out and I always thought I would, but it took some believing at times. I brought all 15 out alive.'

Sergeant-Major Bob Hobbs, 2 Column

THE JAPANESE were determined to punish Wingate's force. They established three north-south patrol lines (Irrawaddy/Mu Valley/Chindwin) to snare the returning Chindits.[1]

Major Fergusson, 5 Column's Commander, watched reactions as the news spread that they were returning to India.[2] He worried that this might put the men in a dangerously over-cautious frame of mind. 5 Column joined Brigade HQ and 7 and 8 Columns on the Hehtin Chaung. Everyone realised this was now a fight for survival, with no supply drops until the Irrawaddy was crossed and no foraging in villages for security reasons. The Brigade would move back *en masse* to Inywa, around 40 miles away, where Wingate and 7 and 8 Columns had crossed just recently. Wingate assumed (wrongly, as it happened) that the Japanese would not expect him to return the same way.

Bernard Fergusson's men slaughtered some mules on the way back to the river. Rifle Platoon Commander Philip Stibbe was among the very few who found mule acceptable: 'Mule meat is very tasty. We tried various ways of cooking it. It seemed to keep best when roasted and each man put a good sized steak in his pack for the march.'[3]

Wingate wanted most mules slaughtered, to speed up the return. Food was a by-product. In *Beyond the Chindwin*, Fergusson described how his Animal Transport Officer (ATO) supervised the shooting of animals in groups of six: 'Poor Bill Smyly marched that day with a white face, slipping away every now and then to despatch a few more and rejoining the Column with tears on his cheek.'[4]

According to Fergusson, Wingate eventually halted the slaughter due to the noise. Smyly's recollections differ from Fergusson's account (which appears to document what should have happened, rather than what actually took place). Firstly, Smyly recalls being ordered to kill the mules silently:

'Vets can do this with a special spring knife, by clipping a large vein about elbow length up the rectum. I had been shown how (in conversation, rather than formal training) by the Chief Vet, Colonel Stewart, when he supervised the 'silencing' of mule vocal chords in Jhansi. I had felt the pulse in this vein but did not have the gadget and would not have tried it anyway without supervision.

'The regular way to kill a mule is a pistol shot to the forehead. This is also where a poleaxe or humane killer is used to stun. I tried to kill one mule holding a bayonet to this point and getting a British armourer (a very strong man in the Engineering Section) to drive it in with the butt of a rifle. The bayonet went in about four inches and the animal stood looking at me. I shot him quickly with my pistol. Five rounds left and no spares!'

Bill Smyly solved his problem with as much care as pragmatism allowed: 'All the other mules had their saddles taken off and were left in the jungle, in halters. I hoped the Japanese would be kind to them.'

Orde Wingate led the way as they set out on 27 March 1943. He planned to cross the river at Inywa on the night of 28 March. All non-essential kit was abandoned. Philip Stibbe reluctantly threw away his Milton and divided the contents of a medical haversack between members of his Platoon. He began taking a cod liver oil capsule and a biscuit as a meal.[5]

EVEN   OUR   MOST   FAITHFUL   FOLLOWERS   FOUND
THE   ROAD   TOO   TOUGH   AND   MANY   WERE   LEFT
ON   THE   TRACKSIDE

Point of no return: many mules were overcome by hunger, thirst and exhaustion. They collapsed and were unable to continue. (Tony Wailes)

Wingate always made great demands on himself and generally saw no reason to treat others differently. An observer from his days in Palestine wrote:

> Wingate's theory was that as long as a man is conscious, his willpower must force him to go on. If you pity him too much, not good. If consciousness [is] gone, he must be given every help and comfort. When we came to water, he gave everyone to drink and he drank last.[5]

Major Gilkes' 7 Column made for China – a way out seen as longer but safer. Some Columns dispersed. A number of dispersal groups came very close to safety, only to be undone by the fact that IV Corps had pulled back from sections of the Chindwin's west bank. Consequently, they were captured or killed by Japanese patrols.[6] Fergusson:

> Our troubles arose from the fact that all seven Columns eventually found themselves, in late March and early April, in a great bag formed by two wide rivers – the Irrawaddy and the Shweli – and across the mouth of this bag ran a motor road. The Japanese were able to bring up substantial reinforcements, to patrol the road, to confiscate all the boats they could find on the rivers, and to occupy all the villages where we hoped to victual and many of the Columns, like my own, had lost in action the wireless sets on which we depended for supplies from the air.[7]

There were mixed fortunes during the return. Major Gilkes' 7 Column eventually split into three dispersal groups. One took supply drops and succeeded in reaching Fort Hertz, in the far north. A second group, including the less fit, made for the Chindwin. Gilkes' own group headed for China. They crossed the Shweli on 17 April and reached Chinese forces around Yunnan on 1 May. They were feted as heroes. Gilkes even received a loan of US$7,000, allowing him to pay his men and give them the opportunity to buy presents for their families! The Americans flew them back to India.

Michael Calvert's 3 Column, 20 miles south of the main body, proceeded independently and his men suffered terribly on the return. One officer (Lieutenant Jeffrey Lockett) later said he kept going only with heavy doses of Benzedrine, adding that he was taking up to 12 tablets daily as they neared the Chindwin. Yet Calvert's inner fire still burned. When his party reached the railway he couldn't resist one final series of demolitions.[8]

Having taken its final supply drop near Taunggon, receiving food, ammunition, boots and other stores, 3 Column had divided into its dispersal groups. Calvert respected Wingate's view that each party should not exceed 40 in number, so offering more opportunity to live off the land. They then took their chosen routes towards the Irrawaddy and Chindwin. Rooney wrote:

His orders to the group leaders are a model of sound sense, built on wide experience, and probably account for the fact that a high proportion of 3 Column arrived safely home. First he tackled the problem of tiredness, saying: 'Tiredness makes cowards of us all' and he ordered them to march methodically and not to get overtired. Then he added, with homely and sound sense, 'If you are really up against it, sit down and make a cup of tea, and the problem will usually get solved'. Then, on another plane, he warned them not to let the hunted feeling get to them. He advised them not to go so far out of their way to avoid Japanese patrols that they suffer more casualties through drowning or through the lack of food and water.[9]

There were many rivers to cross and, here too, he gave sound advice: 'If you can't get boats in one place, then get them in another and, if all else fails, make big rafts of bamboo and push off at night. Remember, it doesn't matter how far you drift downriver.' Realising that the new groups might themselves be split up, he ordered the unit commanders to ensure that every man had a map giving directions and distances.[9]

Calvert took the Commando Platoon, cooks and orderlies south, to draw the Japanese away from the other groups. They then turned north-west, successfully crossed the Irrawaddy and reached the railway south of Nankan. Calvert forgot himself that night. He had failed to score the time pencils required to detonate the explosives. This would have allowed him to select, in the dark, those with the appropriate time. He found a solution but won only grudging compliance from Jeffrey Lockett, a Scot who always wore his kilt. Calvert ordered him to oblige with some tartan cover, so allowing him to strike matches and select the time pencils required without showing a light.[10]

8 Column also suffered grievously. Scott's men went far to the north, hindered by growing numbers of sick, wounded and exhausted men. Meanwhile, 5 Column pressed on, hoping to reach Inywa by around 18.00 the following day, 28 March. Wingate told Fergusson to throw a defensive screen around the crossing area. The 5 Column Commander became confused by a reference in his orders to setting an ambush. He decided to distract the Japanese by creating a false night bivouac and lighting fires near the occupied village of Hintha.[3]

Now within a mile of Hintha village, Fergusson put his plan into action. A force was to be sent into the village to attack any Japanese in residence, as the rest of the Column proceeded along the chaung. Unfortunately, the main body then found the way blocked by prickly bamboo. Bill Smyly describes what he terms 'the most impenetrable wall in Nature':

'Imagine a bamboo in the middle of such a clump growing up vertically like a telegraph pole. Cover this with horizontal branches sticking out straight at one foot intervals and defend these all over with very sharp six inch spikes and a few bamboo leaves, so that you aren't sure where the spikes are.'

Fergusson had no choice but to take his entire Column through the village. Suddenly, Hintha was before them. Fergusson and two Burrifs entered the village, the Major with grenade in hand. He saw four figures seated around a fire, assumed they were Burmese and approached. He said a few words, suddenly realised they were Japanese, tossed the grenade into the fire and fled. Fergusson then ordered Philip Stibbe to go in with his Rifle Platoon and clear Hintha with the bayonet. During the advance Stibbe was hit in the left shoulder. He was then ordered to pull back. As one of his Platoon applied a field dressing, Stibbe had sufficient presence of mind to remove the remaining rations from his pack and stuff them down the front of his shirt. Fergusson was also wounded, with grenade fragments in the hip. A Column Platoon then attacked and managed to clear the track.

'Doc' Aird dressed Stibbe's wound while under fire: 'The bullet had gone in through my chest just below my left collar bone, leaving only a very small hole which I had not noticed; the hole at the back, where it came out, was considerably larger and it was from this that I was losing all the blood'.[3]

They continued to take casualties and were unable to punch through. They found a way round the enemy positions but Fergusson was now under extreme pressure as it grew light. He made his decision and 'Second Dispersal' was sounded. Groups within the Column broke away and set out independently towards a pre-agreed rendezvous.[3] When the fighting began, ATO Bill Smyly took cover with his men on the track:

'We were there a long time. I nodded off. We hadn't slept for 20 hours and didn't sleep again for another

Last chance for salvation: statichutes were quickly arranged to form the words 'PLANE LAND HERE NOW'. Three days later a Dakota put down in the clearing and evacuated Major Scott's wounded and sick, despite the fact that it was only a few minutes flying time from a Japanese fighter strip. (Trustees of the Imperial War Museum)

20. It wasn't a deep sleep, just nodding off from time to time. The Japanese were making a lot of noise. I think they had the Platoon idiot in some safe place, hooting and calling out in English. They did not attack. Nor did we. We waited for someone to stand up, so we could shoot him. The Japs did the same.

'The men were around me on the ground, facing various directions. They all had rifles, of course – Lee Enfields and 20 rounds. That's not a lot and we didn't want to waste them. There were cat-calls in the dark: 'Hey! Hey! Tommy! Tommy!' I can't remember how long we were there. The waiting came to an end with the Dispersal. It was sounded by trumpet. Wingate had given this to our Bugler – a beautiful instrument, of which he was very proud.

'It was a wonderful, stirring call in the middle of the night. It was supposed to tell us to break up and go off in every direction, circle round and meet up at a pre-set rendezvous. Trouble was we didn't have the rendezvous and very few of us had maps. We were on our own from that moment unless we followed others. I followed others! When dawn came we could see planes coming in to a dropping zone and we made for that.'

Philip Stibbe's Platoon covered the withdrawal. Stibbe was put on a pony, led by Private Joe Boyle. They had trouble keeping up with their dispersal group and soon discovered why – the horse itself was wounded. Stibbe decided he couldn't continue at a point around one and a half miles from Hintha. A Burrif volunteered to stay with him: 'Finally, Sergeant Whitehead of the Support Platoon sprang to attention and saluted me. Then they went on down the track and left me, but not, thank God, alone.'[3]

His companion was Rifleman Maung Tun, known to all as 'Moto'. He did what he could to make Stibbe comfortable:

> Although my wound did not hurt me while I lay still, every movement was painful. I also found that when I lay on my left side the blood seemed to collect there, so every time my heart beat there was a squelching sound, like a small sponge being squeezed out.[3]

Maung Tun left Stibbe to search for food. Stibbe took two morphia pills and slept. When he awoke he was alone, but Maung Tun then returned. He intended to

Survivors: the wounded and sick on their way to safety. A cup of water is passed to Corporal Jimmy Walter, suffering from dysentery and an infected hip. He fell behind the Column but managed to catch up at the clearing. (Trustees of the Imperial War Museum)

Good to be alive: Sergeant Len McElroy, from Seegley, Manchester, and Corporal Jimmy Walter, from Berwick-upon-Tweed. McElroy's right arm is bandaged. (Trustees of the Imperial War Museum)

leave Stibbe with the villagers once the Japanese left Hintha. The following morning Maung Tun left to keep a rendezvous with a villager and this time he failed to return. After waiting 48 hours Stibbe went in search of water. It was 31 March. On approaching Hintha he walked into a party of Japanese. Later, he discovered that Maung Tun had been taken and tortured but had stubbornly refused to betray him. The Japanese then shot him.[3]

As Bernard Fergusson's dispersal group neared Inywa they heard shooting and concluded that the Brigade's crossing of the Irrawaddy was being opposed. Indeed, elements of Major Gilkes' 7 Column had come under fire as they attempted to cross. Two Platoons, using boats apparently collected by the Japanese, were in mid-stream when fired on from the opposite bank. Men watching on the other bank returned fire. In this exchange the six rowing boats in transit were virtually ignored. They reached the far bank downstream from the enemy, but never rejoined the Column.[11]

Wingate favoured dispersal groups no more than 40 strong. Fergusson, now missing many members of 5 Column at the rendezvous following the Hintha action, took a different view. He felt that his relatively large force, if kept together, would be sufficiently powerful to overcome any likely opposition. He decided that his depleted Column would do better heading north and east, well clear of any threat in the Inywa area. He would cross the Shweli and enter the relatively friendly Kachin hills. Sadly, however, he was to lose many more men, who were unable to cross the formidable and fast-flowing Shweli.

5 Column ATO Bill Smyly had no knowledge of Fergusson's rendezvous but had joined others heading for a supply drop taking place in the distance:

'I reported to the officer running the drop. We were then attached to the large group commanded by Major Ken Gilkes. They planned to cross the Shweli at one of its narrowest points. An engineering team prepared the crossing. A line was fired across and secured to tree roots on the far bank. Transport was by rubber dinghy, with six men holding the rope, standing on a sandbank on the near side.'

Following the Hintha fighting and the abandonment of the Irrawaddy crossing, Gilkes' 7 Column had divided. His party was now swollen by members of 5 Column, including Smyly's group. Burma Rifles officer George Astell and his party were first across. Bill Smyly:

'There were just 60 of them and it took all night! As dawn was breaking I was called to the head of the Column and Major Gilkes asked me if I would like to take over the dinghy. I said we would. He, poor man, had this huge crowd depending on him and he had to reduce the number somehow. Also, the crossing did seem possible – the going had been slow, but it looked possible.

'We were on a sand spit, on the inside of a bend in the fast-flowing river. This side was flat sandbank. The other side was a steep bank. Engineers had secured a rope to the far bank and it was held this side by six British soldiers. Six of my men took over. Two men were needed as boat crew, to help get the loaded boat over, secure it when it reached the other side and bring it back again for the next load. I should have asked the British Engineers for a couple of volunteers to man the dinghy, but thought of that too late. Gurkhas do not normally play with boats.

'So here we have 28 men to be ferried over the fast-flowing narrows and I reckoned it would take at least three trips, say 20 minutes each. The dinghy held about eight men with their gear – six passengers and two crew to stay with the inflatable and bring it back for the second and third loads. The dinghy had a ring of rope loops around the outside. We would carry as much gear as possible in the early loads and, on the final trip, non-swimmers inside and the rest in the water, hanging onto the ropes. I expected to be with them and to launch out into the stream till we lost our foothold and then allow the current to swing us like a pendulum to the east bank.

'My orders were to report to Astell, for whom a supply drop had been arranged. He would give me the map reference. I went over with the first load and raced up the bank to get the map reference and let him know we were joining his party. It was full daylight by now and Astell was fretting to be off. His men were Karens and Kachins eager to reach home. Gilkes however, planned to head for China with the rest of his party and fly home over "The Hump", which he did!

'I got my map reference and returned to the shore, at the base of the bank. The rope was taut and the holding team was in place on the other side. The Havildar had ordered his men to fan out in a defensive position. That was good. But ... no dinghy! There were just six men this side, so we must have lost two. Maybe they had lost their grip on the rope and been whirled downstream. Boat and crew had vanished. Some members of the holding team had put their boots, rifles and packs in the dinghy on my orders and now they were on the other side – with bare feet and their boots, rifles and packs gone.

'Astell's very courageous Batman then crossed to me on the rope, hand over hand – an extremely dangerous feat. My men were silent at first and then

began to curse. No-one followed the Batman. They turned away from the river, to rejoin Gilkes' force. My group of 28 was now reduced to six Gurkhas. We were on the east bank and with no need of a map reference, as Astell's Batman tracked the party ahead as if he were walking down his own village street. We were with them inside the hour. Gilkes' group, meanwhile, crossed the river the following day, headed east for the Burma Road and into China. They were flown out to India from Kunming.'

Bernard Fergusson's experience of the Shweli was even more traumatic. His group of around 120 was carried across by Burmese boatmen, who betrayed them during the night. They discovered that they had been marooned on a huge sandbank, probably better described as a jungle-covered island, with a fast-running channel separating them from the far bank. Fergusson gave a graphic description of what it was like to cross that stretch of river:

> There was no word for it but 'nightmare'. The roaring of the waters, the blackness of the night, the occasional sucking of a quicksand were bad enough, but the current was devilish. At its deepest I suppose it was about four feet six or a little more. I am over six foot one and it was more than breast-high on me. The current must have been four or five knots. It sought to scoop the feet from under you and, at the same time, thrust powerfully at your chest. The only method of progress was to lean against the current, to attempt to keep an intermittent footing, to maintain your angle against the stream, and kick off the ground whenever your feet touched it. If once you lost your vertical position, you knew as a black certainty that you would disappear down the stream forever.
>
> It was not until almost within reach of the bank that the river shallowed to a couple of feet and, even then, it was all one could do to make one's way upstream against it. Although the crossing could not have been more than 70 or 80 yards, one finished at least 40 yards farther downstream than the point of the sandbank.[12]

This ordeal was compounded by a terrible decision now thrust into Fergusson's hands. There were no boats and over 40 of his men refused to attempt the crossing and stayed put on the sandbank. Fergusson made it clear that they could either wade or stay where they were. As dawn neared Fergusson had to leave them. He wrote movingly of that dreadful moment:

> I made the decision to come away. I have it on my conscience for as long as I live, but I stand by that decision and believe it to be the correct one. Those who may think otherwise may well be right. Some of my officers volunteered to stay, but I refused them permission to do so.[13]

A total of 46 men were left behind. Some subsequently drowned trying to cross. Fergusson added a comment which underlines the fact that war inflicts more than physical wounds: 'The crossing of the Shweli River will haunt me all my life and, to my mind, the decision which fell to me there was as cruel as any which could fall on the shoulders of a junior commander.'[13]

The Shweli also challenged Major Walter Scott's 8 Column, now with Lieutenant-Colonel Sam Cooke's Headquarters, Northern Group. Scott attempted to keep the main body of his Column intact, although two parties had been permitted to proceed independently. The main body reached the Shweli on 1 April.[14] Engineers rigged an endless pulley system to work the Column's few dinghies. For some reason an NCO cut the rope after only 35 men had crossed and the dinghies were lost. The party already across was told to proceed as Engineers began to build rafts. Unfortunately, all sank immediately upon launching.[15] The party already across the river was then ambushed, leaving only one survivor.[14]

A request for more dinghies was answered; six more were dropped on 3 April. This drop, however, produced only one day's food ration per man. They crossed the river, keeping only a wireless mule, and continued north towards the Irrawaddy. Three days later this Column skirmished with Japanese manning a strongpoint. They drove out the enemy but reinforcements arrived by truck. The vehicles were engaged with concentrated Bren fire and four were destroyed but a Sergeant and a Section of seven vanished during this action.

Scott took another supply drop on a high ridge some 15 miles to the north. His men were exhausted and out of rations. He called an officers' conference and reviewed the options: to go north, regardless of the appalling country and lack of water; to make for China, despite lack of maps and uncertainties over the distance involved; or to return the way they came in, crossing the Irrawaddy and Chindwin. The officers were told to put it to the men. The majority had had enough of rivers and elected to go north.[16]

Scott's Column then broke into small dispersal parties, with the leader of each group free to choose his own route. Three wounded men, two British and one Burmese, were left with villagers. Sergeant Tony Aubrey was a member of the party taking the wounded in. After a terrible struggle through dense jungle they reached the village, only to find it abandoned. The Burma Rifles officer, Captain Whitehead, knew of another village six miles on and the wounded were left there. The party split in two. Sergeant Aubrey's group went back, to reach Scott before he moved off and explain the reasons for delay. Aubrey pushed on ahead for the last leg and spent a miserable hour hopelessly lost. Then he reached his destination but found that Scott and HQ had already left. He wrote a note and made a directional arrow for those behind him, set off again and was greatly relieved to be reunited with the main body just a mile further on.[17]

It would be difficult to overstate the hardships borne by Orde Wingate's men during the return. 'Few men have ever suffered such prolonged privations as the Chindits endured during the next weeks. They had gone into Burma as outstandingly fit, strong men and the majority came out as emaciated skeletons hardly able to walk, their muscles wasted away, leaving brittle skin and bone.'[18] Starvation overshadowed the return. During the long march in over the Burmese hills Sergeant Major Bob Hobbs bought rice in the villages:

'It took about a month to get used to jungle living, but we were quick to learn. For one thing, we found it best to under-cook rice. When you eat under-cooked rice it swells up in your stomach and keeps you going for 24 hours or more, slowly releasing energy.'

Hobbs was a strict disciplinarian, always reminding his men to take salt and use the water-purifying tablets:

'It was important to use both water purification tablets. The first tablet 'killed all known germs', but you couldn't drink water in that state. The second tablet made it palatable. As for Mepacrine, I'd heard the usual rumours but it didn't do me any harm. I went on to have three sons!'

Bob Hobbs' Column included many young Gurkhas. Over six decades later, his right forearm carries a reminder – a large tattoo of crossed kukris. His men did well:

'We were good at looking for and finding the enemy. I came under fire quite a few times. We often heard the Japanese call out in English at night. It was always obvious they were Japs. I killed at least three during an action in a goods yard near a railway station. We got into a goods shed full of Japanese. The men with me killed many more in that building. We attacked it at night.'

Utter relief: Lance Corporal Fred Nightingale, still wearing his sweat-rag and very happy to get out. Some of these photographs were published in *Life*, Vol. 14, No. 26, 28 June 1943. (Trustees of the Imperial War Museum)

As *Longcloth* progressed Hobbs grew accustomed to going hungry for long periods. He took things in his stride: 'We crossed and recrossed the Chindwin and Irrawaddy rivers. We always crossed in the hours of darkness. You'd die trying to cross in daylight.'

When the order was given to disperse for the return, Bob Hobbs was put in charge of a group of 15 men. After 65 years, there was pride in his voice as he described his response to this challenge:

'I was determined to get them out and I always thought I would, but it took some believing at times. I brought all 15 out alive. We carried an inflatable dinghy to cross the big rivers. Most dispersal groups had at least one good swimmer. Our worst problem at that time was the state of our boots. Mine just fell to bits after the Chindwin crossing. On reaching the west bank I threw the remains away and bound my feet in an old pair of shorts. I marched the rest of the way in rags.'

Hunger ground them down. There is food in the Burmese jungle and fish in the rivers and lakes. Yet much of the wildlife – iguanas, snakes and tortoises – is unpalatable to Europeans. Bob Hobbs:

Comradeship: these 13th King's (Liverpool) men, pictured with a Gurkha soldier, were among those flown out. The Chindit on the right is Jim Rogerson – deep jungle sores are visible on his left forearm. (Trustees of the Imperial War Museum)

'I did try snake but it was no good. I went from 13 stone to seven stone. All I thought about was getting home. In our starved condition, hundreds of miles behind enemy lines, the strain began to show. Eventually, I got to such a state that I became frightened of my own shadow. It was just lack of food. There were times at that stage when I began to doubt whether we would get out, yet we did! We all had private thoughts that kept us going. I used to dream of going to the chiropodist! This seemed to me to be the height of luxury.'

One man in Sergeant Tony Aubrey's group made an amazing discovery near the Irrawaddy – a cave full of British Army petrol cans containing rice. It was the food hoard of a nearby village. Tony Aubrey: 'Our need was greater than theirs. We were told to take what we could

of it, every man of us, and we willingly complied, stuffing our socks ... and any other possible receptacle, to the limits of our packs' capacity. For every tin of rice we took, we left in the tin five silver Rupees.'[19]

Major Scott now faced a dilemma. Two nearby villages were occupied by Burmese forces collaborating with the Japanese. His options were to storm one or other village and secure boats for the Irrawaddy crossing, or to continue north. The men favoured attacking a village but preparations were interrupted when two large Japanese motorboats called at the more northerly village. Scott left the vicinity and marched 10 miles north.

On reaching the river again Scott took the initiative. He stripped, jumped in, swam to a passing boat and used his revolver to commandeer it and ferry everyone across. It made three crossings, with some men in the water, hanging on to the sides. The surviving mule and wireless also crossed, but this animal was on its last legs. The Major gave the boat owners 500 silver Rupees. They sank to their knees, overcome with gratitude.

Scott's men took their last drop when the remaining mule died. They had reached an unusually large area of paddy. As the stores came down, they decided to persuade the pilot to land and fly out the seriously ill. They quickly used retrieved statichutes to spell out the message PLANE LAND HERE NOW. The Dakota could not get in and the men on the ground subsequently laid out a longer run (but still extraordinarily short for such an aircraft). Three days later, on 28 April, a Dakota piloted by Flying Officer Vlasto got in and evacuated the wounded and desperately ill, together with Lieutenant-Colonel Cooke, who was described in the resulting *Life* article as having 'intestinal trouble and jungle sores'. On board both flights was an American war correspondent, William Vandivert, who took photographs. Vlasto, escorted by

four Mohawk fighters, had put his aircraft down on a run of only 700 yards. He stayed on the ground just 12 minutes. The ragged Chindits hoped for more aircraft, to fly everyone out, but the clearing was just 20 miles away from the nearest Japanese fighter strip. They set off again, resigned to getting out the hard way but consoled by 10 days' rations, clothing and boots.[20]

Bill Smyly, 5 Column's ATO, makes some interesting observations on the differences between the Fergusson and Scott approaches to river crossings:

'This was a good example of how important it was to understand the position of the Burmese. Scott did. Fergusson didn't. Many of these people had accepted the Japanese and were at pains to please them. Scott took his pistol, commandeered a man's boat, made him do what he required and then rewarded him like a prince. Indian silver Rupees were 98 per cent pure silver, Britannia Metal. There is no such currency as that in the world today. Scott handed over a fortune.

Feeling lucky: tired, ragged but alive – two of the rescued pictured during the flight to safety and hospital. (Trustees of the Imperial War Museum)

Just enough energy for a joke: Private William Crowhurst of South Norwood and Sergeant Tony Aubrey display a souvenir – Burmese paper money. (Trustees of the Imperial War Museum)

'Poor Bernard Fergusson treated the boatmen like gentlemen, arranged a fair price, as if he were negotiating something in the market, and was tricked. He was landed with all his men on an island in the middle of a dangerously fast-flowing river. I bet the boatmen knew exactly what the situation was and went straight to the nearest Japanese outpost.'

In their weakened state, Wingate's men were haunted by the fear of ambush. George MacDonald Fraser described how men could smell the presence of Japanese: 'I can no more describe the smell than I could describe a colour; but it was heavy and pungent and compounded of stale cooked rice and sweat and human waste and ... Jap.'

The Japanese, of course, also had a sense of smell. J.P. Cross wrote: 'Smokers find it hard to realise just how much they stink compared with a non-smoker. I have smelt cigarette smoke one hour after a Platoon had moved off after a rest. The men had sat down near a swamp and the smell of the smoke had not moved.'[21]

The major challenge was to survive without air drops. Many groups making for India or seeking safety in another direction were soon in dire straits. Bernard Fergusson had just 74 men following the losses at the Shweli. He said his group existed in a state of 'despotic socialism', adding:

Nobody fared better than anybody else and offences against the community were to be treated severely.

I had warned all ranks that I would shoot them for any theft of rations among themselves, or for any act against the local population which might inflame it against us, such as pillaging or theft or offences against women. I had told them that I would pass judgement and carry out sentence myself, so that any illegality would lie at my door only. On two occasions I administered punishments not recognised in the Army, for offences against the community, and public opinion on both occasions (I made it my business to learn) approved. Both men concerned were good men who bore no ill-will and pulled their weight as well and in one case better than the average.[22]

Fergusson's troubles were far from over. A few days after the Shweli crossing they obtained food at Zibyugin village, but quickly retreated when warned that Japanese were approaching. Lieutenant Duncan Menzies then volunteered to return to the village with a small party to pick up more food. Menzies and another man were captured, shaved, dressed in Japanese uniform and used for live bayonet practice. Duncan Menzies was still alive when the village was cleared and he asked for a lethal dose of morphia.[23]

Fergusson's 70 men now divided into three groups for the return to India. They were led by Fergusson, Commando Platoon leader Captain Tommy Roberts and Flight Lieutenant Denny Sharp. As Fergusson's dispersal group made for the Irrawaddy, he saw them weaken by the hour:

I had to grant a halt every 20 minutes or half an hour, owing to the weakness of the men. Some ... were frequently fainting. I still insisted that nobody should part with his rifle or grenades, although that extra 10 or 12 pounds was pain and grief, but before we ever set out for India I had sworn that I would leave behind anybody who lost his arms. I allowed packs to be lightened a bit that morning, not that there was much left in them that we could dump.[24]

Orde Wingate ordered the dispersal groups to avoid clashes with the Japanese. Fergusson commented: 'The men were in such a pitiful physical condition that they could barely stumble along, let alone fight. Every man was supporting himself on a stick and we looked more like a collection of Damascus beggars than a fighting force.'[24] Most minds focused on food. Bernard Fergusson: 'Everyone had hallucinations about sugar, differing only according to their background. The craving for sugar was really agony and I cannot convey its intensity. It dimmed even the craving for solid food and that was cruel enough.'[25]

Sergeant Tony Aubrey became so desperate that he ate a fragment of soap, on the grounds that it must contain fat. He only succeeded in making himself violently ill. He found it easier after eight days without food, as his stomach then had no expectations:

Everything began to assume an aspect of slightly comic unreality. I found I couldn't, for instance, judge distances at all, and would take an enormous step into the air to get over a root four or five inches high, while the next moment I would walk straight into an overhanging branch which I had thought to be still five or six feet away.

Things improved marginally when Aubrey ate a piece of bullfrog. His next meal was snake. Then his party stumbled across a bullock, which they killed with their dahs: 'Some of the men, losing their self-control, hacked off portions of the carcass and devoured them raw.' They paid a heavy price the following day, with raging headaches and legs refusing to obey commands.

An unusually detailed knowledge of jungle lore could help to some extent. After the war, during the Malayan Emergency, J.P. Cross sought out jungle food: 'The way I used to test if a plant I did not know was poisonous was to rub it gently on the inner side of my lip and if it burnt I would not touch it further.'[26] Most members of Wingate's dispersal parties, however, were far too concerned about the potential consequences to experiment with unfamiliar jungle plants.

Bernard Fergusson saw his relationship with the men change as they reached the boundaries of endurance: 'I felt that now, when it was a question simply of getting them out, with no military success at stake, I was commanding them principally for their direct benefit and it seemed to me they had a right to know how their interests were being looked after.'[27] The men perked up when three water buffalo were shot. They gorged on the meat and this gave them the energy to wash in a stream. Fergusson was transfixed:

They had no chest muscles at all. Their arms and legs were strings and spindles, their skin seemed so brittle that the ribs looked like bursting through it and they had cavities instead of stomachs. We were all in the same condition. I had no idea that men could have pined away so far and still kept going.[28]

Fergusson's bedraggled group were lucky when they reached the Irrawaddy. They crossed in a boat manned by two young teenagers who treated the experience as a great adventure.

Treasured possession: Jim Rogerson holds up the spoon used for dividing up what little food remained. (Trustees of the Imperial War Museum)

It was not so much that our boots were falling to pieces and that many men were now marching in tattered rubber shoes. The two days of splashing through the Chaunggyi had, despite every precaution, brought on many cases of footrot and it was a matter of time whether the affected feet lasted out. We had nothing to put on them and they were already in a painful state where the sufferer could hardly bear them to be touched ... now every stream was a definite setback.[31]

ATO Bill Smyly continued with Astell's party after they crossed the Shweli. This group consisted of a full Platoon of Burma Rifles, a British Lieutenant of the King's, six British ORs and Smyly's Gurkhas. They covered several hundred miles in three or four weeks. Bill Smyly:

'I can't remember how long I was with this party. The hill ranges run like waves from Burma into China, the line of crests and valleys running north to south. We crossed several ranges of hills and then headed north. At one point I noticed my ankles and feet were beginning to swell – the skin tight and smooth like a

Some returning parties were struck down by disease. Almost everyone had something, with the usual skin complaints receiving little notice. Skin disease plagued men during both Chindit expeditions. Such problems were still evident in mid-1950s Malaya. J.P. Cross wrote: 'Every person who went into the jungle for the first time was noted to have been affected. The chief troubles were ringworm on the feet, secondary infections from abrasions or bites, boils, impetigo and prickly heat.'[29]

Fergusson worried about his fast-dwindling stock of Mepacrine, fearing a catastrophic collapse in health:

For some days past, all ranks had been taking suppressive tablets to ward off malaria but the supply was very limited. As it was, we were taking only three tablets a week, instead of the statutory one a day and, even at that rate, they would barely see out the month of April. If the suppressive treatment is stopped, the suppressed malaria breaks out with increased virulence ...[30]

As they struggled on towards the second major river barrier, the Chindwin, Fergusson was appalled by the condition of his men's feet:

The saviour: Flying Officer Michael Vlasto in the cockpit of his Dakota. He put his aircraft down in a run of just 700 yards and was on the ground for only 12 minutes. War Correspondent William Vandivert was on board. Vlasto was an experienced pilot and a member of the Bengal Flying Club, Calcutta. (Trustees of the Imperial War Museum)

blown-up balloon – and I had trouble seeing. I had beri-
beri. My peripheral vision was OK but my central vision
was blurred in the way TV Producers now blur the faces
of people they don't want recognised.

'*In the line of march I and my six were at the end*
of the Column and I was the one holding them up.
I found I could run downhill – no problem – but
when going up I had to walk at times sideways or
backwards. My feet were like blocks and my ankles
wouldn't bend. This worried my men. They kept
holding back to look after me and I drove them on
to keep up with the others, then came racing down
after them on the downslope. It was on one of these
downhill tumbles that I missed a turning and lost the
track and my company. I was alone.'

Ian MacHorton, who had reported to 2 GR at Jhansi
in the company of Alec Gibson and Harold James,
also reached the point of crisis. The young 2nd
Lieutenant was with Major Emmett's 2 Column when
it was ambushed on 2 March, as it approached to
attack Kyaikthin railway station. The second Southern
Group Column, 1, was operating 10 miles to the north
at the time. Nearly a month later 1 Column was near
Mongmit when the order came to disperse and return.
MacHorton and other survivors from 2 Column had
joined this Column on 5 March. In turn, 1 Column was
attacked on 2 April by a Japanese force, having crossed
the Irrawaddy. MacHorton was hit in the leg and left
behind when the Column withdrew as night fell.[32]

The fighting took place on a ridge near Japanese
positions around Mongmit. Nineteen-year-old
MacHorton was propped up on a grassy bank, revolver
at his side. He reviewed the options: 'Should I shoot
myself or wait until the Japs come to take me?' He
rejected the first course of action: 'After all, while
there was life, there really was hope. I was still alive,
even if I could not walk.'[33]

MacHorton had been wounded by a mortar fragment.
Southern Group Commander Colonel Alexander and
Major George Dunlop, MC, 1 Column Commander, came
to talk to him before he was left. After going through
all the inner horror of being left and finally alone, he
fell asleep. On coming round, MacHorton reflected:
'When it came to leaving behind your wounded and the
"wounded" turned out to be oneself, it was terribly difficult *not* to feel that the rule should not always apply!'[34]

The Japanese failed to find MacHorton, who remained
determined to live. He set himself the goal of 'walking'
one mile a day. He would walk to China and freedom.
He sorted out his kit, keeping only the essentials, made
a crutch (the top padded with a Balaclava helmet) and
eventually succeeded in raising himself up. In agony
from his wound he set out, taking 'shuffling side-steps'.
His inspiration was the text sent by his mother in her
last letter to him. It was the quotation used by King
George VI in his first Christmas Broadcast of the war: 'I
said to the man who stood at the gate of the year: "Give
me a light that I may tread safely into the unknown."
And he replied: "Go out into the darkness and put your
hand into the hand of God. That shall be better than a
light and safer than a known way."' MacHorton covered
three miles that first day.

On 14 April Flight Lieutenant Robert Thompson's
party was around three miles from the Chindwin
when challenged by a Sikh sentry. They were the first
to arrive back from the Irrawaddy.[35] Calvert's group
crossed the Chindwin the next day. Wingate's party
returned on 25 April.

The reception arrangements at Imphal were a great
improvement on the poor care received by survivors of
the 1942 Burma campaign. Michael Calvert wrote: 'The
hospitals were ready for us and we were bathed and
shaved and tucked up in clean sheets in no time at all.
We slept like logs. And we woke up to find that we were
heroes.'[36]

Bernard Fergusson expressed his gratitude for the
help his starving band had received from the Kachin
people:

> They had shielded us from danger and given us a
> mental relief of which we had been sorely in need.
> They had taken us into their keeping without hope
> of reward, when the hand of every man was against
> us. They had fed us and given us rest and put new
> heart into us for the dangers ahead.[37]

Fergusson found room to be amused by the difficulties of breaking long-held jungle habits. When his men
reached safety they refused to be parted from their
small personal hoards of rice. They insisted on cooking
a little rice every few hours, 'to the astonishment of all
beholders'.[38]

Notes

1. Allen, L. (1986), *Burma: The Longest War 1941–45*, 139
2. Fergusson, B. (1971), *Beyond the Chindwin*, 137
3. Stibbe, P. (1995), *Return via Rangoon*, 112–126
4. Fergusson, B. (1971), 143–144
5. Hay, Alice Ivy (1963), *There Was a Man of Genius: Letters to my Grandson, Orde Jonathan Wingate*, 81
6. Fowler, W. (2009), *We Gave Our Today: Burma 1941–1945*, 98
7. MacHorton, I. (1958), *Safer Than a Known Way*, introduction by Bernard Fergusson
8. Rooney, D. (2000), *Wingate and the Chindits: Redressing the Balance*, 93–99
9. Rooney, D. (1997), *Mad Mike*, 58–60
10. Calvert, M. (1996), *Fighting Mad*, 127–128
11. Halley, D. (1945), *With Wingate in Burma*, 96–98
12. Fergusson, B. (1971), 170–171
13. Ibid, 173–174
14. Chinnery, P.D. (2002), *March or Die*, 77
15. Halley, D. (1945), 100–104
16. Ibid, 105–112
17. Ibid, 113–119
18. Rooney, D. (1997), 59–60
19. Halley, D. (1945), 120–127
20. Ibid, 133–147
21. Cross, J.P. (1989), *Jungle Warfare*, 35
22. Fergusson, B. (1971), 193
23. Chinnery, P.D. (2002), 73
24. Fergusson, B. (1971), 189–190
25. Ibid, 188
26. Cross, J.P. (1989), 191
27. Fergusson, B. (1971), 192
28. Ibid, 195
29. Cross, J.P. (1989), 39
30. Fergusson, B. (1971), 220
31. Ibid, 234
32. Chinnery, P.D. (2002), 66
33. MacHorton, I. (1958), 14–27
34. Ibid, 35–43
35. Chinnery, P.D. (2002), 70
36. Calvert, M. (1996), 130
37. Fergusson, B. (1971), 221
38. Ibid, 239

5

A COSTLY YET CONVINCING DEMONSTRATION

'To those who took part in it, the Wingate expedition was a watershed in their lives. Before it, one's appreciation of values was only half developed. Now we have new standards and new touchstones.'

Bernard Fergusson, Commander, 5 Column

OPERATION *LONGCLOTH* yielded modest palpable returns yet demonstrated the potential of Wingate's new way of jungle fighting, independent of conventional supply lines. Air drops *were* a viable alternative for LRP warfare. As Allen commented: 'Wingate had changed the nature of jungle campaigning for good.'[1]

Post-expedition publicity focused on the positive, rather than the substantial human cost. *Longcloth* had a highly positive impact on British morale and, more significantly, on Japanese strategic thinking in relation to Burma and India. The enemy's defensive strategy was abandoned in favour of offensive action across the Burmese border with India. This was to have unforeseen consequences. On the matter of British morale, Charles Carfrae (who would command 29 Column during the 1944 Wingate expedition) wrote:

In succession we had lost ... Malaya, Singapore and Burma and, as a result, thousands of British and Indian troops lay rotting in jungle prison camps. We had failed to defeat the Japanese in a single major battle. Wingate alone, in 1943, had demonstrated on any scale that British and Gurkhas, properly trained, could use the jungle to advantage.[2]

Robert Thompson, an RAF Officer with the Chindits who, in later life, became an internationally recognised counter-insurgency expert, summed up *Longcloth's* outcome:

In local terms it was quite true to say, as all Wingate's detractors have delighted to repeat, that the first Chindit expedition did not achieve very much. We blew up some railway, which was of little consequence because the front it supplied was inactive. There is not much gain from blowing up communications which can be repaired within a few weeks, unless, at the time of their destruction, their use is vital to heavily engaged forces requiring reliable daily supplies.[3]

He went on, however, to spell out *Longcloth's* broader consequences:

The Japanese considered that the expedition was a reconnaissance into North Burma and that a major offensive could be expected to follow. The Chindwin and Zibyu Range could no longer be regarded as an impenetrable barrier. They could not hold such a large territory with dispersed forces. The answer was to push the front further west, across the Chindwin and into the Naga Hills. If the British could penetrate through such a barrier, so could they. The new Commander of the Japanese 15th Army, Lieutenant-General Mutaguchi, stationed at Maymyo, a former British hill station near Mandalay, was more ambitious. He wanted to cut the Dimapur-Imphal road at Kohima, capture Imphal, destroy IV Corps and debouch into Assam.

Fortunately for the Allies, the Japanese were unsuccessful in their endeavours – a failure which would lead, in due course, to their destruction in Burma. According to Thompson, General Wavell told Brigadier Calvert, much later, that he feared such a Japanese attack in 1943 and one of the reasons why he allowed *Longcloth* to proceed was to keep the enemy busy.[3]

The long-term and positive consequences of *Longcloth* for the reconquest of Burma could not have been foreseen. In the immediate aftermath, the focus was on the much-needed boost to morale, rather than the grievous cost in killed, missing, wounded, sick and captured. Fowler wrote:

> The operation was controversial. Critics said that Wingate was a self-publicist who had destroyed a Brigade. Of the men who reached India, 600 were unfit for any further service. All that Wingate could show for it was some damage to railways in Burma that within a month were operating again. It would be many months before 77 Indian Infantry Brigade could be reconstituted as an effective force with fresh troops.[4]

Sergeant-Major Bob Hobbs was among those whose health had been undermined. He was skin and bone when he reached safety. His feet were bound in rags. Suffering from malaria and a cocktail of other ailments, Hobbs went into hospital. He was repatriated as soon as he was well enough. On arriving in Britain he went straight into hospital once again.

Bernard Fergusson recorded the grim toll within 5 Column. He went in with 318 men and there were just 123 survivors. Only 95 reached India; a further 28 survived captivity. According to Allen the unit which suffered most was the 13th King's (Liverpool); of the 721 men who went in, just 384 returned.[1]

Fellow Column Commander Michael Calvert remained convinced that *Longcloth* was worthwhile, although just 2,182 of the 3,000–strong force returned. He wrote:

> The view is still held by some people that, apart from its morale-raising contribution, the first Chindit operation was pointless. This amazes me ... General Numata, Chief of Staff of the Japanese Southern Army, said on interrogation after the war that during Wingate's first campaign, the Japs had found the territory of Northern Burma difficult to defend against guerrilla troops. Therefore, they had decided that 'it would be best to give up defensive tactics'.

It was this switch to an offensive strategy that provided the Japanese context for the 1944 attacks on Imphal and Kohima. This offensive failed and the Japanese became too weak to hold the counter-thrust which eventually developed into the reconquest of Burma.[5] Allied forces, however, were hard put to hold the Japanese assault on Imphal/Kohima and it might, of course, have gone the other way. (For the full story of the extraordinary,

horrifying battle of Kohima, see *Kohima: The Furthest Battle* by Leslie Edwards.) Presumably, had the Japanese offensive succeeded, this narrative would be considering Operation *Longcloth* in the light of a subsequent Allied disaster in Assam!

Orde Wingate's critics, meanwhile, were relentless. Much later, in the 1950s, Slim himself caused much discomfort among Chindit veterans with his surprisingly dismissive remarks, in *Defeat into Victory*:

> They had blown up bridges and cuttings on the Mandalay-Myitkyina railway that supplied the Japanese northern front and attempted to reach across the Irrawaddy to cut the Mandalay-Lashio line. Exhaustion, difficulties of air supply and the reaction of the Japanese prevented this and the Columns, breaking up into small parties, made for the shelter of IV Corps. About a thousand men, a third of the total force, failed to return. It gave little tangible return for the losses it had suffered and the resources it had absorbed. The damage it did to Japanese communications was repaired in a few days, the casualties it inflicted were negligible and it had no immediate effect on Japanese dispositions or plans.[6]

This is a strange conclusion from a great General choosing not to exercise the wisdom of hindsight (unless one places an unusual degree of emphasis on his use of the word 'immediate'). It has been suggested that this dismissive attitude towards Wingate and the Chindits, in *Defeat into Victory*, reflects Slim's contact with the authors of the *Official History of the war against Japan* – who were hostile towards Wingate.[7] In any event, Slim continued:

> The abandonment of a projected enemy offensive through the Hukawng Valley was not due to this raid, but to the fact that the Japanese 55th Division, which was to take part in it, had to be diverted at the end of 1942 to meet the British threat in Arakan. If anything was learnt of air supply or jungle fighting, it was a costly schooling.[6]

Even so, Slim then goes on to suggest that the price *was* worth paying, in terms of public relations benefit. Acknowledging his own negative remarks, he reflected:

> These are hard things to say of an effort that required such stark courage and endurance, as was demanded of and given by Wingate and his men. The operation was, in effect, the old cavalry raid of military history on the enemy's communications,

which, to be effective against a stout-hearted opponent, must be made in tactical coordination with a main attack elsewhere.

Originally, Wingate's raid had been thus planned to coincide with an advance by Chinese forces from Yunnan. Later, although it was clear that this Chinese move would not materialise, General Wavell sent Wingate's force in alone. It was a bold decision and, as it turned out, it was justified, not on military but on psychological grounds. It cannot be judged on material results alone. Whilst, like the Arakan offensive, it was a failure, there was a dramatic quality about this raid which, with the undoubted fact that it had penetrated far behind the Japanese lines and returned, lent itself to presentation as a triumph of British jungle fighting over the Japanese.

Skilfully handled, the press of the Allied world took up the tale and everywhere the story ran that we had beaten the Japanese at their own game. This not only distracted attention from the failure in Arakan, but was important in itself for our own people at home, for our Allies and, above all, for our troops on the Burma front. Whatever the actual facts, to the troops in Burma it seemed the first ripple showing the turning of the tide. For this reason alone, Wingate's raid was worth all the hardship and sacrifice his men endured and by every means in our power we exploited its propaganda value to the full.[6]

Richard Rhodes James offered a less jaundiced view. He said of *Longcloth*:

It had achieved few tangible results – some bridges blown, some stretches of railway damaged, some Japanese killed – had suffered fearfully and had sustained considerable casualties. But the operation made an enormous impact: through its sheer audacity, through showing that the British could operate in the jungle at least as effectively as the Japanese, and through the exciting possibilities it opened up for air supply. For a defeated and jaded army, it was a wonderful shot in the arm.[8]

Certainly, this boost to morale was important but the impact on Japanese strategy was far more significant. In simple terms, the Japanese concluded that they could do the same and better.

As the public relations machine moved into high gear, Wingate's men were still paying *Longcloth*'s price. Emaciated, exhausted and sick survivors continued to struggle towards safety. Newly commissioned Neville Hogan, now recovered from his wounds and the trials of the 1942 Burma campaign, joined one of the parties sent to the Chindwin, to help bring them in:

'I had passed out from Dehra Dun, the 'Sandhurst of the East', in March 1943. I put my heart and soul into it, did well and carried the Academy Standard at the Passing Out Parade. As a 2nd Lieutenant I joined the 2nd Battalion The Burma Rifles, but I was just too late to take part in Wingate's first expedition.'

Hogan was one of a group of five young officers arriving at the Battalion. The Adjutant, Captain P.A.M. Heald, had only recently returned from *Longcloth* and this experience may well have coloured his subsequent remarks to the new boys. He offered them the opportunity to help bring in stragglers. They were given until the following morning to decide whether to go. He warned that anyone wounded and unable to march would be left with a water bottle, spare clip, two hand grenades and whatever rations could be spared. Neville Hogan and one other accepted the challenge:

'We two set out with a party of 20 Karens, Kachins and Gurkhas. We were sent to the Chindwin. We found no stragglers, but stayed on the west bank for some weeks and killed a lot of Indian National Army men, most of whom were thieves and rapists.'

Bill Smyly was alone at this point. His small group of Gurkha Muleteers had joined George Astell's party of Burma Rifles, moving north towards China. Smyly had fought to close the gap that opened up repeatedly as they marched. He caught up on the downhill stretches, but beri-beri undermined his ability to maintain the pace. He then became separated:

'With my central vision gone it was very easy to mistake the track and at one point, when running down, I missed a bend and ran off into the jungle. I pressed on, hoping to find a track somewhere. I did find some traces, only to discover I was in a circle, following my own feet. Now it was evening and getting dark. Night comes down fast in the Tropics, but it never ceases to surprise and this is not the best time to find a place to lie down. Yet I found a pretty little stream of clear water and made a fire and tea, had a biscuit and lay down.

'In the morning I discovered that this was about the worst place I could have chosen. A leech swims in water. Its sucker flattens out into a tail and it swims like a fish. They came in swarms from that stream and I must have had 100 of them on me, as fat as grapes. I stripped and shaved them off with my kukri. They dropped – plop, plop – into the water. Most of them were small but

there were three big ones. We called them "bull leeches", six inches or more and as thick as your thumb in the natural state, but swelling up as big as a large plum. I must have lost a lot of blood, yet they may have done me some good. I was rested, my ankles and sight were much better and my central vision was restored. This blindness tended to come and go. I retraced my steps, found the original path at the place I had run off it and went north.

'To my surprise I was not in the least frightened to be on my own. It was a relief to go at my own pace and not have my men worrying about me. I climbed the next hill for the best part of the day. I don't remember eating but, at one point, the locals had driven a half bamboo pole into the hillside, where there was a rivulet. A trickle of clear water fell from the end of it onto stones by the road. Here I sat for a while on a mossy bank, in the greatest luxury, sipping the water slowly from a bamboo cup. Then an old lady came up with a very pretty daughter. I can't remember what we used for language but they stopped and smiled and took some water from my cup, then went on. About half a mile on I met them again. They had been home, on the edge of the village, and had returned with a bowl of fermenting rice – sweet and slightly sparkling, like champagne. This was supposed to restore the weary and it did. They led me to the house of the village Headman, where I stayed three days till my feet went down.

'From this time I never slept in the open. The path went north from village to village. When I came to a village around evening I was taken to the Headman's house. When I took off my boots my feet swelled up and I did not move on till I could get my boots on again.

'On this journey I had no compass and no map – just a rough sketch in my notebook, along with the names of all my men and details about them, like the best snipers – with high scores on the rifle range – and those who could swim. This sketch showed the Irrawaddy on the left, the Salween on the right and Fort Hertz at the top. If I kept going north, avoiding a big river, I should reach Fort Hertz. Maps can't get much simpler than that.

'All villages in the Kachin Hills are on hilltops. I would walk to the next village and ask for the Headman's house. They would invite me in and I would take off my boots. After a day's march my feet were swollen with beri-beri and it could take two or three days for them to go down, allowing me to put my boots on again.

'We slept around the fire in a large room which occupied most of the building. The long room ran the whole length of the hut but women's quarters, where the cooking was done, was partitioned off on one side. The Headman and his guests sat round a floor fire in the middle of the room. Sometimes they smoked a mixture of opium and tobacco. The meal came out on bamboo carriers – packets of rice wrapped in banana leaves, a bowl of hot water with boiled dried chillies in it and, occasionally, salt. I sometimes pleaded for the washings of the rice, which, for some reason, they generally threw out. Conversation was an important part of the proceedings. Village affairs were sorted out here and news discussed. At one point the ladies would come in and join the party, then withdraw. The Headman went in to sleep with his wife. The guests settled down around the embers of the fire.

'In the morning I would try to put my boots on. If that failed I spent the day alone till around 4.30, when the children came racing back from the fields to make up the fire. The house was built on stilts and the fire was on a built-up mound that came up from the ground below to floor level. Three tree trunks lay across the floor of the built-up fireplace, forming a grate. The trunks burned away slowly and kindling was added each evening. This fire never went out. At night it burned brightly, to light up the faces of those around it. By day it smouldered secretly, so that anyone would think it had gone out, till the children returned from the fields with kindling to revive it. Next morning, with the fire barely visible in the logs, I would struggle with my boots. I generally felt pretty fit when I thanked my hosts and set out again on my journey north. Later, I was told that a rumour had moved ahead of me, eventually reaching Fort Hertz, that a lone British officer was walking out.

'I was well looked after at every village. They had no meat and almost no vegetables, just rice. Boiled rice with nothing else is hard to eat. I was also given the soup of chillies and sometimes salt. Everyone had the same. In one place I saw a salt "factory". They would boil it up in large earthenware bowls until the brine was thick. Pure salt settled on the bowl and became thicker and thicker. It seemed to go on, layer after layer, like lacquer rather than crystallising. When this liner around the clay pot was half an inch thick the bowl was smashed and chips of salt separated. These were the colour of terracotta and very valuable. A man with a chip of salt would take it out at meals and scrape it with a knife.'

Dispersal parties from 3 Column – Calvert's men – were still heading west towards the Chindwin. Some were killed or captured on the way. Cypher Officer Alec Gibson, Lieutenant Ken Gourlay and 2nd Lieutenant Denis Gudgeon were among those destined not to reach India. Rooney's comments on the high proportion of Calvert's men reaching sanctuary must be taken in a relative sense. In fact, only 205 of 3 Column's 360 men crossed the Chindwin to safety.[9] Alec Gibson was stopped by the Irrawaddy:

'We had about two days' food each but were used to getting by on half rations. Whatever happened, however, it would be impossible to reach the Chindwin without more food. I wasn't very hopeful at that point. Everyone worried about the Irrawaddy. There were virtually no swimmers in my party and there was no bamboo on our route – ruling out the possibility of building rafts for the river crossing. As we began the two-day march to the Irrawaddy, it was obvious that our only real hope was to find boats. As we got closer to the river, the Burmese with us discovered that the Japanese had ordered all boats to be moved to the west bank. We found a bivouac close to the river and the swimmers prepared to make an attempt to reach the far bank and negotiate for boats.

'We selected a point on a river bend, hoping the current would sweep us across to the other side, the best part of a mile away. This didn't work and the current swept several swimmers too far round the bend. I made two attempts myself to cross the river. During the first I was swimming with Ken Gourlay when I suddenly developed severe cramp. I told Ken I had to return. He turned with me, to ensure I reached safety. Later, I discovered that only one of our six or seven swimmers reached the other side; some had drowned.

'We returned to the bivouac, only to find it deserted. Fortunately, we still had our kit, tied into groundsheets. We quickly accepted the need to make another attempt immediately. I have no idea what happened during my second attempt to swim the Irrawaddy. I must have lost consciousness at some point. I came to on the sand – still on the eastern bank – in broad daylight and quite alone. Subsequently, I heard that Ken Gourlay had survived but as a POW, spending most of his captivity in Singapore.'

Alec Gibson struggled to recover:

'Remarkably, I still had my kit. It was close by, on the sand. I felt poorly, as the failed river crossings had weakened me. Shortly, however, I came across a Gurkha. We joined forces and decided that our priority should be to find food. We stayed close to the bank in the hope that we might find a small boat.

'There was a village ahead and we approached with the usual caution. We wouldn't have gone in but for the fact that we were desperate – we hadn't had anything to eat for three days. We took a close look. Were the village women moving around freely? They would be indoors if any Japanese were in the village. There were plenty of women visible and we

IS MINS HALT FOR SMOKE AND DRINK

Catch your breath: the Column stopped for a short break during every hour of marching. (Tony Wailes)

decided to go in. Almost immediately, however, we were surrounded by half a dozen members of the so-called Burmese National Army. They didn't beat us but our hands were tied behind our backs and we were marched to a Japanese jungle outpost a few miles away. I was in a pretty weak state at that point, my woes including severe bouts of dysentery.'

As men continued north and west in their attempts to reach safety, others faced the immediate possibility of torture and death at the hands of their Japanese captors. The fortunate survivors already back in India were digesting practical lessons from *Longcloth*. Some issues were beyond dispute and had a strong influence on the planning of future operations. Others appeared significant at the time yet, somehow, were ignored or deliberately set aside for reasons of expediency when Orde Wingate's 1944 expedition began. A number of lessons were chronicled by 5 Column Commander Bernard Fergusson. On the effects of lack of water he wrote:

Real thirst leads quickly to madness and death. A man can go two days without water and still keep marching, but at some time on the third day his spirit will break. I have been astonished to find how

long a man can carry on marching without food and
no less astonished to find how short a time he can
carry on without water.[10]

Fergusson added that fast-flowing water was usually
safe. Slow-running water was often dangerous. Mules
will not drink polluted water, unless desperate:

> I have often filled our water bottles from pools
> which the animals have rejected. Most of our
> water was consumed in the form of tea and boiling
> remains the best way of dealing with it. The sterilis-
> ing tablets were only used for the bottles. Even black
> or yellow water is tolerable in tea, although, occa-
> sionally, it has a nasty tang of buffalo or elephant.[10]

Some lessons were obvious only when comparisons
between the 1943 and 1944 operations became possible. Fergusson, for example, noted that the men of
Operation *Longcloth* remained relatively free of malaria
and he attributed this to the avoidance of villages:

> In 1943 we were on the go from 25 January until
> 25 April, a period of 93 days. Up to 28 March, when
> my Column dispersed in the Shweli Valley, we had
> taken no malarial precautions of any sort and yet
> we had only six cases, all of which were relapses. Not
> until 8 April did we start taking Atabrin and by then
> I only had enough to issue three a week instead of
> the statutory one a day.[11]

Yet, Fergusson's dispersal party saw no fresh case of
malaria until they crossed the Chindwin on 25 April.
Then, after 10 days without Atabrin, 29 out of 30 men
went down with malaria.

He noticed how rest had a negative effect on men
already pushed to the limit. Limbs and muscles soon
stiffened. This was apparent during both expeditions:
'after several months of marching, even three days' rest
does you as much harm as good'.[12]

Longcloth's Columns suffered severely from lack of
food. Nevertheless, the viability of air supply was proven
and this laid the foundation for the support of a much
larger Chindit force in 1944. The problems in 1943 were
due to the handful of aircraft available for the supply
task. Two of the five, the Hudsons, were unsuited to the
role as they were too fast on the dropping run. Yet the
Dakotas showed the way. They flew 178 sorties and all
but 19 were successful. The Columns received some 300
tons of supplies from the air.[13]

One key lesson from *Longcloth* was the importance
of recognising that Chindit warfare had inherent limitations. Force capability must not be overreached and

Wingate's obvious transgression during *Longcloth* was
the decision to cross the Irrawaddy. Some years later,
Robert Thompson of 3 Column acknowledged that the
outward crossing of the Irrawaddy was

> ... a tactical error because we became boxed in an
> area between the Irrawaddy and Shweli rivers, on
> which the Japanese could bring to bear elements of
> three Divisions. We did not realise what an obsta-
> cle the Shweli would prove to be and thought that
> beyond the Irrawaddy we would have almost a free
> run into the friendly Kachin Hills bordering China.[14]

Ian MacHorton was among those left behind. He
remained determined to survive and struggled on alone,
plagued by fever and the pain of his wound. In his par-
lous state he came across two Shan charcoal-burners,
mistook them for Japanese and fired at them with his
revolver before passing out. Fortunately, he missed.
He awoke to find himself washed, his wound freshly
dressed and a large platter of curried chicken and rice
before him. MacHorton was hidden in a small room
below a village pagoda. A Japanese patrol arrived, but
he went undetected. His clothes were washed, repaired
and pressed. He then found he could walk, albeit awk-
wardly, on both legs.[15]

Ian MacHorton's saviours were of Nepalese origin;
the Headman had been a Naik in the 4th Gurkha Rifles.
MacHorton was bewitched by the beauty of the village
and the serenity of its inhabitants.[15] He stayed for two
weeks. He had planned to cross the Shweli but changed
his mind when told that parties of 1 Column had
clashed with the Japanese while attempting a crossing.
He decided to return to India by crossing the Irrawaddy
and Mu rivers and, finally, the Chindwin. He was invited
to stay but was determined to attempt the 300-mile
trek. He now walked with a stick, rather than a crutch.[16]

MacHorton headed for the Irrawaddy but his
strength, built up over his fortnight in the village,
rapidly ebbed away and the wound grew more painful. There were signs of a British party ahead and
MacHorton realised that he would fail to cross the
Irrawaddy unless he caught up with them. He parted
company with his guide and pressed on but his condition deteriorated in the wide 'sand belt' approaches to
the Irrawaddy, with its dense patches of elephant grass
and swarms of flies.[17]

At one point he came close to being trampled by
a herd of elephants in a hurry. He managed to kill a
lizard. He hung it from his belt, until the flesh dried,
before eating it. On the third day he emerged from
the elephant grass and gazed across a sandy waste-
land. Somehow he found the strength to continue,

reaching scrub and, finally, teak jungle. He came upon a stream and more traces of the British group ahead. Ian MacHorton reached Tagaung village just as the British force was completing the river crossing. He boarded one of the last two boats. It was 23 April – 10 days after his twentieth birthday. A Japanese machine gun opened up as they neared the far bank. MacHorton's boat capsized; he held on at the far side, shielded by the hull. The survivors drifted downstream, climbed the bank and entered cover.

MacHorton and a Corporal moved off to the west and soon ran into a group of wounded led by Sergeant Hayes of the RAF Section. Hayes had searched methodically for the wounded and collected them together while under fire. They set out with two stretcher cases, a rifle and 30 rounds for everyone and a total of four pounds of rice – one cupped handful per man. They left the two wounded on the stretchers in a village and began the long trek to the Chindwin.

Alec Gibson had a brutal introduction to life as a prisoner:

'I was questioned forcefully about the Column. I gave them something when the officer held his sword blade to my neck. I gave them a false heading for the Column and they sent a patrol in pursuit. I said they were heading east, rather than west. Beyond the threats during interrogation we were treated fairly well. We were fed, but we were also told that we would be shot if we attempted to escape. I made sure my fellow captive understood what had been said. We spent the rest of that day and the following night at this jungle location before being led away to Wuntho, on the railway, and handed over to troops holding more prisoners. We were then packed into cattle trucks and transported to Maymyo. This move took the best part of a day.'

Maymyo was a holding camp. Gibson was reunited with many members of 3 Column and other Columns. He spent five weeks at this camp, enduring repeated beatings during interrogation. The second-line troops guarding them beat prisoners routinely, without provocation. A favourite pastime was to line up the prisoners and engage in ritualised face-slapping:

'The officers got together to talk about tactics during interrogation. We agreed it would be best to offer some information which was either misleading, or genuine but essentially valueless. Nevertheless, I was badly beaten on several occasions. Our guards were willing to kill without excuse. The interrogations were led by an officer and an interpreter. I was very nearly caught

out. I had been asked to describe something that had happened in India and gave a different version when next questioned. I was challenged but dealt with it in a way that appeared to satisfy the officer.

'Food at Maymyo Camp was not too bad at that stage, with enough rice and vegetables to keep us going. We were taught to line up at the cookhouse and recite the Japanese for 'I have come for my food'. Any mispronunciation resulted in a beating. We learnt a little Japanese very quickly!'

Lieutenant Philip Stibbe of 5 Column also had a brutal first confrontation with his Japanese captors. He had been wounded at Hintha village. His interrogators asked whether he would prefer to be beheaded or shot. The Japanese seemed unaware that dispersal parties were now returning, most making for India. Stibbe was beaten for refusing to disclose the Brigade's heading. Tortured by having an endless stream of water passed down his throat, he made a show of giving in and told them the Brigade was heading south. This appeared to satisfy his tormentors. In his account, Stibbe refused to demonise the Japanese. Indeed, he was careful to note occasional acts of kindness:

> During the night one of them brought me a captured British Army blanket ... The Japs were quite friendly. At mealtimes I was given my share of rice and a very unpleasant sweet soup. If there was anything left over at the end of the meal, they always offered it to me. My enormous appetite seemed to amaze them and, after watching my attempts to eat with chopsticks with considerable mirth, one of them gave me a spoon, which I was allowed to keep.[18]

The Japanese Commander, a Major, had been wounded by grenade splinters at Hintha and he was carried in a chair. Stibbe saw him drinking brandy from what was recently his flask: 'The Jap Major was obviously enjoying the brandy but he had the decency to send over a small tot for me and asked about my wound, so I felt rather better about him.'[18]

Philip Stibbe was shocked to learn that the Japanese had the typewritten names and addresses of the next of kin of every man in 5 Column, until he realised they had found the office box carried by one of the mules. More prisoners were brought in during the night of 2 April. They included Joe Boyle, who had helped Stibbe get out of Hintha. During the following day the Japanese became very excited and Stibbe learned that they now knew that Wingate's men were returning to India. He made a show of surprise.

The Japanese and their prisoners returned to Hintha, continued on to the Shweli and crossed the river by boat. A Japanese Lieutenant enquired about Stibbe's wound, which was improving with daily dressing. More prisoners joined the group and they were taken to Bhamo. The treatment deteriorated as they moved away from the fighting. Their new guards stared into their cages 'and indicated, in dumb show, that we were going to be bayoneted'.[18]

Bill Smyly continued north. He had no idea what 'Fort Hertz' was, but the Hill people were friendly and seemed to think it was the right place to go. His total possessions consisted of a pistol, five rounds, a grenade, half a blanket and a stick of 'male' bamboo. 'Female' bamboo is hollow. 'Male' bamboo is very difficult to find; it is strong, hard and makes a very fine walking stick. His progress was not without incident. In one village he was sitting in the Headman's house when a group of 'Japanese' soldiers entered. Smyly had the half-blanket over his knees. Under the blanket he pulled the grenade's pin and waited:

'Suddenly, everyone began laughing, as if the joke had gone far enough. They told me they had killed some Japanese in an ambush and had decided to surprise me by dressing up in their clothes. They stopped laughing when I took the grenade out from under the blanket and – rather shakily – started twisting the pin back in.'

In another hilltop village five British soldiers came to see him at the Headman's house:

'I think they had settled down for a holiday but the villagers probably expected them to move on with me. They could not have been in a more pleasant place. The air on the hilltops was clean and cool and there were fine rockpools and waterfalls in the valleys below. I told them that if they joined me we would become a military unit. I then showed them my little map. I was heading for Fort Hertz and, I hoped, an aeroplane to India. Speaking frankly, I told them I did not recommend myself very highly. If they joined me and I fell out on the march, they would be expected to press on without me to Fort Hertz. It was entirely up to them whether they joined me or not.

'They told me they were having a good time living in the village, so I wished them luck and off they went. The Headman was shocked. He really wanted them to move on. Curiously, I met some of them again a year later, as we were leaving Burma after the second campaign: three British soldiers with their wives – babies strapped to the girls' backs. They had treated that village as a holiday resort and had returned family men!'

Smyly's route north must have been to the east of low-lying, Japanese-garrisoned towns such as Myitkyina. He arrived at Fort Hertz in July:

'During all this trip I was never frightened. I walked whenever I could get my boots on. There were times when I simply couldn't walk, but there were other times of sheer delight. One of my worst moments was the first day on my own, in the grip of beri-beri. The slope seemed to get steeper and steeper. In fact, I was leaning further forward, until the point where I slipped and hit the floor. Outside my house in Bedford there is an old man who walks down the road bent almost double. I think his boots must be in the middle of his field of vision and I suppose I could have been walking like that. Yet this was beautiful country, full of great trees and clear running water and largely free of Japanese.

'In particular, I remember that meeting at the watering point. When that old woman and her pretty daughter came along, it was a moment of pure delight. I also remember a very dark patch of jungle. There was a gap in the canopy and a shaft of sunlight pierced the jungle and focused on a great bunch of purple orchids.'

Lieutenant Ian MacHorton's party, having survived the Irrawaddy crossing, found a guide for their approach to the railway. Friendly villagers gave them rice. Women washed them and tended their wounds with herbal ointments before bandaging them. MacHorton was tormented by the knowledge that the Monsoon was just two weeks away. They still had around 150 miles to go. They managed to evade the Japanese patrols along the railway and made for the next challenge, the Mu river. They marched west during the night hours and rested during the day. MacHorton, fretting about the pending Monsoon, then changed tactics. They marched day and night, resting only when someone fell out. Suddenly, they came upon a village and found the main body once again. MacHorton was reunited with Colonel Alexander, Major Dunlop and many others. His party received a mess tin of raw rice each as they prepared to cross the Mu.[19] Sadly, they were ambushed as they made ready and those surviving the initial bursts of fire rushed the river. MacHorton remembered this crossing as relatively orderly, given the circumstances, with the enemy firing from both banks. The Mu was swift-flowing but shallow and the men waded across in waist-deep water. On reaching the shallows, they charged the Japanese waiting for them ashore. MacHorton and four other survivors from his group hurried away. He saw Colonel Alexander, wounded, carried over the shoulder away from the enemy.

Ian MacHorton had been wounded yet again, this time in the leg and face. He passed out, then woke to find himself a prisoner. He was taken by truck to the Chindwin's east bank. He was in a very poor state and later described an 'out of body' experience:

> Out there in the moonlight I was not hungry any more. I felt young and strong in body and soul. I felt sorry for that pain-wracked creature that I knew was me, back there in the hut. Then, abruptly, I was back in that body. And my body opened its eyes and a flood of determination and strength welled up within me: 'I am not dead. I will live!' I said: 'I will cross the Chindwin.'[20]

He fell asleep again, but came to as firing broke out some distance away. The guards left the hut and MacHorton had the opportunity to make a break for it. He had to cross 25 yards of open moonlit ground to reach cover. He succeeded, entered the jungle and climbed away from his captors. Sick, starving and without food or compass, he was determined to cross the Chindwin. On reaching an escarpment, he had around 20 miles to go but was close to dying of thirst. He held on until he entered green jungle and found water. Progressing along the chaung's bank he came across a small group of officers and men from 1 Column. Soon after they shot and butchered a water buffalo, drinking the hot blood. Before they could eat a group of Burmese appeared and demanded their surrender, warning that the Japanese were in the jungle behind them. Major George Dunlop, 1 Column's Commander, told his men to make up their own minds and suddenly made a break for it. MacHorton and others joined him. By now every member of this group had been wounded at least once.

Dunlop now decided that their only chance was to break into much smaller parties of two or three. Each man had the option of surrendering or carrying on. MacHorton wrote: 'My own resolution was firm. Nothing, no-one, would dissuade me from going on to the Chindwin.' Indeed, everyone with Dunlop decided to go on.[20]

Ian MacHorton and his companions reached the Chindwin: 'There before me were the last 800 yards of my trek of more than 300 miles achieved since that fateful hour of dusk at Mongmit, when I had been left behind, too badly wounded to walk. Left behind to die. I had achieved my goal.'[21]

Taking off his torn shirt and wrapping it round a bundle of bamboo, MacHorton went to cross the river. He was called back and warned he wouldn't make it if he left the group. They planned to go upstream and attempt a crossing at Auktaung. MacHorton wouldn't

be thwarted and refused to comply. One man then made a remarkable sacrifice. He gave him a pair of water-wings he had carried for 1,000 miles. The water-wings deflated in use but MacHorton got over and was alone once more. His troubles then continued. On reaching the west bank he was almost immediately shot in the foot by a Sikh civilian. The bullet failed to penetrate but the foot was injured. MacHorton had no choice; he killed his attacker by crushing his head with a hefty piece of teak driftwood.

MacHorton headed off but was delirious and eventually wandered back to the Chindwin. Too exhausted to continue, he collapsed into sleep. When he awoke he set out again for the British lines, easing his hunger by killing a python and boiling some of the flesh. The last hours were full of confusion and MacHorton was close to the end. He lost his boots in a swamp. He came across a track, saw bootprints and followed them, stopped to look back and could see only the prints of his now naked feet. Deeply disturbed, he re-traced his steps and found bootprints once again. He came to a river, saw soldiers, assumed they were Japanese and passed out. When he came to, a young British officer offered him a mug of tea. When he was strong enough to ask for the date, he was told it was 16 May.[21]

Many of Orde Wingate's men were now in Japanese hands and faced a future of brutality, sickness, slave labour and, often, the closure of death. Alec Gibson was moved to Rangoon Central Gaol. Upon arrival, all officers were placed in solitary confinement:

'I was luckier than some. I had only five weeks' solitary. The idea was to soften up the prisoner for interrogation. Eventually I was moved to the Officers' Block. The treatment in Rangoon Gaol was slightly better than at Maymyo, but we were beaten occasionally.'

Gibson's family had received notification that he was 'missing, presumed drowned' during the attempt to cross the Irrawaddy. They never knew he was alive and a prisoner.

Around 60 of Wingate's force were now held in Bhamo Gaol, including 20 Gurkhas of Fergusson's 5 Column. This group included men who had failed to cross the Shweli and stayed on the sandbank. Lieutenant Philip Stibbe was the only officer and he did his best to impose order. A Japanese medical orderly and a Burmese doctor made occasional visits and the wounded, including Stibbe, began to recover.

In *Return via Rangoon* Stibbe recognised good as well as bad in his captors. While at Bhamo, he recalled the companionship offered by one enemy officer:

IT WAS OFTEN NECESSARY TO PUT
MULES OUT OF PAIN BY WAY
OF REVOLVER

Act of mercy: the usual way of killing a mule was a bullet to the forehead, but a silent method was often necessary, due to the proximity of the Japanese. (Tony Wailes)

A Japanese Lieutenant used to come and see me often; he was much bigger than the other Japs and had been a champion wrestler. Sometimes he would stay for over an hour talking to me in his broken English and sometimes he would bring a few tomatoes, or a cake or cigarettes. He had quite a sense of humour and seemed as amused at some of my comments on the Japanese as I was by his remarks about the English.[22]

Philip Stibbe's wound healed completely in six weeks. On 12 May the fit prisoners were told they were to march 200 miles to Lashio, where they would entrain for Maymyo. The Japanese warned that anyone falling out on the march would be shot. In the event the worst cases were allowed to ride on the ration lorry. Others unable to march found riding a mule bareback a very painful experience.

One night a car drew up. Inside was the Major responsible for Stibbe's capture: 'He had now fully recovered from his wounds and seemed pleased to hear that I had too. He apologised for the conditions at Bhamo, gave

me some cake and cigarettes, wished me good luck and drove on. I found this piece of courtesy and consideration genuinely pleasing.'[23]

Stibbe, however, also saw the sharp contrasts in Japanese behaviour. On the day-long train journey from Lashio to Maymyo, he watched his Japanese guards amuse themselves by torturing a small puppy: 'Their favourite trick was to apply a lighted cigarette to the most tender parts of its body.'[24]

Philip Stibbe was introduced to Maymyo's harsh regime, with its daily round of beatings. The men were beaten until they learned Japanese commands:

Nearly all the guards carried a club or wooden sword, which they used whenever they saw the slightest reason for doing so. If they were in a good mood you had your face slapped. If they were feeling a bit liverish, they struck you with a clenched fist; on bad days they would use a rifle butt or kick you on the shins.

The most common trigger for violence was the failure to bow or salute a sentry: 'As often as not, a man who was being beaten up would not have the slightest idea of what he had done wrong; the least thing seemed to provoke the Japs.'[25]

Daily work parties went into Maymyo town. When paraded, prisoners were required to number in Japanese at roll call. They had three meals daily:

The food was well-cooked but there was never enough ... Every meal consisted of rice and vegetable stew, with sometimes a little meat or fish; all the time we were at Maymyo we never lost the feeling of hunger.'[25] When the prisoners were moved to Rangoon Gaol in early June, they were reunited with many familiar faces: 'In a strange way, the atmosphere was almost like that of a homecoming.'[26]

Bill Smyly flew out from Fort Hertz after his remarkable feat of survival in the Burmese jungle. In complete modesty, in his discussions with the author he argued against the term 'remarkable'. The reader must draw his or her own conclusion as to whether the use of this word is justified. Smyly weighed just six stone on admission to Chabura Hospital, Assam. This was a rural Anglican hospital founded by the Society for the Propagation of the Gospel – the very society which had employed his father in China. It was still run by its prewar missionary staff, British and Indian.

As the Chindits reached sanctuary they were deloused, washed, examined by doctors and shaved, losing their thick, matted beards. Bill Smyly:

'It was strange for some officers to see a Private, whom they had accepted as an elderly, rather stooping figure, to whom they had grown to show some respect as an elder statesman, emerge as a pink-cheeked 20-year-old.'

Smyly had a six-month beard and wanted a photograph before he shaved, but this was not possible:

'In hospital we got everything we needed, even free issue 'V' cigarettes, but there was no Paymaster for officers, no chequebook, no bank and no photographer.'

It was not until Smyly was discharged from hospital and sent for two weeks' rest in the beautiful hill station of Shillong that such things were possible. His six stone frame had been likened by someone to Jesus Christ, but his weight then ballooned to 12 stone and a wispy beard emerged from stubble:

'I grew disgustingly fat; I couldn't stop eating. It certainly wasn't hunger – perhaps it was psychological. Eat when you have the chance! Food was security! I didn't gobble; a biscuit might last in my mouth for several minutes. It was just the pure pleasure of food. I ate continuously, even waking in the middle of the night for a bite. Yet, by the same token, I was never hungry. When I had a tapeworm and had to go for a week without food I felt no distress.'

That tapeworm may have contributed to Bill Smyly's new eating habits:

'This creature was quite spectacular. I went hungry for a week and then they gave me a potion. I passed all 22 ft of this tapeworm in one go. It had a tiny black head with spikes on. These helped it lodge in the gut and its length probably depended on how far up the intestine it had lodged. The head produced a trailing body, thin as a thread at the top, then thicker in short-banded segments, which got thinner and longer and finally dropped off, to pass out in the stool. It wasn't hard to know if you had one. The segments were full of eggs, ready to infect a scavenging pig. We did eat pork on one occasion after dispersal, when Astell bought a pig from villagers. It must have had tapeworm cysts. I was treated for two tapeworms at different times. I think this big one, at 22 ft, was the champion.'

Astell bought that pig with local currency. Wingate's Brigade HQ Column had a large amount in silver Rupees and some brick-sized blocks of opium. Bill Smyly:

'The purpose was to supplement rations which came in by air with local purchase and, possibly, to give our Burma Rifles liaison people more leverage in their negotiations. I don't know what happened to the opium, but when the Brigade was ordered to break up, I distributed our heavy 500 silver Rupees equally amongst 30 men. I did this in front of them, explaining that it was Army money, not pay, and might be required from time to time to buy rice.

'When I took my wrong turning on the journey north, George Astell was under the impression that I had all the Gurkha silver. He was not aware that I had distributed it. When he bought the pig he had asked me for a contribution, to which, of course, the men were happy to subscribe. When I lost the track, however, he told others that this was a heavy loss to the Column because Smyly had all this money with him. Not so!

'Local purchasing was more practical on the first show than the second, as we moved in smaller units. Our rations were more easily supplemented by local purchase, particularly of rice – the ideal emergency ration. It is lightweight, bulks up large and is filling when cooked.'

Beyond the orchestrated public relations frenzy, no great euphoria surrounded *Longcloth's* survivors:

'Some said we had walked a long way and done nothing, which, I suppose, was very much what I thought myself. I didn't, however, unlike a lot of British Brass, question the idea of Long Range Penetration. We thought the Wingate show was, perhaps, too expensive and, if we couldn't afford it, it would soon be forgotten. It probably would have been forgotten but for Churchill.'

After convalescence in Shillong, Smyly received a Movement Order for the return to Dehra Dun:

'This kind of Movement Order – it worked instead of a ticket – must have been designed in the days of travel by bullock cart. You could take any train you wished and were allowed a day for every hundred miles of your journey. Of course, you were supposed to be travelling in the general direction of your destination. What would any schoolboy do with a First Class ticket and very little money? I wanted to see India, off the beaten track or on. I spent the nights on the train. I got off as early as possible in the morning, wherever I happened to be, and wandered. It didn't matter where. It was a joy to be back in India. Wherever you were, you met someone worth meeting. I got back to Dehra Dun in five days and turned up in the Mess for dinner, ready for another job.'

Smyly got his wish.

The experience of Chindit warfare had a profound impact on the survivors. 5 Column Commander Bernard Fergusson made a short but moving statement on how Operation *Longcloth* changed outlooks:

> To those who took part in it, the Wingate expedition was a watershed in their lives. Before it, one's appreciation of values was only half-developed. Now we have new standards and new touchstones. In my case, at least, things I had previously taken for granted I can now appraise and value in a truer perspective – diverse things, ranging from the human character to water supply, from a cup of tea to food and shelter. I learned how much of what we think to be necessary is superfluous. I learned how few things are essential and how essential those things really are.
>
> I had never before known hunger or thirst in the sense that I know them now, or appreciated the vital differences between day and night, moonlight and starlight. I had always before supposed that to be cooped up for a long time with the same people meant to quarrel with them. I had supposed that after a long period of strain one would see people at their worst and best, but I had never guessed how, when all the layers are stripped off one by one, far more people are basically good than bad. I did not

know how closely linked food and morale really are. I did not know what it was to be hunted, nor the marvellous relief of deliverance.[27]

Bill Smyly knew he owed his life to the Kachins: 'They looked after me without thought of payment or reward. Our war was their war.'

Orde Wingate held a press conference in Delhi on 20 May 1943. The Reuters' report cranked up the propaganda machine: 'This must surely rank as one of the greatest guerrilla operations ever undertaken ... the Japanese were harassed, killed, bamboozled and bewildered through a vast area of Burma.'

Rooney wrote: 'At a time when news of nothing but defeat and disaster was coming out of Burma, it was natural that the press latched on to this one great success and perhaps overdid it.'[28]

Operation *Longcloth's* outcome was dismissed by the *Official History*, now regarded as heavily biased against Wingate and the Chindits. It claimed the expedition had no strategic value. In fact, as discussed earlier, it had immense (albeit largely unintended) strategic consequences, deeply influencing the Japanese. After the war, 15 Army Commander Lieutenant-General Mutaguchi said *Longcloth* disrupted his 1943 campaign plans and caused a rethink of the entire Japanese strategy in Burma. The Chindits of 1943, in effect, were instrumental in the failure of the Japanese Imphal/Kohima offensive in 1944.

Notes

1. Allen, L. (1986), *Burma: The Longest War 1941–45*, 148
2. Carfrae, C. (1985), *Chindit Column*, 89
3. Thompson, Sir Robert (1989), *Make for the Hills*, 33–34
4. Fowler, W. (2009), *We Gave Our Today: Burma 1941–1945*, 97–101
5. Calvert, M. (1996), *Fighting Mad*, 131–132
6. Slim, Field Marshal Viscount (1999), *Defeat into Victory*, 162–163
7. Rooney, D. (2000), *Wingate and the Chindits: Redressing the Balance*, 225–234
8. Rhodes James, R. (1981), *Chindit*, 8
9. Chinnery, P.D. (2002), *March or Die*, 69–71
10. Fergusson, B. (1946), *The Wild Green Earth*, 195–196
11. Ibid, 197–200
12. Ibid, 249
13. Nesbit, R. C. (2009), *The Battle for Burma*, 85
14. Thompson, Sir Robert (1989), 26–27
15. MacHorton, I. (1958), *Safer Than a Known Way*, 50–59
16. Ibid, 147–151
17. Ibid, 158–186
18. Stibbe, P. (1995), *Return via Rangoon*, 132–141
19. MacHorton, I. (1958), 192–196
20. Ibid, 200–225
21. Ibid, 226–245
22. Stibbe, P. (1995), 142–144
23. Ibid, 147–152
24. Ibid, 154
25. Ibid, 155–157
26. Ibid, 161
27. Fergusson, B. (1971), *Beyond the Chindwin*, 13
28. Rooney, D. (1997), *Mad Mike*, 61–62

6

OPERATION *THURSDAY* TAKES SHAPE

'Everything was all very different from our training for the first Chindit campaign. We were so much bigger now, not one Brigade of 3,000 men but several Brigades totalling more than 20,000.'

Michael Calvert, Commander, 77 Brigade

Special Force, Operation *Thursday*

THE CHINDITS became Special Force by expanding from one Brigade (77) to six Brigades, with the addition of 111 Indian Infantry Brigade, three Brigades (14, 16, 23) from 70th Division and 3 (West African) Brigade.

Commander: Major-General O. C. Wingate, DSO (succeeded by Major-General W. D. A. Lentaigne).
Deputy Commander: Major-General G. W. Symes (succeeded by Brigadier D. Tulloch).

3 (WA) Brigade ('Thunder')
Brigadier A.H. Gillmore, succeeded by Brigadier A. H. G. Ricketts, DSO

Headquarters	10 Column
6th Battalion Nigeria Regiment (6 NR)	39, 66 Columns
7th Battalion Nigeria Regiment (7 NR)	29, 35 Columns
12th Battalion Nigeria Regiment (12 NR)	12, 43 Columns

14 British Infantry Brigade (ex–70th Division) ('Javelin')
Brigadier Tom Brodie

Headquarters	59 Column
1st Battalion The Bedfordshire and Hertfordshire Regiment	16, 61 Columns
7th Battalion The Royal Leicestershire Regiment	47, 74 Columns
2nd Battalion The Black Watch	42, 73 Columns
2nd Battalion The York and Lancaster Regiment	65, 84 Columns
54th Field Company, Royal Engineers	(Support)

16 British Infantry Brigade (ex–70th Division) ('Enterprise')
Brigadier Bernard Fergusson, DSO

Headquarters	99 Column
51st/69th Field Regiments, Royal Artillery (as infantry) (51/69 RA)	51, 69 Columns
2nd Battalion The Queen's Royal Regiment (Queen's)	21, 22 Columns
2nd Battalion The Royal Leicestershire Regiment	17, 71 Columns
45th Reconnaissance Regiment, Royal Armoured Corps (as infantry) (45 Recce)	45, 54 Columns
2nd Field Company, Royal Engineers	(Support)

23 British Infantry Brigade (ex–70th Division)
Brigadier Lance Perowne, CBE

Headquarters	32 Column
60th Field Regiment, Royal Artillery (as infantry) (60 RA)	60, 68 Columns
2nd Battalion The Duke of Wellington's Regiment	33, 76 Columns
4th Battalion The Border Regiment	34, 55 Columns
1st Battalion The Essex Regiment	44, 56 Columns
12th Field Company, Royal Engineers	(Support)

77 Indian Infantry Brigade ('Emphasis')
Brigadier Michael Calvert, DSO

Headquarters	25 Column
1st Battalion The King's (Liverpool) Regiment (King's)	81, 82 Columns (to 111 Brigade in May)
1st Battalion The Lancashire Fusiliers	20, 50 Columns
1st Battalion The South Staffordshire Regiment	38, 80 Columns
3rd Battalion 6th Gurkha Rifles (6 GR)	36, 63 Columns
3rd Battalion 9th Gurkha Rifles (9 GR)	57, 93 Columns (to 111 Brigade in May)
Mixed Field Company, Royal Engineers/ Royal Indian Engineers	(Support)
142 Company, Hong Kong Volunteers	(Support)

111 Indian Infantry Brigade ('Profound')
Brigadier 'Joe' Lentaigne, CBE, DSO (succeeded by Lieutenant-Colonel Jack Masters, DSO, Brigade Commander)

Headquarters	48 Column
2nd Battalion The King's Own Royal Regiment (King's Own)	41, 46 Columns
1st Battalion The Cameronians	26, 90 Columns
3rd Battalion 4th Gurkha Rifles (4 GR)	30 Column
Mixed Field Company, Royal Engineers/Royal Indian Engineers	(Support)

Morris Force
Brigadier J. R. Morris, CBE, DSO

4th Battalion 9th Gurkha Rifles (9 GR)	49, 94 Columns
3rd Battalion 4th Gurkha Rifles (4 GR)	40 Column

Bladet Force
Major Blain
Commando Engineers

Dah Force
Lieutenant-Colonel D.C. Herring
Kachin Levies

Other Units
2nd Battalion The Burma Rifles (Burrifs)
R, S, U Troops, 160th Jungle Field Regiment, Royal Artillery (25 Pounders)
W, X, Y, Z Troops, 69th Light Anti-Aircraft Regiment, Royal Artillery (Bofors)
1st Air Commando Group (USAAF) (Colonel Phil Cochran)

Orde Wingate's exhaustive report on *Longcloth* included 16 appendices reviewing all aspects of the operation. Winston Churchill read the report and wanted to know more. The Prime Minister, recalling Wingate's exploits in Palestine and Abyssinia, found him a welcome contrast to many commanders in the Far East theatre. He minuted: 'In the welter of inefficiency and lassitude which has characterised the operations on the India front, this man of genius and audacity stands out and no question of seniority must obstruct his advance.'[1]

On arriving back in Britain, Wingate was summoned to dinner at 10 Downing Street in early August 1943. Not surprisingly, he made the most of this unique opportunity to explain his concept of Long Range Penetration to a war leader already favourably disposed towards irregular warfare. Churchill decided to take Wingate with him to Quebec, to the 'Quadrant' conference of the Combined Chiefs of Staff, scheduled for 17–24 August. Wingate was accompanied by his wife. Churchill ordered an express stopped and a startled Mrs Wingate was escorted from the train to a waiting car. They boarded the *Queen Mary* for the voyage across the Atlantic. Standing before the Quadrant delegates, Wingate sold his ideas with masterful conviction. As Richard Rhodes James commented in *Chindit*, this was 'an astonishing achievement for a Brigadier.'[2]

Orde Wingate outlined his plan to deploy three LRP groups in early 1944. One would assist General Stilwell's advance. Another would assist Chinese forces pushing forward from the Yunnan. The third would attack and destroy Japanese communications centred on Indaw and serving enemy forces opposing Stilwell and IV Corps at Imphal/Kohima. He set this plan within the wider context of an anticipated Japanese attack on Imphal/Kohima – ironically, an offensive his 1943 venture did much to trigger.[1]

Wingate carried the day. Delhi was informed that six Brigades were to be trained for LRP warfare in Burma. Wingate's unusually persuasive personality had worked its magic. Rhodes James wrote:

> He got most of what he wanted. The idea of Long Range Penetration had been greatly enlarged to include several Brigades, with American air support. Wingate had captured the imagination of the Americans and they were prepared to supply air support on a huge scale. Wingate was now a Major-General and was promoting his old Column Commanders to positions of responsibility under him. 70th Division was turned over completely to the new force ...[2]

It should be said, however, that Wingate preached to the converted in Quebec. The obvious Allied strategy in Burma – an amphibious attack and the capture of Rangoon – was impossible due to the lack of landing craft.[3] Wingate had a fresh option. The Americans then went one better, offering capacity for an air landing *en masse*. Wingate, in turn, was quick to recognise the potential of large-scale airborne assault. He continued to push his mind in increasingly ambitious directions.

American priorities differed from those of the British and this explains their enthusiastic backing for Wingate's ideas. The Americans wanted to extend the Ledo Road from India, taking it over the hills to connect with the northern section of the old Burma Road.[4] This 'land bridge' would help keep the Chinese fighting.[5] Sixty Chinese Divisions could be equipped to confront the 25 Japanese Divisions in South China. New airfields would become available for America's strategic bombing of Japan.[1] The American Chiefs of Staff saw Wingate's plan as a contribution to the main task – ejecting the Japanese from North Burma.

In contrast, the British were more interested in reconquering the whole of Burma, with recaptured Rangoon as the key supply hub.[4] In the event, however, the Allies agreed that the construction of the Ledo Road should continue and that other options should be set aside.

Wingate's coup at Quebec included the remarkable pledge of a dedicated air force to support the Chindits. Rhodes James commented: 'American air support did, in fact, make the whole operation possible. It was our close tactical support, our heavy artillery, our lifeline.'[6]

Bill Towill, an Intelligence Officer with 3rd/9th Gurkha Rifles (111 Brigade), paid tribute to Wingate's achievements at Quadrant:

> 'By skilful oratory he gained the support and promise of help from the Americans. They formed the 1st Air Commando for this purpose. Now he would take a much larger force – six Brigades (though one was later detached), the equivalent of two whole Divisions of infantry – well behind enemy lines.'

General (later, Field Marshal Viscount) Slim later described Wingate's dedicated air force as a 'unique luxury'. He had sympathy, 'in principle', with the Air Staff view that it was wrong to commit precious air resources on such a scale to 'one subsidiary operation'. Yet in 1944 Slim was a robust defender of 1st Air Commando's exclusive tie to Special Force and, after the war, he acknowledged that the balance of the argument was in favour of respecting the original intention of exclusivity.[7]

Training begins: men of B Company, 1st Bedfordshire and Hertfordshire Regiment, cross an Indian river during a 100-mile march prior to Operation *Thursday*. (John Riggs)

Known as 3rd Indian Infantry Division for security reasons, Special Force had British, Gurkha, Burmese and African troops, but no Indians. It consisted of: a reconstituted 77 Brigade; 111 Indian Infantry Brigade (raised and trained while *Longcloth* was still under way); 3rd (West African) Brigade, for garrison duties; and three Brigades from the break-up of 70th British Division, a formation with a proud record in the Middle East.[8]

This Division's Battalions were almost all pre-Second World War Regular units. They were involved in dealing with the Arab insurgencies of 1936–38. Some units later took part in major confrontations in East Africa, Greece, Crete, Syria and the Lebanon. 70th Division was established in the third quarter of 1941 and deployed to relieve the Australians at Tobruk. In November 1941 the Eighth Army mounted Operation *Crusader* to push back the Germans and 70th Division units saw plenty of action in the break-out from Tobruk.

70th Division was rushed to India in 1942 with a view to holding Rangoon, but the Japanese moved too quickly. During 1942–43 many 70th Division elements were in Eastern India on internal security duties and preparing to counter any Japanese attempt to land on the east coast, south of Calcutta.

Much reorganisation was required in order to join Special Force. Each Infantry Brigade required four Battalions, rather than the usual three. The units gave up their transport and heavy weapons, acquired mules and concentrated at Gwalior, Jhansi and adjacent areas for jungle training. Many additional men were required to bring the Columns up to strength.

The break-up of 70th Division had caused real anger and Slim had been presented with a *fait accompli*. At one point 70th Division had been part of Slim's command. Now it was back, but in a new guise. Later, Slim did not mince his words:

> I was convinced – and nothing I saw subsequently
> caused me to change my mind – that a battle-tried,
> experienced, well-knit British Division, like the 70th,
> would have more effect against the Japanese than
> a Special Force of twice its size. Moreover, the 70th
> Division was the only British formation trained in
> jungle warfare. It was a mistake to break it up.[7]

Slim's suggestion that 70th Division was already jungle-trained, at the time of its break-up, is an overstatement. General Claude Auchinleck, Wavell's successor, argued vigorously against the break-up of 70th Division at the time, but to no avail. Operation *Thursday*, as then envisaged, would be spearheaded by three Brigades – two commanded by Wingate's outstanding Column Commanders of 1943, Michael Calvert and Bernard Fergusson. The operation would open with Fergusson's 16 Brigade marching into Burma from Ledo, ahead of the main body. Around four weeks later, Calvert's 77 Brigade and Brigadier W.D.A. 'Joe' Lentaigne's 111 Brigade would fly into clearings around 150 miles behind Japanese lines. The other Chindit Brigades would follow later.

Operation *Thursday* required four large jungle clearings. Dakota-capable strips would be created by glider-borne first waves, including combat engineering teams. The clearings were codenamed Broadway (35 miles east-north-east of Indaw), Piccadilly (40 miles north-east of Indaw), Aberdeen (27 miles north-west of Indaw), and Chowringhee (35 miles east of Indaw). Under the plan, 77 Brigade would fly into Broadway and Piccadilly (the large clearing from which Vlasco's Dakota flew out a number of sick and wounded Chindits during *Longcloth*). In the event three of the four strips were used: Broadway and, to some extent, Chowringhee were used by 77 and 111 Brigade Columns and, subsequently, Aberdeen was opened to fly in more Special Force units. The fly-in would commence in early March 1944 and the first priority would be to establish a heavily fortified Block astride the railway supplying the Japanese northern front.

The remaining Special Force Brigades deployed for Operation *Thursday* were 3 (WA), led by Brigadier A.H. Gillmore, and 14 British Infantry Brigade, commanded by Brigadier Tom Brodie. Their Columns flew in after the initial landings by 77 and 111 Brigades, when Aberdeen was also in use. 23 British Infantry Brigade, led by Brigadier Lance Perowne, was detached from Special Force and deployed in a Chindit role with IV Corps, on the Imphal/Kohima front.

The Chindits had various special elements: 'Morris Force' (three Columns of Gurkhas under Lieutenant-Colonel (later, Brigadier) J.R. 'Jumbo' Morris); 'Dah Force' (a unit of Kachin Levies commanded by Lieutenant-Colonel D.C. 'Fish' Herring); and 'Bladet Force' (a unit of glider-borne demolition specialists led by Major Blain). There were also the Burrifs (2nd Burma Rifles) and the guns: three Troops of 160th Jungle Field Regiment, RA, and four Troops of the 69th Light Anti-Aircraft Regiment, RA.

Before leaving for England, Wingate promised Calvert he would soon be fighting in Burma once again. He also told Calvert he would be made up to full Colonel and would probably go on to lead the reconstituted 77 Brigade. In Wingate's absence, Calvert wasted no time. He found a suitable Chindit training base at Orchha, in the Central Provinces.[9]

1st Air Commando – Colonel Cochran's 'Chindit Air Force' – made Operation *Thursday* possible, at least in the form it eventually took. The assault glider was the key. Without glider landings, rough jungle clearings could not be turned into airstrips, allowing the Dakotas to bring in the main body of Special Force. Cochran and many of the men surrounding him were larger-than-life characters. Cartoonist Milton Caniff had known Cochran at Ohio State University in the mid-1930s. Later, he based his character Flip Corkin, in the newspaper cartoon strip 'Terry and the Pirates', on Cochran.[10]

In June 1941 the United States War Department held a design competition for a cargo/transport combat glider. The WACO (Weaver Aircraft Company of Ohio) design team won with the CG-4A. Around 14,000 of these externally braced, high wing monoplane gliders were built. The CG-4A, constructed of fabric-covered wood and steel tubing, had a wingspan of 83 ft 3 in, a 'useful load' of 4,060 pounds, a tow speed of 120 mph and a stall speed of 50 mph.

There were some bizarre early ideas for stopping gliders immediately after touchdown, including fuselage-mounted ploughshares and a tail-mounted bazooka-like device firing spikes into the ground, attached to ropes. Even more alarming suggestions included explosive charges, to blow off the tail section! Not surprisingly, no-one was keen to fly assault landings in gliders rigged with explosive charges. In the event, a saner solution was found: the designers settled on a powerful wing spoiler system.[11]

The CG-4A carried 13 troops and equipment, together with Pilot and Co-pilot. The glider was surprisingly complex, having 70,000 parts, and was the only US aircraft of the Second World War able to carry more than its own weight. Sixteen companies built the CG-4A. Ford, for example, produced 4,190, at a unit cost of US $15,000.[12]

The other aircraft which made Special Force truly airmobile was the Douglas C-47. The military version of the DC3 airliner carried 28 paratroopers, or 18 stretcher cases and three medical personnel, or 10,000 pounds of cargo. Another twin-engined transport, the Curtis C-46 Commando, also participated in Operation *Thursday*. It had a greater range and higher speed than the C-47, carrying 12,200 pounds of cargo.[13]

During the Quadrant conference in Quebec, Roosevelt promised that wounded Chindits would be flown out by light aircraft. General 'Hap' Arnold, the USAAF Chief of Staff, then said he could do better. He could provide Wingate with a self-contained air force, including bombers, fighters and light aircraft for casualty evacuation. Most importantly, he offered sufficient transport aircraft and gliders to turn the Chindits into an air landing force. Phil Cochran and John Alison were given joint command of 1st Air Commando. P.51 Mustang pilot Olin B. Carter recalls:

'Both were fighter pilots and didn't want the job, at least at first. They changed their minds when things were explained. They realised that not many military ventures get the personal backing of the President of the United States and the USAAF Chief of Staff! They had joint command, but that didn't work out. Alison

Men who made things happen: Wingate, with his trademark sun helmet, talks with Colonel Phil Cochran, Commander of 1st Air Commando. (Trustees of the Imperial War Museum)

suggested that Cochran take command. Alison became his deputy.'

1st Air Commando had over 300 aircraft on strength and more than 500 aircrew, including some 300 pilots. The aircraft included 30 fighters, 15 bombers, transports, gliders, communications aircraft and 100 light aircraft, together with the first helicopters to be used in a combat zone. These aircraft carried five white diagonal stripes on the fuselage, behind the cockpit. 1st Air Commando's motto, 'Any place. Any time. Anywhere', originated from the pen of a British officer. He wrote to Cochran following an air accident – two gliders had collided, killing three Americans and four British soldiers. His note to Cochran pledged: 'Please be assured that we will go with your boys, any place, any time, anywhere.'[14]

Privately, Wingate must have been amazed at the magnitude of his success at Quebec. He even received a personal letter from Churchill authorising him to contact the Prime Minister direct, should his plans be frustrated by others. Nevertheless, Wingate had a frosty reception in Delhi on his return to India and he began to threaten to make use of his direct access to Churchill.[1]

Orde Wingate realised that 1st Air Commando transformed Special Force's capabilities. His Chindits would

be able to receive much more than food, small arms ammunition and mortar rounds. Cochran's force could deliver close support and fly in field artillery and anti-aircraft guns. Building on this new reality, Wingate continued to develop his 'Stronghold' concept, with the airstrips allowing the Chindits to create heavily fortified bases for Brigade-strength forces. Chindit warfare in 1944 would become a complex blend of mobile warfare, in Columns, and the garrisoning of fortresses designed as killing grounds. Strongholds would be located where the Japanese would find it difficult to bring up heavy weapons. There had to be enough flat ground for the essential C-47 strip and a good supply of water. Each Stronghold would be held by a well-supplied garrison force, with 25 pounders and light anti-aircraft guns. The garrison would man interlocking strongpoints, defending a very heavily wired perimeter.[5]

Rooney wrote: 'From this secure base Chindit columns would range far and wide, destroying the Japanese lines of communication, transport and supplies to all their Divisions in North Burma.'[5] These bases would be exploited to attack the supply lines of 18th Division, opposing Stilwell, and the 15th, 31st and 33rd Divisions during their attack on Imphal/Kohima.[15]

Wingate's plans for Operation *Thursday* evolved far beyond the classic model of mobile Chindit warfare, as described by Lieutenant-Colonel Philip Graves-Morris, who would lead the 2nd York and Lancaster Regiment during the 1944 expedition:

In general, its task was to sow seeds of confusion among the enemy, by keeping him in constant doubt as to where he would be harassed next. The general principle of application was one of 'tip and run' and 'hide and seek', living, moving and existing in dense jungle and suddenly breaking cover, doing one's task and as quickly moving off again to hide and move on in the jungle.[16]

Although a fair definition of Chindit warfare in the style of Operation *Longcloth*, this was much modified for the more extensive 1944 campaign. Wingate's new blend of mobile and fortress warfare, in the setting of the North Burmese jungle, made good sense within a rapidly developing strategic context.

The 1943 Quadrant conference produced new thinking on the war in the Far East. Lord Louis Mountbatten became Allied Supreme Commander, South East Asia Command (SEAC). Plans were made for a three-pronged attack on occupied North Burma – by IV Corps from Imphal, by Stilwell's forces from Ledo and by the Chinese from Yunnan. It was hoped to force the Japanese out of Burmese territory north of Indaw. Special Force would fight behind the lines, disrupting Japanese communications and reducing the enemy's ability to counter the offensive thrusts.

When Burma was overrun in 1942 the only link with China was the air bridge over 'The Hump'. Robert Thompson wrote: 'The ultimate objective was to open a new land route to China from the railhead at Ledo, in northern Assam, down the Hukawng Valley to Mogaung and Myitkyina and thence over the Kachin Hills, to join the old Burma Road to Kunming.'[17]

On 15 November 1943, the newly established SEAC assumed responsibility for operations in Burma, Thailand, Malaya and Sumatra, together with the defence of north-east India and Ceylon.[18] General Stilwell became Mountbatten's Deputy and was told to take North Burma up to the Mogaung-Myitkyina area, 'so as to cover the building of the road and to increase the safety of the air route to China'. According to Slim, this required action to prevent the Japanese reinforcing 18th Division, opposing Stilwell. It was against this background that detailed plans emerged to use Special Force to cut Japanese communications on the northern front.[19]

By the early weeks of 1944, however, it was apparent that any Allied advance into North Burma would be modest in scale. As in 1943, this placed Wingate's venture in doubt. Now, however, the stakes were higher, given the much larger scale of Wingate's Special Force. There remained much bitterness over the break-up of 70th Division and, on this occasion, Wingate's critics were able to point to the heavy losses suffered by the Chindits in 1943.

These arguments died away, however, when the enemy provided Special Force with a new *raison d'être*. It became clear that the three Divisions of the Japanese 15th Army were concentrating for an offensive across the Chindwin, to threaten Imphal and the huge network of supply bases to the rear. This active Japanese threat greatly strengthened Wingate's case for proceeding with Operation *Thursday*. He argued that the Japanese advance would stretch their supply lines and make them all the more vulnerable to Chindit attacks in their rear. There would also be more room behind the front line, due to the concentration of force in the main area of fighting.[20]

Within this new, essentially defensive context, it was decided that Stilwell's advance on Myitkyina and Wingate's LRP operation should still proceed, together with an advance by IV Corps to the Chindwin.[21] Wingate's Stronghold concept, in addition to mobile attacks on lines of communication, now came into its own. The Japanese Command, almost certainly, would have to divert substantial forces to crush such a major

challenge behind the front line. Indeed, this proved to be the case.

Orde Wingate's initial proposals were for 16, 77 and 111 Brigades to cut Japanese communications to 18th Division, opposing Stilwell, and 56th Division, confronting the Chinese in the Yunnan area. With the capture of Mogaung and Myitkyina, the Ledo Road to China could be completed. Then Allied offensive plans were scaled back and it became clear that the Japanese would do the attacking. Wingate's ideas changed. Special Force would operate against 18th Division's lines of communication *and* attack the rear of the three Japanese Divisions assaulting Imphal/Kohima.[20] The Strongholds, bastions for the mobile Columns disrupting Japanese communications, would present a challenge to the enemy which could not be ignored.

In January 1944 the Japanese opened an offensive in the Arakan, to draw in British reserves prior to the Imphal/Kohima offensive. Meanwhile, Stilwell's three Chinese Divisions (later expanded to five), together with a Chindit-trained American Brigade, advanced slowly – with Mogaung as the main objective.[22] The 3,000-strong American force was dubbed 'Merrill's Marauders' by *Time/Life* war correspondent James Shepley. Its formal title was less evocative: 5307 Composite Unit (Provisional), known as 'Galahad'. On 11 January 1944, Mountbatten agreed that they be deployed.[23]

Merrill's Marauders began an 18-day march to their operational zone. Their first brush with the Japanese was at Lanen Ga. Fowler wrote: 'In an ambush, Private Robert Landes, who was at point, was killed in a burst of machine gun fire. He became the first American infan-

Hooking up: a tow-cable is secured to a WACO CG-4A glider, which carried a crew of two and 13 troops and equipment. (Trustees of the Imperial War Museum)

tryman to be killed in action on the continent of Asia since the Boxer Rising in Peking in June-August 1900.[23]

Stilwell planned his advance into North Burma, drawing the Ledo Road behind and driving the Japanese 18th Division down the Hukawng Valley. The Kachin Levies, meanwhile, would operate from Fort Hertz and fight as guerrillas in the southern area towards Myitkyina. It was also hoped that Chinese forces from Yunnan would eventually advance into Burma and attack the Japanese 56th Division.

Stilwell's advance received the go-ahead on 14 January but had stalled by 29 January, largely owing to Chiang Kai-shek's machinations (he was fighting the Chinese Communists as well as the Japanese). Nevertheless, Merrill's Marauders helped secure the Hukawng Valley.[24]

Wingate, meanwhile, explored the possibility of capturing Indaw and its airfields. Success at Indaw would allow a Regular Division to be flown in. Fergusson's 16 Brigade would make the main attack on Indaw, with Calvert's 77 Brigade blocking the northern approaches and Lentaigne's 111 Brigade preventing Japanese reinforcements coming up from the south.[25]

Wingate returned to India in mid-September 1943, following Quadrant. Planning for Operation *Thursday* began in earnest. Wingate and his wife spent time together at the London flat before they said farewell. Lorna's mother wrote:

> This time, alas, for ever. I did not see him on his return from Quebec as I was in Scotland, but we spoke more than once on the telephone. He seemed to have a presentiment that he would not return.[26]

HQ Special Force opened at Gwalior on 25 October 1943. On Wingate's return Michael Calvert was promoted to Brigadier (just two months after becoming a Colonel). Calvert noted how the atmosphere differed from the preparations for the 1943 expedition:

> Everything was all very different from our training for the first Chindit campaign. We were so much bigger now, not one Brigade of 3,000 men but several Brigades totalling more than 20,000. Although the close comradeship of a comparatively small group could no longer be achieved, it says a lot for Wingate's special magnetism that he managed to impose his personality on every unit in Special Force.[9]

Over 50 Chindit columns would enter Burma in 1944, as against just seven the previous year. The various Brigades started preparing for the second campaign at different times and with different levels of experience. 77 Indian Infantry Brigade had been much reduced by Operation *Longcloth* but had been reconstituted by July 1943. 111 Indian Infantry Brigade had been in training for some time. This Brigade's LRP training began as early as April 1943, when *Longcloth's* dispersal parties were still attempting to reach safety. The three 70th Division Brigades – 14, 16 and 23 – were in the process of establishment. A sixth Brigade, 3rd (West African), did not arrive in India until late November. It was decided to allocate 3rd (WA) to Stronghold garrison duties, as it was the last Brigade to join Special Force and the least trained in LRP tactics.[27]

Each Special Force Brigade had four Battalions. Training focused on getting the three frontrunner Brigades – 77, 111 and 16 – ready for action by the early New Year 1944. The original intention had been to introduce Columns from other Brigades to relieve them later in the campaign. By December 1943 the three spearhead Brigades had completed the main programme of training. Instruction in special weapons use – such as PIATs, Lifebuoy flamethrowers and American lightweight carbines – had yet to be completed. The weapons had yet to arrive. The force had also to be trained in the use of Ranger boats and special engineering equipment.[27]

December was busy. 1st Air Commando built up its strength and Cochran's advance party reached Special Force, to begin joint training. Merrill's Marauders had also arrived for their Chindit jungle training.[27] Wingate was in no position to oversee training. He became seriously ill with typhoid, which came close to killing him. This has been linked to a display of petulance. On his way to India, Wingate arrived at an airfield and, thirsty and in the absence of service, he threw out flowers from a vase and drank the water. His absence at this critical time was filled by Major-General Symes of 70th Division. He showed considerable generosity in the circumstances and ensured the necessary progress was made.

Wingate ignored the doctors and declared himself fit to resume duties on 1 December. He met Slim the next day and was informed that no Division would be available to fly into Indaw, should its airfields be captured. He then met with Stilwell and Chiang Kai-shek. Stilwell agreed to 16 Brigade's entry into Burma from the Ledo Road but, as a *quid pro quo*, demanded that the Chindits attack Lonkin town on the way to their operational area. This commitment by Wingate was to have unfortunate consequences.

Slim and Wingate conferred again on 3 January. Now Wingate was warned that just one Battalion could be spared to hold Indaw, if the town was seized by Fergusson's 16 Brigade. Furthermore, there would be no IV Corps advance to the Chindwin. Naturally, Wingate stressed the value of Special Force operations behind enemy lines during a Japanese offensive against Imphal/Kohima.

The life-saver: light aircraft were used to evacuate wounded and sick from small jungle clearings. (Trustees of the Imperial War Museum)

During January 1944 16, 77 and 111 Brigades moved forward from Jhansi, prior to operations. The PIATs and Lifebuoys arrived and last-minute weapons training began. It was during the move forward that Special Force received the cover name 3rd Indian Infantry Division. Its Advance HQ was established next to IV Corps at Imphal on 10 January. Rear Headquarters was established next to 14th Army at Comilla, with Administrative HQ at Sylhet Airbase.[27] Wingate, meanwhile, found the time to ensure that his Chindits' spiritual welfare was catered for. A Chaplain would accompany each Column on operations. Those unfit for Column work were assigned to Airbase and Special Force HQ.

The final plans for Operation *Thursday* were reviewed at a Brigade Commanders' Conference at Advance HQ on 31 January–1 February 1944. Final orders arrived three days later, just before 16 Brigade began its long trek into Burma. Everyone realised that much had still to be done if the main force landings were to take place as scheduled, in early March.[27]

The 'Joint Operation Instruction' issued by 14th Army and Eastern Air Command on 4 February set the Commander of Special Force three objectives. The first was to contribute to Stilwell's advance on Myitkyina, by drawing off and disorganising enemy forces and preventing their reinforcement. The second was to create a situation favourable to a Chinese advance westwards, across the Salween. The third was to inflict the 'maximum confusion, damage and loss' on Japanese forces in North Burma.

Orde Wingate planned for 16, 77 and 111 Brigades to converge on Indaw and cut the communications of 31st Division, opposing IV Corps, and 18th Division, opposing the Ledo sector. This would demand a well-coordinated concentration of effort in the decisive zone – the area within 40 miles of Indaw. The operation would last around three months, with the Brigades relieved just before the Monsoon.

Wingate found time to make contingencies. Mindful of the likely power of the Japanese threat, he made plans to move his Advance HQ from Imphal to Sylhet, should this prove necessary. In the event this was necessary and Advance HQ operated at Sylhet from 21 March.

Regardless of what he might have been told, it seems Wingate still believed forces would be found to fly into Indaw, should his Columns take the town and its airfields. In the event, Indaw's airfields were found to be fairweather only and of little use. There would be no

time to improve them before the onset of the Monsoon. Furthermore, Wingate's own reserve would be unavailable for Indaw. 23 Brigade was detached from Special Force, for a new role in the defence of Imphal/Kohima.

The 4 February Joint Operation Instruction was cast into Brigade-specific orders:

• 16 Brigade: march south from Ledo, cross the Chindwin on about 18 February and move towards Haungpa. Two Columns were to attack Lonkin in the 1–10 March period. The balance of the Brigade was to move from Haungpa to Banmauk and Indaw, reaching Banmauk not later than 14 March. During the descent of the Meza river, the Brigade was to recce a suitable site for a Stronghold (Aberdeen). 16 Brigade was to deny the enemy possession of key areas such as Indaw and Banmauk, using road blocks, a Stronghold with 'floater' forces and other LRP methods.

• 77 Brigade: was to arrive in the Kaukkwe Valley during 6–9 March. The landing ground was to become a Stronghold garrisoned by 9 GR, one Troop of field artillery and a Troop of light anti-aircraft guns. 77 Brigade was to cut all road, rail and river communications of 18th Division between the parallels 25° and 24°. Dah Force and one Battalion of 111 Brigade was to operate in Kachin country east of the Irrawaddy, to block northwards communication to Myitkyina.

• 111 Brigade: the initial task was to sever road and rail communications between Wuntho and Indaw.[27]

Special Force's air component took shape. Originally, the main air base was to be at Agartala, with a subsidiary air base at Sylhet. Airbase parties were in position by 11 January 1944. The 2nd Indian Air Supply Company, RIASC, together with one Section of 61 Air Supply Company, RASC, were to maintain 16, 77 and 111 Brigades, having trained with them at Lalitpur. At this late stage, however, Troop Carrier Command insisted that the main Airbase should be at Sylhet, to shorten the carry. The move began on 24 January, under extreme pressure. They had to be ready to begin supply dropping to 16 Brigade by 6 February. Sylhet was designated No. 1 Airbase.

Initially, 315 and 27 Troop Carrier Squadrons, USAAF, were to support 16 Brigade. For a 10-day period in March, during the fly-in of 77 and 111 Brigades, they would be relieved by 31 Squadron, RAF, operating from Agartala. Aircraft were then allocated as follows: 117 Squadron, RAF, 77 Brigade; 27 Squadron, USAAF, 16 Brigade; and 315 Squadron, USAAF, 111 Brigade.

1st Air Commando aircraft were based at Lalaghat and Hailakandi. RAF fighters and fighter-bomber aircraft (221 Group) were based in the Imphal area, together with Vengeance dive-bombers operating from the Surma Valley. Brigades and Columns in the field were to request air support by wireless to Advance HQ. Requests were normally sent in clear, with map references scrambled using a simple code.[27]

Notes

1. Rooney, D. (2000), *Wingate and the Chindits: Redressing the Balance*, 102–106
2. Rhodes James, R. (1981), *Chindit*, 22
3. Calvert, M. (1974), *Chindits: Long Range Penetration*, 12
4. Nesbit, R.C. (2009), *The Battle for Burma*, 149
5. Rooney, D. (1997), *Mad Mike*, 64–66
6. Rhodes James, R. (1981), 33
7. Slim, Field Marshal Viscount (1999), *Defeat into Victory*, 216–219
8. Calvert, M. (1974), 15
9. Calvert, M. (1996), *Fighting Mad*, 134–135
10. Larson, G.A. (2008), *Aerial Assault into Burma*, 94
11. Ibid, 20–25
12. Ibid, 34–40
13. Ibid, 13–16
14. Fowler, W. (2009), *We Gave Our Today: Burma 1941–1945*, 104
15. Rooney, D. (2000), 112–113
16. Graves-Morris, Lieutenant-Colonel P.H., unpublished MS (via Bill Smith and Corinne Simons)
17. Thompson, Sir Robert (1989), *Make for the Hills*, 42
18. Fowler, W. (2009), 101
19. Slim, Field Marshal Viscount (1999), 251
20. Thompson, Sir Robert (1989), 44–46
21. Slim, Field Marshal Viscount (1999), 214
22. Calvert, M. (1974), 16–19
23. Fowler, W. (2009), 107–108
24. Allen, L. (1986), *Burma: The Longest War 1941–45*, 321–323
25. Calvert, M. (1974), 21
26. Hay, Alice Ivy (1963), *There Was a Man of Genius: Letters to my Grandson, Orde Jonathan Wingate*, 105
27. Report on operations carried out by Special Force, October 1943 to September 1944

7

THE MEN WHO BECAME THE CHINDITS

'With all that talk about bivouacking, sleeping in the open and cooking on campfires, it sounded almost like going to a Scout Jamboree!'

Fred Holliday, 82 Column, 1st King's (Liverpool)

MANY CHINDITS joining Wingate's second expedition had already seen action. In 1940 some were caught up in the debacle in France and Operation *Dynamo*, the evacuation from the Dunkirk beaches. Their experiences reflect Britain's dismal fortunes during the first three years of war.

Those destined for Burma included Ronald Swann, born in Leicester in 1919. Europe drifted towards war and Swann joined the Territorials in July 1939, intending to serve with the Royal Artillery. He was mindful of his father's experiences in the trenches (seriously wounded, he had been taken prisoner during the Second Battle of the Somme). Ronald Swann joined 115th Field Regiment, RA, armed with 13 Pounders of Great War vintage, converted to 18 Pounders:

'We took these ancient peashooters to France in late April 1940, as part of the British Expeditionary Force (BEF). We went into action against the Germans at St. Maur, near Tournai, and fell back until we reached Mont Kemmel, where we established anti-tank positions. We were then ordered to withdraw and spike the guns, to prevent them falling into enemy hands. We removed the protective caps from shells and rammed them down the muzzles. The guns were then fired with the long lanyard, destroying them. We were told we would re-equip back in England.'

Swann, then a Sergeant Gunner, was extremely lucky to escape from France:

'My Troop Commander, Captain Robin Winchester, found his way into the Dunkirk canal system. He drove through the defence lines and got our vehicles to within 200 yards of the harbour in Dunkirk by waving a paper stating that he was to report to the Quay Commandant. We boarded the destroyer HMS Codrington, the last to load alongside the last surviving mole. We reached Dover and safety but Codrington was sunk afterwards at Ramsgate.'

Swann's unit went to Okehampton, Devon, then to the Midlands and the north-east before moving south to reinforce London's defences. They now had elderly 4-inch naval guns, deployed in the Bexleyheath-Beckenham area of south-east London. Swann's gun was mounted on a reinforced double-decker bus chassis. It was to be sited at the rear of a well known pub, the Black Prince, ready to fire on German tanks advancing on London along the main A2 road.

When the 'invasion imminent' codeword (Cromwell) was issued, the 4-inch naval gun stationed at Beckenham was moved to the Black Prince. The gun had to be loaded, with an armour-piercing shell in the breech. There was some confusion over the exact meaning of 'Cromwell'. Swann telephoned Beckenham from the pub, seeking orders. He was told to stand down:

'I prepared to unload the gun. The men were untrained and had no idea how to extract the shell. I used the ejector. I warned them to catch the shell as it came out of the breech but they dropped it and it clattered onto the reinforced steel platform. They immediately jumped for it, convinced it would explode!'

Subsequently, Swann's Troop was posted to Norfolk and re-equipped with modern Mk. II 25 Pounders. They were bewitched:

'These marvellous weapons were still used in the 1990s by the Honourable Artillery Company for Royal Salutes at the Tower of London. The 25 Pounder, a dual purpose gun/howitzer, had a maximum range of 13,000 yards. Charges were supplied in bags with three colours: red, white and blue. 'Charge 3' (using all three) was for maximum range. This weapon was very different from other guns I had fired. The 25 Pounder rotated on a platform, giving a 360 deg. field of fire. We fired high explosive (H.E.), armour-piercing and smoke rounds, the latter with a time fuse.'

115th Field Regiment went overseas in March 1942; on arriving at Bombay they went to Bangalore, completed a training programme and moved to Ceylon:

'The tremendous firepower of our 25 Pounders became apparent. Our guns were 'surveyed in', fired by order and the fall of shot recorded, to achieve absolute accuracy. These muzzle velocity tests were carried out on salt flats at Hambantota, on the south coast. The object was to achieve accuracy when firing more than one gun at the same target – important if one or more Troops or the whole Regiment were to fire on the same target. The accuracy was remarkable. One gun fired 10 shells and three fell into the same hole!'

On New Year's Day 1943 Swann left Ceylon for India and OCTU. He was commissioned in June and posted to 160th Jungle Field Regiment at Chittagong. One Troop saw action in the Arakan but Swann's Troop was held in reserve and spent some time in Cox's Bazaar. Then the entire Regiment underwent a thorough medical examination:

'We didn't know much, only that three Troops were allocated for 'special services' and that we were wanted at Lalaghat, an air base near the border with North Burma, complete with four 25 Pounder guns per Troop, designated R, S and U.'

U Troop would not be held in reserve on this occasion.

Tony Howard's long journey to Special Force also came close to a premature end at Dunkirk. He was born in 1920 and his family lived at Salcombe, Devon. Two very different men – his Uncle and Adolf Hitler – shaped his future. The former helped launch a life-long Post Office Telephones career; the latter was responsible for his seven years in the Army. Before the outbreak of war Howard and many thousands of other young men joined the Territorials. Tony Howard:

'When the Germans invaded Poland I packed my things and reported to the 1st/7th Royal Warwickshires. This led to some embarrassment. In my haste I failed to tell the Post Office and an Inspector called, asking my parents where I'd gone!'

In January 1940 Howard's unit crossed to France with the BEF. It returned a few months later, rescued from Dunkirk's beaches:

'We remained an organised fighting unit to the very end. We were one of the last Battalions through the perimeter and a destroyer, HMS Malcolm, took us off the mole. I was just 19.'

There was an air of unreality back in Britain. Howard's Signals Section used flags and lamps, rather than wireless, and their equipment was of Great War vintage. They travelled in a commandeered 'Corona' lemonade lorry. For 18 months Howard moved around the country with 143rd Brigade (attached to 48th Division) in the coastal defence role, but then fell victim to a lung condition. By January 1942, however, he was fit again and volunteered to join a draft to Singapore. They sailed on the Dutch cargo vessel *Sibajak*: 'When Singapore fell we diverted to Colombo. Japanese air raids started just as we arrived. The stevedores disappeared and we had no choice but to unload our own ship!' He joined 16 British Infantry Brigade, based near Kandy: 'By the time we had marched to the centre of Ceylon, we all had malaria.' He transferred to the Royal Corps of Signals in late 1942 and was attached to 16 Brigade's HQ. Howard recalls that malaria was not the only health problem. VD was rife: 'Every week a new batch of unfortunates was taken to the "college" – the local clap clinic – where they received the dreaded "umbrella treatment".' Howard would serve as a Signaller NCO with 21 Column, 2nd Queen's.

Many men with the Special Force Chindit columns had been battle-tested in the Western Desert. They included Lawrence 'Lou' Lake. He was born in 1919 and his family lived in London's Notting Hill Gate. He was named after 'Lawrence of Arabia' (his father, a Boer War veteran, went on to serve in the Middle East with T.E. Lawrence).

Lake worked as a shorthand typist. He found it dull and a friend urged him to consider the Army. He joined the Royal Engineers in November 1938 and was in Egypt a few months later:

'It was a culture shock for someone who had been no further than Southend! I had no idea of what was before me: three years in Egypt, 18 months in Ceylon and Burma, my return to the UK, then more active service in Europe. I took part in the 1945 Rhine Crossing.'

Men of Special Force: from top left, clockwise: Captain Ronald Swann, RA, Gun Position Officer with U Troop, 160th Jungle Field Regiment; Corporal (later, Sergeant) Peter Heppell, the King's 82 Column; Corporal Jesse Dunn, Commando Platoon, the South Staffords' 80 Column; Lieutenant (later, Major) Harold Pettinger, MC; Vickers gunner Frank Anderson, the King's 81 Column; and Private Jack Hutchin, 80 Column.

Discontented with his lot as a Pay Corporal, Lake remained bored. Egypt however, gave him his chance. He became a Sapper with 2nd Field Company, RE (the Army's oldest Field Company), and left his desk far behind. Lake's days were now filled with bridge-building and mine clearance:

'I enjoyed the desert. It was hot, sandy and romantic. One street trader in Damascus even had the audacity to offer me a piece of the 'True Cross'. Later, I was part of Tobruk's garrison. We were dive-bombed constantly, especially at night. I was stationed at Outpost 88 and my main job, every morning, was to check 22 booby traps and a buried 500 pound bomb. One day a 'flowerpot' mine went off during my inspection. 'Jumping Jacks' spring up and explode. This one did

just that – it went clean over my head! I installed a 69 Grenade to replace it.'

Lake's unit was attached to the Dragoon Guards for the Tobruk break-out. They fought their way through the German lines in armoured cars. Lou Lake was alongside the Signaller/Wireless Operator when their vehicle was struck by a shell:

'It penetrated where I usually sat. This shell buzzed around inside the car, glowing red hot, then exited without hitting anyone. We were also blown up twice but, once again, our luck held and no-one was hurt.'

Subsequently, 2nd Field Company joined other 70th Division elements at Suez and embarked for Ceylon:

'Ceylon was a beautiful place but, unfortunately, we arrived during the Monsoon. We were housed in disused tea warehouses. We were told to mine the main bridges, including the bridge at Trincomalee, due to the threat of invasion. We nearly blew that big bridge! We got a signal to detonate the charges, but without the codeword 'prop'. Happily, someone checked.

'We were very popular in the local village. We used guncotton blocks to fish the nearby tidal river. We would get enough fish to feed the entire village. Meanwhile, I had acquired a pet Rhesus Monkey, "Sheila", who had almost human characteristics. She would stay in a tree when we were out of camp. On our return I would always find her in a local teashop, begging bananas.'

Life was about to become more challenging for Lou Lake, as a Chindit Wireless Operator with 17 Column, 2nd Leicesters.

Corporal Ted Treadwell also saw bitter fighting in the Desert. He served with the Leicesters as well but in sister Column 71. Treadwell was born in 1916 and grew up in south-east London. He left school at 14 and became a butcher's errand boy. Called up in 1940, he was sent to an infantry training centre in Dorset, was posted to Egypt within 10 weeks and took part in heavy fighting around Bardia and Tobruk.

Treadwell's unit then went to Crete, to stiffen Maleme airfield's defences. They were evacuated by the Royal Navy when the Germans took the island. Having avoided capture at Tobruk and Crete, Treadwell's next destination was Abyssinia, to fight the Italians in Eritrea. By early 1942 he was back in Egypt. The Leicesters sailed for Singapore and once again his luck held – the vessel diverted to Colombo as Singapore fell.

Corporal Arthur 'Tom' Turvey had much in common with Treadwell. Turvey was from a village near Brackley, had left school at 14 and had seen action at Tobruk. He also joined 71 Column of Special Force, as a member of the Recce Platoon: 'After Tobruk we went into Syria to fight Vichy French African troops. We soon saw them off. Our Battalion then sailed for Ceylon.' Turvey, a talented cricketer who had had a number of County trials, played for Battalion, Brigade, Division and Corps. He began jungle training during the third quarter of 1943.

John Riggs also fought at Tobruk and against the Vichy French in Syria. He had an interesting childhood. He was born in Essex in 1920 and his family went to China when he was still a small child. His father, a Master Mariner, took a shore job in Shanghai. Young Riggs returned to England in 1926 to go to school. He joined the Territorials in 1938, was commissioned shortly after the outbreak of war and was posted to Palestine early in 1940. He joined the 1st Bedfordshire and Hertfordshire

Regiment and spent the best part of a year in Palestine. The Battalion then went to the Greek island of Lemnos, returned to Egypt and was at Alexandria during the Crete evacuation. They had been preparing to reinforce Crete but moved to Syria in July 1941, to help neutralise the Vichy French:

'There was real concern that they would allow the Germans to reach Iraq and the Gulf oilfields. There was considerable fighting but we were involved in only a minor way before an Armistice was signed. We soon returned to Egypt and in the October we joined 70th Division. We were taken by Royal Navy destroyers from Alexandria to Tobruk, to relieve the Australian garrison.'

Tobruk, the best port between Tripoli and Alexandria, was heavily besieged by the Germans and Italians. Riggs' Battalion took part in the breakout, to link up with the Eighth Army driving westwards from Egypt in Operation Crusader. The siege was lifted after some 250 days. Subsequently, 70th Division was sent to India, arriving in Bombay shortly after Rangoon fell to the Japanese. Captain John Riggs served as Recce Platoon Commander with 16 Column, 14 British Infantry Brigade.

Corporal John Henry 'Jack' Goldfinch was another future Chindit who had fought with distinction at Tobruk and in Syria. Born in Ramsgate, Kent, in 1920, Goldfinch joined the Army in September 1940. Following basic training he boarded the troopship *Orontes*, bound for Egypt. Goldfinch joined units of the Queen's fighting in Syria.

Following some hard fighting around Damascus, the Queen's moved to Beirut and boarded the cruiser HMS *Neptune* for the voyage to Alexandria. They then transferred to an Australian destroyer and sailed for Tobruk, where the Australian 9th Division had been holding out against the Germans for many months. Goldfinch took part in the Tobruk breakout. Later, his unit was promised leave but the men were then given one more job. There had been a particularly vicious engagement between enemy tanks and New Zealand Gunners. Jack Goldfinch and the others found themselves digging up hastily buried bodies for more formal interment. He described this as the worst two weeks of his life.

The Battalion then went to the Far East. Goldfinch boarded the troopship *Nieuw Amsterdam* at Port Tewfik, bound for Rangoon, but the ship diverted to Ceylon as the Japanese overwhelmed Burma. Corporal Goldfinch eventually joined the Mortar Section of the Queen's 21 Column.

Another Tobruk veteran, Harold Pettinger, won the Military Cross during the fighting. Pettinger was born in

Dulwich, South East London, in 1920. As a teenager he joined Alleyn's School OTC, followed by the Territorials in 1938:

'I remember comparing my Attestation Form with that of my Uncle. The form hadn't changed since 1914! In any event, I was too young. I had to wait until I was 19. Eventually, I joined The Buffs and reported to Canterbury Barracks.'

Pettinger was commissioned in the York and Lancaster Regiment, went to the Middle East and joined the 2nd Battalion in its short, vicious campaign against the Vichy French. Subsequently, the Battalion became part of 70th Division and went to Tobruk to relieve the Australians. They went without Pettinger, however, who was in hospital at the time. He finally arrived at Tobruk on board the destroyer HMS *Jackal*. On 12 November 1941, 2nd Lieutenant (later, Major) Pettinger celebrated his 21st birthday sitting in a slit trench within Tobruk's perimeter. The Commander of 13 Platoon, B Company, sipped his 'Tobruk Tea' – an unpleasant concoction tainted by brackish water. During the breakout B Company was ordered to capture a fortified position beyond the perimeter:

'Our assault went in on 23 November 1941. It was like a First World War attack. We had to cover around 800 yards of open ground immediately after the artillery barrage lifted. We were supported by the 3rd Royal Tank Regiment's Matilda tanks. We took around 60 per cent casualties and I was the only officer left. Fortunately, my Platoon was on the right and most of the heavy mortar and machine gun fire was directed at the centre. Due to the casualties, C Company came up in support.'

The citation for Pettinger's MC reads: 'Though under continual heavy fire, 2nd Lieutenant Pettinger showed a complete disregard for his personal safety and it was largely due to his personal example and leadership that this attack by his Company was a success.' Fate, however, would deny Pettinger his chance to go into Burma.

H.M. 'Bill' Williams also served in the Middle East. He was born in 1918. His father's family was from Anglesey and his mother was born of British parents living in Argentina. The couple had settled in Cumberland:

'My father was a Tank Corps officer. He met my mother while in hospital, recovering from a wound. He must have made quite an impression, as she was engaged to someone else at the time. Future Labour Prime Minister Clement Atlee was among my father's friends and became my Godfather. I don't remember him playing

any significant part in my upbringing, beyond the arrival of an occasional birthday present.'

As a Territorial – a Trooper in the Staffordshire Yeomanry – Williams was called up the day war broke out. He was sent overseas before the year's end and spent six months in Palestine before being commissioned into the South Staffords:

'I joined them in the Western Desert in November 1940. We took part in Wavell's first offensive, which resulted in the capture of thousands of Italians. I had no personal involvement, as my Company was held in reserve.'

2nd Lieutenant (later, Major) Bill Williams' Battalion then had the job of escorting Italian POWs to India:

'As a young 2nd Lieutenant I found myself O/C troops on a Dutch ship with 800 POWs and their escort. It turned out to be a very pleasant voyage. We stayed in Bombay for a couple of months and then sailed back to Egypt, completing a rather enjoyable interlude in my war service. When back in Egypt some Battalion elements went to Tobruk. I didn't go. Instead, I was attached for six weeks to the Coldstream Guards, who were short of officers at that time.'

Eventually, the reunited Battalion sailed for Bombay. After six months' training in the Central Provinces they deployed to the Arakan, where one Company of South Staffords saw action. Bill Williams, however, became Animal Transport Officer (ATO) with the Chindits of the South Staffords' 80 Column:

'I remember attending a lecture on Wingate's 1943 expedition. This was the first indication of our intended role, as part of Michael Calvert's 77 Brigade. It was suggested that Wingate's second expedition would take place in late 1943. I can't say we were terribly enthusiastic; it seemed a very dangerous undertaking. After all, half the men participating in his first venture had been killed, wounded, captured or just plain lost.'

Some first expedition survivors participated in Wingate's second operation. Most 'new' Chindits, however, lacked jungle experience, having played no part in *Longcloth* or the earlier fighting when the Japanese overran Burma. A few, however, had some jungle expertise, including John Pearson, born in Portsmouth in 1922. Pearson had studied electrical engineering at university and the syllabus included wireless communications. This was to have some significance during his service in the Far East.

During early 1941 the Air Ministry engaged Professor C.P. Snow to head-hunt graduates with a wireless communications background. They included Pearson, who joined a six-month Cranwell course for Signals Officers. He was then posted to the Far East, arriving in Bombay in September 1942.

The Japanese in Burma now occupied airstrips formerly used by the big logging companies. Calcutta was under threat of air attack and a rudimentary early warning system was to be established. John Pearson:

'Radar wasn't really mobile at that time, certainly not mobile enough for use in jungle areas with few roads, so we established a chain of observer posts along the East Bengal/Burmese border. Obsolete aircraft morse transmitters were used to report enemy air activity. These posts were set up at 10-mile intervals, running north-south from the Akyab area to just west of the Chin Hills. Each post was manned by three Wireless Operators and three Observers, all trained in aircraft recognition, together with a mechanic. The idea was to maintain a continuous watch by two men, over three eight-hour shifts.

'Establishing each post required at least 10 men and three mules. The party included Muleteers. The animals carried in the wireless, batteries, generator, fuel and other equipment. These "establishment groups" were protected by infantry Platoons.'

Flying Officer Pearson was closely involved in this early warning network until mid-1943, when responsibility for it passed from the RAF to Indian Army Signals. He was then drawn into preparations for Operation *Thursday*, becoming RAF Signals Officer for 111 Brigade, Special Force. It was familiar ground: 'I had spent much time in the jungle setting up the observer posts. I also had experience of mules, as the Indian Army unit responsible for supplying the posts used the animals.' Pearson began training Wireless Operators for Special Force Columns and the base station at Rear Brigade HQ: 'These men were already trained Wireless Operators, but they needed instruction in the specific communication needs of Chindit columns.'

Some Chindit officers had a rather genteel background. Peter Allnutt OBE was born in 1917. His father was an Army doctor and an overseas posting took the family to Bermuda during the 1920s, where they enjoyed an idyllic lifestyle: 'Our home was just 100 yards from the sea and we really did have a "Surrey with the fringe on top". Allnutt joined the Colonial Service and was sent to Nigeria as an Administrative Officer:

'I arrived at the very end of the 'Sanders of the River' era. I went on tour for three weeks at a time, accompanied by 20 carriers head-loading my gear, including a comfortable camp bed. I would rise in the morning for my bath (a tin bath was carried on tour) and then catch up with the advance party in time for the breakfast stop. We would go on till noon. After a rest, I would deal with complaints during the afternoon and hear Native Court cases the following day.'

These echoes of Victorian empire soon crumbled under the pressures of 20th-century warfare. The 12th Nigeria Regiment was raised at Kano in 1940. 12 NR was one of three Battalions making up the 3rd (West African) Brigade. 2nd Lieutenant Allnutt was not entirely successful in severing associations with 'Sanders of the River'. 12 NR went north to patrol the border with French Equatorial Africa: 'We had horses and camels and, occasionally, we would meet mounted Free French troops. It was like something out of a film.'

The Brigade sailed for the Far East in 1943. They crossed India by train and boarded a Brahmaputra steamer during their long journey to war in Burma. Peter Allnutt became a Platoon Commander with 43 Column. He had no qualms about Special Force:

'I had always disliked regimentation. The Chindits offered scope for using one's own initiative. I admired Wingate and regarded Long Range Penetration as a brilliant new concept.'

Captain (later, Colonel) K.M. 'Richard' Stuckey OBE became a Rifle Platoon Commander with 43 Column. Stuckey was born in 1920, into a Somerset family of yeoman farmers with origins traceable back to the 1200s:

'My father was the fourth son – there was no farm for him. In 1914 he joined the Yeomanry and served in France throughout the Great War. He went in a Trooper and came out a Corporal. The other side of the family was more entrepreneurial, founding Stuckey's Bank, with 120 branches in the West Country. It is now part of the Royal Bank of Scotland.'

Dick Stuckey joined Bristol Grammar School's OTC and later went to Sandhurst:

'I was commissioned in late 1939, joining the South Staffordshire Regiment. I had wanted the Somerset Light Infantry but that would have required a private income of around £500 a year – a huge sum at that time. My father had already met the costs of my education and Sandhurst and I was unwilling to ask for more.

Men of Special Force: from top left, clockwise: Driver Peter Fairmaner; Lieutenant (later, Major) Cyril Baldock, Animal Transport Officer with 45 Recce's 54 Column; Cypher Operator Norman Campbell, with the Cameronians' 90 Column; Captain Tony Wailes, with 23 Brigade's 60 Column; Captain (later, Colonel) Dick Stuckey, with 12 NR's 43 Column; and Lieutenant Peter Allnutt, also with 43 Column.

'It happened that Bernard Fergusson, then a Captain, was my Platoon Commander at Sandhurst. He was always a very grand fellow, fully rigged in his Black Watch uniform. Fergusson gave me some advice. He had been ADC to Wavell when commanding the Aldershot Brigade. He remembered Wavell saying that the South Staffords were the best. I took the hint, applied and was approved by the Colonel of the Regiment.'

Stuckey was at Lichfield Depot when orders came to drop everything and prepare to receive survivors from Dunkirk:

'Train-load after train-load arrived. They were fed and settled into barracks, tightly packed and sleeping on mattresses on the floor. I remember opening the door of the Officers' Mess and being shocked. They looked like a lot of dead bodies, sprawled on the floor, exhausted and oblivious.'

Dick Stuckey was posted to the 10th South Staffords, a wartime Battalion engaged in airfield and coastal defence. At one point they were stationed east of Dundee. On one Saturday evening Stuckey, the C/O, the Adjutant and the Quartermaster were the only ones who hadn't gone into Dundee:

'The Adjutant, Fred Brady [later killed in action], handed the C/O the signal 'Cromwell'. Invasion imminent! When the chaps arrived back at 10 o'clock, they were all half-drunk and it was difficult to get them to take things seriously. They thought I was pulling their legs. Off we went to defend the beaches. At dawn we had just finished digging slit trenches when the 2 i/c turned up. He said we were too close to the water and ordered us to do it all again, higher up the slope. Comments from the soldiery can be imagined!'

In the absence of Germans, Stuckey was given an unpleasant task:

'Apparently, a chap had blown himself up on Troon Golf Course. I was told to take my Platoon and sort it out. One old soldier gave me advice: 'You had better take groundsheets with you; he's bound to be in bits.' The victim had been part of a four playing golf on Sunday morning. The ball had gone over the Dannert wire, into a mined area. He thought he'd be OK, as the ground had been sown with anti-tank mines. These cannot be detonated by a man's weight. He had insisted: 'I know. I was in the Royal Engineers in the last war.' Sadly, he had failed to realise that anti-tank mines are usually interspersed with anti-personnel mines. He really was in bits!'

During late 1940 volunteers were being sought for African service and Commando training. Stuckey went to Africa:

'I thought they meant North Africa, but that wasn't the case. I was among 400 officers who boarded an Elders & Fyffe banana boat at Glasgow. We called at Freetown, Sierra Leone, then sailed on to Takoradi on the Gold Coast and, eventually, Lagos. I was an innocent, unaware that I would spend the next two-and-a-half years in Nigeria.'

A.M. 'Larry' Gaines also went to Africa. Born in Clapham in 1919, his studies at the London School of Economics were interrupted by war. He was commissioned into the Sherwood Foresters in 1940 but later contracted scarlet fever and missed his unit's embarkation for the Far East the following year. Kicking his heels in Lichfield Isolation Hospital, he had no idea just how fortunate he had been. His Division became prisoners when Singapore fell.

Lieutenant (later, Captain) Gaines recovered from his illness, but then broke a leg and spent another six months in hospital. It was a long haul to return to A.1 fitness but Gaines succeeded and he then volunteered for service in West Africa. He sailed for Nigeria on the *Highland Princess* and joined 6 NR, then jungle training in tropical forest. He was to see a lot more forest in Burma, as Commander of 66 Column's Vickers Platoon.

Denis Arnold arrived in West Africa and joined 7 NR. He was born in 1918 in Chiswick. Arnold's family has a proud military tradition. His great uncle, David Embleton, won the VC on 5 August 1882 during the Arabi Pasha rebellion in Egypt, while serving under the *nom de guerre* Frederick Corbett. Two uncles served in the Boer War and other uncles fought in both World

Wars. His father, a Royal Engineer, had served in Nigeria and this influenced the direction of his son's military career.

Arnold studied chemical engineering and joined Associated Portland Cement (later Blue Circle). When war broke out he was in the Militia, having completed his basic training with a Royal Artillery searchlight regiment. Subsequently, he served in Northern Ireland, made full Sergeant and was commissioned in late 1942, joining the 13th Royal Welch Fusiliers. He then responded to the call for volunteers to serve in Nigeria. Earlier in life he had been captivated by his father's stories of West Africa. He arrived in Nigeria in October 1942 and stayed until September 1943, when he sailed to India with his unit. Lieutenant (later, Major) Arnold became a Platoon Commander with 29 Column and subsequently added to his family's tradition of bravery in the field. He won an immediate MC in North Burma.

Edward 'Ted' McArdle also had a VC in the family. Born in Liverpool in 1923, he left school at 14 and was 16 when war began. He stayed in the city throughout the bombing, joined the Home Guard and volunteered on reaching 18:

'One of my uncles, Albert White, won the VC in the Great War. A real tearaway – a tough guy on the street – he died charging a German machine gun nest. All the men in my family were in the Army during the First War, with the exception of another uncle, who was in the Navy.'

McArdle wanted to join the King's and he got his wish. He arrived in Bombay in 1943 on the Athlone Castle and travelled to Deolali. He became a Muleteer with 82 Column and was fated to become a prisoner of the Japanese.

Many other Chindits came from relatively modest backgrounds. John Simon, born in 1919, was the youngest son of a large family of four sons and four daughters living in Birkenhead. His father joined up at the start of the Great War but was called back to the shipyard, where he was in charge of launchings. Later, he supervised the keel-laying of the battleship *King George V* and the liner *Queen Mary*.

Simon's father died following injuries suffered on board a coaster; he was burnt by a falling bucket of boiling pitch. His widow received compensation of 10 shillings a week. Fourteen-year-old John became the breadwinner, stuck in a dead-end job as a Co-op delivery boy for two years. He graduated to milk deliveries and stood that for another two years but then found himself out of work. He went to sea, completed some coastal voyages and then joined a cruise ship as a cabin boy. Subsequently, he worked ashore for this company until war broke out. Jaded with his lot, he had joined the Territorials in 1938. When called-up he reported to 70th Heavy AA Regiment and spent nearly a year with the guns protecting Scapa Flow naval base. His Battery then moved to Manchester. John Simon sailed for the Far East in March 1942:

'A TA unit is like a family and instinctively tries to stay together. Postings away tend to be blocked. Such concerns were brushed aside when we were given the choice of serving as Gunners in the Middle East or staying in the Far East as members of a 'Long Range Penetration Group'. That sounded a bit like the famous unit in the Western Desert, so I volunteered.'

Simon became a Chindit Bren gunner with Bernard Fergusson's 16 Brigade HQ Column.

The author's father, John 'Jack' Redding, was another Bren gunner. He grew up in difficult circumstances in the Peckham area of south-east London. Jack, one of four children, was born in 1917. He was still a teenager when his father died. Walter Redding was out of work. The family story is that he broke a leg escaping from an angry farmer, having helped himself to some vegetables. He died shortly afterwards from a blood clot. The family then lived hand-to-mouth; occasional 'moonlight flits' avoided the rentman and, at one point, both boys went into care.

Jack Redding never forgot his harsh treatment in care and, throughout his life he retained a sense of the value of money known only to those who have experienced what it means to have none. After trying various poorly paid jobs, including that of pedal-powered ice cream salesman, he got a steady position as a railway porter at Lee Station, south-east London. He met his future wife, Emily, and they married in December 1939. Jack Redding was called up and posted to The Duke of Cornwall's Light Infantry. During the summer of 1940 he spent some weeks on Pevensey beach, housed in a large section of concrete pipe half buried in the shingle, waiting for the Germans and watching enemy raiders fly in so low that the pilots could be seen in their cockpits.

Jack Redding went to India in 1942. With the 2nd King's Own Royal Regiment, he would land by assault glider on Broadway jungle clearing in early March 1944.

Deolali was one of British India's more significant military centres. No-one had a good word to say about this huge, desolate transit camp. Deolali offered masterclasses in *ennui*. Its name became synonymous with 'going round the bend' – or 'going Deolali'. Many Chindits spent time there. Deolali encouraged men to volunteer for other duties in the hope of escaping the place.

From Peckham to Burma: the author's father, Private Jack Redding of the King's Own, 111 Brigade.

Londoner Fred Holliday, born in 1922, left school at 14 and went to work. Called up in January 1942, he was posted to the Royal Warwickshires and joined an overseas draft in early 1943. On arriving in Bombay he discovered that Deolali was the next stop. The draft included his close friend, Tom Pickering:

'Tom was from Nuneaton and six or seven years older than me. We were both Corporals and wanted to remain together. Having attended talks about Burma at Deolali, we visited the Orderly Room and offered our services. With all that talk about bivouacking, sleeping in the open and cooking on campfires, it sounded almost like going to a Scout Jamboree!'

They were posted to the King's, then bivouacked near Jhansi. Corporal Holliday and his pal found active service with 10 Platoon, 82 Column, very different from a Scout Jamboree.

Peter Heppell also volunteered for the Chindits. He was born in 1920. The family's roots were in Northumberland, but he grew up in London. His father was a successful commercial artist and the director of a large London Agency. Peter attended Art School then joined his father at S.T. Garland Advertising Agency, with day release to continue his studies at St. Martin's. Life changed completely in May 1940, when he joined the Royal Engineers and served with a chemical warfare unit: 'Gases were not used in WWII but were certainly stockpiled. Gas would almost certainly have been used, had the Germans invaded.' First Group Chemical Warfare carried out exercises on the East Coast with newly issued equipment, including rocket-fired gas canisters: 'It was all very hush-hush. The components were always referred to by cricketing codenames. The rocket was the "bat" and the canister the "ball".

They moved to Lynmouth, where comments from the locals – 'Oh! You've got that new rocket thing!' – caused consternation. Heppell's Section then became an anti-tank Platoon armed with makeshift weapons: 'sticky bombs' and oil drums filled with flammable liquid and dug into the roadside.

In 1942 Heppell went to the Far East with 67 Chemical Warfare Company. On reaching Deolali their gas munitions were put in store, but the high temperature caused mustard shells to 'sweat'. Fortunately, at this delicate point the RAF and Royal Artillery were given responsibility for chemical warfare. Peter Heppell's unit became 67th Field Company. They moved to Cox's Bazaar, with the job of improving the airfield. Heppell and a friend, Ron Fletcher, volunteered for 'special duties' when they discovered they would not be allowed within 10 miles of the front due to their knowledge of chemical warfare:

'We knew all about the dangers of volunteering, yet this seemed the only way of escaping the "10-mile rule". We felt we were not really involved in the war and wanted excitement.'

Lance Corporal (later, Sergeant) Heppell found more than enough excitement with the King's and 82 Column, behind the lines in Burma.

Frank Anderson was a Vickers gunner with 81, the King's sister Column. Born in 1914, Frank lived in Morecambe. He left school at 14, began a five-year apprenticeship as a plasterer and he was called up in late 1939:

'I joined the King's Own at Lancaster. I was there for just three weeks before being posted to Penrith for traffic control duties; I spent two years there. I was back with the King's Own in late 1941 and went to India in 1943. I then transferred to the 1st King's and began jungle training near Jhansi.'

Horace Howkins was born in 1923 and became a factory worker on leaving school at 14. He joined the Home Guard in 1939 and was called up in 1942, joining the Royal Warwickshires before transferring to the Leicesters. He went to India in early 1943 and moved to the South Staffords while at Deolali. His Battalion was busy training and also had internal security duties. Private Howkins saw action as a Rifleman with 80 Column.

Other future members of 80 Column then at Deolali included Jesse Dunn, who became a Corporal in the Column's Commando Platoon. Dunn was born in Wordsley, Amblecote, in 1920. His father had been gassed in the Great War and died young, at 58. Jesse was a keen motorcyclist and had a natural flair for all things mechanical. He became a toolmaker and his post-war career saw him advance to the post of Technical Director of a large company. Dunn was called up in February 1940, did his infantry training with the Worcesters and stayed with them until late 1942, when he went to India and transferred to the South Staffords.

Private John 'Jack' Hutchin saw hard fighting with 80 Column. He was born in 1924. His family lived in Cardiff and the paternal family was extensive. They had arrived from Ireland in 1849 as Potato Famine refugees. Hutchin's grandparents had 11 children; nine survived and were reared. His father escaped both World Wars, being too young for one and too old for the other:

'My parents married in 1923 and divorced in 1939. Father married a woman of great passion but they were totally unsuited and family life was volatile. I was just 15 when war came. Father left home, passing on his responsibilities to me. He looked at me and said: "Well, Jack! It's up to you now!" As a young man I was full of anger. I had been forced to take sides and I went to my mother's defence, as the eldest son. Yet, looking back, without my father and some bitter early experiences, I would never have survived my time as a Chindit.'

Jack Hutchin worried that the war might end before he became old enough to fight. Repeated British setbacks during the first three years of war ensured that his fears were groundless. When his call-up papers finally arrived, in July 1943, his father attempted to keep him out of harm's way. He went so far as to 'volunteer' his son for non-combatant ground duties with the RAF. These efforts came to nothing. Jack joined the South Wales Borderers and his training included a punishing Commando course:

'No-one knew where we were going. I got so fed up waiting I decided to shave off my hair. We then went to India and ended up at Deolali. One night Ginger Davies and other friends arrived in my tent. They had just returned from Battalion HQ. Davies announced: "We've just joined the Chindits." Without giving it any thought, I said: "Well, if you're going, I'm going." I knew nothing about the Chindits. In fact, I had never heard of Special Force, but we were soon on our way, spending 13 days on trains as we headed for 77 Brigade's base in Assam.'

Ian Niven was another young Chindit, also born in 1924. Niven's father came from Dunfermline, but the family subsequently lived in Manchester. Ian Niven had just one ambition, to be a professional footballer: 'I had this one great asset – I could play football. At 14 I was selected for Manchester Boys.' The war then gave rise to another ambition. Niven volunteered for aircrew and spent three days at London's Aircrew Selection Centre:

'I passed the tests, only to be told that I would be on deferment for six to nine months. I told the officer: "The bloody war will be over by then." He wasn't impressed and snapped back: "Stand up straight when you talk to me!" He proceeded to give me a severe bollocking for my cheek. Next day I stood before the Recruiting Sergeant at Manchester Depot and joined the Royal Scots.'

With his basic training completed, Niven boarded a troopship for India:

'My first stop in India was Deolali, where I was soon enjoying myself again, playing football. It was a strange place. People really went "Deolali". Some just lolled around the place, almost as though they were drunk. They were "tapped", having lived like that for years.'

Ian Niven became a Regimental Signaller with 20 Column, 1st Lancashire Fusiliers.

Deolali also failed to impress Norman Campbell, from Birmingham. He had volunteered for aircrew but had been turned down. Called up later in 1942, having just reached 19, he joined the Army. Campbell sailed for India in July 1943 and was posted to Deolali:

'The place was huge but there was nothing there. During my stay I read Dostoevsky's Crime and Punishment! Others turned to drink. Fortunately, I was soon posted to the 1st Cameronians, who had already split into two Columns for Chindit service.'

Campbell became a Cypher Operator with 90 Column.

Nineteen-year-old A.H. 'Tony' Wailes completed a 12-month engineering course at Cambridge University before volunteering for the Royal Engineers. He was commissioned and went to India with 12th Field Company, part of 70th Division. They were responsible for battlefield tasks such as mine clearance and demolition. 2nd Lieutenant (later, Captain) Wailes joined 60 Column (60th Field Regiment, RA).

Eric Sugden was called up in September 1942. His father was Private Secretary to Sir Maurice Holmes, Permanent Secretary at the Ministry of Education. This conferred at least one advantage. The Sugden home at Old Malden (now part of the London Borough of Kingston) had priority for a telephone line. Sugden intended to become a Chartered Surveyor and was then an Articled Pupil:

'It was common practice for anyone connected with the building industry to go into the Royal Engineers. I joined No. 1 RE Training Battalion for a 12-week course, one module being concerned with explosives. I appeared before a Board, but was refused a commission on grounds of immaturity.'

Eric Sugden was still 18 when he arrived at No. 5 RE Training Battalion at Blacon, on the Dee near Chester:

'We were told we were all "volunteers" for a special operation. The training was intense, with route marches, assault courses and more instruction on explosives. We also practised crossing the Dee in small inflatables. At the end of two weeks we were given 13 days' embarkation leave. We were going abroad.'

The Blacon course was very tough and around 20 of the 60 in Sugden's group were returned to unit, judged unfit for the trials ahead. Sugden's ship, meanwhile, docked at Bombay on 27 November 1943. It had been an uncomfortable voyage; thousands had been crammed into the *Strathmore*, the convoy flagship. Eric Sugden took to sleeping on deck, but sleep was interrupted off Gibraltar when they were dive-bombed. *Strathmore* escaped but three other transports were hit and damaged. On reaching Bombay the troops boarded trains for the journey through the Western Ghats to Deolali. Sapper Sugden would serve with 61 Column, 1st Bedfordshire and Hertfordshire.

Jim Unsworth was a few years older than Eric Sugden and Tony Wailes. He was born in 1916 into a large family living in the Yorkshire town of Littleborough. He never knew his father, who died when he was just nine months old. Jim and his two brothers all saw service:

'I was working in a market garden when my papers came. My call-up was a mistake, as food production was a Reserved Occupation. This was an error I never bothered to put right.'

After basic training and a miserable winter on coastal defence around Lowestoft, Unsworth went to India:

Troop transport: Lancashire Fusilier Harold Shippey left England in July 1943 and later joined the *Empire Pride* at Gibraltar for the voyage to Bombay. (Harold Shippey, via Ian Niven)

'I took a real dislike to the country. It was filthy and Bhopal was the worst, with a sewer-like river running through the centre. I got to know the huge Military Hospital very well. I spent seven weeks there, suffering from dysentery.'

Private Unsworth served with the King's Own's 46 Column.

Cigarette manufacturers W.D. & H.O. Wills' contribution to the war effort included a booklet produced to help new arrivals in India. This publication, 'Wild Woodbine', offered useful tips and encouraging messages for the Woodbine smoker, such as 'Everyone likes them'.

The booklet included essential phrases, such as choop ra-ho (shut up) and char bun-now (make the tea). There was advice on the dangers of dog bite: 'Much alarm is generally occasioned by this, though quite unnecessarily if the dog is *not* mad when it bites. If, however, the animal is known to be mad, wash well the wound immediately with warm water (if available) and a solution of Permanganate of Potash, or strong carbolic soap, then bandage, after which return to barracks, or the nearest large station, for "Pasteur" treatment.' Permanganate of Potash was also recommended for snake bite: 'Tie the limb (above the bite) with a tight ligature ... Then have the wound sucked by one who has no sores, cuts or blisters on the lips, or in the mouth. If suction is not possible, make incisions in the flesh of the limb across and around the site of the bite with a very sharp knife or razor blade. Encourage

bleeding and apply to the open wounds a strong solution (or raw crystals) of Permanganate of Potash. If incisions cannot be made because of the presence of a vein or artery, a red-hot coal, cigarette end or red-hot wire should be applied to the bite, after which Permanganate of Potash may be used...'

Presumably, after reading these words, the novice to India would immediately want to light up! The booklet adds a final warning: 'Don't smoke everything that comes your way. "Woodbine" cigarettes are the British Army's old favourites.'

Some medical judgements on fitness, taken at that time, look ludicrous in the context of subsequent Chindit service. R.P.J. 'Paddy' Dobney was commissioned into the York and Lancasters in March 1940. He was shocked when a Medical Officer said he had flat feet and would be transferred to the Service Corps or Ordnance Corps. Lieutenant (later, Major) Dobney took evasive action and arrived in Bombay in March 1942. Later, in a lengthy personal account, he reflected: 'I wonder what happened to that Doctor? I hope, for the sake of his patients, that his powers of diagnosis improved for, in the next five years, I was to march several thousands of miles on one of the best pairs of marching feet in the British Army.'

Many of those miles were completed with the York and Lancaster's 84 Column. This Column's Chindits also included NCO Reg Smith, a Londoner from Walthamstow. He sailed to the Far East on board the SS *Otranto*, arriving in July 1942.

Wingate's second expedition could not have taken place in the form it did without Colonel Phil Cochran's 1st Air Commando providing air landing, air support and casualty evacuation. Cochran's pilots included Olin B. Carter, born in 1921 and raised on a farm. His ancestors, two brothers, reached America before the *Mayflower* colonists; one settled in Massachusetts and the other in Virginia:

'I had wanted to be a flyer from the age of six, when I used to look up at an old biplane overflying our farm. When I was 12 I found a $5 bill. That was it! I bought myself a ride in an airplane. I joined the USAAF in 1941 – before the war started – and stayed in for 25 years.'

In 1942 Carter was flying the P.38 Lightning fighter. Life took a new direction when he was called by a friend who had just joined 1st Air Commando:

'Robert T. Smith had flown with the Flying Tigers in China. He was one of the first pilots recruited by Cochran. We knew each other from our last assignment and he asked me if I'd be interested. Every 1st Air Commando pilot was a volunteer. I said yes, knowing that I would soon be posted for combat and that it would be better to be with people you know.'

1st Lieutenant (later, Captain) Carter became one of this elite group's fighter pilots. Cochran and his Deputy, Colonel John Alison, set up shop initially at the Hay Adams Hotel in Washington DC. Room 281 became their office. For this reason the new venture became known as Project CA 28–1. It became No. 1 Air Commando in December 1943 and 1st Air Commando in March 1944.

Carter sailed for India one month after his wedding in San Diego. Having exchanged the twin-engined P.38 Lightning for the single-engined Mustang, he was apprehensive at first:

'We were flying the early Mustang variant, the P.51A. This had the same engine as the P.38. Well, I'd made over 20 single-engined landings in the P.38 and the P.51A had only one of those engines! To be fair, we were instructed to shut down an engine when flying the P.38, if it began to run rough, to avoid unnecessary damage. Even so, I was concerned.'

Carter preferred the P.51B and P.51C variants, both having the Packard-built Merlin:

'That Rolls Royce engine made all the difference – performance and reliability were much improved. The range was increased with the addition of an 85-gallon

tank immediately behind the pilot. The only problem was that it sat right on the centre of gravity. Until it drained it felt like you were riding a basketball. We always used that tank first; the aircraft then had a much more stable feel.'

The P.51A had four .50 guns. The P.51B and P.51C had six .50 guns and carried an impressive mix of stores:

'We could carry up to two 1,000 lb bombs, on racks built for a maximum load of 500 lb, plus six rockets. We carried three rockets beneath each wing. These weapons were very large and the early type came with fibre launch tubes. There was a folding fin at the back, for stabilisation during flight. They packed a hefty punch, with the explosive power of a 75 mm shell. The problem was that the rockets' flying speed fell off very quickly. This meant we had to get in close, to fire with accuracy at the target. One B.25 equipped with these rockets and flying operationally over Germany, as a locomotive-buster, attacked a train and blew the engine's boiler high into the air. This aircraft flew under the boiler and survived!'

As a child, Carter wasn't the only future member of Cochran's Air Commando watching aircraft with longing eyes. Charles J. Campbell, born in 1924, lived in the Los Angeles area. He finished High School in 1943 and went into the USAAF:

'I was interested in flying. As a kid I always went outdoors to watch the occasional aircraft fly over. I also went to the Air Races but never had the money to buy a pleasure flight.'

Campbell began flight training but suffered from sinus problems:

'They told me I'd never fly but I then heard about 1st Air Commando's call for volunteers. I made up my mind to say nothing about past setbacks. I met Phil Cochran at Goldsboro, North Carolina. I walked in and saluted. He looked up and said: "OK. Put that in your pocket. We don't do that here." To my young eyes he was a really neat guy. I had been to Air Training College and had gone through Engine School. Cochran accepted me for aircrew and I became a C-47 Engineer.'

Some flyers fought on foot with the Chindits. Flight Lieutenant John Knowles trod a long road to join the Queen's 22 Column as RAF Officer. His 18th birthday approached in June 1941. Knowles had been inspired by 'The Few' of the Battle of Britain. He left his clerical job at The Macmillan Company and his Brooklyn home for Montreal, to enlist in the Royal Canadian Air Force. Thousands of Americans did the same before Pearl Harbor brought the USA into the war on 7 December 1941. Virtually all transferred to the US Armed Forces as the opportunity arose. Knowles, however, tended to do things his way. He was accepted for pilot training, received his wings in due course and reached the UK as a Sergeant-Pilot. He flew Hurricanes at Annan OTU, Dumfriesshire. To their surprise and delight, he and two other RCAF Sergeant-Pilots, Allyn Kerr and John Gibson, received commissions as Pilot Officers: 'This was totally unexpected. There was no Board, no interview, nothing – like manna from heaven, out of a clear blue sky.' The three were among a dozen or so RCAF pilots posted to India. John Knowles:

'I had ample time to go to London, be kitted out as a Pilot Officer at Austin Reed, get laid and get to Liverpool to board the SS Dominion Monarch.'

On arriving in India and following a refresher on Hurricanes, Knowles, Kerr and Gibson went to 146 Squadron, flying Hurricanes mainly in the ground attack role. They found none of the romance associated with their Battle of Britain role models:

'During the 1943 Monsoon the Japanese were smart enough to pull back into Siam and Malaya, but we were dumb enough to continue with our silly sorties. These "Rhubarb" operations, flown from Feni and, later, Comilla, consisted largely of flying through horrible weather for ammunition-wasting attacks on unoccupied sampans. It was all very depressing, extremely dangerous and not at all what I had joined up for. I never saw an enemy aircraft until I was a Chindit in the jungle. We lost a number of good men in unreliable machines, in terrible weather, on pointless missions. They included my close buddy "Gibby" Gibson, a farm boy from Caledonia, Ontario.'

In late 1943 it was decided that the Squadron would re-equip with P.47 Thunderbolts. This meant it could be non-operational for up to six months. John Knowles, meanwhile, had hit a bad patch; nothing seemed to go right. One incident involved an indiscretion in a letter home and he was required to fly to Chittagong, to be reprimanded personally by the Group Captain. On returning, he landed at Comilla and made for the wrong end of the strip. Having got there, he had to turn around and taxi back to his squadron's end.

In an act of self-mockery Knowles arranged for a talented airman to draw on his Mae West a picture of

the famous, feckless RAF cartoon character, Pilot Officer Prune – dutiful but dumb, willing but wet. Knowles was in the right frame of mind for something different. He certainly found it with the Queen's, footslogging in the Burmese jungle as a Chindit Column's RAF Officer.

Walter Longstaff also became a Chindit RAF Officer. Born in Darlington in 1919, he joined the RAFVR, began pilot training but had persistant problems with his landings. He retrained as an Observer and was drafted to the Far East. He was to join the York and Lancaster's 65 Column.

Longstaff, known as 'Hector', completed operational tours as a Navigator in Sumatra until it fell to the Japanese. Subsequently, he was stationed in Ceylon and India. He flew with 100 Squadron, equipped with ancient Wildebeest torpedo bombers – ungainly biplanes with a top speed somewhat short of 100 mph. Longstaff was in Singapore when it fell to the Japanese and only just managed to get out. A left-handed golfer, he always regretted leaving behind a set of new left-handed clubs.

Flight Lieutenant Longstaff, in common with Knowles, was looking for something new:

'There was a call for volunteers for Special Force and, in the best service tradition, I was "asked" to volunteer. I hadn't heard of Wingate and the Chindits, but I was curious. I was told that the job would be arduous – extremely physical. That didn't put me off. I was a rugby player, young and very fit.'

————•————

Some men gave up their aircraft to fight with the Chindits. Others, including Cyril Baldock, gave up their vehicles. Lieutenant (later, Major) Baldock was born in 1921 and grew up in Tunbridge Wells, Kent. His father was a stud groom, specialising in breaking and training hunters, polo ponies and carriage horses. During 1940 Baldock joined the Royal West Kents as a 19-year-old volunteer, fresh from school. He became an NCO and eventually went before a Board:

'I was in the first intake for a special OCTU for The Reconnaissance Corps – light armoured regiments equipped with scout cars and Bren carriers. I was commissioned in October 1941 and joined 45th Reconnaissance Regiment. Our role was to support the infantry Divisions. We went to India in 1942 and joined 70th Division as its Recce Regiment.'

45 Recce continued to train for motorised warfare until the second half of 1943, when it was included in Special Force, adding 45 and 54 Columns to 16 Brigade. Baldock became Animal Transport Officer with 54 Column,

his family background proving more than useful. He remembers Bernard Fergusson visiting 45 Recce to introduce Special Force:

'Fergusson made it clear "just how lucky we were". His talk was a bit of a shock – we had no marching experience and we were to give up our vehicles! He had a powerful personality. This 33-year-old Brigadier cast a spell over his audience. By the time he had finished we considered it an honour to join him! I got to know Fergusson over the coming weeks. For some reason he remembered my name from the first. I also met Wingate on two occasions, once when we were jungle training around Jhansi and, secondly, when he landed on a sandbar as we were crossing the Chindwin. He struck me as eccentric and brilliant.'

GHQ India was stunned by the break-up of 70th Division. Many of those directly involved were also amazed. Philip Sharpe, with 45 Recce, set the scene in *To Be a Chindit*:

The news of the new role of 70th Division was eventually made known to the Regiment at a special parade on Tuesday 7 September, when the Divisional Commander, Major-General Symes, spoke enthusiastically about our future. We were stunned, of course, almost to disbelief. After training for two years as a mechanised unit, we were to revert to infantry ...

Richard 'Dick' Hilder gave up his tank:

'I had intended to go to Sandhurst but war changed everything. We were told to join the ranks and apply for a commission later. I joined the Life Guards as a Trooper. Life Guards and Horse Guards still had horses in 1940 and a composite regiment had been deployed overseas and was serving in Palestine. Things were changing rapidly and the Household Cavalry was soon motorised. I was commissioned in The Armoured Corps and joined a draft for India in early 1942.'

Lieutenant (later, Captain) Hilder would return to tanks in due course, but not before he had completed his service with the HQ Column of 14 Brigade, Special Force.

Edward 'Ted' Meese switched from Bren carrier to mule. Meese, a bricklayer from Stourport, Worcestershire, was 17 when called up in late 1942. He had trained on Bren carriers before going to the Far East. When in India he transferred to the 2nd Leicesters and began jungle training. He became a Muleteer with 17 Column, part of Fergusson's 16 Brigade.

Andrew Sutherland was to fight in the Burmese jungle with 23 Brigade. Born in Medicine Hat, Alberta, he had moved to England at the age of five. Sutherland and his friends tossed a coin to select their wartime service. It was 'heads' for the Army and 'tails' for the Navy, with the Air Force at longer odds – requiring the coin to stand on edge. Sutherland's coin came up heads and he decided on the artillery rather than the infantry. Ironically, the one man who saw his coin stand on edge already intended to join the Air Force. He was the only one of this group to die on active service.

Andrew Sutherland reported to 227 Battery, 113th Field Regiment, at Shoreham on 1 September 1939. They had two Great War vintage guns and shared a solitary truck with a neighbouring Battery. Soon, however, they were operating an impressive fleet of requisitioned vehicles, including a red Coca Cola van, a Watmoughs Biscuits pantechnicon and a Graham-Paige luxury saloon. The Battery suffered its first casualty during the summer of 1940, when a passing German aircraft machine-gunned the biscuit van, which caught fire and burnt out. By way of compensation, within a few weeks the Battery received brand-new Mk II 25 Pounders.

In 1942 Sutherland attended officer training in India. He graduated from the Indian School of Artillery, Deolali, and joined B Troop of 60th Field Regiment, Ranchi, as Troop Leader. He had an eye for the curious and noted how Monsoon flooding flushed out the snakes holed up in the bund walls: 'Our MO collected the poison sacs from captured kraits, to produce antidotes in case anyone was bitten.' He was to see stranger sights when with 60 Column, 60th Field Regiment, RA, fighting the Japanese with 23 Brigade in the Imphal/Kohima area.

Percy Stopher joined those supporting 23 Brigade's separate campaign. Born in West Ham, he was a veteran of fighting in the Western Desert, including Tobruk. Stopher did not set out to join the RAMC but that is where he ended up. He was among a group of 25 men taken to a requisitioned school in Hitchin, where newly formed medical units were trained in the treatment of battlefield casualties.

Medical Orderly Percy Stopher arrived in India in February 1942 and stayed in the Far East for three years. He served with 200th Medical Unit, B Company, attached to 23 Brigade during the Imphal/Kohima battles.

Special Force operations were supported at Rear HQ and the air bases by an extensive organisation. The men involved included drivers Peter Fairmaner and Ray 'Lofty' Newport. Fairmaner had been a student at Guildford Technical College and the School of Art until his call up in April 1941. He saw an opportunity to indulge his love of cars and driving. He already had a claim to fame: a car race with future world champion Mike Hawthorn, a fellow pupil at the Technical College. Fairmaner lost the race.

Fairmaner went to India in 1942 and became a nomad. Driving assignments took him to bases across India, from Delhi and Deolali to Bangalore and Cawnpore. Much of the time he ferried trucks. He settled into service life but it came as something of a raw shock early on. Letters from his mother survive and hint at a background which did little to prepare him for the rigours of military service. One letter warned him to avoid the perils of damp underwear. Another asked: 'Who is washing your underclothes? Who darns your socks? ... There is nothing worse than badly darned socks.' Many Chindits who suffered in the jungle of North Burma would beg to differ with Fairmaner's mother!

Lofty Newport was an Air Force driver. As a young man he was part of the family business, a butchers in the East Kent village of Littlebourne:

'My older brother was in the Navy and I wanted to do my bit, so I volunteered for the Air Force. After basic training at Skegness I moved to Blackpool for a driving course before RE training at Old Sarum in late 1942. Soon after I had a shock. There was a terrible road accident – three lorries were in collision. The people involved included WAAFs and many were killed. I was detailed to help clear up the mess. It was horrific.'

Newport also followed a nomadic lifestyle in India: 'We reached India in late 1943 and travelled all over the northern regions, mainly driving lorries in military convoy. We went from one job to the next and lived quite rough.'

Lofty Newport continued to do his bit. During the second Wingate expedition he flew operational sorties on Dakotas, dropping food, ammunition and other essentials to the Chindits below. His long legs were ideal for kicking out the loads.

8

TRAINING FOR WAR IN THE WILDERNESS

'Here I was, just 19 – I had never had a beer, or a woman. I may have been small but I was full of aggression. I had no fear; nothing seemed to frighten me.'

Private Jack Hutchin, 80 Column, 1st South Staffords

TRAINING FOR Operation *Thursday* was a vast under- taking. The three 70th Division Brigades (14, 16 and 23) had a large training area near the Ken River and 77 and 111 Brigades trained at Dukhwan Dam, 25 miles from Jhansi. 3 (WA) Brigade also trained in the Jhansi area. The training air base was at Lalitpur. The British Brigades were to move to the Lalitpur-Saugor area for their final exercises.

The battle to take Burma from the Japanese was already under way. During October 1943 the Chinese 38th Division advanced south from Ledo but had made slow progress. It was urged on and had reached a point over 100 miles from Ledo by the year's end, helped by a 22nd Division Regiment. The remainder of 22nd Division then joined the advance south, together with 'Galahad' – Merrill's Marauders.[1]

As the Chindit training progressed, the men were transformed. Richard Rhodes James wrote: 'The troops were beginning to shake off their natural distaste for discomfort and hard living. They were beginning, in a faltering way, to regain some of the qualities of which they had been deprived by their own civilisation.'[2]

The Column was Special Force's basic unit. The heart of the Column was an extra powerful Rifle Company.[3] In January 1944 Eric Sugden was among the late arrivals reaching the Ken River:

'I joined 54th Field Company as a Sapper. They had already split up among 14 Brigade's Columns. I was attached to 61, one of the two Bedfordshire and Hertfordshire Columns. My Section of eight was led by a Yorkshireman, Corporal Earnshaw. There were three Sections of eight in the Platoon. Each Section consisted of a Corporal, Lance Corporal and six Sappers. Our Section was organised into two groups of four, each consisting of two pairs of "muckers". My group included Earnshaw and Sapper Jock MacDonald. I paired up with H.H. McDonald, known as "Mac".'

Major (later, Lieutenant Colonel) Barrow, DSO, com- manded 61 Column. The Sapper Platoon was led by Captain Turner, a South African. Eric Sugden:

'The training was hard but we coped as we were extremely fit. Yet everyone bent forward when carrying that heavy pack. I liked the idea of being a Chindit – going to war with mules and bullocks. I had a taste for adventure. When I finally got out, however, I thanked God for the experience and begged him never to put me through such an ordeal again.'

Romantic notions of jungle life evaporated under the crushing weight of the Chindit pack. Some got on better than others. Tony Wailes had been promoted to Captain by the time he arrived at Jhansi:

'I got on well during the long marches, despite the heavy pack. I was slim and very fit. There is a well-known book entitled "The jungle is neutral". Well, it isn't! I spent four months living Chindit-style with 23 Brigade and it was a pretty dreadful experience. Despite the hard going, carrying all that weight, I adapted well. I had always been an outdoor type and that helped. In common with most, however, once in I looked forward to my return to civilisation.'

Wailes joined the Commando Platoon of 60 Column, 60th Field Regiment, RA (fighting as infantry), one

Consultation: a Medical Officer chats with a patient during Operation *Thursday*. (Walter Longstaff)

of 23 Brigade's Battalions. This Brigade was commanded by Brigadier Lance E.C.M. Perowne, CBE, who had known Wingate at the Royal Military Academy, Woolwich, in 1921. He had shared a room with him. Perowne was determined to make the most of his wireless equipment and developed the habit of maintaining radio contact with his mobile Columns while orbiting in a light aircraft.

Perowne's Brigade brought together elements of the Essex Regiment, the Border Regiment, the Duke of Wellington's and the Gunners, with engineering support. This Brigade was held in reserve when Operation *Thursday* began and was later detached to fight the Japanese attacking at Imphal/Kohima. Tony Wailes:

'Our training was very effective, despite the usual complaints. Practice air drops went well and we got used to K-rations without too much moaning. I was fortunate in my Batman, a South Londoner known to everyone as "Comrade" Shead. Some years older than me, he was a magnificent chap and a great cook. He looked after me like a father.'

By June 1943 Neville Hogan was back at Dehra Dun and the 2nd Burma Rifles eventually began training as part of Special Force:

'All Burmese-speaking ORs were sent to us. We ended up with between 1,800 and 2,000 men, equivalent to two Battalions. When the training ended we divided into individual Recce Platoons and joined the Columns.'

Captain (later, Major) Hogan would lead the Recce Platoon of 46 Column, 2nd King's Own. When training began he had two problems. Firstly, he was very young and unusually fresh-faced (which would get him into trouble later). Secondly, he was a 'townie' from Rangoon:

'Karens are naturals in the jungle, but I'd lived my life in the city. I was more of a townie than a village lad. Everyone assumed I could take them anywhere in the jungle without getting lost! Fortunately, I could draw on the services of Subedar Johnny Htoo, a Governor's Commissioned Officer. He was a totally fearless character, steadfast, happy-go-lucky and more than willing to share his jungle knowledge with me.'

The Jhansi area was ideal for Chindit training. Neville Hogan:

'It had everything, including fast-flowing rivers – to practise river crossings – and plenty of thick jungle. We did everything at the double. We worked up a real hatred of the enemy. Japanese faces were pinned on trees. We were encouraged to slash them with our knives during exercises. We were told we were killers, whereas the Japanese were murderers – an important distinction.'

By Christmas 1943 Hogan was attached to the King's Own. He had his leg pulled on occasion. He was dozing when he heard one soldier say to another: 'Hogan's a *bacha* (baby).'

'I spoke suddenly, telling them in a loud voice that this baby had gone through the entire first Burma campaign. This produced a quick "Sorry, Sir!" Yet it was true that I was baby-faced. I never shaved. We Karens don't need to shave a lot. On another, much later occasion, while on leave in Calcutta, I was arrested for wearing crowns. The Military Police thought I had dressed up to impress the girls and kept me in a cell for the night, refusing to accept that I was an Acting Major. Their attitude changed when my story checked out. I was just 23 years and five months at that time.

South East Asia Command HQ in Ceylon felt I was too young and inexperienced for the rank, but my Colonel felt otherwise.'

Ian Niven 'volunteered' for the Chindits in the traditional British Army manner. Niven and many other Royal Scots were transferred to the 1st Lancashire Fusiliers, bringing that Battalion up to strength for Operation *Thursday*:

'We had heard of Wingate and his first expedition. At one point we paraded and an officer said: "Anyone who doesn't want to volunteer for the Chindits, step forward." Obviously, no-one moved. We were young, ready for anything but apprehensive. Anyway, we were jungle training at Jhansi within the week.'

Twelve weeks of jungle training at Jhansi began in September 1943, followed by a further 12 weeks in Assam. Niven became a Regimental Signaller with 20 Column:

'I got on well, being young and fit to professional footballing standard. My pack was half my body weight but I got used to it. After my service in Burma I bless my feet every morning. They gave me no trouble whatsoever; all I had to do was give my toes a good rub every morning. I found it easy to adapt to jungle life. I was more frightened of the mules than the prospect of fighting the Japanese. I hated the way the mules reared up. I got on OK with K-rations. It sorted me out regarding any "fancies". Today, I'll still eat anything, with the exception of syrup of figs.

'Before going in we went on leave to Bombay. We had plenty of money, having drawn extra pay. Six of us went together, looking for a good time, but that was difficult. Generally, the Indians didn't like us and the British in India were very snobbish, especially towards British ORs. I'd come from a good working class background and had been brought up with manners. Consequently, I took exception to their rude attitude.'

Beyond accepting physical hardship, some men found it difficult to make the mental adjustments required for service with Special Force. It was particularly hard for those trained for motorised warfare, who were suddenly expected to march. Dick Hilder arrived in Bombay in 1943 and was posted to the 26th Hussars. Fully equipped and trained as an armoured regiment, they were disbanded. Subsequently, Lieutenant (later, Captain) Hilder was attached to 14 Brigade's HQ Column:

'Half the regiment went to the 3rd Carabiniers and took part in the Imphal fighting. The other half (including

yours truly, unfortunately) became Chindits. The Chindits didn't mean much to us at that time – we were still tank men. The disbandment of our regiment had been traumatic and it was still on our minds. Speaking personally, I wasn't impressed with the Chindit concept. Producing a good armoured regiment is time-consuming and expensive; scrapping our regiment and turning us into infantry didn't make sense. On the other hand, I didn't mind the mules. Father always had plenty of horses around and I was very accustomed to animals.'

Brigadier Brodie's Brigade Major ordered Hilder to train a group as infantry:

'The essential qualification was to carry the heavy pack and march long distances. Fortunately, the Troop Sergeant was an infantryman before he transferred to the Armoured Corps. I was a 22-year-old Lieutenant. He was a more experienced man.'

The Sergeant had served for many years in India and he was used to wild country, having spent time on the North West Frontier. The training included 'Brigade Schemes', living rough in the jungle. The Brigade Major then gave Hilder another job – training 100 mules:

'I just got on with it, having long concluded that all associated with this venture were barking mad. That was my opinion then. Today, of course, I am proud to have been a Chindit and have grown fond of my Chindit comrades.'

Dick Hilder found this new task demanding:

'These mules had never had a saddle on. I had to break them in before training them! As for the Muleteers, most were former 70th Division drivers who knew nothing about animals. They had surrendered trucks for mules. I had to train the Muleteers to work the mules. Fortunately, some were former Hussars, with a sound cavalry background. They were a great help.'

The thought of operating behind enemy lines with mules failed to put Hilder in a more positive frame of mind:

'I thought they were all crazy. I then heard that Wingate was planning to visit Brigade HQ. I took care not to be around when he called. Orde Wingate was brilliant but ruthless – a complete eccentric and exactly the sort of man I always took pains to avoid. Yet, looking back, something like the Wingate phenomenon had to happen. We had to stop the Japanese invading India.'

The training became no easier as the weeks passed:

'Things were very tricky. It is not easy to turn cavalrymen into infantrymen in just a few months. The only thing we had no worries about was the quality of marksmanship. The main challenge was to get feet and backs strong and sort out the mules.'

Gordon Hughes was also much preoccupied with mules. Commissioned into the South Wales Borderers, he had sought a posting to the 6th Battalion, then in the Arakan. Instead, he found himself on a train from Deolali, to join the Queen's at Bangalore. He was introduced to mules at Babugarh, a depot just north of Delhi, while the Battalion moved to Jhansi for jungle training. Hughes would command a Platoon and act as a reserve ATO.[4]

Hughes attended the Animal Management Course organised by No. 2 Animal Transport Mule Training Regiment. He spent a month at Babugarh, passing with distinction despite his past lack of experience working with animals. Gordon Hughes wrote:

> We used an Austrian method of handling that proved successful. It was bribery, essentially – touching the animal with a long stick, and, immediately after the touch, rewarding it with sugar. It was not long before you were able to groom the animal and even pick out its hooves.

Hughes then reported to Battalion HQ near the Ken River. The Queen's officers received instruction from specialists in LRP tactics:

> If the enemy was encountered on the line of march a dispersal signal would be blown and the Column would melt away in the jungle, leaving the Point Platoon to take care of the opposition. Should the opposition prove too strong, the Point Platoon would take on the role of 'Fire Platoon' and the Rifle Company would attack on an appropriate flank. If the opposition proved too strong for the Company, then a second dispersal would be blown and the enemy disengaged, to allow the Column to move away by units, to rendezvous at a pre-determined map reference.[4]

Typically, the first rendezvous would be open to 23.59 the following day, with a second rendezvous open until 23.59 on the third day after dispersal. The rendezvous was a six-figure map reference on a two miles to the inch map.

The jungle training routine mirrored the march discipline of a Column on active service. The men grew accustomed to jungle living. Gordon Hughes:

Getting acquainted: mule lines at Urili Camp. Ted Meese, a Muleteer with the 2nd Leicesters' 17 Column, is walking up the centre of the lines, towards the back. Meese had a longer walk ahead of him. (Ted Meese)

There was no water to spare for washing or shaving, so your daily toilet was reduced from a 'shit, shave and shampoo' to a shit. The next few months saw us change from ordinary troops to hardened men who could put minds and bodies to anything. No obstacle would delay us for long. We became expert at mule handling at river crossings, even to the extent that we used the animals to float poor swimmers across the widest of rivers. We were proficient at taking supply drops and distributed supplies quickly after the drop, to enable a fast getaway from the danger area. We rehearsed ambushes, attacks on airfields and blockades on roads and railways, to deny the enemy their use.'[4]

The Nigerians adjusted well during training. Charles Carfrae, Commander of 7 NR's 29 Column, wrote: 'The black Rifleman, accustomed to living simply and demanding little, adapted easily and without complaint. Making no effort to fight the jungle, they surrendered to it.'

Lieutenant (later, Major) Denis Arnold, MC, was a Platoon Commander in Carfrae's Column. He confirms this positive view:

'Later, Japanese sources described the West Africans as the fiercest jungle fighters in Burma. Our men were Muslims, from the north of Nigeria. They proved to be excellent physical material and their condition further improved with a combination of good diet and hard exercise. They did extremely well during jungle training, but they had to be closely led and they recognised this.'

Donald Mackay, Padre with the 1st Cameronians, recalled one exercise that pitted his Battalion against the West Africans: 'They ambushed us neatly as we passed through a village and what began as a friendly scrap nearly ended up in a bloody battle as the Africans tried to take away the Jocks' rifles.'[5]

Captain (later, Colonel) K.M. 'Dick' Stuckey was a Rifle Platoon Commander with 12 NR's 43 Column. He was also encouraged by the way the Nigerians took to the jungle. Having docked at Bombay in September 1943, they were soon training with Special Force. He recalls the explanation given of how Chindits should operate:

'It was likened to submarine operations. The Chindits would emerge, hit their targets and then 'submerge' back into the jungle. The British, Gurkhas and Nigerians learnt their jungle craft together.'

Pat Hughes commanded 12 NR and led 43 Column. The sister Column, 12, was commanded by Major 'Skip' Taylor. There were some changes in 3 (WA) Brigade's Command. Dick Stuckey:

'The Brigade Commander during training was Brigadier Richards, from the West Yorkshire Regiment. Wingate regarded him as too old to go into Burma, although he was later to achieve fame at Kohima. Justice was done for this very professional and charming officer of the old school.'

Brigadier A.H. Gillmore took over from Richards. His tenure was marred by later events. As for Pat Hughes,

Stuckey remembers him as 'an affable chap', in his early thirties and newly married to a girl in Kenya:

'Hughes was an excellent sportsman but not a natural soldier. He was perhaps too sensitive as a Column Commander. Chindit warfare was not his cup of tea but he certainly pulled it out of the bag when we went in. He left the Army a Brigadier and went on to become a District Commissioner in Kenya. We met again in 1963, when I was commanding my Regiment in Kenya.

'As for our Nigerians, they were naturals in the jungle. They had sworn allegiance to King and Emperor and they took that oath extremely seriously. They had instinctive abilities in the jungle. They could see and hear things that would be missed by most Europeans. I learned my fieldcraft from the Nigerians and our attached Burrifs, mainly Karens. They all had an extraordinary ability to get a fire going under the worst possible conditions. The Nigerians were fearless.'

Those Columns unfamiliar with infantry warfare struggled to adjust. They included 54 Column of 45 Recce. The Column Commander, Major Bill Varcoe, gave Cyril Baldock the job of ATO:

'I had been brought up with horses and I used to ride in the Regiment. I had a Sergeant, a couple of Corporals and the Muleteers. This was a sizeable responsibility for a young man: I had charge of 60 mules, 12 ponies and one Brahman Bull. The latter became our mascot. At times we were close to starving but "Oscar" was sacrosanct. No-one would have dreamt of eating him! Oscar was excused all heavy work and was not expected to carry a load (although he did carry a token pack of armourers' tools and later did sterling service carrying wounded). At all times Oscar remained too affectionate to abuse in any way.'

Lieutenant (later, Major) Baldock progressed well during jungle training:

'I was young, fit and healthy. That pack was bloody heavy but I got used to it. I accepted the hardships, as did all the others. However, this was a young man's style of warfare. Anyone much over 30 tended to leave us. Being a Recce Regiment, each Troop had two officers and that was too many for our new role as Chindits. Some officers were posted out to other Battalions. Human nature being what it is, this was used as an opportunity to get rid of the unpopular and inept.

'Bill Varcoe was a nice chap but I'm not sure he was cut out for the job of Column Commander. This requires sound tactical decision-making and a natural ability to be seen to be in charge. After our first clash with the enemy Varcoe and the CO, Lieutenant-Colonel Dick Cumberlege, were flown out. Cumberlege was another good man but perhaps too old [over 40] for the immense demands of this type of warfare.'

On Friday 22 October 1943, 45th Reconnaissance Regiment, Royal Armoured Corps, made the transformation. On the Monday it reappeared as 54 and 45 Columns of 16 Brigade, Special Force. Philip Sharpe, a Wireless Operator with 45 Column, received his jungle kit, including underwear dyed a dark green colour. In *To Be a Chindit*, Sharpe described his initiation, a jungle exercise beginning on 17 November:

Up at 4 am, loaded mules, shouldered packs and rifles and marched two hours in the dark before breakfast. Off again at 07.00, weight of pack real purgatory and all I can see, now it is light, is the backside of one of our mules and the scrub and bamboo each side. This is already the hardest day of my life. Column halt from 12.00 to 15.00 hours, mules unloaded. Contacted Brigade signals and passed messages while most of those around us had a sleep. Then off again until 18.00 hours. Unloaded mules for night. Passed more messages, all in cypher. Completely shagged out but writing up diary.

The Column practised calling up and receiving supply drops. All needs were listed in code. Philip Sharpe: 'There was a code for what was called a standard drop. This covered the basic needs of a Column for five days, mainly food and fodder. Extras could always be added to the basic request, which was based on a Column strength of 450 men.'[6] The message calling for a drop was known as the 'QQ', confirmed by the return signal 'QK'.

Many men were in close contact with animals for the first time in their lives. They often named the mules and ponies after wives and girlfriends. The author's father, Private Jack Redding of the King's Own, named a mule 'Emily'. When the campaign was over, he wrote to his wife, apologising for the fact that this animal had been shot and eaten.

Much of 111 Brigade's training focused on mules. Brigade Cypher Officer Richard Rhodes James:

We spent days endeavouring to persuade mules to cross rivers, beating, cursing and threatening them. We tried different types of bank and widths of stream, catapulting the animals into the water with ropes or standing on the far bank making tempting noises and holding out bags of grain. But, usually, we had to resort to riding the animals across ourselves. This was hectic though not as dangerous as it might sound. Mounting a mule which is lashing about in shallow water, in company with several others, is not easy but the water seems to absorb much of the power of their kicks.[7]

The mules needed careful watching in the hills, as steep climbs shifted much of the weight onto their rear quarters. The mules had been 'debrayed', to keep the noise down when operating in the jungle. Vocal chords were crushed, rather than cut, by Veterinary Officers. Rhodes James recalled that, instead of resonant braying, 'all that could be heard now was a hoarse rush of wind, like the sound of a mighty bellows, or perhaps it could be better described as whooping cough.'[7]

Some animals gradually regained their voices, to the unspoken satisfaction of many. Bill Williams, ATO with the South Staffords' 80 Column, drew heavily on his past experience in a cavalry regiment: 'The animals were as surprised as we were when, after many weeks, they recovered the ability to bray. They gave every sign of being amazed.'

The South Staffords were jungle training near Jhansi:

The best of mates: the author's father, Private Jack Redding (centre), pictured with 'Nobby' Evans (left) and Dave Davies.

'Mostly the training consisted of jungle marching, but it also included an operation against Merrill's Marauders. We became firm friends with this American unit. During the scheme we trekked 400 miles in four weeks. My feet held up well. At that point we were still expecting to march in. I took advantage of my job and stayed mounted for at least part of the time!'

Williams was taken aback when told he was now part of an Air Landing Brigade:

'I had never flown before. We now had to find out how to fly in mules and ponies. We were not encouraged when we first succeeded in getting a mule into a WACO glider. The animal showed intense displeasure and promptly demolished sections of fuselage. In the Dakotas we could load five animals per aircraft – three abreast forward, with two behind. That left enough space for us and the equipment.

'There were four categories of mule: MA (Mountain Artillery – large animals otherwise known as "Argentine Mules"), E1 (Equipment 1), E2 (Equipment 2) and AT (Animal Transport). Some mules, even those with otherwise pleasant temperaments, could be absolute sods when the time came to enter the aircraft.'

Any man already sorely tried and exhausted could lose patience with an obstinate mule, yet strong bonds would be forged in adversity. Bill Williams:

'I became very fond of the mules, which were far tougher than ponies. Before going in, I went on a short veterinary course. I had had some experience in the Yeomanry, where I trained as a shoesmith. With the load-carrying mules we had to be very careful about sores under the saddle. When we took our 10-minute break every hour on the march, the Muleteers had it rough. By the time they had unloaded their mules, it was time to load up again. When we had longer halts, the Muleteers had to go out and cut fodder.'

Private Ted McArdle was among the many Muleteers with no previous experience of animals:

'The job didn't bother me but I was cautious around the mules. I watched some lads jump on the mules' backs. I would never have done that – I never had the courage to try! When I was given my mule it was still pretty wild. I couldn't tame it and it wouldn't take a load on its back. I couldn't do anything with it and it refused to calm down. A more experienced Indian Muleteer had a

go and he failed too. Finally, they took the troublemaker away and gave me another. This mule was very different – as calm as anything. I named him Joey. He had a good temperament and a soft nature. You could do anything with him; if you wanted to look at a hoof, he'd lift it up for you!'

McArdle was a Muleteer with the King's 82 Column, commanded by Major Dick Gaitley. The Battalion Commander, also leading 81 Column, was Lieutenant-Colonel Walter Scott. McArdle knew nothing about the Chindits when he began training:

'I hadn't even heard of the first expedition, but I did see Wingate when we were still in Assam. He walked up and down our lines. He looked just like one of us. He already had a beard and a rather scruffy appearance. I never saw anything of Calvert, the Brigade Commander, but I met Mountbatten, who also came to visit us in the jungle.'

Lieutenant Andrew Sutherland shared in the general dismay when the news broke that 60 RA was to lose its guns and serve as Chindit infantry. The regiment had won laurels opposing German armour around Tobruk. Many specialists were posted out and a new CO arrived, Lieutenant-Colonel du Vallon. Sutherland saw him as an old school Regular and a strict disciplinarian: 'He was also an athlete and an expert horseman. He had already won the Military Cross in France, in 1940, and was to be awarded a DSO after the Chindit operation.'

Sutherland joined 60 Column and got to know his mules – Maisie, Millie and Nelson, each with their particular eccentricities: 'Maisie was tough and willing, but would not take a load that rattled in any way. The slightest rattle resulted in her bucking until she had kicked the offending load all over the countryside. Get rid of the rattle and Maisie was as good as gold. When approaching a mule from the rear, we would run a hand along the animal's rump and flank, so that it knew where we were. Millie was a cow-kicker: she didn't kick backwards but sideways, so a hand running along the rump was safe but the flank was not! Nelson was blind in one eye. He was the best-tempered, the most docile of creatures. He didn't need to be led: he responded to voice command! When he was being groomed he practically purred.'

With the training completed the Battalion went east, by truck and then by train, to reach Gauhati, on the Brahmaputra. They travelled by ferry east to Jorhat and took the narrow gauge railway to Mariani, near the Patkai Hills, where leeches were a serious hazard for men and animals. Andrew Sutherland: 'The leeches attacked the mules, whose nostrils were their most vulnerable parts. Blood dripping from a mule's nose usually meant the leeches were at work. Salt thrown into a nostril made the pests let go.'

Only the very fittest could tolerate a Chindit load in tropical heat and humidity, when crossing steep, jungle-covered terrain. The formidable weight carried was equivalent to two heavy suitcases. This was more than double what a mule would be expected to carry, in proportion to bodyweight. The weight of clothing and basic equipment carried by each man was officially calculated at 38 lbs 6 oz. The Rifleman's typical load was 56 lbs 10 oz and a Bren gunner 68 lbs 2 oz. These figures do not include rations. Five days' K-rations weighed 15 lbs 10 oz, bringing the total load of a Bren gunner, fully rationed, to a back-breaking 83 lbs 12 oz.

The basic equipment for each man (excluding clothing, as worn) included: two pairs of socks, two pairs of laces, a pullover, identity discs, rubber-soled canvas shoes, towel (dyed green), green enamel mug, dubbin, lightweight blanket, groundsheet, clasp knife, water sterilising kit, field dressing, elastoplast patches, anti-lice powder, aluminium mess tin, entrenching tool, 'panic map', escape compass, canvas water chagul, 36 Type grenade, water bottle, Bergen rucksack, waterproof matches and machete.

The clothing, including boots, weighed 8 lbs 8 oz. The basic equipment weighed 29 lbs 14 oz. A Rifleman's weapon, 30 rounds of ammunition, bayonet, a Bren magazine and other items added another 18 lbs 4 oz. The Bren gunner's extra load totalled 29 lbs 12 oz. Officers carried additional items, such as two compasses, binoculars and torches, together with a .38 pistol and 18 rounds.

Personal arms varied. Some officers and NCOs were eventually armed with the American semi-automatic carbine (when these weapons became available); others had Bren guns, the much-despised Sten or the heavy Thompson sub-machine gun. Most men, however, had the classic infantry weapon, the bolt-action Lee Enfield rifle.

Jesse Dunn, a Corporal in 80 Column's Commando Platoon, had charge of three 'Lifebuoy' flamethrowers:

'The weapon was very effective, with a range of about 30 yards. It looked like a big tyre – hence the name – with a pressurised sphere and a flame igniter. The tank was pressurised by undoing the valve. The real weakness was the batteries; they were always losing charge.'

Chindit column Commander Charles Carfrae's description of carrying a full pack after a supply drop captures the pain:

Scarcely able to stir a step under loads so intolerable, at first we found training marches agony, sweat streaming from our faces, backs and spirits alike near to breaking, legs buckling under us. But, with practice, pack-toting capacity began to improve and in a month we had developed into satisfactory beasts of burden. Unless of herculean physique, however, no soldier could run more than a few paces with a full pack. The best he could do was to shamble along like a bear.[8]

Richard Rhodes James wrote that no-one forgot their first experience of shouldering a pack:

We felt for the first time the full weight of our operational kit and we loathed it. Never, through all the long training marches or the muddy scrambles over the hills, did we accustom ourselves to the enormous weight we had to carry.

I pitied most of all those who had to carry service rifles and those thrice wretched men whose turn it was to carry the Bren gun. Having carried one for only short periods, I marvelled that anyone could survive under such a load.[9]

Most of the weight was carried on standard British Army webbing: a wide belt taking two ammunition pouches, water bottle, bayonet, machete and the small pack (usually holding eating, drinking and washing items, together with medical and personal kit). The large pack, with a further two large ammunition pouches sewn on the side, held most of the rest of the kit. Anything left over was strapped to the packs. A full chagul of water could be carried in whichever hand was free.[10]

The Chindit uniform included the distinctive felt bush hat, with leather liner. The brim could be folded up and secured by a press-stud, giving it the familiar 'Australian' look. When in the Burmese jungle, however, most Chindits preferred the full protection of an unsecured brim. Typically, Chindit clothing was made in India and supplied in 'jungle green' rather than khaki. The lightweight wool flannel shirt was a pullover type, with half button front fastening. The buttons were often made from coconut fibre. The trousers and shorts were of heavy grade cotton drill. The men wore standard ammunition boots, with quality varying according to country of manufacture; Indian-made boots were generally ill-fitting and unpopular.

The 'Indian Light Scale' training rations for Wingate's Columns were despised by many. Rhodes James wrote:

They consisted of biscuits, raisins, dates, bully beef and cheese. The raisins and dates were almost

invariably weevil-ridden and we had to content ourselves, as sustenance for one day's hard march, on a small tin of bully beef, cheese and a few biscuits. We were saved by our daily brews of tea.[11]

Rhodes James also described the pain of jungle training with the heavy pack:

The sweat begins to collect under the pack and flows in great, salty streams from the forehead through the eyes and down the chin. All the aches and pains of yesterday appear again, to be joined by the peculiar discomforts of today. The ill-adjusted pack, the rubbing of the water bottle or haversack, that place where the belt fails to coincide with the contours of the body, the place you long to scratch but cannot reach. And then the boots, pinching, slipping, rubbing, the socks sliding down the foot and collecting in an abrasive bundle at the heel.[11]

Many men took deep pride in their membership of Special Force. They included Private Jack Hutchin. When he arrived at 77 Brigade he had had no jungle training:

'I was A.1+, however, and super fit. I had taken part in some very hard marches and had practised river crossings. At the age of 19 I was among the youngest of the Chindits. The Brigade Commander, Michael Calvert, made a strong impression. Like Wingate and the other big names of Special Force, he had a huge personality.'

Jack Hutchin joined the South Staffords' 80 Column:

'I took tremendous pride in such company. I was a small chap, weighing less than 10 stone, but I felt twice that weight. These were hard Black Country men; some had fought the Italians in Abyssinia. Here I was, just 19 – I had never had a beer, or a woman. I may have been small but I was full of aggression. I had no fear; nothing seemed to frighten me.

'Our Column Commander was Colonel Ronnie Degg. Captain Hilton was Company Commander and Lieutenant Scholey commanded our Rifle Platoon. Apart from Scholey, our officers were a fierce bunch – competent, hard and totally lacking in compassion. "Scott" Scholey was different. He was eccentric. He had a butterfly net attached to his pack. One day he turned to me and said: "Good news! Today is May Day. The 1st of May!" I had no idea what difference that made in the middle of the Burmese jungle. During the campaign he won the MC, in the same attack on Pagoda Hill that led to the award of the VC to Lieutenant Cairns.'

Scholey came from a farming family. Sadly, along with so many others, he would be killed in action during 77 Brigade's savage struggle to take Mogaung.

The men of another 77 Brigade Battalion, the King's, were surprised by the sheer number of animals around when they arrived at the camp near the Betwa river. Corporal Fred Holliday was with 82 Column:

'There were around 200 mules tethered opposite each other and in a long line, plus a dozen or so horses. Some of our lads would become Muleteers but we all needed training, to some extent, in handling these animals. The Battalion was camped over a wide area of scrub, rocky slope and thinnish jungle, though in due course we discovered thick jungle, hills and ravines in what can be described as "difficult country".'

The men were kitted out in jungle green, received their equipment and arms and were allocated to Platoons. Fred Holliday and Tom Pickering joined 10 Platoon, commanded by Lieutenant (later, Captain) Fred Freeman, with Joss Aitcheson as Platoon Sergeant. Fred Holliday:

'Aitcheson, a "Scouser" through and through, wanted the BEST Platoon. He certainly put us through our paces. The Battalion CO was Lieutenant-Colonel Walter Scott. "Scottie" was held in high esteem, having risen from the ranks. He was with Wingate's 8 Column during the first campaign. His only interests were beating the enemy and looking after his men. He called everyone "Laddie" and insisted that orders and campaign news were passed on to every individual. On the battlefield and in times of stress he was cool, calm and collected. His attributes endeared him to his troops and, in consequence, he got the best out of everyone.'

The King's divided into two Columns, each of around 450 men. A Column consisted of HQ, three or four Rifle Platoons, a Commando Platoon, a Recce Platoon and an attached Section of Burrifs. The HQ included Signals personnel, RAF Liaison, MO and medics, Intelligence and Cypher Officers, Veterinary Officer and an Engineer with Sappers. Holliday and Pickering, as Section Leaders, were astonished when issued with Thompson submachine guns: 'Shades of James Cagney! As you can imagine, there were many ribald comments from the men. Thankfully, they were replaced later by American lightweight carbines.'

Initial exercises lasted up to five days, with the men expected to complete up to 20 miles or more daily. Fred Holliday:

'Along the way we learnt how to live in the jungle – how to move, how to fight and how to bivouac. We trained in river crossings, laying ambushes, demolition and, of course, handling the mules. Nothing stopped for the weather. If it rained, it rained and everything carried on. I was young and healthy but, even so, at times I was knackered! We all were. Tom and I no longer thought we were "Scouting".'

Laurence 'Lou' Lake trained as a Signaller before being posted to Sylhet to join the Leicesters for Special Force training. He became a Wireless Operator with 17 Column. The Battalion was commanded by Colonel C.J. 'Jack' Wilkinson and was part of Bernard Fergusson's 16 Brigade – the only Operation *Thursday* Brigade to walk in. Lou Lake: 'The Americans were busy building the Ledo Road. I remember one Yank pointing to the Naga Hills and saying: "You won't get up there!" He was wrong.' At the same time, Lake found the jungle training very hard:

'It was terrible, in a word! We cut our way up each steep slope, all covered in thick jungle, went down the other side and forded the river at the bottom. Then we went up again. It was absolutely vital to get your heavy pack positioned correctly.'

This harsh training paid off during 16 Brigade's punishing trek into Burma, across the Patkai Hills.

The Battalions of 14 British Infantry Brigade now under training included the Bedfordshire and Hertfordshire's 16 and 61 Columns. Captain John Riggs, 16 Column's Recce Platoon Commander, found some aspects of Chindit training rather unusual:

'We discovered that over half our Battalion couldn't swim, although we knew we would probably have to undertake major river crossings with all the animals and equipment. Swimming lessons were organised in local rivers, but we were uncertain about the presence of crocodiles.'

John Riggs had other worries. He took charge of training his 30-strong Recce Platoon – three British infantry Sections, a Burrif Section, two Signallers and three mules carrying the Platoon's wireless, batteries, charging engine and fuel:

'A heavy, powerful wireless was needed, as our signals were often relayed to the Column via Rear HQ in Assam, hundreds of miles west. Our reconnaissance activities frequently took us many miles away from the Column Commander.'

Once inside Burma Riggs' job would be to see but not be seen, often operating days ahead of the Column's main body. He would try to stay out of trouble while searching for suitable drop zones, river crossings and water in dry terrain. The Recce Platoon's responsibilities also included locating and gauging the strength of any Japanese units:

'Burrif officers taught us how to use their Section. Given our forward role, we needed first class NCOs. They were not specially selected but were carefully trained into the job. The key to everything was to train each man to be self-confident in the jungle, as parts of the Recce Platoon operated alone much of the time. We became acclimatised by the simple act of going out, living in the jungle and becoming part of it.'

The men were taught to operate quietly:

'This took some getting used to and, initially, we found it hard to maintain. Many men were edgy at first when operating at night in the jungle. Much time was spent sending out small detachments alone over a wide area of forest, to give everyone the confidence to fend for themselves, over a period of days, and then find their way back.

'I can still feel my pack. Our kit was awful, of course – nothing like today's equipment. They were standard issue Army packs, with extra pouches but no shoulder padding. I was only about 10 stone when I went in and, after a supply drop, my pack weighed around 70 pounds. Fortunately, officers and NCOs had plenty of things to occupy their minds. A few men were simply unable to cope with the physical demands. No-one over 40 remained with us. Our Battalion CO had been replaced by Lieutenant-Colonel Pat Eason. Earlier, Eason had served on Eisenhower's staff during the planning for Operation Torch, the invasion of North Africa. Sadly, Eason was to go down with scrub typhus and was to die in a field hospital in Assam.'

Lieutenant-Colonel Philip Graves-Morris commanded another 14 Brigade Battalion, the 2nd York and Lancaster Regiment. He led 84 Column and his 2 i/c, Major Downward, commanded sister Column 65. They had been based at Bangalore, where they became bored with repetitive 'JEWTS' (Jungle Exercises Without Trees). On moving to the Ken River, however, they found plenty of real jungle and ample opportunities for river crossing training. The move north was made in a five-day, 80-mile exercise.[12]

The York and Lancaster men spent October and November 1943 hardening their bodies on long marches, adapting to jungle living and practising battle drills. Graves-Morris wrote: 'The men all showed excellent spirit at the thought that, at last, they were training for some definite operation. Throughout training there developed a rivalry, at times a little too pronounced, between the two Columns, which fostered *esprit-de-Colonne* rather than *esprit-de-Battailon*.'[12]

They sought to cover 16–18 miles daily, but this was rarely achieved in such difficult country, with a shade temperature of 110–112 deg. F. Once inside Burma and burdened with sickness and Monsoon conditions, they would often have only three or four miles to show for a day's toil. They learned quickly and shared their new-found knowledge. The men experimented with ways of making brew-up fires with minimal smoke. Bad habits were curbed. Philip Graves-Morris: 'The thoughtlessness that led to a trail of cigarette packets, paper, match-boxes and tins ... was hard to eradicate, until individuals who had personally taken trouble started to exercise their influence on their friends and, slowly, taking pride in doing things properly grew.'

The men were silent most of the time, their eyes fixed on the man in front as the Column Snake progressed. Those who couldn't take the training were removed but some, subsequently, were called back to fill gaps in the Columns just before their deployment in Burma. The Battalion Commander saw the injustice in this: 'Not only were they not quite up to the physical requirements, but had been denied the hard, thorough training which all others had undergone. Most of them fell by the wayside in Burma and only got themselves to an evacuation strip by dogged determination and the assistance of their more fortunate comrades.'[12] 84 Column Administrative Officer Paddy Dobney described this as

... a piece of criminal staff work by someone in a distant headquarters. We were told to make up our shortage by using those who had failed to pass the demanding physical standard five months ago. So all those unfortunate storemen, orderlies and some cooks, about 30 of them, were absorbed back into the two Columns.[13]

Chindit training was comprehensive and diverse, demanding extreme fitness and new combat skills. It focused on march discipline, jungle drills for moving in and out of bivouac, dispersal, compass marching, taking supply drops, night operations, watermanship and river crossings, animal management, first aid, sanitation, individual cooking and a great deal more. Training was divided into four broad sections: fitness, weapons proficiency, discipline and welfare. Lieutenant-Colonel

Adapted to jungle living: B Company of the 2nd York and Lancaster pictured in the last weeks of 1943, after some tough marches. (Harold Pettinger)

Graves-Morris summed up the prevailing philosophy: 'It is no good being able to march if you cannot fight and you cannot fight unless you obey orders and have been properly fed and learned to look after yourself.'[12]

Paddy Dobney recorded the discouraging debut of the mules during training – the long march to the Ken River:

Fifteen minutes before move-off time the two Columns stood ready, with the mule loads paired for loading. From the direction of the mule lines a struggling string of men and animals approached us. Clearly, a complete *entente* had not yet been established between men and beasts. But with coaxing and cursing, most of the animals were persuaded into the correct positions for loading. The loading began. Five minutes later, Muleteers and mules, many with half-hanging loads, were careering out of sight in all directions. The Colonel, rather heartlessly, I considered, looked at his watch and announced it was time to move off. We left the unfortunate handlers to sort out the mess and join us later.[13]

A Column Snake of over 400 men and their animals stretched back over half a mile. Control was far from

easy. Battle tactics concentrated on the ability to fight, disperse and re-form at pre-agreed rendezvous points. Paddy Dobney: 'If the stakes had not been so high, our training was not unlike a huge game of "Cowboys and Indians" – we being the Indians. We were required to hide and strike when and where we chose. In order to do this, we had to learn to use jungle lore.'[13]

This included an understanding of what can be eaten and what must be avoided and the use of bamboo for beds, stretchers and as an emergency source of water. It was vital to blend into the surroundings. Paddy Dobney:

Nothing we possessed could be white. Our handkerchiefs, underpants, towels and drinking pots were all stained brown or green. The Doctor's bandages and dressings were all brown. White markings on our ponies were stained. Officers ceased to wear insignia.

At the end of each day's march the Column had to curl itself into a tight ball, to be best organised to defend itself during the night ... It must be stressed that we would never really feel safe from detection and attack. We would be constantly on the alert, often looking over our shoulders, rarely able to drop our guard. Villages had to be approached with caution for fear of being betrayed, as many Burmese could not be trusted. All noise had to be minimal at all times. Our cooking fires must be restricted and often totally forbidden.[13]

Early on in the training the rations came in a 10-man pack, with large tins of bully beef, cheese and bacon, together with porridge and biscuits. 84 Column's Paddy Dobney described these rations as 'heavy, bulky and difficult to break down and distribute equally in weight amongst a Section of soldiers.' Individually packaged K-rations solved this problem. Each meal came in a book-sized pack. The K-ration pack was waxed. It was waterproof and also made an ideal fuel, providing just enough heat for a hot drink. Dobney gave his verdict on K-rations: 'In Burma, we liked it for the first 20 days, tolerated it for the next 20 days and for the remaining 100 days loathed the sight of every packet.'[13]

14 Brigade's training entered a new phase in December 1943. Support Platoons underwent three weeks' intensive training with Brigade instructors. Exercises included Column attacks on prepared 'enemy' positions, using all available weapons and air strikes.[12]

Christmas Day at the York and Lancaster's Ken River camp was marked by a 'Country Fun Fair', with the Battalion's officers manning the various booths. The NCOs took over on Boxing Day. Activities included a fancy dress football match between officers and Sergeants. The Battalion Commander enjoyed it: 'The old year was finished off with a Brigade Gymkhana, inter-Battalion football matches, mule and pony shows, fun fair, boxing and sports and, finally, on New Year's Eve, 70th Division Concert Party produced its show, "Christmas Crackers", for the Battalion.'[12]

The fun was over on New Year's Day. 84 Column marched out to take a night supply drop. Two days later both York and Lancaster Columns moved by dispersal groups to Barukpur and the next fortnight was filled with river crossing training and weapons practice. The new location met with Graves-Morris' approval:

The area near Barukpur Dam provided first class conditions as, here, the river flows slowly, is 800 yards wide, and narrower streams leading to the dam provide stronger currents. Every effort was made to teach all ranks to swim and to practise the improvisation of boats. Major Ken Robertson, RE, ran a course for all officers in the art of making a boat from groundsheets and bamboo, how to work outboard motors, methods of crossing rivers and how to handle infantry assault boats. These lessons were then handed on to the men and, on 10 January, both Columns carried out a silent river crossing without mishap.

Nevertheless, there was disappointment at the mules' behaviour. Once in the water they tended to develop a follow-my-leader procession back to the near shore.[12]

The two Columns came together for Battalion-strength simulated night attacks on strongpoints. The Column Commanders were always relieved when these attacks were over and no-one had been hit.[12] Column wireless equipment had been issued. The Column HQ wireless detachment communicated with Brigade HQ and the Recce Platoon operating forward. The RAF Section wireless communicated with Airbase and with aircraft engaged in supply drops and air strikes. New battle drills were introduced for attacks on airfields and installations. Special attention was paid to ambush drill and sabotage techniques. Paddy Dobney felt on top form: 'To say we were fit and hard was an understatement. I have never been fitter and I am sure that most others in the Battalion would say the same.'[13]

Every effort was made to attend to details. For example, there would be no dentistry behind enemy lines. Teeth were inspected. Fillings were not available at the Field Dental Unit; all suspect teeth were removed, as a precautionary measure. Paddy Dobney waited in line for his turn. He listened to the unpleasant noises behind the screen: 'We were all rather pale now and a tough-looking Corporal next to me, wearing the Military Medal, is starting to sweat.' When it was the Corporal's turn, Dobney listened to the commentary: 'Sit down! Open! Open, I said! Fetch him back, Percy. Quickly!' It was then Dobney's turn. He had three teeth pulled.[13]

The author's father, Private Jack Redding of the King's Own, had a lifelong loathing of dentists, following his experience of Army dentistry – to the point where he would seek to escort any member of his family requiring dental treatment (even when his eldest son reached his fifties!).

Men became accustomed to low rations and high levels of physical work. On 16 January 1944, 84 and 65 Columns began a five-day scheme, 'Exercise Steeple'. 84 Column was briefed to assault an imaginary airstrip defended by 65 Column. The location was selected for its inaccessibility. 84 Column was expected to cover 35 miles in four days, including taking an airdrop, making a river crossing and ascending a steep escarpment – all concluding with a night approach march. Meanwhile, 65 Column would make its own approach march and prepare to attack 84 Column, complete with air support.[12]

The next exercise, 'Peahen', began on 1 February and involved a 20-mile approach march for a joint night attack by 84 and 65 Columns on 'Japanese' positions. After the extreme demands of 'Steeple' the York and

Lancaster men found 'Peahen' a rather easy-going affair.[12] Realistic training confirmed the viability of air supply. 111 Brigade Cypher Officer Richard Rhodes James described the first air drop he witnessed:

> We watched enchanted as the parachutes floated down ... Then the next morning we examined our new K-rations. We tore open the double packing, excitedly, like children, and gaped in wonder at the neat little tins and cellophane wrappings. Beside our previous rations, this was a feast. We ate it with relish.[14]

The novelty, unfortunately, soon wore off.

The training of Operation *Thursday's* air component involved RAF squadrons and 1st Air Commando. The latter provided the lion's share of air landing and support capacity. Captain (later, Major) Paul Griffin was Wingate's G-3 (Air) – a Liaison Officer attached to Cochran's Air Commando: 'I left the 3rd/6th Gurkha Rifles before they went in. I went down with malaria and developed jaundice. As a result, I was downgraded to Category B at the crucial moment.' Griffin went to Special Force HQ, where his air-related duties underwent a rapid evolution:

'*Wingate had a couple of communications aircraft on hand at that time, an Anson and a Fairchild Argus. I had the job of looking after them. It didn't take long for the idea to take hold that I knew something about aircraft. It was only a short step to being regarded as a leading expert on glider landings in jungle terrain!*'

Griffin and Frank Barns, the G-2 (Air), occupied an Operations Room at Lalaghat. Wingate had cast a spell over them. Paul Griffin:

'*I idolised him. Frank and I were young and impressionable. Orde Wingate made a deep impression – he was a genius. Later, it was Frank who found Wingate's body on that hillside.*'

When 1st Air Commando was established, Griffin went to Lalitpur as Air Liaison Officer: 'I met Phil Cochran, a man with great charisma. I also met Jackie Coogan, who was outgoing and pleasant.' Griffin got to know a lot about the C-47, or Dakota:

'*In my view it was the greatest aircraft ever built. It could land in a short space and take a large load, including mules. Travelling in a Dakota was about as safe as riding a bike. I had a similar feeling about*

the WACO glider after my first trip in one. I do think, however, that the dual tow idea was rather optimistic.*

'*The air supply set-up was marvellous. It was commanded by Peter Lord, who had a real gift for air supply organisation. The air support function was also superb. Close air support meant CLOSE, down to 100 yards! We were pioneers in this area, with RAF Officers attached to the Columns.*'

Key personalities in the air support and supply organisation took up their posts in late 1943. They included Robert Thompson, then a Squadron Leader who commanded 77 Brigade's RAF Sections. Thompson (later, Sir Robert Thompson, KBE, CMG, DSO, MC) was one of many 'old hands' from the first expedition who joined the second.[15]

There were some early doubts about the claims upon which Operation *Thursday's* air support and supply expectations were founded. Cochran's pledges concerning precision air strikes were questioned. It seems such doubts arose due to the lack of certain radio equipment in RAF aircraft operating in the Far East theatre. American aircraft had both VHF and HF. This allowed Chindits with Type 22 HF wirelesses to communicate directly with aircraft overhead.[16] Thompson and Griffin had similar views on the dual tow of gliders. Thompson wrote:

> This was a mistake, as it turned out, but we thought we would need that number of gliders to get enough in on the first night, including troops to defend the sites, and there were not enough Dakotas if they hauled only one glider each. As it was, some of the Dakotas were required to make more than one round trip if all went well.[17]

Undamaged gliders could be retrieved – once they had landed in clearings or on sandbanks – by the so-called 'snatch' technique. Thompson described this alarming procedure:

> We sat in the glider on the ground, with two slender posts in front with lights on the top and with the tow rope draped across them, so that it looked like a high goal post. The DC3 [*sic*] with a hook underneath (rather like a large gaff), fixed to a winch in the aircraft, flew over from behind very low and, with luck, the hook caught the tow rope. The strain was taken partly by the nylon tow rope (12 pairs of stockings a foot, I was told) which was stretchable and partly by the winch, which was set to pay out line above a certain pressure. Even so, you went from stationary on the ground to 20 ft up at 70 plus

mph in about a second. You were advised to remove your false teeth before you swallowed them.[18]

Paul Griffin experienced a 'snatch' drill at Lalitpur:

'It took many pretty terrifying passes close to the ground before my superb pilot hooked on. It was clear that, excellent as the manoeuvre was, it could only be of limited use because anyone attempting it had to be a fine pilot, specially trained, and because the sort of situation requiring the feat would seldom present itself, jungle clearings and light aircraft being available.'

Nevertheless, glider-snatching was used occasionally when Special Force entered Burma.

The Chindits had no assault landing capability without the gliders, required to land advance parties and engineers, who would then create airstrips for the C-47s flying in the main body. The USAAF originally sought 1,000 glider pilots, but this requirement eventually expanded to 12,000. Recruitment was slow, perhaps reflecting the obvious risks of combat flying in such aircraft.[19] Glider pilot training had three phases: 60 hours light aircraft instruction, 30 hours in civilian gliders and 60 hours instruction in the WACO CG-4A.[20]

The entire glider construction programme came under scrutiny following an accident involving a CG-4A built by Robertson Aircraft Company. Robertson was a relatively minor builder of gliders, having completed just over 60 when a major accident occurred at the beginning of August 1943. A VIP flight was arranged. Larson (*Aerial Assault into Burma*) described what happened:

> Company executives decided to organise a flight demonstration of their glider, carrying the Mayor of St. Louis, Missouri, the President of the Chamber of Commerce, a Judge, along with Robertson's President and Vice-President. A USAAF C-47 hooked up to the glider, took off, climbed to 1,000 ft and the glider pilot released the tow-rope. During a climbing standard turn the left wing collapsed, wrenching the aircraft, ripping off the right wing. The glider crashed nose-first into the ground, killing everyone.[21]

Despite this high-profile setback, glider construction and pilot training continued. In normal flight the CG-4A was flown just above the tug aircraft, clear of the propwash but not high enough to cause the tow-cable to become taut. A pupil pilot was taught how to keep station by fixing the tug aircraft's position by reference to the fourth or fifth rivet up on the side of the WACO's front panel.[22] Most pupils tended to over-control. The glider training manual warned: 'The cargo glider tends to oscillate while on the tow, which is a characteristic not found in sailplanes and other light gliders. If one wing drops, the student pilot tends to over-correct, with the result that the other wing will drop. This swing from side to side will continue, with increased amplitude, unless the proper correction is made.' It then adds a rather obvious piece of advice on release from the tug, downwind of the field: 'The student pilot should stay on tow until a position is attained from which he can make a safe landing in the designated area.'[23]

The syllabus required the pupil to fly the 'ideal' circuit, entering the downwind leg at 1,200 ft, passing the landing point at 1,000 ft and starting the base leg at 800 ft, with final approach commencing at 400 ft. Airspeed for landing was 70–90 mph, with 90 mph required when fully laden. The glider would be held a few feet above the ground until settling at about 60 mph. With supreme irony (which can be appreciated fully only by those who landed by glider at Broadway and other jungle clearings), the training manual added: 'Extreme care should be used in avoiding rough spots on the field, as some training landing gears are easily damaged.' The manual went on to acknowledge the British assault glider tactic of the dive approach, reducing exposure to ground fire, but ruled this out for the CG-4A: 'Any manoeuvring close to the ground after level flight seriously decreases the remaining amount of distance that can be travelled.'[24]

1st Air Commando's strength included 30 P.51 Mustangs, 12 B.25 Mitchell bombers, 100 light aircraft (the majority Vultee L.1 Vigilants, together with a few Stinson L.5A Sentinels), 12 Noorduyn UC-64 Norseman utility aircraft and a fleet of C-47s.[25] Cochran also received 100 WACO gliders. Liberty ships reached Calcutta in early December 1943 with the CG-4As, together with 25 training gliders.[26] Later, another 50 CG-4As were shipped to India. Gliders were no use without tugs. The extra gliders increased Cochran's requirement for C-47s. His original allocation of 13 was doubled by involving Tenth Air Force Troop Carrier Command aircraft. Pilots and co-pilots of 27 Troop Carrier Squadron were trained in glider-towing.[27]

The C-47 or Dakota – the military variant of the DC3 airliner – had a crew of four. The Pilot sat on the left, with the Co-pilot alongside. The Engineer sat immediately behind the Pilot. The Radio Operator sat across from the Engineer. Charles J. Campbell was the Engineer of C-47 'Assam Dragon':

'Our crew stayed together throughout the missions over Burma. Our Pilot was Major Orio "Red" Austin

*and the Co-pilot was Captain Donald I. Erickson. Both
were career officers before the war. Austin was a very
conservative pilot but, when the chips were down, he
could really fly that C-47.*

*'The C-47 was an airplane that could do anything.
As a variant of a commercial aircraft it was good to
start with. The Engineer's main job was to manage the
fuel. We had two very reliable 1,200 hp Pratt & Whitney
R–1830 Twin Wasp radials. They were excellent,
commercial grade engines.'*

Austin's crew, together with all the C-47 crews involved,
trained for several roles, including glider towing, supply
dropping and the fly-in of troops and cargo into rough
jungle strips. Charles J. Campbell: 'In fact, Austin trained
on dual tows and glider snatch retrieval back in the
USA, so these things were not exactly last-minute expe-
diencies.'

The success of the air landings hinged on the
capabilities of the American airstrip construction
specialists. On 10 August 1943, the 900th Airborne
Engineer Company arrived in India. This unit had a wide
range of glider transportable construction equipment,
carried fully assembled and ready to work. The 900th
reached Lalaghat airfield on 7 February 1944. The airmobile equipment included bulldozers, wheeled tractors
and towed graders.[27]

Orde Wingate tended to 'move the goalposts' as
training progressed and his plans crystallised. He
became increasingly ambitious. Slim noted the change
in his thinking:

> His original idea had been that of a force, which,
> penetrating behind the enemy lines, would operate
> in comparatively small, lightly equipped Columns
> to harry his communications and rear establish-
> ments, while our main forces struck the decisive
> blows elsewhere.[28]

What changed was Wingate's growing appreciation
of the potential of the dedicated air force now at his
disposal. He now saw the Chindits as a heavier armed,
larger penetration force, according to Slim 'not only to
hold landing ground bases against major attacks, but
to assault strongly defended positions.'[28] Some would
challenge this assertion by Slim, regarding the eventual deployment of Chindits in conventional attacks
on fortified positions as an abuse of Special Force and
Wingate's strategy and tactics. Slim's comment could
be seen as an attempt to link Wingate himself to the
unfortunate decisions, taken *after* his death, which
eventually led to the decimation of Special Force in
wasteful conventional infantry assaults.

Slim suggested that Wingate was 'strangely naive' in
his views on fighting the Japanese. The picture is further
clouded by Slim's observation that 'Wingate's men were
neither trained nor equipped to fight pitched battles,
offensive or defensive.' Perhaps this was supposed to
imply that Special Force was left unprepared for a role
Wingate himself came to envisage for his command and
that, therefore, he should at least share responsibility
for the severe losses in later battles such as Mogaung
(despite the fact that this fighting took place months
after his death). The true motives behind this commentary remain unclear but, at the same time, it is certainly
correct to say that Wingate's demands continued to
escalate. He asked Slim for 26th Indian Division but
was refused. Slim wrote: 'He already had more troops
than we should be able to lift and supply by air.'[28] In the
event, Wingate had to be content with five Brigades:
two flown in immediately, two flown in later and one
to march in.

As the first wave Battalions of Special Force moved
up to their forward positions, Wingate continued to
develop his jungle 'Stronghold' concept, with requirements for artillery and anti-aircraft defences. Slim
later questioned Wingate's attitude towards Japanese
fighting qualities: 'I went over with him his ideas of the
defence of one of these Strongholds and found that he
had little appreciation of what a real Japanese attack
would be like.' Slim suggests that it was he who recommended the 'floater' model of Stronghold defence, with
each garrison having a mobile force ready to attack the
rear of an attacking enemy.[28]

Wingate's late proposals for relatively static Chindit
warfare caused some disquiet. Lieutenant-Colonel
Graves-Morris, commanding the York and Lancaster
Battalion, recalled one of the more outlandish ideas
from Wingate:

> Some wonder and trepidation was raised by a small
> pamphlet issued by the General on 'Strongholds'. In
> this, the General considered the possibility of the
> defenders taking in cattle and even learning the art
> of growing crops, particularly rice. One wondered
> just how long he imagined his troops would be
> besieged![12]

Chindit warfare had need of many specialists. They
included John Knowles, with the Queen's 22 Column. He
had been sufficiently fed up to look for something new,
at the very time Wingate was recruiting RAF Officers
for his Columns: 'When on leave in Calcutta I met some
survivors of the first Chindit campaign. They looked
awful but this daring, long range commando raid really
caught my imagination.'

Knowles volunteered, was promoted to Flight Lieutenant and arrived at Gwalior in December 1943. He and an equally bored Australian, Flight Lieutenant Douglas 'Singe' St. John – another 146 Squadron volunteer – were assigned to 23 Brigade's 34 and 55 Columns, 4th Border Regiment. Within a few days, however, Knowles was reassigned to the Queen's 22 Column, part of 16 Brigade. He arrived 'cold', when the Column had already finished jungle training. 'Singe', in contrast, had time to complete his training, stayed with 23 Brigade and survived the campaign.

The term 'RAF Officer' was shorthand for Royal Air Force Air Liaison Officer. This role was similar to the more recent Forward Air Controller, although the job in the Columns was much broader. John Knowles:

'Calling up air strikes was just one aspect and something I never had cause to do. Air supply, usually at night, was our main concern. The RAF Officer advised on the selection of drop zones and supervised the marking of the DZ with fires. Typically, a DZ layout would consist of five fires in an L-shape, with the short leg turned away from any high ground in the immediate area, as a guide to low-flying aircraft. The RAF Officer was also responsible for selecting casualty evacuation sites for L.1 or L.5 light aircraft.'

Tony Howard, with the Queen's sister Column, 21, had put his Post Office Telephones experience back in Britain to good use. So far, most of his time had been spent at 16 Brigade HQ, manning the switchboard. Life was now more exciting as NCO i/c of 21 Column's Royal Signals wireless detachment. Howard had done some jungle training around Gwalior and the Ken and Betwa rivers, but he still worried that he might be left behind when 21 Column finally moved out. He told 16 Brigade's Signals Officer, Major 'Shiner' Moon, that he wanted to go in rather than stay at HQ. He got his wish:

'My training concentrated on the Type 22 wireless. I don't remember doing much jungle training. As a Corporal Signaller I did what I was told. I remember spending a couple of hours practising getting in and out of a glider but even that was irrelevant, as our Brigade was to march in.'

Others had even less training. Howard's Royal Signals detachment included Wireless Operators George Hill and Albert 'Geordie' Beaton. This small team was completed by Instrument Mechanic George Baker. These men were late arrivals. They joined 21 Column on 27 December, only a few weeks after they arrived in India. George Hill was one of a group of 150 'white-knees'

– Signallers newly arrived from the UK. His troopship, *Strathmore*, docked at Bombay on 27 November. He reached 21 Column near Jhansi four weeks later.

Tony Howard himself had arrived only days earlier. His Battalion Commander was Colonel John Metcalf:

'The Colonel came to visit his Signallers. I remember him having a long chat with me. He said: 'Whatever you do, look after your boots!' He'd had the same pair of boots for 22 years and they looked as good as new. I remembered his words when we were on our last exercise, a two-week scheme including a march of 100 miles. I recalled them again, when in Burma. My boots wore out very quickly. I hoped for a new pair of South African or Australian boots, the best and most comfortable. Indian boots were not made for English feet. Following a supply drop I had a new pair of Indian boots issued to me in the dark. I put them on and when it became light I found I had put them on the wrong feet! They were very wide and shapeless, but I was stuck with them until the next supply drop.'

Back at Rear HQ Flying Officer John Pearson prepared 111 Brigade's RAF communications. He remembers the equipment:

'The wireless was a 1082/1083 set. The receiver and transmitter were mounted side-by-side. When on the mule the wireless box was balanced by the batteries. This equipment was more reliable than any other wireless I have ever known. A similar but slightly bigger set was in use back at Air base. The 1082/1083 was hardly new, having been introduced in the 1920s, but this valve wireless was very simple and designed to stand up to the rigours of aircraft use – in other words, to survive heavy landings. Its components were protected in shock-proof mountings. We carried a few spare valves and had a coded list which allowed us to request other components.

'Time and again this wireless was used successfully to order up supply drops from a range of up to 300 miles. The aerial consisted of 40–50 ft of wire, stowed in the box when not in use. Wireless Operators tied the end of the wire to a weight and threw it over a handy tree branch. Getting the aerial down was trickier and, occasionally, an agile local would be encouraged to do the job.'

The petrol-driven generator for the RAF wireless had many names, the most polite being the 'piggy'. John Pearson: 'It was carried in a frame with two tubular hoops, forming a shape that could be secured to the mule. The generator was balanced by petrol cans on the other side.'

Percy Stopher was a Medical Orderly with 23 Brigade. He experienced all the rigours of Chindit training, finding it hard but not without its moments of amusement:

'The week before we finished training was devoted to getting the animals sorted out. At one point we had the idea of holding a Gymkhana. We dressed all the mules and horses, using whatever we could lay our hands on – hats, old pyjamas and so on. We cried with laughter!'

The mood was more sober when Wingate and Mountbatten visited the Special Force Brigades before they went in. These visits often provoked some blunt exchanges. Norman Campbell, a Cypher Operator with the Cameronians' 90 Column, had missed 10 days' training due to enteritis:

'We did our jungle training in country nothing like Burma, in a fairly flat part of India. The Battalion then moved to Imphal. We knew we were going into Burma and we heard more when Wingate came to visit. We had just completed a difficult, 60-mile trek from Silchar to Bishenpur, up and down a series of 6,000 ft "hills", then marched to Imphal and an area close to the airstrip. We were dumped at that place with absolutely nothing. There were no buildings and no beds. The food was appalling. Wingate asked us about conditions and one soldier, Rifleman Cooke, didn't hold back. He told Wingate straight: 'It's bloody awful. The place is not fit for pigs!' That got results. Things changed overnight and the food improved.

Saving life: a light aircraft ticks over on a jungle clearing as casualties are loaded for evacuation. These aircraft were nicknamed 'flying mess tins' by the Chindits. This particular aircraft carries the legend 'Chunky'. (Walter Longstaff)

'I remember Wingate as a lean, ascetic-looking man, wearing his trademark pith helmet. His speech worked, giving us vast confidence. He was very single-minded. There was only one way to run the jungle war and that was his way. Mountbatten made less of an impression in his over-crisp Navy Whites.'

Norman Campbell knew how to look after himself in the jungle, having adapted well:

'I coped with the pack and never had problems with my legs and feet. There was a knack to carrying that pack. You had to get it high on your shoulders. If it sat well down, it would drag you back. Looking back, I must have been pretty naive at 19. I knew we were going in, but it never occurred to me that I could be killed or captured.'

111 Brigade RAF Signals Officer John Pearson also witnessed a Wingate pep talk:

'He looked like a fanatic – someone you just could not argue with. In fact, the very thought of questioning his orders would never enter your mind. Before the fly-in Masters was Brigade Major and effectively ran all the training. He was a wonderful character and I got on well with him. Major Briggs – "Briggo" – was 111 Brigade's Senior Signals Officer and Squadron Leader "Chesty" Jennings was Brigade Senior RAF Officer, attached to Forward HQ. Jennings had been a Navigator on flying boats. I knew him during training at Jhansi, when he was RAF Officer with a Column before being promoted, to replace the original Senior RAF Officer.'

During his talk Wingate introduced Cochran and outlined plans for casualty evacuation by air. John Pearson:

'A demonstration of evacuation was arranged for the following day. One Brigade would call for a casualty fly-out, using the opportunity to bring out an officer who had to return to Special Force HQ. 14 Brigade provided the 'casualty' and Air Commando wanted someone to go along and help the pilot locate Brigade HQ. I got the job and showed up early that morning at a small strip. Cochran and a couple of Sergeants stood around two L.5 light aircraft. I introduced myself. Cochran looked me up and down and said I would be accompanying him in the lead aircraft.'

At Rear HQ Pearson worked closely with the Brigade's team of four Air Quartermasters, each representing a Battalion. They were responsible for making up the loads according to the air drop requests by wireless.

'Gather round!': SEAC Supreme Commander Lord Louis Mountbatten addresses the Nigerian troops of 7 NR, training in the Central Provinces. Beside him is Special Force Commander Orde Wingate. On his left is Brigadier Richards of 3(WA) Brigade. (Peter Allnutt)

The Air Quartermasters supervised the loading: 'Special items would be catered for, from Brigadier Fergusson's replacement monocle to an additional wireless for Blackpool Block.'

Lieutenant-Colonel W.J. 'Bill' Henning, the Cameronians' Battalion Commander, led 90 Column. Sister Column 26 was commanded by Major B.J. 'Breezy' Brennan. 90 Column's Norman Campbell:

'Henning, a tea planter in Assam when war broke out, had a distinct manner and talked in a quick, staccato way. Brennan, in contrast, had a rather plummy voice. Both were excellent officers and saved lives by avoiding unnecessary risks. They led their Columns with impeccable map-reading. In our Column, Henning's second in command was Captain Neil McLean. He was a great bloke, with a special way of treating people.'

Campbell was attached to Column HQ as a Cypher Operator but, as with every Chindit, above all else he was an infantryman: 'The CSM knew I had been a clerk and I was told to work in 90 Column's office. I then got a second job as Cypher Operator, working alongside Cypher Corporal Eddie Walsh. Eddie was a few years older than me and friendly enough.'

Orde Wingate continued to tour the Brigades and his talks remain fresh in many minds, over 60 years later. Private Horace Howkins of the South Staffords' 80 Column used the word 'eccentric', the term most commonly used to describe him. Wingate's blunt style was not to every taste and he put plenty of emphasis on hardship and suffering. He usually included the claim: 'You will go down in history' – an assertion which proved accurate enough. Captain Dick Stuckey of 12 NR's 43 Column:

'We saw Wingate from time to time. He and Mountbatten would arrive in an American jeep – driven by Wingate. After a five-minute pep talk Wingate would finish with the words 'Everything depends on you' and an alarm clock would then sound off in his pocket. 'Well, time waits for no man!' And that was that. Mountbatten was different. Lieutenant-Colonel Pat Hughes, our CO, lined up his officers. Mountbatten had excellent social skills and he had a few words with each man.'

Lieutenant Denis Arnold, a 29 Column Platoon Commander, remembers Wingate visiting the Nigerians:

'He walked along the ranks and delivered a very blunt address. He told us there was every possibility we would be killed, adding the dry comment: 'You know what happened during Longcloth!' He then asked those who couldn't face it to fall out!'

Very few men of 6 NR's 66 Column had any combat experience. Lieutenant (later, Captain) Larry Gaines led the Vickers Platoon: 'The vast majority had no idea what to expect. They were simple peasant people, mostly

Hausas from northern Nigeria, and some from Bauchi – easily recognised by their sharp, filed teeth.'

Corporal Ted Treadwell, of the Leicesters' 71 Column, attended a Mountbatten talk:

'He said: "I know exactly what you are going to call me. But you are going to Burma. You are going to be Chindits. And we are going to give you the air support you need." He told us straight – exactly what we could expect. No bullshit.'

When in the jungle, Treadwell enjoyed trying to live off the land, although this was to be next to impossible in the North Burmese wilderness: 'We were told we could shoot peahens but not peacocks, as they are sacred. Peahens taste very good. We also shot young deer. I used to do some of the cooking for the boys.'

Mountbatten made a favourable impression on Tom Turvey, also with 71 Column:

'Mountbatten told us to gather round. I stood just a few feet from him. He pulled no punches: "Some of you won't be coming back." He knew how to talk to soldiers. He asked me: "Where do you come from, Corporal?" I said my home is a little village near Brackley. I didn't expect him to know it but he replied immediately: "I know that part of the country very well. I have hunted over it many times." It was remarkable. Every time he spoke to someone, he had something to say about where they lived.'

Turvey served with 71 Column's Recce Platoon, led by Captain Percy Lake of The Burma Rifles. Tom Turvey:

'Major Daniels was the Column Commander – a big fellow and a very decent man. I also met Fergusson, who was known by all as a very good soldier. I saw Wingate during the march in. He was a wonderful man. If you had a broken leg and he said you hadn't, you'd end up believing him! Mind you, if I'd thought we were going in by glider I wouldn't have gone. Being towed in a glider? Not bloody likely! I wouldn't have had that.'

As part of 16 Brigade Turvey and the rest of 71 Column walked into Burma. Turvey's 'mucker' was Freddie Finch, from Market Harborough:

'We got on fine together. The training continued and we carried 65 pounds plus on long marches. When we were on high ground it got surprisingly chilly. We got used to the weight with five days' K-rations up – not that we often had five days' food when we were in. Attention to detail was important. I made up my mind to carry

plenty of woollen socks when we went into Burma. They had to be pre-shrunk, otherwise the heel would end up in the middle of your foot.'

Frank Anderson, a Vickers Gunner with the King's 81 Column, coped well with the physical strain of long training marches: 'I had been hardened by my trade as a plasterer. The work was very physical and I was accustomed to putting up with things. Chindit training wasn't that different from a hard day's work.' Anderson saw Wingate during the training and described him as the 'absolute leader'. As for Brigadier Michael Calvert: 'He looked the part and was very strong. In those days men led by example. Calvert set a good example; he was a lion.' Battalion Commander Lieutenant-Colonel Walter Scott had a different style:

'He was a gentleman, in every sense, with an ardent personality. He was just as much a leader as Wingate, but they had very different approaches. Wingate upset a lot of people. Scott was a gentle type but strong, nevertheless. He'd come up from the ranks and had worked for Liverpool Corporation before the war. He was a good fellow.'

—————————

111 Brigade prepared for the long train journey to Sylhet, Assam, prior to the fly-in. Cypher Officer Richard Rhodes James wrote:

> Those last few days before we got on the train were unreal. We were continually trying to think about the future, yet we could never bring ourselves to understand what we were in for. Wingate gave a final talk to our troops, of which the theme was 'Life is fleeting'. It was most depressing but I think the troops appreciated it in a grim sort of way. We had trained together for seven months and achieved a sense of unity that I have never seen before or since.[29]

The York and Lancaster Columns moved to a new camp at Deogarh on 5 February. It had been occupied by Merrill's Marauders and was in a poor state. Four days later, 84 and 65 Columns began a final, harsh test. 'Exercise Orange' was a 140-mile trek, ending on 23 February. It included air drops, independent Column operation, a major river crossing, a Battalion rendezvous on 18 February, separation and establishment of a block on the road from Saugor.[12] They returned by truck to Lalitpur. Battalion Commander Lieutenant-Colonel Graves-Morris described the latter as 'a more sanitary, though rat-infested camp', much preferred to the filthy Deogarh.

Philip Graves-Morris was satisfied with the Battalion's performance during Exercise Orange: 'Both men and animals had proved themselves capable of hard going and ready for the real thing.' Leave arrangements were curtailed in early March. The Battalion then assumed a 'Japanese' identity, protecting supply dumps and rail communications against attacks from 23 Brigade Columns still completing their training.[12]

The training had a heavy air component. Richard Rhodes James of 111 Brigade watched two Dakotas land on a rough strip near the camp: 'We spent days getting in and out of these planes and pushing mules up the bamboo ramps, coaxing, swearing, threatening. For the most part the animals were quite amenable, provided it was all done in an orderly manner.'[30]

Then a WACO glider landed on the strip. The Gurkhas regarded an aircraft without an engine with much suspicion.[30] Glider 'snatches' were practised. Larson described the C-47's glider snatch gear: 'a large, energy-absorbing drum with two pulleys, a large torque table and an hydraulic cylinder containing 950 ft of high tension steel cable. An emergency cable cutter was installed, to chop the steel cable if a problem developed.'[31]

Chindit warfare was a strange mixture of primitive, hand-to-hand combat and mid-1940s high technology. Cochran's Air Commando took on strength six Sikorsky YR-4 helicopters. Two were lost during training in India, but the remaining four flew 23 operations.[32] The YR-4 made its first flight on 14 January 1942. It had a range of 130 miles and had a maximum speed of 75 mph.[33] A number of Chindits owe their lives to the YR-4.

The final phase of training included large-scale demonstrations of glider landings. Wingate watched one simulated assault landing involving 20 gliders. In this exercise, however, the gliders carried no heavy equipment. Had they done so, the observers might have gained a far more accurate impression of the operational realities.

Gliders were of no immediate interest to 16 Brigade, now about to begin its march into Burma. They were to set out a month before Operation *Thursday's* air landings. The Queen's final exercise in India included a crossing of the Betwa River, which was too deep to wade. 21 Column Corporal Signaller Tony Howard paired up with Wireless Operator Geordie Beaton for the crossing. They would swim across, towing and pushing a 'sausage' of packs, equipment and rifles:

'To make a sausage, a groundsheet was laid out. The two packs were placed about a quarter way in from either end, leaving a space in the middle. Into this space we

The way forward: Wingate studies a map with Lieutenant-Colonel Walter Scott (right), of the King's, and Major Gaitley. (Trustees of the Imperial War Museum)

put all our clothes and equipment, except for boots and rifles. The rifles were now placed along the sides of the packs. The ends of the groundsheet were then twisted and tied together with parachute cord, which we all carried. The sides of the groundsheet were then laced up as tightly as possible, to make a long roll. This was then placed upside down onto the second groundsheet and this, likewise, was laced up tightly with cord.'

Their boots were tied to the sausage before entering the water. They had been given Indian-made condoms to keep watches, compasses and other such items dry: 'These condoms worked OK as they were like inner tubes for cars!'

Gordon Hughes, a Queen's Platoon Commander, described his last exercise, an approach march on an 'enemy' airfield, followed by its capture and consolidation. The Nigerians provided the opposition and their outposts failed to detect the approach. The airfield was captured.[4]

During this exercise Hughes became increasingly unwell. His temperature soared and he was taken to hospital. Fergusson's Brigade left by train on 10 January 1944, Hughes' 24th birthday:

You can well imagine my feelings at being left behind. A day or so later Bernard Fergusson and Lord Louis Mountbatten inspected the tented hospital and, on passing my bed, they stopped to talk. Fergusson asked if there was anything I required.

I replied: 'Could you arrange for my early discharge, Sir, so I can rejoin the Queen's at Ledo?' Two days later I picked up other discharged patients and we were on our way by train to Ledo. I had sufficient medicine to complete the anti-malaria treatment whilst on the train.[4]

This journey involved travel by train to Dimapur and then 90 miles down the Ledo Road by truck. Tony Howard of the Queen's recalls Wingate and Mountbatten at Saugor railhead, after the last exercise:

Wingate was complete with his funny old hat. He was quite short and had a rather high, bell-like voice that was most unusual. When he told the officers to return to their Columns, one very dignified Colonel started to march back. Wingate noticed this and barked an order that forced him to break into a run.

When the Queen's Commander, Lieutenant-Colonel Metcalf, talked with Howard, he told him that all Column wireless groups were to be led by Sergeants. As a result, Howard was made Acting Sergeant. Wireless Operator George Hill, never a great fan of authority, was amused by his casual promotion: 'He always made a point of continuing to call me "Corporal", with plenty of emphasis on the word. This was not unjust, as I still had just the two stripes up.'

By late January 1944 16 Brigade had concentrated at Tagap Ga, on the Ledo Road. George Hill was among those with very little jungle experience:

'I was to learn the hard way. It was very much a case of "sink or swim". It was not a very satisfactory introduction to the art of being a Chindit. My jungle training was limited to the final training exercise around Jhansi.'

This got off to a bad start for Hill. On the first morning a mule bolted and ran him down. To his acute embarrassment he found he could not get up. He was firmly pinned to the ground by his 70 pound pack. Hill was not the only one knocked over and requiring help to get up. He quickly learned the facts of life about mules:

'They do not like noises behind their ears, coming from sources they cannot see. They do not like loads of uneven weight upon each side of their backs and they do not like loads of uneven bulk, even if the weight is the same.'

As for the main air-landing force, Corporal Fred Holliday of the King's 82 Column didn't have much of a 21st birthday:

'Before Christmas 1943 a 10-day exercise involved the whole of Special Force. We then had seven days' leave. I was sent to Bombay and my fellow Section Leader, Tom Pickering, to Lahore. There was no choice in the matter. I felt a little sad. I had to spend my 21st birthday on my own.'

On their return, as they prepared to move forward, it was announced that they would go in by glider: 'None of us had ever flown in a plane, let alone a glider.'

One Muleteer, concerned about his charge, enquired about future plans for his mule and was shocked by the reply that the animal would be joining him in the glider, as part of Operation *Thursday*'s spearhead. Fred Holliday:

'We saw Wingate once more. He thought we were on a great adventure. He wished us good luck and said: "Some of you are going to die in Burma." That was a good send off! Little did he know that he would be among the first to die.'

All personal belongings were left behind when they entrained for the seven-day journey to Assam. The going was slow and uncomfortable. Eventually they left the train, boarded a Brahmaputra river steamer and then joined another train for Silchar, where they bivouacked until late February. The training had changed and now included liaison with aircraft, supply drop drill, close-quarters air support and 'get to know you' sessions with 1st Air Commando. They also took the opportunity to go over the fundamentals of Chindit operations: laying

The only way to travel: a mule ready to be loaded. This animal is part of the 'Living History' Chindit display. (Bill Smith)

ambushes, demolition, jungle living, water and sanitary discipline and personal protection against mosquitoes, leeches, ticks and other pests. Fred Holliday: 'We began taking our malaria suppressants, which turned us various shades of yellow. We were also told to complete the Form of Will in our paybooks before handing them in.'

'Airgraph' letters were sent to nominated family members, advising that the men would not be able to write for some time, but that families should continue to write to them. Holliday recalls only one 'perk' to being a Chindit: 'We were excused shaving and many grew the most wonderful, luxuriant beards. I only managed "bum fluff".'

Three Troops of 160th Jungle Field Regiment prepared for action in North Burma. U Troop's Gun Position Officer, Lieutenant (later, Captain) Ronald Swann, RA, found the prospect challenging:

'The guns would have to be completely stripped down for the fly-in. This meant removing the piece, or barrel, then the recuperator, shield, breech block and wheels, finally leaving the carriage platform standing free. On landing in Burma these would have to be put together again, possibly under fire! There were some old soldiers in my Troop who didn't like the idea of taking the 25 Pounders to bits and made it clear that certain parts could not be freed. I made my mark by demonstrating how to release the carriage from the wheels by the simple use of a brass drift and hammer. The old Reservists took the hint and I had no further reaction.'

On 1 March 1944, the King's Own was at Saiton Camp, with the men already busy checking their weapons, equipment and kit. On 5 March Divine Services were held and briefings given on the landings and the route to the first objective. An advance party of King's Own would fly in with the assault gliders. The main body moved up to the airstrip a couple of days later, on 8 March.

Private Jim Unsworth was a late arrival, having just recovered from dysentery. He had been posted to the York and Lancaster Regiment but was switched to the King's Own:

'The King's Own needed more men to increase Battalion strength in readiness for Burma. I was one of 25 posted to Imphal. It was quite a journey – by train to Calcutta, by paddle-steamer on the Brahmaputra River, then more trains north and trucks for the last stretch to Imphal. We arrived just in time for the final days of jungle training. We took a quick look round. HQ was alongside the airstrip, with gliders and Dakotas parked up. We were very hungry and eventually found the

dining hall, a huge marquee. We had had nothing much to eat for two days but were turned away with the words: "You'll get nothing here tonight." Service wasn't much improved the following morning; we breakfasted on a slice of bread and a scoop of beans.'

Extra equipment was issued to 41 and 46, the King's Own Columns. Jim Unsworth, with 46 Column, received ammunition, a couple of Bren magazines and two grenades, together with five days' K-rations.

Peter Heppell had volunteered for special duties to escape the tedium of life with 67th Field Company at Cox's Bazaar. After several months' wait he was posted as a Lance Corporal (later, Sergeant) to the King's. He coped with the heavy pack during jungle training, despite his past habit of bulking out his pack with cardboard before route marches. Heppell went to the other extreme during his Chindit training, filling his pack with bricks: 'We Sappers formed a Section of 82 Column's Commando Platoon. Our main concerns were booby-trapping and assisting supply drops and river crossings. We got the jobs the others didn't like.'

82 Column received a final briefing a few days before going in. Peter Heppell:

'I should have felt fear but I don't recall that. I do remember feeling exhilarated. I had already learnt a lot. We made the transition from RE to infantry. In addition, of course, most of the men were from Liverpool and I had to get used to the accent and humour. It came as a shock to realise that many NCOs were poorly educated – they had got their rank with their fists. During training some went out on a Saturday night looking for Cameronians to beat up. And the Cameronians did the same. In contrast, we REs were supposed to be gentlemen.'

During the final preparations Heppell packed a small sketchbook and made a brief will (using AB64). His family received the standard letter warning that he wouldn't be writing for some time, but that they should continue to write to him.

Bren gunner John Simon was on his way, with 16 Brigade's HQ Column. Simon hadn't heard of Wingate but had volunteered for Special Force. He saw Fergusson on the Ledo Road, as they were going in: 'What a guy! He knew how to talk to troops. He really came over well.'

The Column's HQ Rifle Platoon carried small arms and light machine guns only, with no mortars. They were led by Sergeant Peter Dorans, Fergusson's Batman during the first Chindit expedition. On at least one occasion Dorans saved Fergusson's life. He was awarded the DCM for his service during the 1943 operation. He

On the river: many Chindits on their way to war in Burma enjoyed a brief interlude on a Brahmaputra paddle steamer, to reach the narrow gauge railway leading to the final concentration areas in Assam. (Jim Unsworth)

had lived on Fergusson's estate, where his father was a gamekeeper.

Fundamental errors were made during the training for Operation *Thursday*. The results were high sickness levels and undernourishment. Richard Rhodes James wrote:

> Our object was to harden ourselves to jungle life, but we made the mistake, in our excess of zeal, of imagining that hard training meant bad quarters and indifferent food. It was fortunate that the high morale of the men was sufficient to overlook, or at least to tolerate, a serious defect in our training.[34]

A 111 Brigade 75-mile training march underlined the vulnerabilities of Chindit soldiering. Rhodes James:

> The rot set in with a march to the Betwa River and, once again, we followed blindly the principle of physical exertion which had led us through our training. The previous year Wingate's men had trained in the same place and at the same time and they had been decimated by malaria. The lesson was lost on us, as were most of the lessons of moderation, and we set out on a period of intensive training in the sticky heat and malaria of September. The Brigadier even conceived the idea of living by the

Betwa without tents, but he was compelled to change his decision by the unanimous protest of COs and Medical Officers. When we arrived at our new camp we found we had lost a quarter of our personnel.[35]

The author's father, with the King's Own, was hospitalised twice prior to Operation *Thursday* in early March. Jack Redding had two bouts of malaria, but recovered A.1 fitness.

Paddy Dobney, with the York and Lancaster's 84 Column, missed his Battalion's 100-mile approach march to the training area. He was hospitalised with jaundice. He returned as they re-deployed to Calcutta to meet the threat of Japanese invasion. In this low-lying area men struggled with the extreme temperatures and high humidity. Most suffered the scourge of prickly heat. Paddy Dobney:

> When a white body continually sweats and never dries, the pores of the skin become so overworked, tender and sore from the body's salt, large areas erupt in a blazing mass of red inflammation. The torso is the worst affected. Gusts of pain, as if a thousand red hot needle points were pressed against the skin, can cause the worst affected to cry out during hot, airless tropical nights.'[13]

Dobney's Battalion took part in the Arakan fighting during 1943, but became more concerned about malaria than the Japanese. The Monsoon broke just two weeks after their arrival in the Arakan. On returning to Chittagong, Dobney went into hospital once again, this time with malaria:

> On my last evening in Chittagong Hospital a group of us discussed the war's progress. I had no reason at the time to record in my memory any part of that conversation but, as clearly now as if it were yesterday, I can hear one of the group in that far away hospital say: 'This chap Wingate seems to have achieved something, anyway'. I had never heard of Wingate and had no idea just what he had achieved and recall showing little interest in the matter. Destiny must have meant that remark to lodge in my memory, however. Within a few months the name Wingate and all he had achieved were made very clear to me and to thousands of others. Each of us, as we followed his star, was to be left with physical and mental reminders, to be borne for the rest of our days.[13]

Some men had been undermined by the strain of carrying the heavy pack over long distances. Paddy Dobney:

> From a strictly medical opinion a man should not carry more than a third of his own weight – a mule or horse not more than a quarter. So, an 11-stone man should not carry more than about 50 pounds. Of course, many strong men in industry and agriculture can, and often do, carry up to one hundredweight, but not permanently on their backs for long hours each day.[13]

Dobney's Battalion Commander, Lieutenant-Colonel Philip Graves-Morris, added:

> The total weight was somewhere near 70 pounds and even more when the rains came and all the kit was soaked. It was this grinding drag on one's back and shoulder muscles that finally led to the intense fatigue which overtook all Columns, which governed their movements and which eventually sowed the seeds of exhaustion and sickness that was to be the destruction of so many splendid men.[12]

Elements of 111 Brigade's final training had to be cancelled due to the collapse in health. Richard Rhodes James: 'Men were being carried off dozens at a time to Jhansi Hospital, 25 miles away. Battalions were left with barely enough men to look after their mules and training came to an abrupt halt'.[36]

Eventually, the High Command acquainted itself with the situation and was horrified. General Auchinlech himself wrote to enquire why 77 and 111 Infantry Brigades, which were due to enter Burma in two months' time, were in such an appalling condition. 'There developed what the Army describes as a "first-class flap".'[36]

The Brigades were visited by doctors: 'Nutrition experts examined our food and were not impressed. Malariologists took one look at our camp and raised their hands in hygienic horror. We conceded to them by moving one Battalion away from the river's edge. What had been a fine fighting force was now a collection of convalescents'.[36]

Effective action was taken, though very late in the day. The food improved but the men hated the mandatory shark's liver oil prescribed by the nutritionists: 'Rather belatedly, we went through a course of Mepacrine which, if it had been given to us a month earlier, might well have prevented 90 per cent of the malaria'.[36]

Some men could not go in due to injury, rather than sickness. Lieutenant (later, Major) Harold Pettinger, MC, was jungle training with the York and Lancaster Regiment near Jhansi when an accident cut short his career as a Chindit:

> 'It happened while I was leading the Company through the jungle on a night march to compass bearing. I fell down a steep chaung bank covered in foliage. I injured my knee and ended up in 119 Indian General Hospital at Ranchi. I hoped the knee would improve quickly and allow me to go, but it turned out to be a cracked patella. That was that!'

Pettinger was posted to Sylhet Air base.

South Staffords Rifle Section Leader Les Grainger had been an anti-aircraft gunner in Assam in late 1943. His unit protected the railway linking the huge supply dumps around Dimapur. Sergeant Grainger was bored and volunteered for the Chindits:

> '"Never volunteer" is a good maxim in the Army, but we would never have won the war if everyone had felt that way. Some people didn't settle with Regular units, but I liked the South Staffs. This was a well-established County Regiment and the men were a rugged, no-nonsense bunch. They had been overseas – in the Middle East – when war broke out. In the end they did a total of six years abroad, an illustration of what Britain demanded of its soldiers. I think US Army personnel could expect to go home after two years.'

Grainger never entered Burma. He was injured after the training, as the Battalion marched to the airfield for the fly-in:

'I developed what was known as a "march fracture" – a broken metatarsal in the left foot caused by the weight we carried. I was not the only one. The problem began with a slight pain and this became steadily worse, until it reached an excruciating level. I hobbled along and managed to reach the bivouac. The Medical Officer came to see me and ordered an X-ray. It turned out to be a fracture rather than a sprain.

'I was very disappointed, as I had been training hard for just over four months. At that time I thought I could fly in later but, as anyone with the experience of a broken bone will know, things are never back to normal immediately the cast comes off. Anyway, I found myself heading for a convalescent hospital, rather than Burma.'

Notes

1. Nesbit, R. C. (2009), *The Battle for Burma*, 149–150
2. Rhodes James, R. (1981), *Chindit*, 12
3. Carfrae, C. (1985), *Chindit Column*, 77
4. Hughes, G., unpublished MS
5. Mackay, Rev. Donald, 1st Cameronians, 'A Padre with the Chindits', *Dekho*, Autumn 2000, 20–25
6. Sharpe, P. (1995), *To Be a Chindit*, 130–131
7. Rhodes James, R. (1981), 28
8. Carfrae, C. (1985), 83
9. Rhodes James, R. (1981), 13
10. Gerrard, F. (2000), unpublished MS (via Bill Smith)
11. Rhodes James, R. (1981), 14–17
12. Graves-Morris, Lieutenant-Colonel P.H., unpublished MS (via Bill Smith and Corinne Simons)
13. Dobney, Major R.P.J. 'Paddy' (1981), unpublished MS (via Bill Smith and Corinne Simons)
14. Rhodes James, R. (1981), 31
15. Thompson, Sir Robert (1989), *Make for the Hills*, 40
16. Ibid, 43
17. Ibid, 47
18. Ibid, 42
19. Larson, G. A. (2008), *Aerial Assault into Burma*, 41
20. Ibid, 44
21. Ibid, 39–40
22. Ibid, 48–49
23. Ibid, 50–53
24. Ibid, 54–57
25. Ibid, 96–97
26. Ibid, 108
27. Ibid, 120–121
28. Slim, Field Marshal Viscount (1999), *Defeat into Victory*, 217–218
29. Rhodes James, R. (1981), 34
30. Ibid, 48
31. Larson, G. A. (2008), 98
32. Ibid, 97
33. Fowler, W. (2009), *We Gave Our Today: Burma 1941–1945*, 250
34. Rhodes James, R. (1981), 10
35. Ibid, 24–25
36. Ibid, 26–27

9

THE TOUGHEST MARCH

'After we took a supply drop our packs were full and our backs were bent almost double under the weight. Slowly, over the next eight or so days to the next supply drop, we straightened up as we ate the weight off.'

Flight Lieutenant John Knowles, RAF Officer, 22 Column, 2nd Queen's

ORDE WINGATE'S second expedition, Operation *Thursday*, began on Saturday 5 February 1944, when Brigadier Bernard Fergusson's 16 Brigade, code-named 'Enterprise', began its long penetration march into North Burma.[1] It would take a full month for all Brigade Battalions to cross the Chindwin. Fergusson would then, in effect, lose part of his force, due to the agreement between Wingate and General Stilwell that exchanged a two-Column attack on the town of Lonkin for entry into Burma from the Ledo Road. Fergusson was not consulted. Taking Lonkin, in the Kachin Hills 20 miles west of Kamaing, should have been the responsibility of Stilwell's slow-moving Chinese. The detachment of two Columns would contribute to 16 Brigade's eventual failure to take Indaw.

These must have seemed distant concerns as several thousand men and the mules began their strange, symbiotic existence under the forest canopy. Ted Meese had no past experience with animals but was now a Muleteer with the 2nd Leicesters' 17 Column. The new Muleteers had collected their animals and moved from camp to camp in India, learning the many aspects of animal care. Meese felt sorry for one man who never had a chance to rest – he was a qualified farrier. They travelled in covered rail wagons, five animals to each side and a bed of hay running down the middle:

'During the night a Muleteer would stay in each carriage, watching over the animals. You started off sleeping on a generous pile of hay but by morning, after 10 animals had feasted on your mattress, you found yourself on the floorboards.'

Whenever a stop was reached the animals were always impatient to be led into the sunlight. They often came close to stampeding:

'You just couldn't hold them. There were ponies and mules everywhere, with men scattered around, ducking to avoid the high kicks from strong hind legs that were being fully stretched at last.'

Christmas 1943 found them at Shargarha Camp and the Muleteers celebrated with mule racing and mule wrestling (two Muleteers would mount up and attempt to wrestle their opponent to the ground). Ted Meese:

'Most mules and ponies had been sourced in Afghanistan, were new to Army life and were only partially "broken in". The men who handed them over were the roughest looking bunch of brigands I had ever seen. I was concerned that my jungle career might end before it began. If they didn't finish me off, breaking in a wild mule might.

'Each mule had a unique personality. It was not a good idea to get on the back of my mule, affectionately known as Buck, or to hang on to his tail. That was asking to be kicked. In fact, hanging on to a mule's tail was strictly forbidden, as was loading any part of your own pack or equipment on to the animal. You'd be in trouble if caught doing that. Buck would readily accept any load on his back but would never allow a human to climb on board for more than a couple of seconds. Some men tried to ride Buck and all failed.'

Meese was never kicked during training. He developed real affection for Buck and for other mules, including

Muleteer: Ted Meese, with the 2nd Leicesters' 17 Column, came to appreciate that each mule had a unique personality. (Ted Meese)

Last Chance, Peggy, Chico and Harry the Devil. Yet he had found the training hard going:

'I didn't get on with the heat and humidity and those hills are more like mountains. When we started out Buck was carrying dinghies for our river crossings. Later, he carried explosives and detonators. The mules required very little veterinary attention. Saddle sores were the most common problem. Captain Leyland was in charge of our mules and he would ride along the Column from time to time, taking a look at each animal. Our mules always came first. When we got into night bivvy, they were always fed and watered – if that was possible – before we had our meal. If there was no corn we cut young bamboo for them.'

Fergusson's Brigade's concentrated at Tagap Ga, on the Ledo Road in the Brahmaputra Valley. Ledo's main attraction as a jumping off point was that it minimised the likelihood of early confrontations with the Japanese during a southerly march of over 300 miles to the operational area around Indaw. The first leg of the march involved crossing the Patkai range of the

Naga Hills, to reach the small outpost of Hkalak Ga. The Patkai Hills were to be crossed by the lowest available pass. The Queen's Columns, 21 and 22, took the lead, cutting through dense jungle and revetting the worst slopes. Some steep, muddy gradients forced the men onto their hands and knees, in torrential rain. It took the Columns to the rear up to nine days to cover the 35 miles to Hkalak Ga.

The order of march (and, much later, the order of battle at Indaw) was not pre-planned. It resulted from the order in which the Battalions reached the railhead for the move forward, on completing their final exercises. The Queen's happened to be the first to reach Tagap Ga. They were ready to set out up the first hill on 5 February. Brigadier Fergusson was not encouraged at the end of the first day:

Of the two Columns, something over half the mules had reached the top of the first hill, barely a mile from the road; most of their loads were still at the bottom of the hill, or at various points on the way up. All except the first few loads had had to be man-handled. The elaborate steps and traverses were in ruins and the whole hill was one unsavoury chute.[2]

There were some 350 miles to go. The Queen's Columns tackled the steep climbs by sending the mules up light and manhandling their loads. A Leicesters Column – the third on the track – tried another idea. They stationed Muleteers at points up the slope, to catch and rest mules which were allowed to go up free but laden. This method worked well and became standard throughout the Brigade.[3]

21 Column took the lead from the jumping off point, starting out on the track known to the Americans as the 'Salt Spring Trail'. Fergusson picked this track after extensive air reconnaissance. This Column included Acting Sergeant Tony Howard and his small group of Signallers. They had the dubious honour of being the first Royal Signals Detachment to enter Japanese-occupied Burma for Operation *Thursday*. 21 Column began the initial 3,000 ft climb, the first of countless struggles up and down steep, mud-clogged slopes. This first ascent took the entire day. Tony Howard: 'Many men lost their footing in the deep mud. Heavy loads, including wireless equipment, had to be offloaded and manhauled to the top.'

Given the significance of the wireless equipment, mules carrying such loads were carefully selected. One of Howard's Signallers, George Hill, wrote:

It was always necessary to use what one hoped was a relatively docile mule for carrying the 12 volt battery, known as a 'dag', and the battery-charging engine. While they were of roughly equal weight, they were certainly not of equal bulk. The battery was neat, small and rectangular, while the chore-horse was bulky and ungainly, creating the possibility of load-slip, anathema to any mule!

Load-slip was a persistent problem when negotiating very steep slopes. Hill noticed how the capacities of man and mule became better understood as time went by: 'A principle began to be accepted that where a man could negotiate a slope without the use of his hands, then a mule could also manage it without being offloaded.'

Hill was meticulous. Every evening he took out his orange silk 'panic map' of North Burma and pencilled in the Column's route and dates of reaching key locations. These were still legible over 60 years later, complete with sweat-ingrained dirt on the outside and a neat line of bloodstains inside: 'These resulted from the activities of a most impertinent leech, which had penetrated to that area of my anatomy covered by my back trouser pocket, which was where I always kept the map.'

Gordon Hughes, a young Queen's officer, received an object lesson in what the Burmese jungle can do, virtually overnight, to a fit man:

One morning I was surprised when Private Pritchard reported sick. He was no malingerer and I must confess that he looked terrible. His skin had quite a death-like pallor. He opened his shirt and said, dryly, 'I think I've been bitten, Sir'. His body was one mass of leech bites. He must have rested in a bed of these blood-sucking creatures and, while he slept, they'd had a leeches' banquet. The effect on Pritchard's physique was severe. He had lost all his strength and his mind was confused. I talked to the Doctor, who said there was little to be done except to put his pack and weapon on a mule and relieve him of all duties. Other than this he had to march like the rest of us. It took, I suppose, the best part of two weeks for Pritchard to replace his depleted blood system, but recover he did and was none the worse for it.

Flight Lieutenant John Knowles, 22 Column's RAF Officer, saw similar cases. He led a small section – an RAF Signals Sergeant, a Corporal and several ORs – responsible for the RAF wireless. Knowles had little jungle training prior to going in. His experience consisted of just one two-day exercise with 23 Brigade:

'I was moved to 16 Brigade to replace an officer who could no longer cope with the training, due to a wound received in the Middle East. Trained only on booze and
cigarettes, I worked my way into the rigours of the march. I found that even the best of jungle-trained men, in top physical condition, can lose their edge. One athletic man with very short hair – we called him "Curly" – folded up quickly and had to be flown out. The "booze and cigarettes" men did much better, rapidly working their way into shape.*

'After we took a supply drop our packs were full and our backs were bent almost double under the weight. Slowly, over the next eight or so days to the next supply drop, we straightened up as we ate the weight off. The real problem was the extra weight beyond the 70 pound pack. When you add in extra rations, rifle, pistol, grenades, water bottle, water-filled chagul and all the rest, the total weight could exceed 100 pounds. My shoulders took the strain but the skin where the webbing cut became totally insensitive and still is. I think the nerve endings just gave up. The experience did give me a very strong back, which I also still have.'

Corporal Jack Goldfinch, with 21 Column, marched drenched in sweat and thought longingly of the motor transport that had taken them to Tagap Ga. Lieutenant-Colonel John Metcalf, leading the Column, took a couple of Platoons ahead to explore the way to Hkalak Ga. He found the going appalling. It included an ascent of Saya Bum, a large mountainous feature. The map showed the track skirting Saya Bum but Metcalf found this to be incorrect. On the challenge of a direct climb, John Metcalf's message to his Brigadier was terse: 'No choice.' Bernard Fergusson:

This march was the heaviest imaginable. The rain was torrential and almost continuous, the gradients were often one in two, no single stretch of level going a hundred yards in length existed between Tagap and Hkalak and few thereafter. Many mule loads had to be carried by hand up steep slopes and the path had to be remade, or the traverses rebuilt, two to three times during the passage of a Column.

The cold was intense, particularly at bivouacs over five thousand feet. The 70 pounds which men were carrying was greatly increased in weight due to saturation with water. A dry bivouac was practically unknown.[3]

The much-bitten Private Pritchard might well have disagreed with Fergusson's added comment: 'Leeches, which were innumerable, were the least trying of the conditions ... wireless communication was difficult and the supply dropping on the whole atrocious, up to forty and fifty per cent of the supplies dropped falling hundreds or thousands of feet down the cliffs and becoming a dead loss.'[3] This depressing start did not brighten when free-dropped bales of hay killed two very unlucky Chindits during an early supply drop.

Despite (or, perhaps, because of) their pioneering position, 21 Column covered the 35 miles to Hkalak Ga in a week, arriving on 11 February. They rested, waiting for the other Columns to catch up. Tony Howard found enough energy to go exploring while at Hkalak Ga:

'I climbed down the track from the bivouac for half a mile or so, surrounded by jungle and, eventually, very tall elephant grass. I was quite unconcerned, having already settled into jungle life. Yet we did have some uncomfortable moments. Once we had a load slip on a mule. We pulled over to one side and the Column had gone by the time we had sorted it out. We had no map or rendezvous point and no-one came back to see where we had got to. We worked hard to catch up. Something similar happened on another occasion, on the march to Saugor railhead. It took until the lunch bivouac the next day before we caught up with the Column. It was a worrying night (and that is an understatement).'

45 Recce's 45 and 54 Columns drew the short straw. At the rear of the huge Brigade Snake, they endured countless amplified stops and starts, struggling through deep mud churned up by the thousands of heavily laden men and hundreds of animals ahead. Even worse, they had little time to rest when they finally struggled into Hkalak Ga. 45 Recce had been unlucky from the first. Lieutenant (later, Major) Cyril Baldock, Animal Transport Officer with 54 Column, recalled the awful march through thick mud for 70 miles along the Ledo Road, while others were trucked up by the Americans.

On Friday, 28 January 1944, the men of 45 Column had boarded a train at Teharka station, 25 miles east of Jhansi, to begin their journey to Tagap Ga.[4] Security was tight in 16 Brigade's concentration area. Arriving trains entered 'Jungle Siding', on a spur line, and these units were brought up by truck under the cover of darkness. Even so, according to Bernard Fergusson, Japanese-controlled Radio Saigon broadcast a personal message to him twice in one day: 'Monocled Fergusson! We knew all about you and your Australians at Ledo. You got out last time, but you won't get out this. We will bomb you day and night.' The Brigadier assumed this was a bad joke, until several men, including an officer and NCOs, said they had heard it. Presumably, the reference to 'Australians' was prompted by the Chindits' bush hats.[5]

Trooper N.P. Aylen noted down his impressions of Wingate when he gave a farewell address to 45 Recce on 5 February: 'Piercing, observant eyes, unfriendly look, no puttees, three days' growth on chin, red band round cap, about 5 ft. 9 in. General impression: tough, determined and ruthless.'[6]

45 Recce set out from Tagap Ga on 12 February. Bringing up the rear, they found the Salt Spring Trail reduced to a steep mudslide. The steps and traverses constructed by the Columns ahead had been destroyed in their passing. While waiting for the forward elements to improve the track, Wireless Operator Philip Sharpe watched those close to him experiment with a novel way to quickly light a fire. A small tin can was half filled with sand, and petrol added from the chore-horse supply. Two wires, running from batteries still on the mule's back, were touched to create a spark: 'In seconds we were heating our water...'[7]

Walkie-Talkies were issued, to tighten up the Column Snake on the march. They were carried by 45 Column's Point Platoon and by other Sections back along the Snake. Philip Sharpe described the SCR 536 Walkie-Talkie as bulky – its popularity waned long before they reached the Chindwin.[8]

Many officers had concerns about what Sharpe referred to as Wingate's 'violent and archaic' code of discipline:

A man found sleeping on guard or stealing rations, either from his comrades or during a supply drop, would be given a severe flogging in front of his Platoon. Should he transgress again he would be given a rifle and five rounds of ammunition and banished from the Column, to fend for himself. Furthermore, all officers had been briefed that in the event of the slightest sign of mutiny or cowardice among the men, the offenders would be shot without exception or hesitation.[9]

The Brigade resumed its advance on 17 February. The Leicesters took the lead at Hkalak for the second stage, the descent into the Hukawng Valley and the march to the Chindwin. As the Queen's continued, Tony Howard and his comrades in 21 Column spent little time thinking about the Japanese. They concentrated on keeping up:

'I remember reaching the top of an escarpment at Gum Ga and looking across the vast expanse of jungle below. In the distance the sun glinted on the Chindwin. It would be another fortnight before we reached the river.'

The men rested at the top of this escarpment for a couple of days. Signaller George Hill needed this break. One morning he had found it difficult to walk and the reason soon became apparent: 'At least half a dozen ticks were firmly embedded under the surface of one heel.' Fortunately, his foot improved rapidly with rest.

Sitting in the night bivouac, 22 Column Platoon Commander Gordon Hughes took a dirty signal pad and pencil and wrote a short note to his future wife, Trudy, proposing marriage. Rather surprisingly, this message was delivered.

Corporal Ted Treadwell was marching with 71, one of the 2nd Leicesters' Columns leading 16 Brigade. He recalled the grim struggle to keep moving: 'Everyone became completely knackered. I could never understand why we had to march in. Some men became so exhausted that they grasped the mules' tails, to help keep their legs moving.' A number of mules were lost. Ted Treadwell: 'One just disappeared in a bog and another fell over a steep hillside.' Lou Lake was a Wireless Operator with sister Column 17:

'We had to revet steep slopes to get our mules to the top. I remember one mule losing its balance and plunging back down. Somehow, my feet stayed in good condition. The going was hard but we settled into a routine. The Signals Group consisted of myself, Walter 'Wally' Nichols, a curly haired carpenter from Hitchin, and Eric Cook, from the North of England. Eric was an electrician by trade and that came in handy later.'

Corporal Tom Turvey, out ahead with 71 Column's Recce Platoon, noticed how life became more informal as they advanced some distance from the main body. Recce Platoon Commander Percy Lake developed his reputation as a voracious smoker of other people's cigarettes. Tom Turvey:

'I got used to his constant cadging of fags from our K-ration packs. We had five cigarettes in each pack – 15 a day. We ignored rank at the Platoon level when in Burma. Percy would come along at every rest and say: "Got any fags?" I used to tell him to piss off but he'd always come back and try again. If you handed him a fag, he'd smoke it immediately.

'The forest was now so dense that it was sometimes difficult to cover more than four or five miles a day. I accepted the situation. We had enough K-rations to allow us to survive as our stomachs shrunk. I noticed how I now felt full after just a few mouthfuls. It was all a strain and most of us were bloody terrified most of the time.'

A careful watch ensured the men took their Mepacrine. Their bodies then took on the yellowish hue induced by the malaria suppressant. Medical Officers worked hard to dismiss claims that Mepacrine's side effects included impotence or sterility. John Simon was No. 1 on a Bren with 16 Brigade's HQ Column:

'The Bren was a fine weapon. It was a two-man job – one to fire and one to change mags – but you could carry it and fire from the hip. Its weakness was a magazine holding just 28 rounds. When running to attack a position, 28 rounds doesn't go far! You have to stop to change mags. The Bren was very reliable, provided it was kept clean. We put a canvas cover, fastened with poppers, over the barrel when in damp jungle and not expecting opposition.'

During the hard march to the Chindwin, the men made do with K-rations but welcomed the occasional drops of bread and bully. John Simon:

'I don't remember being very hungry at this stage. It was a case of 'keep going'. My mucker was Les Martindale, a butcher from Liverpool. He was amusing company – very witty and a natural mimic. Things worked out very well between us. He did all the cooking and I made up the beds. We weren't fussy. We were bone weary by the end of the day and always ready to get our heads down.'

The extreme physical effort on the march drained energy and left men permanently soaked in sweat, white lines of salt appearing on their clothes and webbing. Their sense of taste changed as salt leached out of their bodies. Baty (*Surgeon in the Jungle War*) observed: 'When the body is lacking salt, a drink of tea laced with several spoonfuls of salt, instead of sugar, does not even have a salty taste.'[10]

The order of march was five Columns ahead of Brigade HQ and three behind, with 45 Recce still at the rear. Fergusson acknowledged their sufferings:

To be tail Column of a long line of Columns is misery and to be in that position for a period of two months an abominable cruelty, which I should have avoided inflicting could I possibly have done so. But to pass Columns ahead of each other was impossible without loss of time and time was all-important.[11]

45 Column fell behind. Due to the appalling state of the track they were only 12 miles from the start point on the morning of the fifth day. Their first supply drop had been deferred. When it eventually took place many loads floated out of reach and the men received just two days' rations, rather than five. Wireless Operator Philip Sharpe consoled himself with a biscuit porridge, flavoured with K-ration bouillon. This soup was extremely salty on its own, tasting rather like Marmite, but they were grateful: 'Our hunger had been acute and this broth tasted absolutely delicious.'[12]

One parachute failed to open and the broken container's contents were welcomed by a nearby Platoon. This was noticed and resulted in an NCO being reduced to the ranks and all were deducted one day's ration later on.[12]

Trooper Aylen, with No. 1 Section of 45 Column's Recce Troop, had a happier recollection of that first air drop: 'we received Delhi Light Rations and in the evening we had a feast of bully stew, bread (now a luxury), tinned fruit, jam, etc'. The Recce Troop would be less fortunate in the days and weeks ahead. Operating well ahead of the main body, they could not afford the extra weight of 'luxury' rations. They also often reduced the usual three-hour midday halt to one hour.[6]

It took 45 Column fully nine days to cover the 35 miles to Hkalak Ga, where the men were rewarded with more rations, including bully and tinned tomatoes.[13]

———— •◦• ————

According to Bernard Fergusson, Wingate failed to pass on the news that no force would be available to fly into Indaw, if taken: 'This modification in the plan was not made known to General Wingate's Brigade Commanders. Perhaps he thought it would discourage us; perhaps he hoped to create such a favourable situation that the original plan would be switched on again.'[14]

The next leg of the march-in was from Hkalak Ga to Lulum Nok. The country beyond Lulum was little known; Fergusson's maps showed large white areas with the discouraging annotation 'unsurveyed'.[15] There was almost no interaction between the men as they marched deeper into the Burmese wilderness. Acting Sergeant Signaller Tony Howard, with the Queen's 21 Column:

'I never learnt much about the others and their personal lives. There wasn't much in the way of chat, as we marched in single file, with noise down to a minimum. We were too busy and tired to talk much in bivouac.'

Forward vision was almost always very limited. Signaller George Hill didn't think much of his view: 'My far horizon, normally, was the back end, legs, feet and swishing tail of the mule I spent my whole life, or so it seemed, dragging myself along behind'. The mood switched from appreciation of K-rations to one of tolerance. Tony Howard found the lunch meal the least appetising, with its lemonade powder, dextrose and cheese (usually an unattractive mix of processed cheese and chopped ham). This was not improved by the fact that most lunch meals were eaten cold. Everyone welcomed the occasional drop of bully:

'The bully beef was cooked in its tin. All you had to do was use your bayonet to make holes in the tin's sides, top and bottom, then put it in the hot ashes of your fire. All the fat would run out and burn, so helping the cooking. When done and taken out of its tin, it looked like a nice chunk of roast beef. This was probably the best meal we could have and it went down well with rice, if we were lucky enough to have some.'

It rained heavily most of the time and the men were soaked for long periods. Howard recalled being told at school that this area of North Burma has the heaviest rainfall in the world:

'We didn't bother too much about hygiene. In fact I can only remember washing once and that was when we reached "Aberdeen". At the same time, I recall one man being taken under escort to a chaung, having been ordered to wash. He smelt so badly that the people marching immediately behind him complained.'

Those who had not been hardened by lengthy jungle training suffered in silence. Signaller George Hill: 'Putting one's pack on after any halt was always absolute agony. Some of the men tried to ease this by padding the straps with shock-absorbing packaging from air-dropped supplies'. Hill became accustomed to Chindit deportment:

Our usual method of proceeding was with head down and shoulders hunched forward – which earned for itself the soubriquet 'The Chindit Stoop'. One's posture was even more forward sloping when climbing. We might have been likened to snails, in that we also carried our 'homes' on our backs. During a short halt we usually kept our packs on and propped them up with our rifles, to take the weight off our backs for 10 minutes.

The Rifle Platoon leading the Column rotated on a daily basis at the exposed point position. Howard and Hill had quickly picked up the fundamentals of jungle living – splitting bamboo before using it for fuel (so avoiding it going off like a rifle shot) and making no other unnecessary noise. The punishment for indiscretion by a smoker (coughing or litter) was the denial of cigarettes. Smoking was confined to lunch and evening bivouacs. Memories of K-ration cigarettes differ. Some recall packets of five; others say their cigarette rations came in fours. George Hill remembered packets of three American cigarettes, the main brands being Philip Morris, Chesterfield and Lucky Strike. The author's father, Jack Redding, shared the almost universal hatred

A view all too familiar to every Chindit: a mule's rear. (Bill Smith)

Column Wireless Operator Philip Sharpe described his feelings after walking that river bed for three miles:

> Making headway in these conditions was very demanding ... The bed of the stream was solid enough, but stones and small boulders below the surface caused problems and several early baths. The alternative of ploughing through the sand of the banks was even worse. Our boots sank into the dry loose grains and filled with grit. We were glad when this initial ordeal was over and the track took us uphill, away from the valley.[16]

They arrived at Lulum Ga during the evening of 25 February.

The Leicesters – leading 16 Brigade – reached the Chindwin on 29 February, having covered around 110 miles. Their reward was a signal from Wingate: 'Well done, Leicesters. Hannibal eclipsed!' They now faced a river several hundred yards wide (with the jungle-to-jungle distance double that). Rules for successful river crossings included the examination of the proposed location by a Recce Platoon. Several factors might spoil an otherwise attractive crossing point, including the close presence of the enemy, nearby villages with potential informers, poor cover on either side, high banks and strong currents. An opposed crossing should never be attempted.

Bernard Fergusson stood on the Chindwin's bank on 29 February and took stock. He was five miles downstream from the intended crossing place, at Ninghkau Ga, and five miles closer to a Japanese garrison at Singkaling Hkamti. They could not spare the two days required to reposition. Fergusson didn't hesitate:

> As a crossing place, the spot where we were seemed nearly perfect. There was ample cover on both sides of the river. The bank on which we were was high, but there were plenty of places where mules could get down. At the foot of the bank was a broad beach and, on the opposite side, shingle jutted out at least 600 yards. The actual width to be crossed cannot have exceeded 300 yards and the current was no more than a knot – far less than at my crossing places of the previous year, 100 miles to the south.[17]

The Brigade Commander took precautions. He sent a party to block the track the Japanese would have to use if they were to oppose the crossing. In addition, a diversion was organised along the river, to distract the Japanese.[17] The night before the crossing, 21 Column came up and bivouacked some distance away from the

of British issue 'V' cigarettes – smoked only when there was nothing else.

Before the early morning start all rubbish had to be buried, including the animal droppings. Men did their business cat-like, scraping a hole in the ground, then burying it. There would be a short girth-tightening stop after about 30 minutes, followed later by the breakfast halt. Special precautions were taken when crossing a track, road or railway. Tony Howard:

'It took 15–20 minutes for the Column to pass a single point. When we approached a crossing point, we stopped about 50–100 yards away and formed up parallel to it. On a signal we then turned and faced the track, etc, and groups of 4–6 men plus one mule crossed in around 20 seconds, with very little disturbance to the jungle or the track. The last man in each group made sure there were no mule droppings or other signs visible.'

The 45 Recce Columns were the last to leave Hkalak Ga for the Chindwin. They set out on 22 February. On one stretch, the map carried the note 'Path follows bed'. 45

Getting across: two men swim a chaung, pushing before them a 'sausage' of kit and weapons. (Trustees of the Imperial War Museum)

others; no fires were allowed. Sister Column 22 was nearby. It was 25 days since the first elements had left Ledo.

The Leicesters decided to have a go almost immediately. Corporal Ted Treadwell of 71 Column saw the best swimmers set off with a rope:

'Mules had to be accompanied when swimming, to hold their heads up. If they went under, they never came up. The Chindwin is a huge river and I was a bit dubious about it, but at least I could swim. When some men began to cross, they encouraged the others to try.'

Wingate arranged for the Dakotas of 117 Squadron, RAF, to deliver boats and outboard motors for 16 Brigade.[18] Forward elements on the river sent the codeword 'Trip', to bring in gliders and boats but no aircraft arrived. Fergusson fumed as most of his men took advantage of the rare opportunity to rest and bathe. Suddenly, the Dakotas and gliders appeared an hour before dusk. The gliders landed on the shingle bank and assault boats

were in operation within minutes. The Leicesters continued their crossing in boats.[17]

Gordon Hughes, Platoon Commander with the Queen's 22 Column, saw the boats in use but found no space for his men. They crossed by swimming, towing and pushing groundsheet 'sausages' holding packs, equipment and weapons: 'My Batman was no swimmer and I towed both him and the sausage across. Needless to say, the current took us well downstream.'

They rested on the sand near two gliders. The pilots were inside, waiting for a 'snatch':

The first aircraft came in very low, with a large, rigid steel hook protruding from the fuselage, and with one pass over the gliders was able to hook the loop and snatch a glider into the air. The second was not so lucky, having to make many passes before it was able to complete the recovery.[19]

The crossing continued throughout the night. One of the Queen's Columns, 21, was exceptionally well trained in river crossings. It set the record – all 400 men and 60 animals were across the Chindwin in just two hours and 10 minutes.[17] They moved on almost immediately, continuing in a southerly direction and finding it increasingly difficult to locate water. Those with any lingering desire to wash soon realised that water was far too precious for such a frivolous activity.

Bernard Fergusson's big worry was the fact that he was late: 'My original orders from Wingate had been to arrive in the Banmauk-Indaw area about 5 March. In a few hours it would be March 1 and I had well over 200 miles to go...'[17] In North Burma, of course, there is a significant difference between 'map miles' and 'track miles' – the latter exceeding the former by 20 per cent or more.

The condition of the men played on Fergusson's mind. They were not as fit as they should have been, given that they had been in for just over three weeks. Later, he complained that his men had been under-rationed during training. No K-rations were available and normal rations were too heavy for hard marching. The obvious solution was a 'feed-up' between exercises but extra rations were not made available. Two specific requests for more rations, based on medical assessments, were rejected. Fergusson remonstrated and was then blamed for 'underdrawing' entitlement. He protested and the sole concession, at that point, was an insulting issue of two ounces of cocoa and some extra milk per man. Fergusson concluded:

We could have been 20 to 30 per cent fitter for our task had our representations been accepted and honoured ... You sometimes hear it suggested that troops should practise living and working on short commons. This is a fallacy and troops who are likely to have to go short of food must not be stinted during their training period.[20]

Brigadier-General Frank Merrill, leading his three American Battalions of Chindit-trained infantry, also became aware of how quickly the North Burmese jungle could undermine fit, strong men. During February his force, 'Galahad', also entered Burma. They were to suffer grievously from hunger, disease and battle casualties – worked without pity by the ruthless Stilwell.

Wingate flew in when 16 Brigade reached the Chindwin. When across, Fergusson entertained Wingate with a dip:

Then, by bad luck, we met one of the opium-growers on the beach, selling turtles' eggs. Wingate bought the lot, amounting to 20 or 30, and distributed them to men whom he met on the beach, standing over them while he made them eat the horrible, jelly-like substance raw, declaiming that it was good for one.[17]

During this visit, Wingate gave Fergusson his paper on Strongholds, with instructions to study the contents and then destroy it. This paper stated that a Stronghold should have a secure water supply and be dug, ditched, wired, mined and strongly defended. It must cover (if it could not safely include) a Dakota strip from which fighters could also operate.[21]

Fergusson warned Wingate that his best date for arriving in the Banmauk-Indaw area was now around 20 March.[17] Before 21 Column left the river, Signaller George Hill had watched the two men strolling along the Chindwin's beach. They looked incongruous. Fergusson wore nothing except a towel round his middle and his monocle. Orde Wingate kept his trademark sun helmet on his head.

45 Recce's Columns continued to bring up the rear. 45 Column reached the Chindwin at 16.00 on Saturday 4 March. It had taken them 21 days to cover some of the wildest, toughest country in the world.[22] 16 Brigade's crossing of the Upper Chindwin was completed the next day and the Columns continued south.[23] Taken overall, the crossing was successful. 45 Column Wireless Operator Philip Sharpe had been relieved to find that boats were available for them. He had gazed in amazement as repeated crossings were made by assault boats equipped with outboards. He had been watching elements of 51 and 69 Columns (51/69 Field Regiments, RA) cross the river as his Column prepared to follow

them.[24] Many others had shared Sharpe's relief. Lou Lake, a Wireless Operator with the 2nd Leicesters' 17 Column, had been among the first to look out across the Chindwin:

'The crossing looked very nasty. We rolled our kit into groundsheet "sausages", in readiness for a long swim. Suddenly, everything changed. I saw the gliders land on a sandbank. They were carrying boats. I crossed the Chindwin in comfort, on an inflatable. The mules didn't think much of the river – they were snorting, blowing and otherwise complaining. My mule, Betsy, was very unhappy but swam across safely. Betsy was very important. She carried our heavy Type 22 wireless. We then watched the empty gliders snatched off the sandbanks by Dakotas. That was an amazing sight.'

Cyril Baldock, 54 Column's ATO, felt pleased with his mules: 'The animals did well. Most mules can swim and most swam the Chindwin.' Muleteer Ted Meese, with 17 Column, recalled that most animals were compliant during the crossing, but there were exceptions:

'One pony caused a fuss when it attempted to board one of the small boats and sank it. Unfortunately, this boat contained non-swimmers. Some learnt to swim very quickly and most made it back to the bank and were ferried across on another boat.'

As the Columns moved on, the men felt a new sense of commitment, with the Chindwin behind them. There was no escape, however, from the constant nervous strain. Column Commander Charles Carfrae described these emotions:

No Chindit soldier could at any time consider himself secure from enemy ambush or night attack ... nor could he hope for periods of rest and recuperation ... It became a joke that one might meet Japanese round the next corner, but it was literal truth and when one corner had been negotiated, another appeared just ahead ... stress manifested itself as a constant, nagging sense of unease, varying in degree, for which neither palliative nor cure could be offered.[25]

Men became accustomed to jungle noises. Trooper Aylen of 45 Recce:

We became familiar with different bird calls. One, a woodpecker, made a noise resembling that of a distant machine gun. Another had a high-pitched 'peep', like that of a wireless set transmitting morse.

Other birds had calls which seemed to fit into certain phrases. One seemed to be continually calling 'Sergeant-Major! Sergeant-Major!'[6]

The pace was relentless and the going tough in the extreme. Bernard Fergusson:

> So it went on, day after day. It was no unusual thing for a Column to sleep in two halves, with one of those major hills dividing the two. Supper was often a dry meal, with no water within reach, save that which we caught in our mugs or groundsheets from the rain. A dry bivouac was unknown and all bivouacs over 5,000 ft were bitterly cold. There was an unpleasant plague also in the shape of the Polaung Fly: a tiny creature, no bigger than a sandfly, with a particularly vicious bite which drew blood and hardened, with those most allergic to it, into a septic spot as tough as a wart.[3]

As they trekked in single file, each man had his own thoughts for company. Flight Lieutenant John Knowles, the RAF Officer with the Queen's 22 Column, was plagued by a song that buzzed inside his head. It was a popular recording by Webster Booth:

> 'All the way this goddam song filled my head – "I'll walk beside you." It nearly drove me nuts. This was an actual auditory hallucination, heard as clearly as any other sound. I couldn't turn it off. Years later, Bernard Fergusson told me that his hallucination was visual. He actually saw trees festooned with Christmas lights.'

Perhaps some 45 Recce Chindits, missing their vehicles, also had that song in their heads as they staggered on under the crushing load of pack and weapons. On 1 October 1942, 'I'll walk beside you' had been the first record played on a request programme for 45 Recce on board the troopship *Dominion Monarch*. John Knowles travelled on this ship the following January.

Tony Howard, with 21 Column's Signallers, had reached the conclusion that mules were extremely intelligent:

> 'Our lead mule was "Taxi" – an ex-Artillery mule built like a cart-horse. Yet this huge animal allowed his rather dour Muleteer, Paddy Myers, to lift a back leg to inspect a hoof. Taxi carried the Type 22 wireless and battery.'

Taxi was peculiar, in that he had an obvious and anarchic sense of humour:

> 'When loading or unloading, Taxi would occasionally lean towards the man standing at one side. Someone else would go on that side and push. Taxi would respond by leaning more. We would get to the point where three of us were holding him up. Taxi would then make a noise that sounded a lot like laughter!'

The Signals Detachment's other three mules included Nellie, with Frank Archer as Muleteer. Nellie carried the chore-horse and petrol. There was also Chota, partnered by Muleteer Dowsett. Chota was small and could carry very little. Dextrose was led by cheerful Muleteer Frank Holmes. This mule carried the spare batteries. Tony Howard:

> 'The mules were great judges of distance. If they thought two trees were not far enough apart for them to get through with their loads, nothing would make them attempt it. Our saddest moments included occasions when a mule was hurt and had to be killed, sometimes in circumstances where a shot could not be fired. Then the throat had to be cut. Its meat would then be shared out between the Column.'

Howard's Detachment often found it difficult to make contact with Rear HQ, due to the terrain and poor atmospheric conditions. 21 Column's transmissions were received by operators at Imphal (and, later, at Sylhet, when the Japanese offensive necessitated a move). There was little direct Column-to-Column contact, especially in the deep valleys. Messages for other Columns were transmitted to the rear and then forwarded on. Howard, in common with all Operators, had his own morse key:

> 'These were guarded like gold dust. Each Operator adjusted the key to his own particular likes. I used a rather large RAF key. The key itself was about six inches long. The length of movement made sending a bit slower than with smaller keys but, as conditions were usually so bad, our speed was never above 10 words per minute. Reception was best if the so-called "Collins Aerial" was fixed 20–30 ft up, pointing in the direction of the distant station.'

The aerial was usually rigged by tying one end of the wire to a length of parachute cord, tied in turn to an unfused hand grenade, which was thrown over a branch. When in night bivouac, Mechanic George Baker dug a small hole to accommodate the chore horse. This deadened the noise it made. 21 Column had two call signs, the principal being BBJ. Weak signals and poor reception put a great strain on the ears. The eyes were also strained, as most transmissions were made at night,

The 'Commander's Tree': briefing for officers. (Jim Unsworth)

by dim lamplight. The Signallers used four-digit groups from a 'one-off pad'. Each day, sender and receiver used a fresh page, with the same unique four-number groups identifying the correct word. The Signallers would finish at around midnight, leaving just five hours before another sweat-soaked march.

Signaller George Hill had much to say about sweat: 'It could be felt trickling down almost everywhere and our clothing was usually saturated with it. We could tolerate it dripping off the ends of our noses and our chins, but didn't care much for it running down our foreheads, into our eyes. It made it very difficult to see!' The salt sweat made the eyes sore and painful.

Frequent heavy rain was a major problem. Tony Howard:

'This was some weeks before the Monsoon, yet it rained heavily on most days. Sometimes the downpours were so heavy that it was impossible to open up the wireless equipment. Water was the indirect cause of another problem later on. We couldn't get the chore-horse to start. Then we halted to collect supplies following a drop. George Baker tried to sort out the problem. He found that the petrol dropped to us was contaminated. The fuel had been delivered in two-gallon water cans and this was a mistake. Water and fuel came in the

Up you come! A laden mule struggles on a steep slope during the February 1944 march in of 16 Brigade. (Cyril Baldock)

'It was as hard as a plank and full of bugs. It was terrible but we regarded it as a treat at the time. I noticed that a lot of watercress – or what looked like watercress – grew near some of the streams. We used to pick a lot of that. It was good. I don't remember ever being very thirsty, except when it was my turn at the front of the Column, hacking a way through the undergrowth.'

Platoon Commander Gordon Hughes, with the Queen's 22 Column, had a grim duty to perform two days after leaving the Chindwin. He was ordered to examine a body discovered during a 10-minute halt:

At first, all I saw was a British steel helmet but, on moving the undergrowth back, a complete skeleton of a soldier became visible. He was in a foetal position, with a Thompson sub-machine gun across his legs. We took his identity tags and, later, they were sent to records, together with a map reference. Was he wounded and died of wounds? Did he die of thirst and hunger? Or did he lack the will to live and crawl into the undergrowth to meet his maker? We will never know.[26]

Corporal Treadwell's high level of fitness and robust constitution continued to withstand the rigours of the march. He had avoided jungle sores, dysentery and malaria. He had been hospitalised with malaria while training in Ceylon, but suffered no attacks while with 71 Column as they struggled over the Naga Hills. Nevertheless, there was no escape from leeches and red ants:

'There were plenty of leeches. You'd never feel them, but then you'd look down and see your leg all bloodied up. If you had a cigarette on, you could burn them off. If you tried to pull them off, their heads would stay in. As for red ants, they would fall off the trees, often in hundreds, land on your body and bite. That was very painful.'

It was impossible to keep clean: 'It was terrible. On a 10-day drop you might get some shirts come in and you would get a chance to change. We'd throw the filthy clothing away – it was buried.' When Treadwell finally took off his pack in night bivouac, he always kept his boots on: 'After all, we never knew who might be round the next corner.' Discomfort, in every form, was the daily round: 'I've tried to sleep in four inches of water in a waterlogged bivouac. I was glad enough just to rest for a couple of hours. We rarely had the comfort of a fire.' There was always the possibility of becoming separated from the Column:

same type of can, but water cans had an internal coating of pitch, to prevent them going rusty. The petrol had dissolved the pitch, clogging the engine with tar. Fortunately, one of our officers took a pony, reached another Column and brought back some clean fuel for the charger.'

Fergusson's Chindits lost their inhibitions about food. Some Columns fared better than others. Luck certainly played a part in the reception of supplies. Corporal Ted Treadwell remembered that 71 Column 'didn't suffer too badly'. They had received occasional conventional rations – mostly bully – during the march-in. Later, the K-rations dropped were regarded as a poor substitute. 'Tread' Treadwell retained his love of bully and, over 60 years later, often sat down to a plate of corned beef and chips. In contrast, the author's father, Private Jack Redding of the King's Own, loathed corned beef for the rest of his life. Some drops included bread. Ted Treadwell:

'I never got lost but I was afraid in the jungle. Everyone was afraid. Yet we had some very good officers. They were hand-picked for behind-the-lines jungle fighting and the unsuitable were weeded out. We all had inner doubts, however, about our ability to survive. We'd been warned before going in. Mountbatten told us face to face: "You may never come out of Burma." I remained confident in our officers. I even had a brief talk with Fergusson himself one day. We had a chat and a laugh. He said: "Well done, boy!" He was a great bloke.'

Notes

1. Rooney, D. (2000), *Wingate and the Chindits: Redressing the Balance*, 109
2. Fergusson, B. (1946), *The Wild Green Earth*, 40–41
3. Ibid, 44–49
4. Sharpe, P. (1995), *To Be a Chindit*, 143
5. Fergusson, B. (1946), 30–31
6. Aylen, Trooper N. P., *A British OR in Burma*, Imperial War Museum, 80/49/1
7. Sharpe, P. (1995), 162
8. Ibid, 175
9. Ibid, 176
10. Baty, J.A. (1979), *Surgeon in the Jungle War*, 44
11. Fergusson, B. (1946), 42
12. Sharpe, P. (1995), 177–179
13. Ibid, 181
14. Fergusson, B. (1946), 14–19
15. Ibid, 33
16. Sharpe, P. (1995), 181–185
17. Fergusson, B. (1946), 57–69
18. Rooney, D. (2000), 158
19. Hughes, G., unpublished MS
20. Fergusson, B. (1946), 192–193
21. Ibid, 72–80
22. Sharpe, P. (1995), 190
23. Calvert, M. (1974), *Chindits: Long Range Penetration*, 21
24. Sharpe, P. (1995), 192
25. Carfrae, C. (1985), *Chindit Column*, 136–137
26. Hughes, G., unpublished MS

10

WHEN SUNDAY BECAME THURSDAY

5 March 1944

'Privately, I hoped for a very big earthquake. This seemed the only way such a huge operation could be stopped. I remember everyone smiled too much.'

Major Neville Hogan, 46 Column, 2nd King's Own

BRITISH ENGINEERS prepared two fairweather airfields to fly in and support Wingate's force. Lalaghat and Hailakandi were 12 miles apart and 100 miles from the Burmese border. Lalaghat's graded strip was 6,000 ft long and 300 ft wide. Lalaghat accommodated the C-47s and a fleet of WACO CG-4A assault gliders. 1st Air Commando's P.51 Mustang fighters and B.25 Mitchell bombers were based at Hailakandi. The large pool of light aircraft was divided between the two strips until deployed forward.[1]

Final preparations for the fly-in were under way at Lalaghat during the morning of Sunday 5 March 1944. Most of the first wave gliders were for 77 Brigade. The crowded airfield shimmered in the heat. Alongside the long ranks of aircraft and gliders were thousands of troops, checking weapons and equipment, tending animals, listening to final briefings, loading gliders and struggling to complete other tasks in the final hours before the first wave began to take off at 17.00 hrs. Everyone lent a hand, including the Gunners, who until now had remained somewhat isolated from the rest of Special Force.

There were 83 RAF and USAAF C-47s and 80 gliders ready at Lalaghat. Long, complex patterns were formed by the tow ropes, carefully laid out and ready for hook-up. The first wave had been allocated 26 tug aircraft and 52 gliders.[2]

Some men were struck by the scale of Wingate's enterprise, all achieved through the sheer force of one man's personality. Those waiting to emplane that morning included 3rd/9th Gurkha Rifles' Intelligence Officer Bill Towill:

'It must be remembered that the greatest invasion of all time, Operation Overlord – the D-Day invasion of

Normandy on 6 June – was just three months away. It was miraculous that Wingate got these huge resources turned over to him.'

Advance elements of 111 Brigade would also fly in by glider. While waiting at Lalaghat, Captain Neville Hogan's mind drifted back to the bitter days of 1942 and his desperate struggle to reach safety and carry on the fight after the Japanese overwhelmed his country. That hard-won experience had been recognised. He was made Captain within nine months of joining The Burma Rifles. Hogan now commanded the Burrif Recce Platoon attached to the King's Own's 46 Column. He watched his 2i/c, Johnny Htoo, talking to Platoon members. His small force consisted of three Rifle Sections, two Royal Signallers and two Royal Engineers specialising in demolition. The Platoon strength was completed by Hogan's Orderly and a runner. Hogan went over the briefings that had defined the Recce Platoon's role:

'I was told never to remain with the Column but, rather, to stay at least five hours ahead and occasionally go forward by as much as two days' march. One of our main roles was to seek out water. I was told to try to reach water at least once a day. We also had the job of searching out potential supply drop sites and light plane strips. We were to gather local intelligence, find the enemy and, when possible, gauge their strength. Naturally, we were also to keep a sharp lookout for rice and other food.'

Nothing in Neville Hogan's training and past experience had prepared him for the vast scale of the enterprise unfolding at Lalaghat. He was transfixed:

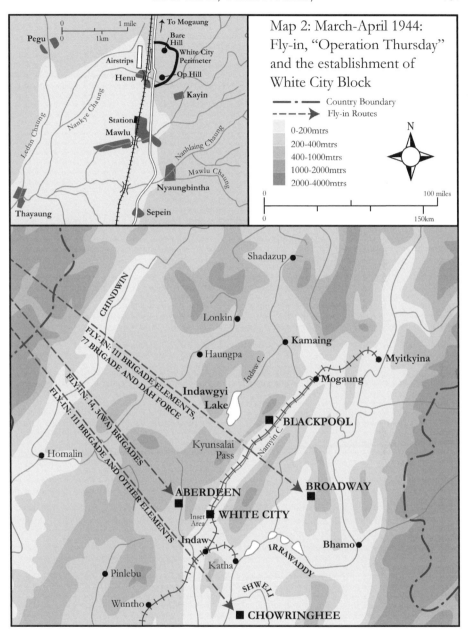

Map 2: March-April 1944: Fly-in, "Operation Thursday" and the establishment of White City Block

Glider line-up: Lalaghat on Sunday 5 March 1944. Ground crews lay out tow-cables, ready for the fly-in to Burma. (Trustees of the Imperial War Museum)

'I had never flown. I had never seen a glider before. I watched the American ground crews laying out more tow ropes. Privately, I hoped for a very big earthquake. This seemed the only way such a huge operation could be stopped. I remember everyone smiled too much. They all wore identical "bravado grins". I know I was saying my prayers.'

Some men drew comfort in a 'big feed'. Lance Corporal Peter Heppell, of 82 Column, 1st King's (Liverpool), helped to ensure that all available rations were consumed:

'We used a two-gallon ghee tin as a cooking pot, filling it with a seven pound tin of bully beef and plenty of vegetables. We had a huge feed. Our Padre then said he was going to hold a brief service. I was never very religious but I liked him and didn't want to let him down. I attended. It was very straightforward – no sentiment.'

The operation had been timed to begin four days before the full moon, so allowing aircraft landing over a number of nights to benefit from moonlight. Among those getting ready that Sunday was the film star Jackie Coogan, now one of Phil Cochran's pilots. The author's father remembered seeing Coogan on the airstrip that afternoon.

Ian Niven, a Regimental Signaller with 20 Column, 1st Lancashire Fusiliers, would fly in the second wave. He had two surprises that day:

'Major Monteith gave me a very responsible job: completing the loading manifest for a Dakota and
its two gliders, including accurate weights for men, animals and weapons. I was then presented to General Wingate as one of the youngest Chindits going in. I thought Wingate looked a bit weird, with his beard and pith helmet, yet we idolised him. He said: "Are you looking forward to it? Are you fit?" I told him I was a footballer. He replied: "Well, you should be fit then ... and you'll need it. Good luck to you!" I vividly remember those brief moments and his pleasant words.'

Some were less impressed. When Wingate arrived at Lalaghat that Sunday his agenda included a pep talk for Cochran's C-47 and glider crews. C-47 Engineer Charles J. Campbell: 'I saw him just that once. I didn't speak to him personally. I got the feeling he was talking down to us. Anyway, I didn't take to him – he was no Cochran with the men.'

111 Brigade's Operations Order had been prepared by the Brigade Major, Jack Masters. Loading tables had been compiled. Kit was weighed, but not the animals. Weights were assumed in three classes: ponies, small mules and large mules.[3]

There was some ill-feeling within 111 Brigade when it heard that most of its elements would not fly in for a couple of days. Wingate and Michael Calvert were very close and there was a view that 111 Brigade always deferred to 77 Brigade – Wingate's original Long Range Penetration force in 1943. One officer later wrote: 'We always had a sort of feeling that we were playing second fiddle to Wingate's old Brigade.'[4]

Men laboured throughout the morning to stow supplies, ammunition, engineering stores, signalling equipment and personal kit in the gliders. Many succumbed to temptation. Ignoring declared weights, they smuggled on extra food and ammunition. Those who stayed busy during those last, tense hours were grateful. Others, their work done, sought diversion. Bill Towill found solace in a book, *Daily Light*, given to him by his mother. It offered passages from the Bible for each morning and evening of the year. He looked up the evening of 5 March and the morning of 6 March and found the readings appropriate and comforting:

> The Lord your God ... went in the way before you, to search you out a place to pitch your tents in ... to show you by what way ye should go ... As an eagle stirreth up her nest, fluttereth over her young, spreadeth abroad her wings, taketh them, beareth them on her wings ... With us is the Lord our God to help us and to fight our battles.[5]

Others grappled with practical problems, including coaxing difficult mules into gliders. Signaller Ian Niven escaped the tension by watching a film; *The Man Who Came to Dinner* starred Bette Davis in one of her few comedy roles. Niven had never flown before; nor had anyone in his immediate company:

'We weren't exactly nervous, just apprehensive. The main feeling was excitement. There was plenty of adrenaline in the air. Things were hectic on the strip. Everyone mucked in, although it all looked a bit haphazard.'

There was nothing haphazard about Michael Calvert's thinking. 77 Brigade's Commander knew exactly where he stood:

> My job was to cut, and keep cut, all the communications of the Japanese Divisions facing Stilwell, in order to help his advance south. My plan was to do this first by establishing a 'Stronghold', which would be our base. My main force of 77 Brigade would advance from that base immediately to establish and maintain a Block across the road and railway between Mawlu and Hopin. A third job was to deny the use of the Irrawaddy to the Japanese. Fourthly, Lieutenant-Colonel Herring, with his Dah Force and the 4th/9th Gurkhas, was to cut the other route to the Japanese in the north — the Bhamo-Myitkyina road.[6]

The moment approaches: Chindits wait to emplane at Lalaghat. This photograph has a note attached by a grandson, dated April 2003: the soldier at the bottom of the ramp, on the left, is William (Bill) McEwan, the King's (Liverpool) Regiment. (Trustees of the Imperial War Museum)

Emplaning the mules: some required a great deal of encouragement. (Trustees of the Imperial War Museum)

1st Air Commando was prepared and briefed to tow up to 40 gliders into Broadway clearing and another 40 into Piccadilly. The first four gliders landing at each clearing were pathfinders, carrying airstrip marker and communications teams. These parties had been warned that they had just 40 minutes to lay out flares to mark the landing zone, with a second cluster directly below the glider release point. After 40 minutes glider pairs would start to land at two to five minute intervals.[7]

During the afternoon, the more observant at Lalaghat noticed that something odd was going on. Wingate, Slim, Cochran and other senior officers were having an increasingly animated discussion. Corporal Fred Holliday felt something was wrong:

'Of the two King's Columns, 81 was due to fly first. Although with 82, I was asked to go in with 81's Commando Platoon, to help make up numbers. We were sitting by our glider, watching Wingate and other high-ranking officers, including our own CO. There seemed to be a lot of comings and goings. Then someone walked over and said take-off was delayed for half an hour. Apparently, a last-minute flight over the two landing sites had shown Piccadilly blocked by tree trunks, although Broadway seemed OK. In no time at all the rumour spread that the Japs were waiting for us. This

rumour rapidly gained momentum and we became very apprehensive. I tried to reason with those around me. If the Japs were waiting, why put logs on the site and prevent the landing? Then we got the news: Broadway here we come!'

Bill Towill was among those expecting to fly into Piccadilly:

'Clearly, something was very wrong. My own glider was at position five in the line-up. I was part of a Section, including the Colonel, acting as the advance party. The rest of the Battalion would fly in later. About 50 yards away, a group of big-wigs had assembled to see us off. This group was now in turmoil. Piccadilly was covered in enormous teak logs and landing there would have been a total disaster. After some discussion it was decided to land everyone at Broadway, which the Americans jocularly accepted as being "much more attractive" than Piccadilly.'

Corporal Fred Holliday's hard-headed logic, dismissing the ambush rumour, escaped the Commanders when they were first confronted with the aerial photographs. Wingate had banned photographic sorties over Broadway, Piccadilly and a third clearing, codenamed

Chowringhee, to avoid raising Japanese suspicions. Nevertheless, there was a last-minute overflight by a B.25 Mitchell. The photos were developed just 40 minutes before the first tugs and gliders were due to take off. The photos arrived at 16.30 by light aircraft, as the first wave (77 Brigade HQ, leading elements of British and Gurkha infantry and American airfield engineers) were actually boarding. A jeep crossed the strip at speed and reached Slim, Wingate and the others. The photos had been taken just two hours earlier.

In a letter to Bidwell, the author of *The Chindit War* (Imperial War Museum, Misc. 140, 2180), Charles Russhon suggested that these photos were the product of 'private enterprise' on his part. Russhon, who also featured as a character with Cochran and others in the *Terry and the Pirates* strip cartoon (he was dubbed 'Charlie Vanilla', a reference to his extreme love of ice cream), explained:

I came in the service (USAAF, 10th Combat Camera Unit) as an American from Hollywood. It was easy to see what a great project was being done and therefore I thought it was most important to get pictures of both places (Broadway and Piccadilly) *before* the invasion, to go along with what I was hoping to get in photos of everything that would take place after the invasion, to show both sides ... before and after ... [The photos] were not taken as a military requirement, even if I said directly to General Wingate, after he saw my pictures, that nobody ordered me to take them, but that it was normal American procedure to take last-minute photos before an operation. I was careful to say nothing about Cochran telling me NOT to take them and then getting Alison to go along with my request.

No special flight was set for this mission. I was in a plane piloted by R.T. Smith and after performing a bombing mission we broke away from the Flight and went on our own to both locations and flew like we were lost, so that it would look like we were not going to any *special* place ... Wingate wrote me up for a British DFC ... I was never a photographer. I was a Hollywood soundman ...

Slim's book, *Defeat into Victory*, gives a disparaging description of Wingate's behaviour when the photos arrived. This conflicts with accounts by everyone else present. According to Slim, Wingate was 'in a very emotional state', immediately concluding that the operation had been 'betrayed'. He said Wingate wanted to cancel the fly-in, as the Japanese would be waiting for them. Piccadilly might have been compromised by its use during Operation *Longcloth* in 1943. Photos of a Dakota

on this clearing had been published in an American magazine. At that time, of course, there was no anticipation that a potential security issue could arise the following year.

Slim portrayed himself as the calming influence, pointing out that if the operation had been compromised, one would have expected all three sites to have been obstructed.[8] Slim's account may put Wingate in a poor light yet the others present remember him showing cool and solid leadership.[9]

Slim weighed up the pledges made to the Americans and General Stilwell. He had to take into account the fact that 16 Brigade had been marching into Burma for the past month and, in addition, the Japanese offensive against Assam was about to break. Three Japanese Divisions would advance on Imphal and Kohima: 'I calculated on Wingate's operation to confuse and hamper it. "The operation will go on," I said'.

Wingate stated that *he* did the persuading, rather than Slim. According to Slim, Wingate decided that all units due to fly into Piccadilly should switch to Chowringhee. Slim wrote: 'I very much doubted the wisdom of this. Chowringhee was on the east of the Irrawaddy; the railway and road to be cut were on the west'.[8]

In any event, Air Marshal Sir John Baldwin warned that there was no time for such a drastic change. What soon emerged was a decision favouring Brigadier Calvert's view: the fly-in would be to Broadway alone. These discussions unfolded at a furious pace. The start of the fly-in was timed at 18.12 hrs, just 72 minutes late!

Subsequently, it was discovered that the obstructions at Piccadilly had nothing to do with the Japanese. They were merely the consequences of normal logging activities. Teak logs had been left out to dry. Everyone soon discovered that Broadway itself was far from free of obstructions. Long grass camouflaged logs and the deep ruts caused by dragging trees out of the jungle during the wet season. Yet Robert Thompson, 77 Brigade's Senior RAF Officer, later claimed that Piccadilly's obstruction *was* a deliberate act by the Japanese. He maintained that 'villagers had been instructed to do it and had used elephants to move the tree trunks', but gave no source to support this view.[10]

Phil Cochran had reduced the delay to a minimum. He told his C-47 and glider pilots that he had a 'new and better plan'. Mustang pilot Olin B. Carter attended this briefing, also watched by Wingate and other Special Force senior officers:

'He ended it with words I have never forgotten: "Nothing you have ever done, nothing you are ever going to do,

counts now. Only the next few hours. Tonight you are going to find your souls".

A few hours later Carter and his fellow fighter pilots were briefed to fly continuous daylight Combat Air Patrols over Broadway clearing, beginning at dawn. Captain Neville Hogan and his Burrif Recce Platoon flew in with the first wave. He watched a mule being coaxed into his glider; he and his men then followed:

'Our cargo included a small bulldozer, for use by engineers building Broadway's Dakota strip. The men settled down on the box-type seating along each side of the glider. We found it difficult to keep our seats during take off. The flight was unpleasant and frightening.'

They flew across the hills, entering Burmese airspace in darkness. The men tried to ignore the stomach-churning succession of violent air pockets. Hogan's mood was not improved when he realised how much the glider was yawing on the tow. From time to time, as the glider lurched from one side to the other, he caught sight of the brilliant exhaust flames of the Dakota's engines.

Back at Lalaghat, some gliders beginning their ground runs were in danger of tipping up due to overloading. Troops were quickly organised into teams of four, to hold down the tail during the initial ground run.[11]

It has been suggested that the Chindits themselves were largely responsible for the pilots' difficulties that night: 'Chindits disrupted planned glider load weights by taking extra ammunition, weapons and food, causing towing problems. There were premature releases with crash landings into the jungle and, at Broadway, glider pilots had to maintain a steeper dive to land, with disastrous results.'[12] Surely, however, it should have been expected that men facing long months in the wilderness, confronting a vicious enemy, would attempt to increase their chances in every way possible. In any event, there would have been far fewer losses that night with more C-47s and single, rather than dual glider tows.

It would be simplistic to seek one cause of the glider losses that night. Beyond overloading and the strain of dual tows, Calvert, for example, mentions a failure to reload gliders with due care following the decision to go to Broadway alone and the fact that around one-third of the tugs were crewed by RAF aircrew who had had only two or three days' instruction in glider towing.[13]

One glider pilot, Earl Waller, wrote a vivid account of his terrifying experience as a see-saw motion developed between tug and tows, in extremely poor visibility:

Suddenly, I developed vertigo. I had never had it before. The tow ship looked like it was diving

straight down and the air speed sounded like it had built up to a very high speed. I had one hand on the wheel and started to reach up for the cut-off because I could see the Irrawaddy River. I glanced down at the air speed and it was setting on normal, around 150 mph. It was definitely vertigo. The co-pilot encouraged me to stay on the tow. He had no way of knowing that my vision and hearing were not right and the situation was very bad.

I am unable to remember more until we got to Broadway. The next thing I remember is being in a tight turn to the left and my glider started to stall. I cut off and headed down. We were too high but had no choice, so a violent slip got us onto the edge of Broadway at about 120 mph, not much control here. We hit a log buried in the elephant grass and tore off the left landing gear and swerved right, missing the piles of wrecked gliders by sheer luck! Someone in the glider came forward, slapped me on the back and said, 'Good job!' I think he was the British doctor. I was completely exhausted but somehow got out of the cockpit seat and outside the aircraft. Things were bad, gliders piling into each other.[14]

In brilliant moonlight more C-47s and gliders flew east over the Chindwin and towards Broadway clearing, 130 miles behind Japanese lines. Their engines laboured as they fought for altitude to cross the hills, attached to overloaded dual tows.

Major Orio 'Red' Austin's C-47, 'Assam Dragon', had been one of the first away from Lalaghat. Austin's Engineer, Charles T. Campbell:

'We were pulled into position and hooked up. We were third or fourth in line. We had two gliders, on short and long tow. The pilot of the long tow glider spent the entire flight yawing from side to side. This caused our pilot all sorts of problems. It was a real threat – this can whip a C-47 into a crash. Anyway, Austin, being the man he was, persevered and took them all the way.

'Our gliders were supposed to cut loose when they saw the two main sets of markers laid out in Broadway clearing and took the time needed to get their bearings, but the long tow glider pilot cast off as soon as he glimpsed the lights. He was too far out at that point and went straight into the trees. I understand that everyone on board was killed. He shouldn't have been flying that glider – or anything else for that matter! Happily, our other glider then cast off and got in safely. He waited until he was within range of the clearing. It was a really rough night.'

The moment of decision: Wingate (second right), with Calvert on his right, takes in the unpleasant surprise of aerial photos showing Piccadilly obstructed by teak logs. Phil Cochran (third from left) has his back to the camera. On his right, his Deputy, John Alison, holds a map with Walter Scott of the King's. (Trustees of the Imperial War Museum)

In fact, Red Austin's night was only a quarter over. They had been briefed to return to Lalaghat, hook up a second pair of gliders and fly straight back to Broadway!

Many gliders failed to reach the jungle clearing. Frank Anderson, a Vickers gunner with the King's 81 Column, experienced an abrupt end to his glider flight:

'We were on dual tow and overloaded. Our glider was in the long tow position. We got up OK but conditions were very turbulent. We were aloft for about an hour when the two gliders suddenly began to sheer into each other. The short tow cable parted and then ours went. Our lives now rested with our American glider pilot, Captain Randles. Instinctively, everyone clasped hands. We gripped so tight that the fingernail impressions remained for some time afterwards. There was no panic as we went down and no time to do any thinking. I just felt: "Well, we're done with it!" Suddenly, I could see water and heard Randles shout: "It's a lake!" Then – bang! We were in the lake. We ploughed in and everyone tumbled down into the nose. The Vickers fell on me and I was trapped as the water came in and the fuselage flooded. Luckily, they managed to get me out in time. That was my first and last flight in a glider.'

The men waded ashore through shallow water and moved towards some bashas at the lakeside:

'The occupants had been fishing and were cooking their evening meal. They took off when we suddenly descended. We took advantage of the situation and bedded down for the night. During the following morning we found we were on the Indian side of the Chindwin and made our way to a road. We were soon back at Lalaghat. I then flew out again, but by Dakota this time.'

According to Larson, the first glider into Broadway was piloted by Captain William H. Taylor: 'The glider hit the ground, skidding to a stop without damage to the glider or injury to those inside.' Taylor and his co-pilot began setting out flares to mark the landing zone for the following gliders.[15] Flares were laid out in a diamond pattern to mark the landing area. Other flares were set out at the glider release point, one mile in front of the clearing. The briefed release height was 1,000 ft.[16]

Just 35 of 61 gliders reached Broadway. In many cases, overloaded dual tows proved too much. Nine of the 26 gliders failing to arrive were less fortunate than

On the tow: a glider at 8,000 ft, on its way to Broadway. Note the question mark badge of 1st Air Commando on the C-47's fin. (Trustees of the Imperial War Museum)

balance them off with throttle changes to slow or accelerate my aircraft, to keep them from over-running us. On a particularly hard pull my two gliders broke loose. I made a climbing right hand turn to see where they were. I looked down, located the Chindwin river and, in searching the area, we could see large sand bars in the river which stood out in the moonlight and expected the glider pilots could also see the sand bars and make a normal landing on them.[11]

This pilot was nervous at the prospect of explaining things to Cochran, on returning to Lalaghat. He need not have worried. He had to join a queue of C-47 pilots reporting losses. 'Colonel Cochran assembled us and told us to go hook-up a single glider and leave for Broadway immediately, not risking any more double tows.'

Cochran also told the C-47 pilots to show their navigation lights, to help the glider pilots keep station.[11] He had been warned that the glider pilots were having severe problems when their tugs reached 8,000 ft and settled into the cruise. At that point they lost their key reference – the bright exhaust flames of the C-47s' engines, which had been at maximum power. They were then left with only the indistinct silhouette of the tug ahead.

Tugs and tows continued to leave Lalaghat. Bill Towill and 9 GR CO Lieutenant-Colonel Noel George were among an advance party in the port glider of the fifth pair to leave the ground. The starboard glider had Peter Fleming on board, together with an attached RE Officer, Lieutenant Leigh-Mallory, son of the renowned mountaineer and nephew of Air Marshal Sir Trafford Leigh Mallory.[18]

Towill and his Gurkhas sat on hard benches in their glider, packs between their knees. They were not going far. Towill sat forward and looked over the pilot's shoulder. He found the view not to his taste:

Frank Anderson's. They crash-landed in Japanese-held territory.[17] About half of those on board eventually reached safety. Eight, including Anderson's, landed in friendly territory. Others were recalled.

The C-47 pilots were briefed to climb out from Lalaghat for 10 minutes, turn left and continue for another 10 minutes, turn left again and then make a final left turn to arrive back over the airfield at 4,000 ft. This wide circuit allowed them to stay within safe distance of Lalaghat as they climbed. The C-47s needed full power to reach the cruise altitude with their heavy burdens. At 4,000 ft, they had still reached only half the height required to clear the hills.[11]

Not all tugs and gliders made it to 4,000 ft and there were more premature releases at cruising height. One pilot described his experience:

As we started over the Chin Hills the two gliders began to surge and we were constantly trying to

He was wrestling with the controls and trying to trim the glider, while the glider on our starboard kept swinging in towards us dangerously. Suddenly he reached up and punched at the lever above his head, the tow line fell away and the glow of the tug's exhausts receded into the distance while we banked steeply and, in total silence, apart from the sound of the wind rushing past the fuselage, headed back along the flight path we had been following.

Below us, in the brilliant moonlight, I could see the open paddy fields, with the paddy bunds lying directly across our path, rushing up at us at 70 miles per hour. I saw the pilot put his feet up on the dashboard and he then yelled out 'Hang on

... there's going to be a bump!' Spreadeagling my hands above my head, I hung onto two convenient struts – we had no seatbelts – lifted my feet in the air, indicated to my men to do likewise and waited in this ungainly posture for the crash, expecting any moment to end up with my backside ploughing the fields! Then we hit the ground. In a rending, drumming, tearing, grinding, crashing tumult of sound we bucketed and bounced our way over the paddy bunds, hanging on for dear life as we were violently jolted around and the glider filled with choking dust until, after a few seconds which seemed like an eternity, we came to a juddering halt. Apart from being shaken up and a little bruised, most of us had suffered no harm, though one man at the rear of the glider sustained a broken arm.[19]

Interviewed over 60 years later, Towill added:

'A red Very light and the wireless soon brought transport to our rescue. We were only a few miles from the airfield. We were quickly back at Lalaghat and joined the end of the glider lines, hoping for better luck next time.'

Neville Hogan's men made it all the way, having been somewhat subdued during the flight:

'As we came in at Broadway, our right wing hit another glider and the landing was very hard. Somehow our mule broke both front legs and my first duty on the ground was to shoot the animal. That mule was our only casualty. I sent my 2i/c, Johnny Htoo, off to find the other two gliders with the rest of our Recce Platoon.'

The occupants of other gliders were much less fortunate. 82 Column's Peter Heppell sat forward in his WACO:

'As the pilot cast off over Broadway I got an excellent view of the entire strip when the glider banked sharply. I saw that some gliders were already down and men were unloading stores along the edge of the strip. As these gliders were not in neat rows, as per instructions, our pilot assumed the worst and muttered: "Christ! Japs!" By then we were nearly down. The wheels came off on impact; we swung round and ended up facing the jungle edge. Getting out in the bright moonlight felt dodgy — we had no idea what or who was waiting for us.'

Now safely down, Heppell took stock. Broadway was a shambles. He and the others began unloading the glider, taking their stores to the jungle perimeter:

'As I went back to the fuselage, something made me run for it. Then another glider hit ours. Its cockpit ran down our left hand wing, causing a number of casualties. The incoming glider's wing also knocked off my Bush Hat. I found it, put it back on and returned to the open door of our glider. All I could see was a collection of rifle muzzles. It appeared that some of our blokes had been forced underneath. I can't remember anything else. I've got a complete blank from almost immediately after the collision. I was told later that some people got out of the wreck through the floor.'

Alison, Cochran's deputy, landed safely in the third glider. He tried to avoid more collisions by ordering flares to be moved after each pair of gliders landed, so helping the next pair avoid wrecks and obstructions.[14]

Neville Hogan, of the King's Own's 46 Column, began to orientate himself:

'I believe we landed at over 100 mph. Our pilot must have wanted something in reserve, to get in safely over the trees at the perimeter. When we got out of the glider I heard men screaming for help in the darkness around me. The casualties mounted as more gliders came in and piled into the wrecks. I was told to take my Platoon to the north side of the paddy and dig in, against the possibility of an immediate Jap attack. That was good. It is better to be busy in such situations.'

Sitting in his glider, looking down at the hills, Brigadier Michael Calvert remembered that it would be his birthday in just a few hours. If he survived the landing he would be 31. His glider had been one of the third pair to take off. Calvert thought back to those critical minutes at Lalaghat, when the aerial photos were examined and Operation *Thursday* hung in the balance. Wingate gave him his chance and he took it, on the understanding that he could keep his Brigade together and go into Broadway.[20]

As men around him dozed off his mind stayed active. The Chindwin passed below and then the railway, followed by the Irrawaddy. They began a turn, approaching the Kaukkwe valley. Calvert caught sight of Broadway as the tow was slipped. They landed with a huge bounce. Their glider pilot had traded speed for height and just scraped over the wreck of another glider.

On the ground the advance parties were finding it impossible to clear gliders from the strip. Most could not be moved across the deep ruts hidden in long grass. Three of the original six were still obstructing the clearing when the next wave of gliders arrived overhead. '... several of this batch were also wrecked by the ditches and became immovable in their turn, adding to the hazards for those still to come.'[20]

Moment of impact: a WACO CG-4A glider, airbrakes deployed, hits the water in an emergency landing. (Trustees of the Imperial War Museum)

It was chaos on the ground yet some men had a remarkably trouble-free flight and landing. 82 Column Muleteer Ted McArdle was one of the lucky ones:

'Our mules remained quiet and the flight was without incident. I hadn't flown before but wasn't nervous. In the Army you do what you are told. Our landing at Broadway was very bumpy. My job was to get Joey the mule out of the glider but, for some reason, I have no recollection of doing so.'

Another 82 Column Chindit, Corporal Fred Holliday, had a more disagreeable flight:

'We were on the long tow. One minute we were well above both the tug and the lead glider, then we were far below. We were all over the place. Anyway, our landing was reasonable. When I got out the first thing that struck me was the lack of firing. The landing was unopposed. But there was plenty of noise, with men shouting orders and lots of activity. The first move was to send out patrols. It wasn't long before we realised there were no Japs in the vicinity of our landing site.'

Ian Niven noted that the Lancashire Fusiliers in his glider showed no nerves after take-off:

'I suppose the main worry was not knowing whether you would be fired on upon landing. When our glider went in we hit really hard. When I got out I could see wrecks and bodies strewn in the trees near us. Yet I felt fantastic: I was in one piece! We moved off to help form the perimeter. We settled in and got what sleep we could.'

There was no rest for Mike Calvert at that point. The 77 Brigade Commander gazed over the devastation, highlighted in the moonlight: 'I knew that many of the first wave had not turned up at all. I saw quite a large number of men in front of me killed or wounded. The glider path was jammed with broken gliders. A second wave was due to take off. Our communications with base were unpredictable. I sent the fateful message 'Soya Link'.[21] Beyond the wrecked gliders, Broadway clearing had two other obstructions: a pair of trees in the very centre of the strip and a pair of ditches – drag paths for elephants moving teak logs.[22]

With some understatement, Slim described the period after the first wave left Lalaghat as an unpleasant wait. 'Soya Link', the code for an unsuccessful landing, referred to a wartime substitute sausage made from soya beans. The signal was sent in clear and caused much dismay. Back at base, many assumed this meant an opposed landing. It took some time before it was appreciated that the problem was the inability to take more gliders, owing to the wreckage and other obstructions.[17]

'Soya Link' brought a breathing space at Broadway. Peter Heppell had been stunned by the collision of a glider with his own aircraft, already on the ground. Now he began to recover:

'My next memory is of yet more gliders coming in, with the sound of them hitting the ground or crashing into the jungle. When 'Soya Link' was sent, that called a halt to the landings that night. It quietened down at around 5 am. We settled into some bushes and got our heads down.'

This was frustrating for those still waiting at Lalaghat. The 9 GR advance party had already survived a crash-landing only a short distance from Lalaghat. Now the Gurkhas went to the end of the queue, steeling themselves for a second try, only to learn that flights had halted.

Some men were extraordinarily determined to get in. Calvert noted: 'One keen officer took off three times in different gliders, but each time either crashed or landed nearby.'[23] Before Calvert sent his signal, C-47 crews landing back at Lalaghat had hooked up to more gliders. C-47 Engineer Charles J. Campbell remembered the fast turnround:

'We were about 45 minutes into our second flight when we received the recall. In their damaged condition at Broadway, the gliders were just too difficult and heavy to move in the time available.'

Notes

1. Larson, G. A. (2008), *Aerial Assault into Burma*, 110
2. Rooney. D. (2000), *Wingate and the Chindits: Redressing the Balance*, 113
3. Rhodes James, R. (1981), *Chindit*, 54
4. Ibid, 56
5. Towill, B. (2000), *A Chindit's Chronicle*, 16–17
6. Calvert, M. (1974), *Chindits: Long Range Penetration*, 27
7. Larson, G. A. (2008), 135–136
8. Slim, Field Marshal Viscount (1999), *Defeat into Victory*, 260–262
9. Rooney, D. (1997), *Mad Mike*, 70–71
10. Thompson, Sir Robert (1989), *Make for the Hills*, 47
11. Larson, G. A. (2008), 149–151
12. Ibid, 145
13. Calvert, M. (1973), *Prisoners of Hope*, 23–24
14. Larson, G. A. (2008), 159–160
15. Ibid, 9
16. Ibid, 152
17. Slim, Field Marshal Viscount (1999), 264
18. Towill, B. (2000), 15
19. Ibid, 18–19
20. Calvert, M. (1996), *Fighting Mad*, 139–143
21. Calvert, M. (1974), 29
22. Calvert, M. (1973), 28
23. Ibid, 31

THE FLY-IN CONTINUES

6–15 March 1944

'To see the Dakotas coming in was an amazing, uplifting experience. It was difficult to believe that, just a few hours earlier, this had been nothing more than a virgin open clearing in a vast teak jungle.'

Major Bill Towill, 3rd/9th Gurkha Rifles

AT DAWN on 6 March 1944, Olin B. Carter was flying a Combat Air Patrol, as one of a section of four Mustang fighters over Broadway clearing. Keeping a close all-round watch for Japanese aircraft, he dropped down to 2,000 ft and took a good look. He was shocked at the chaos below.

'It was a scene of complete devastation. There was not a single glider capable of being recovered. The plan was to put some of our glider pilots into the gliders and begin to snatch them out. It was obvious that this wasn't going to happen.'

Thirty-seven gliders had landed at Broadway and just three remained in flyable condition.[1] Lance Corporal Peter Heppell's Sapper section, with 82 Column, 1st King's (Liverpool), had been divided between two gliders. Heppell was asked to take on a traumatic job:

'Our second glider overshot the strip and landed in the trees. Two or three at the very back of the glider got out but all the rest were killed. During the morning Lieutenant Johnny Long, our Section Commander, asked me to set fire to that glider. This was not an order but Long said it was the best we could do for them. I declined. I told him I wanted to get on with my duties. I always felt guilt about that. Decades later, on returning to Burma, I found the names of the men in that glider. They now rest in Rangoon Cemetery. I drew comfort from the fact that they had received proper burial.'

This was not always possible. When Gurkha Intelligence Officer Bill Towill finally arrived at Broadway, after an abortive first attempt and the 'Soya Link' delay, he was among a group of officers gathered round Wingate, who flew in on 7 March:

'Just as he was speaking, what appeared to be a savage firefight broke out behind us. One of the gliders had landed high in the treetops, killing everyone. Since it was impossible to disentangle the bodies from the mangled wreckage, it was turned into a funeral pyre. As the flames reached the ammunition, the firefight erupted.'

Lieutenant Norman Durant, MC, with the 1st South Staffordshire's 80 Column, was in no mood for pep talks, having had a difficult flight into Broadway. The Platoon Commander saw Wingate arrive in a B.25 Mitchell: 'Already he had a large beard – quite unnecessary in view of the fact he was directing operations from Assam, where he had every facility for shaving ... everyone melted away and pretended to be engaged in some work of vital import.'

Durant was no fan of Wingate. Writing to his family after Operation *Thursday*, he commented: 'He was the worst dressed officer I have ever seen. He was a man in whose presence anyone, from Lieutenant General to Private, felt uncomfortable and aware of his faults and shortcomings. He spared no-one in his criticisms and never used soft words to his victims. He had absolute mental and moral courage allied with a complete lack of pity, so that he said what he liked, to whom he liked and where he liked.' At the same time, Durant also acknowledged: 'There was something awe-inspiring in his certainty and dogmatism.'[2]

Men like Heppell and Durant were keen to get busy after the chaos of the initial landings. 77 Brigade

The morning after the night before: Chindits and American personnel pictured beside tangled glider wreckage at Broadway. (Trustees of the Imperial War Museum)

Commander Michael Calvert had sent the 'Soya Link' signal at 0400 on 6 March 1944. His 31st birthday got off to an unhappy start.[3] When the landings paused, as a result of this signal, there was time to take a more measured view. Calvert even snatched an hour's sleep. Lieutenant Brockett, leading the US Army Engineers at Broadway, talked with Calvert as dawn broke. He told him that, given the manpower, he could have a Dakota strip ready for action that evening. Calvert, much encouraged, sent the success signal, 'Pork Sausage', to HQ at 06.30 – to the immense relief of the recipients.[4]

Sixty-six men were lost in the gliders failing to reach Broadway.[5] Twenty-three men died and 30 were injured in the Broadway landings. The first wave assault gliders landed 539 men, 29,972 pounds of equipment (including four mini-bulldozers), airfield lighting, a few mules and other gear.[1]

Some gliders carrying airstrip construction equipment crashed at Broadway. Two gliders carrying bulldozers overshot and smashed into trees. Their pilots lived thanks to a life-saving design feature. The WACO's cockpit was designed to swing up, to facilitate loading and unloading. This worked well at Broadway! In both crashes the bulldozers shot clear – under the nose of each glider as it abruptly hinged. Only one of the four men in the cockpits was hurt. Sergeant Joseph A. DeSalvo, struck on the head as his glider's bulldozer was propelled out by the impact, was evacuated to Lalaghat.[6] Fortunately, enough equipment, including a scraper, had survived.[5]

One priority was to evacuate the injured by light aircraft. There was simultaneous working on a light plane strip and the main Dakota landing area. They could not wait for construction plant to be recovered; the Chindits set to work by hand. Peter Heppell had to face the fact that the Commando Platoon's Sappers had lost half their strength and much of their equipment. It was essential to get on with the strips and infantry parties worked with picks and shovels in long shifts. They carried on alongside a small tractor and scraper. Heppell told his Section they would get no cha until they had done their share:

The race is on: Monday 6 March and Chindits set to work on what would become Broadway's C-47 strip. A bulldozer is in action to the right of the photograph. (Trustees of the Imperial War Museum)

'I found water in a buffalo wallow at the end of the strip. When tea was brewed it was the same colour as the water. No-one knew the difference! We still had plenty of work ahead of us. As at Piccadilly, Broadway clearing had been scarred by foresters dragging logs across sodden ground during the Monsoon. The logs had cut deep furrows which had to be filled before the Dakotas could land. These ruts were hidden in tall grass at Broadway.'

Lieutenant Brockett of 900th Airborne Engineers had just nine surviving members of his team to work on the strip:

> At 6 am, while Colonel Alison and I were on ground reconnaissance, grading was begun in the general direction of the flight strip. When the direction had been determined, we ran a base line with a jeep pulling a grader the length of the field, missing as many buffalo wallows as possible. At this time there was one grader, one jeep, two bulldozers and one carryall in operation.[7]

Brockett and his team stayed at Broadway for over a month, being relieved by another engineering team on 10 April. Work continued on improving Broadway's C-47 strip until 20 April.[8]

During the afternoon of 6 March the engineers and the Chindits worked on a rough strip 2,000 ft long and 300 ft wide. Subsequently, this was greatly extended, to assist night landings. 'The main job consisted of filling in the log ruts ... In the dry season these were now as hard as stone, some 16 in deep, two to four feet wide.'[7]

Captain Neville Hogan's Recce Platoon kept busy:

'Our next job was to mark out and dig shallow pits for the fires that would mark out the airstrip as the Dakotas started to come in. We dug a fire pit every 50 yards. Men were detailed to collect firewood. A bulldozer was trying to break up the paddy bunds. This was no easy task. Those bunds had been there for years and were like cement. I worried about the noise – that bulldozer was loud enough to alert any Japs for miles around.'

USAAF Major Andy Rebori led an initial group of light aircraft to Broadway, to fly out injured.[9] They flew in medical supplies and food and evacuated six severe cases. It was decided to leave the less serious for evacuation by C-47.[7]

Work on the defences made Broadway a Stronghold of the type envisaged by Wingate. Broadway was commanded by Colonel Claude Rome. Its defences included mobile Columns acting as 'floater' forces.

Frank Anderson was a Vickers gunner with the King's 81 Column:

'We were detailed as floaters around Broadway, which was to be garrisoned by the Gurkhas. We were to disrupt any Japanese attempt to concentrate and attack the still incomplete perimeter.'

Inside the Stronghold, men dug in at a frantic pace. They were creating a refuge for mobile Columns and a Chindit bastion – a killing ground for Japanese attackers. Bill Towill:

I remember digging all night without a break. The individual foxholes were of a keyhole shape, the long portion roofed in with substantial timbers from the almost inexhaustible supply in the jungle all around us and covered with earth, to afford a shelter which would be proof against mortar fire, and with the round part of the keyhole recessed to form a fire step.[10]

Sixty-five years later, Towill added:

'Following the talk by Wingate, Brigadier Calvert led our small party to the other side of the landing ground, to show us where he wanted 9 GR to set up its positions. Just about 50 yards inside the edge of the jungle was a shallow depression in the ground, through which ran a substantial stream of beautiful, clean water, sparkling in the morning sunlight and quite adequate for all our needs. We were then left to lay out our defences, so that when the Battalion arrived that night it could be led straight to its position. It would not be a simple trench, but a series of individual weapon pits, giving fire support to each other. When our wire arrived, we could be wired in and a formidable defensive position would result.'

The Dakota strip had to be ready by early evening, to bring in the essential stores needed to complete the defences.

Grading at Broadway was minimised – only mounds over 3 in high were removed. Brockett was as good as his word. The first C-47 landed at 7.10pm.[6] Peter Heppell's surviving Sappers had been among those who slaved in the sun to make it happen: 'Within an hour or so of completion Broadway strip was an amazing sight, with flares blazing and planes coming in with their lights on. It gave us a lot of satisfaction.' Bill Towill was awestruck:

'To see the Dakotas coming in was an amazing, uplifting experience. It was difficult to believe that, just

a few hours earlier, this had been nothing more than a virgin open clearing in a vast teak jungle.'

Many men at Broadway were mesmerised by this sight. In his own account, Towill wrote:

In the few hours available to them, the small force at Broadway ... had achieved little short of the miraculous in building a rough airstrip which that night received no less than 61 Dakotas and their loads ... To stand alongside the strip and see the aircraft landing and taking off again, just as if it were a busy civil airport, brought a sense of exultation I shall never forget.[11]

Calvert was awarded a second DSO for his outstanding leadership during the landings.[12]

A few hours earlier, back at Lalaghat, Corporal Jesse Dunn and other members of the Commando Platoon of the South Staffords' 80 Column had made their final preparations. They had expected to fly in the day before. Some men shaved their heads. Others watched a Bing Crosby film and made a conscious effort to think of nothing else. Late on 6 March, their mules loaded, the soldiers boarded the Dakotas. They took their places, backs against the fuselage walls. Jesse Dunn:

'It was chaos when we arrived. There were wrecked gliders all over the place and we were ordered to help clear up. We soon moved on, however, and began our march to establish what became White City Block.'

During the final hours of waiting, some men had considered their intellectual needs. Captain W.F. Jeffrey, Administrative Officer with 50 Column, 1st Lancashire Fusiliers, spent precious time wrestling with his selection of books: 'I made my final choice: *The Shropshire Lad*, a selection of five of Shakespeare's plays and some of his sonnets and Logan Pearsale Smith's *Treasury of English Prose*.' Later, his Batman, Walker, brought him down to earth. When they landed by Dakota during the night of 6 March, Walker suddenly appeared, brandishing a loaf of bread and tinned jam: 'He sat down and, muttering something about "This being Burma and not thinking much of it," began to prepare a meal!'[13]

Vickers gunner Frank Anderson was making his second flight in 24 hours. The first ended in an emergency glider landing, fortunately on the Indian side of the Chindwin. Now he was sitting in a Dakota:

'There really was no point in thinking about what might happen when you arrived. We landed after dark. It was

still very chaotic at Broadway, with a good deal of glider and aircraft wreckage around. We didn't stay long.'

Corporal Fred Holliday landed by glider with elements of the King's 81 Column, but was pleased to be reunited with 82 Column, when they arrived during the evening and night of 6/7 March: 'It was a wonderful sight. We couldn't believe what we were seeing – Dakota after Dakota coming in. Eventually, they even brought in 25 Pounders.'

Four troops of 160th Jungle Field Regiment, RA, were preparing to fly in to support the Chindits. R Troop flew into Broadway, S Troop went to White City and U Troop eventually went to the northern Block, 'Blackpool'. T Troop was not deployed. This Troop was to have flown in later, into the 'Aberdeen' Stronghold, but this plan was abandoned (Captain S.R. Nicholls, Imperial War Museum, 80/49/1).

Private Jack Hutchin, with the South Staffords' 80 Column, had an uncomfortable flight over the hills:

'Air pockets made it very bumpy but I still managed to fall asleep. When our Dakota circled to land I had trouble waking up; I poured some water over my head, to shake myself out of the stupor. We were surrounded by chaos on landing. Wrecked gliders were strewn all over the area. Large bits of glider were jammed into nearby trees. Broadway looked a terrible mess, but our Column formed up quickly. God knows how, as this wasn't something you could rehearse with any realism.'

One of the first C-47s to land that night was Major Red Austin's 'Assam Dragon'. This time his aircraft was not towing gliders but, rather, carrying a Section of Chindits, their kit and stores. Engineer Charles T. Campbell:

'We helped bring in men, guns, ammunition, equipment and mules. A cargo of boxed ammunition was best, as it could be unloaded quickly. Mules were very different; it took some time to get the animals out of the airplane.'

Most animals gave no trouble during the flight. Bill Williams, Animal Transport Officer (ATO) with 80 Column, anticipated trouble when emplaning the mules. Not surprisingly, they became increasingly unsettled as the roar of aero-engines filled the air:

'I reminded the Muleteers that any serious misbehaviour by mules during the flight should end only one way, if it could not be controlled. The animal must be shot. In the event, the fly-in went smoothly, at least from my standpoint. One mule started careering around. A couple of men wrestled it to the ground and sat on its head until it calmed down.

'When we took off I can't remember being disturbed by uncomfortable thoughts. Some men appeared to treat the flight like a holiday – an adventure – but I do remember one Sergeant saying aloud: "This doesn't seem to be a very safe thing to do." The landing was not too bad.'

On 6 March, 80 Column Machine Gun Platoon Commander Norman Durant supervised the loading of his aircraft with eight South Staffords, four mules and a Vickers machine gun and ammunition. He described this as a 'rather unpleasant man-mule ratio.' The fourth mule refused to board. The problem was solved by putting sacking over its head, confusing it by leading it very fast around in circles and pushing it up the ramp before it had time to work out what was happening.[2]

Take-off was problematical: 'As the plane rushed forward the most truculent of the four mules leant to the side, his hooves got off the floor matting and onto the aluminium. He slipped and was down on the floor, thrashing about, before we could do anything. This naturally upset the other three and they began lashing out until the place was bedlam and I had visions of having to ask the pilot to turn back. By superhuman efforts we got the mule on its feet again, soothed them with soft words and corn, tightened the lashings and peace was restored.'[2]

Assam Dragon's Engineer: Charles J. Campbell and his flying jacket, emblazoned with 1st Air Commando's question mark badge. (Chuck Campbell)

Occupational hazard: flying into jungle airstrips meant inevitable losses. This C-47 ran into a paddy bund. The wreck was probably at Aberdeen. (Jim Unsworth)

When 9 GR arrived to garrison Broadway, their advance party briefed them and took them to where the defences were to be prepared. The Gurkhas started to dig weapon pits. Intelligence Officer Bill Towill made his own preparations:

'I had dragged into the Stronghold a wing from a crashed glider and lashed it upright between two trees. On one side I pasted over one inch maps of the district and, on the other, our quarter inch maps. I overlaid the maps with perspex windows from the gliders. With chinagraph pencils I could then indicate where our men and the enemy were and, as might be expected, this became a meeting point for all and sundry.'

The 2nd King's Own Columns flew into Broadway. The main body of 41 Column flew in during the night of 9/10 March. The first aircraft were airborne at 22.30 and landed at Broadway at 23.50. 46 Column's main body arrived the following day. Private Jim Unsworth of 46 Column was detailed to accompany 2nd Lieutenant Littlewood, commanding a Rifle Platoon:

'All the big names were present when we set off. We sat on the Dakota's floor, backs against the fuselage sides. It was light when we landed at Broadway. We didn't hang around. I was first out, jumping from the door while the aircraft was still rolling. I sprinted to

the perimeter, despite my heavy kit, and waited for everyone else. Things were very quiet; there was no-one about at first. Then an American Mustang fighter appeared overhead, attempted to land and cartwheeled twice. I was amazed to see the pilot emerge in one piece. He got out of the cockpit double quick and made for cover at the perimeter. Other than that, the airstrip had been cleaned up by the time we arrived, although there had been plenty of accidents. There was a swamp at one end of the strip and numerous aircraft were now in that bog.'

On 6 March Wingate decided to open Chowringhee, to compensate for Piccadilly's loss. He felt uncomfortable relying on just one jungle airstrip. Gliders were prepared to secure a second clearing, for the landing of Morris Force and 111 Brigade's HQ and the Columns of 3rd/4th Gurkha Rifles. Morris Force consisted of 49 and 94 Columns (4th/9th Gurkha Rifles) and, eventually – by force of circumstance – 40 Column of 3rd/4th Gurkha Rifles (the sister Column to 30 Column).

Late that Monday, at dusk, tugs and tows left Lalaghat and 12 gliders soon landed at Chowringhee, named after Calcutta's main street. This clearing was 60 miles south of Broadway. One aircraft was piloted by Jackie Coogan. Unfortunately, the glider carrying the bulldozer crashed.[14] This glider was piloted by First Lieutenant Robert L. Dowe. He overshot, attempted a

180-degree turn, struck a tree and cartwheeled across the clearing. The pilot and two engineers died. The heavy bulldozer ripped their glider apart as it careered across the landing area.

A short, rough airstrip was carved out manually, allowing an American Combat Engineering Team to land. A replacement bulldozer arrived and Dakota flights soon began.[14] With construction equipment on site it took just four hours to prepare a 3,000 ft strip. Chowringhee's surface was in better original condition than that of Broadway. The first C-47 landed at 01.30 hrs on 8 March.[15]

111 Brigade HQ Cypher Officer Richard Rhodes James sat in his Dakota with 12 Gurkhas, two large mules and a pony, bound for Chowringhee:

> The three animals were led right forward, until their heads were touching the back of the radio operator's cabin. Bamboo poles were fastened between each of them and then behind them, stretching across the plane. The pilot came to have a look and was not very impressed. The previous night a pony in his plane had had to be shot, and would we please fasten the animals a bit more securely. We did.[16]

Rhodes James' aircraft crossed the Chin Hills at 10,000 ft, then the Chindwin, followed by the Irrawaddy. They soon saw 'a brilliantly lit flarepath cutting a long, narrow path through the jungle clearing.'

Chowringhee was abandoned almost immediately, when the fly-in was completed. On the morning of 10 March, the last Column to land at Chowringhee left the strip. It was bombed by the Japanese a few hours later. There was no intention to hold this clearing as a base, as it was on the 'wrong' side of the Irrawaddy. Meanwhile, 111 Brigade's British Battalions, the Cameronians (26 and 90 Columns) and King's Own (41 and 46 Columns), had arrived at Broadway.

On Thursday 9 March, Lieutenant Larry Gaines checked his Section's equipment and readiness to fly into Broadway. Originally, they were to fly into Chowringhee. The switch was good news – now they would be on the correct side of the Irrawaddy and this was fortunate as 6th Nigeria Regiment had had no river crossing experience. Gaines commanded 66 Column's Machine Gun Platoon. Both 6 NR Columns, 66 and 39, were due to fly in that day. There was some heavy whisky drinking the night before:

'We finished up shaving each others' heads with mule clippers! I looked awful with hair 1/16th of an inch long. At 10.00 hrs we paraded, with 66 Column leading. The

heat was terrific – I almost passed out. Captain Tigne, our Quartermaster, had organised a wonderful meal of eggs, bacon, fried bread, tea, fruit and rum.'

Aircraft loading weights were based on an average man-load of 240 pounds, with mules at 800 pounds and other equipment to make up a total load, per Dakota, not exceeding 5,500 pounds. As mentioned earlier regarding the gliders, this was often exceeded due to 'extras' smuggled on board. Emplaning was well organised. The men were briefed by Battalion CO Lieutenant-Colonel Day. Each Column formed up at one end of the strip, in rows of flights of six aircraft, the first plane-load to the right. As aircraft became available, each party filed through a checkpoint, receiving a number corresponding to the allocated aircraft. Lieutenant-Colonel Day's group moved off in the mid-afternoon. Larry Gaines and his men followed to 'Stage 31' at 17.00 hrs. The Dakotas began to take off an hour later. Gaines was told to be ready by 20.00 hrs; he decided to make an early start by getting the mules in. 'They proved to be bloody awkward.'

The aircraft climbed slowly to 10,000 ft and the men began to feel the intense cold. Gaines watched men and animals settle down and then fell asleep. He stirred once, looked down and saw the Chindwin far below. His next memory is of being woken by Sergeant Abdalla Lai:

'We were landing. The scene on Broadway strip was fantastic, even at night. Planes kept coming in at short intervals. Everything seemed well-organised, but I never really got a good look at the strip in daylight.'

Squadron Leader Robert Thompson, 77 Brigade's Senior RAF Officer, said that air movements at Broadway were limited only by the available parking space – sufficient for around seven aircraft at a time. A huge cloud of dust rose into the air as each Dakota took off. Air Marshal Baldwin, Third Tactical Air Force, visited Broadway. Later, he commented: 'Nobody has seen a transport operation until he has stood at Broadway, under the light of a Burma full moon, and watched Dakotas coming in and taking off in opposite directions on a single strip all night long, at the rate of one landing or one take-off every three minutes.'[17]

Cypher Operator Norman Campbell, with the Cameronians' 90 Column, recalled the mood of introspection during the final hours before emplaning for Broadway on 10 March:

'We were immersed in our thoughts. Our aircraft carried three mules, tethered at the front. We sat on the Dakota's floor. I dozed off and later stirred, seeing the moon from the window. Then I saw it again and realised we were circling, preparing to land at Broadway.

'When I jumped out of the aircraft, two of my 'muckers' were waiting. Bill Stanton and Fred Tatham grabbed me and headed towards the Column area. I had a K-ration supper meal: biscuits, a tin of meat and a packet of bouillon powder with water, followed by a bar of chocolate. I brought it up as soon as I had finished – perhaps it was nerves! When dawn broke Broadway was revealed as a large area of paddy with the bunds flattened to create the strip. I don't recall seeing any glider or aircraft wreckage.'

Those flying in during the night of 9/10 March included Captain W.H. Miller, the King's Own Chaplain. Miller pointed out that every officer acted as a plane commander. He was responsible for 13 men and three mules. It was an uncomfortable flight, made more so by a hard steel seat and the icy blast from a missing window near his head.[18] A few hours earlier, on the airstrip, Miller had been approached by a soldier seeking Baptism: 'The Baptism was as simple as it could be; a mess tin filled with water from somebody's water bottle served as our font. A few of his personal friends stood with him.'

As the landings continued, Slim noted the lack of Japanese reaction. They had no wish to be deflected from the Imphal offensive. The Chindit landings were to be dealt with by scratch formations. The only Japanese action so far had been the air raid on the freshly abandoned Chowringhee strip.[19]

Most men trekking with Brigadier Fergusson's 16 Brigade would have given much for a Dakota seat, regardless of flying conditions. Instead, they continued their epic march across some of the hardest country in the world. Many asked the obvious question: 'Why are we walking in?' Philip Sharpe, a Wireless Operator with 45th Reconnaissance Regiment's 45 Column, later wrote:

At the time, many of us began to consider the absurdity of the hazardous march we were making ... it was to be over virtually unknown country, before we could reach our objective around Indaw ... We were all suffering from malnutrition, some men had lost a great amount of weight, and many were mentally and physically debilitated. It naturally followed that our fighting ability would be dulled.[20]

In sharp contrast, other Special Force Brigades were fresh and already in their operational areas, having spent just an hour or so in the air. It is difficult to avoid the uncomfortable thought that Wingate saw 16

Brigade's early march in as insurance against the late cancellation of Operation *Thursday*. Indeed, Slim himself wrote that when considering options at Lalaghat, on finding Piccadilly obstructed, one factor he took into account was 16 Brigade: 'We could hardly desert it.'

16 Brigade continued their slow advance. 45 Column ran out of rations on 9 March and the next supply drop yielded just a couple of K-ration packets per man. The following drop, by a solitary Dakota, did little better – one day's ration of three packs. An exchange by wireless then revealed that 45 Column's stores had been dropped in error to another Column. They had to wait until 15 March for a successful drop.[20]

On 10 March 16 Brigade approached Haungpa. Honouring the British commitment to Stilwell, Fergusson detached two Columns to attack Lonkin from a southerly direction. On 12 March Fergusson received orders to take Indaw's airfield facilities, destroy surrounding communications and supply dumps and, in addition, establish a new Stronghold. The Brigade went south, moving parallel to and west of the railway.[21] The changes to the original orders now called for a direct assault on Indaw, rather than going past and swinging back, to attack from the south-east.[22] The retention of the two Columns detached for Lonkin might well have led to a more positive outcome at Indaw.

The race was on to garrison and fortify Broadway Stronghold against ground attack, deploy the mobile Columns landed at Broadway and Chowringhee and establish a strong Block on the main north-south road and railway. In addition, Morris Force's 49 and 94 Columns (9 GR) went north-east from Chowringhee, to cut the Bhamo-Myitkyina road. Lentaigne's HQ and 30 and 40 Columns (4 GR) left Chowringhee and marched towards the Irrawaddy. 111 Brigade's British Battalions, the Cameronians and King's Own, had flown into Broadway and then marched south to link up with Lentaigne around Nankan. This Brigade's main task was to stop Indaw being reinforced from the south, by means of road and rail blocks.[23] 41 Column's Recce Platoon set out on 11 March, followed by the main body the next day. By 14 March 41 Column had reached Yihku and 46 Column was at Thayetta. By 17 March they had progressed to a position west of Kaka and Naung Pein.

During the march the King's Own Padre, Captain Miller, took an active dislike to K-ration dextrose tablets. He began to feed them to a nearby mule: 'This beast of burden delighted in dextrose tablets and would often swallow them complete with cardboard carton in one mighty gulp.' Meanwhile, Miller's Batman, the appropriately named Dick Cook, became recognised as a 'champion maker of chocolate duff.'[18]

With the King's Own: Captain W.H. Miller, Padre to the 2nd Battalion. (Trustees of the Imperial War Museum)

So far, Calvert's entire 77 Brigade and half of 111 Brigade had landed at Broadway and Lentaigne's HQ and other Columns were down at Chowringhee. In addition, 16 Brigade would establish a new Stronghold site, to be known as 'Aberdeen'.[24] The air landings behind enemy lines had been a great success. They had been unopposed, bringing in over 9,000 troops and nearly 1,400 animals.

Broadway's defences grew stronger. Bill Towill: 'As supplies arrived, we wired ourselves in with a double wall of triple Dannert barbed wire entanglements. By the time we finished, we had an almost impregnable fortress comprised of dozens of bunkers covered by an interlocking fire plan, with its western flank along the edge of the jungle overlooking the airstrip. The strip, lit by paraffin flares, hour after hour throughout the night, resounded with the roar of aircraft ceaselessly landing with more men and animals and supplies ... This truly astonishing flight plan was controlled from a centre set up in one of the crashed gliders.'[25]

Michael Calvert led major elements of his Brigade towards Mawlu, to establish the road and rail Block. Meanwhile, Lieutenant-Colonel Hugh Christie took the 1st Lancashire Fusiliers' 50 Column to cut the road and railway between Kadu and Mawhun. In addition, half of 20, the sister Column, led by Major David Monteith, went south to the Irrawaddy to close the river to enemy traffic.[26]

Captain Jeffrey, 50 Column's Administrative Officer, took time to record his growing admiration for his Batman, Walker, who met the many trials of life with serenity:

> When a mule ran amok or someone gave an order which caused temporary confusion, he would nudge my elbow and mutter: 'Ere, he wants to get a grip', then pull a wet cigarette from his pocket, give me half, and sinking down on the ground advise everyone around him to get 'cush' while they could. But in times of danger none acted more swiftly and sensibly and I owe my life to him. He cared for me as a child. He was more than a Batman. He was the best friend I ever had on those marches.

Regimental Signaller Ian Niven was with the other half of 20 Column, led by Major Shuttleworth, briefed to cut the railway between Mawlu and Pinwe:

'Shuttleworth was a big man. I was 5ft 6in. Shuttleworth was 6ft 6in and looked like a film character. He wore a monocle throughout the campaign. Our Column demolitions group cut the railway as we continued to the Block which eventually became known as White City.'

Back at Broadway, the defences continued to progress, with anti-aircraft guns now in place. The Stronghold was garrisoned by 9 GR and the King's 81 and 82 Columns were operating as floaters beyond the perimeter.[27] The King's Battalion Commander, Walter Scott ('Scottie'), led 81 Column towards the Bhamo area. Sister Column 82, under Major Dick Gaitley, made for the Kaukkwe valley. Brigadier Calvert had set out on 8 March to form the Block at Henu village. His force consisted of the South Staffords (80 and 38 Columns) and Gurkhas (6 GR). 80 Column ATO Bill Williams:

'We spent that first night at Broadway and set out the following morning to the site of White City. Our Column Commander was Ron Degg, later to command the Battalion when our CO was killed. Major Degg was a remarkable man. He served in the South Staffords in every rank, from Private to his ultimate rank of Colonel. I had tremendous respect for him.'

During the march towards Henu, Corporal Jesse Dunn, with 80 Column's Commando Platoon, settled into the rhythm of things. He had total confidence in his Brigadier:

'Calvert was a fabulous man. I'll never know why he didn't get hit. He was tough – a very popular fighting leader.'

Private Jack Hutchin was also with 80 Column. He was carrying grenades and four Bren magazines. He took his turn carrying heavy items not on the mules, including parts of a stripped down Vickers machine gun. It took several days to reach Henu:

'I kept my pack well up on my shoulders during that trek. If you let it sag, it was impossible to march properly. The pack's web straps clipped into my belt. There was a sort of rhythm to the march. Every now and then I would grab my straps and hoist the pack higher.'

80 Column Rifleman Horace Howkins found the going tough:

'Our march to White City was very tiring. I got fed up with the K-rations after a few days but liked the cigarettes. I got on well with my mucker, who was slightly older than me. He was a Regular from Northampton.'

Captain Norman Durant judged the struggle to the top of Loimaw Peak, at 4,500 ft, the toughest climb. They started heavy, with six days' rations up. By 15 March, after a week, they were just four miles from Henu and the Recce Platoon went ahead. By first light they reached the site of the Block.

Lieutenant Denis Arnold was a Platoon Commander with 7th Nigeria Regiment's 29 Column. 7 NR were to fly into Aberdeen. The two Columns, 29 and 35, were to operate as floaters around White City. Once in and on the march, his men made adjustments as and when they could, but some changes had to wait: 'Tommy guns were found to be too heavy and were discarded later on.'

Many men were to exchange their British weapons for the American semi-automatic M30 carbine. It was shorter and lighter, with a 15-round magazine. Bill Towill was an enthusiast: 'Although the cartridge was much smaller and it was not as good as our rifles for long range work, it could be, with its semi-automatic action, very deadly for close-quarter action – and many of the engagements in the jungle fell into that category.'[28]

The West Africans who landed at Broadway also moved out. 6 NR's 66 and 39 Columns headed west, for the railway. Lieutenant Larry Gaines, leading 66 Column's Machine Gun Platoon, recalls they left

Broadway at about 14.00 hrs the day after their arrival. They were heading for the site of the new Aberdeen Stronghold:

'Our main objective, after crossing the north-south road and railway, was this Stronghold at Manhton. The Africans talked too much in the Column but, otherwise, the going was good.'

When the King's Own's 46 Column left Broadway, its Recce Platoon had gone ahead. The Recce Platoon was led by Captain Neville Hogan, who was heavily laden:

'I had 15 K-ration packets, for five days, together with a Tommy gun, four magazines, four grenades, map case, water bottle and First Aid kit, plus all the other equipment. Typically, we positioned ourselves one or two days' march ahead of the main body.'

Morris Force's 49 and 94 Columns (9 GR) were to operate east of the Irrawaddy but 111 Brigade HQ and 30 and 40 Columns (4 GR) had to cross the Irrawaddy and link up with its two British Battalions, landed at Broadway on the other side of the river. They reached the Irrawaddy at Inywa, where four gliders delivered boats during the night of 11 March.

Cypher Officer Richard Rhodes James watched them land on a large sandbank. They overshot: 'I was at once struck, as I believe everyone was, by what appeared to be a big defect in these American gliders. They came in at a very shallow gliding angle, so that any slight overshoot would mean landing a long way from the strip. It also meant that a low approach was essential and this was not always possible in Burma.'[29] Nevertheless, C-47s later managed the 'snatch' recoveries of two of the four gliders.

Even with the boats in use the crossing was slow. Brigade HQ and 30 Column had crossed but dawn was fast approaching. Lentaigne ordered 40 Column, still on the far bank, to turn back and join Morris Force. This left Lentaigne with HQ and half a Battalion, his two British Battalions being some way ahead.[23]

Morris Force, now with 40 Column, found the country beyond Chowringhee extremely dry. The men learnt not to be too fussy whenever they had an opportunity to drink. Rhodes James noted that men were 'surprised but grateful' when 111 Brigade Medical Officer 'Doc' Whyte said they could drink Irrawaddy river water without sterilising it.[30]

Broadway's first serious challenge came from the air on 13 March, with an enemy raid by 20 'Oscar' fighters. Unfortunately for the Japanese, six Spitfires from

Mustangs on the loose: a Section of P.51s on a Chindit support mission. A B.25 is on the airstrip. (Trustees of the Imperial War Museum)

81 Squadron had flown into Broadway the day before and a mobile radar gave them a few minutes' warning.[31] Four Oscars fell to the Spitfires, for one loss. Broadway's AA guns were credited with a 'probable'.

As the Columns made for their objectives, the officers nursed private concerns. Captain Jeffrey of 50 Column tried to gauge the mood on the march:

> The men had been keyed up to fight from the moment they jumped out of their gliders, finger on trigger and, as each day passed without a shot being fired, except in error by a nervous sentry, the keen edge was taken off their enthusiasm and watchfulness. Also, there were many weak links in our efficiency and morale which a successful skirmish, however small, would have put right at the beginning, but which became difficult to cure after a long period of immunity from attack.[32]

As the Columns advanced, 1st Air Commando launched a wave of attacks to keep the Japanese busy, hitting bridges, railyards and supply dumps. Cochran's pilots scored a major success within a couple of days of the first glider landings at Broadway, when the three Japanese airfields at Anisakan, Onbauk and Shwebo were attacked.[33]

Olin B. Carter's Mustang was 'Little Kitten' – his wife's nickname – and carried Squadron Number 23:

'We numbered our Mustangs 1 to 28. Cochran flew No. 1. When not flying close support, we attacked Jap airfields. I destroyed 15 aircraft on the ground in Burma. On 8 March one of our American-born Japanese Nisei was monitoring enemy frequencies and heard that Japanese fighters, returning from a strike up north, were being flown into the three airfields. We caught them on the ground and destroyed around 25 per cent of the Japanese Air Force strength in Burma at that time.'

According to Rooney, these attacks on Japanese-held airfields destroyed 78 aircraft. Carter claimed three aircraft strafed on the ground and outran another that got onto his tail: 'We flew three missions that day and everyone got at least three on the ground. My total time in the air on 8 March was nine hours.'

Meanwhile, Calvert's main force neared Henu, anxious to block the main road and rail link from Indaw/Mawlu to Mogaung/Myitkyina, the main supply route for the Japanese 18th and 56th Divisions.

Notes

1. Larson, G. A. (2008), *Aerial Assault into Burma*, 160
2. Durant, Captain Norman, MC, 80 Column (1st South Staffords), letter to his family
3. Rooney. D. (1997), *Mad Mike*, 73
4. Calvert, M. (1974), *Chindits: Long Range Penetration*, 34
5. Calvert, M. (1996), *Fighting Mad*, 146
6. Larson, G. A. (2008), 156
7. Ibid, 161–162
8. Ibid, 163
9. Towill, B. (2000), *A Chindit's Chronicle*, 20
10. Ibid, 26
11. Ibid, 23
12. Rooney. D. (1997), 74
13. Jeffrey, W.F. (1950), *Sunbeams Like Swords*, 49–52
14. Towill, B. (2000), 31
15. Larson, G. A. (2008), 172–174
16. Rhodes James, R. (1981), *Chindit*, 61–63
17. Thompson, Sir Robert (1989), *Make for the Hills*, 50–51
18. Miller, Rev. W.H., *A Chaplain with the Chindits*, Imperial War Museum, 80/49/1
19. Slim, Field Marshal Viscount (1999), *Defeat into Victory*, 266
20. Sharpe, P. (1995), *To Be a Chindit*, 203–208
21. Calvert, M. (1974), 59
22. Fergusson, B. (1946), *The Wild Green Earth*, 74–75
23. Calvert, M. (1974), 62–63
24. Slim, Field Marshal Viscount (1999), 265
25. Towill, B. (2000), 26
26. Chinnery, P.D. (2002), *March or Die*, 127
27. Ibid, 113
28. Towill, B. (2000), 69–70
29. Rhodes James, R. (1981), 67
30. Ibid, 66
31. Calvert, M. (1974), 80
32. Jeffrey, W.F. (1950), 57
33. Larson, G. A. (2008), 164–165

12

WHITE CITY: ESTABLISHING THE BLOCK

16–21 March 1944

'The actual area of fighting was not much bigger than a tennis court. There wasn't much shooting. People were using swords, bayonets and knives.'

Major Bill Williams, Animal Transport Officer, 80 Column, 1st South Staffords

WITH THE attack on Imphal and Kohima in progress, the Japanese were reluctant to be sidetracked. Their slow response to the air landings gave Calvert's 77 Brigade freedom to strike out from Broadway and establish the main Block astride the road and railway linking Mandalay and Myitkyina. With this in place, Special Force's first task was accomplished. Road and rail communications supplying Japanese forces fighting General Stilwell's Divisions were blocked. Slim remarked: 'It was impossible for the enemy to ignore this.'[1]

The Japanese in the locality agreed. They responded vigorously, giving Calvert's force immediate attention. They attacked on the first night and followed up with another assault the next day. A 6,000-strong scratch force was being assembled to crush Special Force and its Block, but these efforts were to end in failure, heavy losses and withdrawal.

With Broadway established, Brigadier Calvert and 77 Brigade's main body marched west to 'Railway Valley'. They left Broadway on 8 March, making for Henu village, close to Mawlu and around 20 miles north of Indaw. This force consisted of Calvert's HQ (25 Column), the Gurkhas (6 GR's 36 and 63 Columns) and the South Staffords (38 and 80 Columns). Two Columns of Lancashire Fusiliers (20 and 50) were to be deployed as floaters. They were to cut communications to either side of Mawlu, giving Calvert's force more time to establish a heavily fortified Block.[2] 50 Column would guard the northern approaches, while 20 Column protected the south. The idea was to keep the Japanese at Indaw and Mohnyin fully occupied.[3]

Bill Towill described the country in the Chindits' operational area: 'For a distance of some 60 miles northwards from Mawlu, the road and railway which comprised the main supply route for the Japanese 18th Division facing Stilwell and his forces in the Hukawng Valley ran side by side through quite a narrow valley, hemmed in on the east by the Gangaw Range, rising in places to 4,500 ft, and on the west by a tangle of hills.' It was difficult going: '... steep slopes intersected by a multitude of steep-sided valleys, carrying rivulets and streams which feed into each other until they become substantial watercourses. This craggy, jungle-covered terrain is traversed only by footpaths – and even they are few and far between.'[4]

A Japanese garrison of around 500 second-line troops was based at Mawlu, only a mile from Henu. Calvert planned his approach with care. He sent Major Freddie Shaw and his 6 GR Column towards Nansiaung (where they skirmished with the Japanese), while the South Staffords and 77 Brigade's Defence Company, under Captain MacPherson, continued towards Henu.[3] Bill Williams was Animal Transport Officer (ATO) with the South Staffords' 80 Column:

'It took us about five days to march from Broadway to Henu. The going was tough. In effect, we were crossing a mountain range, ascending precipitous slopes, going down, crossing chaungs and climbing up another 2,000 ft to 3,000 ft. When we arrived our Column was told to capture and hold one of the hill positions in the Block. 38 Column had been given a floater role. This high ground became known as "Pagoda Hill". We soon discovered we were overlooked – to our utter amazement, Japs were still in Henu village and they were firing down on us.'

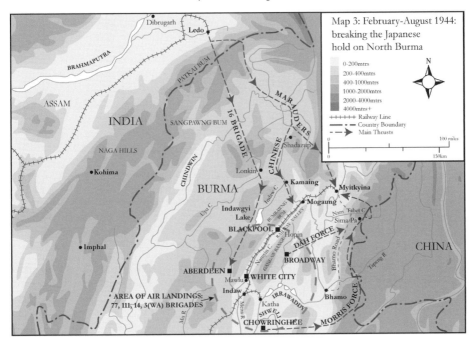

Map 3: February-August 1944: breaking the Japanese hold on North Burma

Major Degg's South Staffords had been the first to arrive at the railway near Henu.[3] Degg called for a large air drop, including wire, but this fell wide and took a week to retrieve. The enemy reacted swiftly, before his men could dig in. On 16 March they began to infiltrate between the Columns attempting to establish the Block. When Calvert arrived with his HQ during the following day, he concluded that the Japanese must be thrown off Pagoda Hill.[5]

80 Column's Machine Gun Platoon Commander, Lieutenant Norman Durant, was on a hill with the road and railway at the bottom, just 200 yards away. There was an unoccupied hill 100 yards south and Durant was ordered to occupy this feature with two Platoons and two Vickers. They managed to dig in before dark. Just across from them was Pagoda Hill, but there had been no time to occupy it that first night.

At dawn there was shouting on the hill opposite and Durant was surprised to see a party of six Japanese walking down towards the road. In his excitement he grabbed a Bren and fired from the hip: 'I missed the lot but it certainly gave them the surprise of their lives.'[6]

Durant then heard firing behind him. He was warned that the Japanese had infiltrated on to the hill first occupied. Durant got a Vickers into position and sprayed the offending area. Two Japanese fell and four more fled. Later, he spotted Japanese crossing open paddy from the Mawlu direction. His Platoon inflicted many

casualties with the Vickers but the surviving Japanese eventually reached the safety of dead ground, behind the hill.

At around 11.00 heavy rifle and machine gun fire opened up from Pagoda Hill, together with mortar fire and grenades from a Japanese Platoon newly arrived on an adjacent hill to the east. Casualties mounted over the next few hours. Durant remembers Calvert arriving at 16.00. By that time, a third of the men were casualties. The firing intensified and it appeared that the Japanese were planning to rush the road and attack from Pagoda Hill. Michael Calvert:

> It seemed to me that shock tactics were needed if we were to succeed in ejecting them from the Henu area and setting up our Block. If we could get them off that hill we would probably win the day, but if we allowed them to stay there and consolidate their position it would take God knows what to shift them and might easily wreck the whole operation.[7]

Norman Durant heard Calvert asking how many men could be spared to attack Pagoda Hill. He was told: 'About 20.' He then replied: 'Right, we'll go straight up.' Durant and Mortar Officer George Cairns prepared themselves, picking up grenades and checking their revolvers: 'We had been shot at all day and everyone felt like getting into the Japs and exacting a bit of

NOTHING STRONGER FOR MEN OR
MULES THAN WATER

The fundamentals of survival: men and animals can last
for some time without food, but must water regularly in
the tropical heat. This caption is not quite correct. The men
enjoyed the occasional tot of rum. (Tony Wailes)

*resulting in the posthumous award of the VC to
Captain George Cairns of the Somerset Light Infantry,
attached to the South Staffords.'*

Williams and others saw Cairns lose his arm to a sword-
wielding Japanese officer. Cairns had also been bayoneted
twice. He repeatedly bayoneted his opponent, discarded
his weapon, picked up the sword and continued to fight
with it until he collapsed. This was also witnessed by
Norman Durant. Durant went up the hill 'like a two-year-
old', took the path about 12 ft below the Pagoda that led
to the houses, rounded a corner and was confronted by a
Japanese Section getting out of their trenches under the
nearest house and coming straight for him, 'the leading
two with bayonets fixed and rather unfriendly expressions being about 20 yards on my right.' He attempted
to fire his revolver twice but nothing happened – the
hammer had worked loose. With no-one to help him,
he threw a four-second grenade over the heads of the
two leading Japanese and dived off the hillside. He was
shot in the leg as he jumped but was unmolested when
he landed. His Sergeant rounded the corner and shot
the two leading Japanese. Durant's grenade had caused
casualties and the remaining Japanese moved back. The
Sergeant, seeing no sign of Durant, thought he had been
captured and 'went quite berserk, grenading like a lunatic
until the area of the huts was clear.'[6]

Durant now saw the fighting in progress farther up
the hill. He watched Cairns and a Japanese struggling
on the ground. He climbed towards them, picking up a
Japanese rifle

*'I saw George break free and, picking up a rifle,
bayonet the Jap again and again like a madman. It
was only when I got near that I saw he himself had
already been bayoneted twice through the side and
that his left arm was hanging on by a few strips of
muscle. How he had found the strength to fight was
a miracle, but the effort had been too much and he
died the next morning.'[6]*

As this description suggests, the Pagoda Hill encounter had a special kind of savagery, later described as
medieval. The Chindits had charged upslope and the
Japanese had run down, meeting in an explosion of
fighting across that small, flattish area. Bill Williams was
surprised at the Japanese reaction:

*'I was amazed that the Japs left their relatively secure
position. The actual area of fighting was not much
bigger than a tennis court. There wasn't much shooting.
People were using swords, bayonets and knives. I had
my carbine but used my kukri. Afterwards, I took a*

retribution.' Durant was ordered to take a party to the
left and clear the houses on the hill. Another officer was
told to go right and clear the Pagoda.[6]

Calvert ordered his men to fix bayonets, yelled
'charge' and ran down into the valley before Pagoda
Hill. He stopped to demand that the half of the South
Staffords who had frozen get going, then carried on
and reached the slope of Pagoda Hill.[7] Later, with some
tact, he wrote that his orders 'were not immediately
understood in the uproar of firing, as they were rather
unusual.'[3] They were met by the Japanese, who charged
down and fought a vicious hand-to-hand battle in a
small, relatively flat area only some 50 yards square. Bill
Williams saw Calvert come forward and suddenly shout:
'Charge! Charge the hill!'

*'I can remember thinking: 'This really doesn't have
anything to do with me. I'm an Animal Transport
Officer.' Nevertheless, I took part in the charge up
Pagoda Hill and, as a result, I witnessed the action*

sword from a Japanese officer. I still have this weapon in my possession.'

The Japanese were pushed off the hill, towards Henu village. Later, they withdrew into Mawlu as Henu was set ablaze by 80 Column's flamethrowers. Many Japanese were cut down as they crossed an area of open paddy.

Norman Durant had his wound dressed: 'The hill was a horrid sight, littered with Japanese dead. Already, the ones who had been killed there earlier in the day were black with flies.' The casualties included Lieutenant Noel Day, a Platoon Commander, shot through the back of the head by a Japanese feigning death: 'On trying to repeat the ruse he was spotted by Noel's Platoon Sergeant, who promptly kicked his head in.'[6]

1st Air Commando flew close support during the day. Calvert's Senior RAF Officer, Squadron Leader Robert Thompson, called up air strikes. Some Japanese were conveniently situated on a ridge easily identified by smoke. According to Thompson, one strike was delivered by RAF Vengeance dive-bombers: 'Not one of them missed. It was a shattering attack and any survivors just vanished into the jungle. This was the only occasion on which we had RAF close support. We never again had such a precise target for them.'[8]

Securing the Block had been expensive. Calvert's casualties included three dead and four wounded officers out of the 14 participating in the charge. Twenty ORs died and 60 were wounded. Japanese losses were heavier, with 42 dead counted on Pagoda Hill alone.

77 Brigade's Commander later remarked: 'Victory for a unit in its first scrap is a great morale-builder and lays the seeds in the minds of all for further successes.' Nevertheless, the Japanese had fought ferociously and it was sobering to discover that, in fact, they were members of an engineering unit! Calvert reflected: 'We were lucky to have been bloodied against second class opposition.'[7]

The battle on Pagoda Hill was described by Allen as 'characteristic of much of the Chindit fighting. The philosophy of the Columns was to avoid frontal encounters and the men might march for days without seeing or hearing a Japanese. Then, when the battle broke, it was a question of bloody hand-to-hand combat of the most ferocious kind.'[9] Corporal Jesse Dunn, with 80 Column's Commando Platoon:

'When we went to help on Pagoda Hill, some of our men were killed by Japanese who had pretended to be dead and had fired at their backs, including my old Platoon Commander, Noel Day. These were sharp lessons and on one occasion we finished off 10 Japanese wounded, to avoid similar incidents.'

White City was at a point where the road and railway ran along the edge of the hills, on the eastern side of the valley. On 18 March Calvert's force took a very substantial night drop, including the wire and entrenching tools needed to turn the Block into a fortress. The profusion of white parachutes, draped high in the trees, gave White City its name.[7] Calvert later claimed that he had christened the Block. This drop included stocks of mortar rounds, small arms ammunition and extra rations. Calvert now had the Gurkhas (6 GR), the South Staffords, Brigade HQ and the Brigade Defence Company within the newly established perimeter.[10]

When taking a drop, one zone would be marked for parachute-dropped supplies and a second for free drops.[11] The standard 'AMSAC' (American Sack) container was widely used for air drops over Burma, although many other container types were available for specialised loads such as medical supplies. Parachutes of cotton (and, later, Rayon) ranged from 24 ft to 48 ft in diameter. When dropping heavy loads, multiple chutes – up to four – were used, delivering weights of up to 4,200 pounds. Loads could be webbed together, for a tightly concentrated drop.[12] A basic AMSAC/24 ft chute combination delivered up to 465 pounds.[11]

Ray Newport was an RAF driver attached to three units during his service in the Far East: 31 Squadron, 62 Squadron and, later, 94 Squadron – all flying Dakotas. His main job was refuelling aircraft and bringing up stores for loading. Newport got a new job when Operation *Thursday* began:

'I was 6 ft tall and my long legs were ideal for a "kicker" – a member of the team dropping stores from the Dakotas. Supplies were secured by lashings to rings in the aircraft floor. The loads were prepared as we approached the drop zone. There were three of us: two standing on either side of the hatch and me with my back against the fuselage wall and feet braced against the load. When we got the green light I pushed against the load, helped by the men to each side. We all wore safety harnesses, just in case.'

Michael Calvert kept everyone working hard on improving the defences. White City became a maze of slit trenches and bunkers, roofed with heavy timbers and proof against anything but a direct hit from a heavy shell.[13]

It takes time, however, to construct a fortress. The Block was well covered to the west but was more exposed from other directions, especially the east, where the hilly terrain hid a series of chaung beds offering cover right up to the perimeter wire.[14]

Private Jack Hutchin, with the South Staffords' 80 Column, occupied a position at the bottom of Pagoda Hill, less than a quarter of a mile from the chaung where they drew their water: 'Platoons went out to destroy the railway line. Some sleepers were hauled back to our lines, to reinforce slit trenches on the lower slopes of the hill. My trench was close to the very bottom.' Hutchin described a Japanese assault at White City:

'Hundreds attacked us at about 07.00, with the last daylight assault at around 16.00. Night attacks then followed. Their bugle calls made us laugh. Bizarrely, they sounded like Tiger Rag. *We cut fire lanes on the approaches to the hill, but had no wired defences at that stage. Nevertheless, our Vickers, Brens and 2 in. mortars were sufficient to slaughter the Japs.'*

White City became a powerful concentration of force. Calvert's three Battalions were steadily reinforced. Eventually, given the strong garrison in place and a heavily wired perimeter, the rest of Calvert's substantial force became available for mobile action.

Classic Chindit warfare was founded on flexibility and mobility. Calvert wrote that a Chindit Brigade could penetrate any type of country in eight Columns of about 400 men each, like the fingers of a hand, then come together, concentrating in a clenched fist at an important objective.[15]

Ian Niven, Regimental Signaller with the Lancashire Fusiliers' 20 Column, had marched from Broadway with Major Shuttleworth's detachment – briefed to cut a section of railway:

'It took us 10 days to get to White City. We were the last to arrive and I don't think Calvert was best pleased. Shuttleworth wasn't top of the pops with the Brigadier. Anyway, we settled down and dug in. During the march I began to suspect that Shuttleworth had got us lost. His style was to keep things close to his chest. We would be put in the picture, but only if there was the possibility of battle.'

Shuttleworth, on reaching Pinwe, became snared in the Kaukkwe Valley's dense jungle. On one occasion, showing humour in adversity, he wirelessed for a path to be dropped to him.[16] Ian Niven remembers the Lancashire Fusiliers' warm welcome at White City:

'We were greeted with enthusiasm when we eventually arrived. At that time the defences were still incomplete. Everyone worked like beavers, digging out bunkers and slit trenches, reinforcing the wire and setting booby-traps. White City had a commanding position. I spent

part of my time at Shuttleworth's headquarters, as a Signaller, and the rest of the time digging trenches.'

Others were impressed by White City's layout: a series of small, jungle-covered hills with valleys sheltering animals, medical facilities and other vulnerable assets. Captain Jeffrey, with the Lancashire Fusiliers' 50 Column, later wrote:

The position chosen for the Block could hardly have been better. It consisted of a group of hills set back a few hundred yards from the road and railway line. The defenders of each hill were able to support their neighbours with fire during attack. In the centre of the position the RAP (Regimental Aid Post) and stores depots were being established, and the Sappers had already dug wells to ensure that water would be available if we were cut off from our normal water point. This was perhaps the one weakness in the position, for to reach the water point we had to go out of the main Block and walk along the road a couple of hundred yards to a small ford.[14]

Michael Calvert described White City as

... ideally situated around a series of hills about 30ft to 50ft high, with numerous little valleys in between, with water at the north and south. I brought the village of Henu into our defended area, so that we would have a good field of fire across the paddy to the south. I also brought into the perimeter what we called 'OP Hill', a feature slightly higher than our own little hills, to give us good observation. Our perimeter was now about 1,000 yards long, mostly along the railway, and 800 yards deep.[10]

The Japanese probed White City's perimeter for three days, beginning on 18 March. The main defences were completed by 19 March.[9] All positions were now wired in, telephone lines were buried and mortar and machine gun fire plans ready. Sections received their stocks of ammunition and grenades. Calvert wrote: 'I detached one Company as a floater Company, to carry out short patrols around the Block, outside the perimeter wire, keeping in touch with me by wireless, so that it might attack in the rear any enemy attacking the Block. This was a nerve-wracking job and the Company was frequently relieved.'[17]

A light aircraft strip was cleared, shielded by the hills and the railway embankment. Calvert now had 2,000 men in his well-stocked Block and floater Columns operating to north and south.[10] He also had a sizeable force protecting Broadway, with the King's

81 and 82 Columns and 9 GR's 57 and 93 Columns as garrison.

Calvert called in air strikes to punish the Japanese in Mawlu. Inside White City's perimeter, Signaller Ian Niven maintained a habit picked up during the march to the Block: 'During the trek we all developed habits that stayed with us. I took to hoarding milk powder, mixing it into a paste and snacking on it.'

While those who entered the Block found it offered few attractions, Private Horace Howkins, with the South Staffords' 80 Column, remained confident: 'When we got into White City we were constantly shelled and charged by the Japs, but I felt sure we could hold them. They never got through our wire. The Vickers guns saw to that.' At one point, during a patrol near Mawlu village, they were jumped and Howkins was wounded:

I was shot in the shoulder. The bullet hit the Bren and was deflected into me. It didn't do a lot of damage. Our MO got the bullet out with tweezers and cleaned up the wound, finishing with the comment: "Carry on. You're alright now." Fortunately, the wound stayed clean.'

Howkins was lucky. The Japanese bullet had a smaller calibre than its British counterpart but had a higher velocity. As the Gurkhas' Bill Towill remarked: 'if it hit anything solid, like bone, it tended to turn turtle and inflict a larger wound.'[18]

White City had functioning light plane and Dakota strips by 21 March and the wounded were being evacuated.[5] The bulldozers then went to work to improve the tracks within the perimeter, making it easier to move around.[19] Late on 21 March the Japanese launched a major night attack and fighting continued for some 48 hours. The perimeter held, with the help of air support.[7]

80 Column's Jack Hutchin took part in the South Staffords' savage fighting to throw back the Japanese attacking their section of perimeter. He fought in his slit trench at the foot of Pagoda Hill:

'There was a golden rule on Pagoda Hill: no-one moved after dark. We had a catchphrase that included the Urdu word for 'OK'. We would say: "Thik Hai" and wait for the reply: "Thik Hai, Sahib". Anyone moving was presumed hostile. The Japs then got onto the hill and had to be driven off in hand-to-hand fighting.'

Jack Hutchin waited quietly for the next attack:

'Much of the undergrowth on Pagoda Hill's lower slopes had been flattened early on. In our slit trenches we could see each night attack develop, with the advancing Japanese silhouetted against the sky. I

spent seven weeks at White City. The hand-to-hand fighting continued. We used bayonets, machetes and knives. Having spent a long time under these appalling conditions, our nerves became frayed. I remember one chap — a large, ginger-haired bugger — give out a big sigh. I turned and said: "Is that how you feel?" He replied: "What the f***ing hell has it got to do with you how I feel?" There was no real animosity in his response. He was just tense.'*

Hutchin shared that tension:

'I had only one fight, other than with the Japanese. When visiting the chaung, we always watered the mules and did our washing downstream from where we drew drinking water. On this occasion I saw a chap washing his pan upstream from the drinking water point. He was a bit bigger than me but that didn't stop me having a go. I had suffered plenty of good kickings when I was a kid and it was not in my nature to keep my views to myself. I broke my hand on him.'

The first full-scale assault on White City started at about 6.45pm on 21 March. It struck the northern sector. The Japanese lost heavily and the few enemy inside the wire were thrown out with the bayonet in the early morning. It was during this bayonet charge that the South Staffords' CO, Lieutenant-Colonel Richards, was wounded in the chest and flown out. Calvert ordered Major Shaw's Gurkhas to attack the Japanese rear. An air strike was also called in against the attackers — four Companies of the 3rd Battalion of the 114th Regiment, 18th Division (Stilwell's opponents).[17] 80 Column Commander Ron Degg took over from Richards, who later died of septicaemia in a Dacca hospital for want of penicillin.

Corporal Jesse Dunn helped bring in his CO: 'Richards was a brave man. Three of us tried to get him out. The one holding his legs was killed.' The earlier casualties at White City included Jesse Dunn's close friend, Corporal Fred Lee:

'Fred came from the Evesham area. We got to know each other on the boat to India and played chess together. He was a bit younger than me, just 20 years old, and had married two weeks before going overseas.'

Many years later Jesse Dunn stood before his young friend's grave in Rangoon Cemetery:

'Fred was not alongside me when he was killed, but I saw his body. He was wrapped in parachute silk. Today, he is buried alongside George Cairns, VC. I returned

A young friend's grave: Jesse Dunn, of the South Staffords, took this photograph at Rangoon Cemetery. (Jesse Dunn)

to Burma three times, visiting Fred's grave on each occasion. Michael Calvert was with us in 1997. Fred's brother accompanied me in 2003 and I was able to show him where he had fallen.'

White City's defences had been tested and had held. Even so, Calvert ordered urgent work to improve the wire and this continued for another six days.[5] He was quick to draw lessons. The booby-traps were effective, as was the telephone control system allowing any Section to call for mortar support. Air strikes could be laid on at 2½ hours' notice during daylight. The one major change was to the floater role. The floater force was either embroiled in fighting, without the benefit of wired defences, or too far away to help. Calvert issued fresh orders: 'We decided that the floater Company should try to find the enemy's base or gun area and attack that while his troops were away and not mix in the immediate battle on the perimeter.'[17]

Inside the perimeter, Lancashire Fusiliers' Signaller Ian Niven spent most of his time in a foxhole, waiting for the next assault. He had been with Major Shuttleworth during the big attack of 21 March:

'My job was to relay messages requesting mortar fire to break up the Jap attacks. Everything went well until, suddenly, communications with the mortar teams broke down. There was nothing for it – I got out of my trench, ran towards the mortars and gave them the message in person. Shuttleworth let me have it when I returned: "You bloody fool! What are you doing? Are you trying to win a VC in your first action? Get back where you belong! Don't be so impetuous." I didn't know what "impetuous" meant and I didn't tell him I'd done the

first thing that had entered my head. Anyway, I must have overdone my excuses as he barked at me: "Don't procrastinate, Niven!" This was another new word for my vocabulary.'

During the fighting Niven received grenade fragments in his arm:

'It didn't bother me at first – I was too fired up. Later, however, the wounds began to fester and needed attention. I saw two of our lads hit on my section of the perimeter. One was killed and the other wounded. The dead man was Fusilier Bamford from Manchester and I was in the burial party the next day. I was detailed to dig his grave.'

Wingate flew into White City on 20 March. He gave Calvert an overview of the wider situation, which was volatile enough to temper the Brigadier's first flush of success:

He told me that IV Corps, in the Imphal area, was in quite a state and he had had difficulty in seeing that we were sufficiently supplied. He said Stilwell's advance was slowing up because the Japanese thrust towards Kohima was threatening his own rail communications and he did not want to involve himself too deeply in case his own communications were cut in turn. This lessened the effect of our cutting the Japanese communications, because fighting had ceased at the end of them.[17]

Initially, 77 Brigade had been opposed by Japanese administrative and railway engineering units. Then, however, 15th Army Commander General Mutaguchi ordered the 18th, 56th and 15th Divisions to contribute one Battalion each to an Indaw-based anti-airborne forces Brigade led by Colonel Hashimoto. 18th Division's 3rd/114th Regiment was available early on, reaching Indaw on 17 March. It took 15th Division's 2nd/51st Regiment another 10 days to reach the town. The 56th Division's 2nd/146th Regiment, from the Salween, was diverted to operate against Broadway Stronghold.

The Japanese gained flexibility when they realised that the Allies were in no position to mount simultaneous airborne and seaborne assaults. This freed up four Battalions of 24th Independent Mixed Brigade from deployment in southern Burma against possible Allied landings. Further additions were to be made: 2nd Division's 4th Infantry Regiment, from Malaya, and 2nd/29th Regiment from lower Burma.[20]

These forces were grouped under the command of Major-General Hyashi, of 24th Independent Mixed

Brigade. He took command at Indaw on 18 March. Three Battalions managed to reach their new operational area before 111 Brigade cut the railway eight days later (followed by similar action by Bladet Force near Kyaithyin on 30 March).[20] Lentaigne's 30 Column blew a railway bridge south of Nankan on 20 March and the two King's Own Columns crossed the Indaw-Nabu branch line that same day. By that time, however, the swift Japanese reinforcement of Indaw already had sufficient weight to frustrate Brigadier Fergusson's best efforts to take the town.[21]

As Calvert turned White City Block into a fortress, the Japanese massed against Broadway Stronghold. There was a successful Japanese air attack against Broadway on 18 March. With little early warning, four Spitfires could not get off in time. Three were destroyed on the ground and another was shot down. Two Japanese aircraft were claimed, but the strip's mobile radar was destroyed and the surviving aircraft were recalled to India.[22] Writing after the war, Air Marshal Sir John Baldwin confirmed that the decision to withdraw the fighters was prompted by the inadequate warning given by the mobile radar of the day.

The 18 March air raid destroyed Broadway's stock of medical supplies but these were quickly replaced.[23] A follow-up raid then took place, involving medium bombers with fighter escort. Mobile Columns moved out from Broadway as soon as possible. Lieutenant-Colonel Herring's Dah Force set out immediately, crossed the Irrawaddy and had reached the Bhamo–Myitkyina road by 21 March.[24] The King's 82 Column

Keeping in touch: a Column Signaller at work. As the size of the set suggests, a powerful mule was required to carry the wireless. Typically, they were 'Argentine' mules, rather than the smaller Indian mules. (John Riggs)

stayed put in the area. They had a floater role – providing active defence beyond Broadway's perimeter. Lance Corporal Peter Heppell:

'We stayed at Broadway for some weeks, missing out on White City – probably just as well! We took numerous drops and some stores fell in the trees and into the chaung. On one occasion some bread fell into the river. It was retrieved and "poured" into our mess tins. I just added milk powder and sugar and it tasted great! The American pilots had a tendency to drop high and we often struggled to recover the supplies.

'As for the K-rations, many disliked the processed cheese but I didn't mind it. Being a non-smoker also helped – I traded my cigarettes for chocolate bars. I used to make a cake with mashed up biscuits and Hershey Bars. Those biscuits often had weevils inside, but they became invisible in the mix. This "cake" would keep during the next day's march. Occasionally, I even used powdered dextrose tablets to make a sort of "icing" for my cakes.'

Men became very attached to the mules. Heppell remembers losing 'Rosie':

'The mules varied tremendously in looks and build. Rosie looked like a small pony. She was light on her feet and very careful. Many mules simply barged through jungle. You would have to be careful, ready to dodge branches whipping back. On this occasion we were marching along the edge of a ravine. Suddenly, Rosie went down on her haunches to avoid something. She lost her footing and went over the side. Her Muleteer, a tough guy from the Midlands, went down after her. Some days before we had come across the wreck of an American light aircraft. The pilot's remains were still in the seat. This Muleteer had recovered the pilot's Colt 45. He used the weapon on his mule. We heard a single shot. When he climbed back on the track, his eyes were filled with tears.'

On 19 March Fergusson's 16 Brigade neared Manhton village and prepared to establish Aberdeen Stronghold. 77 Brigade was already well entrenched at White City Block and two Battalions (57 and 93 Gurkha Columns (9 GR) and the King's 81 and 82 Columns), remained at Broadway to defend the first of the Strongholds.

Lentaigne's 111 Brigade HQ and 30 Gurkha Column (4 GR) were in the lower Meza area. This Brigade's two British Battalions (the Cameronians' 26 and 90 Columns and the King's Own's 41 and 46 Columns) were around 10 miles south-west of Mawlu/White City. In addition, Morris Force's three Gurkha Columns, 49 and 94

(9 GR) and 40 (4 GR), together with Lieutenant-Colonel Herring's Dah Force, concentrated on the Bhamo–Myitkyina road. Meanwhile, Major Blain's glider-borne Commando engineers of Bladet Force landed in the Meza Valley during the night of 19/20 March. They were to operate with 111 Brigade and destroy a rail bridge and a section of railway.

Captain Miller, the King's Own Chaplain, recorded the Battalion's first casualty: 'At nightfall or on about 20 March we were safely in harbour. I remember there was moonlight. In the dead of night a shot rang out. Everybody stood to ... nothing happened.' A nervous sentry had heard rustling in the undergrowth and had fired; the round ricocheted off a tree and killed a man sleeping nearby. He was buried at dawn.[25]

Nerves may have been sharpened by their first encounter with the enemy earlier that day, when 41 Column crossed the railway and road. Two Platoons attacked Japanese positions, killing five and wounding 12 without loss. There was great relief the next day, 21 March, when 41 Column found water after going thirsty for 30 hours. Meanwhile, sister Column 46 crossed the road and railway without incident.

The two 6th Nigeria Regiment Columns, 66 and 39, were among units landed at Broadway. Having set out for the area where Aberdeen Stronghold was to be established, they suffered a significant setback. The Battalion was scattered by elements of a Japanese Battalion from 146th Regiment (56th Division).

Their intention had been to destroy an ammunition dump just north of Mohnyin, before continuing on to Aberdeen. It seems that the lead Column, 66, bumped a Japanese patrol, rather than ran into an ambush. What happened next demonstrated the vulnerabilities of Chindit warfare. The men had prepared to cross the main north-south railway and road. They were moving over open paddy before the moon rose. The lead Column came under fire and subsequently the entire Battalion scattered. 39 Column withdrew to make another attempt to cross the valley at a narrower location to the south. Dispersal groups of 66 Column, meanwhile, continued towards Aberdeen. The majority of 6 NR had reached Aberdeen by late March and then garrisoned the Stronghold.[26]

Lieutenant Larry Gaines of 66 Column recalls events immediately prior to this encounter, only a week after landing at Broadway on 9 March:

'My machine gun Section consisted of 12 men and four mules. We had two Vickers guns. The mules seemed quite well behaved. The Nigerians had recovered from the bewildering experience of their Dakota flight. The Recce Platoon was already well ahead, guarding the crossing of the Kaukkwe Chaung. On reaching the chaung it was important to let the mules find their own way up its steep bank. The animals refused to cooperate if their Muleteers attempted to lead them from the front. Our men then moved into night harbour well away from the chaung.'

During the following morning 66 and 39 Columns came together for a supply drop. This went well. Every man got at least four days' rations and a few welcome luxuries: bread, rum and tinned fruit. Meanwhile, the Recce Platoon had reached Lamong and began looking for a crossing of the Namyin Chaung, while keeping the railway corridor under observation. Both Columns rested near Lamong when it got dark. They moved off again at 20.00 hrs, with 66 Column leading. Chinnery quoted Captain Robert St John Walsh, at the head of 66 Column when firing erupted: 'Total confusion reigned, the rear platoons and 39 Column behind us not knowing what sort or strength of opposition lay ahead.'[26]

Larry Gaines remembers that the fire-fight developed as they crossed the Namyin Chaung. The Africans and mules turned back. The Support Platoon moved away a short distance to the left as Gaines attempted to create order out of confusion. More firing then broke out at 66 Column's rear, with the head of 39 Column returning fire. 66 Column's rearmost Platoon was pinned down. They marched back to Broadway. Later, they were ordered to proceed to Mawlu and eventually entered White City Block. Gaines pressed on: 'I managed to sort out my group of odds and sods. I decided to head west and then southwards, to our 24-hour rendezvous. I had 24 Nigerians and 14 mules for company.'

Sergeant Mower was unaccounted for. Gaines had no other European in his Platoon. He was not looking forward to crossing the railway, but this proved trouble-free. A train came down from the north but Gaines favoured discretion and let it pass. Namket Chaung was another challenge. It took some time to find a way up the steep bank on the other side:

'The rendezvous was on a north-south track, west of a marshy area bordering a lake. Eventually, we came across other elements of 66 Column, preparing to leave after a midday break. More men joined this large group, which then set out for Kadu, the 10-day rendezvous. Ten officers and 140 ORs, plus some 40 mules and ponies, were still missing.'

Wingate was livid. He assumed the two Nigerian Columns had allowed themselves to be ambushed due to sloppy security on the march. Bill Towill, an

Intelligence Officer with the Gurkhas (9 GR) and then at Broadway, later wrote:

> Wingate was outraged and furious that this had happened and gave strict instructions that they were to be given no help or succour – if they came to us, they were to be turned away. I gathered that he took the view that this could not possibly have happened had strict march discipline been observed. To bump into a party of the enemy was one thing, but to give them sufficient notice of your approach to lay an elaborate ambush was quite another.[27]

Had this been the case, surely even a small Japanese force would have inflicted catastrophic casualties? In all probability, the real damage was done by confusion in the dark, although Chinnery notes a suggestion that the Nigerians could have been betrayed by their Shan guides.[28] This possibility did not stand in the way of Battalion Commander Lieutenant-Colonel P.G. Day's subsequent return to India. Larry Gaines reflected on the immediate implications for his group:

'Wingate decided we would get no more rations until we reached Aberdeen, which we were to garrison. Aberdeen was 80 miles away. I felt for our Nigerians. They were isolated, in a strange country and living in a very alien environment. The ban on air drops was immaterial – when we separated, we lost our radio. We were on our own and I explained to the Nigerians that it was absolutely vital that we reach Aberdeen as soon as possible.'

Notes

1. Slim, Field Marshal Viscount (1999), *Defeat into Victory*, 267
2. Chinnery, P.D. (2002), *March or Die*, 127
3. Calvert, M. (1974), *Chindits: Long Range Penetration*, 45–49
4. Towill, B. (2000), *A Chindit's Chronicle*, 45–47
5. Rooney. D. (1997), *Mad Mike*, 75–80
6. Durant, Captain Norman, MC, 80 Column (1st South Staffords), letter to his family
7. Calvert, M. (1996), *Fighting Mad*, 150–158
8. Thompson, Sir Robert (1989), *Make for the Hills*, 53
9. Allen, L. (1986), *Burma: The Longest War 1941–45*, 330
10. Calvert, M. (1974), 51–53
11. Larson, G. A. (2008), *Aerial Assault into Burma*, 114
12. Ibid, 112
13. Towill, B. (2000), 63–64
14. Jeffrey, W.F. (1950), *Sunbeams Like Swords*, 65–66
15. Calvert, M. (1973), *Prisoners of Hope*, 39
16. Ibid, 55
17. Calvert, M. (1974), 55–57
18. Towill, B. (2000), 56–57
19. Larson, G. A. (2008), 188
20. Calvert, M. (1974), 59
21. Ibid, 63
22. Ibid, 80
23. Larson, G. A. (2008), 168–169
24. Calvert, M. (1974), 122
25. Miller, Rev. W.H. *A Chaplain with the Chindits*, Imperial War Museum, 80/49/1
26. Chinnery, P.D. (2002), 136–137
27. Towill, B. (2000), 35
28. Chinnery, P.D. (2002), 138

13

ABERDEEN GARRISONED
... WHITE CITY HELD

22–23 March 1944

'When the wounded came out, some just had a piece of cloth tied around their waist. Their kit had rotted away in the jungle.'

Percy Stopher, Medical Orderly

AT FIRST light on 22 March six gliders landed on the jungle clearing named 'Aberdeen', bringing in American engineers and plant needed to prepare a C-47 strip. Lead elements of Brigadier Brodie's 14 Brigade began to arrive during the early evening of the next day. His two Black Watch Columns, 42 and 73, were to block the Indaw-Banmauk road. The Brigade would also block the southern approaches to Indaw and White City. Meanwhile, 111 Brigade would stop Japanese movement along the Pinlebu-Pinbon road. Fergusson's 16 Brigade would attack Indaw, a key garrison town on the railway.

Having crossed the Chindwin, 16 Brigade took what was said to be a 'special' route. Fergusson's men found it special for all the wrong reasons. Gordon Hughes, a 22 Column Platoon Commander, recalls one appalling stretch: 'After some miles on this route the jungle became more and more dense, the bamboo changing to a horrible, prickly type. Before long we had to resort to cutting, to form a passage for the mules. Our rate of progress was now down to a mere 100 yards per hour. We were on the point of giving up and retracing our steps when we heard a trampling noise some distance in front, which turned out to be a small herd of elephants. They conveniently trampled down the thick bamboo and we followed their tracks until we were clear of this difficult area.'

Brigade elements then reached the site of Aberdeen, some 60 miles west of Broadway. It was at Manhton, just east of the Meza river and 25 miles from the railway supplying the 18th Division, fighting Stilwell's Chinese, and the 56th Division, opposing the Yunnan Chinese. Slim paid tribute to Fergusson's men: 'The Brigade had covered 450 miles of about the most dif-

ficult country in the world in just over six weeks – a magnificent feat of endurance.'[1]

Aberdeen encompassed three villages: Kalat, Manhton and Naunghmi (where the airstrip was located). Fergusson chose this site during a reconnaissance flight which included the valley around Manhton:

It had much to commend it. On three sides were high hills, inhabited by Kachins to the north-east, where we could form them into a sure warning screen, to guard against surprise from that quarter ... On the east lay the waterless hills ... On the west, save for one pass at the head of the valley, leading to the reputed garrison of Mansi, there was the thick jungle of the Chaunggyibya Reserved Forest. Only from the south, from the main Banmauk-Indaw road, could the enemy move against us in force ...[2]

In *The Wild Green Earth*, however, Fergusson acknowledged that Aberdeen did not meet a crucial Wingate requirement for a Stronghold, as it was 'highly accessible' to the enemy. Yet, he felt its advantages outweighed this. Aberdeen was only two days' march from Indaw and 14 miles from the Banmauk-Indaw road. It was positioned at the junction of the Meza River and the Kalat Chaung, with the airstrip on the east side of the river. The dominant feature was a hill at the northern end, where the permanent garrison would be located.

A few days earlier Flight Lieutenant John Knowles, the RAF Officer with the Queen's 22 Column, had been ordered to ride a pony back up the track to meet Wingate, who had flown in by light aircraft:

Levelling: American engineers at work on a C-47 strip. (Trustees of the Imperial War Museum)

'He and a few others were in a basha. I went in and saluted. The floor was covered in maps. Wingate was very curt and stiff. He asked: 'Where are we?' I asked permission to look more closely at the maps. I was halfway to the floor when he snapped, 'Never mind. We're here,' pointing with a stick. He then ordered me to look at a particular area and assess its suitability for a Dakota strip. This became Aberdeen.'

A light aircraft landed safely on Naunghmi's clearing during the afternoon of 21 March. An Airstrip Construction Supervisor closely examined the flat area earmarked for Aberdeen's landing ground. Some Chindits worked all night to prepare a glider strip. The gliders landed at dawn and the construction team went to work. They had two bulldozers, a carry-all, a grader, a tractor and a jeep. The Chindits continued to help prepare the 3,600 ft C-47 strip, which was ready by the evening of the next day.[3] It was operational within 36 hours of the pathfinder glider landings.[4] Some 700 sorties would be flown into Aberdeen in the six weeks until its closure in the first half of May.[5] The early arrivals at Aberdeen had included elements of the Leicesters' 17 and 71 Columns. They took up defensive positions around the clearing and organised work parties to help the glider-borne engineers.[6] The Queen's officers at the

scene included Flight Lieutenant Knowles, who had assessed Aberdeen and was now busy directing soldiers to chop away paddy bunds: 'We soon discovered that this job couldn't be done with entrenching tools. We needed that machinery.'

During the morning Knowles saw Phil Cochran arrive in a Norseman. Conscious of his bearded, malodorous condition and ragged appearance, Knowles approached, saluted and introduced himself as 'Flight Lieutenant Knowles from Brooklyn, N.Y.'

'Cochran gave me what I can only describe as a long, fish-eyed stare, then deliberately turned away to address a remark to his equally spic-and-span, clean-shaven US officer colleague. That was it. I could only turn and leave. I understand that the late Phil Cochran had a good record and was highly regarded by both his superiors and his subordinates. Unfortunately, I have no golden words from this famous American Commander, to record for posterity ...'

Early arrivals by C-47 included Bill Smyly, a veteran of Operation *Longcloth* the previous year. Having recovered from his lone walk-out to Fort Hertz, Smyly had rejoined the 3rd/2nd Gurkha Rifles in southern India:

'We were equipped with Bren carriers. I couldn't see the relevance to jungle fighting and kept testing them to see what they would do ... and they frequently didn't! They were always getting stuck and REME help was needed to retrieve them. My Colonel was relieved when I applied to go back to the Chindits and their mules. One of Bernard Fergusson's Animal Transport Officers (ATOs) had dropped out and I filled the vacancy.'

Bill Smyly became 22 Column's ATO.

Many of Fergusson's men experienced extreme hunger. On 19 March, 45 Column took a drop near Mezam village and left half the supplies cached for sister Column 54, bringing up the rear of 16 Brigade. Wireless Operator Philip Sharpe wrote:

> It was at this drop that a Lance Corporal and three men were caught stealing rations and charged. Certainly, they were not the only party on collection who had done this but, according to the grapevine, they had been suspected previously. Before we moved off they were flogged by the CSM in front of their Platoon and the Lance Corporal was reduced to the ranks.

Floggings were rare but did occur from time to time for serious offences, such as sleeping on sentry duty or stealing rations.

The Queen's Columns, 21 and 22, arrived at Aberdeen on 19 March. Tony Howard, an NCO Signaller with 21, recalls that they had only a brief stay, moving on the following day to support the main Brigade assault on Indaw and its airfields. Elements of the Queen's were briefed to ambush the Banmauk–Indaw road at Milestone 20. The Leicesters and 45 Recce would attack Indaw from the north, in line with Wingate's new orders of 12 March. The original plan required Fergusson to orbit Indaw and swing round, to attack from the south east. Now there would be a direct assault. When the Queen's left Aberdeen, it was still little more than an overnight bivouac.

Wireless Operators and Muleteers got little rest on the march. Exhausted at the end of the day, the Muleteers had to water, feed and groom the animals, while the wireless team offloaded the equipment, set up the wireless and aerial and dealt with all traffic before closing down for what was left of the night. They were also busy during the three-hour lunchtime halt. The wireless was carried in a 'Yakdan', a large leather case around 3 ft long and 20 in. deep. Tony Howard welcomed the later issue of aluminium carriers, painted green: 'These were lighter than the leather ones and, being rigid, gave more protection to the contents. You could also use it as a table, for resting the wireless on when we were set up and operating.'

Shortly after leaving Aberdeen 21 Column Wireless Operator George Hill went down with dysentery:

> 'This is one of the most debilitating afflictions. It is absolutely essential to "answer the call" immediately, since there is very little warning of, and even less control over, the impending discharge of very hot, virtually liquid matter – which can be, and usually is, a very painful experience! In the early stages of the problem I once didn't make it in time and spent that night operating the wireless set standing up, a distinctly awkward procedure. I carried the results of that episode around with me until we arrived back at Aberdeen some three weeks later, the first opportunity I had to do anything about it.'

His discomfort was aggravated by another unfortunate complaint: 'Not exactly a "malady", it was caused purely by dirt, sweat and friction but, being a "private" affair, I will go no further ... As time went on I was leaving the Column more and more often to relieve myself and finding it increasingly difficult to regain my allotted space in the Column, immediately behind the battery mule ... I was getting to the point of not being able to carry on. For this reason I was relieved of my pack, which was carried on a pony.' This was to have unfortunate consequences.

Lancashire Fusilier Ian Niven, with 20 Column, agrees with Hill's description of dysentery:

> 'It is the most debilitating affliction. It feels like a syringe has extracted every ounce of energy in your body – not a problem if you are in a comfortable situation but the pits if you are required to be an all-action Chindit!'

45 Column approached Aberdeen on 21 March. When they moved out two days later they had five days' rations up. During the approach to Indaw they could hear fighting at White City from their night bivouac to the west, near Nyauggon village. It was at this point that wireless problems began to dog 45 Column and other Brigade elements. This was due to the relocation of Special Force HQ to Sylhet, as Japanese pressure on Imphal increased. It added to Fergusson's difficulties in coordinating his Columns.[7]

Philip Sharpe wrote: 'The big Royal Signals transmitters closed down, remaining silent for one full week. Admittedly, back in Sylhet, temporary 22 sets began to operate, but they did not have enough power to be effective at a sufficiently great distance.' In Sharpe's view, given that the seriousness of the Japanese threat to Imphal was known, it had been an error to site Special Force communications so far forward.[7]

It is likely that Wingate pressed for 14 Brigade to be flown in as quickly as possible (even before Aberdeen's garrison Battalion) to pre-empt any attempt to take this Brigade away from him. Nevertheless, it took time to bring in 14 Brigade's four Battalions. The two Black Watch Columns were ready to fly in during the night of 24 March but bad weather caused delays. 3 (WA) Brigade was also to fly in; two Battalions were earmarked for White City and the remaining Columns would garrison Aberdeen.[6]

14 Brigade's York and Lancaster Columns, 65 and 84, entrained at Lalitpur during the third week of March and arrived in North Assam eight days later. They continued by train to the Brahmaputra river, completing the journey with a day-long voyage upriver and a further two days on the narrow-gauge railway. Battalion Commander Philip Graves-Morris recalled a stop at a tea station in Assam. The ladies had organised tea for the troop trains and 65 and 84 Columns were their first customers: 'They eagerly asked permission to give tea to the troops and rallied to the carriages with half a dozen puny household jugs of tea, to find 900 pint mugs waving from the windows, all down the train.'[8]

On reaching Lalaghat airfield the Columns drew stores and grouped into plane-loads. Each man had to decide what was vital to carry in. Everyone went through his kit, which might include toggle rope, mae

west, cardigan, gym shoes, spare shirts, shorts, socks, pants, groundsheet, blanket, mess tin, knife, fork and spoon, towel, soap, machete or Dah, spare laces, mosquito cream, Mepacrine, clasp knife, two grenades, chagul, five days' rations, weapon and ammunition. These decisions were far from easy. Graves-Morris: 'Experiments in personal loads had been made throughout training but, when packing up for the last time, everything seemed so important that one felt that one should leave nothing behind.'

Graves-Morris led 84 Column. His Column officers included Major R.D. Shiell (Staff Officer), Captain N.R. Douglas (Adjutant), Captain R.P.J. 'Paddy' Dobney (Administrative Officer), Lieutenant F.H. Luxa (ATO), Captain F. Lockett (MO), Flight Lieutenant J.C. Franks (RAF Officer), Captain (Rev.) C.M. Johnston (Padre) and Burrif Recce Officers Lieutenant K.A.P. Liddy and Captain G.C.O. Boug.[8]

Shiell and his 65 Column counterpart, Major J.C. Bruce, MC, struggled with the C-47 manifests. Capacities varied and changes in aircraft allocation forced them to repeatedly re-calculate the distribution of men, animals and stores. The weather was stormy but 84 Column's lead elements took off from Lalaghat during the evening of 1 April. Some mules resisted their opportunity to join the adventure. Graves-Morris: 'Periodically, a wayward mule had broken away and gone careering across the airfield. It was an offence for a Muleteer to let go of his mule and many of them

That knowing look! A 45 Recce Chindit passes the village maidens at Nyauggon. (Cyril Baldock)

stubbornly hung on, being swung round in the air like the weight on a bolas.'

1 April was an appropriate date. Aberdeen was made unserviceable by torrential rain and all aircraft had to return to Lalaghat. They set out again the following day, this time with success.[8]

Fred Gerrard of 84 Column landed at Aberdeen on 2 April, at the second attempt. He fell asleep during the flight and woke to the shout: 'We're landing!' He looked out, saw lights everywhere and immediately assumed the aircraft had turned back during his doze. He was wrong. On touchdown the door was opened and brisk orders given: 'Mules out! Load them up. Put on your packs. Move into the jungle at the side of the runway. Bed down until daylight.'[6]

Bad weather and the shortage of aircraft slowed 14 Brigade's fly-in, which took until 4 April. The fly-in of Aberdeen's garrison took a further week. Aberdeen would be closed just over three weeks later, on 6 May. Until then, Aberdeen would be garrisoned by the Nigerian 39 and 66 Columns (6 NR). Aberdeen's garrison was never challenged. Bernard Fergusson wrote: 'Except from the air, it was never subjected to attack, for the Japs had so much to worry about elsewhere that they could never amass a ground force strong enough to take it on.'[5] Fergusson must have had in mind the intense fighting around White City.

Bren gunner John Simon, serving with 16 Brigade's HQ Column, worried about his 'mucker':

'Les Martindale went down with malaria at Aberdeen. I did my best to look after him. Jap fighters regularly strafed the strip. They would come in between two hills and try to destroy the light planes parked up. We were told not to fire, so as not to give away our positions. Morale was good at Aberdeen. The only casualty I saw was a fellow caught in a free drop. A bale of fodder hit him and caused injuries.'

White City had already held a series of powerful Japanese attacks. The Block's defenders included Private Jack Hutchin of the South Staffords' 80 Column:

'We were doing well. I didn't think we would hold the Japanese that long, but we took a lot of punishment, with many killed and wounded. One man died in my trench. Shrapnel cut his stomach open.

'The supply situation at White City was excellent. Our defences were now very heavily wired and we withstood repeated assaults. Besides the wire, the airdrops included lime, as the stench of dead men and mules became overwhelming in that heat. The Japs tried to blow gaps in the wire using Bangalore Torpedoes – long lengths of bamboo filled with explosives. We had plenty of ammunition and food and a highly regarded leader in Calvert. He was extremely hands-on, with a very obvious presence. Calvert was an engineer who could blow up anything. He was a powerful man in every sense, physically and in his role as 77 Brigade's Commander.'*

White City's defences had survived a severe test on the night of 21 March, with a savage fight lasting nearly eight hours. The Japanese broke through at one point but were then ejected. Around 300 were killed. Even when things were relatively quiet, the daily round at White City carried the risk of instant death. Ian Niven, a Regimental Signaller with the Lancashire Fusiliers' 20 Column:

'Life in the Block was horrendous. They never left us alone. Air raids were routine. We didn't worry too much about the bombing, as their aim was lousy, but the shelling was different. As darkness fell we knew what was coming. On some occasions they attacked the Block on three sides. One side was secure, as the slope was too steep to assault. To my knowledge the perimeter was breached on just the one occasion and the enemy was soon pushed out.'

Niven had the impression that the enemy was confused over the strength of White City's garrison. The Japanese began to call in reinforcements. Casualties continued to mount as the wire was stormed time and again and shelling continued. Niven remembers Fusilier Leo Conroy, killed at White City at this time. He had been a trainee Signaller in Niven's class at Inverness. Niven himself had a close call:

'We were being shelled by a heavy mortar. There was a tremendous explosion near me. The blast hit me from the left and I was blown into the trench. Then someone else jumped in and landed with their legs over my shoulders. I knew we were safe in that "hole" but the back of my neck was wet. I thought he'd been wounded. In fact, he'd pissed himself as he jumped into the trench. I was just happy he wasn't wounded.'

Others were much less fortunate. Some wounds were very severe and the Burmese climate tended to reduce the efficacy of some drugs. For example, the heat and inadequate fluid intake could have serious consequences for patients treated with Sulphanilamides. The drug could crystallise out in the kidneys, suppressing urine production.[9]

On recovering from the initial shock of the heavy mortar blast, Ian Niven checked himself for damage:

'The hearing in my left ear was down to five per cent after this episode. It only annoys me now that my right ear is much less efficient.'

As casualties increased jobs were reallocated. Signaller Niven became a Battalion Runner, replacing a man who had been killed. He was now the link between Major Shuttleworth and Brigade HQ:

'This was a lonesome job, but I did it only twice. I handed messages to Calvert and took his orders to Shuttleworth. There was no conversation. I gave Calvert a smart salute. I think this was the only time I saluted during my entire time in Burma.'

Wingate had visited Bernard Fergusson at Aberdeen. Fergusson wanted to rest his Brigade after the exhausting march in but Wingate told him to press on immediately, before Indaw could be further reinforced (a task, unfortunately, already largely accomplished by the Japanese). The Indaw plan was confirmed and implementation began during the night of 24 March. The 2nd Leicesters and 45 Recce would attack Indaw from the east and north respectively. One Column of the Queen's would block the Banmauk–Indaw road and the other would attack on the west. The Leicesters would take Inwa village, one mile north of Indaw and 45 Recce would occupy the north end of Indaw Lake.[10]

At this point the scale of the now substantial Japanese response to the second Chindit incursion was not appreciated by Special Force. Around 20,000 Japanese troops were massing in the main Chindit operational area of Indaw–Mawlu. Later, Calvert reflected: 'The 14th Army, fighting for its life on long land lines of communication, but now supplied and reinforced by air, also never appreciated that the Chindits eventually absorbed the strength of two Japanese Divisions while they themselves had only three and a half Divisions to counter.'[11]

There are conflicting accounts of the date and outcome of the last meeting between Wingate and Fergusson. The exact date (23 March or a day or so earlier) could have a bearing on the validity of differing views on the extent to which Fergusson believed 14 Brigade would support his attack on Indaw.

Most of Fergusson's weary men left Aberdeen on 24 March. They were still without 51 and 69 Columns, detached earlier to attack Lonkin following the pledge to Stilwell. These Columns were returning, but were 10 days behind – too far away to influence the outcome at Indaw. On 16 March this detached force had entered Lonkin, dealt with limited opposition, destroyed supply dumps and withdrew the following day. Before the attack they had captured a Japanese soldier who

subsequently escaped and alerted Lonkin's garrison. This had the happy result of prompting the Japanese to withdraw, leaving only a small unit still in residence. Nevertheless, the two Columns suffered casualties at Lonkin and the remaining Japanese defenders had to be overcome with the help of a Lifebuoy flamethrower. It would take these Columns over three weeks to reach Aberdeen; they arrived on 10 April.

The 2nd Leicesters' Columns led the advance on Indaw. It seems that Fergusson did set out with the understanding that 14 Brigade would help, but he was to be disappointed. Whatever transpired between Wingate and Fergusson at their last meeting, any plan to use 14 Brigade at Indaw was not progressed (perhaps because Wingate had no opportunity to issue orders before his death). Clearly, on his side, Wingate still hoped that the capture of Indaw's airfields would prompt the fly-in of additional forces, despite all warnings to the contrary.[12] In reality, success at Indaw was a forlorn hope, given the now sizeable Japanese reinforcement of the town.

As 16 Brigade continued, the dry country caused much suffering in the Columns. Indeed, lack of water largely shaped the course of events. The Japanese now covered all obvious watering places on the approaches to Indaw. 16 Brigade would have to fight for its water.

Lieutenant-Colonel Graves-Morris, commanding 14 Brigade's York and Lancaster Columns (84 and 65): 'The problem of water was always with us and in the very early stages largely governed our movements and even operations. Water had to be reached at least once every day ... It was estimated by the medical staff that the men should drink at least 12 pints a day to replace the loss of sweat. Except when near good streams, of course, this was seldom possible. Every evening, on arriving in bivouac, the first question as officers came up to the "Conference Tree" was: "Is there any water in the area?"' As often as not, Graves-Morris could only reply that the Burrifs were out looking for water. Men resorted to digging out dry river beds – 'a slow and laborious task, taking half an hour to fill a water bottle and of no use to a thirsty animal.'[8]

Living under extreme strain at besieged White City, men found solace in companionship and the stolid behaviour of the animals. Six days after the establishment of White City, shortly after the first full-scale assault on the perimeter, a pony gave birth to a foal in the middle of another attack and a ferocious mortar barrage. The garrison was captivated by this new arrival, christened 'Minnie' after a nearby mortar post. During yet another heavy attack a mule broke loose and kicked Minnie above the right eye. A Lancashire Fusiliers' NCO fought to save the eye. Calvert ordered periodic reports

On their way: Nigerian troops board an RAF Dakota for the flight into Burma. (Trustees of the Imperial War Museum)

on Minnie's progress to be circulated to all forward positions. Minnie made a real contribution to morale as her
condition improved. When recovered she took to 'doing
the rounds' of the mortar positions, on the scrounge for
tea – which she would drink from a pint pot. Minnie's
antics chased away grim thoughts from men who knew
they were fighting for their lives.

Minnie survived White City and further battles
and went on to enjoy a distinguished military career.
'Chindit Minnie' features in Evelyn Le Chene's book
Silent Heroes, a tribute to the courage of animals in
war. Minnie became the Lancashire Fusiliers' Mascot,
returned safely to India, travelled on to Britain and
subsequently joined the Regiment on a tour of duty
in Egypt.

16 Brigade's advance on Indaw may have been compromised inadvertently by movements of 111 Brigade.
One of the latter's British Battalions, the Cameronians,
moved in a wide sweep west of Indaw and crossed the
Banmauk road on 22 March.[13] This Battalion had landed
at Broadway and then set out for the Mawlu–White City
area. With the Japanese offensive against Imphal, however, they were then ordered to cut the Indaw–Homalin
road. They marched through the night and bumped a
Japanese patrol. Donald MacKay, the Cameronians'

Padre: 'After crossing the road safely we had to run
across a wide, shallow ford with mules, under light fire.
Two were wounded and others had very narrow escapes
as they strove to rescue some of the wireless loads
which had fallen into the stream.'

An RAF Officer was shot through the lung and an
NCO badly wounded in the arm. They were flown out by
light aircraft the following morning: 'Half an hour later
the lads were in Broadway and by nightfall safely back
to the base hospital at Sylhet, where they both made a
good recovery.'

Meanwhile, the King's Own Columns were fast developing a reputation for being unlucky with supply drops.
Three successive attempts, on 21, 22 and 23 March, all
ended in failure. K-rations were finally dropped at 10.00
on 24 March. There was some concern that nothing had
been heard from 41 Column's Recce Platoon.

Medical Orderly Percy Stopher was involved in Dakota
casualty evacuation flights, primarily in support of 23
Brigade during the Imphal/Kohima fighting. Stopher
hadn't flown before but he took all new experiences in
his stride. He had a naturally straightforward outlook:

*'When I needed help, I asked for it. We got the job
done and I kept out of trouble as much as I could. We
were a small unit of 60 men, with three officers and a*

few NCOs – about 70 in all. We were in for around five months, evacuating as many of the lads as possible to our depot. Some engineers built a casualty reception area equipped with showers and baths. When the wounded came out, some just had a piece of cloth tied around their waist. Their kit had rotted away in the jungle.'

Some Chindits took to modifying their dress, to ease discomfort, especially after the Monsoon broke. The first item of clothing to wear out was trouser bottoms, almost always wet and caked with mud. The men also found that wet webbing would abrade and fail, the straps being under constant pressure. Some men with wounds had clothing removed to gain access to their injuries. Percy Stopher described the reception of the less serious cases:

'As they came off the aircraft all clothing was removed. They had hot showers and changed into clean clothing. We couldn't give them much to eat, as proper food would have killed them. These men had often gone many days without a drop.'

The badly wounded and seriously ill received immediate care and were then moved on to military hospitals. Some serious cases, on making further progress, were flown to South Africa to continue their treatment. Stopher's unit became expert, working swiftly on hostile ground:

'You couldn't afford to hang around. The turnround was very fast whenever possible. Our engineers continuously cleared new jungle strips, to keep us close to the fighting. The wounded took priority. We would take the sick if there was room, but the wounded always came first.'

There was little interest in the Japanese wounded – other than the obvious precautions in the interests of personal safety and the need to avoid a last, desperate throw of a grenade:

'We'd just walk by Japanese casualties. We didn't see any wounded; they were all dead. They were fanatical and fought to the death. The operational area was usually cleared by the time we arrived.'

In some circumstances Medical Orderlies had to stay put for several days:

'Occasionally, we went hungry ourselves. At one point we tried to recover panniers that had been out of reach

for eight or nine days. We didn't worry about the mould on that bread.'

Percy Stopher tried to look after himself. There were no food shortages back at Airbase and he stayed fit, although suffering bouts of malaria. Ironically, the greatest threat to his future came earlier on, shortly after his arrival in India. He came close to losing a leg to septicaemia, probably caused by a small but deep puncture wound from a jungle thorn:

'My leg was red from toe to thigh. When three officers did their rounds I heard them discussing the need to take my leg off. They then decided to try a treatment using heated paste. It was on my leg for five days and it did bloody hurt, but the red line on my leg began to recede.'

Some of the small parties resulting from 66 Column's dispersal (during a night action involving both 6 NR Columns) now came together. Landing at Broadway on 9 March, they had set out for Aberdeen after three days. The night engagement happened a few days later. A week had passed and Lieutenant Larry Gaines, with a large group of 66 Column, was heading south to avoid bad terrain. Larry Gaines:

'On the way down one African went haywire. He fired two rounds at the man in front of him, wounding him in the bottom. I thought we had bumped into Japs in the process of climbing up. Our casualty had to be carried on an improvised stretcher. His attacker was handcuffed.'

Discipline was vital if the men were to stay alive. Some were flogged for losing rifles or kit. Gaines recalls the occasion when a Nigerian soldier lost his rifle: 'He was given another rifle, some rations and told to bugger off.'

At about 17.00 on 22 March they reached Pinmadi village. Larry Gaines:

'Despite the rain we settled down to the comfort of a good meal of chicken curry, rice and rice wine. The latter was easily the best I tasted in Burma, being sweet and full of kick. Our rations were running very low and the Africans used their "danger money" to buy rice. Considering the Japs were so near, the villagers were very kind and helped us as much as possible. Our Burmese in the Column were extremely good at ferreting out rice and other food. I was glad that, in addition to everything else, I had held on to my precious tin of curry powder. It didn't last long but it was very useful, as it gave K-ration stew an entirely different taste.'

They made an early start on 23 March, heading north for Natmah. There was trouble with the mules. A bamboo stake had pierced one animal's groin and another had developed an infection. Both had to be shot. Larry Gaines, meanwhile, continued his education in jungle warfare:

'By this time I had learnt quite a lot. In particular, on a future show I would do my best to be with the Recce Platoon and share in the rice and other food they acquired in the villages, before the main body arrived!'

The men of 66 Column were now very thirsty. On 24 March they headed south for water at Malim. They watered on the Natmawk Chaung and the men then began to think of their stomachs. Larry Gaines: 'During one halt I wasted valuable energy knocking down what appeared to be red apples on a tree. I discovered that they were hard-skinned, with sticky, evil-smelling centres.'

The men no longer had a wireless and could not request a drop. Captain Peter Crews, leading 66 Column's Support Platoon, consoled himself with a local cigar when they reached Namakyaing village, on the Nami Chaung. They moved on after a short rest. The K-rations were virtually exhausted; but villagers had provided rice, potatoes, tomatoes, chickens, eggs, water melons and other food – all eagerly purchased.

They continued to follow the strict drill for night bivouacs, putting out sentries, stand-to, making small fires to heat up supper and, finally, stand-down. Larry Gaines:

'If boots were taken off, plimsolls were put on at once, in case a quick getaway was needed. One evening I decided to dubbin my boots. I put my hand inside, felt something, dropped it and saw a snake rearing up. Luckily, one of my men reacted quickly and sliced off its head with his machete.'

Notes

1. Slim, Field Marshall Viscount (1999), *Defeat into Victory*, 258–259
2. Fergusson, B. (1946), *The Wild Green Earth*, 72–80
3. Larson, G. A. (2008), *Aerial Assault into Burma*, 183
4. Towill, B. (2000), *A Chindit's Chronicle*, 36
5. Fergusson, B. (1946), 84–85
6. F.E. Gerrard, unpublished MS, October 2000 (via Bill Smith)
7. Sharpe, P. (1995), *To Be a Chindit*, 210–215
8. Lieutenant-Colonel P.H Graves-Morris, unpublished MS (via Bill Smith and Corinne Simons)
9. Baty, J.A. (1979), *Surgeon in the Jungle War*, 67
10. Calvert, M. (1974), *Chindits: Long Range Penetration*, 69
11. Ibid 59–60
12. Allen, L. (1986), *Burma: The Longest War 1941–45*, 339–343
13. Calvert, M. (1974), 63

14

ENGAGING THE ENEMY

24 March–1 April 1944

'The aircraft dropped jellied petrol on the Japanese strongpoints. One man close to me had his fingers shot off. It was my first attack and afterwards I began to develop a feeling that I wouldn't get out of this alive.'

Corporal Ted Treadwell, 71 Column, 2nd Leicesters

BY THE last week in March Wingate's Chindits were fighting for their lives, as the Japanese now realised the significance of this major incursion and attempted to crush it. White City's garrison expected more big attacks and stiffened the Block's defences. With the Dakota strip operational, most supplies were flown in rather than dropped. The early Dakota loads included four 25 Pounders, six Bofors anti-aircraft guns and four two-pounder anti-tank guns.[1]

Brigadier Fergusson's 16 Brigade found little to encourage them as they edged towards Indaw. They had been in Burma for six weeks and were exhausted by a penetration march of several hundred miles. Their fighting capacity had been reduced by the strain of walking in and by the detachment of two Columns for the Lonkin attack. Furthermore, the Queen's 22 Column was needed to block the Indaw–Banmauk road. The Japanese had reinforced Indaw, with particularly strong defensive positions around Thetkegyin. Taking account of the dry country, they covered all the obvious locations for watering. There was no immediate prospect of help from 14 Brigade.[2] Wireless difficulties made things worse. 45 Column Wireless Operator Philip Sharpe later suggested that a nine-day period of disrupted wireless traffic, caused by the move from Imphal to Sylhet, was the major contributor to 16 Brigade's failure to take Indaw.[3] This may be going too far but, clearly, it did nothing to help.

The Indaw attack ended in frustration. 22 Column was successful on the Indaw–Banmauk road but sister Column 21 was less fortunate. Briefed to march west of Indaw Lake and attack Indaw East airfield from that direction, it was itself attacked in bivouac (which had encroached on a dirt road used by Japanese trucks).[2] In

addition, 45 Recce's two Columns, 45 and 54, became involved in hard fighting without water and suffered heavily as they extricated themselves. They fought for their water at Thetkegyin on 26–27 March. Only the 2nd Leicesters' Columns, 17 and 71, reached their objective. They held on grimly at Indaw, but were eventually ordered to withdraw. Most 16 Brigade Columns then returned to Aberdeen to regroup.

Orde Wingate didn't live to see his plans unravel. On 23 March the Special Force Commander flew into Broadway, then travelled on by light aircraft to meet Calvert at White City. Squadron Leader Robert Thompson saw Wingate for the last time at White City: 'In spite of his pith helmet and Lee-Enfield rifle, his bearded figure always appeared to have stepped straight out of the *Book of Joshua*. I travelled with him over to Manhton ... For the short, 30-minute flight in an L.1 we lay on the length of board behind the pilot's head.'[4]

Wingate had a meeting in Imphal with the 3rd Tactical Air Force Commander, Air Marshal Sir John Baldwin. After the meeting, Wingate and his ADC, George Borrow, accompanied by two war correspondents, took off for Sylhet in a B.25.

Captain Bill Towill of the 3rd/9th Gurkha Rifles watched Wingate climb into the B.25 for the flight to Imphal:

'He landed safely. The weather was atrocious and, as I understand it, he was strongly advised to wait for the storm to pass before continuing on to Sylhet. Disastrously, his very worst characteristic then came into play. He would never take advice from anyone. He was always, always, incontestably right! So, he insisted

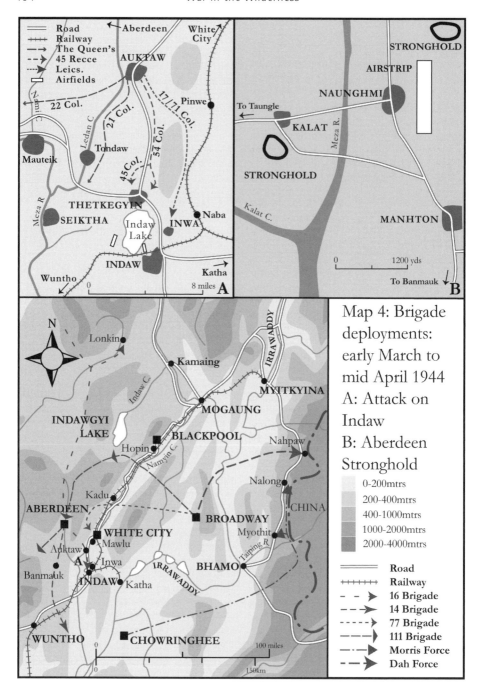

Map 4: Brigade
deployments:
early March to
mid April 1944
A: Attack on
Indaw
B: Aberdeen
Stronghold

on flying and the almost inevitable happened. In the appalling weather, his plane flew straight into the side of a mountain and all the occupants were killed. Rescuers arriving at the crash site found his much derided ancient sun helmet lying clear of the wreckage.'

Accounts differ on the state of the weather but the fact remains that the bomber hit the slopes of the final range before the Sylhet Plain. Strangely, one report states that his aircraft was flying *east* when it went into the *western* slope of the hill (*Major R.D. van Wagner, Air Command and Staff College, 86–2580*, April 1986). Baldwin, flying in his own aircraft at the time, later claimed he saw Wingate's B.25 flying a level course just six minutes before the crash. Subsequently, he suggested that the weather may not have been the cause. He claimed that the B.25 pilot might have left the trailing aerial out. The static shock could have been powerful enough to have knocked him unconscious when he switched on to talk to Sylhet Control. He would have slumped forward, putting the B.25 into a dive. Wingate was in the Co-pilot's seat and the Co-pilot would not have had time to regain his seat before impact. Of course, this must be pure conjecture on Baldwin's part.[5]

There are several theories concerning the cause of the accident, including poor weather, Wingate's insistence on flying immediately despite the adverse conditions and possible problems with one of the B.25's engines (a factor perhaps set aside when Wingate demanded to fly without delay). There is also the alternative explanation put forward by Master Sergeant Charles N. Baisden, USAF *(National Archives, CAB 101/182)*. Baisden had written to Field Marshal Viscount Slim shortly after the publication of *Defeat into Victory* and had received a reply. This prompted a second letter from Baisden, dated 1 August 1962, which sets out another theory concerning Wingate's death.

Eighteen years earlier, Charles Baisden had been serving with 1st Air Commando's B.25 unit. They received a message to fly Wingate on the day of his death: 'Prior to this order we had bombed up our Mitchell bombers for a strike mission into Burma. We were loaded with a mixture of fragmentation cluster bombs and incendiaries. A normal load was 12 clusters, or 72 fragmentation bombs.'

According to Baisden, when these bombs arrived at Hailakandi, they were 'in very poor shape', with the binding wires rusted in. The pilots made a point of never landing with these cluster weapons on board. Baisden added: 'My crew (I flew with Lieutenant-Colonel R.T. Smith, as Armorer-Gunner) was the crew scheduled to pick up General Wingate, as we had flown him before; but for some reason another crew took off at short notice to do this job.'

The other aircraft was piloted by First Lieutenant Brian F. Hodges: 'This crew took off with the load of fragmentation clusters, such as I have described. They did not download, probably due to short notice or for reasons I do not know. They made a landing to pick up General Wingate (they did not salvo their bombs prior to this).' Baisden then set out his theory to Slim:

Three or more fragmentation bombs broke away from the cluster, either during the loading or in the air turbulence of the weather front. There was always some air currents in the bomb bay which could cause the arming vanes to spin off and the bomb or bombs rolled into the fuselage and detonated. Proof that this happened? I have none, but until someone, some place, some day, comes up with a better explanation, this is what I really believed happened.

On the face of it, it is hard to believe that an experienced B.25 crew would fly an air communications mission combining a British Major-General *and* a full bomb load! Some descriptions of the crash site portray a scene of complete devastation. Certainly, no human remains could be identified prior to burial. Equally, according to Major van Wagner, the evidence at the crash scene suggested that the aircraft nosed in, with the wreckage 'severely confined', which would argue against a mid-air explosion.

Bill Towill, of 9 GR, described Wingate's loss as 'a profound disaster, greater than any we could ever remotely contemplate.' Until that point Chindit casualties had been far fewer than those inflicted on the enemy. Michael Calvert wrote: 'It was only when Slim reversed Wingate's theories and practice, and returned to the old stereotyped warfare, that the Chindit casualties began to mount.'[5]

The feeling persists to this day that everything fell apart when Wingate died. The shock of the loss certainly unbalanced Special Force. After all, it was the creation of one man, to the point where the loss of that man caused significant damage, made all the more serious by the way the Chindits identified themselves with him alone. When Wingate died on that hillside, the Chindits lost more than their Commander.

Richard Rhodes James offers a perceptive description of the effect on 111 Brigade: 'It was the start of a new frame of mind in the Brigade; if, in future, things went wrong they would say, "Wingate would not have done that." We became, in a sense, a Brigade looking at the past and criticising the present.'[6]

Calvert described his reaction in *Fighting Mad*: 'It is difficult to express in words the horror and dismay we felt. The Chindits would fight on, but they would never be quite the same again without the man who created and inspired them.'[7]

Chindit training and resolve rose above this grievous loss, but the efforts of Brigade and Column Commanders to carry on were not assisted by Slim's choice of successor.

On hearing the news of Wingate's death, Churchill said of him: 'Here was a man of genius, who might well have become also a man of destiny.' When the news reached Palestine, all flags from Jewish national and municipal buildings were flown at half-mast. Wingate's wife, Lorna, was pregnant when he left for the Far East. Their son, Orde Jonathan, was born on 11 May 1944, just over six weeks after the fatal crash. Haile Selassie, Emperor of Abyssinia, became one of Orde Jonathan's godfathers. Wingate's mother-in-law later wrote that Wingate was convinced he would never die on the battlefield. Alice Hay also recalled that Wingate never liked flying.[8]

In early 1959 Orde Wingate's Hagana Medal was presented to his son at the Israeli Embassy in London. During the ceremony Colonel Yuval Naman said: 'We, who live in the State of Israel, guard well the memories of the heroes of our history – Joshua, Yiftach, Gideon, Joav and others. With them we guard the memory of Orde, Hayedid ("The Friend").'[9]

In one of his last letters home, Orde Wingate was in a reflective mood: 'I feel rather like an ill-tempered dog, when the world suddenly begins patting it.' Much later, Alice Hay wrote: 'Years of disapproval, hostility, even persecution, had left their mark; it was not surprising. I personally always found that he responded quite normally to courtesy, friendliness and affection, both from myself and from others.'[10]

It may be that the family's judgement of those who opposed Wingate hardened when they heard that a senior General, surrounded by others in the Mess at Delhi, remarked: 'Well, thank God that fellow Wingate is dead!' Apparently, Mountbatten overheard, rebuked the General and added: 'Wingate was my friend.'

Most Chindits had no time to think deeply about the death of their Commander. They were too busy trying to stay alive themselves. In the week immediately following Wingate's death Special Force Columns fought a series of vicious engagements.

The Queen's 22 Column prepared to block the Indaw–Banmauk road. They established a bivouac on The (pronounced 'Tai') Chaung – a haven for the Column's 'soft skin' elements. The fighting Platoons formed a Battle Group and moved rapidly to the planned ambush site at Milestone 20, a stretch of the Banmauk road running parallel to the river. It had been recognised for some time as the perfect site for an ambush.

Gordon Hughes commanded 22 Column's 14 Platoon. He liked the look of the Milestone 20 site:

> We reckoned that lining the roadside with our men would produce a curtain of fire at any convoy passing through and at each end we would position a Lifebuoy flamethrower and a Vickers MMG firing along the road, to seal the ambush. The only possible escape for the enemy was to the south, but this was a precipitous, rocky slope ending up in the river.[11]

The Battle Group spread out and took up positions for around 1,000 yards along the higher side of the road. The other side was strewn with trip-wired grenades. They were ready on 26 March. On the night of the ambush the men waited quietly in their positions along the road. At about 0300 the far-away drone of trucks was heard. Gordon Hughes:

> Then, as if out of nowhere, we saw trucks loaded with enemy soldiers in our midst. As the leading truck reached our MMG and the flamethrower, we heard the rattle of the machine gun, followed by a huge gush of flame from the Lifebuoy and the lead truck burst into flames. Our second machine gun and flamethrower joined in, sealing the road at the other end. It was all hell let loose, the machine gun fire supplemented by a full complement of Brens, rifles and carbines lining the roadside. For good measure, dozens of hand grenades were hurled into the inferno. The enemy had no way of escape and they were virtually annihilated, as our later inspection was to prove.

It appears that some 21 Column elements also took part in this ambush. Flight Lieutenant John Knowles, 22 Column's RAF Officer, teamed up with Lieutenant Douglas Walker-Brash of 21 Column at the western end of the ambush. They could hear the calls of Japanese survivors attempting to regroup. Knowles threw a grenade but it failed to detonate. His companion had better luck. When firing ceased the screams of Japanese wounded could be heard. The Chindits stayed in their positions until first light. Gordon Hughes was surprised to find that the Column's casualties totalled only one officer and two ORs killed and a small number of wounded, now being tended by the MO.

The ambush had been a complete success. Many Japanese had been killed at little cost to the Chindits. This, however, turned out to be just the prelude to the battle proper, fought a few hours later. With hindsight, it would have made good sense for the Queen's to

Last hours: Wingate boards an aircraft on the fateful day. He always said he would never die on the battlefield. (Trustees of the Imperial War Museum)

have moved on immediately, rather than stay put and offer a target to the larger Japanese force now bent on retribution.

Gordon Hughes' Platoon joined others inspecting the wrecked, burnt-out Japanese vehicles. 14 Platoon was detailed to fire any trucks which had escaped damage and, in addition, to bring up water for the rest of the men:

On reaching the road the ambush scene was quite staggering. Each truck appeared to have a drum of petrol on board which had either exploded or caught fire. As a result the trucks were a complete write-off and lying alongside were dead Japanese in all sorts of weird positions. Some had obviously attempted to penetrate our positions, only to be cut down by small arms fire. Others had tried to make for the river side of the road, to collapse in a hail of shrapnel from exploding grenades. Strangely enough, we saw no live enemy and could only surmise that if there were any they had managed to crawl away into the thick undergrowth.[11]

According to Hughes, however, there was at least one Japanese survivor still close by. He shot and killed 22

Column's Lieutenant Harry Sparrow as it grew light. Hughes remembered him as 'a mild-mannered man on whom you could always depend.'[11] Flight Lieutenant Knowles has another recollection of this young officer's death: 'Those closest to him told me he moved into the line of fire just as a Bren opened up, the burst killing him instantly.'

By around 0830 the Column, buoyed with success, prepared to march back to The Chaung. They moved off thirty minutes later, with 13 Platoon at point. Almost immediately they came under sudden, intense small arms and mortar fire. Hughes' Platoon was at the rear and took the brunt of it. Later, Hughes claimed that the Milestone 20 ambush had not been 'closed'. One truck in the convoy was lame and had lagged behind. When the ambush was sprung, it was far enough behind to turn round, head back to Indaw and raise the alarm. 22 Column now faced a strong and determined enemy force.[11]

The Japanese attacked the Chindits' hastily re-occupied positions and suffered many casualties to the Brens and the remaining trip-wired grenades. The attackers were then caught on the open ground between road and river. Gordon Hughes:

The first attack came in frontally, the enemy as usual screaming their war cries like a troop of baboons, led by an officer brandishing his two-handed sword and accompanied by an NCO with an Army flag tied to his rifle and bayonet. The attack failed under our intense, accurate fire and they withdrew after sustaining heavy casualties. Again and again they launched furious frontal attacks, with no deviation in their tactics. God knows how many of their men were killed. While they were able, on occasion, to force their way into our positions, they were quickly evicted by some excellent bayonet work.

There was a 45-minute lull. It seemed as though the Japanese had had enough. Column HQ ordered all elements to prepare to pull out but a fresh attack soon developed on the left flank. This was stopped by concentrated fire and volleys of rifle grenades, yet it was pressed to within 20 yards of the Chindits' positions.

RAF Officer John Knowles remembers the long line of 22 Column HQ officers and Riflemen on their stomachs, looking down the slope and waiting for the next attack. Most of the Riflemen were positioned further down, dug in among the brush at the foot of the rise. There was around 30 yards of relatively open ground between the two lines of positions. John Knowles:

'A young soldier, Private "Chippie" Wood, was downslope and wounded. I was stretched out prone at the top, six or seven men to the right of the Column Commander, Lieutenant-Colonel Terence Close. The men with Wood were calling for help but no-one went down. We were still under fire and the man on my immediate right, Private Potter, suddenly got it from a sniper high in a tree on the other side of the road. He gave a short, sharp cry of pain and arched and twisted his body. The bullet entered at a point over his left kidney.

The medic, meanwhile, declined to go down to Wood under heavy fire. I asked Close for permission to go but was refused. I decided that, for once in my life, I would do something brave and soldierly. I pretended to have misunderstood Close, called out "Thank you, Sir" and went anyway. It wasn't difficult to find Wood, as a couple of his mates were with him and calling. He was conscious but could barely walk. Unfortunately, he was far too big for me to carry upslope.'

Knowles made slow progress up the hill, with Wood's left arm draped over his shoulder, both somehow evading the gunfire. On reaching the top Knowles tried to comfort the man but Wood knew he was dying. Flight Lieutenant Gillies, DFM, 21 Column's RAF Officer, was with the group. John Knowles:

'He took charge of Wood. He took him to a nearby dry chaung and called up an L.5 to fly him out. The aircraft appeared, made a couple of passes and then flew off. Gilly was furious with the American pilot, claiming that the L.5 could have got in. Perhaps that was so, but Gilly was an exceptional pilot and not every man had his skills. Wood had been hit somewhere in the torso. Dying from internal bleeding, he could not be evacuated. He had to be shot, so as not to fall into the hands of the Japanese. As a matter of force majeure, this unhappy duty was performed by 22 Column's Padre.'

The Japanese withdrew and 22 Column took the opportunity to 'melt' into the jungle. The Battle Group broke into smaller parties, each taking a different route back to The Chaung bivouac and Column HQ.

According to Gordon Hughes, Private Potter was shot in the stomach: 'Some of his gut was pushing out of his abdomen, with extensive bleeding. We put a large field dressing on the wound and managed to stem the bleeding, but the poor chap must have gone through hell as he rocked to and fro on the saddle of a casualty pony.'[11] John Knowles clarifies this by noting that Hughes was describing the exit wound, Potter having been shot through the back by a sniper above and to his front.

Hughes had been shocked by the earlier death of George Britnell, the first member of 14 Platoon to be killed. Gordon Hughes: 'I recall writing to his parents in Aylesbury. His mother replied with the most poignant of letters. She had two other sons away fighting and lived in fear for their lives.'[11]

Later, John Knowles heard that some 22 Column officers felt that his recovery of Private Wood under fire warranted formal recognition but the Column Commander refused to consider the idea. Knowles and Close were not the best of friends.

Hughes led 14 Platoon away from the ambush site. They zig-zagged east and only went west towards The Chaung when sure that they were not being pursued. They reached the RV at 19.00, to find things well-organised. Hot tea was distributed as the MO took over the wounded. Hughes tucked into his biscuit 'burgoo', made tastier with the addition of tinned pork loaf: 'We felt as if we were in heaven. It was better than dining at the Ritz.'

Finishing his food, Hughes then began his rounds with the Platoon Sergeant-Major: 'I checked each man, to see that all was well.' He then visited the MO and spent time with Potter, who had been given morphine: 'He was cheerful and talkative, telling me about his family in Wales.' Potter was flown out from Aberdeen but, sadly, died on the operating table in India.[11]

Disaster could overtake a Column ambushed in night bivouac. York and Lancaster Chindit Fred Gerrard wrote: 'Most attacks on a Column's bivouac area came about because normal routine was not followed, by bivouacking near water or on a main path, or excessive noise or smoke from cooking fires – so betraying your position. When this occurred the Japanese infiltrated the defensive circle during the night with a small group, who would then open fire, especially against the centre, with as much firepower as possible. This, of course, had the effect of causing casualties among the senior and essential personnel who were normally positioned in the centre, as well as destroying mules and communications equipment. This created mayhem among the defenders, who couldn't tell whether the firing within their midst was friend or foe.'[12]

Being surprised in bivouac was the cardinal sin, but luck could suddenly desert any Column. During the evening before the Queen's fought its successful action at Milestone 20, the main body of 21 Column was heading for Indaw as planned, Lieutenant-Colonel John Metcalf wanted to cross the Sedan Chaung before nightfall. This chaung, flowing into the southern end of Indaw Lake, was found to be more of an obstacle than expected. It was decided to defer the crossing until morning.

The night bivouac first chosen was found to straddle a track and was moved. It seems, however, that the track took an unexpected sharp turn, returning into the edge of the final bivouac area. The Column was still coming into bivouac when three lorry-loads of Japanese infantry suddenly turned up. In the *mêlée* Metcalf was wounded. NCO Signaller Tony Howard was nearby:

'All hell broke loose when the Jap trucks arrived. There were grenades going off and machine gun fire everywhere. We Signallers had unloaded one of our mules. I was putting up the aerial and only 20–30 ft away from the Japs as they drove in. I had no weapon, so I moved back and grabbed my rifle, getting off a couple of rounds. Then the dispersal bugle sounded.'

Subsequently, Metcalf was criticised for the 'loss' of 21 Column's wireless equipment. Howard sheds light on what actually happened:

'It takes three people to unload a mule and four to load it. The wireless set and batteries weighed 100 pounds on each side. The Muleteer held the animal's head during loading and the others manhandled, supported and secured the loads, standing on both sides of the mule. Our wireless pannier was open, as I was setting up the aerial. Somehow we retrieved the aerial, shut the pannier, reloaded the mule and led the animals into the jungle, away from the fighting.'

Signaller George Hill confirmed Howard's account. In the darkness, Hill heard who he thought was Metcalf shout: 'My God! Stand to!' as the trucks appeared. Hill's story, although written many years later, continued his ingrained habit of calling Acting Sergeant Tony Howard 'Corporal':

Our Corporal was on the far side of the track, hurling our 40 ft aerial over a tree branch ... Our Corporal arrived back like a scalded cat — he hadn't carried his rifle! This was when I confirmed what I had already suspected: that it is just not possible to load a mule from one side only. Nobody wanted to be on the side from which the bullets were arriving.

These accounts suggest that some men were aware that the track still intruded into the bivouac but the enemy vehicles arrived before matters could be put right. Tony Howard even suggests that there may have been two tracks:

'The other track was not on the map and probably ran parallel to our track, cutting the bivvy at part of the perimeter. It was pure bad luck, with the Japs arriving at exactly the wrong moment.'

In the darkness and confusion George Hill heard another voice shout: 'The CO's been hit!' It sounded like the Adjutant, Major Achieson. The Signals Detachment should have been at the *centre* of the bivouac but they were exposed, towards the front, when the enemy arrived. The dispersal signal gave Tony Howard a major problem:

'I didn't know the 24-hour rendezvous. By the time we had loaded the mule and collected the rest of them, everyone else had disappeared. We were alone but fighting was still going on and it was very dark. There was no-one on hand to give advice. I led my little group away from the noise. In a few minutes we came to the chaung. The water wasn't deep but the banks went down 50 ft and had a slope of 45 degrees. It would be impossible to get down with the mules under these conditions. When I realised we couldn't get across, I wasn't sure what to do next ... and it was up to me! So I led them back from the chaung. Then we bumped into another, larger dispersal group along the river bank. God was with us that night. I can't describe the tremendous feeling of relief when we found them.

Feeling the heat: the Mortar Platoon of the Queen's 21 Column on the march. Third from the left is Sergeant 'Smudger' Smith. Behind him (with the pipe) is Corporal Jack Goldfinch. This photograph was taken in early May, during the march to Broadway and evacuation to India. (The family of Jack Goldfinch)

'Now part of this much larger group, we managed to get our mules down the steep bank and across the waist-deep chaung. We then climbed the other side, which was not quite so steep at that point. I was then challenged. All our passwords began with the letter "R", as it was widely believed that the Japanese would mispronounce them. Anyway, I couldn't remember the password and just shouted: "It's me! Sergeant Howard! Signals!" We had found more of the Column.

'Feeling slightly more secure, we caught our breath for an hour or so. I was a bit shaken up but still thinking clearly. I can only put this down to my lack of imagination. As for that "lost wireless" business, I can only say that our dispersal procedure was to join the HQ group and its two Cypher Sergeants, but I recall no orders to actually do this when we bumped into the Japanese (or, rather, when they bumped into us).'

In all probability, this was because the Signals Detachment was 'out of position', towards the front rather than at the Column centre with HQ – which was in broadly the right place but with no idea that the track ahead still cut the bivouac's perimeter.

Tony Howard and his Signallers had joined a group led by the Column Intelligence Officer, Lieutenant Phillips, who had thought the wireless was lost. Yet its 'loss' (if that is what it was) lasted only a brief time.

George Hill was fed up as he had lost his pack. Weakened by dysentery, Hill had been told to put his pack on a pony. This animal disappeared during the night encounter with the Japanese. Pony and pack were gone forever. Howard quietly shared his rations with him.

The dead were buried early the following morning. By this time George Hill felt more positive. His dysentery had disappeared at a stroke, cleared up by the traumas of the night: 'Odd, as I would have thought the opposite to be more likely. My dysentery never returned.'

Most men took this fight in their stride. Tony Howard:

'We didn't see Japs under every bush after that. I think we were too tired to be worried. We were soon on the move and returned to the usual preoccupations: how long did we have to go before the next stop and what did we have to eat when we did stop?'

21 Column's fighting capacity, however, was greatly reduced. Many men and mules had been lost, as had much of the heavy equipment. Tony Howard reflects on Metcalf's evacuation:

'Metcalf was a first class officer and a very nice person. Whenever he visited the Signallers he would hand over the odd tin of bully or pineapple. A Jap bullet *struck his revolver and injured his hand. As far as I'm concerned his wound, rather than the handling of the engagement, was the reason why he was flown out.'*

This point was confirmed later, in a letter of 6 December 1957, from Bernard Fergusson to Major-General Kirby, then preparing the *Official History of the War Against Japan*. George Hill described 'the largest defaulters' parade I ever saw while in the Army – around 60 to 70 men drawn up in three ranks in a small clearing just about big enough for the purpose. These were the men who had lost weapons, equipment or animals in the skirmish ...' Almost certainly, Hill was watching a roll-call rather than a 'defaulters' parade'.

Many Chindit columns were heavily engaged at this point, yet news of Wingate's death spread rapidly. Captain Bill Towill:

> We found it difficult to believe that fate could have been so cruel to deprive us of our leader less than three weeks into an operation which had enjoyed such great success. No matter who was appointed to succeed him, he could never be replaced and a sudden gloom descended upon us all.[13]

This was the problem in a nutshell. No-one – with the possible exception of Calvert – could stand in Wingate's shoes. 111 Brigade's Richard Rhodes James understood the peculiar vulnerability of special forces aligned too closely with a charismatic commander:

> We had been devised as a special force with a special mission and an independence of operation. The idea, conceived by Wingate, had been fostered by Churchill. We would subordinate ourselves to no other commander; only one man knew how to use us. Now that man was dead we were to be at the beck and call of anyone who felt in need of help and our strategic plan would be discarded. Already, we heard that 23 Brigade, one of the reserve Brigades, had been taken over by the 14th Army for the Kohima operations in the Naga Hills. Were we to become the plaything of 14th Army?[14]

The reality, of course, was much worse. They would become the plaything of Stilwell, a notorious anglophobe.

Wingate's actions in life made things no easier after his death. It fell to Slim to name his successor. He wrote: 'It is an interesting sidelight on a strange personality that, after his death, three different officers each informed me that Wingate had told him he was to be his successor, should one be required. I have no doubt at all that they were speaking the truth.'[15]

Brigadier Joe Lentaigne was named as the new Special Force Commander and was promoted to Major-General. This was a surprise to all and brought comfort to few. Bill Towill:

> He was not at all in tune with Wingate's ideas, he lacked his charisma and flair and, equally importantly, his high-ranking contacts (for which, of course, he couldn't be blamed) and also his 'hands on' control.
>
> In direct contrast to Wingate, he hardly ever visited his troops in the field, but was content to deal by remote control and he didn't have the weight required to stand up to General 'Vinegar Joe' Stilwell, whose pathological hatred of all things British was legendary. As a consequence, in the closing stages of the campaign the Chindits were remorselessly run into the ground, instead of being relieved.[13]

Lentaigne took over Special Force on 30 March. To many, he was 'a Chindit who appeared not to believe in Chindit ways'.[12] In the month immediately following Wingate's death, 14, 16 and 111 Brigades appeared to lack direction. They stayed around Indaw, ambushing the Japanese and destroying supply dumps but with no firm focus on a major objective. This did not change until late April, with the concerted move north. Meanwhile, the Imphal/Kohima battles approached a decisive phase. Dimapur's huge stores dumps were the prize. Mutaguchi's three Divisions intended to capture them and take the railway supplying Stilwell's Divisions and supporting air operations over 'The Hump'. The Japanese knew Dimapur was lightly defended. They had taken a huge gamble as, unlike Special Force, they had no air supply organisation. They had set out with three weeks' rations and would starve unless they captured stores at Kohima and Dimapur.

Jack Masters took over from Lentaigne as 111 Brigade Commander. He was ordered to intensify operations north of Pinlebu, to block enemy communication to the Chindwin and the Imphal/Kohima front. Brigadier Morris should have taken over 111 Brigade, but he was detached with Morris Force. Lieutenant-Colonel Masters, the Brigadier Major, got the Brigade but not the rank. He was another controversial figure. The man who later became the best-selling author of *Bhowani Junction* and other works, including a vivid portrait of war in Burma, *The road past Mandalay*, had few fans. Bill Towill: 'Though those who knew him well spoke warmly of him, I did not find him a likeable person, when we were later transferred to his Brigade, and that view seems to be shared by several of my old comrades. He seemed cool and distant.'[13]

There was genuine puzzlement over the choice of Lentaigne. In describing the week following Wingate's loss, Towill told the author:

'For us, the wound was almost physical and made worse by the choice of successor. Beyond any doubt, it should have been Mike Calvert, Wingate's staunchest supporter and closest confidant and a grand fighting soldier in his own right.'

111 Brigade's Richard Rhodes James wrote that Lentaigne

> ... always regarded Wingate as something of an upstart. He did not resent his rapid rise, but he thought his ideas were dangerously unsound and totally unproven. This, added to the fact that, physically, he was not up to the rigours of the campaign, had made those first few weeks a very testing time for him and for the officers in his headquarters an embarrassing glimpse of senior officers at logger-heads. That such a man should take over Wingate's job posed problems of its own.[16]

How did Lentaigne get the job? It has been suggested that Calvert was made too much in Wingate's image to be considered. Major Denis Arnold, MC, has another perspective on the matter:

'I spoke to Calvert about this when near Pagoda Hill, at White City, during the 1997 Royal British Legion visit. Calvert dismissed the idea of his taking over Wingate's Command and was adamant that he was not and had not been trained for the job and would not have accepted the Command even if offered to him.'

Slim asked Derek Tulloch (the Brigadier, General Staff) for advice. Tulloch then suggested Joe Lentaigne but is said to have regretted this for the rest of his days. He may not have been aware of concerns within 111 Brigade about Lentaigne's performance as a Brigade Commander, although Tulloch certainly should have known that his choice was no disciple of Wingate.[17] Wingate's deputy, General Symes, was overlooked in the selection process and asked to be relieved. Denis Arnold comments: 'Wingate, according to many, should have appointed Symes as 2 i/c. He was a proven commander in North Africa. He was also loyal to Wingate and believed in him.'

In fairness to Slim, it should be remembered that he had his hands full. The Imphal battle was in progress. If

Wingate's surprise successor: Major-General Joe Lentaigne – 'not at all in tune with Wingate's ideas.' (Trustees of the Imperial War Museum)

the enemy thrust succeeded, IV Corps could be throttled. Slim may have felt that Lentaigne, at the least, would be much easier to handle than Wingate. Rooney expresses pungent views on Wingate's successor:

> Lentaigne had completely failed as a commander in the field and had lost the confidence of his own officers; his inadequacy and his failure to block the railway south of Indaw contributed to the defeat of 16 Brigade and he was so out of touch with Chindit beliefs that, even before he had taken over, he thought that White City and Broadway would be overrun immediately.[18]

Slim now had to decide whether to fly in Wingate's second wave Brigades, given the threat to Imphal and Kohima. When these additional Special Force Brigades were committed, there was then the question of whether to focus the entire Chindit effort on the Imphal/Kohima struggle, supporting IV Corps. Later, Slim said he was wrong not to make this change: 'Imphal was the decisive battle ...'[19]

Slim sought Tulloch's views on the Chindits and Imphal. Tulloch warned that Fergusson and Calvert were too heavily engaged to break away. The compromise was to leave White City in place but deploy 14 and 111 Brigades to cut communications supplying the Japanese 18th and 31st Divisions. Later, Tulloch was much troubled. He came to feel that he should have argued for a complete shift of emphasis away from Stilwell, as this may have saved Special Force from being taken over and 'so misused by him that 90 per cent of its casualties were incurred under his command'.[20]

During the final week of March Fergusson's Indaw attack lost cohesion. What remained of 21 Column, following its night encounter with Japanese trucks, had concentrated by 27 March. They had been due to join the Indaw attack but plans were changed. The 16 Brigade Columns advancing from the north had run into trouble and were suffering from lack of water. On 26 March the Leicesters Columns, 17 and 71, took Inwa and reached water on Indaw Lake but a fighting patrol was ambushed the next day. Inwa changed hands several times on 27 March and access to water became increasingly difficult. Water parties visiting the Indaw Chaung came under fire but air strikes helped to contain the situation. 45 Recce also suffered a check at Thetkegyin, to the north of Inwa. They failed to take strong Japanese positions in and around the village and were forced to withdraw owing to lack of water.

Subsequently, the Queen's 21 Column was ordered to return to Aberdeen, arriving during the second week of April. The long march into North Burma and subsequent trials had taken a heavy toll among the men. The animals also suffered – many now had cuts, sores and saddle galls. The physical and mental burdens were also evident in sister Column 22. Platoon Commander Gordon Hughes described the key symptoms of deterioration: 'Our digestive systems were beginning to revolt at the monotonous diet and we were eating less than 50 per cent of our daily ration. We were all underweight and losing further pounds as the days went by.'

22 Column took no direct part in the Indaw fighting. Instead, they were ordered to patrol the low hills between the Ledan and Nami chaungs, to take pressure off Calvert at White City. They reached a village and attempted a deception, claiming to be the forward elements of a much larger force bound for White City. Although desperate for water, they waited until they were south of the village before watering on the Nami Chaung. They then came under fire and marched into the darkness to evade the enemy. Eventually, they bivouacked and sat through an uncomfortable night following a torrential downpour.

22 Column took the track east in the morning but the going was slow as five men had gone down with cerebral malaria. Gordon Hughes: 'They were very sick

and the Doctor was not hopeful of their recovery, so we bivouacked earlier than normal, in the hope of doing something for them. The Doctor was right and the five men died through the night. We buried them and I remember thinking how sad and forlorn the short row of graves looked, with each man's bush hat perched on the top of a small bamboo cross.'

22 Column continued to 'demonstrate', attempting to draw Japanese units away from White City. The Column's main body circled round and entered the recently visited village once again, claiming to be the 'much larger force', while its Recce Platoon went north on an offensive patrol. Gordon Hughes' 14 Platoon, meanwhile, took part in a successful night operation to blow a bridge across the Meza. The sentries were disposed of and the men sweated for an hour as charges were prepared. They were rewarded when the bridge went up with 'a God almighty roar'.[11]

The Leicesters' Columns came together to clear Auktaw village with the bayonet before a final push against Indaw, to the south. Ted Meese was a Muleteer with 17 Column. His mule saved his life during the fighting with Japanese and Burma National Army (BNA) soldiers at Auktaw:

'Buck went down, having been hit twice – with bullet wounds in the shoulder and neck. The bullet in his neck would have probably hit me but for the fact that I was on the other side. He was still alive and Captain Leyland had a look at him. Both bullets had gone straight

Simple crosses, bush hats and a map reference. (Trustees of the Imperial War Museum)

through – the round in the neck still missing me! Leyland packed a large tablet into each hole and dressed the wounds. Buck was then loaded up and carried on.'

17 Column Wireless Operator Lou Lake witnessed the capture of some BNA men:

'They were put on a plane to India. They were very reluctant to board, being convinced that they would be thrown out at the first opportunity. At one point we also caught a former Sepoy who was on his way back to India with a bagful of Japanese propaganda.'

Initially, some men in the returning Platoons were shaken by the ferocity of the fighting. Ted Meese:

'One of our officers was shot in the leg and his position was hopeless. The MO put him to sleep! On occasions like this there is a lot of tension in the night bivouac. I remember trying to sleep in teak jungle. Teak leaves are as big as buckets and made one hell of a racket when stepped on. Was it friend or foe making the noise?'

According to Corporal Ted Treadwell of 71 Column, Battalion Commander Jack Wilkinson was the first battle casualty. Wilkinson was hit in the arm. Nevertheless, the assault went well, with the resident Japanese and BNA caught off balance. Some were at their ablutions when the firing started. Ted Treadwell: 'When we moved into the village we ate the Japanese troops' food. We discovered, to our surprise, that they were dining on captured Australian tinned foods, including peaches.' They reviewed the fight during the meal. A determined Japanese charge had been stopped with a flamethrower: 'One of our Sergeants was a nice bloke but he wasn't good at giving rapid orders. So I stepped in and snapped: "Get that flamethrower out quick."'

Treadwell and those around him had trouble sleeping that night:

'We felt terrible. They had given us hell when we went in. The fighting was very close-quarters and we had to call in an air strike to overcome them. The aircraft dropped jellied petrol on the Japanese strongpoints. One man close to me had his fingers shot off. It was my first attack and, afterwards, I began to develop a feeling that I wouldn't get out of this alive.'

Treadwell refused to discuss his experiences during this attack in any detail:

'I will never talk about this, because I am a murderer. That's how I look at it. We were all murderers. Killing

people. It was kill or be killed. Before we went in Mountbatten told us, in effect, not to take prisoners. He said: "Do what you have to do and look after yourself." In any case, we couldn't take prisoners. We had no means of getting them out.*

'When we came face to face with the Japanese in that village, we found out that not all of them were little blokes! I was with one of our Sergeants, Joe Chandler. He got wounded and so did some of the others. One officer was severely injured. The badly wounded were a serious problem. We couldn't get them out, so our MO gave them morphine and they were then shot. There was nothing else we could do. It was horrible but there was no choice. The MO had to kill his own mate, a Lieutenant, together with a couple of Privates.'

Happily, Sergeant Chandler survived his stomach wound. He was evacuated by light plane – the pilot was former film star Jackie Coogan. Treadwell exchanged a few words with Coogan: 'He looked at me and said: "Got any souvenirs?" I told him: "Sod that! We don't have time to look for bloody souvenirs!" Coogan then tossed us some cigarettes, in a big American pack.'

Treadwell never saw direct evidence of Japanese atrocities against Chindit prisoners but he was fully aware of what could happen: 'Eight of our men went out with a Lieutenant on a night recce. They were ambushed and found slashed to death. I remember that this officer came from Croydon.'

Corporal Tom Turvey, with 71 Column's Recce Platoon, recalled that Jack Wilkinson had a shattered elbow. The Colonel's Batman was also wounded. This man was known for his pronounced stutter:

'He was hit in the mouth. The bullet smashed teeth and emerged through his cheek. He was flown out by "Flying Mess Tin", our nickname for the American light aircraft used for casualty evacuation. Strangely enough, when the Batman eventually returned to the Battalion his stutter had disappeared completely. That bullet cured him and his speech was perfect!'

Wilkinson carried on for a few days. The MO set his arm, encasing it in plaster. The Battalion Commander remained determined to reach Indaw and its airfields. The combined fighting elements of both Columns pushed forward during the night. In the late afternoon of 26 March the Leicesters reached a spur overlooking Indaw Lake's eastern shore. They prepared to take Inwa village. The plan then required the Battalion to head north towards 45th Reconnaissance Regiment (following its occupation of Thetkegyin). The enemy would be trapped between them. There was no time to lose, as the men were suffering from extreme thirst and had to reach water within a few hours. After a short pause the fighting Platoons moved off, took Inwa and secured an area of lakeside and the Indaw Chaung. The Japanese responded vigorously. 17 Column's Lou Lake:

'I remember using the wireless with bullets zipping through the trees around me. It was hard to focus on the Morse key with all that going on. Later, I remember the CO taking time to thank the three of us for a good job during the action.'

The Japanese were determined to push them away from the water and dominate the situation. Inwa changed hands repeatedly. Corporal Tom Turvey, with 71 Column's Recce Platoon, survived an ambush:

'We were going through a clearing and Percy Lake was leading. Suddenly, there was a loud bang behind us. Oddly, the Japs had a little dog with them. It ran out at us and I fired at it instinctively, missing the animal. Everyone took cover in just a second or two. I never saw any Japanese. The fighting was soon over. We took no casualties but 23 dead Japs were found. There was a chaung close by, with a boat tied up on the bank. The Platoon ferried itself across. My Section was last, of course, and I was the last one to board. I immediately lost one of the oars and then fell in. We had a good laugh about that later. Fortunately, the Rifle Platoons were just behind us. They then returned to the Column and we were left to ourselves in this strange area. The jungle was dense and very dark and everything was bathed in a dull green light. I wasn't sorry when we went back the following morning.'

As 17 Column marched on, tempers wore thin. Lou Lake:

'On one occasion one of my mates was detailed with another man to go to the Column rear and clear the track of any signs of our passing. The bloke who went with him refused to do his share and my mate thumped him. He then got down to it.'

———————

Before setting out for Indaw, Brigadier Fergusson had used Aberdeen as a base for light plane reconnaissance to the south and east. He took every opportunity to visit his Columns. With an eye to the future, 16 Brigade's Commander also requested a surgical team and blood plasma.[21] These resources were to be needed in the days ahead.

While the Leicesters cleared Auktaw, 45 Recce's 45 and 54 Columns continued south. They were to pass through Thetkegyin village and link up with the Leicesters. 45 Column Radio Operator Philip Sharpe recalled 'an air of foreboding' as they advanced on Thetkegyin. The scrub thinned and the going was very hot. Auktaw Forest was dry and all streams were waterless. The next water was at Indaw Lake itself.[22] They stopped at the edge of open paddy on 26 March, with Thetkegyin visible on the other side. The Indaw–Banmauk dirt road was just 30 yards in front of them. They suddenly drew fire and exchanged machine gun bursts with the Japanese occupying the village. Mortar bombs fell behind them. More mortar bombs then rained down; they got closer and one exploded between two signal mules. One animal was torn apart by the blast and the wireless was destroyed. Philip Sharpe:

Simultaneously, two yellow lorries sped in a cloud of dust from the direction of Indaw, passing by us and pulling up no more than 50 yards away. How the Japanese failed to see us was amazing, because we were not in solid jungle. Jumping off the tailboards, they ran into the thickets behind us, presumably to encircle the rear of our Column.'[23]

Sharpe was impressed at their appearance and size: 'huge fellows, nothing like the Japanese we had expected.'

They then saw Colonel Cumberlege and a group of men on the other side of the road, moving away. Philip Sharpe: 'Most of the HQ Section around us were petrified and I said, "Let's join the CO". They went unnoticed as they tagged along, having escaped harm crossing open ground.

Unfortunately, the fight was sharp enough to disperse 45 Column. The group led by Cumberlege headed west for the 24-hour RV fixed before leaving Auktaw that morning, but only 60 men out of 450 gathered there. Philip Sharpe checked his watch when he had the chance: 'It was exactly five o'clock in the afternoon, just two hours since our first brush with the enemy. The 45th Reconnaissance Corps had ceased to be commanded and no longer existed as an integral unit.'

Sharpe suddenly became aware of a minor shrapnel wound to his arm. He saw Colonel Cumberlege begin his rounds, talking to the men in small groups: 'He was obviously very distressed, looking tired and haggard. He was one of the very few officers who had managed to evade the over-forty age limit decreed by Wingate ... No doubt he had been physically exhausted by the privations on the march from Ledo, not to mention today's catastrophe.'

The men could hear more fighting in progress around Thetkegyin and Indaw. That night, desperate for water, they reached the Ledan Chaung. Cumberlege decided to

All the comforts: Bernard Fergusson's 16 Brigade HQ at Aberdeen Stronghold. (Jim Unsworth)

take as many Riflemen as possible to join the Leicesters east of Indaw. Two fighting Platoons were hastily organised and moved off. Lieut.Tony Musselwhite took charge of the rest, including Royal Signals. They were to head back to Aberdeen. They bivouacked away from Ledan Chaung and Philip Sharpe dined frugally on a 3 oz. tin of corned pork loaf he had exchanged for five Camel cigarettes. Eventually, they neared Aberdeen. When just outside Manhton they saw Brigade HQ arrive. Fergusson stayed to talk with Musselwhite. The group then followed Brigade HQ into Aberdeen. They enjoyed specially flown-in rations but were shocked to learn of Wingate's death. More 45 Recce elements then arrived. Many 45 Column men fought on after Cumberlege pulled back. They then dispersed and made for Aberdeen. Varcoe's 54 Column fought extremely well but took heavy casualties. They continued to fight throughout the night and into 27 March but shortage of water eventually forced them to withdraw. When the Battalion's survivors came together, they had a strength equivalent to one Column.[23]

As ATO, Cyril Baldock was in charge of much of 54 Column's 'soft skin':

'Some mules carrying weapons were sent forward, but others stayed put. The Japanese had strong positions on the track leading to the lake shore. We had to win this battle for water, but 54 Column never made it to the lake. We had no choice but to continue with frontal attacks and we pushed and pushed again, taking many

casualties. Then it became apparent that 45 Column had dispersed.

'I saw horrific sights. At one point I sent a mule forward with containers of flamethrower fuel. This animal was hit and the fuel ignited. It ran around, just a ball of galloping fire, dripping burning fuel on the wounded on the ground. I realised the seriousness of our position when I was told to gather everyone up and get out. Our first priority was to reach higher ground capable of being defended. We went back and climbed hard, going higher and higher. Unfortunately, the going was completely dry – no water anywhere!

'Many of our wounded were left behind in the confusion of battle. They could not be extricated. All that could be done was to leave them the means to kill themselves. One wounded man in terrible pain had been hit in both legs. We strapped him to Oscar the bull. Another casualty had been hit in the genitals and was in a bad way. We put him on a pony and he survived the ordeal. We were pursued by the Japs but our fighting Platoons had rejoined us and, in contrast to 45 Column, we were still a coherent unit. We were now led by Captain (later, Lieutenant Col.) "Jimmy" White, who was awarded the MC for this action.'

Those men suffering most from acute thirst began to lose control of their limbs. Wobbly legs were the first sign of collapse. 54 Column *had* to find water and find it quickly if it was to remain an effective force. Cyril Baldock:

'The ponies rapidly lost condition. They began to fall over and we had to leave them. We lost all the ponies. We couldn't shoot them as the Japanese were too close. The fighting continued the following day. Much of the action was close-quarters bayonet fighting. Every so often we were confronted by groups of Japs. A wonderful Irishman, Trooper M.J. "Paddy" Flynn, did excellent work with the Vickers in these engagements. He ended up with a second Military Medal.'

Lieutenant Roger Brewer, with 54 Column's 13 Troop, reported that his men were now so desperate for water that they had begun to drink their own urine. Then a party led by Burrifs found a dry chaung and began to dig. Sufficient water was found for the wounded and some of the others. The Column officers, including Cyril Baldock, took stock:

'We knew 45 Column had dispersed. Our Column had taken around 20–25 per cent casualties and we were in poor condition due to lack of water, the burden of significant numbers of wounded and our earlier exhausting march of several hundred miles. It was obvious that a return to Aberdeen was essential. We took no air drops after this action but we did begin to find water. In fact, the mules found it — they just pricked up their ears and went!'

Returning to Aberdeen was no easy matter. The Japanese began to close in. Jimmy White took a Section and punished the pursuers in a rearguard action. Cyril Baldock: 'I remember Jimmy as a man without fear. He was brave, resolute and a great friend to me.'

Trooper N.P. Aylen of 45 Recce kept his diary, despite the ordeal at Thetkegyin. On 27 March he wrote: 'Attack by Column on Thetkegyin village (held by Japanese). Recce Troop guarded baggage while the Column attacked the village. Got my first Jap this morning with Bren — water shortage.'

Aylen's diary entry for 28 March offers a terse summary of the grim, two-day confrontation: 'Spotted by Jap patrol – under MG fire for three hours – no cover except bushes – three men wounded (who died) in No. 3 Section – Sgt. Carter wounded in 4 places – got water – moved out under fire to better position – attacked with 2 in. mortar and rifle grenades.'[24]

The attack on Thetkegyin came in from east and west. Aylen was with the Recce Troop guarding stores, mules and HQ personnel. They heard the fighting during the morning. Some Japanese then headed in their direction:

I had just stood up to stretch myself after a long period of waiting when someone waved me to get down. As I dropped down a bullet whistled overhead and I observed two Japs running up the track. There was an exchange of shots and the two Japs were temporarily hidden from my sight by a clump of bushes. Only one running Jap reappeared from the other side of the clump but I was ready for him with the Bren. Aiming "one width ahead", according to rule, I saw him run dead into my sights, stop and dive off the track, into the woods.[24]

This Japanese soldier was found dead. The survivor was discovered and also received a Bren burst. The Recce Troop went forward to make contact with the main body:

We reached a clearing where the ground was littered with abandoned equipment. The jungle had been on fire and the ground was blackened and still smouldering. Two dying mules lay in the middle of the track. As we reached the mules we were greeted by a burst of machine gun fire.

Corporal Cole was killed outright as abandoned grenades and mortar rounds, cooking in the smouldering undergrowth, began to explode around them:

Presently, we received the order to move on again. The enemy machine-gunner had cleared off. The next sight that greeted us was a row of dead Japs ... I counted 26 bodies. Two of our own casualties lay beside a fallen log. The sight of the dying mules and of our two casualties, together with the smouldering earth and the feeling of death in the air combined to form a nightmarish atmosphere.

The Recce Troop guarded a section of perimeter, then acted as rearguard when the Column withdrew. They waited half an hour and followed. During the night they became desperate for water. Trooper Aylen:

A man's normal requirements, undergoing the exertion we did, in the tropical heat, was 10 to 12 pints daily. And we had had only one water bottle, about 2½ pints, all day. We had also used up a lot of ammunition. So, next morning we were given orders that if a Jap patrol appeared we were not to open fire, but to let it pass.[24]

The next morning, however, brought a terrifying encounter. An hour after sunrise a 30-strong Japanese patrol was seen advancing. They were almost out of earshot when a mule brayed. The patrol then turned. Aylen's Section was in a poor position — a hollow in a small clearing. Another Section occupied the adjacent ridge. The men in the hollow could not be seen by the Japanese but they had no cover. A machine gun began to fire down into the hollow. They stayed quiet and did not return fire.

The machine-gunner then fired bursts at the ridge to the left of the hollow and a wounded man began to shout. Some Japanese attempted to move round on the left but were stopped by fire from the ridge. The machine-gunner then fired into the hollow and at the ridge alternately. Aylen heard him call out in English: 'Come on, Johnny! Come up here! I've got something for you!' The trapped men in the hollow remained silent. As the sun rose higher, their thirst became harder to bear.

Aylen saw a bullet hit the pack at his side. He moved and got behind a clump of bamboo:

A second later the spot I had just vacated was furrowed with machine-gun bullets. At the same time the Section Sergeant (Sergeant Carter), who lay at my right side, uttered a groan. Three bullets had gone through his ankle and foot. He managed to suppress his agony and kept quiet and, for the moment, no further bursts came in our direction.

After a while the wounded Sergeant could not entirely suppress his groans and the sound brought another burst in our direction. Two more bullets went through the Sergeant's foot and, in a rage, he fired his Sten in the direction of the enemy machine gun. We all thought our last moment had come but, to our surprise, there was no answering fire. The Jap machine-gunner had evidently run out of ammunition at this critical moment.

Three men on the ridge were severely wounded and all died shortly afterwards. The men with Aylen were dismayed when the Japanese machine-gunner resumed firing at the ridge and into their position. This continued until midday, when the enemy finally departed. The Section in the hollow had survived the action with just one casualty.

Other Column elements found a little water by digging a dry chaung, but Aylen went foraging, dissatisfied with water shared out in spoonfuls. He found a small banana tree and cut the trunk into slices. On the way back he ran into men from another Troop who had been out on patrol rather than in defensive positions. Aylen wrote: 'It was heartbreaking to see their gaunt and bearded faces, with eyes protruding from shrunken flesh.' One asked for a share of the banana tree and Aylen gave him half.

The Japanese returned with reinforcements during the afternoon. This time the Vickers was ready and silenced the Japanese machine-gun. The enemy left the scene after another hour of fighting. Three men died manning the Vickers; the survivor was Paddy Flynn.[24]

The men were still desperate for water. They returned to the chaung bed, to dig deeper. Aylen's Section drank their fill and found they could eat a little. During the late afternoon they took up a stronger position by a small stream, moving under intermittent fire and protected by a rearguard. The new position was on a steep slope protected by a horseshoe-shaped ridge. This was soon attacked but the Japanese were silenced by a few mortar rounds. Everyone stayed awake during that long night, soaked in the light drizzle. Orders were then passed to prepare to pull back to Aberdeen. They moved out during the morning of 29 March, carrying their wounded, but soon ran out of water. Trooper Aylen: 'The little water we had was reserved for the wounded. To add to our troubles, we were feeling weak from lack of food.'

Fortunately, they found a stream and bivouacked for the night. The men felt better the following morning, but lack of water took its toll once again as the day unfolded: 'In the afternoon some dirty rainwater was found in a muddy stream bed littered with rotting leaves and branches. This was rationed out, boiled and took away the edge of our thirst.'

Later that day they made contact with Brigade HQ, then reached the very spot on a chaung where they had bivouacked five days earlier, just before their first brush with the Japanese:

For the first time in five days we were able to brew up to our heart's content. After slaking our thirst with three or four mugfuls of water, we spent the evening brewing up tea, coffee, soup and making lemonades. Throughout the night I kept waking up and taking gulps out of my water bottle. Out of curiosity, I counted the number of mugfuls I consumed that evening. It came to 15 pints.[24]

The morning of 31 March found Aylen so weak he could barely stand. After half an hour's marching and another brew-up he felt better, although a swollen foot troubled him. At meal halts the fitter men cooked for the exhausted and wounded. On 1 April they took an emergency light aircraft drop of one day's K-rations. They reached Aberdeen the next day. These events had left just the Leicesters Columns to gallantly press the fight for Indaw.

———◆———

Colonel Jack Wilkinson, the Leicesters' wounded Battalion Commander, knew the Japanese held Indaw in strength. He organised his men into a powerful fighting force, concentrating their firepower, including the Vickers and mortars. Rooney wrote: 'This excellent Battalion, with firm fire discipline, repulsed constant Japanese attacks, causing very heavy casualties for the loss of 11 killed and six wounded.'[25] The isolated Columns, 71 and 17, held on for three days and two nights of intense fighting. Brigadier Fergusson ordered them back to Auktaw on the morning of 29 March, where they were joined by elements of 45 Recce. Fergusson wrote frankly about Indaw:

I made at least three mistakes at Indaw. One was in not insisting on a rest for my troops before we assaulted. One was in failing to assess accurately, after all the practice I had had, the Jap reaction to the news they must have had of my approach. The third, and the least excusable, was in losing touch with my Columns. There were good reasons for all three, but all three were bloomers.[26]

The key issue was Fergusson's inability to bring his forces together, forming a 'clenched fist'. Rooney: 'Fergusson had clearly forgotten Wingate's dictum "Concentrate, concentrate, concentrate".'[25] It is more likely, in fact, that Fergusson knew exactly what he wanted to do, but circumstances worked against him. The separation of the 45 Recce and Leicesters Columns undermined his efforts. Earlier, Fergusson had planned to combine the Queen's and Leicesters for the main attack (in recognition of their infantry fighting expertise), but the order of march ruled this out.[26]

111 Brigade had been expected to cut the Wuntho-Indaw road and railway before Wingate's death. Lentaigne was about to do so when he became Wingate's successor. According to Rooney, 111 Brigade 'should have demolished the main railway south of Indaw, in order to prevent Japanese reinforcements from the south coming up to strengthen the town's defences, but they failed to do this, with grave consequences for Fergusson's 16 Brigade.'[27]

Morale remained firm within White City Block. Corporal Jesse Dunn was with 80 Column's Commando Platoon (infantry and Engineers):

'The mood was very good and supplies were no problem. At the personal level, however, I didn't expect to get out alive. In time I came to accept that. There were even some amusing episodes, such as the time the rail bridge was blown again after the Japs were driven off Pagoda Hill and out of Henu village. A camera team had arrived and the bridge was blown a second time for the benefit of audiences at home.'

Most attacks came in at night. Jesse Dunn:

'Flares illuminated the wire and the attackers were pushed back with grenades and machine gun fire. Occasionally, the Japs tried to trick us, with calls in English such as "Commando coming in!" Over the weeks the wire in front of us became clogged with Japanese dead. The stench was unbearable.'

The garrison's own dead were buried in shallow graves and there were worries about the activities of scavenging animals. The only solution was to dig deeper. During his seven weeks at White City Dunn was hit in the right arm by shrapnel from a mortar round. The wound was minor and healed within a fortnight.

Brigadier Michael Calvert was ready to take the offensive. White City and Broadway were well defended and the main road and railway were blocked. His opening move was to order an attack from White City against nearby Japanese-occupied Mawlu. The Lancashire Fusiliers of 50 Column and the Gurkhas of 63 Column (6 GR) attacked Mawlu from three sides on 27 March. They took the village and burnt it out with flamethrowers. The remaining strongpoints were taken with kukri and bayonet and at least 50 Japanese died.

The Chindits received round-the-clock support from the Special Force air supply organisation. Airbase driver Peter Fairmaner:

'I spent much of my time fuelling Dakotas for Chindit supply drops. I also brought up the loads, including the large fodder bales that were free-dropped. I spent a lot of time with mules in the back of my truck. Before the operation began I had driven a staff car. My passengers included Fergusson and Calvert. I remember Bernard Fergusson, in particular, as friendly and easy to get on with.'

The base was crammed with C-47s and with Mitchell bombers:

'I used to sit on the wing with a huge refuelling funnel, using a large piece of chamois leather for a filter. Contact with the Americans was always interesting but one man did ruin a nice plate of eggs and bacon by adding syrup. On occasion I went in, delivering mules, supplies and reinforcements. I kept my head down. You are OK if you can hear the bullet – by then it had already passed you! In many ways it was exciting rather than frightening.'

It fell to Lentaigne, having succeeded Wingate, to balance two priorities. According to Tulloch, Wingate and

Slim had agreed that two Brigades (16 and 77) would block Japanese communication to forces opposing Stilwell and two others (111 and 14) would disrupt the communications of 15th Army attacking at Imphal/Kohima. 111 Brigade was positioned to cut the Wuntho–Pinlebu road – one of three main supply routes for 15th Army. As operations unfolded, 111 and 14 Brigades disrupted two of 15th Army's three main lines of communication. Calvert wrote: 'With road blocks and ambushes they succeeded in putting the northerly route completely out of commission.'[28]

On 27 March the Recce Platoon of the King's Own's 41 Column jumped a Company of Japanese infantry bivouacked near the Kaukkwe Chaung.[29] These troops were advancing on Broadway, a remote location requiring a long approach march. It is likely that the author's father, Private Jack Redding, took part in this action. He was among a group who surprised a large Japanese party bathing in a river. During the action he remembered hitting a naked Japanese 'in the behind' with a rifle round. The Recce Platoon then met up with the King's 82 Column north of the Irrawaddy.

The King's Own Columns had received fresh orders on 29 March to operate along the Pinlebu–Pinbon road. Two days later, both 41 and 46 Columns were to the east and north-west of Nankan railway station. They needed resupply before commencing their new mission.

The first ground challenge to Broadway began on 26 March, when an 82 Column floater patrol ambushed a 150-strong Japanese force, killing 31. During that night Broadway's defenders held a Battalion-strength attack on the wire. Bill Towill, with 9 GR, heard what seemed to be a working party returning from the airstrip and under English words of command:

'They halted in front of our section of the perimeter and the command was given – "Right turn!", followed immediately by "Charge!" They came at us screaming our password – "Mandalay!"

'We were not taken in by these theatricals and reserved our welcome until they hit the wire, when we really let them have it. Our defences held firm. I saw only one man get through. He was killed by a grenade, rolled along the ground, which exploded under his chin. It splayed out the bottom half of his face, giving him a strange, frog-like appearance. His emergency rations consisted of a sock full of rice and a lump of raw sugar, wrapped in brown paper.

'The following night there was an electrical storm of unbelievable intensity – continuous thunder and lightning, rain coming down like a waterfall and huge tree branches falling down upon us from the canopy above. The Japs were attacking fiercely, mortar bombs

and shells were showering down incessantly, our men and the enemy were shouting and screaming at each other and the noise was out of this world. It seemed as if the enemy would be in among us in no time and I began crawling along a narrow, shallow slit trench to get to my men and see how they were doing. I lifted my head to take a peek. At that very instant two bombs dropped, either side of and very close to my head, bashing me to the bottom of the trench, as if from the clout of a giant hand. I just could not stop vomiting. I struggled to bring myself under control and eventually managed to do so, but only after a lapse of many seconds. It had been a close call. If I had lifted my head a split second earlier, it would have caught the full blast and that would have been curtains – no doubt about it.

'We decided to clear out the Japs. With the help of our attached RAF Officers, we called for air support, which arrived and flew a "cab rank" above us. We located targets for them by coloured smoke from the 3 in. mortars. We then met no resistance; the enemy fled when our aircraft arrived.'

During 27 March two Companies of Japanese had occupied the jungle around Broadway. This put a stop to light aircraft movements and denied the main airstrip to the C-47s. The Japanese attackers were fanatical and totally oblivious to their losses. Close air support was essential to the survival of Broadway's garrison. The cab rank pilots above the Stronghold included Mustang flyer Olin B. Carter:

'Broadway's defenders were known as "Tommy". We would get the call from "Tommy" advising they were laying smoke of a given colour in so many seconds. We would attack on the smoke. We would dive-bomb to within 50 yards of Tommy's positions. We never scratched a Chindit!'

As one air strike developed the P.51 pilots became suspicious. They were contacted by an obviously Japanese voice, giving instructions in English to bomb what were thought to be Chindit positions. Olin Carter: 'Our leader just said: "OK boys. Let's take them home!" We didn't drop.'

For the most part the air support required to defend Broadway's wire was much too close for a weapon like napalm. 1st Air Commando, however, did make occasional use of jellied petrol and naval depth charges when supporting Chindit infantry attacking well dug-in, heavily fortified Japanese positions. Olin Carter:

'Conventional bombs have a low explosive content in relation to casing weight. Depth charges are different.

The strain shows: a Bren team at Broadway Stronghold, Bren magazines at the ready. (Trustees of the Imperial War Museum)

Their thin casings are full of powerful explosive. The concussive effects were tremendous, but they could be used only if the Chindits pulled back to a safe range. We used depth charges to blast out the Japanese, in some cases sealing them within caves. These weapons were also particularly effective for killing snipers tied to trees.'

Broadway's defenders began to encounter evidence of Japanese atrocities. Bill Towill did. He was with a group who went forward, through clouds of dust and smoke, towards some Japanese weapons pits hit by an air strike:

'We saw a grisly sight which filled me with rage and despair. A Section of our men – eight of them – had been outside the wire, guarding one of the aircraft. They had been overrun and taken prisoner. With their hands tied behind their backs, they had been summarily butchered and their bodies stacked like a pile of logs. Later, on patrol around our base, we often came across the body of one of our men – body and head separated, as a Japanese officer had practised his swordsmanship and displayed his true colours.'

This killing of a group of helpless prisoners happened at the south-western corner of Broadway's perimeter,

beside one of the light aircraft bays. This Rifle Section had sent back a Runner at the start of the attack, warning that they were short of ammunition but would hold as long as they could. The decapitated individuals, however, were members of 9 GR's D Company, commanded by Major Irwin Pickett. There are unresolved questions concerning D Company's fate. It had a floater role yet, for some reason, fought in exposed fixed positions just *outside* the wire. Pickett was killed during a night assault. B Company then attacked this Japanese force just north of the airstrip.[30]

Bill Towill described the events leading to Pickett's death:

'I don't know what orders were given to him, but in true Chindit fashion he should have been moving freely as a large fighting patrol. When the Japs attacked the perimeter, he could then have attacked them from the rear, like a sledgehammer crushing them against the anvil of Broadway and its defences. Instead, he positioned each of his three Platoons in defensive positions just outside the wire. This enabled the Japs to attack and overrun each position in turn. The survivors fell back to Company HQ, which finally came under attack itself. Sadly, a grenade fell into Irwin's slit trench, landing in his lap and mortally wounding him.

The survivors fought their way through the encircling enemy and reached the safety of the Block.'

The following morning a strong fighting patrol recovered Pickett's body, killing about 20 Japanese in the process. Pickett was buried just outside the south-eastern corner of the wire. Some men of D Company were captured and beheaded. Bill Towill: 'Such were just some of our experiences of the vaunted Japanese concept of "Bushido" and thousands of similar or much worse experiences could be related by anyone who had anything to do with the Japanese during the war. It is not at all surprising that so many of our men who fought against the Japanese are of the view that, whatever came to the Japanese later by way of horror and retribution, no-one deserved it or earned it more than they.'[31]

The author's father was with a patrol who came face-to-face with Japanese depravity. On entering a village they found three prisoners tied to a tree and bayoneted to death. They had been left hanging, with their severed genitals stuffed into their mouths.

Broadway's defenders developed some unconventional tactics. Bill Towill:

'I was enlisted by the Brigade Major to attempt an "air raid" on Japanese positions. The plan was to go up in two of the light aircraft, which our RAF pilots had managed to fix by cannibalising some wrecked aircraft, and toss grenades onto the heads of the Japanese. Since this crazy idea emanated from the Brigade Major, I had to accept despite very strong reservations. We found no enemy but did locate one of our Columns and the pilot, in a sort of feu de joie, flew almost vertically down at them! I could see them scattering in all directions and, though I couldn't hear them, it took little effort to guess what they were saying. Flying alongside, the Brigade Major grinned at me, but it was all too much for my stomach. I turned away and, as discreetly as I could, threw up!'

Mustang pilot Olin Carter had more serious business in the air. There were occasional opportunities for air-to-air combat:

'Sometimes they turned us loose to go hunting. I saw Japanese aircraft in the air on at least six missions. Most Japanese air activity was farther south, in the Mandalay–Rangoon area. I had a couple of pretty wild fights. I shot down two in combat. This was an attack on the regular Japanese photo reconnaissance flight. For some reason, British Spitfires were unable to intercept that day. The recce was flown by a "Betty" bomber with

Zero fighters as escort. I ran for my Mustang fighter but it wasn't prepared. It needed ammunition and gas and had a defective oxygen system. I took off anyway.

'The British radar was excellent but not so good at giving altitude. I made the interception at 26,000 ft and told Control I couldn't see anything. They suggested I look below. There they were – 3,000 ft below me. Lack of oxygen then got to me and I did a stupid thing. I rolled right over and went straight through the Japanese formation without firing a shot! I pulled up, turned left and looked over. I was above them and still had plenty of speed. No aircraft had detached to challenge me. I made a firing pass and some of the Zeros lifted their noses to fire at me. I went low to get some oxygen into my blood. I saw two Zeros detach but they weren't very aggressive and soon returned to the formation. I shot down two Zeros and turned for home.

'Alison and Cochran debriefed me and said I should have got a third. They said I was over friendly territory, so I should have got behind another and chewed its tail off with my prop before jumping and walking home. I don't know if they were kidding!'

Broadway's Commander, Colonel Rome, had been warned by a Kachin scout on 26 March that a large Japanese force had crossed the Kaukkwe and was heading south to attack the Stronghold. Operation *Longcloth* veteran Major (later, Lieutenant Col.) Astell and a party monitored their progress. Rome knew Broadway's defences should be stronger; but White City had the priority for wire and other key stores.[32]

The wounded were flown out during the evening of 27 March, despite the close proximity of the Japanese. At 10.45pm heavy firing broke out from the floater Company's area but things quietened down just before midnight. The 2nd Battalion of the 146th Regiment (56th Division), however, then advanced across the airstrip and attacked Broadway's lightly defended western perimeter. The fighting continued until dawn on 28 March. The garrison suffered 60 killed, wounded or missing (some of whom returned later).[32]

During the morning of 29 March the Japanese were digging in north of the perimeter. The King's 82 Column was ordered to return and assist in the defence of the Stronghold. Major Gaitley had his hands full elsewhere, but sent a Company led by Captain Coultart. They attacked the Japanese positions along the perimeter at around 4pm but this did not go well. They were heavily outnumbered and withdrew as night fell. Corporal Fred Holliday of 82 Column:

'The Japanese had got into the slit trenches at the end of Broadway's airstrip. Our main attack was a bit of

a shambles. It was the first time most of us had been under fire and we really didn't know exactly where the Japs were.'

According to Chinnery, Coultart was among 36 killed and wounded from 82 Column.[33] His force was far too small to take on the Japanese 2nd/146th Regiment. Three days of hard fighting at Broadway concluded with counterattacks by the Gurkhas (9 GR) and 82 Column on 31 March, following concentrated air strikes to dislodge the enemy. The guns – R Troop of 160th Jungle Field Regiment, RA (Captain Guy Hepburn) – fired in support of the counterattacks. The Japanese pulled back from the northern area and now concentrated south of Broadway. Unfortunately, the King's couldn't keep up the pressure due to ammunition shortages. 82 Column pulled back and took a replenishment drop.[32]

A powerful combination of counterattacks and air strikes persuaded the Japanese to pull back. Michael Calvert estimated that the Japanese of 2nd/146th Regiment suffered one-third casualties in the Broadway fighting.[34] Their losses might have been much higher, but for premature 3 in. mortar smoke, which gave them just enough time to abandon their positions and escape an unusually heavy air strike.

Broadway's position had been consolidated. Further counterattacks found only a small Japanese rearguard. More patrols went out on 1 April and swept the entire area around Broadway. They found no Japanese.[32] Broadway remained free of enemy ground interference until it closed on 13 May.

According to 82 Column's Fred Holliday, it was after a bayonet charge in the final push to throw back the Japanese around Broadway that an unforgettable photograph was taken. The official caption claims that it shows men of 45 Recce after the fighting at White City. Fred Holliday:

'I know this is a photograph of The King's 82 Column, taken after the Broadway battle at the end of March. My friend, Tom Pickering, is third from the left in that picture. From the left is Sergeant Patterson, Sergeant Joss Aitcheson, Corporal Tom Pickering (head only), someone known to me but I can't retrieve the name and Corporal (or Sergeant) Farrel. The man on the stretcher is Captain Ronnie Hurst.'

Meanwhile, the 3rd/9th Gurkhas' Colonel, Noel George, fell ill and was evacuated. This had consequences for Bill Towill:

'We were concerned to learn that he had contracted polio. His successor had been serving with our 4th

Battalion on the Myitkyina front. Major Alec Harper was a Regular officer commissioned, I believe, in 1930 or thereabouts but with no Gurkha background. A cavalryman from The Royal Deccan Horse, he was disappointed that his own Regiment had not been in action and, there being no immediate prospect of change, he decided to put this right by joining the Chindits. He was ferried over by light plane to take command.

'He regarded our Adjutant as too edgy and called together the Company Commanders to seek their advice on a replacement. They voted me into the job and I found myself in a cheek by jowl relationship with him. He was ill-tempered and, much worse, very sparing in his thanks or words of encouragement. In this way he immediately distanced himself from the men. If one of my men did something well, I always made a

Saving a life: this photograph has been attributed to 45 Recce but Corporal Fred Holliday, of the King's 82 Column, maintained that it was taken after the bayonet charge to clear the Japanese from Broadway and shows men of his Column. From the left: Sergeant Patterson, Sergeant Joss Aitcheson, Corporal Tom Pickering (just visible), an unidentified man and Corporal (or Sergeant) Farrel. Captain Ronnie Hurst is on the stretcher. (Trustees of the Imperial War Museum)

point of thanking him for it and offering words of encouragement which, so to speak, would make his day.'

Lieutenant-Colonel Herring's Dah Force crossed the Irrawaddy and had reached Nahpaw, in the Kachin Hills, by 25 March. Stores were dropped, to arm and equip Kachin guerillas. Dah Force, however, was then pursued by the Japanese and pushed out of Nahpaw. They took refuge in the jungle. Herring awaited the arrival of 49 and 94 Columns – Morris Force's 4th/9th Gurkhas. 94 blew a bridge on 1 April. Major Blain's Bladet force had also blown a bridge and was now in search of fresh demolition targets. Morris Force had landed at Chowringhee, crossed the Shweli, destroyed bridges and otherwise disrupted the supply lines to Myitkyina and the Japanese 56th Division on the Salween. The three Morris Force Columns endured great hardship as they operated at extreme range; drops were few and far between.[35]

14 Brigade's Columns continued to fly into Aberdeen. On 1 April, immediately before his abortive first attempt to fly into Aberdeen, Richard 'Dick' Hilder, with Brigade HQ, recalled an encounter in the final hours before take-off: 'Another 26th Hussars officer, a Dutchman, came to see me. He said: "Cheerio, Dick. I'm never going to see you again." I replied: "Quite likely, but don't dwell on it."' The Dutchman's prediction was accurate.

Aberdeen strip was out of action on 1 April due to torrential rain. Hilder's Dakota would have returned anyway, having been severely shaken by a sudden, extremely violent air pocket. Over 60 years later, Hilder and several other former members of 14 Brigade HQ still telephone each other on 1 April, to ask each other whether they are 'going in'.

The events of 1 April included moments of high comedy. Men in the first Dakotas returning to Assam, having been unable to land at Aberdeen, were unaware they were landing back in India. Paddy Dobney, Administrative Officer with the York and Lancaster's 84 Column, remembered with amusement how they poured out of the doors with weapons ready, prepared to fight for their lives. Gales of laughter erupted from those still waiting patiently to emplane.[36]

14 Brigade's eight Columns received their final orders. Six Columns (Bedfordshire and Hertfordshire, York and Lancaster and 7th Leicesters) were to block the southern approaches to Indaw and White City, while the two Black Watch Columns were to block the Indaw-Banmauk road.

Dick Hilder's Dakota landed successfully at Aberdeen on 2 April. On touchdown Hilder peered out, jumped from the door and dived for cover as a Japanese Zero strafed the strip.

During 2 April Paddy Dobney's Dakota was being loaded with 12 men, three mules and equipment, together with wireless sets. A sudden roar of Dakota engines startled a mule. She bolted, stumbled on wet, slippery grass and broke a leg. Dobney had to shoot the animal in the head with his pistol. Saddened, he turned to walk away, only to hear one of the men shout: 'Sir, she's getting up again!' Dobney turned and was horrified to see the animal standing. He fired again but the matter was still unfinished: 'Fortunately, at that moment "Stormy" Tempest, the Brigade Veterinary Officer, rushed up in a jeep. He snatched a rifle from a nearby soldier, slammed a round into the breech and shot the unfortunate creature in the neck. It was not a happy start.'

Just before they emplaned the Quartermaster sent the cook's wagon to each aircraft, giving the men a final large helping of 'all-in' Army stew. Paddy Dobney: 'For many of us it was our last good meal for over 10 weeks. For some, it was their last ever.'[36]

According to Eric Sugden of the Bedfordshire and Hertfordshire's 61 Column, his aircraft managed to get into Aberdeen during the night of 31 March/1 April: 'It's funny how things stick in your mind. I remember, for example, the Poet and Peasant Overture playing over the loudspeakers at Lalaghat.'

Dick Stuckey, a Rifle Platoon Commander with the West African 43 Column (12 NR), watched his men get ready:

'We were due to take off at 8 o'clock. The CO and a few other officers were to fly together in a Dakota. We shared a tot or two of rum. For some reason our American pilot was very late and he found us sitting there, snoozing. As the Colonel's Staff Officer, I went to wake Pat Hughes. I think he'd had one tot too many.'

Stuckey settled down and dozed off again during the flight:

'I was at peace. Everything was in the lap of the Gods. All too soon I awoke to the words: "Landing in 10 minutes." Looking out, I soon saw Aberdeen's lights below. During the landing we hit a huge bump but all was well. The engines screamed as we pulled up just in front of a large hill. When it grew light, I saw that Aberdeen was just a paddy field with its bunds levelled in strategic places.'

Paddy Dobney's aircraft took off and climbed to over 8,000 ft, to clear the mountains. Men shivered in their light tropical kit. The sky grew dark as the engines settled into the cruise. Suddenly it became warmer as the descent began towards the jungle clearing below. Things happened quickly on landing. The door opened, a ramp was run up and the mules were led out and stores unloaded. The pilot appeared and offered a terse 'Good luck!' 84 Column went into bivouac and settled down for their first night under a Burmese sky. The men fell asleep without difficulty. Sister Column 65 was due to arrive the following night. When they were safely down, the Battalion Commander, Lieutenant-Colonel Graves-Morris, called his first Order Group. He was only halfway through when interrupted by a Japanese air raid.

Eric Sugden of 61 Column shared his Dakota with another Sapper, a machine gun team and their mules:

'We landed at one o'clock in the morning and formed up with the rest of the Platoon a few hours later, after some sleep. Initially I had a Sten – a weapon that was both useless and dangerous – really cheap and nasty. During training, one of our officers lost an eye when a Sten burst. Oddly, I ran into him many years later. He turned up at the London County Council Planning Office; he had become an architect. Anyway, I exchanged the Sten for a Lee-Enfield rifle. Later, the bolt seized as we had no oil. I then found that fat from a tin of K-ration processed meat was a passable substitute.'

The arrivals at Aberdeen included 43 Column's Dick Stuckey. His stay was short and not especially sweet:

'The Column formed up at dawn. We were preparing to commence our march to White City when Japanese Zero fighters flew over, dropping 50 lb anti-personnel bombs. Together with five other foolish virgins I got under a tree. A bomb hit this tree and killed four of the six outright. 12 Column's RAF Officer was badly wounded.

'Later, I was informed that all six had been written off. Our Medical Officer was Leon Gonet, who was to become a renowned London surgeon. He told me: "We saw the four dead. You were motionless on the ground with blood coming out of your ears. That looked like brain damage. I didn't even stop to look at you. On the way back, however, I noticed that you had moved. To cut a long story short, you were put on a stretcher and flown out that same night".'

Almost exactly 24 hours after landing at Aberdeen, Stuckey was in hospital back at Airbase, under the care of the redoubtable Matron Agnes McGeary – recipient of a gallantry award for services at Dunkirk in 1940. Matron McGeary had looked after the survivors of Operation *Longcloth* in 1943. She had also nursed

Wingate himself in October of that year, when he had almost succumbed to typhoid. Dick Stuckey:

'Basically, I was OK. I was a bit deaf and had a bomb fragment in my right shoulder. Three of us were evacuated that night. My companions were Captain John Findlay of the Queen's and a Captain in the Reconnaissance Regiment. We put the case to Matron McGeary for our immediate return to Aberdeen. She was sympathetic but insisted that our next stop was the Rehabilitation Centre.'

Those tending the wounded at Aberdeen included Medical Orderly George Fulton. During his jungle training, Fulton was surprised on being handed a weapon. He shared Eric Sugden's loathing of the Sten:

'This was a first for the British Army, in that Medics were armed. We were given Stens. Perhaps this was because the Japanese did not acknowledge the Red Cross. I hated the Sten. It would go off at any excuse. You had plenty of opportunity to kill yourself by accident.

'Our lads had been asked to volunteer to provide support to the Chindits. That's how I came to be an Orderly at a Casualty Clearing Station for Aberdeen. Our unit was commanded by a Doctor, Major Cresswell. We also had a Scottish Sergeant who was a pharmacist. The rest were Orderlies. Our total strength was around 25. We tended the wounded and cleared them for evacuation.'

A week had passed since Wingate's death. Some Special Force Brigades may have lacked direction during the short interregnum and critics maintain that this continued when Lentaigne took over on 30 March. John Riggs, Recce Platoon Commander with the Bedfordshire and Hertfordshire's 16 Column: 'The initial task of our Columns was to operate around Indaw. By the time we arrived at Indaw we were almost immediately turned round, to head back to the White City area.'

Sister Column 61 set off from Aberdeen on 3 April. Eric Sugden:

'We were carrying four days' rations. Trained as fighting troops, we Sappers took our turn as lead or rear Platoon. Initially, the terrain was fairly open forest and scrub. The heat was intense and I developed symptoms of heat exhaustion. The MO carried some rock salt. It was brown and looked unappetising, but I got to like it. The symptoms soon disappeared with some rock salt under the tongue.'

There should have been eight mules with Sugden's Platoon. Instead, they had seven and a bullock:

Packs off: settling into night bivouac, the mules in the background. (John Riggs)

'A mule walks at the same pace as a man, but a bullock's speed is about half a mile an hour slower. The last thing anyone wants in a marching Column is a gap. We tried everything to speed up the bullock, from twisting his tail to prodding him with a bayonet.'

This bullock had the last laugh. It came into its own later – making light of the Monsoon mud as the mules slithered. Rude messages then arrived from the Column head, requesting the RE to retrieve their bullock, now making better speed than the competition.

Lieutenant-Colonel John Barrow, leading 61 Column, described the daily challenges of the Column Commander: 'You will have to think on available information and plan five days ahead for supply drops, three days ahead for the tasks of the Recce Platoon, two days ahead for general line of march, RVs for stragglers or for reassembly if the Column is dispersed for any reason. Watering points or alternative if source is dry. Have in mind areas for landing light planes if we get casualties. Plan next day's march in detail.'

43 Column's Dick Stuckey, meanwhile, was going nowhere. Evacuated from Aberdeen after just 24 hours, having been injured in a Japanese air raid, he and two companions were still trying to avoid the 'Rehabilitation Centre':

'We continued to press for our return to Aberdeen. We told the Rehabilitation Centre CO, Major Munn, RAMC, that we were highly trained, fit and merely the victims of a most unfortunate setback. The Major was intransigent: "I'm sorry. You will all follow an eight-week regime of convalescence, finishing up with an assault course!" We pleaded once more, but in vain. We then decided to do a midnight flit.

'We made discreet enquiries about the local bus service. The airfield was around 90 minutes' drive from the hospital. The best time to make our move would be after breakfast, when we should be making up the beds. We absconded from the Rehabilitation Centre and boarded a bus full of locals, together with their children and chickens. We got off at the nearest military HQ to Lalaghat. We asked for the CO but got his deputy. Unfortunately, he turned out to be a Captain in the Military Police. We were somewhat disconcerted when he addressed us by name.

'The Rehabilitation Centre had second-guessed us and telephoned ahead, ordering our arrest. We appealed to him and, fortunately, he was made of different stuff. He said: "I haven't seen you!" He then told us to turn up at the airfield that afternoon. A Dakota was taking mules and ammunition into Aberdeen and we hitched a ride, having spent the day hidden in bushes!'

Aberdeen airstrip was built between two hills and the run was too short for comfort. Flying Control was housed in the fuselage of a wrecked C-47. Dick Stuckey was back:

'I had been away about eight days and our Columns had since moved on to White City, to reinforce the garrison. Major Gordon Upjohn helped us reach White City. We got a lift in an American L.1 light aircraft. Lieutenant-Colonel Pat Hughes was surprised to see me. He asked me what I had been up to. Apparently, he had received a signal stating that Captain Stuckey had gone AWOL! It soon became clear that he found the entire episode very amusing. He was happy to have me back, provided I could still do my job. My shoulder remained painful but my ears troubled me more. I had been lucky. The shrapnel had virtually shaved off one side of my bush hat.'

Three West African units flew in: 7 NR and 12 NR to Aberdeen and 6 NR to Broadway. The latter's two Columns, 66 and 39, had then suffered a major setback in a night action on the way to Aberdeen. On 26 March a group from 66 Column followed the chaung to Nami, with Aberdeen airstrip to the west. During the afternoon they entered the Meza Valley and halted just south of the airstrip. It was at this point that they learned of Wingate's death. They were digging in when they received further discouraging news – a force of 500 Japanese was reported to be advancing on Aberdeen from the south-west. During the night, at around 04.00, heavy firing broke out but it was found that this 'battle' had been triggered by noise from a restless bullock!

On 29 March Japanese aircraft bombed and machine-gunned the Nigerian positions, causing some fatalities. They returned the following morning. During the lull Larry Gaines watched his Vickers Platoon take the opportunity to bathe in the river. Things looked up on 31 March, when the balance of 66 Column and the complete 39 Column finally entered Aberdeen's perimeter. Major Alistair MacKenzie, the Company Commander, warned Gaines and his men not to be cocky with the stragglers. 39 Column occupied a long hill to the north of the strip, just above 66 Column's positions.

The normal unpleasant conditions associated with jungle living now affected almost everyone. Skin infections were rife. John Baty described one common dark red fungal growth that produced no disease, despite spreading in the hair of the armpits and pubic area.[37] Footrot and prickly heat were more serious. Footrot can reduce the sufferer to the point where he can no longer march. As for prickly heat, scratching can open a sore which may spread at a catastrophic rate. Footrot was countered by applications of Gentian Violet, although 16 Brigade Commander Bernard Fergusson favoured Sulphanilamide.

Many men carried personal medical kits. Fergusson named six essentials: disinfectant, Gentian Violet, Sulphanilamide, adhesive plaster, suppressant tablets and morphia.[38] Chindits of European origin took on a distinctive yellow tinge, caused by the malaria suppressant Mepacrine. There were worries that liver damage might result from its prolonged use, but no evidence to support this was found.[39]

On 1 March 16 Brigade Chindits began taking Mepacrine – one tablet daily, plus a 'crash course' of three a day for five days, once every three weeks. The Brigade began to see primary cases, as opposed to relapses, during the final week of March. One 16 Brigade Column, denied Mepacrine for three days having missed supply drops, soon reached 30 per cent malaria. Even Columns taking Mepacrine regularly reported cases. Bernard Fergusson, not surprisingly, rejected claims that it was impossible for anyone taking Mepacrine to develop malaria.[40]

Fergusson remained concerned about man-made hazards - booby traps - having tried and failed to persuade Wingate to ban them: 'I have no notion how many Japs were killed on our booby traps; I know that I lost over 20 killed and wounded on traps set by other Chindit Brigades.'[41]

Men grew tolerant of many discomforts, including the ever-present leeches. Yet the leech's ability to find any home on a soldier's body sometimes caused dismay. John Baty, with No. 7 Indian Mobile Surgical Unit in the Arakan, wrote of such a case: 'a leech had attached itself to a man's tonsil, thus demonstrating one of the disadvantages of sleeping with the mouth open.'[42]

Special Force Brigade Commanders, even the Column Commanders of the preceding year, continued to learn from experience. One important lesson was the need to avoid the abuse of signal priorities. Bernard Fergusson: 'In this matter, Wingate himself was the chief offender. He never sent a signal with any priority lower than "Most Immediate". He had an awkward habit of despatching circular signals to all Columns, either of exhortation or (more often) of reproof. There was an occasion in 1944, when Mike Calvert had completed his fly-in, when Wingate decided to send out a flamboyant and eloquent "Order of the Day", which completely and utterly jammed all my wireless sets throughout the whole Brigade for 48 hours.'[43]

On 31 March, the day after taking over Special Force, Lentaigne flew to Comilla to meet Slim. He was told that 23 Brigade, his only reserve, had been taken away to help defend the Dimapur bases. There is some irony here. 23 Brigade was detached from Special Force to fight Chindit-style in the Naga Hills and disrupt the Japanese attack on Imphal/Kohima.

The irony turns on the highly successful nature of 23 Brigade's operations, using traditional Chindit tactics of extreme mobility, rather than the 'hybrid' mobile and static fighting now characterising Special Force activities.

RAF Officer W.A. Wilcox wrote that his 23 Brigade Column received orders 'to work south through the hills, behind the Japanese main positions, and to attack and destroy such units as we might find. We were to harass and ambush their food foraging parties and, wherever possible, prevent their occupation of Naga villages.'[44]

Meanwhile, the failure to take Indaw had consequences for Special Force. Given 16 Brigade's exhausted state, the Japanese build-up against White City and 111 Brigade's commitment to the Pinlebu–Pinbon area, 14 Brigade was given a new role. It was to stop enemy reinforcements attacking 77 Brigade from the south and west. To this end, 14 Brigade's Black Watch Columns were ordered to block the Indaw–Banmauk road. The rest of the Brigade was to operate in the Meza area. 74 Column was held back to protect Aberdeen in the floater role.

Notes

1. Towill, B. (2000), *A Chindit's Chronicle*, 63–64
2. Rooney, D. (2000), *Wingate and the Chindits: Redressing the Balance*, 160–163
3. Sharpe, P. (1995), *To Be a Chindit*, 173
4. Thompson, Sir Robert (1989), *Make for the Hills*, 53
5. Calvert, M. (1974), *Chindits: Long Range Penetration*, 85–89
6. Rhodes James, R. (1981), *Chindit*, 95
7. Calvert, M. (1996), *Fighting Mad*, 159
8. Hay, Alice Ivy (1963), *There Was a Man of Genius: Letters to my Grandson, Orde Jonathan Wingate*, 107
9. Ibid, 135–136
10. Ibid, 108–109
11. Hughes, G. unpublished MS
12. Gerrard, F. (2000), *Wingate's Chindits*, unpublished MS (via Bill Smith)
13. Towill, B. (2000), 50–52
14. Rhodes James, R. (1981), 92
15. Slim, Field Marshal Viscount (1999), *Defeat into Victory*, 269–270
16. Rhodes James, R. (1981), 87
17. Rooney, D. (1997), *Mad Mike*, 82–83
18. Rooney, D. (2000), 125–126
19. Slim, Field Marshal Viscount (1999), 268
20. Allen, L. (1986), *Burma: The Longest War 1941–45*, 348–350
21. Fergusson, B. (1946), *The Wild Green Earth*, 89–92
22. Sharpe, P. (1995), 220
23. Ibid, 221–232
24. Aylen, N. P., Trooper, *45th Reconnaissance Regiment*, Imperial War Museum, 80/49/1
25. Rooney, D. (2000), 164
26. Fergusson, B. (1946), 97–100
27. Rooney, D. (2000), 132–133
28. Calvert, M. (1974), 63–67
29. Bidwell, S. (1979), *The Chindit War*, 127–128
30. Towill, B. (2000), 53–56
31. Ibid, 59–60
32. Calvert, M. (1974), 80–83
33. Chinnery, P.D., (2002), *March or Die*, 178
34. Calvert, M. (1974), 72–73
35. Ibid, 122
36. Dobney, Major R.P.J. 'Paddy', unpublished MS, July 1981 (via Bill Smith and Corinne Simons)
37. Baty, J.A. (1979), *Surgeon in the Jungle War*, 84
38. Fergusson, B. (1946), 200–201
39. Baty, J.A. (1979), 79
40. Fergusson, B. (1946), 197–199
41. Ibid, 216
42. Baty, J.A. (1979), 82
43. Fergusson, B. (1946), 237
44. Wilcox, W.A. (1945), *Chindit Column 76*, 7

15

REINFORCING SUCCESS

2–8 April 1944

'The Japanese were very persistent. It was obvious that they regarded their own lives as of no consequence.'

Dick Stuckey, 43 Column, 12th Nigeria Regiment

BERNARD FERGUSSON'S 16 Brigade HQ arrived at Aberdeen on 3 April. The main body of 45th Reconnaissance Regiment's 45 and 54 Columns had reached the new Stronghold the day before, following the fighting at Thetkegyin. 14 Brigade completed its fly-in to Aberdeen on 4 April, but many 3 (WA) elements had yet to arrive. Daily Japanese air attacks on Aberdeen caused little fresh damage – they repeatedly hit the same wrecked aircraft. Newly appointed Special Force Commander Joe Lentaigne called a Brigade Commanders' conference and the outcome included a decision to reinforce White City. Five gliders with engineering equipment landed at White City and a C-47 strip was operational by 4 April. The weather caused a brief delay but the first C-47 landed the following day, the initial sorties bringing in 25 Pounders, anti-aircraft guns and anti-tank weapons. The Japanese would find White City impossible to break.

S Troop, 160th Jungle Field Regiment, RA, arrived at White City on 5 April, brought in by eight Dakotas. The guns were reassembled and towed to the eastern side of Thazi Wood. The Bofors guns and their crews also arrived that night *(Captain S.R. Nicholls, S Troop Commander, Imperial War Museum 80/49/1)*.

On the morning of 6 April the gun platforms were chosen and a line laid to the South Staffords' mortar OP, on OP Hill. It was felt that this OP was too exposed, with some remarking that it looked like a submarine conning tower. It was then decided to lay another line east of Pagoda Hill, to a reserve OP.

Troop Commander Captain Nicholls described the scene: 'The gun position was in a small valley, which was a continuation of that down which the Napin track ran. All guns could fire from 160 deg. to 210 deg. The right

section could fire further round to the left, up the Napin track. We later found that No. 4 gun had a zone of fire to the north, but this was never used.' The guns were in action during the afternoon of that first day, when an air raid was followed by mortaring and shelling from Sepein. Nicholls spotted the flashes and engaged with the right Section.

Brigadier Michael Calvert's 77 Brigade was to be reinforced. They would be joined by 16 Brigade's 2nd Leicesters Columns, to operate as floaters around White City. Meanwhile, 14 Brigade's 74 Column (7th Leicesters) was released from its floater role, as reports of an enemy threat were found to be without substance. 111 Brigade was in action on 6 April. A road block manned by the Cameronians' 26 and 90 Columns was attacked in Company strength but the Japanese lost heavily, with at least 30 killed and 70 wounded. Fighting continued into the following day and claimed another 21 Japanese lives. The Cameronians lost three killed and 11 missing.

Morris Force switched from 77 Brigade to Special Force HQ command and received orders to attack the Bhamo-Myitkyina road as soon as possible. The Gurkhas of 40 Column (4 GR) soon found success. On 7 April they sprang an ambush on the Bhamo-Lashio road, killing 30 Japanese. Elsewhere, 14 Brigade's 47 Column (7th Leicesters) blew up a road bridge. At White City a fierce battle ended in defeat for the Japanese. Repeated attacks were stopped by White City's heavily wired, mined and entrenched positions. White City's success was due to its power to attract repeated suicidal charges into perimeter areas covered by Vickers machine guns. Light aircraft pilots could smell the corpses on the wire as they flew over. Those trying to clear them from the wire were left with the smell on their hands and bodies.

———————◆———————

RAF Officer Walter Longstaff arrived at Aberdeen during the early days of April, to join the York and Lancaster's 65 Column. The Column Commander was Major Downward, 2i/c to Battalion Commander Lieutenant-Colonel Philip Graves-Morris. Longstaff, a latecomer, had received little jungle training. He was warned of tough times ahead. He would shed three stone over the next few months:

'I didn't mind K-rations, but there was not enough variety and I didn't care for the processed cheese. On one occasion a party was detailed to get rid of all the rubbish after a supply drop. The main body moved out and we hadn't gone far when we heard explosions behind us. A Section went back and found the clean-up group had lit a fire to burn some of the waste. Hundreds of abandoned tins of processed cheese were exploding in the heat.'

The fly-in of 84 Column and the lead elements of 65 Column was completed by 03.00 on 3 April. The rest of 65 Column was due at 19.00. They arrived just five minutes after an attack on Aberdeen by 10 Japanese Zeros. The optimistic Dakota pilots identified the Zeros as British fighter cover and, fortunately, they were not attacked.

Battalion Commander Philip Graves-Morris later wrote: 'It was uncanny and not a little unreal to sit on the hillside overlooking the strip and watch the Dakotas coming in to land with landing lights full on, plus also the ground landing lights, brought in by Control as if they were at Croydon Airport.'[1]

84 Column's Recce Platoon, led by Lieutenant Liddy, moved out on the first day. They headed south to explore the Indaw-Banmauk road and Meza river area. Graves-Morris noted:

This was the start of the day we had been waiting for. This was the actual beginning of the real test, after all our weeks of sweat, toil and hard living. This was the first venture into the unknown but it was heartening to see this well-trained Platoon moving off with a grin (perhaps sometimes a little forced, but it was there) and looking so fit and confident.[1]

The two Columns moved out independently on 4 April, making for the first target, the Wuntho-Indaw railway about 80 miles south.[1] Paddy Dobney, 84 Column's Administrative Officer, appreciated three days of relatively good conditions before moving east into dry country. He felt for the heavily laden mules. They were not unloaded during the brief hourly halts and their heads hung down in the steaming heat. The men suffered with them, having been forbidden to drink during the hourly stops: 'At any brief check along the way everyone leant forward, with hands on knees, trying to ease our equipment straps from cutting painfully into aching shoulders. Then the sweat would stream from faces and run from noses and chins, to drop onto the dusty track.'[2]

At the midday halt the mules were unloaded but remained saddled. Paddy Dobney described a halt in teak forest:

Around us the forest boiled in the heat. This was not dense jungle, which can shut out sunlight. Instead, the sun's heat directly overhead burst through the trees and there was rarely even the slightest breeze. Nothing stirred. There was scarcely a sound. It was as if every living creature had crawled under the nearest patch of shade, to lie there, panting.[2]

The York and Lancaster Columns crossed the Indaw-Banmauk road and Meza river on Thursday 6 April. On Good Friday the Padre held a service. Graves-Morris' Battalion followed strict rules on silence but as the Battalion Commander himself later admitted, 'it is very depressing always talking in a subdued voice.' There was some debate as to whether hymns should be permitted. Graves-Morris recalled: 'The Padre ably conducted his service *sotto voce* though, perhaps, a little singing would have heartened the men.'[1]

During the night of 8 April the Battalion took its first supply drop. Graves-Morris: 'In all our drops we were never once attacked, although we often had to move fast and on occasions we were actually watched by Japanese.'[1]

Local villagers helped bring in supplies and were rewarded with hand-outs of prized statichute cloth. There were angry outbursts from the Chindits when the first containers were opened. Graves-Morris: 'All ranks were distressed to discover that many of the K-rations had been tampered with by the Indian packers at Airbase and that the goodies of chocolate, fruit bars and cigarettes had been removed from many of the packages. One was inclined to weep with rage at this mean theft that could not be made good, particularly as it was the first supply drop and there seemed no guarantee that this state of affairs would not continue throughout the expedition.' Happily, however, this crime was not repeated. With three days' rations up, the Columns continued south through dry jungle, heavily laden with full chaguls of water.[1]

As 14 Brigade's Columns advanced, Aberdeen Stronghold continued to develop. Its defences were strengthened and reinforced as the West Africans settled in. Platoon Commander Lieutenant Larry Gaines, with 6 NR's 66 Column, made sure his men did not go hungry:

'Food was plentiful, including tinned fruit. Our Nigerians were Muslim for the most part and couldn't eat pork. The Emir of Katsina, however, gave them special dispensation. Our Nigerians could eat K-ration chopped pork. They loved it and were most disappointed when returned to normal rations later on.'

Gordon Upjohn, 3 (WA)'s Brigade Major, arrived on 7 April to take command of 6 NR's 66 and 39 Columns. More wiring of positions was under way and the defences were stiffened with machine guns and mortars. The two York and Lancaster Columns were ordered to 'operate aggressively' against enemy lines of communication south of Indaw. Flight Lieutenant Longstaff, 65 Column's RAF Officer, led a team including two Wireless Operators. Longstaff got on well with men and animals:

'I liked the mules carrying our gear, but you had to be careful. On one occasion I grabbed the tail of a Medical Section mule, to help me up a slope, and received a powerful kick in return. My elbow was very badly bruised.'

'Hector' Longstaff had other problems, including repeated bouts of malaria and dysentery. He was also plagued by prickly heat. Yet his feet held up well. He stopped marching on only one occasion, when a foot became badly blistered:

'I rode one of the ponies for a couple of days. It amused me to see how the natives reacted. They would pay their respects, assuming that anyone riding a horse had to be important.'

Paddy Dobney, with sister Column 84, recalled that the York and Lancaster bivouacs were always well away from water, an obvious precaution in dry country. On arriving at the 'bivvy', water parties would assemble with their mules, ponies and an armed escort. They had been marching for four days but were still a long way from their objective. A drop was requested. Paddy Dobney:

All normal requirements – our rations, animal grain, clothing, boots, equipment, explosives, petrol for battery-charging machines, medical supplies,

brandy (medicinal comfort for sick and wounded), Communion wine (for the Padre), rum (for everybody) – were all listed and coded, as were all those small items like toothpaste, mess tins, bootlaces and extra silver Rupees. Arrangements had even been made for those soldiers who wore spectacles to hold spare pairs for them.[2]

Extreme care was needed when encoding and transmitting: '... a single incorrect letter or figure could have serious results.'

Signallers were under constant pressure. When setting up they were always pressed: 'Are we through yet?' Lieutenant-Colonel Graves-Morris wrote: 'Only those who have waited through the long hours of darkness for a "break" in the air, to try and get away a long coded message, can appreciate what a tedious and nerve-racking affair it can be. In fact, it was soon discovered that the Signallers were the first to show signs of stress and fatigue.'[1]

The Recce Platoon usually selected or confirmed the drop site. This was then screened by a Rifle Platoon as 84 Column's RAF Officer, Flight Lieutenant Franks, decided on the best approach for the aircraft – the fires being set accordingly. The aircraft then made its run along the long side of the 'L' formed by the fires, following an exchange of recognition signals. 'Collectors' retrieved the containers. Several runs were made to complete the drop. Paddy Dobney: 'The initial drop consisted largely of K-rations, but some statichutes were coloured, to indicate mail or other special items – including the all-important drop manifest. This ensured the retrieval parties knew exactly what to search for.'

The main stockpile grew rapidly and was broken down into manageable piles. Any 'goodies' were shared out with care. Paddy Dobney: 'This was not easy as we rarely received more than one container of tinned fruit, which worked out at two or three tins to a Platoon of 35 men. Tinned fruit became so precious that the greatest care had to be taken to convince everyone they were getting a fair share.'[2]

This drop was successful but yielded just three days rations. The best of the statichutes were wrapped in blankets and put on mules, for use when bartering for food or labour.

14 Brigade's arrival at Aberdeen before most of the Nigerian garrison troops reflects Wingate's priorities at the time of his death. He wanted 14 Brigade flown in before it could be taken away. Consequently, some West African Columns were still arriving at Aberdeen during the second week of April. Lieutenant (later, Major) Denis Arnold, MC, was a Platoon Commander with 7 NR's 29 Column. His flight into Burma was not without incident:

Keeping contact: a Royal Signals Detachment and wireless. (Peter Allnutt)

'A Japanese fighter decided to have a go at us in bright moonlight. It was "interesting" to see the glowing rounds pass through the cabin. Fortunately, no-one was hurt, although one man had a very lucky escape – a bullet struck his mess tin.'

Shortly before this encounter, Arnold looked out as his aircraft crossed the Chindwin in brilliant moonlight:

'We had several mules and they were surprisingly well-behaved during the flight. My feelings were of relief rather than apprehension. We had been training for a very long time and I felt glad we were on the move at last.'

Charles Carfrae, Arnold's Column Commander, described the departure from Lalaghat: 'The pilot smiled and shook my hand and one by one we stepped into the dark stomach of his aircraft. After dumping our great packs by the door, we sat on metal seats, facing one another. It was the first time any of the Africans had been inside a plane, but the Dakota might have been another three-ton lorry, for all the impression it made upon them.'[3]

The plan was for 12 NR (commanded by Lieutenant-Colonel Pat Hughes) and 7 NR (led by Lieutenant-Colonel

Peter Vaughan) to march to White City. 6 NR would garrison Aberdeen. 6 NR landed at Broadway on 9 March and one of its Columns, 66, had been dispersed on the way to Aberdeen. Brigade Major Gordon Upjohn took over from Lieutenant-Colonel P.G. Day.

The Commander of 3 (WA), Brigadier Gillmore, took command at White City on 9 April. The way was now clear for 77 Brigade's Brigadier Calvert to begin offensive operations outside the Block. Later, Gillmore would be succeeded by Brigadier Ricketts.

Peter Allnutt was Staff Officer to 12 NR's Pat Hughes, who led 43 Column. Allnutt was among those delayed for 48 hours at Lalaghat due to rainstorms, which turned strips into mudbaths. Allnutt struggled with successive late changes to the loading manifests. Eventually, most 12 NR elements flew in over three successive nights. Allnutt snatched rest when he could. His only comfort was the constant 'cha' produced by his Orderly, Alijebba Dumel. As for the American aircrew and ground personnel at Lalaghat, Allnutt couldn't help noticing that they appeared to subsist entirely on a mixed diet of ice cream and movies.

Those waiting at Lalaghat heard on the grapevine about the heavy fighting at White City. This was confirmed by the arrival of growing numbers of wounded, flown out from Aberdeen. In the language of the time, men still kicking their heels at Lalaghat were 'browned off'. Peter Allnutt heard Sergeant 'Dapper' Brown, a machine-gunner from Liverpool, sum up everyone's thoughts: 'The whole ******* war will be over and all the rest of the ******* Battalion killed before we get out of this ******* place.'

Allnutt had his own worries, not least the problem of 'Horace'. This goat had wandered into the Battalion's jungle training camp and had since led a charmed life. It was fortunate indeed to have survived the huge feast prepared to celebrate the end of jungle training. The Battalion Commander took a shine to Horace. Pat Hughes told Allnutt to take the goat on strength. The animal relished its new-found status as Battalion Mascot, refusing to recognise rank and adopting an impudent, overbearing attitude:

'Horace was now a member of the Battalion. For that reason, I decided that he must fly in with us. I told Sergeant Gadsby to put him in with the mules. The goat appeared on the loading manifest as "1 box, 3 inch mortar bombs".

In a Dakota at long last, Allnutt and his companions sat on their packs. The men were quiet, their features occasionally highlighted by flashes of lightning away to the north. Suddenly, Aberdeen's lights came into view as the aircraft banked sharply. In common with so many others, Allnutt was startled to see two lines of brilliant white lights in the inky blackness, so far behind enemy lines. Once down they joined the buzz of activity on the strip. Aircraft landed and took off every few minutes. Ground teams struggled to unload aircraft as quickly as possible. 12 NR's bivouac was a length of shallow ditch. Within a couple of hours Peter Allnutt had his first look at Aberdeen in the dawn light. The strip occupied the nearby village's paddy fields.

29 Column Platoon Commander Denis Arnold arrived during the night:

'Aberdeen looked like a well-organised base, although it wasn't easy for the Dakota pilots. They had to go into a steep climb immediately on take-off, to avoid coming to grief.'

29 Column was briefed to move out the next morning. 29 and its sister Column, 35, would make for the area south of White City and patrol aggressively as floaters. They would operate well clear of the Block's perimeter.

Peter Allnutt was glad to leave Aberdeen, having been bombed and machine-gunned twice by Japanese aircraft in the space of a few hours. The two West African Battalions followed the Meza river valley. 12 NR would enter White City Block and 7 NR would operate as floaters. As they began climbing steep gradients in the extreme heat and humidity, Allnutt saw many men throw away unnecessary items from their heavy packs: 'To my amazement, one man just ahead of me jettisoned hair brushes, a bottle of hair restorer and two bottles of patent medicine!'

They reached the ridge summit by mid-afternoon and began the descent taking them into the rail corridor and on to White City. There was a brief alarm caused by 'rifle fire', but this turned out to be bamboo exploding in a forest fire. They crossed the river the next morning and entered railway valley, 15 miles wide at that point. Peter Allnutt:

'43 Column then met troops coming the other way on the narrow track. Two Columns from 16 Brigade were marching out, having spent two months in the jungle. They were an unforgettable sight. They had marched hundreds of miles through some of the worst country on Earth and had then fought two hard battles. They were bearded, lean and gaunt, their clothing in rags. They walked with a peculiar slouch, effortless and automatic. Faces wore a set, strained look but their eyes were bright and alert as they grinned and mouthed an occasional word of greeting.'

The new Special Force Commander, Joe Lentaigne, had met Mountbatten, Slim and Stilwell on 3 April. Stilwell worried about the Japanese threat to his communications and offered a Chinese Division to help defend Imphal. The Japanese attack on Imphal/Kohima now developed into a bitter struggle that lasted until the second week of May.[4] Stilwell's offer was declined. Slim took Chindit-trained 23 Brigade to strengthen the Kohima sector. It was agreed that elements of 14 and 111 Brigades should be deployed to ease the pressure on IV Corps.[5]

During Lentaigne's discussions with his Brigade Commanders, Calvert and Fergusson argued against entanglement in the Imphal fighting. Calvert was anxious to preserve White City and Broadway and Fergusson wanted a second try at Indaw. Yet it appears that Calvert also appreciated that 77 Brigade would have to move north soon to link up with Stilwell's Chinese before the Monsoon broke.[6] Lentaigne stressed that Broadway's airstrip could not be made all-weather within a few weeks. Fergusson then pressed the case for another attempt at Indaw, a town with two airfields.[7]

It was decided that Calvert should attack Mohnyin, 25 miles along the railway from White City – opening a drive on Mogaung.[7] This plan was soon set aside, however, when a large Japanese force – 24th Independent Mixed Brigade – approached White City. Luckily, the Block's C-47 strip had been completed and the guns were flown in just before the Japanese attacked.[8] The Japanese forward elements were encountered at Sepein and the main body closed with White City on 5 April.[6]

Orders were changed after another conference between Mountbatten, Slim and Lentaigne. Special Force was to be confined to its original role, supporting Stilwell. Furthermore, Special Force would transfer to Stilwell's command. Stilwell didn't want the Chindits and favoured holding White City. If the Chindits went north they would bring more Japanese in Stilwell's direction and his forces were struggling against the hard-fighting 18th Division. Furthermore, the Chinese forces in the Yunnan sector were still reluctant to advance. Nevertheless, the new arrangements were implemented. Lentaigne set up an Advance HQ at Shadazup, alongside Stilwell's Northern Combat Area Command HQ. White City would be abandoned and a new Block established near Hopin, closer to Mogaung. Allen comments: 'This was not a wise move. Long Range Penetration succeeds only if it is remote from the front … Calvert had not only established a solid position in the Block at Henu, the Japanese had thrown everything they could to dislodge him and had failed.'[5]

Bernard Fergusson's 16 Brigade was spent. On 3 April Trooper Aylen of 45 Recce noted the comments from his Column Commander on the outcome of their operations. They had, at a conservative estimate, killed 100 Japanese for 17 killed and four missing (two of whom turned up later with another Column).[9] Everyone was glad to return to Aberdeen in the first days of April. Lieutenant Cyril Baldock, ATO with 45 Recce's 54 Column, looked forward to a rest but his Brigadier had other ideas: 'Fergusson said: "Cyril! I've chosen you! We have just had the West Africans here. I want you to escort their animal transport to White City and then return."'

54 Column and elements of 45 Column were reorganised into two Companies while at Aberdeen. Their losses had included Major Ron Adams, who was wounded and told his men to leave him as he continued to fight. Cyril Baldock: 'I remember Adams as a very fine man. A devout Christian, he had an extraordinary ability to get people going. He was a big man in every sense.'

16 Brigade's 2nd Leicesters were to have no rest. On 6 April 17 and 71 Columns were attached to 77 Brigade for the floater role around White City. Corporal Ted Treadwell was with 71 Column. Despite the many hardships of jungle living, his remarkable constitution shielded him:

'I was still quite fit after the march in. Some of the others got tick fever but I stayed healthy. Compared to Ceylon, the mosquitoes were not so bad, but prickly heat was a big problem. It made your shoulders twitch despite the pack's weight. Somehow I stayed free of jungle sores.'

The desire to barter crossed the cultural divides. Treadwell remembers his successful negotiations to buy eggs:

'The villagers always had plenty of chickens. Fresh eggs were wonderful and I found the Burmese people very friendly. We also liked Burmese rice. For some reason I was one of the few to lose no weight.'

Treadwell's Column often heard Japanese catcalls: 'Come on, Johnny! Over here!' This would sometimes draw ironic replies: 'We would say: "Don't worry. We'll be there soon. We'll be coming after you!"'

The Japanese were masters of encirclement and air strikes were often required to break up these threats. Discipline was vital if the Chindits were to survive and Column justice remained rough and ready. Ted Treadwell:

'One of our officers was a heavyweight boxer. Some of our blokes would try to climb trees and get more rations for themselves. If they were caught, our boxer administered punishment with his fists. He gave a few of them black eyes.'

Deep friendships were forged within the Column:

'We were all good mates. After the war I bumped into one. I was working on a road resurfacing job in the Croydon area and he was a local dustman. Alf Sullivan was a member of one of our mortar teams. Another mate, Alfie Tucker, returned safely from Burma and lived in Ealing after the war.'

Charles Carfrae commanded 7 NR's 29 Column. He watched his men settle down for the night on reaching White City. Some slept under the wings of wrecked aircraft. Carfrae could hear small arms fire and grenades exploding some distance away. He described the scene at daybreak:

At our backs, we could see nothing but deep jungle. Ahead of us lay the Dakota landing strip and beyond it, distant a quarter of a mile, the tree-clad hillocks of the White City Block rose a few hundred feet above the railway line and attendant road, which

Aberdeen crash: two Dakotas collided on the strip. (Jim Unsworth)

wound from Myitkyina southward through the long valley known to Chindits as the railway corridor. Figures in jungle green with slung rifles moved here and there across the landing ground and over White City floated a thin blue veil of woodsmoke. The defenders were brewing up.[10]

Some men found moments of solace at White City. Lieutenant (later, Captain) Norman Durant, MC, commanding the machine gun Platoon of the South Staffords' 80 Column, found respite for an hour or so during quiet periods beside the small stream on the Block's southern perimeter. There would be very few quiet periods in the days ahead.

Attacks on White City became a nightly occurrence from 6 April. Units of the Japanese 24th Independent Mixed Brigade were determined to blow a way through the thick wall of wire using Bangalore Torpedoes. The 6 April attack began at 22.00 and the Chindits' 3 in. mortars poured fire on the threatened section of perimeter. Even the Bofors anti-aircraft gunners depressed their barrels and joined in. The Japanese attacked repeatedly for the next 10 days.[11] Almost every assault began with shelling and mortaring, often answered by the Block's newly arrived 25 Pounders. The guns helped break up the attacks.

The initial assault hit the Block's south-east corner. The attackers were overwhelmed by heavy Vickers enfilade fire sweeping the perimeter and a dense barrage from 16 centrally controlled 3 in. mortars. Two further attacks, launched on the same 400 yards of wire, were defeated. Calvert called up air strikes for dawn; six

Mustangs arrived and attacked the Japanese forming up area.[12] Captain Bill Towill, with 3rd/9th Gurkhas, described what followed:

> After a pause, the attack would be repeated again in exactly the same spot in a senseless, totally unimaginative way. The only result was to add further corpses to the hundreds hanging on the wire or lying in the minefields. They lay there bloated, rotting and stinking, covered with clouds of gorged flies and quite inaccessible for burial. Attempts to cremate them with flamethrowers only substituted one revolting stench and sight for another.[13]

RAF Officer Robert Thompson added:

> Japanese infantry attacks would go on most of the night in their attempts to get through the wire and breach our defences. They would be countered by a creeping barrage of massed mortar batteries, fixed-line Vickers machine gun fire and hand grenades. At dawn the Japanese would pull back a short distance into the jungle and dig in. Our floating Columns outside the Block could pinpoint where they were, together with the location of any artillery.
>
> Soon after dawn the Mustangs under Lieutenant-Colonel Paddy Mahoney would arrive, loaded with 500 lb bombs. Voice radio contact with them, on an ordinary Army 22 set, was loud and clear. This had the advantage that the Company Commanders could listen in. Again, thanks to Cochran, we all, including the pilots, had a complete mosaic of the

Keeping up: Chindits on the outskirts of a Burmese village. (Trustees of the Imperial War Museum)

area. The pilots would be informed what the target was, in which square on the mosaic, and the line of attack – for example, on a bearing of 200°. This last was dictated partly by topography and sun, but was designed to ensure that the aircraft were attacking parallel to our troops and turning left afterwards, away from them.

A mortar would be ready to fire a smoke bomb marker and Paddy would be told, 'Ten seconds from now'. As he came round on the bearing, down he would go. We knew most of them by name and Chuck would be told, 'Five yards right of Paddy' and down he would go. It would often be necessary to fire another smoke bomb when the air cleared. ... It was all very flexible.[14]

After the bombs had been dropped, the aircraft strafed the area with .5 machine guns. Against infantry in fox-holes the technique was to dive steeply and fire down vertically.

The defenders of White City were extremely well dug-in. Chindit casualties on 6 April were three killed and 11 wounded. The wounded were flown out by light aircraft to Broadway, then on to hospitals in India.

Japanese aircraft were also active. On 7 April medium bombers raided White City, bombing from 3,000 ft. The

Bofors guns engaged the 27 attackers and claimed six kills and six probables. Gaps were blown in the perimeter wire and desperate efforts were made to repair the damage before the next ground assault came in.[12]

At 17.00 that day the Japanese began shelling and the bombardment lasted until nightfall, when more attacks began. Major Freddie Shaw's floater force received orders to attack the Japanese rear but Calvert had no appreciation of the true size of the large enemy force. Shaw's Gurkhas suffered heavy losses in very hard fighting. He was then told to re-enter the Block.[12] Dick Stuckey, with 12 NR's 43 Column, gave his impression of the attackers:

'The Japanese were very persistent. It was obvious that they regarded their own lives as of no consequence. Most attacks came in at dusk and would continue until 9 or 10 o'clock. Hughes liked to do the rounds and visit the South Staffords and Gurkhas. As Staff Officer I had to accompany him, but Hughes was a sensible chap and didn't stick his neck out unnecessarily. On the other hand, he was very brave and didn't mind getting out of his slit trench if the situation demanded. The Japs' 4.2 in medium mortar was a good reason for getting into a slit trench.'

The men holding White City especially loathed the Japanese 6 in. heavy mortar. This monster fired a 4ft 6in. projectile with a 30-second flight time. It could penetrate deep dugouts. Calvert's Intelligence Officer was among those killed by this formidable weapon.[12]

At 03.00 on 8 April T Troop Commander Captain Arthur Mendus (who had entered White City to assist S Troop) heard vehicles in Mawlu. He was acting as Nicholls' OP relief. These trucks brought up the 6 in. heavy mortar, which opened fire at 04.00. Brigade woke Nicholls and asked him to do something about it. The big mortar's flash was visible from the OP, the target was engaged and soon ceased firing. Later that day the guns fired at Japanese anti-aircraft guns firing at aircraft supporting the Block. One aircraft lingered and spotted for the 25 Pounders.

During the periods of very heavy fighting the drops consisted exclusively of ammunition. At one point Calvert received a signal informing him that the next drop would include 50 per cent rations. He replied: 'We can live without food but we can't live without ammunition. Send ammunition.'[12] The mules suffered heavily. Dick Stuckey:

'We tried to dig a mule graveyard but the shelling was incessant and we just couldn't get them all underground. The best we could do for most was to drag them out, just beyond the wire, and leave them to disintegrate in the hot sun.'

There were lighter moments:

'At one point the Japanese made a determined effort to take higher ground. A South Staffords Lance Corporal was busy digging in. Another man downslope was doing the same. The Lance Corporal asked him how he was getting on and the answer came back in Japanese. The Jap got the message and made off. He could have shot him but he let him go.'

The garrison's morale held, bolstered by plentiful ammunition and sufficient food – including tinned fruit and bully. Stuckey saw Calvert from time to time:

'He was dedicated, fearless and a bit mad. I knew his brother in Malaya after the war and I told him: "You're not a bit like your brother." He replied: "Well, he's known as the bonkers one in the family!" Calvert always pushed his luck. He made such an obvious target, riding round on his horse, with his red hat on! He led a charmed life.'

Calvert always had a reason for his actions. Such displays were probably for the benefit of anyone who

might be inclined to spend too much time in his slit trench. It was a signal to get on with daily chores. Bill Williams, ATO with the South Staffords' 80 Column, was unscathed in the Pagoda Hill action which had secured White City. He was wounded, however, when leading a small recce patrol: 'We suddenly came across a group of Japs and one threw a grenade. I received a superficial leg wound, but it rapidly turned into a deep jungle sore and then went gangrenous.'

Before this engagement Williams had endured seven weeks at White City, helping to repel many Japanese attacks. Much of the fiercest fighting took place during the first fortnight:

'I was on a feature known as "Bare Hill". At first, all I had to do was ensure the animals were safe, fed and watered. As we had nothing else to do, half the Muleteers were formed into a Rifle Platoon. When the fighting became intense, there were moments when it looked as though the Japs might break in. Their big mistake was to use the same failed tactics time and again. They always did the same thing, at the same time, every day. You could almost set your watch by them. The Vickers and mortars kept them at bay. Those Vickers gunners were wonderful.

'I don't recall being particularly uncomfortable at this time. We knew exactly what we were doing, although it did seem a bit mad to be totally dependent on air supply. Yet we were never short of ammo. We were using an awful lot of grenades. My position was nearly overrun during the first big attack, when we ran short of grenades. From then on we had boxes of them hauled up to our positions. I looked at one of the boxes and found the grenades had been manufactured by a company which had once employed me. They were better known to me as makers of locks, rather than grenades. It seemed curious that their name found its way, on a box of grenades, into my slit trench in deepest Burma. Many years later I was to own this company, until we were bought out eventually by Chubb.'

Every evening the shelling began at around 17.00, followed by an infantry attack just after last light. The east and south-east perimeter would be assaulted. The area would be illuminated by flares and hit by concentrated fire from the defenders, manning up to 13 Vickers guns. Their weapons became red-hot during the fighting. The concentrated machine gun fire made a continuous roar. The attacks would slacken off as more and more Japanese died on the wire.[8]

White City's wired defences were formidable. The wire was 20 yards thick in places and festooned with mines, booby traps and other anti-personnel weapons.

Zigzag alleyways through the dense wire allowed access for counter-attacks. Over 100,000 yards of barbed wire and 600 50ft coils of Dannert wire were received by White City's garrison.[7]

How did this jungle fortress relate to Wingate's original concept of mobile Chindit warfare? Calvert always held that the Chindits were an outflanking movement delivered by air transport, rather than guerrillas: 'Mountbatten and Stilwell fully understood this, but Slim never did.' Only when the Chindit threat concentrated and produced strong fortress hubs – bases for mobile Columns seizing and destroying vital points – did the Japanese respond in the desired manner and divert forces from other areas.[7]

Having landed at Chowringhee, 111 Brigade HQ and the Gurkhas were in the Lower Meza during the third week of March. The Brigade's two British Battalions, Cameronians and King's Own, had landed at Broadway and were around 10 miles south-west of Mawlu. 111 Brigade was to block the Pinlebu–Pinbon road, but the British Battalions had suffered greatly during their difficult crossing of the hills near Katha. The going was so bad that the King's Own, at one point, had to blast a way through a barrier of trees.[15]

After this experience 111 Brigade's Richard Rhodes James felt disillusioned:

> Coming out of the thick jungle, we were confronted with a small, overgrown track which had not been used for some time. We crossed it and, on questioning an officer, I discovered that this was The Road. It struck us as farcical. We had marched all this way and, arriving at our destination, we found there was nothing to do. I found this an intensely disappointing moment. The efforts of the past two weeks appeared to have led us nowhere.[16]

Rhodes James added: 'It is a peculiar discipline of Long Range Penetration that the design of the whole is often obscured by the frustrations of the parts. 77 Brigade were doing great things and killing many Japs. We were still fumbling in the hot jungle and seeking a role. It seemed to me an expensive way to use all these troops.'[17]

The King's Own's actions were small-scale at this time. They requested a Battalion supply drop on 3 April, in readiness for blocking the Pinlebu–Pinbon road.

Bringing 111 Brigade together would be difficult. As decribed earlier, Brigade HQ and the Gurkhas had attempted to cross the Irrawaddy and link up with the Cameronians and King's Own, but the crossing was only half-complete when dawn broke. 40 Column and many animals were still on the wrong bank. This situation was accepted and 40 Column was ordered to link up with Morris Force.[18]

The two Columns of Cameronians set off independently from Broadway but remained close together. Cypher Operator Norman Campbell, with 90 Column, had no real grasp of where they were:

> 'For several weeks, until we entered Blackpool Block, we floated around Katha, Indaw, Wuntho, Pinlebu and Banmauk, generally heading in a northerly direction. One encounter with the Japs occurred near Banmauk. A Jap was badly wounded. Judging by his uniform he was either a senior NCO or a junior officer. As he lay on the ground he seemed to go for a weapon or grenade and the man on my right stuck his bayonet into him. In such situations you can't hesitate. You have to trust your instincts. Be quick or be dead!'

This was not the first Japanese Campbell had met in Burma:

> 'I had been fed on the myth that all Japs were shortsighted, small men. We bumped an enemy patrol and one casualty gave me a shock. This Jap was over 6 ft tall, well proportioned and tough looking. Fortunately for me, he was also dead, with a bullet in the forehead. Our Intelligence Sergeant, Bill Pullen, searched his body. I took his cap badge – a five-pointed metal star – and wore it on my bush hat as a lucky charm. Had I been captured, this souvenir might have been unlucky. We also recovered our first Japanese sword. It was sent back to base in a light plane, with the intention of hanging it in the Officers' Mess. I suspect it was "sidetracked" in transit.
>
> Another skirmish began when a number of Japanese were surprised as they made breakfast at a small jungle depot. They were dealt with, their breakfast eaten and their rice purloined. Anything we couldn't carry was destroyed.'

As the Cameronians of 90 Column approached the end of each day's march, Colonel Henning and his Batman went forward to select a bivouac. Norman Campbell:

> 'We always knew we had arrived when the Colonel came back down the track wearing only his bush hat and boots, with his rifle draped across his shoulders. He had a habit of immediately hanging up his sweat-soaked shirt and trousers by his tree, to dry out. The Colonel knew me by name. One day he asked me to cut his hair. He insisted, despite my protestations that I could not be held responsible for the result. In fact, the outcome was not bad for a first effort. He may have felt otherwise; I was not asked again.'

Norman Campbell and Eddie Walsh were kept busy deciphering messages and enciphering outgoing signals. This work often filled their lunch breaks and cost them sleep at night, when they worked by torchlight with blankets over their heads. There were two wireless teams. Corporal Needham led the Royal Signals group and a Canadian, Flight Lieutenant McDonald, headed the RAF wireless team. Eddie and Norman smiled whenever they sent requests for drops. They also approved of 90 Column's straightforward way of dealing with supplies snagged in trees – a slab of 808 explosive on the tree trunk.

When the King's Own crossed the railway they used a laborious technique. In his memoirs, W.H. Miller said it took hours to cross, each man being called forward individually. The next challenge was the road. A Japanese working party was nearby. A Rifle Platoon went to deal with them and provide cover for the main body during the crossing: 'No-one was hurt on our side – not even a mule. We learned later that we had aroused 200 Japs in a village nearby, who immediately tried to mortar us. They must have thought we were making for Indaw, as most bombs fell in that direction.'[19]

The King's Own had a lucky escape when attacking Naunglon village. An air strike was late and Mustangs carrying 500 lb bombs came close to bombing the lead elements.[20]

The King's Own's 41 and 46 Columns made a steep climb to the site selected for the supply drop on 3 April. On arriving they heard aircraft circling but the drop was aborted due to thick low cloud. They then called for an emergency run by light aircraft, dropping from an extremely low height.[19]

Lack of water caused severe distress within the King's Own Columns. Efforts to dig out dry chaungs proved fruitless. Miller described a hard lesson: 'No-one in the Burmese jungle should ever yield to the temptation of emptying his water bottle unless and until he is in sight of water.' Messages passing along a Column often became garbled. Word spread that there was a stream ahead. By the time they discovered there was no stream, the CO had given the men permission to take a long pull on their water bottles: 'we then went thirsty for two whole days and nights.'

Things got so bad that Miller felt obliged to give out the sacramental wafers and wine: 'The men I gave it to seemed pathetically grateful.' Fortunately, the lead Platoon then located a mountain stream. Everyone drank their fill, bathed in it and a meal was prepared.[19]

The Column's elephants: men of the King's Own pictured at Mokso Sakan with elephants used for carrying mortar rounds and other heavy loads. The effects of poor rations are evident. In the foreground is Captain Frank Baines, Commander of 111 Brigade's Defence Platoon. Major Frank Turner, 111 Brigade ATO, is on the elephant to right. (Trustees of the Imperial War Museum)

SICK   EVACUATED   BY   'NAGA'
        CARRYING   PARTIES

Helping hands: Nagas carry a sick 23 Brigade soldier to an
airstrip for evacuation. (Tony Wailes)

time trying to the utmost of his power to succour
the dying men. He was able to dress some wounds
but, eventually, he realised there was no hope for
them and he withdrew ...

For many hours we lay up in some thick woods,
all too aware of the fact that a much-used road lay
within a quarter of a mile of our 'hide-out' ...The CO
decided it was too dangerous for burial parties and
the Chaplains to return to the ambush site, to bury
the dead.[19]

The King's Own fixed bayonets before moving out at
noon on 5 April. They crossed the road without challenge and struck out at a good pace. Reaching a
relatively open hillside they were attacked by two
American aircraft. They made two firing passes but
there were no casualties, although many of the mules
bolted once again. There was no third run, as the men
were told to take out their orange 'panic maps' and
wave them. This convinced the pilots.

On reaching the Meza they waded the waist-deep river,
reached a second railway line and crossed safely despite
the close proximity of a Japanese garrison. The block on
the Pinlebu–Pinbon road had been established at 1800
on 5 April. Two trucks carrying infantry drove into the
block and were destroyed by PIAT and Vickers fire.

Miller had a close call. During a supply drop on 6 April
he was with 41 Column's ATO, Lieutenant A.R. Leyland.
Miller moved to another tree, where his kit was. Leyland
stayed put and was struck by a 'free-drop' bundle of
ammunition and boots: 'In spite of every attempt by the
MO to bring him round, he remained unconscious for
many days'. Miller later heard that Leyland had survived,
despite a skull fracture.

Sickness tightened its grip on the King's Own. Miller
wrote of two very bad cases of cerebral malaria: 'I saw
both these men, who were desperately ill, before they
died. We buried them in a patch of open jungle just
outside a deserted village. A few weeks later we had
occasion to pass the same spot. Everyone noticed the
appalling stench. The MO went to investigate and found
that they had been disinterred, their clothes and boots
removed and the bodies left exposed as tempting prey
to the animals of the jungle'.

There were several cases of self-inflicted wounds,
bullet shots through hands and feet. As these
became more frequent, severe disciplinary action
was contemplated against such offenders. We could
only hope for an early chance of evacuating these
'passengers' by light aircraft to Airbase, where, no
doubt, they received the punishment they certainly
deserved.[19]

They covered 15 miles on 4 April and reached a village just before dark. This appeared to be deserted and it
was decided they should rest. Men and mules were still
coming in when firing broke out and the animals stam-
peded. The men spent a nervy night in cover, before
regrouping at dawn. It appeared that a Japanese patrol
had allowed the main body to pass before attacking the
tail. The action began when Captain John Busby, the
Battalion's Adjutant, saw figures crouching at the side
of the track, in the dim light of dusk. Miller wrote that
Busby was

... immediately set upon with sword and bayonet
and fatally wounded. His companions also shared
the same fate. A minor battle was fought out at that
bloody spot. CSM Robson, another most gallant soldier and the holder of the MM, organised resistance
and fought the Japs for quite a while, at the same

The Chaplain was also confronted with 'moral welfare' problems – bad news from home. Matrimonial misfortunes dogged some men. One committed suicide on receiving a letter from his wife, announcing that she had given birth to a son.[19]

The men tried to cope with slow starvation. The Cameronians and King's Own never had more than three days' rations for each five-day period. The need for food and other essentials became so overwhelming that later, some were tempted to play the system. Rhodes James:

> We used to bring in the planes on the wireless and it was part of our very strange game that we should call in as many as we could, whoever they were meant for … In the north end of the Mogaung Valley there were several dropping zones and it was easy for the pilot to be bewildered into dropping on the first Column that got him on the air.[21]

Captain Neville Hogan, Recce Platoon Commander with the King's Own's 46 Column, was ordered to go out and capture a notorious Japanese officer, Captain Murakami, who had been terrorising villagers: 'He personally beheaded anyone suspected of helping us. Unusually, this Japanese officer spoke Burmese.' Hogan realised that, by a strange twist of fate, he had a direct personal connection with Murakami:

'It sounds unlikely but it is true. Murakami was the son of a Japanese man who had lived in Rangoon before the war and who had taught me ju-jitsu at the age of seven! I declined to capture him, knowing just how formidable he would be, but I did promise that I would try to kill him.

'We knew he was in a particular village and that he had the habit of spending his evenings in the 'Comfort Girls' basha, set up for the officers. We kept this village under observation, went in when it was dark and made our way to the basha. We threw in four grenades (two four-second and two eight-second) which blew the place to bits and put paid to Murakami.

'Getting out of that village was more difficult than going in. One of my men seemed drunk with success. He was barking like a dog as we ran through the village. Fortunately, Japanese soldiers tended to keep their bayonets fixed at all times and this did nothing to improve their aim. We got out unscathed. In fact, I can't remember a shot being fired, they were so surprised.'

23 Brigade reached its operational zone north of Kohima, around Mokokchaung, on 6 April – the day the Kohima siege began. Throughout April this Brigade was highly mobile, fighting on the Japanese 31st Division's right flank, skirmishing with enemy patrols and assaulting occupied villages, often helped by intelligence from the supportive Nagas. Gradually, the Japanese were forced to concentrate at the larger centres, where fierce actions were fought. One 1st Essex Column lost 10 men, captured by the enemy. On reaching the position, the Column found the captives tied up, their dead bodies covered in bayonet wounds.[22]

Notes

1. Graves-Morris, Lieutenant-Colonel P. H., unpublished MS (via Bill Smith and Corinne Simons)
2. Dobney, Major R.P.J. 'Paddy', unpublished MS, July 1981 (via Bill Smith and Corinne Simons)
3. Carfrae, C. (1985), *Chindit Column*, 91–92
4. Rooney, D. (2000), *Wingate and the Chindits: Redressing the Balance*, 180
5. Allen, L. (1986), *Burma: The Longest War 1941–45*, 351–352
6. Rooney. D. (1997), *Mad Mike*, 83–86
7. Calvert, M. (1974), *Chindits: Long Range Penetration*, 93–97
8. Rooney, D. (2000), 126–128
9. Aylen, N.P., Trooper, *45th Reconnaissance Regiment*, Imperial War Museum, 80/49/1
10. Carfrae, C. (1985), 93–94
11. Calvert, M. (1996), *Fighting Mad*, 162
12. Calvert, M. (1974), 99–101
13. Towill, B. (2000), *A Chindit's Chronicle*, 65
14. Thompson, Sir Robert (1989), *Make for the Hills*, 55–56
15. Rhodes James, R. (1981), *Chindit*, 77–78
16. Ibid, 82–83
17. Ibid, 85
18. Ibid, 69–71
19. Miller, Rev. W. H., 2nd King's Own, *A Chaplain with the Chindits*, Imperial War Museum, 80/49/1
20. Rhodes James, R. (1981), 103–104
21. Ibid, 188
22. Rooney, D. (2000), 176–179

THE FIRST PHASE ENDS

9–17 April 1944

'Everyone's worst fear was a wound bad enough to cause you to be left behind. That was the nightmare.'

Corporal Tom Turvey, 71 Column, 2nd Leicesters

JUST OVER two months had passed since 16 Brigade began its trek into Burma. Other Special Force Brigades had since arrived by air, landing in rough jungle clearings. Two Strongholds (Broadway and Aberdeen) had been established, together with the White City Block on the main road/railway line. As the first phase of Operation *Thursday* neared completion, Japanese forces reorganised. General Mutaguchi handed over his wider responsibilities in North Burma on 11 April. He would focus entirely on the Imphal/Kohima battles. The Japanese now established the 33rd Army, under Lieutenant-General Honda. His command included the 18th and 56th Divisions, 24th Independent Mixed Brigade and the 53rd Division now entering Burma.[1]

White City's garrison knew a major Japanese assault was building. The Block was difficult to attack as its western and southern approaches crossed open paddy. The northern perimeter was too short to allow the Japanese to deploy effectively. Yet they remained determined to burst through White City's thick wire defences. At one point around 40 unexploded Bangalore Torpedoes were collected, scattered among piles of Japanese dead at the wire.[2]

White City had been reinforced. What remained of 45th Reconnaissance Regiment had transferred to Calvert's 77 Brigade. Meanwhile, the Queen's Columns marched north of the Block. Some elements reached Aberdeen on 10 April to rest and reorganise. The men relished the luxury of clean kit. Many lost patience with the filthy, sweat-soaked clothing glued to their bodies. They tore open their shirt-fronts, making it easier to peel off the rags in exchange for new clothing. Dysentery sufferer George Hill was grateful to exchange his soiled trousers for a new pair.

Major-General Lentaigne flew into White City on 10 April. The Block had held successive nights of heavy infantry attacks. He arrived with 3 (WA)'s Brigadier Gillmore and his 2i/c, Lieutenant-Colonel Degg. Brigadier Calvert handed over command of White City to Gillmore, as he prepared his new, offensive phase, with a powerful strike force to challenge strong Japanese concentrations in the area. At this stage Lentaigne and Calvert still underestimated the enemy's strength.[2] The plan was to kill as many Japanese as possible around White City before the Block was closed, just before the onset of the Monsoon. Special Force would then head north to link up with Stilwell's Chinese.

Two Battalions of Gillmore's Brigade (7 NR and 12 NR) contributed to White City's floating defences and garrison. Other forces at White City included the Lancashire Fusiliers' 20 Column and the South Staffords' 38 and 80 Columns, together with the 25 Pounders and anti-aircraft guns.

The strike force would include 77 Brigade's HQ (25 Column), 45 Recce's 45 and 54 Columns, the Gurkhas of 36 and 63 Columns (6 GR) and, later, 50 Column of the Lancashire Fusiliers, returning from Kadu. In addition, 7 NR's 29 and 35 Columns, led by Lieutenant-Colonel Peter Vaughan, were a few miles south of White City. Calvert ordered 7 NR to establish a strike force base to the west, near Thayaung. To the south were the Leicesters Columns, 17 and 71. They blocked the Mawlu-Pinwe road and had fought several successful actions. The *Report on Operations* states that they killed at least 60 Japanese, without loss.

Perhaps the most touching aspect of war in the Burmese wilderness was the ordinary soldier's determination to make the best of things, regardless of the appalling circumstances. Ted McArdle, with the King's 82 Column, represents the Chindit spirit. On 10 April McArdle celebrated his 21st birthday near Broadway Stronghold. He had hoarded chocolate bars from his K-rations, together with packets of currants: 'I broke up biscuits and used the other ingredients to make myself a birthday cake, which was baked in my dixie, over a fire.'

On Easter Sunday, 9 April, 45 Recce had left Aberdeen, heading for White City after a week's recuperation following the hard fighting around Indaw. They were now led by Major Ted Hennings as Cumberlege and Varcoe had been flown out from Aberdeen. Lieutenant-Colonel George Astell would eventually take command, with Hennings as his 2i/c.[3]

As 45 Recce neared White City Brigadier Calvert flew out in an L.5 to greet them and celebrate the arrival of another 400 men. Those who had suffered badly in recent weeks must have been rather crestfallen when Calvert enthusiastically described his tactics for proactive defence. 16 Brigade Commander Bernard Fergusson had understood that 45 Recce would join White City's static garrison, but Calvert made himself clear: they would be operating beyond the wire, helping to crush the Japanese attackers against the Block's defences. NCO Signaller Philip Sharpe decided to move into Lieutenant Winter's Rifle Section, concluding that he would be better off in their company when confronting the Japanese.[3]

45 Recce Trooper N. P. Aylen's diary notes that the sounds of battle could be heard every night as they drew closer to White City.[4] 77 Brigade's 2,400-strong counter-attack group prepared for action. Calvert ordered the Gurkhas to block the railway south of White City, while the West Africans blocked the road. 45 Recce was his reserve. One key objective was Sepein village, just south of Mawlu and thought to be the main Japanese base.

At 16.55 hrs on 11 April the enemy began shelling White City in preparation for another major attack. This came in at 19.30 and was repulsed, leaving at least 100 Japanese dead at the wire. A Japanese tank appeared at dusk, crawled along the southern perimeter but made no attempt to enter and eventually moved away. The attacks continued on 12 April and 13, with the Japanese making determined attempts to blow open the wire with Bangalore Torpedoes. Each assault was a costly failure.

Sergeant Harold Bottomley, with the Commando Platoon of the Lancashire Fusiliers' 20 Column, won the MM for his courage during a very heavy attack on their positions during the night of 13 April. The Japanese knocked out three Bren weapons pits and Bottomley

recovered the weapons, re-sited them, got them back into action and then went back for the wounded. After the war he sent a note to Fusilier Harold Shippey, a fellow member of the Commando Platoon, thanking him for 'helping to earn this award.'

On 14 April the Nigerians were left to man the road and rail blocks. The Gurkhas and 45 Recce left their packs with them and loaded up with ammunition. They had orders to advance and kill as many Japanese as possible. They accounted for over 300 rear echelon Japanese troops, for negligible loss.[2]

45 Recce rendezvoused with Brigade HQ. Calvert briefed them for another attack the next morning, to relieve the pressure on White City. During the night of 14/15 April, the Japanese launched furious assaults on the perimeter and were beaten back. In the early morning of 15 April Calvert wanted to repeat yesterday's successes. He planned to take the Japanese in the rear and drive them against White City's perimeter wire and machine guns. 45 Recce did well. A large fighting group led by Lieutenant-Colonel Astell caught a Japanese party in bivouac and overran an HQ and a wireless detachment. They surprised some 200 Japanese bathing in a chaung. Subsequently, they took a second headquarters and set up machine gun nests to cover a wide jungle track. These guns then surprised two Japanese Companies.[2]

Aylen was wounded during Calvert's push against the large Japanese force investing White City. Astell had given the Recce Platoon the job of defending Column HQ. Trooper Aylen: 'Firing was regular but not intense and I took the opportunity of having breakfast during a comparative lull. As I sat up to loosen my haversack a burst of automatic fire went into the tree above my head, so I had my breakfast in a prone position.'[4]

Column HQ came under heavy mortar fire. Aylen saw Trooper Flynn in action once again with his Vickers: 'He had taken his gun into an open space, where he was completely unprotected from enemy fire, and was periodically pouring fire into enemy patrols as he spotted them moving round on our flanks.'

Then a Japanese patrol got close enough to rake Aylen's area: 'I felt a sharp pain in my knuckle and a slight tug at my chest. I hugged the earth as close as possible while the storm continued.' When Aylen looked up again Flynn was still working the Vickers, disregarding the enemy fire: 'During the next lull I glanced down, to find my shirt soaked in blood from a gash in my chest.'

As the men withdrew they came across some grotesque sights, including single dead Gurkhas every few yards. They had died at their posts. They passed a mule munching bamboo leaves despite the gaping hole in its side.[4]

Pick-up: a Dakota at Aberdeen ready to receive West African wounded. (Jim Unsworth)

45 Recce's progress slowed as the opposition stiffened. Calvert saw the danger of lost momentum and ordered two Gurkha Companies to sweep 45 Recce's flanks. These moves were blocked by the enemy. Calvert responded by calling up a West African counter-attack from the Block, only half a mile away. He remained determined to squeeze the Japanese against the wire. These manoeuvres provoked a full-scale battle, involving 1,600 Chindits in savage close-quarters fighting. They were hard-pressed and Calvert was wise to call in a maximum strength air strike; 27 Mustangs bombed and strafed the Japanese forming up areas, only 200 yards away.

Calvert now took the opportunity to withdraw. He had over 100 dead and more than 200 wounded. The Nigerians were sent out to help recover the wounded. The search for the missing revealed that the Japanese had pulled back. They had abandoned many of their wounded.[2]

Lieutenant Peter Allnutt has vivid memories of arriving at White City with the Nigerians. Allnutt was with 12 NR's 43 Column. A patrol went forward as the Battalion neared the Block. They failed to contact the garrison but found no Japanese. Battalion Commander Pat Hughes was encouraged; the idea was to reinforce the Block unobserved. During the morning, as they drew closer, they heard firing. Suddenly, every-

thing went very quiet, leaving the more imaginative with the uncomfortable thought that the Block might have fallen. The men passed two empty villages then reached the edge of open paddy. They saw the statichutes that gave White City its name, clearly visible across the tops of the far trees. They took in the scene. The houses visible to the south were in Japanese-occupied Mawlu. The rubble on the southern edge of the ridge marked the ruins of Henu village, which had been flattened. There was no cover between 12 NR and White City's perimeter. Crossing that stretch of open ground in the searing heat was unpleasant; but they reached the wire unscathed. There was a false alarm when aircraft were heard, but they were Mustangs attacking Mawlu.

Peter Allnutt studied White City and its collection of low, denuded hills, with open paddy to the west and south. A small river flowed east to west. Japanese mortar fire had put a stop to the Dakota landings. At that point Aberdeen served as White City's airstrip. Direct supply to White City was almost entirely confined to air drops alone, although Cochran's light aircraft still flew out the battle casualties.

The two 7 NR Columns, 29 and 35, also neared White City. 35 Column's Recce Platoon went forward to explore the route. Denis Arnold was a Platoon Commander with 29 Column:

'I could hear distant gunfire. White City, over 20 miles away, was under constant Japanese attack. Occasionally, there was an unusually loud explosion. This was from a Japanese heavy mortar firing huge projectiles into White City. I was more concerned about the noise we were making, marching through dry teak jungle. We made a terrible racket as the big teak leaves crunched underfoot.'

Denis Arnold was one of many who were disappointed when told of their role at White City: 'We were good in the jungle and we were to show ourselves skilled in the arts of ambush. Had Wingate lived, I am sure he would not have used us in the garrison role.'

The Battalion Commander, Lieutenant-Colonel Peter Vaughan, led 35 Column. The Commander's personality largely shaped the Column's personality. Denis Arnold:

'Peter Vaughan was quite different from 29 Column's Charles Carfrae. Vaughan was a gung-ho extrovert. Carfrae was introspective and academic in style, not the typical Regular soldier. The most important quality of any Column Commander, of course, was personal courage. He must not show even a hint of fear, at any time.'

Charles Carfrae held a high opinion of Denis Arnold. In his book, *Chindit Column*, the 29 Column Commander described him as 'an able and courageous Platoon Commander'. Peter Allnutt of 43 Column:

'Peter Vaughan was a Guardsman who always looked as if he was just about to go on Parade. He was a fine soldier, loved by his troops. On one occasion his men were held up by a Japanese light machine-gun. Peter could stomach it no longer. He drew his revolver, stepped out from cover and shouted to the astounded Japanese: "I say, you fellows! Surrender! Surrender, I say, immediately!" After a few seconds of silence, a burst of fire clipped a bush close to Peter's head. He withdrew at a leisurely pace behind cover.'

Morale remained solid within the Block. The garrison was convinced White City could be held. Slit trenches were deepened. Men made them more comfortable by lining them with statichutes. Nightly supply drops brought in more food, ammunition and equipment. Red Austin's C-47, 'Assam Dragon', operated continually in support of the Chindits and took on many roles. This aircraft was a glider tug during the landings and also flew troops into the Strongholds. Assam Dragon ferried supplies into White City and later took part in supply drops over the Block. Austin and his crew encountered

no enemy aircraft in over 90 missions, but often saw ground fire reaching up towards them.

During one night mission flying in cargo and ordnance they spotted a Japanese truck convoy. Assam Dragon made several low passes and the Engineer threw incendiary bombs out of the cargo door. On their return they received a mild reprimand for 'deviating' from their mission.

Each hill at White City was a distinct fighting position, with heavily wired defences. Any movement beyond the wire at night brought down immediate heavy fire. During the day, however, the tracks linking the hill positions were busy with men and mules.

Peter Allnutt's first night at White City passed without incident. He felt cheered when his Orderly, Alijebba Dumel, arrived with his morning tea. Allnutt was now 2i/c of a Company holding 'Pat's Hill'. This was the final hill on the southern perimeter, directly facing Mawlu. The outer wire defences were immediately in front of their trenches. The inner wire was behind them, with the 25 Pounders just beyond. To the east, the perimeter was completed by OP Hill. This feature was a mess – blasted bare and pitted with shell holes.

Pat's Hill received plenty of attention from Japanese guns and mortars, due to the proximity of the 25 Pounders. Allnutt was shown to his foxhole by Sergeant-Major Potter. He decided to cheer up the officer with a 'funny' comment: 'That's the one, Sir. It got a direct hit a few nights ago. I hope the roof's mended.' The roof was still in its damaged condition. Repairs began as Allnutt took stock of Pat's Hill. Its weak spot was a projection towards Mawlu, at the western end. This might become isolated in an attack. The Dannert wire was just a few yards from Allnutt's foxhole and the river itself only 30 yards beyond. A mile of open paddy then extended to the trees, where jungle-clad hills rose to 6,000 ft.

OP Hill was held by elements of 12 NR and a Section of South Staffords. An adjacent, lower feature was held by a detachment from OP Hill. Further south and even lower was Dummy Hill (named after two dummy bunkers). There were not enough men to occupy Dummy Hill and the Japanese often took advantage and moved onto this feature at night. To the west, set back from Pat's Hill, was Pagoda Hill. It had a 270-degree outlook, from east to north, and was home to the pulverised ruins of Henu village.

Peter Allnutt was new to the realities of White City. Nine of his Company's 12 Europeans would become casualties at the Block. Two Platoon Commanders, George Manuel and Bill Briggs, were killed in action. Allnutt was the only officer to escape injury. With the roof of his new home fully restored, Allnutt was drinking tea in the late afternoon when the Japanese mortars in Mawlu opened up. Then 75 mm guns, low angle AA guns and high velocity 'whizz-bangs' joined in. Peter Allnutt:

'That 6 in. heavy mortar was a real horror. It fired a bomb that made a crater 12 ft across. One of these 'coal scuttle' bombs landed a dozen yards away and lifted me clean off the trench floor. Later, we used this hole as our private rubbish dump.'

Whenever possible, the 25 Pounders of S Troop engaged the heavy mortar teams. On 9 April, for example, there was heavy shelling from Nanthayan Chaung and a 90 mm mortar east of Nyaungbirtha. Captain Nicholls, the Troop Commander, couldn't find the guns but saw mortar smoke and engaged. Later, the 6 in. mortar began firing and the 25 Pounders engaged the flash, spotted at Myothit and fired until it ceased. The guns also suppressed the big mortar the following day.

Shells hit the Block every second or so throughout the major bombardments. As the barrage lifted another ground assault would begin, usually from the jungle fringe facing the east perimeter (the only area favouring the attackers). The noise of small arms fire and grenades was interspersed with slow, steady fire from the Vickers and short, sharper Bren bursts. With the evening attack repulsed, Lieutenant Allnutt tried to settle down but mortaring started again at 2 am. A final attack followed around an hour later. This was beaten off and Allnutt had survived his first night of action at White City. It was nothing exceptional to most of the men around him, who had already spent a couple of weeks defending the Block.

Meanwhile, 54 Column ATO Cyril Baldock had completed the task set by Fergusson. He had returned the West Africans' animal transport:

'I delivered the animals safely, but arrived exactly when the Japanese launched their main series of attacks on White City. I was trapped and remained inside the Block for several weeks. I would not see 45 Recce again until I got back to India!'

Baldock made himself useful at White City: 'On several occasions I went out with the mules and one or two Burrifs to buy produce from the locals. They were prepared to sell fruit and vegetables despite the fact that the Japs were all around us.'

As a newcomer, Peter Allnutt was surprised at the garrison's light casualties at the end of his first night: two killed and five wounded. Fifty Japanese corpses were counted; others had been dragged away during the night. In the morning the Block's 25 Pounders fired into Mawlu for 10 minutes and then laid smoke for

1st Air Commando's B.25 bombers. It was the turn of the Japanese in the afternoon: six Zeros attacked the Chindits' positions.

Before Michael Calvert and his strike force left the Block, 77 Brigade's Commander briefed 7 NR's Peter Vaughan for an attack on Mawlu, to reduce its usefulness as an enemy base. Lieutenant Allnutt observed the mixed results of this operation. Allnutt then saw the wounded taken to White City's 'hospital'. This had been dug into a hillside, reinforced with steel rails and sleepers taken from the railway and lined with statichutes. The two MOs were 'Doc' Wilson and Leon Gonet. The hospital had two spaces, the Casualty Clearing Station and the Operating Theatre; both were fly and mosquito-proofed. The Operating Theatre equipment was dropped to Wilson and Gonet, who saved many lives.

Most wounded on Allnutt's second day at White City were hit during a four-hour barrage aimed primarily at OP Hill. 'Banzai' attacks were sent against the eastern perimeter. There were so many attacks here that troops manning the area were rotated regularly. Men in the slit trenches stockpiled grenades, in readiness for the night's proceedings. Peter Allnutt:

'The Vickers guns played a key role in the defence. At dawn you could see the fresh Japanese corpses spreadeagled on the wire. These were burnt down with flamethrowers. The entire eastern side of the Block was stinking, with that characteristic sweet smell of rotting human flesh. It was all pretty grim.'

The wounded on OP Hill included T Troop Commander Arthur Mendus, who was stationed in the main OP. He was seriously injured and later died. On 13 April the gun position was bombed by Japanese aircraft and then heavily shelled and mortared. No. 3 Gun was put out of action by a direct hit from a 75 mm shell. The Gun Detachment fought hard to control the resulting cordite fires.

Efforts outside the Block to drive more Japanese against the wire and the Vickers guns brought success. White City was a killing ground for the Japanese. Air strikes by B.25s and Mustangs also took many Japanese lives. The B.25s occasionally released clouds of small parachute-retarded bombs over the Japanese positions. Peter Allnutt: 'When hundreds of these small bombs descended, they looked like spawning salmon until they detonated in the treetops.'

Charles Carfrae, 29 Column's Commander, wrote that one day at White City was much like another:

> There would be attacks, in varying degrees of ferocity, every night from the east and south-east, but

Strike from the sky: a 1st Air Commando B.25 Mitchell bomber. The diagonal markings of Cochran's force are visible on the fuselage. (Trustees of the Imperial War Museum)

they failed to pierce through the thick coils of rusting wire. In the darkness Dakotas, flying low, dropped rations and ammunition and also medical supplies for the makeshift underground casualty station, containers crashing through trees ... Many would be caught up in branches and daylight revealed scores of parachutes hanging limp and pallid on the treetops, like linen hung out to dry – perfect aiming marks for Japanese guns.[5]

Airbase ensured that the supplies got through. Les Grainger trained as a Rifle Section Leader with the South Staffords. Unable to fly in due to a fractured foot, incurred during a training march, he was posted to a base in Assam, where he was soon hospitalised with malaria. Having recovered, he was then posted to Airbase and given the job of decoding Chindit supply drop requests:

'I would take the order to the supply dump and oversee its delivery to the airfield. We often received special requests, mostly for bread or onions. The latter were prized for flavouring other foods. I also remember two

signals from Calvert. One read: 'The men are fighting magnificently!' The other said something along the lines of: 'The RAF say they cannot supply because of the weather. It is the RAF who are wet, not the weather!'

Men unable to go in due to accident or illness did all they could to help those fighting in the Columns. Lieutenant Harold Pettinger, MC, had injured a knee during training and was transferred to REME. He joined the 'LAD' (Light Air Detachment) at Sylhet, supporting 14 Brigade Columns:

'Our activities included the supply of outboard engines for river crossings and other river work. We were always careful to run them in. These engines had to start first time in the field. I was always keen on variety, so I volunteered to fly as a "kicker". On one occasion I pushed out a consignment of bullion from a Dakota's hatch. Later, I had to sign a paper stating that I had indeed pushed it out at the correct map reference. I flew on quite a number of supply drops from Sylhet.'

Down it goes! A 'kicker' pushes as a load is dropped to the Chindits below. (Trustees of the Imperial War Museum)

When Calvert's force set out from White City they faced two enemies: the Japanese and disease. Captain W. F. Jeffrey, with the Lancashire Fusiliers' 50 Column, saw malaria strike down nearly 50 men. The planned attack on Mohnyin was cancelled when the Japanese opened their full-scale assault on White City. 50 Column then had the problem of getting back into the Block and recovering the many sick they had left in the care of a Platoon from 20 Column. More men went down with fever and were unable to march. The 10 men were hidden at a rendezvous point but were discovered and bayoneted by a Japanese patrol. Only one man escaped.[6]

A few 16 Brigade Chindits remained surprisingly fit after two months of jungle living. They included Wireless Operator Lou Lake, with the 2nd Leicesters' 17 Column. He was still in relatively good shape:

'I was free of malaria but had a touch of dysentery when marching in. My biggest problem was prickly heat. It was crucifying. My feet were fine throughout. Much later, when back in Britain, I was marked down to A.2 due to the condition of my feet. I had been A.1 fit throughout my service and I took great offence at this. I had marched a thousand miles in Burma and this man had the cheek to inform me that I was unfit.'

Corporal Tom Turvey was with the Leicesters' sister Column, 71. Turvey lived with hunger and constant tension. His place was out in front, with the Column's Recce Platoon:

'Before 16 Brigade started the march in, we had a final briefing in India. We really were told that all Japanese were small, cross-eyed and wore glasses. What is more, they couldn't shoot straight and they never attacked

at night! One bloke stood up and asked the briefing officer: "Did you get all this out of a book?"

'Everyone's worst fear was a wound bad enough to cause you to be left behind. That was the nightmare. We all lived with that dread ... the fear that the moment might come when you would be left.'

The Recce Platoon's Burrifs occasionally supplemented their meagre diet:

'I remember joining our Burrifs for a meal of crocodile (or something like crocodile) stew. I also tried snake at one point. The crocodile tasted fishy but the snake had a flavour quite unlike anything else I have tasted.'

The Recce Platoon was fortunate to have two excellent mules, but one was lost under sad circumstances:

'It was a queer thing. This mule started to drink from a chaung when its front feet slipped. The front legs went and the head went under. We made every effort but couldn't get him out. One Muleteer was a strong swimmer and he made to go in but was stopped — we didn't want to lose him as well. The mule drowned. It still had one pannier on and this had filled with water, keeping his head under.'

Platoon members knew they could 'bump' a Japanese patrol at any time. Tom Turvey:

'Our consolation was Lieutenant Percy Lake. He was naturally funny and had the knack of making us laugh. At the same time he made it clear that, if there weren't too many, "we'll have them buggers!" On one occasion, during the night, a Jap patrol jumped us. We drove them off after four hours or so. Afterwards we had a good laugh, thanks to Rifleman Charlie Lloyd. He was known as "Dandy Charlie" at home. In the Platoon, no matter how filthy everyone else was, Charlie always looked clean. Anyway, during the fight Charlie moved his position and fell into a Jap shit trench. He had to stay in that condition for a couple of days. Even when he managed to clean up, he still stank.'

Turvey witnessed the cruelty of the Japanese soldiery. The Recce Platoon set a watch on a village and then decided to enter. They discovered that the Japanese had visited the day before:

'They had offered the Headman a fag, then poured petrol over his head. I don't remember why but we had an MO with us. He took one look at the Headman and said he would never survive. He gave the victim

morphine. I suppose all the Japanese involved in that episode are dead now, but I would say that they are a bloody cruel race.'

14 April began with a Japanese air raid on White City. During the late afternoon two tanks emerged from Mawlu and were engaged by the two-pounder guns. One was damaged and began emitting black smoke. They retreated and were not seen again. The usual attempts to blow holes in the wire followed, but machine gun and mortar fire killed the attackers.

A major assault on the eastern perimeter came at 04.00 on 15 April. The Japanese gained a foothold on one of White City's hills by sheer weight of numbers. This hill was held by an officer and six men who refused to budge. A swift counter-attack then threw out the Japanese. In all, the enemy lost around 150 killed. Fierce fighting continued the next day, 16 April. Attacks on the perimeter were met by heavy defensive fire, attacks on the enemy rear and highly accurate 'cab rank' strikes by 1st Air Commando's Mustangs and bombing by B.25s.

The guns also played their part. S Troop Commander Captain Nicholls: 'Our guns fired on the 150 mm mortar and quietened it. Later, guns were laid over open sights on the crest of OP Hill, where the Japanese had obtained a foothold. A good view was had of the Nigerian counter-attack which cleared them off.'

On the afternoon of 17 April Nicholls moved into a new and very strong OP on Mugga Hill, just west of OP Hill. The roof had been strengthened with lengths of rail and Nicholls soon found that this rendered the compass useless.

The Chindits were doing severe damage to the Japanese 24th Independent Mixed Brigade and other units of General Hyashi's force of 10 Battalions, assembled to destroy Special Force. According to Calvert, the 24th alone, with a total strength of 5,495 men, suffered over 3,000 casualties at White City. The 3rd/114th (18th Division) also lost heavily on White City's wired defences and in fighting around Mawlu. The 2nd/146th (56th Division) took one-third casualties during its attacks on Broadway. Around Indaw 16 Brigade inflicted 250 casualties on the 2nd/29th (2nd Division) and the 2nd/51st (15th Division). The 1st/146th, confronting Morris Force on the Bhamo Road, took one-third casualties. Yet Chindit losses within White City remained 'remarkably small'. Two weeks of heavy shelling, for example, killed 20 and wounded 40.[2]

All Japanese efforts to crush White City had failed and Calvert had high hopes for his mobile force now operating outside the Block. Yet the Block's Garrison Commander, Gillmore, sent an alarming message to Calvert on 17 April, warning that he might not be able to hold. This controversial signal was sent without the knowledge of Calvert's own officers within the Block. Subsequently, Gillmore was succeeded by Brigadier Ricketts.[7] As it was, Gillmore's warning encouraged Calvert to push even harder towards the Block, which he now assumed to be in danger of falling. In fact, the opposite was the case; that day's big attack represented the enemy's last throw.

White City's defences remained unbroken. Well coordinated machine gun and mortar fire smashed each attack in the long series beginning on 6 April. Deeply buried telephone lines ensured that mortar support was available on call. Supply drops continued and mines and booby traps were relaid on and around the wire every day. After 11 days' fighting over 1,000 Japanese dead were decomposing in the fetid atmosphere. Most lay where they fell, just beyond the wire; others were grotesque in death, suspended on the wire itself. The stench of putrefaction hung in the air. Even flamethrowers and quicklime failed to improve things and there was growing concern about the risk to the Block's water supply.[8]

Michael Calvert already had his hands full when he received Gillmore's warning. On 12 April Lentaigne ordered him to attack Sepein, regarded as the main Japanese base for the attacks on White City. Calvert had around 2,400 men available for mobile operations. He could call up fire support from the Block's 25 Pounders and air support as required. Yet things began to unravel. Initially, Calvert received some good news: the Nigerians had taken Mawlu. But there were also a number of sinister developments. Firstly, the Japanese positions at Sepein were not in the village itself but just outside, about one mile to the south. Thick Lantana scrub made it almost impossible to assault the enemy. Even 25 Pounder bombardments (two 100-round shoots) and Mustang air strikes failed to shift them. The Sepein attack petered out and Calvert pulled back, to regroup at Thayaung. Then came Gillmore's signal.[9]

Calvert had no choice. He attacked the Japanese rear and attempted to force the enemy against White City's wire. Garrison elements could then sortie out and increase the pressure. His Japanese opponents were just too strong. Around 2,000 Japanese soldiers were being squeezed into an area just half-a-mile wide. A well-timed air strike and a Nigerian attack from the perimeter shifted the balance in 77 Brigade's favour, but Calvert's HQ came close to being overwhelmed in the desperate hand-to-hand fighting. As the enemy fell back, Calvert knew his men were in no shape to follow. They pulled back again to 7 NR's base at Thayaung, where a light aircraft strip had been cleared and the wounded and sick could be flown out.[9] Elements of Peter Vaughan's

7 NR had captured Mawlu railway station but were told to pull back. Calvert felt over-extended and was anxious to retain his firm grip on the road and railway.

The Chindits suffered over 200 casualties. Around 100 were killed in battles with 24th Independent Mixed Brigade. Rooney wrote: 'The Chindits had won an outstanding victory, but there was no joy nor elation because the price had been too high and too many close friends and fine soldiers had been killed.'[9] The casualties included 45 Recce Troop Commander Lieutenant Tony Musselwhite, who had to be left after suffering a mortal wound. Major Ted Hennings was also killed in action.

14 Brigade elements attacked Bonchaung railway station and the Bonchaung Gorge bridges during the night of 13/14 April. Bonchaung is south of Indaw, between Nankan and Wuntho. The forces involved included the Black Watch Columns (42 and 73), the 7th Leicesters' 47 Column and the Bedfordshire and Hertfordshire's 16 Column. The main rail bridge and two other girder bridges were blown in the face of Japanese opposition. Over 40 of the enemy were killed.

York and Lancaster Columns 65 and 84 planned to blow railway bridges north of Bonchaung but, given the waterless country, it was decided to make for Bonchaung Gorge.

Some Columns were desperately short of water in the week prior to the Bonchaung attacks. This problem was anticipated. Some men carried two water bottles and a full chagul (around one gallon), but this still fell far short of daily requirements in such extreme conditions. 84 Column's Paddy Dobney described the intense desire for water: 'Many suffered the head and body pains caused by loss of body fluid and salt. Hot sweet tea, however limited, and salt tablets were our saviours.'

Wild elephants were clever at finding water in dry chaung beds, often only a few inches below the surface. Some men claimed abilities as 'dowsers' and attempted to find likely spots to dig. Digging out dry chaungs produced some water but not enough to fill hundreds of water bottles and meet the needs of the animals. Throats became 'brick-dry' and men found it impossible to swallow what little food they had. Yet they continued to advance on the railway and requested a drop for 11 April. The site chosen was some distance from the bivouac (it had been selected in a hurry as night fell) and proved far from ideal. Paddy Dobney asked 'Doc' Luckett for a Benzedrine tablet, to help him remain alert for the drop.[10]

The Battalion Commander, Lieutenant-Colonel Philip Graves-Morris, noted that the water situation on 11 April was so bad that men were collecting rain off groundsheets during the night, to brew tea the next morning. 'It tasted very rubbery.'[11]

Cutting communications: a demolition team prepares to destroy a railway bridge. (Trustees of the Imperial War Museum)

The first run on 11 April left many loads snagged high in the canopy. The men used their last reserves of energy to cut down trees. With supreme effort they recovered around 75 per cent of the drop. Dawn had long passed by the time Dobney headed back to the bivouac. On the way he collapsed on the warm, soft sand of a stream bed and slept off the worst effects of the Benzedrine tablet.[10]

Graves-Morris heard how 65 Column's Recce Platoon fared even worse. The Recce Officer was reduced to sucking dew from leaves to reduce his thirst. The Platoon marched on in hot, dry teak jungle, moving through clouds of dust and 'well beyond the thirsty stage'. They dug a little water in a dry chaung yet remained desperately thirsty.

The results of the drop were reviewed. This drop zone was not a clearing but, rather, an area where trees were relatively widely spread. Yet very few loads hit the ground cleanly. The men moved off and their mood was not improved when they came upon the perfect drop zone just half-a-mile from bivouac.

During the following day they approached the railway, intending to blow a bridge in front of a train and then destroy a second bridge nearby. There were two train movements during the night and the northbound train was full of troops. They would blow the bridges and destroy a northbound train the following night. A special drop of explosives was received within a few hours of sending the request. Major Downward, 65 Column's Commander, and 84 Column's Captain Pearsall worked out the exact requirements for explosives and detonators.[11]

Unfortunately, there was a sudden, brief skirmish with a Japanese patrol. Major Downward and his Staff Officer, Major Bruce, killed two Japanese scouts who suddenly appeared on the track. With surprise now lost they abandoned the idea of blowing the bridge (with a 100 ft central span and two 40 ft side spans) as a northbound train approached. Instead, they went to work and blew the bridge as quickly as possible, disregarding the sniping that went on all night. They then moved on to blow a bridge over the Gorge just to the north.[11] Despite opposition around Bonchaung they succeeded in blowing their targets and destroying station facilities.[10]

Dobney's close friend, Lieutenant Eddie Shepherd, led a Section briefed to explore Bonchaung Gorge and station. They inspected several small bridges but found them easily repairable, so recommended concentrating on the main bridge. Both Columns made their preparations as Major Bruce led the soft skins to safe harbour across the railway, two miles east. They would be joined by the Battle Groups the following day, when the action was over. Unfortunately, they drew automatic fire while crossing the railway and the two Defence Platoons engaged the enemy. It was getting dark. Bruce abandoned the crossing and they moved into the jungle. 84 Column's Paddy Dobney:

> It was so dark that it was almost impossible to see anything at arm's length and each soldier hung on to the back of the equipment of the man in front wherever possible. I, like many others, followed a mule's backside. I grabbed his tail with both hands and hung on tightly. The intelligent beast must have sensed that drastic situations called for drastic measures and never once showed any sign of objecting to this affront to his dignity.[10]

Major Bruce issued brisk orders: 'Halt here. No fires. Stand to 5.30.' Listening sentries were posted as men ate a cold, cheerless meal. Dobney fed biscuits to the understanding mule, in gratitude for acceptance of having his tail pulled. The railway line was just 50 yards east. Somewhere close by were the enemy, covering the crossing place. The Japanese still had the crossing covered at first light. Bruce decided to try another track, crossing the railway half a mile south. He left one Platoon to keep the enemy occupied. Paddy Dobney took the other fighting Platoon and soft skins to attempt an unopposed crossing of the railway at the new location. Later that morning Dobney stood before the track and suddenly heard distant firing to the north. He had no idea whether this was Major Bruce's party or the main Battle Groups.

Dobney crossed the line and returned without challenge. He liked the look of things. The ground was level and there were no awkward embankments or cuttings to impede the mules. The jungle fringes came close to the track, which had slight bends a few hundred yards north and south to limit the line of sight.

65 Column Platoon Commander Lieutenant John Shuttleworth was told to position his two Sections at each end of the crossing, just in case. Mule Officer Frank Luxa crossed first, followed by his Batman, Private Prince. The latter ignored Dobney and Shuttleworth, now standing on the track, and pushed his neck out of the undergrowth. Paddy Dobney: 'Then, having satisfied

himself that the coast was clear, to my astonishment he turned and called over his shoulder to the man following him: "We're at the bleeding railway now. When you come to it, go like bloody hell for the other side."' Paddy Dobney tried but failed to stifle his laughter, especially when the following man's mule refused to be hurried and ambled across sedately.

It took time to get the men and animals across. Paddy Dobney: 'At last, it was over and John signalled to his two Sections to rejoin him. He had no need to add the well-known Army signal "At the double!" by pumping his clenched fist up and down. They came at the quick trot and, giving us grins of relief, marched on up the track after the others.'[10]

The Battle Groups attacked the main bridge close to Bonchaung Station at 08.00 on 15 April. Graves-Morris described this as a messy action, with persistent Japanese interference. Major Downward's 65 Column contributed two infantry Platoons and the Commando Platoon for an assault on the main Japanese bunkers protecting the bridge's eastern approach. They were supported by 84 Column's mortars. 84 Column attacked the bridge and railway station from the west with four Platoons. Lieutenant-Colonel Graves-Morris:

> Unfortunately, the dense jungle and high trees offered no opportunity of getting the mortars of 84 Column into action until just after the attack by 65 Column's Platoons had begun. The denseness of the jungle had also caused a change of plan in 65 Column, who were unable to stage a two-Platoon attack, but had to advance in single file, one Platoon tailing the lead Platoon, up a trail which led into the Japanese bunkers covering the railway bridge.[11]

A sharp assault by 15 Platoon, led by Lieutenant Stewart, captured the blazing main bunker at the cost of an NCO and six wounded. Stewart received grenade fragments in the face. Lieutenant Hewitt's 16 Platoon went through and worked under sniper fire to destroy a stores dump and stocks of small arms ammunition.

Meanwhile, 84 Column made good progress. The two righthand Platoons crossed the railway and cordoned off the southern bridge approaches, as the lefthand Platoons infiltrated the station area. Captain Pearsall and the Commando Platoon laid charges, at the cost of two killed, and Bonchaung Bridge was totally destroyed. Bonchaung had been attacked before, by Bernard Fergusson's 5 Column, during the 1943 Wingate operation.

The York and Lancaster Columns withdrew. Lieutenant-Colonel Graves-Morris: 'At 16.00, after destroying the station buildings and wagons in the sidings with Lifebuoy flamethrowers and PIAT bombs, and mortaring with H.E. the northern approaches to the station, the withdrawal to the east began, covered by one Platoon from 65 Column.'[11]

The bivouac for the soft skin elements proved to be no safe haven. The waiting men were attacked by a Japanese patrol before the Battle Groups returned in strength. The Japanese were thrown back, despite the fact that the direction of the assault was without Bren cover. Lieutenant Shuttleworth came up with a Bren but it jammed on the first round during the next attack and he was killed outright. Philip Graves-Morris: 'He was the youngest officer with the Column and his sad loss was felt by all.'[11]

Paddy Dobney described the circumstances of John Shuttleworth's death. Advance elements of the fighting Platoons had begun to arrive back in bivouac. Their immediate problem was the lack of water. Many water bottles and chaguls were already half empty. The animals had no water and showed little interest in feeding. Suddenly the men faced a more urgent challenge. They heard a distant noise, rather like a muted football crowd. One of the Battle Group parties had been followed back. The noise grew much louder and, with shouts of 'Banzai! Banzai!' the Japanese broke through the jungle and into the bivouac clearing. They paid a heavy price for that noisy approach.

There was just enough space for the Chindits to stop the first charge, as others fell back into cover. Dobney warned the men nearest him to watch their ammunition: 'I knew most of the soldiers were separated from their equipment, as I was, and had only the one full magazine for their weapons. My own pistol was expended in the first hectic 10 seconds and I felt naked and vulnerable.'[10]

RAF Officer Franks lobbed grenades at the Japanese. Dobney nipped back a few yards, grabbed his pouches and joined in. The enemy responded at a range of just 20 yards. Unarmed once more, Dobney grabbed a Sten from a man who had been hit in the wrist. A nearby soldier gave him a 10-second course in firing it. Dobney then heard a cry behind him, turned and found that John Shuttleworth had fallen. He could do nothing for him. Meanwhile, Frank Luxa and the Muleteers led the animals out of immediate danger. Two favourite mules, the inseparable Duke and Duchess, were tethered together and died together. Dobney's favourite pony, Anne, had a shattered leg and had to be destroyed. Dobney told everyone to move back a little for thicker cover, seeking the protection of a small bank and an enlarged field of fire.

Shuttleworth died responding to Paddy Dobney's shout for a Bren team. Dobney couldn't leave Shuttleworth but found it impossible to lift him and hold a weapon at the same time. A soldier helped him drag the body over to their new position.

The firing subsided and the Japanese dispersed when caught in the rear by one of the returning Battle Group Platoons. A miserable night followed. The men were completely spent. They struggled with a cold evening meal and tried to settle down alongside the wounded. The water situation remained acute – the animals had not been watered for 36 hours. The Columns' medical teams worked throughout the night, sterilising their surgical instruments in spirit and doing their best with very little light.

There had been no time to set out proper defences before nightfall. The York and Lancaster's Commander wrote: 'Despite all our training and appreciation of the dangers of our layout, there was nothing we could do in pitch darkness to remedy our position, with our casualties in our midst and the Japanese, for all we knew, hanging around our perimeter. We lay in uneasy lines of bodies on the slope of the hillside, with our wounded in the centre, receiving what little comfort we could give them. We had little water and the needs of the wounded were acute.' One injured man died during that long night.[11]

Paddy Dobney was well aware of the 'awful vulnerability' of a Chindit column when cornered. He had a restless night. Before they moved off Shuttleworth and the other dead were laid in their jungle graves. The Adjutant recorded the grave locations by map reference. The Intelligence Section had been up early and had already searched the area of yesterday's fighting. They found 12 Japanese dead; other bodies had been recovered by the enemy.

As a precaution, Graves-Morris ordered the track back to Bonchaung to be booby-trapped. His priority now was to find a suitable site for a light aircraft strip, to fly out the wounded. He knew of a likely place, but it was some distance away and involved a hot, steep climb. Makeshift stretchers were prepared for the wounded.

Carrying just one stretcher case any distance in these conditions, given the Columns' weakened state, required a large group of men. Stretcher-bearers were relieved after just a short time and progress was slow. Everyone was in real distress by the midday halt, tortured by extreme thirst. Many men had not drawn water for over a day. Some managed to swallow a few mouthfuls of brackish water dug from a chaung bed during the midday halt. Fortunately, they reached the Meza river by late afternoon. Paddy Dobney: 'The animals nearly went crazy at the smell and sight of water.' A steep bank stopped the animals reaching the river. Muleteers and grooms ferried water up to them, using

Something to smile about: this pony gave birth to a foal alongside the Meza river in mid-April 1944. The foal, named 'Freedrop', was carried across the river on the shoulders of RSM Hemmings, then hoisted onto its mother's back. Sadly, both mare and foal did not survive. (Walter Longstaff)

canvas buckets. One man put a stop to this personal service after his charge had drained 15 buckets. A pony then foaled at the river. Her offspring was named 'Freedrop'. The men were amazed to see the hard-bitten RSM Hemmings carrying the foal across his shoulders as they forded the river.

A site was selected for a light plane strip. A supply drop was requested and six Dakotas arrived but the drop was interrupted by a brief skirmish with an enemy patrol. There was further excitement when a container of 3 in. mortar smoke bombs ignited on landing. The men managed to beat out the fire. Light aircraft landed and took out the wounded.

Graves-Morris reviewed the events of the past few days. Later, he wrote that his two Columns 'had attacked, been attacked and the Recce, Support and Commando Platoons had all been employed in their various roles. Throughout a tiring three days, all ranks had acquitted themselves admirably.'[11]

On 9 April Major Peter Cane's 94 Column (4th/9th Gurkhas) – with Morris Force – captured Myothit, 24 miles from Bhamo. They destroyed the road bridge over the Taying river, together with the ferry and a rice mill supplying Japanese forces, before returning to the hills.[12]

Sister Column 49, led by Major Ted Russell, was to block the road beyond Myothit but Brigadier Morris decided to move off without doing so and failed to warn Peter Cane.[13] The third Morris Force Column, 40 (3rd/4th Gurkhas), achieved a success on 10 April. Led by Lieutenant-Colonel Monteith, it set an ambush on the Bhamo-Lashio road, destroying three vehicles and killing 30 Japanese.

111 Brigade received new orders on 10 April. The new priority was to stop reinforcements moving towards Aberdeen and White City Block, via Wuntho and Pinlebu, and, in addition, to destroy supply dumps.

Things were relatively quiet at Broadway, now garrisoned by four Columns: 57 and 93 (3rd/9th Gurkhas) and the King's 81 and 82 Columns. Aberdeen was also free of enemy pressure. Here, the garrison consisted of 6 NR's 39 and 66 Columns.

During the period 11–16 April 111 Brigade destroyed two supply dumps and killed 23 Japanese. In addition, the Cameronians' 90 Column blocked a road and killed a further 24. According to Slim, the now reunited 111 Brigade's activities west of Indaw and several other Chindit operations yielded only modest results: 'These operations did not, as I had hoped they would, seriously disorganise the Japanese communications with the Assam front. Their chief effect, as far as the battle there was concerned, was to delay for a couple of months two infantry and one artillery battalions ... on their way to take part in the offensive against Imphal.'[14] Given the difficulties of stopping the Japanese at Imphal/Kohima, this might be regarded as no mean achievement.

When the starved King's Own Columns reached Aberdeen, the Chaplain received mail, including a large wooden box despatched by his wife's relatives in South Africa. Miller became very popular when he shared out the contents. The box was full of crystallised fruits.[15] Everyone craved sugar.

The King's Own had before them a tough, 80-mile positioning trek – half the distance being along the Meza river: 'Some of us counted the number of times we crossed and recrossed that accursed river. It came to 70 times. For no two minutes were our feet ever dry.'[15]

Miller remembered one man, an Officer's Batman, who 'contrived to get lost in the jungle by disappearing off the line of march for the purpose of relieving nature. When the Column was out of sight, he was said to have doubled back to Aberdeen. After being given a temporary job there, he was, so we heard, flown back to India and court-martialled for desertion.'[15]

Private Jim Unsworth was with the King's Own's 46 Column. This Column had had several Commanders. The last was Major Openshaw, who made a very favourable impression on Unsworth:

'He was a grand chap. After the war I lived in the Preston area, as did Openshaw. He was a senior judge. I was deeply shocked when he was murdered in the 1980s, stabbed to death outside his own home.'

(Judge William Openshaw died in 1981, stabbed 12 times by a man he had sent to Borstal for stealing in 1968. John Smith was held for 18 months when he was 17 but waited until he was 31 before killing the former King's Own Major. He hid in the garage of Openshaw's home in Broughton, near Preston, before attacking him.)

The King's Own Columns, 41 and 46, set off independently but were never far apart. Jim Unsworth:

'We were on our way to a Japanese supply dump on the other side of Indaw, south of what eventually became Blackpool, when we were ambushed. We had been marching hard to reach that dump and had only a 10-minute break around mid-afternoon. I was that tired

River crossing: Chindits and animals make their way across the Meza. The river is low, prior to the Monsoon. The Chindit on the left is carrying the usual length of bamboo, to steady his legs under the load of the heavy pack. The main attraction of this crossing point is the absence of steep banks, presenting no problems for the mules. (John Riggs)

I fell asleep, flat out on the ground. Shouting and firing woke me just a minute or two later. I stayed doggo as one of our Brens opened up. I had no idea what was happening. We took casualties and some of our heavy equipment, unloaded from the mules, was left behind.'

When 46 Column freed itself from this encounter, Lieutenant Littlewood was detailed to take a Section of 10 men, return the two miles to the ambush site and retrieve the most important items among the abandoned equipment. Unsworth accompanied the Section:

'We headed back and found plenty of kit lying around. Then I saw a man slumped against a tree. I couldn't recognise him, he was that white. A Japanese officer had struck him with a sword and he had been cut from shoulder to chest. There was no blood left in him. He was our Quartermaster. We couldn't bury him.'

Littlewood, Unsworth and the rest of the Section continued a few yards and found two dead Japanese close to the fallen Chindit:

'I said to Littlewood: "I thought Japanese were supposed to be small." These two were huge, over 6 ft tall. They were Imperial Guards, hit by a Bren burst. I noticed white powder spilling out from pouches on the bodies. Littlewood said it was cocaine. Apparently, some Japanese took cocaine before an attack. We walked on and found two more British dead, a Lance-Corporal and his mate. This would not be our last ambush experience. Japanese patrols had a habit of following us into night harbour.'

46 Column neared its target the next morning:

'We reached the area at first light. The Column Commander warned us to make no noise. We called up an air strike and a Mustang soon appeared. It dropped several light bombs on the depot, just to upset them. We pressed on, crossed a river and came upon a few huts. We shot up what was left of the small Japanese force guarding the depot. I was one of three who chased the fleeing Japanese into an area of thick bamboo, exchanging fire at regular intervals. Suddenly we came into a clearing. The firing stopped and all was quiet. No-one about. The Japs had left as we came in – all three of us!

'A dog then appeared and began to bark. Sergeant Oakes promptly shot the animal, warning that it could be rabid. We then discovered that this clearing opened into a wider area where trees had been felled. To one side we saw a line of new trucks. Facing them

was a line of bashas, filled with equipment and uniforms. We had blundered into the middle of the Japanese supply base.

'I had a quick look inside the first truck. It was full of machine guns and ammunition boxes. We exchanged a few words and agreed that it would be smart to get out of there double quick. The main Japanese garrison was just up the road. Littlewood drew his bayonet and stabbed the first truck's petrol tank. He then worked his way down the entire line of vehicles. It didn't take very long. I lit a torch and set the pools of petrol alight. It really was time to go.

'As we left the clearing we soon came to the river. It was waist-deep and around 80 yards wide. Littlewood asked me to fill his water bottle as he kept watch. Within seconds we came under heavy mortar fire. Fortunately, the rounds were falling short. We struggled towards the far bank as the Japanese mortars turned the jungle behind us into a bonfire night display. In reality, a lot of the explosions probably came from the trucks. We'd done a good job.'

The three returned safely and 46 Column's main body then moved forward, entered the base and destroyed everything else: 'One of the lads asked me whether I wanted some Japanese socks. I took a few pairs but they were no use to me. The foot size was very small and they were made of a silk-like material.'

———————

For all the success of Calvert's White City Block and the firm establishment of the Broadway and Aberdeen Strongholds, nothing would hold back the Monsoon. The jungle airstrips could not be converted into all-weather fields.[16] There was real concern that the evacuation of wounded and sick by light aircraft would not be possible in Monsoon conditions. This was an important factor influencing the move north. A link up with American-led Chinese forces would be a lifeline for Chindit casualties.

The first phase of Special Force operations was nearing conclusion. The Chindits were expected to continue to disrupt Japanese communications, although the Monsoon would arrive in around four weeks (some long-range forecasters were over-optimistic, allowing an additional two weeks or more). Redeployments were made. Bladet force regained wireless contact and moved towards Aberdeen for evacuation. Lentaigne's main objective was to retain a firm grip on the rail corridor, as Stilwell's forces progressed towards Myitkyina. 111 Brigade would now have the central role — establishing a new Block on the railway and road north of White City. 77 and 14 Brigades would act as a shield and mobile strike force.[16]

The men at White City sensed that the first phase was over. Suddenly, things went very quiet. 43 Column's Dick Stuckey:

'It was eerie. Had the Japanese pulled back? Or were they massing for something bigger and better? Perhaps they were planning a Divisional attack on White City? In reality, however, the Japs had banged their heads so hard against White City's wire that they had decided to by-pass it. They now offloaded the trains, used motor transport to skirt round the Block and then loaded trains on the other side with the vital supplies needed for the Japanese front line.'

As the Japanese pressure on White City eased, 54 Column's ATO, Cyril Baldock, took his chance to leave the Block. He had been trapped at White City by the constant Japanese attacks and was eager to rejoin 45 Recce. He was briefed to take a party of 'odds and sods', separated from their units, to Aberdeen. They numbered a dozen in all and most were in poor condition:

'I was lucky to make it. I have always considered myself a bloody awful map-reader! I regretted the separation from my Regiment. On the other hand, many of our men died during operations around White City. One of those lost in my absence was my best friend, Freddie Holloway, a Troop Commander with 54 Column. He was killed in the fighting around the Block. We were very close and had much in common. We both had fairly working class backgrounds, had made it to Grammar School and went on to get our commissions. I never found out exactly what happened to him; nor did his family.'

Many White City casualties were evacuated from Aberdeen. The garrison at Aberdeen came to appreciate the ferocity of the fighting around White City. Larry Gaines of 6 NR's 66 Column: 'White City became known as the "Tobruk of Burma". Soldiers who had been at both places said the Burmese version was worse.'

There were many grim sights at Aberdeen as the wounded continued to arrive. On 13 April *Life* correspondent William Vandivert flew in. Many photographs were taken. There had been numerous crashes on the airstrip and plenty of wrecks were to be seen. Larry Gaines: 'There was always a race to the crash scene, to retrieve the aircrew C-rations — more substantial and appetising than K-rations.'

23 Brigade, fighting independently from Special Force, was busy disrupting the communications of Japanese forces attacking at Imphal/Kohima. Captain Tony Wailes was with 60 Column (60th Field Regiment, RA). He thought they would be flying in:

'In the event we marched over the Naga Hills. Each morning our Column MO held Sick Parade – firstly the British Sick Parade, followed by one for the Nagas. Many Nagas had terrible sores and few, if any, of the children were free from spots, sores or skin diseases. They were all very grateful for treatment and loved being bandaged up. They even liked a bit of bandage over sticky plaster! Their self-appointed fees ranged from bananas to eggs and the occasional small chicken. In the Column our small Section of Sappers was used in the support role. I spent much of my time with the mules, encouraging them up steep inclines and down steep slopes. We had great respect for them.'

Wailes followed simple domestic rules. He insisted on routines to keep his men relatively clean and healthy:

'Whenever possible we had a quick wash in a chaung. It was important to maintain standards. The air supply organisation was effective – I don't remember being really hungry during the entire four months. My Batman could turn K-rations into a remarkable meal. Somehow, he made even tinned meat taste palatable. We got very little food from the villages. Usually the villagers were hungrier than we were and pressed us for food. What little we did buy was paid for in silver money. The Nagas, given worthless paper money by the Japanese, responded well to real money.

'My health remained amazingly good. I had no malaria. I took my Mepacrine daily, without fail. I was also free of dysentery. I was careful about drinking water, ensuring it came from a fast-flowing source, whenever possible, and that it had not been contaminated by activities upstream. I paid close attention to my men's feet. I took my boots off whenever I could, when we reached night bivouac.'

The threat to Imphal/Kohima had much influence on the deployment of Special Force Columns. Corporal Roy 'Jim' Welland described the central focus of the fighting at Kohima. He served with the Royal Berkshire Regiment, 6th Brigade, 2nd Division. Welland's unit left the Arakan, arrived at Dimapur and prepared to join the battle at Kohima. The 6th Brigade was ordered to reach Garrison Hill and break the siege. Jim Welland:

We were ordered to spread out and keep our eyes peeled. We had already been sniped at a few times, so we didn't need a lot of telling. We climbed very cautiously until we reached the top, but we lost

Write off: standing in front of the wreck is Bedfordshire and Hertfordshire Medical Officer David Evans, described by John Riggs as 'a wonderful guy'. The remains of a paddy bund are in the foreground. These obstructions wrecked the undercarriage of many aircraft. (John Riggs)

three men on the way up. When we finally made contact with the gallant defenders (Royal West Kent Regiment) we got a few 'low-gear' cheers from these unshaven, smelly chaps who you could see had had a very rough time.

Those being relieved vacated their slit trenches without prompting. These were soon filled with newcomers as the sniping increased. During the night, an English-speaking Japanese spent hours trying to convince them that their wives were sleeping with American GIs. They also brought up a wireless and put 'Tokyo Rose' on the loudspeakers.

At daybreak ... the Japanese then began screaming and throwing hand grenades. These were coming from the Tennis Court area. We opened fire with everything we had. I had a Bren and I pointed it in the direction of where most of the screaming was coming from – a good move, as it turned out. We saw shadows appear in front of us. The cheeky buggers were laughing and talking to each other, as if they were going up the pub. I don't think they realised how close they were to us. I opened fire and other positions followed suit. Being in a box formation, small arms fire and 2 in. mortars were very effective. The artillery was brought in to quieten the enemy guns whipping 75 mm shells among us. Everything seemed quieter, apart from the sniper constantly taking pot shots at us. Someone got this chap eventually. He was found by one of our patrols,

hanging from a tree very high up, dead of course. He had tied himself to the tree so securely that if he did get shot he wouldn't fall to the ground, the idea being that we would think he was still alive and kicking. The Japanese were full of tricks like that.[17]

The Japanese shelling increased and a British tank was brought almost to the top of the hill, to provide close fire support. The tank crew did well but then found they could not reverse down towards the road. The tank was abandoned. Welland remembers the casualties:

Our Officer, a Captain, was killed and a Corporal and his whole Section bayoneted in their trenches. It was very disturbing because they were friends and comrades. We must have given a good account of ourselves. A great number of enemy dead were found around the perimeter. There was no opportunity or place to bury our dead. The Japanese cremated theirs and we could smell the fires at night.[17]

Stocks of food and ammunition began to dwindle and the Japanese occasionally shared in the proceeds of air drops. Welland's unit was on the hill for 17 days. When they were relieved they were unwashed, unshaven and pleased to visit a latrine without being sniped at.

As the Japanese attempted to break through at Imphal/Kohima, 23 Brigade struck at their lines of com-

The First Phase Ends 249

munication. The Brigade operated to the east and south of Kohima. As the fighting continued, its Battalions began to take a few prisoners. Tony Wailes:

'I used to worry about them at night. They needed careful guarding, just in case they attempted to do you in when it grew dark. We tied their arms and legs up. In one case I tied a Jap's wrists to mine — perhaps, on reflection, an unwise thing to do. We always passed our prisoners down the line as soon as possible.'

Despite the best efforts of his Batman, Wailes lost weight steadily over a period of four months. In common with everyone else, he fantasised about food:

'I was always fond of scrambled eggs. I thought a lot about scrambled eggs while in Burma. Even today I regard scrambled eggs as a real treat.' Tony Wailes was deeply impressed by the skills of the American light aircraft pilots:

'They could do things that a typical pilot would never dream of attempting. They could get into a 300 yards strip in comfort. They could even squeeze into a run of around 100 yards in extreme circumstances. They took extraordinary risks for the men waiting on the ground. Reluctant to stay down for more than a few minutes, most pilots kept their engines running as the wounded were placed on board.'

Notes

1. Calvert, M. (1974), *Chindits: Long Range Penetration*, 60–62
2. Ibid, 101–105
3. Sharpe, P. (1995), *To Be a Chindit*, 236–248
4. Aylen, N. P., Trooper, *45th Reconnaissance Regiment*, Imperial War Museum, 80/49/1
5. Carfrae, C. (1985), *Chindit Column*, 101–102
6. Jeffrey, W.F. (1950), *Sunbeams Like Swords*, 71–86
7. Chinnery, P.D., (2002), *March or Die*, 167
8. Rooney, D. (1997), *Mad Mike*, 83–86
9. Ibid, 87–89
10. Dobney, Major R.P.J. 'Paddy', unpublished MS, July 1981 (via Bill Smith and Corinne Simons)
11. Graves-Morris, Lieutenant-Colonel P.H., unpublished MS (via Bill Smith and Corinne Simons)
12. Calvert, M. (1974), 122–124
13. Rooney, D. (2000), *Wingate and the Chindits: Redressing the Balance*, 150–151
14. Slim, Field Marshal Viscount (1999), *Defeat into Victory*, 267
15. Miller, Rev. W.H., 2nd King's Own, *A Chaplain with the Chindits*, Imperial War Museum, 80/49/1
16. Allen, L. (1986), *Burma: The Longest War 1941–45*, 353–357
17. Notes by Corporal R.W.J. 'Jim' Welland, Royal Berkshire Regiment (via Bill Smith)

ATTACKING SUPPLY LINES

18–26 April 1944

'A PIAT round hit the first truck. This vehicle was also hit by Bren and rifle fire. Along the road trucks crashed into each other in the confusion, as vehicles trapped in the middle were hit by automatic and rifle fire.'

Captain Denis Arnold, MC, 29 Column, 7th Nigeria Regiment

ORDE WINGATE hoped that Indaw's capture would trigger the fly-in of forces powerful enough to have a decisive influence on the Burma campaign. This prospect vanished when the Indaw attack stalled and the struggle at Imphal/Kohima continued. In any event, Wingate had been warned that the cupboard was bare; Indaw, if taken, could not be garrisoned and 'developed'.

The priority now was to destroy enemy dumps and lines of communication around Indaw, as part of a wider intensification of effort to disrupt supply lines serving the 18th Division opposing Stilwell's Chinese and the 15th and 31st Divisions attacking Imphal. More action around Indaw might also slow up any Japanese attempt to pursue Special Force in strength as it moved north.

Following the reorganisation in April, the main focus for the Japanese was the attack on 14th Army with 15th, 31st and 33rd Divisions. On 18 April, however, 2nd British Division raised the Kohima siege and 31st Division went on the defensive.[1] Chindit-trained 23 Brigade made a valuable contribution to the fighting that turned the tide. This detached Brigade had it no easier than the other Chindit Brigades. They were also dependent on air supply and men often went hungry. Any mishap during a drop caused much anguish. RAF Officer W.A. Wilcox, with 76 Column (2nd Duke of Wellington's), yelled a warning when a statichute failed. The load plummeted down, struck the ground and burst: 'I walked over and gazed at a thick yellow mess which oozed from the battered tins in the basket. Others joined me; there were almost tears in their eyes. "Peaches", someone muttered thickly, "the whole bloody fruit ration."'[2]

The Japanese 15th and 33rd Divisions' advance was blocked before Imphal, as their opponents were rein-

forced. Close air support and air supply were provided by 221 Group, RAF, as the long-range Mustangs were required to support Stilwell and Special Force. All three Japanese Divisions were doomed, eventually facing eight-and-a-half British/Indian Divisions and powerful air and armoured forces.

In late April there were more changes in the Japanese command structure. Lieutenant General Honda took command of 33rd Army, headquartered at Maymyo. He now commanded the 18th Division in the Hukawng Valley and 56th Division on the Salween, together with all units confronting Special Force.

———————

On 18 April two Chindit Brigades, 14 and 16, launched fresh, loosely coordinated attacks on Indaw.14 Brigade pushed from the south and 16 Brigade from the north, with Indaw West airfield a priority target. 111 Brigade took over a block on the Banmauk-Indaw road manned by 14 Brigade's Black Watch Columns.

14 Brigade's York and Lancaster Columns, having successfully attacked the railway and bridges, now crossed the Meza. Battalion Commander Lieutenant-Colonel Graves-Morris wrote: 'In order to safeguard the river crossing, 65 Column was moved to the eastern bank and was followed by the soft skin of 84 Column on the morning of 18 April. The Battle Group of 84 Column remained on the west bank, to evacuate the casualties.' Five light aircraft arrived the following day and flew out 11 casualties.[3] These pilots were old hands, using the full extent of the strip cleared for them and so making the point that the next strip should be no shorter.

The York and Lancaster Columns then headed for Gahe village, around eight miles south of Indaw, to pre-pare for the second assault on the town. They were now free of their wounded and water and food shortages, but they were marching in a temperature of 110 deg. in the shade. 84 Column had trekked seven-and-a-half hours to rejoin 65 Column. They bivouacked alongside a clear mountain stream and the men finally had their chance to rest and recuperate. Echoing the experience of 23 Brigade's 76 Column, they complained bitterly when some air-dropped supplies were damaged due to the failure of inferior cotton statichutes.

An exhausted Paddy Dobney, 84 Column's Administrative Officer, had lost his temper when preparing for this drop. He was with a group who went ahead to select the drop site but had lost daylight just half a mile from the location favoured on the map. Forced to bivouac for the night, Dobney was not in the best of sorts when a loud drumming noise began. Chopping hollow bamboo was strictly forbidden, as the noise could give away the Column's position. Dobney looked for the culprit and saw a Muleteer hacking at bamboo with his machete. He went over and booted the offender in the behind. He regretted this lapse immediately: 'It is just as serious an offence for an officer to strike a junior rank as for a soldier to strike an officer.'[4]

Nine years later the man concerned — then a civilian – sought out Paddy Dobney (then stationed at Pontefract). Dobney recognised him. They shook hands, talked of old times and made no mention of the incident that evening in the Burmese twilight.

Indaw was an important Japanese centre with two airstrips and a network of supply dumps. Earlier, Bernard Fergusson's 16 Brigade had attempted to take it without rest after their debilitating march in. They failed for a variety of reasons, especially lack of water during the approach. Now the second attempt to take Indaw was in progress. Dobney's group prepared a light plane strip and organised a common drop zone for all 14 Brigade Columns concentrating in the area.

16 Column (1st Bedfordshire and Hertfordshire) remained at Gahe to strengthen it as an operational base. Sister Column 61 was briefed to probe Indaw's defences. The fighting elements left Gahe on 20 April and three lightly equipped Platoon patrols set out the next day. Over the next few days, they skirmished with the Japanese and blew up a number of fuel and equipment dumps. Air strikes were called in. As all 14 Brigade Columns then made ready for a concerted attack on Indaw, there was a change of heart. They received orders to prepare to protect White City during its planned evacuation.

Once again the Indaw push stalled. The Japanese were strong and well prepared. In some instances the Chindit dead had to be left unburied on the battlefield. The wounded were flown out by light aircraft.

Brewing up: a typical arrangement — a couple of sticks and a mess tin. Chindits received cotton pouches of tea and powdered milk. (John Riggs)

Nevertheless, Philip Graves-Morris' York and Lancaster Columns, operating south of Indaw, harassed the enemy and attacked dumps. In the period 22 April–26 14 Brigade Columns destroyed over 20 dumps and more than 15,000 gallons of petrol. They cut the railway in 16 places and ambushed a train. Two villages and a railway station were attacked and over 100 Japanese were killed.

The Battle Groups of the York and Lancaster's 65 and 84 Columns marched out on 23 April, heading north towards Indaw and intending to attack a village south of the town on 26 April. Their main target was a complex of petrol and ammunition dumps. 65 Column took up a protective position on 84 Column's left flank. 84 Column's Platoons attacked the dumps following an air strike.

Matters took an unexpected turn when 84 Column's 8 Platoon bumped a Japanese road block and came under machine gun fire. Captain Shepherd led 6 Platoon in a flanking movement but, at one point, he crossed the road and walked straight into the Japanese. 7 Platoon then became embroiled and by 08.30 – when the main attack should have started – everyone was still struggling to reach the start-line. Japanese fighters deflected the incoming air strike. Movement was difficult in the unusually dense jungle, with visibility down to just a few yards. The misfortunes continued when a defective mortar round exploded in the barrel, killing two.

By 10.00 65 Column had a box defence set up in 84 Column's rear. 65 Column's Intelligence Summary noted: 'Jungle very thick and the battle sounded very confusing, for shots seemed to be coming in all directions.' It was just as confusing for 84 Column. Major Downward, 65's Commander, got on the wireless and suggested

RIGHT Enjoying a smoke: York and Lancaster Sergeants Crutchley and Anderson take a rest in teak jungle. (Walter Longstaff)

BELOW Manna from heaven: the aftermath of a supply drop to the Bedfordshire and Hertfordshire Columns. The Chindit right of centre is carrying a box of K-rations sufficient for three or four men for five days. (John Riggs)

ABOVE In rations! The collection point for supplies following a drop to the Bedfordshire and Hertfordshire's 61 Column. The Column would attend, Platoon by Platoon, to receive their K-rations. This photograph was taken by Lieutenant John Salazar. Pictured left is Column Administrative Officer Lieutenant Trevor Mead, with Company Quartermaster Sergeant Danny Bebbington. Danny survived Burma but Trevor did not. (John Riggs)

LEFT Heavyweight and lightweight: RSM Vernon 'Froggie' French with one of 61 Column's two elephants, used primarily for carrying 3 in. mortar rounds. (John Riggs)

that the sister Column was firing on his men. He did not realise that the Japanese had infiltrated the British positions. They would have to fight through another mile of thick jungle to reach their objective and the tracks were defended by bunkers and wire. 84 Column was holding its own and casualties were light, with 65 Column in reserve, but they were still entangled in the outposts rather than the main defences. Battalion Commander Lieutenant-Colonel Graves-Morris: 'The Japanese were obviously strongly contesting the advance and, even if the Columns won through, there would probably have been too much Japanese interference to ensure the demolition of the dumps.'[3]

The target was deemed not worth the likely cost and orders were given to withdraw. There was no Japanese follow up. With the fighting over, the dead included Paddy Dobney's close friend, Captain Eddie Shepherd. Subsequently, Dobney presided over an inquiry into his death. The two men first met in 1940. Shepherd, a teacher from the North of England, then bumped into Dobney in Bombay. They were to join the same Rifle Company.

Shepherd went forward to find out what was holding up the Company. All Dobney learned of the last moments of the man he described as 'almost like a brother' were his final words into a walkie-talkie: 'It is difficult to see exactly what is holding us up. The Japs seem to be firing at everyone else, but they won't fire at me'. Nothing was seen or heard of him again.

14 Brigade's new role was to assist Brigadier Calvert's 77 Brigade at White City, some 30 miles north of Indaw. This required the entire Brigade to cross the railway. One of the 'stops' exchanged fire with a Japanese patrol but nearly 3,000 men and hundreds of animals slipped across successfully and continued north.

14 Brigade would act as a floater shield for White City in the period leading up to the Block's closedown. It was a gruelling positioning march, with midday temperatures reaching 112 deg. and water difficult to find. Graves-Morris issued his two Columns with a stern demand for tighter security against the threat of ambush.

14 Brigade's demolition experts included Sapper Eric Sugden of the Bedfordshire and Hertfordshire's 61 Column. They made rapid progress through teak forest, but found the going harder in the thick, mixed jungle on lower ground. As the leading Section hacked their way through with machetes, Sugden marched on, trying to avoid the large, extremely vicious red ants falling from the undergrowth:

'One day, still near Indaw, Corporal Earnshaw told me to join him on a Platoon strength patrol to locate a Japanese dump. We left our heavy packs with the Column. Shortly after moving out we found ourselves in the middle of the dump. On the way back we entered a village and came under fire. Bullets kicked up the dust in front of me. When I tried to return fire my Sten jammed. Fortunately, our only casualty was a man with a bullet-grazed leg. He was able to walk back with us to the Column.'

As 61 Column went north they carried out demolitions – one target was a railway culvert. Eric Sugden:'While most of the Platoon fixed charges to the culvert, I was told to put explosive on a telegraph pole. We lit the slow-burn fuses and made for cover'. TNT, the highest grade explosive in use at the time, was not favoured by the RE. Guncotton, supplied in one pound 'bricks', was much preferred. Gelignite, widely used in mining and quarrying, was not used as it tended to sweat. Gelignite sweats nitro-glycerine! Guncotton was used to destroy the culvert:

'Each guncotton brick had a tapered hole, shaped to receive the primer. Guncotton requires a primer and a certain moisture content in order to detonate. The one ounce primer was inserted into the hole, followed by a fuse or detonator. Chindit columns used slow-burn fuses. Guncotton was used to cut through steel. A Guncotton brick – slightly thinner than a house brick – could cut through its own thickness of steel. The explosive would be lashed around steel girders. We also used Ammonal, a so-called "slow" explosive, for cratering. One method was to create a hole using Guncotton, then push in Ammonal to blow the crater.'

Bridge-blowing was something of an art, but there was no time for finesse in Burma. Eric Sugden:

'Typically, Burmese bridges had no parapets. They were simple affairs. There might be masonry bank seats, with rails laid straight onto girders. We would blow the girders, but you need to destroy the bank seats to do the job properly. That required drilling into brickwork, to place the explosives, and we were hardly in a position to do that.'

Explosives were also used for unofficial purposes:

'Small quantities of Guncotton served as excellent firelighters. I suspect we may have used more to start the bonfires required to mark dropping zones than we did for demolition work.'

General Hyashi, commanding the 24th Independent Mixed Brigade, was killed during the White City attacks. General Takeda took command and the Brigade was reinforced. These changes took time. Meanwhile, White City stayed relatively quiet.[5] Yet, the Chindits operating around White City continued to suffer. The Lancashire Fusiliers' 50 Column were in dry country west of the Block. The men endured extreme thirst. Administrative Officer Captain Jeffrey: 'The sun rose, our tongues and throats became parched and sore and it was difficult to speak. Suddenly we saw some water buffalo rise up from the ground a hundred yards ahead of us and lumber off in the direction of a village. There we found water, thick, black and evil-smelling, but we boiled it and drank it, sitting in a circle round the swamp and

Teak jungle: 61 Column's RAF Officer, Flight Lieutenant Peter Yorke, has his back to the camera. At one point, Yorke was flown out to ensure targets identified around Indaw were located and bombed. (John Riggs)

laughing with relief. Then, 10 minutes later, we came upon a clear, sparkling stream.'[6]

Air raids remained a daily routine at White City. One bomb fell just beyond Peter Allnutt's Company and put one of the 25 Pounders out of action. When the Japanese were still trying to overrun the Block, mortaring and shelling usually began just after 5pm. Lieutenant Allnutt, with 12 NR's 43 Column, was about to enjoy a fortifying mix of rum and lemonade powder when a 3 in. mortar bomb hit the roof of his foxhole. Fortunately, the repaired and reinforced roof held.

Allnutt was still getting over this when Battalion Commander Pat Hughes demanded his presence. Hughes was fed up with constant fire from a Japanese machine gun on high ground known as Dummy Hill. Allnutt was told to go forward and encourage an officer to silence it.

Men sheltering in the narrow communications trench got in Peter Allnutt's way. He lost patience and told his Orderly that he intended to make a run for Recce Hill. They came under fire but reached Recce Hill's trench

system without harm. Allnutt had a job convincing the officer concerned that he wasn't Japanese. A bizarre exchange in fruity language took place, with a Sten rammed against Allnutt's ribcage. On this dark night the officer's nerves had been stretched to breaking point, but he gathered his wits and poured fire on the Japanese machine gun post when it next opened up. Lieutenant Allnutt, meanwhile, had an equally unpleasant return journey.

Virtually everyone who survived White City had at least one lucky escape. Pat Hughes, for example, was blown off his feet by an incoming heavy mortar round. 'White City' was a slight misnomer, as some statichutes were coloured to indicate special stores such as wireless equipment or medical supplies. All chutes proved extremely useful. Most slit trenches and dugouts were lined with them. Chutes were converted into bedding (two for a mattress, one for a pillow). Some were cut up for handkerchiefs, towels and sweat rags. They were so prized by the Burmese that they were used as local currency.

Fighting at White City had reached a new pitch on 17 April, when the last big attack on the Block came in at first light. The Japanese had occupied Dummy Hill's reverse slope. They brought machine guns to its crest under the cover of darkness and poured fire into the Block's southern area. A ferocious, Battalion-strength assault on OP Hill – held by a single Platoon – then came dangerously close to success. The attackers forced the wire and got halfway up the slope before being repulsed. In a swiftly organised second assault, the Japanese entered the first line of Chindit trenches. A handful of South Staffords fought desperately to hold the second line of defence.

Lieutenant Norman Durant, MC, a Platoon Commander with the South Stafford's 80 Column, described events in a long letter home *(Imperial War Museum, 80/49/1)*:

> From our hill we got a grandstand view of the attack and ourselves mowed down a number of Japs attacking from the north. By sheer weight of numbers they broke through the wire onto OP Hill and only a magnificent show by the Platoon prevented the hill being overrun. Eventually, David Scholey [the platoon commander] and 16 men – all that was left of his Platoon – held off the attack until a counter-attack force of West Africans arrived and cleared the hill.

Peter Allnutt inspected the battle area immediately afterwards:

'It was littered with dead Japs. The attacks cost them around 200 casualties. We buried those within reach. The others were burnt with flamethrowers. One was identified as the Japanese Brigade Commander.'

The next morning opened with depressing familiarity. The Japanese had occupied Dummy Hill during the night and a 7 NR Platoon was briefed to remove them. They lost four men. Later that day Pat Hughes ordered Platoon Commander George Manuel to check Dummy Hill once again. Peter Allnutt:

'He shouted over the locations of Japanese foxholes. We put about 20 mortar bombs down in that area. George said he was going in with grenades but I told him to get back. I called: "OK George, we only want to know if they are there!" Yet he went in again, his Corporal keeping a respectful distance. I shouted: "Don't go back! It isn't worth it!" He took no notice. There was an explosion and a single shot.'

Corporal Tambai Doba reported to Allnutt: 'Mr Manuel, Sah. He is dead!' Doba was experienced but Allnutt pressed him: 'He said George had been shot through the head. Sure enough, we found him and he had been hit in the forehead when 25 yards from the Jap foxhole.'

That night the Japanese started firing again from Dummy Hill. This time they were ignored. In the morning it was Lieutenant Allnutt's turn to check the hill for Japanese. It was unoccupied and the men returned with three of their own dead.

The long series of attacks on White City's perimeter had petered out by 18 April but air raids and patrolling continued. Calvert's floater forces continued to take the fight to the Japanese but nearby Mawlu was unusually quiet and some thought the Japanese had pulled out. Captain Eric Noble was told to take the Recce Platoon and find out. Peter Allnutt:

'We were appalled at this suicidal order. The men began to cross open paddy. They moved on either side of the road and railway, which ran side by side into Mawlu. The suspense was appalling. They reached the halfway point in silence and continued into the outskirts. They were in the main street before the Japs opened a murderous fire. The men lay in the open as bullets kicked up the dust around them. All we could do was get ready to receive the wounded. An officer and eight Africans were killed. Two of the six wounded had to be left behind. Eric Noble was wounded and never really recovered from the events of that day.'

One survivor was CSM Cyril 'Nobby' Hall. He wrote an account at Base Hospital, painting a vivid picture of the constant tension at White City. When the Japanese pulled back after their night attacks, they left snipers in well-concealed positions. Every morning patrols went out on recce and snipers would be waiting. Hall: 'This was a nightmare. At dawn we crawled by dead bodies of Japs killed by our grenades and fire from the previous night, expecting at any moment that lethal shot.'

He described how Noble had been briefed by Brigadier Gillmore for the Mawlu recce: 'Captain Noble forcefully opposed this order, owing to the suicidal outcome of such a movement. The objection was overruled.'

On returning, Noble said he would take the lead and then selected a group of African soldiers, a Lieutenant and CSM Hall: 'We set off in open formation across open paddy. Captain Noble advanced along the railway track, approximately 80–100 yards, where he was very close to the station buildings and we were approximately 150 yards from the outer perimeter of the station grounds.

'We came under heavy machine gun fire and also, I presume, discharger cup fire, but the grenades were exploding well to our right flank. Naturally, we all went down – no cover at all apart from the paddy bunds, to which we crept. We were all within 20–25 yards and we could tell by the accurate firing that the Japs had pinpointed our position. Bullets were hitting the paddy tops, shattering all around.'

The Lieutenant was next to the Corporal with the Bren. Everyone was given a sequence for withdrawal but this became impossible when fire suddenly intensified. The Corporal was killed. The Lieutenant took over the Bren but was then shot in the head and killed outright. Hall glanced to his left, beyond the dead Lieutenant, and saw that another African had been shot: 'We were doomed in this position. I knew White City would know what was required – to give us cover and allow us to move. I gave orders for the remaining Africans to keep low but, at the same time, to keep an eye forward. Grenades were bursting nearer our flank, so near that two more Africans were knocked out. This was the moment I prayed for help.'

Nobby Hall then heard aero engines. An air strike on Mawlu Station had been requested, with the pilots told to avoid the paddy to the north. As the Mustangs made their pass the survivors zig-zagged back to the perimeter. Hall was enraged at an order which could only cost lives in an area virtually devoid of cover.

Peter Allnutt often took out patrols to check if villages were occupied. On one occasion two 12 NR Platoons joined two South Staffords Platoons as a powerful escort for a Burrif Recce Section. They came across a Japanese ammunition dump and recovered around 100 British mortar bombs. The Japanese had been firing them into White City. They continued south, passing through abandoned track ambush positions, and finally arrived at the now empty riverside headquarters of 24th Independent Mixed Brigade, a labyrinth of bunkers and foxholes.

Allnutt was puzzled when one man said he had come across a dead African. No Africans had been operating in this area. Allnutt went over and examined the body. The man was on his back and had been dead for some time. The skin was black but the hair was not that of an African:

'Then I noticed the silk "panic map" knotted round his neck. It was yellow. Those issued to 3 (WA) were white. The corpse was that of a British soldier whose skin had turned black as the body approached putrefaction. The dead man's hair (which was about 2 ft long and fair) and his nails had grown enormously since his death.'

There were more grim sights on the nearby river's far bank:

'Some of Calvert's men had been surprised with their equipment off, brewing tea. I counted 32 corpses. The story was plain to read. They had broken one of Wingate's cardinal rules by bivouacking near water – in this case close to a Jap headquarters! The Japs had crept up in the surrounding jungle and annihilated them to a man.'

Then a survivor was found. He had been without food and water for five days. He was sent back on an improvised stretcher. The recce patrol moved on as the day grew hotter. They were only three-quarters of a mile from the target village at the midday halt. The Burrif Section went ahead to investigate as the others rested. The horror of what they had just seen played on their minds. Peter Allnutt: 'Not only was the heat oppressive, but also the silence. Everyone was tense and keyed up, especially after the scene of carnage that morning.'

Two shots then rang out from the direction of the village, followed by more. The Africans were steady and held their fire but a nervous British Bren gunner fired a full magazine into a thick bush nearby. The Burrifs then returned and told their story. They had rounded a river bend and surprised several Japanese bathing and lounging on the bank. Having answered the principal question – concerning the enemy's presence – the entire patrol then moved back and regained the Block in just three hours. The men were upset when they heard that the stretcher party had disobeyed orders. They had been told to circle round and enter by the 'main gate'. In the event, two men died and others were wounded when they triggered a mine while attempting to enter near Dummy Hill. The ambush survivor was dead by the time they reached the Block.

Many actions were fought at this time. 14 Brigade's 74 Column (7th Leicesters) set an ambush near Bonchaung on 18 April and killed around 50 Japanese before withdrawing under mortar fire.

As 7 NR approached White City, Peter Vaughan's 35 Column ambushed a Japanese force concentrating to attack the Block from positions around Mawlu. Sister Column 29, meanwhile, set its own trap on the Pinwe-Sepein road, south of White City. Column Platoon Commander Denis Arnold had a Very pistol in his hand, waiting to give the signal to open fire on an approaching Japanese truck convoy:

'Unfortunately, I never gave that signal. One of our men – surprisingly, an officer and a Regular at that

Getting out: the evacuation of wounded and sick by light aircraft, watched by well-mannered but curious villagers. (John Riggs)

— opened fire prematurely. That was the end of the ambush. We thought the opportunity had gone.'

Despite this false start, Column Commander Charles Carfrae decided to stay put. Denis Arnold:

'Once in position again we continued to wait. Just after it grew dark, at around 6.30pm, the sound of more trucks was heard. Their approach was hesitant after the earlier, abortive ambush attempt. I was told not to give the signal until the trucks were well into the trap — a section of road with PIATs positioned at either end.

'I fired the Very pistol at the appropriate moment. A PIAT round hit the first truck. This vehicle was also hit by Bren and rifle fire. Along the road trucks crashed into each other in the confusion, as vehicles trapped in the middle were hit by automatic and rifle fire. Sporadic firing continued throughout the night. Each type of weapon had a distinct sound. The Japanese machine guns were relatively lightweight, but the Bren had a deeper, heavier stutter.

'My main concern was to stop the Japanese flanking us. Carfrae ordered Dicky Lambert, his 2 i/c, to clear a stretch of jungle along the track. He then sent for me and told me to do a similar job along the area of track where the trucks were. I had one man killed, a Nigerian who had a tendency to hang back behind me. I had

only just warned Shehu Godabawa that he would be killed if he persisted in this behaviour. I reminded him of my strong "juju". A Japanese bullet then passed under my arm, through my shirt and killed him. On several occasions Japanese fired at me from point-blank range and missed. In this case, the Jap was no more than 10 ft away.

'Mopping up continued the next morning. Japanese wounded had a habit of hiding and firing at your back as you pass. Consequently, they were shot as they were found. What happened at that point has always lived with me. We spent most of the day dealing with stragglers. Most unusually, we took three prisoners who were relatively unharmed — a very rare event. They were roughly handled and a British Sergeant intervened and put a stop to it. What's more, he gave the Japs cigarettes!'

The Column Commander considered what to do with the Japanese bodies. They had collected 41 enemy dead. Carfrae gave orders to cremate them and they were stacked on the wreck of one of the trucks. The Lifebuoy flamethrower proved inadequate to the task. At that point Carfrae became aware that appearances might give the enemy an entirely false and highly negative picture of what had taken place. He left a note for the Japanese Commander, explaining his actions. The three prisoners were taken to White City and flown out for interrogation.

Denis Arnold was satisfied with the performance of his Nigerians:

'I was lucky to have a very fine Sergeant, Umoru Numan. He was a wonderful man. A devout Christian, he would read his Bible at every opportunity. I respected his steadfastness and we made a good team. He won the Military Medal for his part in this and other actions. We had many excellent African soldiers in our Column. I remember Calvert coming up to me after the ambush – the next evening, I think – saying how pleased he was with our efforts. He was tired, having been in action all day trying to clear the Japs away from White City. Michael Calvert was the finest of soldiers, brave and compassionate.'

Most elements of 16 Brigade, who marched into Burma during February, would soon be flown out. On 19 April 45 Recce's depleted 45 and 54 Columns (attached to Calvert's strike force) were combined into one Column (45) and returned to 16 Brigade. They set out for Aberdeen on 23 April. On their way they bumped a Japanese patrol and suffered four additional casualties – fortunately all walking wounded. They were then ordered to make for Broadway, regarded as the safer prospect at that point.[7]

Mustang pilot Olin B. Carter certainly did not regard Broadway as safe. On 19 April he flew his sixtieth mission with 1st Air Commando. As usual, he was in P.51 'Little Kitten', escorting Dakotas into Aberdeen. On one occasion the weather closed in and he and his Section landed at Broadway, to spend the night there:

'We hand-pumped about 50 gallons into each aircraft, got into them and settled down for the night. We opened the cockpits due to the heat and were immediately attacked by mosquitoes. We could hear Japanese calling out in the jungle nearby. We had been warned about Jap patrols surprising dozing pilots and cutting their throats. It wasn't a pleasant night. Our tails were tucked into the undergrowth and men passing by would slap the rudder. This made you jump out of your skin. Were they Japanese? No-one slept.'

The integrated 45 Recce Column, meanwhile, struggled on with over 40 walking wounded and five seriously injured on mules and ponies. The walking wounded included Trooper Aylen: 'I was unable to carry a pack owing to my chest wound and had abandoned everything except rifle, water bottle, half a blanket and a copy

Ten minutes – that's all! The Bedfordshire and Hertfordshire's 61 Column take a break on the march. (John Riggs)

of *Palgrave's Golden Treasury.*[8] They headed north-east towards Broadway, passing through Kachin villages. The men had a surprise on 26 April. They had called up light aircraft to evacuate the serious cases and, instead, were amazed at the arrival of a YR-4 helicopter. Philip Sharpe: 'Just before midday we were flabbergasted when a helicopter circled the clearing and landed.' It took two wounded and returned later for two more. L.5s then took out another eight wounded and sick.[7]

The handful of helicopters operating in North Burma were very active at this point. A few days earlier, on 21 April, First Lieutenant Carter Harmon flew his YR-4 into Aberdeen and evacuated a wounded C-47 pilot and three others.[9]

———•◆•———

To the west, 23 Brigade's Columns were disrupting supply lines to the Japanese forces pulling back from Imphal/Kohima. The men of 23 Brigade experienced every hardship of Chindit life. RAF Officer W.A. Wilcox, with 76 Column (2nd Duke of Wellington's), wrote with feeling: 'A mule's behind is surely the most ludicrous sight on this Earth. I walked many, many miles behind one. It always struck me as being just half an animal; the rumps were there, the tail and the legs, but above the tail there was nothing. Nothing, that is, but the metal contraption on which the panniers were hooked. I could never see the front nor the sides of the mule; they were hidden behind the panniers. To me, the thing in front was just a walking backside upon two stiffly jointed legs that jerked, air-cooled by the never-ending swish, swish of the fly-chasing tail.'[10]

Wilcox appreciated that a little jungle knowledge could save a life. His chagul leaked. He watched as a Naga cut a nick into a tree trunk and spread milky resin on the leaking area. He took a glowing ember from the bivouac fire, held it to the repair and blew until the gum dried. The chagul no longer leaked.[11]

On 21 April 111 Brigade received orders to move (via Aberdeen) to the Hopin area north of White City. The new Block was to be established. Floater defences would be provided by 3 (WA) and 14 Brigades, with 77 Brigade positioned east of the railway and Namyin Chaung, opposite the new Block. This plan recognised the inability to hold Broadway, Aberdeen and White City in the Monsoon, now less than one month away. The Chindits were to stay in and they had to go north, to link up with the Chinese, if their wounded and sick were to survive.

———•◆•———

Some men had already suffered so much that they were losing the will to live. Private Jim Unsworth, of the King's Own's 46 Column, saw something that shook him to the core:

'Four men in my Section, all from Birmingham, were sitting at the side of the track as the Column passed. No-one said anything to them. When I came up I warned them: "You've got to carry on. You've got no food and the Japanese will pick you up. If you stay here, you'll never get out." They argued with me. They said: "We'll make it back." I replied: "Will you 'eck!" I caught up with Major Openshaw as the Column stopped for a 10-minute breather. I told him about the four and he said: "You know the rules. We don't stop for anyone." Later that evening a Sergeant Major came in and asked whether anyone knew what had happened to them. I told him my story. As far as I'm aware, I was the last man to see them. They were never heard of again.'

Until the Monsoon broke 46 Column received regular if infrequent drops. Jim Unsworth:

'On one occasion some lads failed to climb a high tree. A parachute was snagged in its branches. I was pretty good at tree-climbing and went straight up. I reached out to pull down the chute and suddenly changed my mind. In seconds I was covered in ants. They were black, around an inch long and very angry. I didn't climb down – I slid down. They bit me all over and I was covered in large red lumps.'

Major Openshaw had problems of his own. When in night bivouac he went out to relieve himself in an area with an unusually high population of leeches. Some got between his legs and delicate work with cigarettes was needed to get rid of them. Jim Unsworth:

'For me, mosquitoes were the worst. Our Column got lost one day and I looked towards the front, where men were cutting a way through thick jungle with their machetes. In the odd ray of sunlight I saw the huge clouds of mosquitoes surrounding them.'

As for Morris Force, Peter Cane's 94 Column (4th/9th Gurkhas) was operating independently and had identified Nalong village as the key target on the Bhamo-Myitkyina road. Nalong was a major supply hub for 18th Division. He sought to persuade Brigadier Morris and sister Column 49 to focus on Nalong, with its road bridge and maintenance depot, and establish a permanent road block. Cane's Column attacked alone on 22 April and burnt the village. Yet, on 27 April, over 130 Japanese trucks arrived at Nalong. Cane called for an air strike but was ignored. Many more Japanese trucks then arrived, bringing the total to just over 300. Still no air strike materialised. Cane then ordered his Column's remaining explosives to be used to block the road.[12]

This made little impression on the enemy. According to Rooney, Morris had ordered 49 and 40 Columns away, 'ostensibly to make contact with Dah Force.'[13]

14 Brigade took over Aberdeen and 3 (WA) took over White City, to prepare for closure and the move north to support 111 Brigade.[14] On 24 April Special Force Commander Joe Lentaigne issued a warning to the first Chindits coming out:

> You will be asked questions by others about your job and experiences, but there are certain subjects about which you must NOT talk. If you do, you will endanger the lives of those still in Burma and those who go in next time. You must NOT tell anyone what units are part of Special Force. You must NOT talk about the details of how you went in and out of Burma, how you got your rations, how the air helped you, and how your wireless messages were sent and received. You must NOT talk about your special training, equipment and arms. The safety of your comrades in Special Force depends on your loyalty and good sense. I know that I can depend on you to be discreet.

Lentaigne's message included unconscious irony, given that most of Special Force would stay in until August:

> You have shown determination and endurance. You have outmanoeuvred and outfought the enemy. You have every right to be proud of yourself. Now you are tired and need rest and bucking up. I am doing my best to see that you get the rest which is your due.

Notes

1. Calvert, M. (1974), *Chindits: Long Range Penetration*, 107
2. Wilcox, W.A. (1945), *Chindit Column* 76, 85
3. Graves-Morris, Lieutenant-Colonel P.H, unpublished MS (via Bill smith and Corinne Simons)
4. Dobney, Major R.P.J. 'Paddy', unpublished MS, July 1981 (via Bill smith and Corinne Simons)
5. Towill, B. (2000), *A Chindit's Chronicle*, 66–67
6. Jeffrey, W.F. (1950), *Sunbeams Like Swords*, 106–107
7. Sharpe, P. (1995), *To Be a Chindit*, 249–254
8. Aylen, N.P., Trooper, *45th Reconnaissance Regiment*, Imperial War Museum, 80/49/1
9. Larson, G.A. (2008), *Aerial Assault into Burma*, 195
10. Wilcox, W.A. (1945), *Chindit Column* 76, 16
11. Ibid, 23
12. Chinnery, P.D. (2002), *March or Die*, 184–185
13. Rooney, D. (2000), *Wingate and the Chindits: Redressing the Balance*, 150
14. Ibid, 136

18

A SHIFT OF EMPHASIS

27 April–6 May 1944

'It appeared to be our lot to be constantly charging off somewhere, to help another Brigade.'

Paddy Dobney, 84 Column, 2nd York and Lancaster, 14 Brigade.

BY EARLY May the strategic situation in Burma was transformed. The Japanese Divisions attacking Imphal/Kohima had failed. In the Mawlu-Indaw area the Chindits had savaged the 24th Independent Mixed Brigade.[1] At the same time Orde Wingate's death severed Special Force's direct link to its champions in high places. Wingate's hopes for Indaw's capture and the fly-in of fresh forces came to nothing. In fact, 16 Brigade elements had occupied Indaw West airfield on 27 April and found it a disappointment. It was unsurfaced – a fairweather strip useless in Monsoon conditions (and the Monsoon was now just a little more than two weeks away).

With the Japanese falling back from Imphal/Kohima, the focus switched again to support for Stilwell. As Special Force had no further direct responsibility for assisting IV Corps, there was no longer any benefit in staying as far south as Indaw. The case for going north was made stronger by the slow advance of Stilwell's Chinese. Kamaing, Mogaung and Myitkyina remained in Japanese hands. On 28 April Merrill's Marauders and six Battalions of Chinese set out for Myitkyina but their goal was 100 miles distant.[2]

When Slim, Stilwell and Lentaigne met on 1 May it was decided that Special Force should transfer to Stilwell's command. The toxic combination of Stilwell and the Monsoon sealed the fate of Special Force (with the exception of 16 Brigade and the detached 23 Brigade). The exhausted 16 Brigade was to be flown out, while 23 Brigade remained beyond Stilwell's reach. Its Columns continued to engage the Japanese thrown back from Imphal/Kohima.

Aberdeen, Broadway and White City were to be closed before the Monsoon broke. 111 Brigade (reinforced by the addition of the King's, 3rd/9th Gurkhas and 6 NR) would hold centre stage. A new Block would be established to the north, near Hopin, to cut the railway and road to Mogaung. 14 and 3 (WA) Brigades were to be responsible for the final garrisoning and subsequent closure of Aberdeen, Broadway and White City. They would then move north to support 111 Brigade at the new 'Blackpool' Block. 14 Brigade's floater force, the Black Watch Columns, set ambushes to disrupt enemy forces also heading north. They fought a major engagement near Thayaung, south-west of Mawlu, with elements of the newly arrived 53rd Division.[3]

Lentaigne ordered 77 Brigade north. Brigadier Michael Calvert, suffering from malaria, felt bitter about giving up White City and his signals became openly insubordinate. Lentaigne made a rare front-line visit to remonstrate with him. Calvert, threatened with replacement, finally accepted that he and his Brigade were going north towards Mogaung, regardless of the Monsoon.[1]

During the advance ending in the occupation of Indaw West airfield, the Queen's 22 Column moved into Seiktha, a large village on the Meza River, south of the Indaw–Banmauk road and five miles west of the airfield. They dug in, hoping to provoke a Japanese attack, but were ignored. 22 Column's Rifle Company then marched through teak jungle to assault the airfield.

During the initial approach 13 and 14 Platoons led; 15 and 16 then took over to lead the attack. 13 Platoon covered the assault and 14 Platoon was in reserve. 14 Platoon Commander Gordon Hughes, in an unpublished memoir: 'Communication was by fixed frequency walkie-talkie and this provided for instant action and reaction when orders were given. The assault was

Muleteers and their charges: harnessed mules at Aberdeen Stronghold. (Jim Unsworth)

quite a tame affair, for the perimeter workshops were manned by non-combatant personnel who fled in light trucks at the beginning of the action. We destroyed all the workshop equipment and disposed of a couple of ancient training aircraft. It was no big deal and whoever decided that the west airfield was a good target either got the wrong information or drew the wrong conclusion.'

There were no counter-attacks as they withdrew to Seiktha. The Column, complete at this point, immediately went north. There were rumours that they would be flown out from Aberdeen, about 24 miles away. Hughes struggled on, beset with fever. The MO put him on a crash course of Mepacrine (three tablets daily) and he continued marching with difficulty, quietly hoping for firm news of evacuation.

The first priority was a supply drop. Gordon Hughes: 'The drop was uneventful, with a maximum pick-up of 98 per cent. Johnny Knowles, our RCAF flying type, guided in the C-47 in his usual, meticulous way and distribution was swift and efficient.'

They moved on six miles and entered an isolated, relatively safe area about a mile from water – a stretch of the Ledan Chaung well clear of villages. This bivouac became a rest area and the men did their best to unwind. Even the mules appreciated the change and appeared content.

Lou Lake, a Wireless Operator with the 2nd Leicesters' 17 Column, remembers a strange incident during a halt on the way to Aberdeen:

'A large python slithered down a tree and wrapped itself around the legs of Betsy, the mule carrying the wireless. We couldn't shoot it, as that would have given our position away. The snake was dispatched with bayonets. Before we left, some clever chap in the Platoon skinned the snake as he wanted the hide. When we left, the dead, skinned python's body was still moving around. It was all a bit eerie.'

Many Chindits garrisoned Broadway and Aberdeen Strongholds and White City Block, where they were surrounded by their own filth and Japanese dead. Bill Williams, Animal Transport Officer with the South Staffords' 80 Column, was still at White City. Conditions continued to deteriorate: 'It wasn't easy to keep clean as we spent most of our time in slit trenches. American light plane pilots said they could smell White City when they were above it. Many corpses on the wire could not be buried. Meanwhile, I

Raising a smile: members of 16 Brigade's HQ Defence Company. (John Simon)

had problems of my own.' Williams had been wounded in the leg during a patrol:

'I thought little of it at first, having had it cleaned and dressed at the Casualty Clearing Station. Unfortunately, it then started to go wrong. The calf wound became badly infected and I could smell it all the time. I knew it was serious when I developed a lump in my groin.'

Men judged incapable of marching north when White City closed were flown out. Bill Williams:

'I was flown by light plane to Broadway, then on to India by Dakota. I had no idea my condition was so serious. Later, I read a report noting my advanced blood poisoning. I spent five weeks in hospital at Dacca. My leg healed well thanks to M&B. By then the rest of the Battalion was evacuated, having helped Calvert take Mogaung by sheer determination.'

By 5 May 14 Brigade Columns were positioning to shield White City during the Block's closure. Paddy Dobney, Administrative Officer with the York and Lancaster's 84 Column: 'It appeared to be our lot to be constantly charging off somewhere, to help another Brigade.' His Column set out with four days' rations up, facing a tough march across high, steep hills and with little chance of a supply drop. This march was expected to take eight days and the men would have to complete it on half rations.

At this point 16 Brigade had been operating in Burma since the second week of February. The men were reaching the end of their tether. Bren Gunner John Simon was with 16 Brigade's HQ Column:

'I went in at 12 stone 8 pounds and I came out at 9 stone 3 pounds. When we left Aberdeen I succumbed to malaria. My friend, Les Martindale, had become too weak to carry the Bren. That pleasure became all mine. Occasionally, I managed to persuade someone else to take a turn. We were flown out to Sylhet, where the entire Brigade was hospitalised. My Company was the last out. Short of space, the hospital put us in the VD Clinic! Vera Lynn put on a show at the hospital the next day but, for some reason, did not visit us.'

Corporal Jack Goldfinch was with the Queen's 21 Column. He saw the cumulative effects of hundreds of miles of jungle marching and constant stress. Goldfinch's closest friend was Sergeant Harry 'Smudger' Smith, from Southampton. Smith was fighting a private war against a leg injury he had been nursing before he went into Burma. He was a keen footballer and had been hurt during a match immediately prior to departure. The MO told him he was no longer fit to go in, but Smith then told the MO there was no way anyone would stop him.

After the war Goldfinch wrote: 'During the march-in I lost around a stone and a half. Poor Harry kept falling over and couldn't get up. I had to keep lifting him – but it was all about comradeship.' During one engagement Smith's mule made too much noise (it was recovering from 'debraying'). Jack Goldfinch: 'They opened fire and Harry was hit in the mouth by a ricochet. He was airlifted to Calcutta and then returned to Britain.'

Elements of 22 Column proceeded to Broadway for evacuation. This was more distant than Aberdeen. Broadway was 50 miles east, at least four days' march away. They would have to cross the road and railway north of Mawlu, in an area offering only patchy cover and swarming with Japanese. They would then have to climb the Kachin Hills, rising from 400 ft to nearly 4,000 ft in just seven miles, followed by a descent into the Kaukkwe Valley.

Gordon Hughes, 14 Platoon's Commander, recalled that orders to head for Broadway were received at noon. They moved out immediately, intending to reach the vicinity of Henu by late afternoon. The approaches to the road and railway would be explored before dark. If all went well they would cross and reach the base of the Kachin Hills by midnight. After watering on the Ledan Chaung they reached thick jungle just north of Henu and awaited recce reports. The patrols returned at 20.00. The point Platoon crossed the road and railway first, covered by the rest of the Rifle Company. The point Platoon then provided 'bridgehead' cover for the Rifle Company as it crossed, followed by other elements.

Midnight approached but they pushed on and reached the foothills before bivouacking. They stopped at 02.00 and brewed tea before settling down. They rose at 06.00 and moved off without breakfast. The track was good but steep. They had a 45-minute breakfast break at 10.00. Spirits had been lifted by the trouble-free crossing of the road and railway and the thought that Broadway was now two days away.

Jungle navigation in the Kachin Hills was always a challenge. 7 NR's Charles Carfrae, 29 Column's Commander, wrote: 'Man-made features, except for tracks and little Kachin villages connected by narrow forest paths and six or eight miles apart, didn't exist. Sometimes villages might change location or altogether vanish; compass and the brown, ominously closely spaced contour lines printed on the half-inch maps we carried remained the only reliable guides to orientation. Interpreting these lines, comparing them with the little that could be made out through the overlying forest of the physical features of the country – spurs and re-entrants, summits and streams – combined with an accurate judgement of distances tramped (so painfully and slowly), required great skill.'[4]

Gordon Hughes and the other members of 22 Column reached the top of the Kachin Hills, enjoyed the luxury of a relatively level stretch and descended on the third day, reaching a point where they were an easy day's march from Broadway. Tomorrow was to be their last day behind enemy lines. Arriving at the Kaukkwe Chaung at the midday halt, they washed and swam in the river. As they moved off there was some banter about ice-cold beers in India.

Both Queen's Columns flew out in early May. 21 Column Wireless Operator George Hill noted a psychological change when they heard they were being evacuated: 'It was at that point that we suddenly realised that we stank, something we had not really consciously noticed before.'

16 Brigade retained its unique character. It was the only Brigade to march in and the only Brigade to return after three months, as intended by Orde Wingate. As the men had walked in, the return to India by Dakota was the first flight experienced by most. 21 Column arrived at Imphal, spent the rest of the night sleeping alongside the airstrip and then boarded aircraft for the onward flight to Comilla. On arrival, their clothing and personal equipment were destroyed. The thin survivors passed naked through a process of delousing, baths, hair-cutting, shaving and outfitting with new clothes. The majority were confined to a field hospital for at least a week. Those fit enough then went on leave in Bangalore. NCO Signaller Tony Howard remembers nothing of the flights out:

'When we got to Comilla I avoided hospital. I stood outside one of the Reception Centre tents and a young chap came up to me and started a conversation. I didn't know who he was at first. It was none other than "Geordie" Beaton, one of my Wireless Operators! He had had a very impressive Old Testament beard; I couldn't recognise this clean-shaven, pale-faced young man of 20.'

The light was fading as 22 Column elements neared Broadway. They were met by transit staff flown in from India and told they would fly out the next day. 14 Platoon Commander Gordon Hughes prepared to take 10 men and four mules in his aircraft. They emplaned during the early evening. Their flight to Comilla was terrifying:

It was not surprising that I fell fast asleep immediately after take-off. It was a real sleep of exhaustion and, under different circumstances, I suppose I would have slept a full 24 hours. It must have been about an hour after take-off that I was very rudely awakened, being thrown off the seat and landing on the floor. I clambered back and looked out at the most horrific electrical storm. The aeroplane was performing the most hideous gyrations, which was having the most extraordinary effect on my digestive system. I threw up and there was vomit all over the place. All 10 of my party were in the same plight. In front, the mules were no better off. Next moment we seemed to drop hundreds of feet out of control and we began to think that this was the end. The feeling of complete helplessness was appalling, for there was no means of talking to the pilots for reassurance.

I managed to stagger to my feet and made my way up to the four mules. They were panic stricken and thrashing about, trying to break loose from their stalls. I really thought the end was near. I tried to calm the animals but they were in such a state that they were implacable. In fact, the right-hand rear animal was in danger of breaking loose. I decided to shoot the animal and prayed that my one shot would not only kill it but the shock would calm the others. I got one of the men to twitch the mule's ear and put my revolver in the centre of his head, midway between ear and opposite eye. Thank God he dropped dead and there was no apparent rico-chet of the bullet. The other mules were so shocked that they ceased their struggling.

It was over very shortly afterwards. They were safely down:

The two pilots came up and, realising the state we were in, said by way of apology that if we had stayed aloft for a few more minutes we would have crashed. They then led us to the front of the aircraft and showed us the engine cowlings, black with oil. The oil pressure had gone and there was oil all over the place. How on earth they were able to see the approach I do not know.

They had landed at Sylhet rather than Comilla, flew on the next day and were admitted to hospital for check-ups and controlled feeding. Confined to their hospital beds, Hughes and others were in rebellious mood. Washed and clothed, they slipped out and made for the Comilla Club. The four ordered ice-cold pints, took one good mouthful and found they could drink no more. Their shrivelled stomachs were full. They took a few more sips and sheepishly left the bar.

Gordon Hughes was luckier than John Simon, in that he did meet Vera Lynn:

We sauntered into the garden and, to our surprise, saw a rather nice-looking girl drinking lemonade and reading under the shade of a large umbrella.

We joined her and found she was Vera Lynn. We had a long talk and she told us about her various con-certs for troops in forward areas. Notwithstanding the beer fiasco, Vera Lynn made our day and we returned to the hospital well satisfied.

Those not required to stay in hospital left for Bangalore, where the Battalion was reforming. Their personal effects soon arrived and they were due substantial pay following months of active service. Hughes took his leave in the Nilgiri Hills: 'Life was elegant in the Nilgiris. Everyone seemed to be on holiday and the various country clubs were full of Mah Jong-playing females.'

On 26 April 45 Recce's Chindits had watched in amazement as a helicopter lifted out some of the seri-ously wounded, before continuing on to Broadway and evacuation. First Lieutenant Carter Harmon flew 23 cas-ualty missions in his YR-4 helicopter, the last on 4 May.[5]

The 45 Recce survivors reached Ndadaung on 27 April and took a much needed supply drop. They arrived at Laichainkawng two days later and Broadway on 1 May. When they began the march into Burma with Fergusson's 16 Brigade on 12 February, 45 Recce had over 900 men. Seventy-eight days later just over 400 men and 13 officers came into Broadway (and this includes some men not in the original force). Many were in a dreadful condition. Signaller Philip Sharpe found things difficult to the very last. He boarded a Dakota, fell asleep and woke to find himself back at Broadway. His aircraft had turned back owing to bad weather over the mountains. Within hours he was airborne yet again and this time he reached Comilla and safety. It was the early morning of Tuesday, 2 May: 'We were weary but the relief was overwhelming.'[6]

Cyril Baldock, the 54 Column Animal Transport Officer who had been isolated from 45 Recce by the White City fighting, flew out from Aberdeen shortly before the Stronghold closed on the night of 5/6 May:

I went to hospital with malaria. As for the dysentery, my guts have never been the same since. When I recovered I was posted to the South Staffords and began training for a third Chindit operation. Jimmy White had been promoted and I became his 2i/c. Later I joined the Parachute Regiment and did my jump training in India, but the war ended before we were deployed.

The men of the 2nd Leicesters' 17 Column also flew out from Aberdeen. Wireless Operator Lou Lake: 'While waiting for the aircraft we were issued with bread and tins of jam and bacon. We were so hungry we made jam and bacon sandwiches. This may sound ridiculous but they tasted wonderful.'

Safe: members of the Queen's 21 Column prior to the Dakota flight to India. (Trustees of the Imperial War Museum)

Even the crash of an aircraft failed to put them off this feast. Two aircraft were lost during the fly-out of 16 Brigade and 12 men died. Meanwhile, those staying in Burma continued to go hungry. In late April some soldiers had been caught pilfering food by Lieutenant Denis Arnold and his Platoon and were reported. He is emphatic that, contrary to one account, no Nigerians were involved.[7]

16 Brigade's fly-out went well. During the night of 29/30 April the 2nd Leicesters' 17 and 71 Columns and 51 Column (51/69 Field Regiments, RA) began flying out from Aberdeen. This was completed during the night of 4/5 May. The evacuation of 45 Recce, 69 Column (51/69 Field Regiments, RA) and 21 and 22 Column elements (2nd Queen's) began at Broadway on 1/2 May. According to the *Report on Operations carried out by Special Force*, this was completed on the night of 6/7 May.

Ted Meese, a 17 Column Muleteer, was waiting to fly out when his aircraft had a mishap on landing and promptly took off again without him. There would be no more flights that night. He took this in his stride, flew out to India the next day and almost immediately had an accident. He fell down some steps, following the excessive consumption of rum. Apart from a violent hangover he was in surprisingly good shape and avoided the almost obligatory stay in hospital. He was posted for garrison duties in Bombay, where he immediately went down with fever. He was not encouraged

when a well meaning Medical Orderly told him that, by rights, he should be dead. Meese made a full recovery.

Corporal Ted Treadwell, with sister Column 71, was another of the many who met Vera Lynn on returning from Burma:

'When our aircraft tried to get over the hills, the roar of the engines deafened us. I spent just one night in hospital. I felt well and was still relatively fit, but many others were in a terrible state – dead on their feet. I don't know why I stood up to it so well. The next day we flew to Bangalore for a month's recuperation. That was when we met Vera Lynn. She came into the hut and had a chat with us. She didn't sing – just had a laugh and a joke. I had seen her earlier in Ceylon, when I was recovering in hospital from malaria.'

On 26 April Brigadier Fergusson had arrived at Aberdeen to discuss with Major Gordon Upjohn (who succeeded Lieutenant-Colonel Day as 6 NR Commander) plans to evacuate 16 Brigade and close the Stronghold. During the next day orders arrived for the abandonment of Aberdeen by 6 May. The closure of White City and Broadway followed within days.

Both 6 NR Columns, 66 and 39, were now required to support 111 Brigade. They re-equipped before moving out and Major Griffin succeeded Captain Greenway as 66 Column Commander. They left Aberdeen and headed

A chance to recover: 16 Brigade Muleteers at Aberdeen. (Jim Unsworth)

north to join 111 Brigade. Lieutenant Bill Cornish, 66 Column's Intelligence Officer, noted that they left Aberdeen at 04.30 on 6 May. They made for the 111 Brigade rendezvous at Mokso Sakan, established on 28 April. A few hours later they heard Aberdeen's ammunition dumps detonate. The Stronghold had been held for over six weeks and had not been challenged by enemy ground forces.

Wingate's G-3 (Air), Paul Griffin, had spent some weeks at Broadway. The air activity had been intense. Broadway became a busy airport behind enemy lines and Griffin and his small team took steps to further improve its efficiency: 'We organised things so that every aircraft taxied to its designated place and unloaded and loaded as quickly as possible.' Paul Griffin watched 16 Brigade men board the aircraft at Broadway:

'Fergusson's men were still standing, but only just. I have never seen men so tired. Those who were a bit weaker than most complained a little. Overall, their experiences had transformed them into true warriors. It was a most extraordinary change. Even some Padres had become fighting men.'

The men had marched a thousand miles over the worst country in the world. Why were they ordered to walk in? Griffin and others offer no single reason but, rather, a combination of circumstances. Paul Griffin:

'Walking in was an insurance. We were keen on encouraging the Chinese to get moving from the north. 16 Brigade could help if any part of the fly-in went wrong. Committing part of the force earlier than the main body would counter any weakening of support from above. There was also the shortage of aircraft and the opportunity to refine supply dropping before the main effort came.'

Griffin went down with amoebic dysentery at Broadway: 'I flew out on the last plane. I was sent to a convalescent hospital in Assam before returning to Headquarters.' Griffin took part in planning for a third Chindit campaign, as part of Slim's general offensive. He shared in the deep sense of disappointment when Special Force was disbanded.

Morris Force had its successes as April drew to a close. On 1 May Major Peter Cane's 94 Column (4th/9th Gurkhas) saw action. Their block on the Bhamo-Myitkyina road was attacked by two Companies of Japanese. The enemy was held but then reinforced to Battalion strength. The Column disengaged, having killed 60. A further 48 were killed in ambushes set by sister Column 49 and Dah Force.

By 5 May 14 Brigade's Columns were in position to shield White City during the final days leading to closure. The York and Lancaster Columns, 65 and 84, had been operating against rail communications and saw action south of Indaw. An attack on a village had cost two lives and seven men were wounded. At 06.15 the following morning, 27 April, they arrived back at Gahe for a supply drop and the evacuation of casualties by light aircraft.

Battalion Commander Philip Graves-Morris later wrote that this was the only occasion during his Battalion's operations in Burma that the dead were left unburied. The Japanese were too close to allow the safe retrieval of the bodies. He strove to avoid casualties as he knew full well what it took to carry just one wounded man. This attack was no major success but the men were content enough. Philip Graves-Morris: 'The Battalion had been on the operation for 12 long hours and finished knowing they were the equal of the Japanese.'[8]

This area, however, felt uncomfortably like a trap — with the Irrawaddy to the east and the frequently patrolled Bhamo–Indaw road to the north-east. Indaw's garrisoned installations and dumps were to the north and the Meza river and the Wuntho road/railway to the west.[8]

The two Columns left Gahe at 0700 on 28 April, an exhausting, hot march in front of them. Later the Battalion found a suitable night bivouac. Elements of the Bedfordshire and Hertfordshire's 61 Column provided stops for their crossing of the railway and road.

On 30 April Philip Graves-Morris celebrated his birthday and received a remarkable present from CSM Jones. It was a bottle of 'Murree' beer, inscribed with the good wishes of his Columns. The Battalion Commander's birthday had solved a problem for Jones. He had planned to drink the beer on the last night, after 'a few weeks' in Burma. When it became obvious that they would be in for months (in fact, 4 months 24 days) the CSM was in a quandary. What other event could justify its consumption? Jones asked RSM Hemmings to give it to Graves-Morris. Paddy Dobney photographed this presentation, capturing the shock and delight spreading across Graves-Morris' face. That evening, Graves-Morris, the RSM and CSM shared the beer.[9]

Philip Graves-Morris' Columns were fortunate to make an unopposed crossing of the Meza river on 1 May. A nearby Japanese base, big enough for 100 men, was deserted. They then received orders to support White City. 65 Column would shield the Block during

Evacuating casualties: a 'flying mess tin' on a pick-up near Seiktha, for the Queen's. The Chindit on the far left is Intelligence Officer Captain Phillips. Captain Finlay is on the far right. (Tony Howard)

Looking for trouble: this observation post is above what appears to be a blown bridge. (John Riggs)

and 16 Platoon, with the animals, was stationed near Gwegyi village. Some of the men then enjoyed an unusual bounty in the Burmese jungle – a crop of apricots. The fruit was irresistible but somewhat unripe and many paid the inevitable price. Meanwhile, 84 Column had reached positions west of Pinwe undetected. Brigade, however, then cancelled the planned attack and ordered an immediate move north, to assist White City.[8]

Preparations for closure were well advanced within the Block. Some men were producing 'fireworks', combining lengths of slow-burning fuse with a few inches of instantaneous fuse. These devices would sound like rifle shots when detonated. They could also be rigged to grenades and mortar bombs. The idea was to buy time as the garrison disengaged and pulled out, by using 'fireworks' to create the noise of battle and slow down pursuers.

The guns kept a watchful eye on any Japanese build-up. On 5 May, for example, the Japanese were spotted preparing a new gun position. Captain Nicholls' 25 Pounders fired 30 rounds into the target. The guns remained busy. On 6 May they supported the Black Watch, shelling positions north-east of Nathkokyin. Preparations for leaving White City began the following day, with the guns supporting the deployments made to protect the evacuation.

Preparations also continued to establish the new Block. 111 Brigade Columns gathered at Mokso Sakan on 28 April prior to establishing the new Block near Hopin. Cameronians Padre Donald Mackay held an 'Eve of Battle' service at Mokso before his Battalion's two Columns marched off: 'At the close of the service I held a short Communion Service ... one of our best Sergeants came up and asked if he might receive Communion. He was not a Communicant and I had the privilege and pleasure of admitting him there and then to full Communion. How glad I was that I did this, for he lost his life in battle a few days later.'[10]

111 Brigade's other British Battalion, the King's Own, also reached Mokso Sakan on 28 April. By then the Brigade's main body had passed through. The King's Own were told to stay put and rest.[11]

Planners referred to the new Block as 'Clydeside' but, later, this was changed to 'Blackpool' when the original name was compromised. Blackpool was established at Hopin, around 40 miles north of White City. 14 Brigade would protect the new Block to the west of the railway, with 77 Brigade doing much the same to the east. Eventually, 14 Brigade and 3 (WA) Brigade focused on the Hopin area, including the Kyunsalai (or 'Kyusanlai') Pass through the Bumrawng Bum.

Lieutenant Dick Hilder, with 14 Brigade's HQ Column, had an unusual encounter at this time. It happened

its closure, while 84 Column would attack Japanese units near Pinwe, on the road and railway. As 84 Column would be unable to take a drop prior to this attack, 65 Column made up their rations for four days. The two Columns went their separate ways at 15.30 on 3 May.

Major Downward's 65 Column was replenished by a successful supply drop on the night of 4/5 May and reached the new operational area around Thazi village, just north of White City, during the morning of 6 May. The Commando Platoon began preparing a light plane strip.[8]

On arriving at White City 65 Column's Commander learned that closure had been deferred for 48 hours. They used the extra time to dig in. Two Platoons, 12 and 14, were stationed behind heavily wired positions. 15 Platoon's 3 in. mortars were readied for action at Thazi when Brigadier Brodie decided to confer with Bernard Fergusson:

'I accompanied Brodie. A Burrif officer saved us when a wild buffalo squared up to charge us as we progressed along a nullah. The sides were too steep to scramble up. Our saviour persuaded the animal to lose interest by throwing a rock at it.'

As the Monsoon neared, many Chindits recalled Wingate's so-called 'contract'. Special Force would stay in no longer than three months. With 111 Brigade taking the lead role, Jack Masters told them straight:

> There are some of you who think you are nearing the end of your strength. You are wrong. In the past months you have consumed the surplus energy you built up before coming into Burma. Now you are down to scratch and from now on you will be drawing on your strength. You have not reached your reserves and will not do so for some time. There is a big task still to do.[12]

These words did not dispel the widespread belief that, in some way, Special Force had been cheated. Richard Rhodes James wrote of the efforts made to counteract this attitude:

> There must be a firm denial of any rumours of a return to India and, in its place, a promise of blood, sweat and tears. Shame the men of their physical misgivings and in place of sympathy put sharp rebuke. Curse them out of their complex, if necessary, but at all costs do not pamper them. But I am afraid we never overcame this problem.[12]

To the west, 23 Brigade continued its independent, Chindit-style campaign against the Japanese in the Naga Hills. 23 Brigade had been detached from Special Force to help blunt the Japanese incursion. One priority was to block road communications east of Kohima. 60 and 68 Columns (60th Field Regiment, RA) were ordered to proceed to Mokokchaung, perched on a 5,000 ft hilltop. The going was very steep and they averaged only 12 miles daily. Lieutenant Andrew Sutherland of 60 Column remembers a strange encounter with a lone Naga, carrying books, during the fourth day of the march:

'He told us he had left Mariani early that morning and intended to reach Mokokchaung that evening –

Happy Birthday! York and Lancaster Commander Philip Graves-Morris is presented with a bottle of beer on his birthday. 84 Column Administrative Officer Paddy Dobney took this photograph. (Walter Longstaff)

SUPPORT STAGGER FORWARD THROUGH
THE STINKING SLIME OF DEAD
VEGETATION, JAPS AND MULES

Pressing on: the Support Platoon and heavily laden mules struggle in difficult terrain. (Tony Wailes)

48 miles in a day! He was the Headman's son, on holiday from Calcutta University. Nagas, being hill people, have barrel chests and "bicycling" calves. They can lope uphill and down dale at about five mph.'

The Nagas were a tremendous help to 23 Brigade. Their ability to move quickly allowed them to gather timely information about the Japanese. They often ferried water to a hilltop bivouac, situated safely away from water. Andrew Sutherland was amused to see a new game take hold among Naga children. They retrieved fragments of parachute cloth after a drop, made miniature parachutes and played 'supply drops'. Sutherland then saw a party of Nagas arrive with a RAF pilot seated on a chair carried by 'extension poles'. He had crashed and broken both legs, but had managed to persuade them to carry him to safety.

Local villagers helped construct a light aircraft strip at Mokokchaung. A few days later Sutherland suddenly realised that death came quickly in such country: 'Gunner Merrie, a member of 6 Platoon and one of the Muleteers, complained of feeling ill in the evening. He died that same night of tick typhus'.

The men had been tempered by the extremes of jungle living in a combat environment. They became expert at managing the essentials, especially water. Andrew Sutherland:

'Every morning we drank hot tea, filled our water bottles and then drank all the water remaining in our chaguls, forcing it down if need be. Thereafter, no matter how thirsty we became, we would not touch any water for the whole day. For we had very quickly found that even sipping water made the thirst unbearable. It required a certain amount of willpower but was worth the effort. We would keep our mouths moist by chewing gum from our K-rations.'

On 30 April 6 Platoon of Sutherland's Column was ordered to climb a hillside and cover a few miles to the planned site of a supply drop the following morning. They reached their goal – an abandoned Mission School – at midnight. The Platoon relished the luxury of a roof over their heads. There was a successful drop the following morning.

Percy Stopher was a Medical Orderly helping to evacuate 23 Brigade's wounded by Dakotas operating from forward airstrips. Casualties mounted as 23 Brigade became increasingly involved in combat with Japanese units. The terrain in the operational area was extremely challenging. An Essex Regiment Column, for example, took 12 hours to complete a four-mile march. There were frequent landslides and tracks became treacherous in torrential rain. Stopher helped ready more Dakotas for use as air ambulances:

'Everything was stripped out, to turn them into hospital aircraft. We made sure we never came out empty! We were often very close to the front line when picking up wounded. There were lots of them. We were supporting some Gurkhas at one point and they were great soldiers ... good marksmen. Every time they pulled the trigger, a Japanese went down. They could spot snipers in trees by noting that the foliage they were using as camouflage didn't belong to the tree in question. They were that good!'

Stopher spoke of the effectiveness of flame-throwers in dealing with Japanese bunkers: 'There might be 10 to 15 Japanese inside a dugout. They'd come out screaming, to be shot down and left there.'

Evacuations began by flying out casualties to Base airstrips, using return flights to bring in replacements. Percy Stopher:

'On landing we collected the walking wounded and stretcher cases from dressing stations or forward

positions. *Sometimes this required a long trek under infantry protection. We had a system for loading aircraft. Those fit enough to be seated sat up front, with stretchers to the rear. Then we flew back, disembarked the wounded for treatment and surgery and began preparing for the next flight.*

'Their injuries were terrible. Lots had their legs off or arms off – sometimes both. We bound their wounds as best we could. The idea was to get them back as quickly as possible.'

Stopher had been hardened by his experience of war in the Western Desert. There were hectic periods helping medical teams cope with amputees: 'I would change dressings and then go out for a break and cook a meal for the lads. I got used to that sort of life.'

Stopher and the other Orderlies often came under fire, but there were lighter moments when away from the combat areas:

'One of the American cooks asked about 10 of us for dinner one evening. When we arrived at five o'clock, dinner was served. We had a ladle-full of tinned stew, topped with minced vegetables, followed on top by a pancake and a ladle-full of syrup and some cream! We all looked at each other and burst out laughing. Yet dinner tasted good and it was followed by a large, fat cigar to smoke.'

Notes

1. Rooney, D. (1997), *Mad Mike*, 90–93
2. Nesbit, R. C. (2009), *The Battle for Burma*, 155
3. Calvert, M. (1974), *Chindits: Long Range Penetration*, 110–111
4. Carfrae, C. (1985), *Chindit Column*, 146
5. Larsen, G.A. (2008), *Aerial Assault into Burma*, 195
6. Sharpe, P. (1995), *To Be a Chindit*, 254–258
7. Rooney, D. (2000), *Wingate and the Chindits: Redressing the Balance*, 171–173
8. Graves-Morris, Lieutenant-Colonel P.H., unpublished MS (via Bill Smith and Corinne Simons)
9. Dobney, Major R.P.J. 'Paddy', unpublished MS, July 1981 (via Bill Smith and Corinne Simons)
10. Mackay, Rev. Donald, 1st Cameronians, 'A Padre with the Chindits', *Dekho*, Autumn 2000, 20–25
11. Miller, Rev. W. H., Chaplain, 2nd King's Own, *A Chaplain with the Chindits*, Imperial War Museum, 80/49/1
12. Rhodes James, R. (1981), *Chindit*, 109–110

19

MOVING NORTH TO BLACKPOOL BLOCK

7–15 May 1944

'The terrain was very difficult. We were covering only about a mile a day at times. The rain came down like glass rods.'

Captain John Riggs, 16 Column Recce Platoon Commander, 1st Bedfordshire and Hertfordshire Regiment

AS THE Monsoon neared, Stilwell's American Brigade and his Chinese Divisions advanced south towards the line Mogaung-Myitkyina. With the Monsoon now just a week away, the Chindits were moving north, closing with Stilwell's Chinese forces. 111 Brigade had the main role of establishing 'Blackpool', a new road and rail Block near Hopin.

Michael Calvert, 77 Brigade's Commander, almost lost control when ordered to close White City Block. His vigorous protests had almost cost him his command. He had been shocked by the decision to give up Broadway and White City. Allen wrote: 'To Calvert and his Brigade, the idea of abandoning the two positions they had fortified so strongly and defended with such élan and tenacity was unbearable.'[1]

On 8 May Calvert and Lentaigne met at Broadway. Calvert was frank when describing this encounter: 'I was still simmering over the idea of giving up all our gains and marching north into a cul-de-sac between the Mogaung River, the flooded Namyin Chaung and the Japs, in the height of the Monsoon.' Calvert told Lentaigne that these plans were a 'death trap'. Lentaigne responded: 'I have not seen you like this before, Michael. If you really do feel like that I will have to relieve you, which I do not want to do.' Calvert acknowledged, 'That brought me to my senses.'

The Japanese, meanwhile, had undermined White City's effectiveness by unloading and reloading trains on either side of the Block. They also began using a track east of White City to move reinforcements north. On 7 May, 14 Brigade's Black Watch Columns set an ambush on this track and killed 40 of a 200-strong Japanese force. Captain Dick Stuckey of 43 Column (12th Nigeria Regiment) reflects:

'With hindsight it was probably right to leave White City, as it was no longer functioning as a Block. Our primary task was to interfere with Jap communications and White City no longer served that purpose.'

On 8 May Calvert's major elements left White City and marched north towards Mogaung. Lieutenant Peter Allnutt's 43 Column Recce Platoon and Burrifs explored the route out of the Block, especially the availability of water. Returning to White City for the last time they heard the sounds of battle as a final, fruitless attempt was made to clear Mawlu. On the final day of White City's occupation the 25 Pounders fired on Mawlu for the last time. The guns and Bofors were then dismantled and readied for the fly-out that night. At 00.30 on 10 May No. 1 Gun, the last 25 Pounder firing, came out of action and the OP was closed down. Within a couple of hours this last gun was broken down and loaded into a C-47. This flight to Sylhet marked the completion of the evacuation.

White City was closed during the night of 9/10 May. Dakotas flew in during the hours of darkness, taking out wounded and sick, the 25 Pounders, stores and mules. Calvert's displeasure at leaving the Block was not shared by most, following a gruelling, seven-week ordeal at White City. They were glad to see the back of it! Private Jack Hutchin of the South Staffords' 80 Column:

'We were happy to leave. We had the idea we were going home after White City. We were disappointed, of course. White City's evacuation was quick, clean and successful. We were told to head for Mogaung and 80 Column set out independently.'

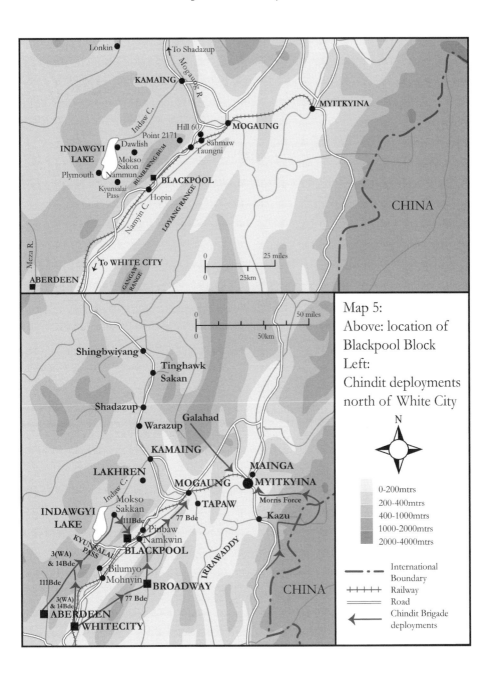

Map 5:
Above: location of Blackpool Block
Left: Chindit deployments north of White City

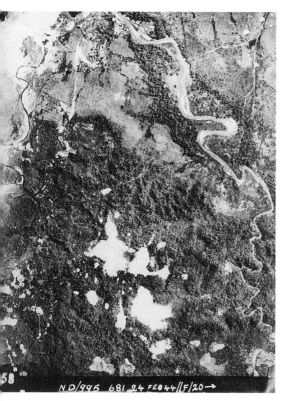

N.D/995 681.24 FEB44//F/20→

The choice: this aerial photograph, taken during an RAF sortie on 24 February 1944, contributed to the selection of the site for Blackpool Block. (Captain Michael Williams, King's Own, via Ronald Swann)

Even the animals were eager to leave White City. Captain Bill Towill noticed the mules 'seemed to sense what was afoot, since they lost all inhibitions about boarding transport and jostled with each other and their drivers to board the planes'.[2]

Many men nursed private hopes of getting out after the hard fighting in and around White City. Ian Niven, Regimental Signaller with the Lancashire Fusiliers' 20 Column, had no idea where they were heading when they left White City:

'As we trudged along we muttered phrases like "only 30 minutes to Broadway", thinking that aircraft would be waiting for us. It soon became obvious that we were not going to Broadway. The news then spread that we were heading for Mogaung, despite Calvert's protestations on our behalf.'

By this time the physical and mental condition of Niven and many others was in sharp decline: 'I think

I had the lot, including two forms of malaria and two types of dysentery, one of which was the often fatal amoebic form.'

The long weeks at White City had seen terrible fighting. No-one knew how long they would be required to hold the Block. The casualties included 12 NR's Major Pat Hughes. He was flown out after being injured in a mine explosion. In the 're-shuffle' Peter Allnutt took on more duties, including inspection of the water point. He stared at its discouraging notice: 'Chlorinate your water! Dead Japs in this river!'

Chatting to another officer, Allnutt learnt of the plans to close the Block. Returning to his position, he passed a mare belonging to 12 NR, standing with a young foal. He was reminded of 'Horace' the goat. Their mascot arrived safely at Aberdeen but disappeared in the confusion of that first air raid. He was never seen again.

Another 43 Column officer, Dick Stuckey, was struck by the effectiveness of the Vickers guns in the defence of White City. One outstanding character caught everyone's imagination:

'I remember a South Staffords CSM known as 'One Belt'. He was wonderful with the Vickers. I watched him in action. When he got the enemy in his sights he fired an entire belt – 250 rounds – in one go.'

The men holding White City and fighting in the surrounding jungle suffered heavily. Stuckey recalls many sad losses, including a 43 Column Sapper:

'Some ground was lost in a fierce Japanese attack and he decided to go out and repair that section of the perimeter. He went out to restore the wire but was blown up by one of our own mines. He died instantly.'

Many wounds left young men maimed for life. After the war Dick Stuckey ran into former White City MO Leon Gonet:

'I asked him why he had become a surgeon. He replied: 'All MOs had trained as GPs, but we were dealing with men who had suffered serious injuries to arms and legs at White City. We became surgeons overnight. I thought to myself, if I can do this in war, I can do it in peacetime. Later, in London, I qualified as a surgeon.'

Attempts were made to confuse and suppress the Japanese threat during White City's abandonment. 14 Brigade Columns had major responsibilities. The Bedfordshire and Hertfordshire's 16 Column and a Company of 73 Column's Black Watch kept the enemy busy at Mawlu, to prevent them firing on the airstrip. They advanced on the Japanese positions and brought down mortar and machine gun fire during 8 May.

These activities continued the next day, with 42 and 73 Columns of the Black Watch moving to the area east of White City. They bumped a sizeable Japanese force and dispersed them with the bayonet. The enemy fled the scene, leaving at least 60 dead.

During 9 May the York and Lancaster's 84 Column reached the Mawlu area, to protect the Block's south-western approaches. They took a night drop in preparation for this operation.[3]

As White City closed down the Gurkhas went first, followed by the South Staffords. The Nigerian 43 Column was the last to leave. Peter Allnutt, leading 43 Column's Recce Platoon, remained dug in on 'Dummy Hill'. His men continued to play their part in deceiving the Japanese. Sitting in his foxhole, Allnutt longed for a return to mobile Chindit warfare: 'Our real job was to operate ahead of the Column, on the march. In effect, this was an independent command. I would be more or less master of my own fate.' Members of the HQ team were the very last to go. Dick Stuckey:

'It was 2 am when we began to cross open paddy, towards the treeline. We were nervous and felt like sitting ducks. The thing that sticks in my mind is the smell of dead mules. That terrible stench stayed in my lungs for four or five days.'

Having demonstrated continued occupancy immediately after evacuation, the rearguard left behind a maze of booby traps and demolition charges with time fuses. They were around 24 hours behind the main body. The Japanese had made no attempt to interfere with White City's closure. On the morning of 10 May the codeword 'Strawberry' was sent, confirming a successful abandonment.

Everything of value was flown out of the Block. According to the *Report on Operations*, between 1,000 and 1,500 Japanese soldiers died attacking White City. The Japanese were now determined to destroy Calvert's command. Elements of 53rd Division pursued them as the spent 24th Independent Mixed Brigade moved to Indaw for garrison duties. As the Chindit redeployment continued, 14 Brigade and the West Africans trekked north to protect the new Blackpool Block from the west and secure the route to Indawgyi Lake. 77 Brigade progressed along a ridge east of White City, to protect Blackpool from the east. Calvert's Brigade was reorganised and now consisted of 3rd/6th Gurkhas, the Lancashire Fusiliers and the South Staffords – reinforced subsequently by around 140 men of the King's,

who were cut off while attempting to cross the railway.[4]

During Lentaigne's visit to Broadway on 8 May – just a few days before that Stronghold's closure on 13 May – he explained why the main effort was moving north. Four Chindit Brigades remained in (23 Brigade had been detached and 16 Brigade had flown out). This left Calvert's 77 Brigade, now on the move, the West Africans leaving White City, 14 Brigade in its mobile role and 111 Brigade also with a mobile role, but heading north to Hopin to establish the new Block. All four Brigades were shifting north towards Stilwell's forces.

Blackpool was established on 7 May. The King's Own's 46 Column were the first troops to arrive. They came under fire as they dug in. The early arrivals requested a large drop, to include picks, shovels and plenty of wire. Fortifying the new Block would be a race against time.[5] The fighting elements of 41 Column arrived on 9 May. The King's Own War Diary *(National Archives, WO 172/4886)* still refers to the new Block as 'Clydeside', rather than Blackpool. The name was not changed until 16 May.

Timing was crucial. The new Block had to be in place just before White City closed and this had to be done before the Monsoon broke. These goals were achieved. Another crucial factor for success was not achieved: the prompt deployment of 14 and 3 (WA) Brigades for floater protection around Blackpool. Floater forces had underpinned White City's outstanding success. Unfortunately, the two Brigades did not take the direct approach to Blackpool followed by 111 Brigade. Instead, they struggled over the Bumrawng Massif.[6]

Aberdeen Stronghold closed on the night of 5/6 May. On leaving Aberdeen, 6 NR's 66 Column followed the Meza valley as far as the Namhkti Chaung, turned east and climbed some 2,000 ft to Pakaw. They took a supply drop at that point, as there was no suitable drop zone between Pakaw and the Indawgyi Lake area. They left Pakaw at 17.00 on 10 May, marched by moonlight until 23.00 and reached Lamai. They left at 06.30 the following morning and arrived at the Namsang Chaung.

111 Brigade reached the Indawgyi Lake area in late April and prepared for the main task. Jack Masters decided to site his Block near Namkwin village, immediately south of Pinbaw. This offered high ground for defensive positions and a flat area for a Dakota strip.[7] 111 Brigade Cypher Officer Richard Rhodes James took a close look at Blackpool: 'The position lay on a series of ridge features jutting out from the lower slopes of the hills we had just crossed. They were small ridges, but very sharp; what might, I suppose, be described as razor-edged. Brigade Headquarters was sited in the middle, at the top of the highest feature, Command Post on the east, facing

the valley, Signals and Intelligence on the west and the Dressing Station a little way down the path. To the west the position eased down into a small valley by a stream, facing the slopes of the mountains in all directions. This the King's Own defended through some desperate days along the ridge that ran north-west by the little valley:

> East were two prong ridges, thrust out into the valley, held by the Cameronians. Below that was the valley or, rather, The Valley. It was our target, the reason for all the battles of the next two weeks. Now it looked peaceful enough. A long, narrow stretch of open country directly below, a river and a railway a mile away. Namkwin village, with its little railway station, a prime target. The road, disappearing north to Mogaung and south to Indaw. On the far side of the valley were more hills and in these hills 77 Brigade was resting after its weeks of fighting at Mawlu; 14 Brigade was away to the south, moving up from Banmauk to protect us and moving, as we thought, very slowly.[8]

111 Brigade Commander Jack Masters had no illusions. He was aware that White City had succeeded as it was in the Japanese rear, in contrast to Blackpool. On the other hand, his selected site offered water, suitable gun positions (although, perhaps, not from a Gunner's perspective) and sufficient space for an airstrip. Allen wrote: 'Unfortunately, 111 Brigade had no time in which to settle in at its leisure. As soon as the King's Own and the Cameronians ... arrived on 8 May [sic], the Japanese attacked them.' The attacking force was a railway unit at Pinbaw, five miles up the line. Although second-line troops, they attacked five nights in succession.[9]

Masters knew he would soon be opposed by first-line troops, yet his site lacked several critical Wingate requirements, including the need to be beyond the reach of enemy heavy artillery. Bill Smyly of the 3rd/9th Gurkhas: 'Blackpool was the best choice under the circumstances but depended on a large body of floaters, which was allocated but did not arrive.'

Blackpool's shortcomings soon became evident. It was obvious that it would be impossible to construct defences as strong as those of White City and Broadway. Furthermore, Blackpool's airstrip was far from ideal, with separate levels and bumps (the paddy had been built as a series of steps).[10]

Nevertheless, 111 Brigade's Chindits worked non-stop on their defences. Rooney wrote: 'For 36 hours every man worked frantically to dig, set up wire, lay cable, collect stores and ammunition and to level the strips.' Despite harassing fire, the C-47s brought in their cargoes, including four 25 Pounders.[11]

Claude Rome's Broadway garrison, meanwhile, was to rejoin Calvert's Brigade for positioning north and to the east of Blackpool, to protect the new Block from that side and also help Stilwell, by eventually attacking Mogaung from the south.[12]

Jack Masters used cricketing terms to name Blackpool's collection of low, steep-sided hills and other features. The central spine, with Brigade HQ, was the 'Wicket', with 'Keeper' to the west and 'Bowler' and 'Umpire' along the spine to the east. Beyond 'Umpire' was a very steep slope down (with very little cover) to what Bill Towill described as 'a waterlogged position carrying the sinister and topographically accurate name of "The Deep".'[13]

The Rev. Donald Mackay, the Cameronians' Padre, described the preparation of a section of Blackpool's defences: 'The paddy fields were levelled out for an airstrip and heavy coils of wire distributed all over the hill, till the whole hill was wired in and booby-trapped. There was little sleep for anyone. Everything depended on the speed with which we could get the Block organised for defence.'[14]

The Japanese were quick to respond to this new threat to the north–south road and rail link. The attack on the first night was repulsed with 20 dead. The enemy began shelling the new positions the next morning. Some 300 shells landed in the Block, killing 24 and wounding 20.[15]

The Rev. W. H. Miller, the King's Own Chaplain, had a grim introduction to life and death at Blackpool. As he neared the Block he could hear Japanese artillery at work. The King's Own elements already at Blackpool crouched in their freshly dug slit trenches, on an exposed ridge.[16] Jack Masters called his Chaplains together. Miller, Mackay and Tom Hawthorn were told that early casualties had been heavy and that the dead should be buried as soon as possible. A suitable cemetery plot was found, away from the main positions. Miller later wrote:

> By dint of much persuasion, I was able to get relays of working parties to dig the graves. Very slowly we carried the dead from the improvised mortuary, opposite the Main Dressing Station. The corpses were normally covered with a blanket, but unidentifiable parts of bodies were put in sacks and buried alongside their comrades in the communal grave. Later, as casualties increased, we had to use shell-holes and disused slit trenches as graves.[16]

Donald Mackay was still digesting an uncomfortable incident during his arrival at Blackpool. They were in bivouac near Namkwin village:

Battleground: the site of Blackpool as it appears today, with low hills in the background. This photograph was taken from the Namkwin Station direction during Ronald Swann's visit to Burma in 2004. (Ian Swann)

I had gone along the bank of the chaung with another officer to swap the cigarettes in my ration for chocolate and, on the way back, stopped for a chat with the CSM. Suddenly, there was a loud cry, 'Look out!', and everyone began rushing towards me along the bank. I turned to run with them in the same direction, tripped over a log and fell with about half a dozen people on top of me. There was a terrific bang – a grenade had gone off by mistake in the middle of the HQ Group. Several officers escaped as by a miracle, but one Rifleman was killed and two officers and Riflemen wounded.[14]

As White City closed, the new Block was strengthened. At first light on 9 May, at around 06.15, four gliders carrying American engineers and airstrip construction equipment arrived over Blackpool. As they cast off and dived for the clearing they came under Japanese small arms fire. One glider stalled and crashed, killing all on board and destroying the load. The others fared little better. The survivors unloaded equipment as best they could and set to work on the strip. Richard Rhodes James:

> One by one the gliders came in and one by one they crashed, until we had four wrecks on the paddy. Of the four pilots, two were killed and the remaining two, badly cut about the face, walked up to Brigade Headquarters. They said they could not see the strip distinctly. One of them said he must go back immediately and fly in another glider with the machinery. He did, a very brave effort. For the moment, we were left with a bulldozer and a smashed grader. We could not build the strip until we had a new grader and until we built the strip we could get no heavy weapons.[15]

According to Larson's account, the first glider got in safely, with the bulldozer still in its restraints, but the second glider – with the grader – stalled at 100 ft. Meanwhile, the first glider, its undercarriage sheared and with both wings gone, came under Japanese fire, with bullets heard striking the bulldozer within.

A team of 50 British troops helped build the Dakota strip. By noon the area was ready to receive light aircraft. With the arrival of more construction equipment a rough C-47 strip of 2,400 ft was ready by 19.00 on 10 May. The first three C-47s arrived that night and made safe landings. A grader was busy improving the strip. The airfield engineers were ordered out later, as Japanese attacks on Blackpool's perimeter intensified.[17]

This account of the initial landings differs somewhat from that of Rhodes James, who wrote that the first C-47 found the strip too short for its liking. An attempted landing was aborted. The second aircraft, however, landed safely. Scraping and levelling continued at Blackpool and subsequent sorties were successful.

The Chindits' *Report on Operations* states that, of the first five movements, one aircraft overshot and burst into flames and two were damaged. It does appear that initial flights were suspended until the strip was further improved. A Dakota flew in on the night of 11/12 May and the strip made a favourable impression on the pilot. It reopened for C-47 landings the following night, 12/13 May.

By 12 May most of the King's had entered the Block (less the 140 men separated in a night engagement and eventually joining Calvert). By way of welcome, the Japanese assaulted the perimeter, following harassing fire to impede work on the defences.

The fly-in priorities included the Block's 25 Pounders. Lieutenant (later, Captain) Ronald Swann, RA, arrived

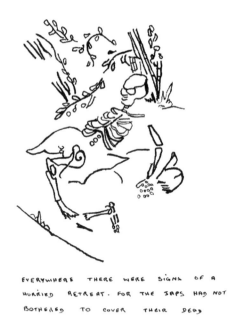

EVERYWHERE THERE WERE SIGNS OF A
HURRIED RETREAT. FOR THE JAPS HAD NOT
BOTHERED TO COVER THEIR DEAD

The retreat from Kohima: 23 Brigade took part in fighting to
destroy the Japanese 31st Division. (Tony Wailes)

with U Troop, 160th Jungle Field Regiment. They landed
at Blackpool on 13 May:

'We landed at the strip, just under a mile from Namkwin
railway station and the road. We soon found the Block
did not accord with Wingate's requirements. A Block
was supposed to be sited at a location where the
Japs could bring up only mortars and light weapons
against it. It was also supposed to be heavily wired,
with floater Columns providing active defence outside
the perimeter. Blackpool had no such floater Columns.
When the Monsoon arrived, the country around was
inundated and 77 Brigade could not reach us.'

On the day the guns flew in to Blackpool, the remnants
of the Japanese were finally squeezed out of Kohima.
2nd Division and 23 Brigade (fighting Chindit-style)
then set about the task of destroying the Japanese 31st
Division, but the road to Imphal would not be opened
until 22 June.[18]

Meanwhile, three of U Troop's 25 Pounders readied
for action at Blackpool. The remaining gun and crew
arrived a few days later. Weight constraints for the
fly-in meant that the Troop had just 25 rounds per gun.
It had been dark when Swann, the gun crews and the
guns landed at Blackpool:

'Some King's Own troops helped us unload early that
morning. During the night the Japs attacked along
another section of perimeter. Anyway, we made a start.
The King's Own chaps obviously didn't know one end
of an artillery piece from the other. When we got to
the breech block I warned them: "Look, this is extremely
heavy. It weighs two or three hundredweight and we
have to be very, very careful." It was awkward, as getting
it out of the Dakota's door meant taking the weight at
chest height. We got it to the edge of the door but one of
the four let go. The breech block dropped and the sliding
breech came up in a scissor-like action and badly gashed
my right wrist, exposing the tendons.

'Having seen all the guns safely in position, towed
into place by jeeps, I visited the MO. He said: "Do you
want to go out?" I replied: "There isn't much point now
I'm here. Can it be handled?" He said yes. Sulfanilamide
powder was sprinkled on the wound and it was bound
up. It was sore for days but didn't hinder me very
much. Meanwhile, more supplies came in and we soon
received plenty of ammunition for each gun.'

Sections of Blackpool's garrison prepared the gun platforms. The 25 Pounders were stationed around 30 yards
apart, two to each side of Swann's Command Post. This
CP was soon moved as it was exposed to incoming
shellfire. Ronald Swann:

'We soon built a very sturdy new Command Post in a
re-entrant almost at right angles to the Japanese line
of fire. The Jap guns were stationed opposite, across the
valley, to the north-east.'

The four 25 Pounders were set into a hill behind the
Blackpool defence position known as 'Wicket'. The
Gurkhas and King's Own were in front of the guns, on
the forward slopes immediately overlooking the airstrip. Not surprisingly, this sector became the centre of
intense, savage fighting:

'The site for our guns was selected personally by 111
Brigade Commander Jack Masters. The guns were
around 1,500 yards from the road and railway station.
We shelled the station, road and rail bridges over the
Namkwin Chaung and many other targets. No Gunner
worth his salt, however, would have sited the guns in
the position chosen for us. The siting of the guns was
suicidal. Strangely enough, I had a similar situation in
May 1940, around Tournai, when a Brigadier placed the
guns just below the crest of a hill. We fired on targets
during the night and the Germans could see the flashes
over the top of the hill. They had marvellous flash-
spotting equipment.'

Flight Lieutenant John Knowles, RAF Officer with the Queen's 22 Column, remembers his relief on reaching Broadway, shortly before the Stronghold was evacuated:

'I was as happy as hell at the prospect of getting out. At the same time, I never really doubted that I would survive. Even then, I realised our life experience is largely an illusion and is really only a prolonged, vivid dream.'

Knowles had good reason to be philosophical, having had his share of close calls. On one occasion he set a new world record for the 50-yard dash:

'We were preparing to take a night drop and started sending "K", our identification letter, but the aircraft engines didn't have that distinctive Pratt & Whitney roar. I had just told Jock to stop signalling when a bomb was dropped. Without thinking, I moved so fast that I teleported out of the danger zone. This was embarrassing. Most of our men were veterans of the war against all four of the King's enemies: the Germans and Italians in Africa, the Vichy French in Syria and now the Japanese in Burma. My comical antics gave them a rare good laugh.

'On another night a parachute failed and an invisible 100-pound pannier landed just an inch from my toes. A couple of inches closer and it would have finished me.'

Having seen many supply drops Knowles was among those who noticed the difference in style between American and RAF aircrews:

'The Americans tended to drop too high, from around 1,200 ft or above, whereas the RAF dropped from as low as a few hundred feet. High drops meant real problems when collecting stores, which drifted all over the place, sometimes took days to recover and were frequently just lost.'

The men of 16 Brigade's Columns were exhausted and now awaited the longed-for Dakota ride. They were completely spent after the long struggle through the Patkai Hills and a subsequent trek of 800 miles or more. The animals had made a big impression on Knowles:

'I loved the mules but had it in for a casualty pony. I couldn't get within three feet of her. This pony had been farting in my face and pissing on my boots for endless miles and, on one occasion, just before we got to Broadway, I got one kick too many close to my testicles and I booted her back. Her handler had to be physically restrained from attacking me. Overall, however, the

relationship between men and mules was remarkable, even beautiful.'

On 13 May, as the guns were flown into Blackpool, Broadway Stronghold was closed. According to the *Report on Operations* by 06.00 on that day Broadway had been completely evacuated. This Stronghold had operated since the first night of the fly-in, almost 10 weeks previously. Beyond the initial air attacks and some days of hard fighting against ground forces, Broadway was left largely undisturbed. Good local intelligence and an effective floater shield contributed much to its security. Some Broadway ammunition and the anti-aircraft guns were ferried over to Blackpool.

When 22 Column flew out from Broadway to Comilla, Animal Transport Officer Bill Smyly stayed on with his mules and moved to the 3rd/9th Gurkhas. This Battalion had seen stiff fighting when the Japanese attempted to destroy Broadway during the early days of its establishment. Smyly's memories of Broadway include the plight of a Japanese captive:

'I remember a Japanese prisoner at Broadway, a small, rather frightened man. He was in a barbed wire cage, made to house him until he could be flown out. The men were curious, wanting a look at a live Jap, and he had a steady stream of visitors. Obviously, most of us were sorry for him and showed it by what happened during the night. I went along quietly myself and threw a packet of cigarettes over the wire. There was a book of matches inside. Next morning I found I wasn't the only one. The floor of his cage was littered with cigarettes, biscuits, cans of cheese and chocolate bars. He had been bombarded with gifts.'

Some days before Broadway's closure the King's 81 and 82 Columns had left and headed north for Blackpool, where they would act as floaters once again. They had patrolled constantly around Broadway, mainly in the Kaukkwe Valley. Their shift north to support 111 Brigade at Blackpool was not achieved without cost.

81 Column led the Battalion north. They approached the road and railway during the night and crossed successfully, arriving safely at Blackpool the following day. 82 Column, however, met the road and railway about an hour later and drew fire as they crossed. Corporal Fred Holliday was in front, with the lead Section:

'When the firing began we had already crossed successfully. Behind us we could hear rifle fire and the explosions of grenades. We stopped but we couldn't return fire without risk of hitting our own men. It was

mayhem. You have to appreciate that there was no moon and it all took place in complete darkness.

'The only officer who took the initiative was our Platoon Commander, Captain Fred Freeman. He was a great character – we called him "Big Ike". He was a Liverpudlian with a mop of red hair. Meanwhile, our Column Commander, Dick Gaitley, was where he shouldn't have been – at the rear of the Column.'

Freeman and his group had yet to cross the road. They stayed put and Freeman organised them into defensive positions. Fred Holliday:

'It was a good effort but hopeless in that situation. It was absolute chaos. It didn't take him long to realise that we were probably firing at each other. It all happened so quickly that there really was no choice but to scatter. Freeman and the others regrouped and later joined Calvert's 77 Brigade, taking part in the fight for Mogaung. We pressed on towards Blackpool.

'One of our officers took charge of our party and we carried on marching. One or two officers went back, to try to get a better idea of what had happened, but they learnt nothing. After a while we stopped and got some rest. This incident is often described as an ambush but I have my doubts. It seemed to me more like an accident, bumping into a party of Japanese on a very dark night. In fact, at times we heard them shouting their heads off. They seemed just as confused as we were.

'There were about 30 or 40 in our party and there were more behind who had crossed safely. The remainder numbered over 100 and Calvert put them in with the Lancashire Fusiliers, calling them the "King's Company".

'We had a rendezvous in case of trouble but, unfortunately, this was on the east side of the road and railway! This was useful only to those who didn't get across. Anyway, those on the western side knew their objective – to reach Blackpool. The new Block wasn't very far away and we reached it just after dawn. Naturally, we were a bit shaken by the night's events. It was bloody awful not knowing what had really happened. On the other hand, it was good to find that Scottie's Column had avoided trouble and had already arrived at Blackpool.'

Before this night encounter, 82 Column Lance-Corporal Peter Heppell heard a rumour:

'There was a story that we were to be flown out from Blackpool. By that time I was suffering from malnutrition and general debility. The Column MO said I would be evacuated but I pleaded to be allowed to stay.'

Heppell was among those who crossed the road and railway unscathed:

'We crossed on our stomachs, moved on and the firing eventually eased up. Lieutenant Long did well – he was a very good officer. Later, a rather pompous Artillery Officer joined us and told Long he was senior to an Engineer and should take command. Fortunately, he saw sense.

'We arrived at Blackpool and found it almost pleasant at first. We took up positions overlooking the airstrip. Later, we discovered that this area was very exposed and moved back. No-one seemed to know what to do with us, so we stayed near the First Aid Post. Then the Monsoon broke.'

Major Gaitley was criticised for 82 Column's disintegration and, subsequently, he was flown out. Fred Holliday believes he was treated unjustly:

'The Column was very unlucky that night. On the other hand, Gaitley should have been more to the front. He had allowed the Column to spread too much and was not in control, as he should have been.'

The Gurkhas' 57 and 93 Columns (9 GR) were also on their way to Blackpool. On 13 May they had left by Broadway's north-east corner, close to where Irwin Pickett was buried. Bill Towill can still picture the scene:

'As I walked past, I remember looking with amazement at a huge cloud of the most beautiful butterflies, which had settled densely over a small area, as if to salute us on our way.'

Towill described the march to Railway Valley:

Following the narrow trail in an immensely long, snaking single file, we soon forded the Kaukkwe Chaung and headed for the Gangaw Range, each carrying a load of around 60 pounds, including rations, equipment, weapons, spare ammunition and grenades.

With all its men and animals a double Column Battalion could extend for over a mile down the jungle track and there was a special bivouac drill, to get everyone into harbour for the night.[19]

As for the Nigerians, 6 NR's 66 Column reached Pahtwe village, where the Headman said they needed arms to protect themselves from Japanese reprisals. Leaving bivouac at 05.30 on 13 May, 66 Column made for Namsai, embarrassed by an ever-expanding party of Kachin

Home from home: 16 Brigade Animal Transport Officer Major Dixon. (Jim Unsworth)

hangers-on, hoping for weapons at the next supply drop. Lack of water required a change of route and difficulties were compounded by the next drop, which was only partially successful, resulting in just three days' rations. More positive was a recce report that the western end of Kyunsalai Pass was clear of Japanese.

The Japanese continued their efforts to quickly crush Blackpool Block. A Company-strength attack on 14 May was backed by artillery support. The enemy was thrown back, with 60 killed, but returned the following morning. Another 50 were killed. 1st Air Commando strike aircraft were called in to punish the attackers. Over the next few days, however, as Monsoon weather took hold, air support and supply became more difficult (Lalaghat and Hailakandi were fairweather fields).

The Cameronians' Padre, Donald Mackay, saw the men take a prisoner during their first week at Blackpool: a small black pony with a long tail and a long face to match. It was adopted by Corporal Norberry and became 26 Column's mascot. This animal's duties included a daily visit to the chaung, to carry up several chaguls of water for the Regimental Aid Post.

Mackay shared in the general feeling of unease: 'We were gravely handicapped by the lack of adequate floater Columns ... the Brigade due to come to our assistance was still many miles distant. Without their help, we could not both defend the Block and control the position in the surrounding jungle.'[14]

Rooney suggests that, on their approach to Hopin, many men of 111 Brigade saw better sites than that eventually selected for the Block. The doubters' early fears were confirmed when the intense shelling began. Jack Masters' officers then heard him let slip some bitter comments about the other Brigades, now unable to reach them.

14 Brigade's progress slowed dramatically when the Monsoon broke on 15 May. Steep slopes required steps and traverses. Men struggled in deep mud and were forced to manhandle the animals' loads. The Columns attempting to reach Blackpool included the Bedfordshire and Hertfordshire's 16 and 61 Columns. Captain John Riggs, 16 Column's Recce Platoon Commander, remembers their struggle through the mire:

'The terrain was very difficult. We were covering only about a mile a day at times. The rain came down like glass rods. The country towards Blackpool, near Indawgyi Lake, was also very steep.'

A few minutes to relax: 16 Column's Recce Platoon rests in a village. On the far right is Karen NCO Saw U, an experienced Burma Rifles soldier. On the far left (foreground) is a Dubliner, Sergeant Tony Byrne. He is taking a chagul from a Platoon member who subsequently fell ill and was revived by John Riggs, who administered intravenous quinine (carried by all Platoon Commanders). (John Riggs)

Lieutenant (later Major) Ronald Bower, RAMC, went in as a replacement in mid-May and became an MO with 16 Column. He had been quietly relieved when told he was to be a 14 Brigade reserve MO, stationed at Airbase to help with returning wounded and sick. His heart then sank on being informed that he would be flying into Broadway in a Dakota, as a 16 Column MO with typhus was being evacuated.

After six weeks at Airbase, Bower was unprepared mentally for the rigours of jungle operations. His introduction was painful. He accompanied a Black Watch Column as he sought to reach 16 Column. He soon developed two large ulcers on the balls of his feet. He learnt that a good MO combined the qualities of doctor and slavedriver: 'If not, many men would have to be left behind, to die or be captured. A weak MO, as I was to witness later on, can have a disastrous effect on his Column.'

Bower learnt that no man could ride unless gravely ill or severely injured: 'which means having a temperature over 104 deg. or being almost unconscious. By not expecting to ride unless nearly dead, many men made that effort, which undoubtedly saved numerous lives.'

At one point Bower was told to go with a party and some ponies to pick up a group of wounded from various units, including the 7th Leicesters:

> Some were severely ill, with high fevers and had no spirit to go any further and only wanted to die. They had been without food for several days and were in poor condition. We got them to the RAP and started feeding them and dosing them with the usual quinine and the odd dysentery with sulphaquinidine. Our hope was to get as many ready to leave with us the next day. The worst, however, were carried a short way to the next village, where some West Africans were hoping to evacuate sick. However, we heard later only a limited number left by air.[20]

14 Brigade reached Indawgyi Lake but a combination of the Monsoon-flooded country and the Japanese blocked further progress towards Blackpool. 47 Column (7th Leicesters) bumped an enemy patrol and suffered nine killed and 20 wounded. They pressed on and managed to occupy the Kyunsalai Pass just ahead of a Japanese force. They then repelled determined attempts to evict them.[21] John Riggs of 16 Column:

'We lacked the strength to force our way through. The Brigade was ordered to stay in the area of the Pass and Lake. A number of attempts were made to force the Pass, but without success. Lieutenant John Salazar of 61 Column led a fighting patrol to its eastern end, attacked a Japanese-held village and captured animals and stores. I knew John very well. He had "liberated" a Leica camera from a German during the fighting in North Africa and, against orders, carried it into Burma. He was awarded a Military Cross for that action and other fine work earlier around Indaw, where he located vast Jap supply dumps of petrol and other stores, which were destroyed by air and ground attack.

'Then Brigadier Tom Brodie, 14 Brigade's Commander, gave me an unusual job. I was told to take the Recce Platoon and proceed along the western side of Indawgyi Lake, survey the terrain north of the Lake and make contact with American-led Chinese forces.'

Lieutenant Ronald Bower, 16 Column's replacement MO, was still trying to reach his unit. He continued to march with the Black Watch. They were climbing a steep slope when the Monsoon broke on 15 May. He used his gas cape to protect his pack and carbine: 'The rain was steadily pouring down and clouds of steam arose from the men's backs. Many had preferred to get wet and now they were halted they were beginning to feel cold. It was very quiet, with no wind, and I felt as if home and the rest of the world scarcely existed. It seemed to have so little relation to us standing there.' The night then offered Bower two options. He could lie on the ground, wrapped in a soaking blanket, or sit on his pack, covered by the gas cape.

On reaching the Brigade area, Bower finally found 16 Column nearby. He reported to Major Phipps, the new CO following the evacuation of Colonel Eason the previous day, who was very ill and died shortly afterwards. Bower was disappointed to learn that 16 Column was to move out that very afternoon, bound for Nammun, in the southern area around Indawgyi Lake. Bower noted that during the march several men suffered cramps and vomiting due to lack of salt.

The 3rd/9th Gurkhas struggled on in the general direction of Blackpool, still unaware of the specific details of their role. Soaked to the skin by the Monsoon rain,

Checking the map: 61 Column Rifle Platoon Commander Lieutenant John Salazar (left) enjoys a smoke. Almost certainly, this photograph was taken using Salazar's Leica camera, smuggled into Burma in his pack. Salazar received the MC for several courageous acts, including a successful raid down from the Kyunsalai Pass, engagements around Indaw and the location of Japanese fuel dumps. In the centre is Major 'Skipper' Franklin, with Red Carter on the right, in characteristic pose with his pipe. Carter is remembered by John Riggs as 'always laughing'. He knew a great deal about animal health and occasionally performed minor veterinary surgery on the Column's animals. (John Riggs)

they fought their way up and down the Gangaw's steep slopes. Bill Towill described the terrible state of the track,

> ... which soon deteriorated into a sea of mud churned up by the mules and men ahead of us. Sometimes we had to leave the track and hack our way laboriously through dense thickets of bamboo...
>
> Sometimes the path climbed steeply up or down, where the mules, blowing hard, struggled to get a footing in the slippery mud, the steam rising in clouds from their heaving, sweating flanks from their exertions under their heavy loads, their sweating Muleteers hauling on their heads and beating the hindquarters of the animal ahead of them, to get them to move ...
>
> We fared no better than our animals as we struggled to keep our balance in the slippery, cloying mud, which denied a secure purchase to our leading foot and yet refused to let go of our rear foot ... we grabbed with one hand or the other at any convenient branch or bush to steady ourselves.
>
> Occasionally, you would miss your footing, or slip in the mud and end up on your hands and knees, under your 60 pound load, and then have to drag yourself painfully to your feet once again and carry on once more.[22]

During the march nerves were stretched. The 3rd/9th Gurkhas War Diary *(National Archives, WO 172/5030)* contains a brief note of a disturbed night – a nightmare in B Company and a trigger-happy C Company sentry who fired at a deer.

The Gurkhas reached Lamai village on the fourth day of this miserable trek. Now high in the Gangaw Range, they rested for 24 hours awaiting a supply drop. It was at this stage that they learnt from 77 Brigade Commander Michael Calvert of their transfer to 111 Brigade and their role at Blackpool, where they would reinforce the garrison.[23]

The War Diary adds: 'In spite of very arduous marching and very heavy loads (the men, in addition to rations, were carrying 100 rounds of small arms ammunition and two grenades), the sick rate has been negligible and the spirit of the men magnificent.'

Another two days' marching had brought them just four miles from Blackpool. The jungle thinned out as they drew closer – the final stretch would have to be crossed in the open. This caused real concern to men long accustomed to the protection of thick jungle. The Battalion was fortunate, however, to have forded the Namyin Chaung just before it ballooned into a Monsoon torrent. It then burst its banks and became a mile-wide

barrier of flooded ground, isolating 77 Brigade from its support role at Blackpool.[23]

More units approached Blackpool but Masters felt uneasy about his Block's prospects. He flew out for a meeting with Stilwell and Lentaigne and asked for 14 Brigade to speed up. Lentaigne told him that Brodie was doing what he could. He added that Masters could abandon Blackpool if he found 111 Brigade on the brink of destruction – not exactly an encouraging comment.

John Riggs' 16 Column Recce Platoon, meanwhile, had a most unpleasant surprise during their exploration of Indawgyi Lake's western shore:

> 'We reached a village about halfway along the lake shore. This was a big village, but with no sign of life and we became cautious. We kept it under observation for about half a day, then decided to move into the outskirts. I took a small party, including a few Burma Riflemen, with me. We kept a low profile for another hour or two, then spotted a Buddhist priest in the local temple. We approached for a chat, only to find that he and the others had smallpox. They were a nauseating sight but we needed answers to the usual questions: "Any Japanese?" "Any food?"
>
> 'We contacted the Column by wireless during the midday halt and reported smallpox in the village, as the entire Brigade would be advancing in that direction. A special air drop then included supplies of smallpox vaccine. All duly received smallpox booster shots and our doctor even vaccinated villagers who emerged from the surrounding jungle. Only the Recce Platoon was not vaccinated! We pressed on and reached the north of the Lake.
>
> 'The going was very marshy. As we left the Lake and moved north a sharp report made us take cover. We had not been fired on. Instead, the Sapper officer following me had stepped on a booby trap. This nasty gadget put a bullet in his leg when he put his weight on it. He hobbled back and we took it in turns to help him along. By the time we were out of the thick jungle area we were covered in leeches. Cigarettes were used to remove around 80 from my body alone. I then awaited further instructions. Eventually, sections of the Column's main body joined us and I was able to hand over our wounded Sapper. That booby trap was American!'

Riggs' Recce Platoon took a fresh route and soon found the Chinese:

> 'They were well dug in. Local villagers assured us that there were no Japanese in the vicinity. We were introduced to the Chinese unit's American Liaison Officers, who then made contact with our Column Commander.'

Fraser (*Quartered Safe Out Here*) described the sudden onset of the Monsoon:

> I was in the act of bending over the brew-tin, stirring in the leaves, when the first big drops landed in the boiling water and I looked up in the gathering dusk at a sky that had suddenly turned dark grey and seemed to be descending slowly. There were cries of disgust and alarm and repetition of the Section's favourite four-letter word.
>
> If you haven't seen the Monsoon burst, it's difficult to imagine. There are the first huge drops, growing heavier and heavier and then God opens the sluices and the jets of a million high pressure hoses are being directed straight down, and the deluge comes with a great roar, crashing against the leaves and rebounding from the earth for perhaps a minute – after that the earth is under a skin of water which looks as though it's being churned up by buckshot.[24]

The longer term effects were even more unpleasant. The constant rain 'puckered the skin in a revoltingly puffy fashion and brought forth a great plague of jungle sores on wrists and ankles.'[25]

Feet suffered badly in these conditions. Fraser commented: 'Your feet are either fine or useless. My soles, by the end of the campaign, were white, spongy and entirely devoid of feeling ... not until 15 years later did they return to normal.'[26] Within the Blackpool perimeter, the Monsoon added to Jack Masters' worries. Allen:

> It turned the foxholes into the trenches of Passchendaele, with trees blown to pieces and human fragments sticking up out of the damp earth, from which rose the smell of putrefaction from the Brigade's dead, or from the spilled entrails of the Japanese corpses hanging on the wire. The proximity of the Japanese artillery, more severe than Calvert had found at Mawlu, was beginning to make Blackpool untenable. It was not the sort of battle for which LRP Groups had been trained.[9]

When the Monsoon rains began to fall on 15 May many men took initial delight in the slightly cooler atmosphere, but constant heavy downpours and thick mud soon changed their minds. South Staffords Private Jack Hutchin and many others were already concerned about the lack of supply drops. They were to find that five days rations would have to last up to 14 days as conditions continued to deteriorate:

'*When the Monsoon broke, we had to accept the discomfort of marching and sleeping wet. Our trek over the hills took some weeks, spent in appalling conditions. Most of the time we were marching at relatively high altitude, but moving down from time to time to raid Japanese supply dumps and communications.*'

Captain Norman Durant, MC, led 80 Column's Machine Gun Platoon. Later, in a letter home, Durant wrote:

> The first four or five days out were absolute hell. We had done no marching and carried no packs for seven weeks ... it was getting near the Monsoon and it was as hot as it could be. We had to climb some very stiff hills and, as the Jap was all around the Block, we had to keep moving pretty fast.[27]

Conditions eased when they were in the hills, where they busied themselves raiding the Mogaung–Katha road and railway. In fact, Durant wrote of feeling good in those last few days before the Monsoon broke: 'By now I was feeling really fit. Up to 3,500 ft it was much cooler, the nights were very pleasant and marching during those days I experienced an unequalled peace of mind.'

Ominously, 1st Air Commando was relieved of its Chindit supply and support duties just a few days after the Monsoon broke. Charles J. Campbell, Engineer with C-47 Assam Dragon's crew, soon found that operating in the Monsoon was much more difficult: 'Our Pilot, Red Austin, used to fly between storms. Our pilots were very sharp on the weather. They seemed to have an instinct for avoiding the worst of the storms.'

In Monsoon conditions supply drops had to be flown in daylight. Charles Carfrae wrote: 'Even then, rain or blankets of low cloud would be apt to hide the best-laid of signal fires from a Dakota pilot's searching eye or foul weather to prohibit flying altogether.'[28]

Some very fortunate men received American jungle hammocks. They made a huge difference to the lucky recipients.[23] Fred Gerrard, of the York and Lancaster's 84 Column, described the lot of the less fortunate:

> The remainder, if they had an extra groundsheet (between two), constructed a shelter to give some protection from Monsoon rain at night. Otherwise, it was sit on your pack, with back to a tree, groundsheet around your shoulders, bush hat on your head and hope for the best.[29]

Small-scale skirmishes with the enemy were often brief and savage. York and Lancaster NCO Reg Smith was a member of a patrol operating ahead of the main body when they suddenly encountered four Japanese. Smith shot one and the remaining three escaped. They were chased, caught and killed by the rest of the patrol as Reg Smith searched the body of the man he had shot. He kept a fountain pen as a reminder of the brief and deadly encounter in the Burmese jungle.

Many men harboured fears of being left behind due to wounds, sickness or exhaustion. Now the arrival of the Monsoon aggravated these fears. The unspoken question in every mind was: 'What will happen if we can't fly the wounded out?'

Notes

1. Allen, L. (1986), *Burma: The Longest War 1941–45*, 356
2. Towill, B. (2000), *A Chindit's Chronicle*, 66
3. Graves-Morris, Lieutenant-Colonel P. H., unpublished MS (via Bill Smith and Corinne Simons)
4. Calvert, M. (1974), *Chindits: Long Range Penetration*, 111–114
5. Rhodes James, R. (1981), *Chindit*, 122
6. Towill, B. (2000), 82–83
7. Rhodes James, R. (1981), 119
8. Ibid, 123
9. Allen, L. (1986), 358–360
10. Towill, B. (2000), 85–86
11. Rooney, D. (2000), *Wingate and the Chindits: Redressing the Balance*, 139
12. Calvert, M. (1996), *Fighting Mad*, 171
13. Towill, B. (2000), 84–85
14. Mackay, Rev. Donald, 1st Cameronians, 'A Padre with the Chindits', *Dekho*, Autumn 2000, 20–25
15. Rhodes James, R. (1981), 127–128
16. Miller, Rev. W.H., 2nd King's Own, *A Chaplain with the Chindits*, Imperial War Museum, 80/49/1
17. Larson, G.A. (2008), *Aerial Assault into Burma*, 190–191
18. Rooney, D. (2000), 180
19. Towill, B. (2000), 72–73
20. Bower, Lieutenant Ronald James, RAMC, memoir, Imperial War Museum, 80/49/1
21. Rooney, D. (2000), 167
22. Towill, B. (2000), 74–75
23. Ibid, 77–79
24. Fraser, G.M. (1995), *Quartered Safe Out Here*, 156
25. Ibid, 164
26. Ibid, 56
27. Durant, Captain N., MC, 80 Column (1st South Staffords), letter to family, Imperial War Museum, 80/49/1
28. Carfrae, C. (1985), *Chindit Column*, 143
29. Gerrard, F.E., *Wingate's Chindits*, unpublished MS, October 2000 (via Bill Smith)

20

111 BRIGADE UNDER SIEGE

16–21 May 1944

'The attacks began with yells and ended with screams as they were stopped by the machine guns. The Japanese never penetrated the wire in our sector. At that stage we were still confident, but most of us felt this was a bloody silly place for a Block. All the Japanese had to do was shell and starve us out.'

Norman Campbell, 90 Column, 1st Cameronians

BLACKPOOL BLOCK was established by 111 Brigade just before the Monsoon broke. Morris Force cut the Myitkyina road to the east and 14 Brigade and 3 (WA) Brigade moved north, to do what they could to help. Calvert's 77 Brigade had the tough dual assignment, to take Mogaung *and* help protect Blackpool (in the latter case he would be thwarted when the rains turned the small Namyin river into an impassable flooded area). 14 Brigade and the West Africans secured the vital Kyunsalai Pass but failed to get close enough to provide significant support for the Block. The future looked grim for 111 Brigade Commander Jack Masters and Blackpool's garrison.[1]

The Japanese took on board the lessons of White City. They were now determined to crush the weaker Blackpool Block. As other Chindit Brigades struggled to provide essential support, General Takeda prepared an all-out assault on 111 Brigade's Block, hampered somewhat by bridge demolition activity.[2]

The Chindit Battalions making for Blackpool included the 3rd/9th Gurkhas, switched to 111 Brigade for defence of the Block. Animal Transport Officer Bill Smyly recalls that the new Battalion Commander, who had succeeded Noel George, had his own style: 'Colonel Alec Harper, a quiet man, was always in control of the situation. He encouraged each Company Commander to put his own stamp on his men.'

Major Jimmy Blaker – who would win a posthumous VC – was among the outstanding Gurkha Company Commanders. Bill Smyly: 'C Company was very much Blaker's Company. He loved it and regarded it much like a treasured sports car.'

Conditions soon deteriorated at Blackpool as the Monsoon took hold. On 16 May Japanese troops pen-

etrated the defences and a counter-attack failed to eject them. Many positions inside the perimeter then came under persistent sniper fire. Shelling that evening heralded another attack. It was beaten back at around 22.00 with 50 Japanese dead. Undaunted, the enemy launched a night attack with two Companies. This was also defeated and an additional 70 Japanese were killed. While the following two days were relatively quiet, sniping and shelling inflicted more casualties.

Wounded Chindits ran the risk of being 'killed by kindness' if they received the traditional British remedy for shock. One surgeon, experienced in the treatment of battlefield casualties, wrote: 'Primary shock certainly responds quickly to a warm drink but in cases of secondary shock from wounds, the patient should only have the fluid supplied intravenously. After having sucked out many gallons of sweet weak tea from the peritoneal cavity, eventually we were able to persuade forward units that those men with abdominal wounds should not be given anything by mouth prior to transference to a surgical unit.'[3] At this stage, of course, many Chindit columns were in no position to get their wounded out to a surgical unit.

Despite the heavy pressure on Blackpool's perimeter defences, patrols went out beyond the wire. On 15 May a King's Own patrol attacked a Japanese unit outside the wire. During the fighting, Lieutenant C.R.A. Jones was killed. On 16 May the Japanese attacked 46 Column elements at 22.00 following a heavy artillery barrage. They were driven off, losing 60 dead.

A wireless-equipped patrol required a Cypher Operator. In the case of the Cameronians' 90 Column, Norman Campbell usually got the job. His luck held despite several close calls: 'I had one near squeak when a burst of machine gun fire hit the tree I was standing against, just a foot above my head.'

Campbell also had a lucky escape of a different kind. He had been just a final trigger squeeze away from shooting a fellow Chindit in the darkness and confusion of a night action on Blackpool's perimeter:

'I saw a shadowy, crouching figure approach during an attack. I was about to fire when he spoke in a broad Scottish accent. If he is still alive, he will never know just how close he came to being shot.'

On arriving at Blackpool, Campbell and Cypher Corporal Eddie Walsh did the sensible thing:

'We dug an L-shaped trench about 4 ft deep, with each arm long enough to provide a "bedroom". There was a ramp at one end, allowing us to run down, rather than jump in and risk injury. When the Jap shelling got worse, we deepened it to 5 ft.

'Tea was always available. There were no restrictions on fires in daylight, as the Japs knew where we were, but no fires were allowed after dark. Eddie and I got familiar with the local layout. Blackpool Block was a range of small hills, like the splayed fingers of a hand. Between the small finger and the ring finger was the Royal Artillery 25 Pounder battery. Looking across the valley, at about 2 o' clock, was the railway station and road. Almost every day, just as we were about to eat our meal, the wind switched to the north and brought with it the smell of the rotting bodies of Japanese who had tried to join us on previous days. I can still smell it.'

Blackpool took on a desolate appearance. Corporal Fred Holliday was among the men of the King's 82 Column who managed to reach the Block after the Column broke up in a night engagement. They were dug in on a forward slope overlooking the airstrip and its collection of wrecked Dakotas. Two or three men occupied each slit trench; the Japanese attacked repeatedly:

'They got through the wire on a regular basis, but never in any strength. We had our Vickers guns on fixed lines of fire. The perimeter defences were quite strong but, at this point, the Japanese were really only probing for weak spots.'

The men got no peace:

'We were supposed to be floater Columns but all hell was going on at Blackpool. Soon, everyone was needed inside the perimeter. Earlier, Scottie had taken out patrols but we soon became "locked in" by

Japanese pressure. For a day or so, however, we were in a relatively quiet position. We had time to get our bearings and appreciate what was going on.

'It was sheer bloody hell at Blackpool, particularly with that 150 mm mortar. Things went from bad to worse very quickly. We didn't regard Blackpool as a "Block" in the true sense of the word. The Japanese brought up a tremendous amount of stuff. Blackpool was clearly unsuitable. Perhaps Masters was unlucky or simply didn't have the time to make a better choice of site. It seemed to me that we couldn't make a move without the Japs knowing.'

As the 3rd/9th Gurkhas neared Blackpool they felt increasingly exposed as the jungle thinned. They abandoned the Column Snake as they approached the edge of the jungle, on the valley's east side, forming up in close column of Companies before starting to cross. Bill Smyly:

'We could see the low foothills and aircraft operating from the airstrip. It had been a scramble setting up the place. I was concerned about bombing and the need to protect the animals. They were scattered among the units they served. I wanted to get them into the valley bottoms, which would give them more protection.

'At Blackpool the mules were shackled for safety in the bottom of steep gullies. Some died there in the shelling and it took three days or less for flies to reduce their flesh to pools of swimming maggots and an indescribable stench of putrefied flesh.'

Captain Bill Towill remembered their arrival at Blackpool on 19 May as a 'greatly welcomed body of fresh troops'. They took up defensive positions around the airstrip, as they could not be accommodated immediately within the perimeter, but moved inside the wire the next day and took over a sector.[2] The War Diary comments: 'Trenches and positions were very inferior compared with Broadway and improvements were immediately started.'

Towill described their highly unpleasant introduction to conditions at Blackpool, which was 'chilling in the extreme':

The morale of the men was at rock bottom – but who could blame them, after what they had been through? The place was pervaded by the overwhelming stench and sight of death, putrescent human remains and desolation. It was a sea of slippery mud, churned up by shell and mortar fire. In 'The Deep', John Thorpe and B Company took over from the Cameronians and Scott Leathart with

D Company took over in 'Pavilion'. As he did so, Scott came across a British soldier sitting in his slit trench and looking out over the valley. He took no notice as Scott jumped into his trench and asked what he was doing and then, when Scott tapped him on the shoulder, he rolled over sideways, stiff with rigor mortis. There was no obvious wound or other indication as to how he had come by his death, but what was equally chilling was that he should have been left there by his comrades or officers, who seemed not to have noticed or cared.[2]

Norman Campbell had a new job. There being no current requirement for his skills as a Cypher Operator, he became a runner and scribe for the Block's newsletter: 'We managed to get some sort of handwritten newsletter out. How far round the Block it went I never knew. I can well imagine it being waylaid for other purposes!'

Campbell and Eddie Walsh were among hundreds within the wire heartily fed up with a Japanese 'whizz-bang' gun. It was sited on a hill at about 12 o'clock from Campbell's trench, around half a mile away:

'You heard the bang as it was fired, the whizz of the shell and the bang as it exploded. The bang-whizz-bang took place virtually simultaneously. This gun fired at anything that moved and could not be pinpointed. Patrols went out to destroy it but failed to find it.'

Their irritation ceased when an aircraft appeared overhead and released a cloud of parachutes. Campbell and his mates then cursed as the chutes drifted over 'Whizz-bang Hill', but attitudes changed when the hill suddenly erupted in a chain of heavy explosions: 'It was an air strike, rather than a supply drop. I don't remember hearing the whizz-bang again.'

Norman Campbell and many others harboured growing fears about Blackpool's prospects. As dusk approached they awaited the next Japanese attack. The evening meal was eaten before dark, then all fires were extinguished as they made ready in their slit trenches:

'The attacks began with yells and ended with screams as they were stopped by the machine guns. The Japanese never penetrated the wire in our sector. At that stage we were still confident, but most of us felt this was a bloody silly place for a Block. All the Japanese had to do was shell and starve us out.'

The four 25 Pounders and frequent air strikes played key roles in Blackpool's defence. Lieutenants Large and Swann had arrived by Dakota with Nos. 2, 3 and 4 guns at around midnight on 13 May. The aircraft flying in No.

1 gun aborted due to bad weather. By 04.00 the three guns were assembled and towed by Jeep into the gun area. Heavy shelling began at 05.25 and eventually found the gun positions. Nevertheless, a line was established to the OP and the three available guns of U Troop, 160th Jungle Field Regiment, came into action after dark on 14 May. During the next morning their positions were shelled and mortared and the Gunners suffered their first casualties, but their guns were in action again that morning. During the evening they received free-dropped 25 Pounder ammunition but found it to be damaged.

16 May was an eventful day for the Gunners. Japanese shelling began at 07.45, followed by another 30 minutes of artillery fire starting at 09.30. Japanese aircraft then bombed and strafed the gun area. Yet casualties were few and the damage was light, according to U Troop's War Diary. The 25 Pounders fired 20 rounds HE per gun at 11.40, followed by smoke rounds from No. 2 gun for air support target indication. During the night of 16/17 May more ammunition was dropped – successfully this time, by means of statichute.

The Troop's outstanding gun, No. 1, arrived during the late evening of 18 May. Blackpool's four 25 Pounders achieved some significant successes. Bill Towill remembered the guns' destruction of an entire train.[4] Lieutenant Ronald Swann, RA, U Troop's Gun Position Officer, recalls casualties from incoming fire: 'They included Captain Philip Young, our OP Officer, who was busy calling down fire when he was killed by a high velocity "whizz-bang" that hit a box of grenades.'

Lieutenant D.A. Large took over but was wounded soon after. Swann and the rest of the garrison became familiar with the enemy's robotic tactics:

'We recognised their routine. It got to the point where we would say: "OK, it's 05.25. Time to stand to. Under cover!" The Japs would then start mortaring for 20 minutes or so. The rest of the day would be quiet until late afternoon when, like clockwork, they would start again. We took some pretty accurate fire and began using smoke shells to make it more difficult for the Japs. We also called down an air strike. The Mustangs blasted the area indicated with smoke shells.

'Crest clearance was very important in a hilly position like Blackpool. We discovered that the Sergeant in charge of one of our guns had not checked clearance when a shell went through a tall tree on the crest and debris fell among the King's Own. Fortunately, no harm was done but you can imagine the language. I never knew exactly where the shell landed.'

How it looked then: a computer-generated representation of U Troop's four 25 Pounders in position on the gun platform at Blackpool Block. (Ian Swann)

A second incident could have ended in serious 'friendly fire' casualties. The Troop received orders to engage target U6 – the village of Leu, south of the Block. Ronald Swann:

'It wasn't until a few years ago, when talking to Major Denis Arnold, MC, an officer in 7 NR's 29 Column, that it came to light that his patrol was to attack Leu. They were about to leave the jungle but were stopped, among other things, by shellfire landing in the area they were to assault.'

The then Lieutenant Arnold was probably not in the best of sorts at that point. Later, he wrote of the first few days of the Monsoon: 'We were wet all the time, day and night. It was difficult to keep the weapons operational and our clothes began to rot on us.'

On the afternoon of 20 May Lieutenant Large joined a patrol of the Cameronians' 90 Column as Forward Observation Officer. They were to set an ambush on the road just north of Kyagigon, with the 25 Pounders in support. U Troop's War Diary records that they found the enemy 'in great strength' at Kyagigon. They moved on, crossed the railway at around 21.00 and then bumped a Japanese patrol. There were casualties on both sides. The Cameronians dispersed and got their wounded away, reassembling five hours later. The ambush was cancelled but the railway was kept under observation. The enemy were using motor vehicles fitted with railway wheels to move stores and ammunition north. These supplies were offloaded at the Namkwin Chaung and carried to the other side. Large was back at Blackpool by 06.00 on 21 May. The guns then had a busy day. A force of 50

Japanese, moving across open paddy towards Kyagigon, received 24 rounds of HE. The guns fired on a variety of 'registered' targets.

Constant torrential rain turned Blackpool into a quagmire. 3rd/9th Gurkhas' Adjutant Bill Towill described a vain attempt to get an injured man on a stretcher up the slope from 'The Deep'. They went down flat into the mud and tried to push the stretcher up alongside them, 'but it was quite hopeless – we'd go up the slope a couple of yards and then slide all the way back, since there was nothing to hang on to.'[5]

Monsoon conditions dominated the fighting at Blackpool and, indeed, the entire campaign in North Burma. In Assam, Monsoon rains turned Hailakandi and Lalaghat airfields into 'mud and flooded lakes'. Air operations moved to an all-weather strip.[6]

General Stilwell's forces enjoyed an unexpected success on 17 May, when Myitkyina West airfield was captured. This could have been used as a springboard for a successful attack on the town itself. Anti-aircraft guns and reinforcements were flown in within 36 hours, but the Chinese 150th Regiment failed to take the town. Morris Force (now on the Irrawaddy's opposite bank) increased the pressure on Myitkyina but the Japanese rapidly reinforced the garrison from 1,000 to 3,000 and held out for another 70 days.[7] According to Rooney, Stilwell had bungled a golden opportunity to take the town when garrisoned by just 700, immediately after the airfield's capture. Within two weeks the Japanese garrison had grown to 4,000.[8]

The British 36th Division could have flown into Myitkyina airfield, but Stilwell didn't want British hands on his prize. Instead, he put together a scratch

American force of non-infantry personnel and green replacements. Apparently, by this stage the much abused Merrill's Marauders hated Stilwell so much that his life was at risk whenever he visited.[9] Certainly, many a British Chindit came to destest Stilwell in the period of great suffering and loss that would follow Blackpool's collapse.

Masters' 111 Brigade was struggling to hold Blackpool, just 40 miles south of Kamaing, Stilwell's next objective.[10] If Blackpool fell, more Japanese would be released and this would make it even harder to take Kamaing and Myitkyina town. Meanwhile, 77 Brigade Columns were positioned in the hills east of Blackpool.

Slim then took a decision that proved catastrophic. Until that point the Chindits had enjoyed considerable success, inflicting thousands of casualties 'at the cost of only a few hundred of their own'.[11] Stilwell's subsequent abuse of Special Force probably led to the death of more Chindits than battle with the Japanese. One example of Stilwell's hostile attitude was his failure to recognise Morris Force's successes on the Bhamo–Myitkyina road. Stilwell subsequently ordered Brigadier Morris to assist in Myitkyina's capture, yet an offer of help at Waingmaw on 20 May, following the Chinese failure to take Myitkyina, was refused. By the time Stilwell told Lentaigne to order Morris Force to take Waingmaw, the river at Kazu was in spate and the Chindits could not get their mules across.[12]

Kazu was 20 miles from Myitkyina. Morris Force was told to take Kazu and Morris ordered an immediate attack. Fortunately, his officers changed his mind. A patrol reported that 1,500 Japanese troops had only just left strong defensive positions. Had that attack gone in, Kazu would have become Morris Force's graveyard.[13]

Slim appeared blind to pending catastrophe. He later wrote: 'It was obvious that, as Special Force came up from the south and the Chinese pressed down from the north, the need for intimate and daily tactical coordination between Lentaigne's and Stilwell's forces would become urgent. On 17 May, therefore, I placed Special Force under Stilwell's direct command'.[10]

Lentaigne and his staff moved to Shadazup on 19 May, joining Stilwell at his headquarters. 111 Brigade Commander Jack Masters visited Shadazup that day and described the situation at Blackpool. While given the flexibility to evacuate the Block *in extremis*, Stilwell expected them to continue to hold. This would assist the drive against Mogaung – to be assaulted by the Chinese 22nd and 38th Divisions from the north and the Chindits from the south, before it could be reinforced.

On 17 May, the day Myitkyina West airfield was captured, 77 Brigade was east of Blackpool, at Naungpong, on the headwaters of the Kaukkwe. They had a total strength of 2,200, but all attempts to help Blackpool's garrison were unsuccessful. They were shut out by the swollen Namyin Chaung. Yet Calvert was not a man to be thwarted and the South Staffords and Lancashire Fusiliers were sent after the guns firing at Blackpool. Conditions were such, however, that only two patrols managed to put in attacks, resulting in some guns being moved.[11] In fact, over 12 attempts were made to cross the mile-wide floods.

The 3rd/6th Gurkhas were sent north and, on 21 May, reported Mogaung held by 4,000 Japanese. Lentaigne, under heavy pressure from Stilwell, told Calvert to order an attack. Wisely, Calvert had already sent the South Staffords north to join the Gurkhas, having accepted that little could be done to help Blackpool. Calvert then brought up the Lancashire Fusiliers and Brigade HQ. It was at this time that he noted that peculiar phenomenon – Chindit reluctance to be seen in the open. In fact, when 77 Brigade began operations against Mogaung, after a long period in jungle with visibility down to a few yards, they were wary of appearing in the open at all. They were suffering from agoraphobia.

According to Rooney, Slim's ignorance of LRP and the best way to use Special Force led to a significant lost opportunity in early May, following the Japanese failure at Imphal/Kohima. The stage was now set for major offensive action by 14th Army. Special Force could have been more effectively redeployed in Monsoon conditions, without squandering the lives of so many Chindits. Ideal conditions had arisen for the use of LRP forces, but Slim 'had no intention of using the Chindits in this role, for which they had been armed, trained and equipped'. Instead, Special Force was given away to Stilwell – who immediately said he didn't want them.

Rooney added: 'Slim, in taking this action, and with the feeble connivance of Lentaigne, was virtually signing the death warrant of many Chindits. After weeks of fighting behind enemy lines, in which they had achieved all that was asked of them, instead of being taken out, restored, re-equipped and used again in their proper role, they were left in the jungle during the Monsoon and launched into an operation in support of 111 Brigade, which offended every military concept Wingate had taught. After that they were used again in an assault on a strongly defended town – Mogaung – which would have been a disaster but for the leadership of Calvert'.[14]

———————•◦•———————

These matters were of no interest to the men of the King's Own's 41 and 46 Columns at Blackpool. They were more concerned with staying alive from one day to the next. Their positions in the sector known as 'The Deep' were under constant heavy attack. Air support helped repel successive waves of attackers. Phil Cochran's Mustangs made high speed runs along the narrow valley separating the King's Own trenches from the enemy. Mitchell bombers arrived and released showers of parachute bomblets on the Japanese. During 18–19 May, 1st Air Commando aircraft were in constant action over Blackpool.

The Japanese were remorseless. They hit the King's Own again in a fierce night attack, rushing the wire with no thought of casualties. 111 Brigade's Richard Rhodes James: 'We were holding and killing, but we were also tiring. The firing used to start at dusk. First the 105 mm, then the 75 mm, which gave us little chance to go to ground, the mortars, the grenades and finally the machine guns. There was an expectancy with each dusk, waiting for the distant thud and whine, the sharp bang and explosion of the "whizz-bang", the more open crash of mortars and grenades.

'Men charged the wire and died as they tried to get over, men blown up on our mines or maimed by our booby traps. With the morning came relief but also an overriding weariness, fatigues on the airstrip, digging and guarding. The King's Own were being steadily worn down and they knew it.'[15]

Ronald Swann, with U Troop's 25 Pounders, saw conditions deteriorate in the Monsoon rain:

'We received few supplies from that point on and our "floater" protection failed to materialise. Meanwhile, the Japs' 150 mm mortar really began to worry us. As usual, it began firing at 05.30, now for around an hour. The incoming rounds had a flight time of about 30 seconds, which gave us the chance to take cover. It would then have another go in the early evening, for about half an hour.'

Men living intimately with violent death took opportunities to find spiritual comfort. Donald Mackay, the Cameronians' Padre, wrote: 'I had the privilege each evening, at the end of Column Orders, of having prayers with the officers and sergeants. I think we all felt the reality and need of these brief acts of worship.'[16]

The King's Own continued to get the worst of it. The 46 Column Chindits crouching in their slit trenches included Private Jim Unsworth. When they arrived at Blackpool, the Column Commander, Major Heap, told Unsworth to stay close:

'I became his Runner. When he wanted to talk to an officer, it was my job to go and fetch him. We settled on a small hill at Blackpool. I didn't know there was a railway at the bottom until the first night, when I heard a train. Our Sappers were busy and several large

explosions soon followed. The Japs then started shelling us. The first shell landed squarely in our Platoon's position. Lieutenant Littlewood asked me about casualties. I told him a Corporal and his pal had been killed. Littlewood then told me to report to the Column Commander.

'Most of our Battalion were dug in below the hill. The King's Own really caught it when the shelling got worse. We were confident, however, as our defences were strong and we had plenty of wire. Yet ammunition and supplies began to run out when the planes couldn't get in due to the Monsoon. After the Japs overran the strip we had no food for around three weeks. We knew we couldn't hold. We did very well to hold them that long.'

Many men remember the hard labour as well as the fighting. When the strip was still operating work continued throughout the night, unloading supplies from the C-47s and distributing them. Between attacks, there was essential work to do — repairing and strengthening defences and restocking with ammunition and grenades.

Richard Rhodes James: 'We were working a supply system which was only just enough to keep us going. It was different in the Column, with 400 troops and no heavy weapons to feed. Here we were 1,500 and encumbered with guns that fired heavy ammunition, mortars that ate greedily everything that was fed to them.'[15]

As the final phase of Blackpool's occupation approached, Bill Smyly was at 'Silly Point', overlooking the airstrip. There were periods of savage hand-to-hand combat. During a particularly determined attack, Smyly saw a sword-wielding Japanese officer hacking at someone in a trench some 50 yards away, to his left:

'It was a Forward Observation Post for our guns and the Jap was in a frenzy. He looked like he was beating a dog with a stick. I was on the Bren at the time and gave him a burst.'

The Gurkhas were dug in on a knoll:

'There was a fairly steep slope in front of us. Behind was a track leading into the Block. 'Silly Point' was the highest point in that area of the perimeter and covered by the Forward Observation Post for the Gunners. We could see the attackers, but not the men in the OP.'

Things would get worse. At 12.00 on 20 May 1st Air Commando ceased to operate in support of the Chindits. Special Force's air support became the responsibility of Northern Air Sector, 10th Air Force, USAAF. On

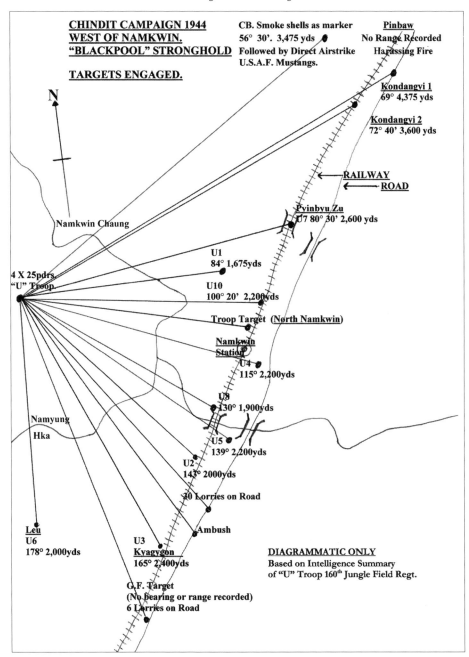

CHINDIT CAMPAIGN 1944 WEST OF NAMKWIN. "BLACKPOOL" STRONGHOLD

TARGETS ENGAGED.

CB. Smoke shells as marker 56° 30'. 3,475 yds
Followed by Direct Airstrike U.S.A.F. Mustangs.

Pinbaw
No Range Recorded
Harassing Fire

N

Kondangyi 1
69° 4,375 yds

Kondangyi 2
72° 40' 3,600 yds

← RAILWAY
← ROAD

Pyinbyu Zu
U7 80° 30' 2,600 yds

Namkwin Chaung

U1
84° 1,675yds

4 X 25pdrs
"U" Troop

U10
100° 20' 2,200yds

Troop Target (North Namkwin)

Namkwin
Station
U4
115° 2,200yds

U8
130° 1,900yds

Namyung
Hka

U5
139° 2,200yds

U2
143° 2000yds

30 Lorries on Road

Ambush

Leu
U6
178° 2,000yds

U3
Kyagygon
165° 2,400yds

DIAGRAMMATIC ONLY
Based on Intelligence Summary
of "U" Troop 160th Jungle Field Regt.

G.F. Target
(No bearing or range recorded)
6 Lorries on Road

Fireplan: a representation of targets engaged by Blackpool Block's 25 Pounders. Ronald Swann was Gun Position Officer, responsible for relaying orders from the Observation Post Officer. The OPO would decide on targets (coded to save time), unless acting on specific orders from the Brigade Commander. 'The Sergeants in charge of each gun would have recorded all the details and the OPO had only to let me know the target chosen and I would give that to the guns. Referring to their records, the Sergeants would then order line, range and ammunition details. Frequently, the OPO would engage a target and then correct line and distance (range) according to the fall of shot.' (Ronald Swann)

19 May Mustang pilot Olin B. Carter flew his last Chindit support sortie. It was his eightieth mission:

'We were pulling back to India. When the Monsoon broke the weather was terrible – up to 10 inches of rain in an hour! My last flight over Burma was a search mission. An Air Commando pilot flying a weather recce had failed to return. Subsequently, we learnt he had got out safely, been captured and later died in Rangoon POW camp.'

Cochran's Air Commando received great praise for its total commitment to Special Force. They would be sorely missed. The new air supply and support arrangements were less responsive. Typically, Stilwell refused to make improvements. From this point on, calls for air strikes around Myitkyina would take priority. In any event, the effectiveness of air support and supply had begun to decline before the Monsoon broke. Over the period 1–20 May nearly one-third of 210 air operations requested by Special Force were aborted due to bad weather.

Bill Smyly watched the intense fighting rapidly consume much of the Block's remaining ammunition and food:

'Monsoon cloud and Japanese anti-aircraft fire reduced drops to a trickle but, at the height of the fighting, we were surrounded by close support fighter-bombers and took a supply drop. Food and bombs rained down from the sky and the noise was terrific and uplifting. If any supplies came near we broke open the containers, pulled the stuff out and passed it round. People helped themselves.'

Bill Towill praised the gallantry of the C-47 pilots:

'Despite their heroism, we were running out of ammunition and had been without food for days. The end was quite close. By now the enemy had got the measure of us and had brought up AA guns to deal with the supply aircraft.'

In mid-May a Met report claimed that the Monsoon was unlikely to break until early June. In fact, it broke very shortly after this over-optimistic forecast was received. During the final day or two at Blackpool, not a single air support sortie was flown. This left the Japanese free to bring up artillery and anti-aircraft guns and allowed them to overrun the airstrip. The lack of floater defences and air support and supply proved fatal to Blackpool and many members of its garrison. During one of the last attempts to drop, 11 of the 12 aircraft involved were hit by AA fire. Night drops were impossible due to the weather. The men inside Blackpool's body-festooned wire knew that supplies of ammunition had reached a dangerously low point.

Driver Ray 'Lofty' Newport joined RAF crews flying those last sorties. He was a 'Kicker', helping to push out the loads. He soon appreciated how difficult it was to fly these operations in Monsoon conditions:

'You have to experience Monsoon rain to understand what it really means. The strong winds were the main problem for the pilots. It was very dangerous flying low along a gully in a heavily laden aircraft. I was fortunate as I never got airsick, despite being thrown about a lot. It was a tall order to find the drop zone in remote country, in poor visibility and success required real teamwork. We knew just how desperately those supplies were needed on the ground.'

Newport is among those who noticed the difference between British and American dropping techniques:

'The Americans were a bit "shit or bust" in their approach. They tended to drop higher. Our blokes treated the cargo like gold, especially ammunition and medical supplies. They would drop at 500 ft or even less.'

Huddled in his slit trench, awaiting the next attack, King's Own Private Jim Unsworth took stock:

'My health had withstood jungle living. My main problem was very typical – a couple of deep jungle sores. I had one on an arm and another on my face, just under the lip. Both had developed from festering bamboo scratches. I also got in the way of some shrapnel during the shelling. A fragment entered my forehead. I happened to be standing next to the Medical Officer when I was wounded. He had a quick look at it, cut my long hair away from the gash and cleaned it up. Fortunately, I had no dysentery. We found that K-ration biscuits helped in that department. When eaten dry they tended to dry you up.'

The King's Own positions were the most unpleasant in the Block. 'The Deep' was at the bottom of a very steep, muddy slope. Much of this area had flooded as the Monsoon rains continued. Bill Towill saw more Japanese attempts to break in: 'We received almost continuous shell and mortar fire and were under heavy attack, day and night. Dog-tired and wild-eyed, we fought desperately to keep them at bay.'

Later, Towill wrote graphically of the sufferings of the King's Own:

Night after night the enemy came in at 'The Deep', no longer in Platoon strength but in Company strength and with set purpose. The King's Own kept holding and killing as one fanatical attack followed another ... on 17 May their positions in 'The Deep' were probed systematically by at least 12 pieces of Japanese heavy artillery and their Second in Command reported that there had been direct hits on his machine gun posts, killing their crews, and he doubted whether they could hold another enemy attack. Masters relieved them with the Cameronians and, as the King's Own passed him, they were walking like zombies, wild-eyed, their jaws sagging wide, obviously right at the end of their tether.[17]

The author's father must have been among those pulling back from the horrors of 'The Deep'.

Luck decided who lived and died. A man could be shot by his neighbour in the confusion of hand-to-hand fighting at night. One man had to take the lead as the sniper ahead took careful aim. Death from mortar bombs and shellfire was entirely random.

Far away from Blackpool, Lieutenant Andrew Sutherland of 60 Column (60th Field Regiment, RA, fighting as infantry with 23 Brigade) had cause to ponder on the role of luck. Before first light on 18 May, three Platoons of 60 Column attacked the Japanese garrison at Jessami. They killed 16 Japanese, found five wounded (all of whom subsequently died) and took three prisoners. The only casualty was 6 Platoon's Wireless Operator, hit by a stray bullet and later flown out. More fighting followed. On 21 May a 5 Platoon patrol encountered a large Japanese force on the Kharasam track, just south of Jessami. When 6 Platoon began an encircling move to Point 5611 they discovered another substantial Japanese position. The men began a four-mile climb at 05.00, finding the going hard in the extreme. Sutherland remembers that rifle slings were knotted together to pull men over vertical rock faces: 'The final approach to Point 5611 was a narrow ridge with near vertical edges and sparse cover. Bdr. Borman, leading the advance Section, was killed — probably by a sniper. A few seconds later L/Bdr. Lloyd was killed while deploying with his Bren Section. Pte Bromnick (1st Essex) found a good position with fallen tree trunks as cover and inflicted most of the casualties on the enemy with his Bren. Everyone carried two Bren magazines and many of these were thrown at him when he yelled for more. The battle lasted two hours. We eventually pulled back when ammunition was running low, including 2 in. mortar bombs — which had been used to advantage'.

When it was over, Sutherland reflected on the losses: 'On separate occasions, some weeks before, both Wally Borman and Norman Lloyd had told me that they knew they would not survive the next action. I wondered about this for years'.

Others were luckier. In an unsuccessful night attack by a 60 Column battle group, an officer, Lieutenant Matthews, was wounded. Andrew Sutherland: 'Because it was the Monsoon season it was impossible for Matt to be air-evacuated. He had ordered his Platoon to leave him by the side of the road as he was being used for bait by the enemy, but Gunner Bert Parker disobeyed the order and dragged him to safety. Afterwards, Matt was carried to the Advance Dressing Station at Phek by Nagas. By then his wounds were gangrenous. He was treated by a doctor who gave him the appropriate shots. By a strange coincidence, one of the doctors on the Permanent Disability Review Board who interviewed Matt in London, some three years later, turned out to be the same chap'.

Back in the squalor of Blackpool Block, the perimeter's interior was now a moonscape of mud and shellholes. Captain Miller, the King's Own Chaplain, struggled to keep up with the burials. Later, he described an horrific experience:

> I was working single-handed at this unpleasant task of transporting the dead or what remained of them to the burying ground when I noticed a body covered over with a blanket which seemed to me to show signs of life. As I gently uncovered the poor, battered face, I could see there was life for he, whoever he was, was still breathing. I ran or stumbled as quickly as I could through the mud and filth to the Main Dressing Station and blurted out what I had found to the Senior Medical Officer. I was told that this particular man had no chance of living and had been placed in the mortuary to await death and his turn for burial. There were so many casualties that bodies had to be left for several days.[18]

In order to keep up their spirits, Miller and his Batman, Cook, indulged in frequent hymn-singing: 'Our great favourite was "Guide me, O Thou Great Jehovah".'[18]

As casualties mounted at Blackpool, some of the men who had failed to reach the Block were trying to come to terms with capture. They included Ted McArdle, a Muleteer with the King's 82 Column, taken prisoner in the confusion when they attempted to repeat the sister Column's successful crossing of the road and railway.

During the night of 11/12 May, his last as a free man, McArdle was unconcerned. There was nothing unusual about marching at night:

'The Column Snake came to a stop. I got the impression that about half the Column was already over the road and railway. We waited our turn. Suddenly, tracers opened up, the mules went into a panic and Joey broke away. I joined the three lads nearest to me and took cover. All of us were without weapons. This small group included a Welsh lad, Taffy Thomas, and Matty Ashton, from Liverpool. Taffy and the third man were shot. Matty and I moved position, staying in cover, and climbed down the bank of a small stream. Shortly afterwards we heard Japanese voices just above us. We were seen and that was it. We were captured.'

The Japanese blindfolded the men and bundled them away:

'They put us on a train to Mandalay and then on to Rangoon Gaol. I was put in an isolation cell. That night I felt an itching sensation on my neck. I put my hand up and my fingers were covered with lice. The following morning Matty and I were taken out of our cells and given a beating with what looked like the branch of a tree. We weren't questioned. The guard seemed to get satisfaction from beating us. It was all very matter of fact. These daily beatings continued for six weeks of solitary confinement. Suddenly, for no apparent reason, the beatings stopped.'

There was food, but rice only — occasionally flavoured with garlic. The new prisoners received two bowls of rice daily. There was nothing in McArdle's cell, other than the old wooden door that doubled as seat and bed: 'There was also a bucket to pee in. We emptied our buckets every morning.'

It was a considerable relief when solitary confinement came to an end. Both men entered the main part of the prison:

'At last we could mix with the other prisoners. We could also get into the yard for some exercise. The prison's Senior British Officer was also the Medical Officer, Colonel MacKenzie [father of television reporter and presenter Jacqueline MacKenzie]. The Colonel made a big impression on me. He'd never say If you get out of here, but, rather, "When you get out of here, we'll get in the beer. That will do you a power of good".'

The diet was just enough to keep a man alive:

'Matty Ashton got a little more after he got a job in the cookhouse. That's why he finished up fitter than me. One prisoner, a Dutchman, attempted to escape but was soon recaptured. They caught him, put him in an isolation cell and knocked hell out of him.'

Beatings took place at random but Ted McArdle managed to avoid trouble:

'Roll call took place daily. We had to shout out our numbers in Japanese. Any mistake, or failure to bow to a Jap guard, would result in a beating.'

In North Burma even the smallest stream became a torrent when the Monsoon arrived. Everyone went hungry — the now desperate garrison at Blackpool and the men of the three other Brigades, 77, 14 and 3(WA). 14 Brigade's Columns had fought to position themselves to defend Blackpool but the terrain, mud, flooded chaungs, lack of food and disease slowly undermined their capabilities.

Lieutenant John Salazar, a Bedfordshire and Hertfordshire Platoon Commander, described his experience on 17 May 1944:

> Rain thunders down onto broad leaves. It's so loud we have to shout to be heard. During lulls, one can hear it approaching across the hills, like a roaring cataract increasing in volume. My Platoon moves off last, carrying cerebral malarial Private Todd on a rough bamboo and groundsheet stretcher. The whole Column has gone ahead, making the track extremely muddy and slippery. Massive great trees are down across the track, making it doubly hard work manhandling the stretcher. Doc. David [Evans] is busier than ever. In a violent thunderstorm (no cover) he gives Todd a saline and quinine intravenous injection. Todd is quite unconscious ... We all shiver in our soaked clothes and try to keep still, so that the water next to our bodies warms up a bit.

Lieutenant-Colonel Philip Graves-Morris' York and Lancaster Columns faced a tough climb — from 600 ft to 3,400 ft over 12 miles — to the north of Tangra, following muddy tracks. The muleloads had to be manhandled over the worst stretches. The men lost count of the small chaungs crossed, as they struggled through the ooze on both banks. Graves-Morris wrote: 'It seemed that no sooner had a mule been loaded on the far side of a sticky chaung, it had to be offloaded to cross the next.'[19]

On 16 May the going was so bad that some mules went rolling down the slopes. The men redoubled their efforts to cut steps. Parties were sent out to find a drop site. The heavy rain was incessant on 17 May and rations were very low. Men became reluctant to eat what they had, knowing that it might have to last double the normal period. Later, Graves-Morris noted: 'Despite this the men were wonderfully cheerful and worked splendidly.' He singled out the sorely tried Muleteers for special praise.[19]

The stress caused by lack of food was later described by Major Paddy Dobney, 84 Column's Administrative Officer. Appetites increased sharply when marching at over 3,000 ft: 'With half rations of only 2 oz of meat hash or cheese and two finger biscuits per meal, we were very hungry.' They were still four days away from the site selected for the next drop. On the second day they met a Column of West Africans and Dobney cadged some food. He brought the small stockpile back to his 15 men. Sixteen small piles were made:

The piles varied in size and quality and the soldiers looked on with special interest as the little heaps were assembled. On these occasions, fairness in distribution must not only be believed to be done, it must be seen to be done and, starting with the junior ranks first, in alphabetical order, each man made his selection. This, of course, meant I had last pick and only had 'Hobson's Choice', my mentally selected pile having long since vanished.

The next day brought another windfall. Dobney managed to buy two eggs in a village. Faced with dividing two eggs between 16 men, he decided to give one egg to each section of eight:

My group of eight then decided to draw lots, but not as a 'sudden death' affair. We decided to split into two fours and then two pairs, like the quarter and semi-finals of the F.A. Cup. Private Heney and I found ourselves facing each other in the final. I rather ungraciously said: 'I hope it chokes you!' as Heney, triumphant in the final, picked up his trophy.[20]

They were half a day ahead of 84 Column's main body on arriving at the drop site. They wirelessed for the drop, but this was delayed. Uncomfortable at the thought of being able to produce nothing when his Battalion Commander arrived, Dobney went 'cadging' once again. He visited another Column in the area. They had just taken a drop and Dobney persuaded them to part with one K-ration meal for 400, on the understanding that the loan would be repaid following 84 Column's drop.[20] When that drop finally came, on 21 May, it included arms for the Kachins.

As for the West Africans, 6 NR's 66 Column reached Lepon on 16 May. They struggled through tall elephant grass towards the open vista of the Indawgyi plain. Heavy Monsoon rain fell all night and the march to Mokso Sakan was very muddy. Lieutenant Larry Gaines:

'We had to stay on the track. It was impossible to get off it in such dense jungle. On the steep, muddy slope in pouring rain, the usual routine went out of the window. There was no question of halting for a nice rest every 50 minutes or so. If the Column head was held up for any reason, we just stayed where we were on the track.

'We started to get real problems with the leeches as we approached Indawgyi Lake. They get everywhere, getting in through the top of your boots and into your flies. One poor bugger got a leech up the penis. The usual remedy, a cigarette end, was no use in this case, but one Burmese knew what to do. The unfortunate victim was told to take his trousers off. Held by four men, stationed at each hand and foot, he was suspended over a heavily smoking fire. This persuaded the leech to release and emerge.

'On a more positive note, one drop included a number of American jungle hammocks with built-in "roofs" and mosquito netting. These were given to those who were really ill. You suspended the hammock between trees, got in and zipped up the netting. They were wonderful and enabled those in them to have a reasonably dry night, with no bites.'

They made contact with 30 Column (3rd/4th Gurkhas), busy lengthening Mokso Sakan's light aircraft strip. With this work completed, 15 sick men were flown out.

Larry Gaines led 66 Column's Vickers Platoon. He nursed a secret. Some days previously, before they had reached Indawgyi Lake, there had been a special drop and he had got his hands on a bottle of South African brandy. Most people rejected any extra weight but Gaines held on to that bottle. In night bivouac, having left the Lake, an exhausted Gaines sat on his gas cape and started on the brandy, to a barrage of comments from fellow officers: 'I said to myself: "Bugger you! I carried it and now I'm drinking it!"'

111 Brigade Commander Jack Masters flew into Mokso Sakan on 20 May. He said there was fighting around Myitkyina and Stilwell's Chinese were held up north of Kamaing. The Japanese were still attacking Blackpool. 30 Column was ordered to recce the Mogaung Chaung, with a view to getting across. 66 Column had orders to attack the enemy north-west of Blackpool and locate and destroy their guns.

The following day, 21 May, 74 Column (7th Leicesters) won the race with the Japanese for the strategic Kyunsalai Pass, overlooking Hopin, Ywathit and the railway corridor. They beat the Japanese with only an hour or two to spare. When the enemy arrived, they were beaten off, leaving over 60 dead.

———•◦•———

For another three months or more the Chindits of 14, 77, 111 and 3(WA) Brigades would experience war in the jungle during the Burmese Monsoon. The effects were disastrous for men and animals. Mules weakened and died of exhaustion. Some sank deep into the mud and could not be freed; they were shot as an act of mercy. Lieutenant-Colonel Graves-Morris feared for his men:

> We were all to see once robust men waste away to skin and bone and to fall from exhaustion and weariness, to die before they could be evacuated. We were all to see the devastating effect continuous rain, jungle gloom, mud and toiling, back-breaking marches were to have on men's minds, as many normal, cheerful men ... collapsed and asked to be left to die or even hastened their end by their own hands.[19]

The York and Lancaster's 65 Column reached Maingthaingyi at 16.45 on 19 May. They were joined by 84 Column the following morning. The eight-day struggle over the hills had been completed on 4.5 days' rations. 84 Column's men were more than grateful for the fruit of Paddy Dobney's efforts – the one meal donated by 61 Column as they awaited the drop promised for the next day. Nerves were frayed – local villagers were jumpy, claiming that the Japanese were near.

Sickness tightened its grip, with more cases of serious malaria and an outbreak of typhus. When the two Columns moved on to Nammun, east of Indawgyi Lake, a party of sick was left, waiting for an aircraft. One duly appeared but damaged its undercarriage on landing. The sick then had no choice but to attempt to catch up with the main body, marching without rations.

As they progressed under the Monsoon deluge, those who had suffered no stomach problems until that point now found their bowels turning to water. Many went on to develop dysentery. The sick and relatively fit together made the four-day march to the Indawgyi Lake area, where they confronted the last series of hills separating them from Blackpool Block.

———•◦•———

When White City closed earlier in May the Nigerians marched north. They reached Nammun, east of the Kyunsalai Pass, on 21 May (just after the Leicesters had beaten the Japanese to it). Subsequently, the 7 NR Columns helped 74 Column of the 7th Leicesters hold the pass against repeated Japanese attacks. At this point Lentaigne seemed unsure of how to use 14 and 3(WA) Brigades.[21]

When Chindit columns were mobile, rather than in the static or relatively static Stronghold or Block role, the Recce Platoon's expertise was fundamental to success. Lieutenant Peter Allnutt now led the Recce Platoon of 12 NR's 43 Column. When this Column left White City during the night of its closure, Allnutt's Platoon led the way. When 15 miles to the north they bivouacked for the day and waited for 12, the sister Column. Everyone was happy to be moving again, but Allnutt was cautious. The Recce Platoon pushed ahead but avoided all villages and trekked in river shallows much of the time, hoping to put any Japanese pursuers off the scent. On reaching the rendezvous on the third day, they settled down to await the main body. They would then strike north, towards Indawgyi Lake.

The Recce Platoon stayed with the main body during the following day, as other Columns were marching ahead of them. They continued to exercise extreme caution, walking in pebbly river shallows, but grew tired of climbing around gigantic boulders and waterfalls. Each detour meant climbing the shallower bank and this often consumed an hour. Just after midday, however, they entered a broad valley and called for a supply drop. They had to wait three days, as Monsoon cloud led to repeated postponements. The men felt starvation grip them. Some gathered jungle roots and attempted to make a meal by boiling them up. Bamboo shoots were very acceptable.

There was huge relief when they finally took a successful drop. The Recce Platoon then set out with five days' rations up. The going was difficult and slippery as they climbed a 2,000 ft gradient. This was followed by a wet, uncomfortable night on the ridge. The morning offered more of the same: slithering down the steep, muddy slopes, crossing the streams at the bottom and immediately beginning the next heart-pounding climb. They stopped for breakfast at 08.00. The Africans, adept at making fire in wet conditions, stripped off sections of wet tree bark and cut slithers from the dry wood underneath. The dry shavings were ignited under the shelter of their hats. Fires of this type would burn even in pouring rain.

The Recce Platoon became alarmed when they came across elephant tracks. This could mean a Japanese patrol ahead. The animals, however, belonged to some Kachins, who said they had seen no Japanese for weeks. Allnutt hoped for a clear run to Indawgyi Lake. The next challenge was a punishing 500-ft, near vertical climb away from the village. Peter Allnutt remembers that grim struggle through the morass:

'Water was rushing down after a recent cloudburst. Progress through the ankle-deep mud was slow and

tiring. We slung our weapons around our necks and hauled ourselves up by main force, using every bush or tree we could see. It took one and a half hours to reach the top. We practically had to crawl up in places.'

Having climbed another ridge, they could see the last hill barrier before Indawgyi Lake. Moving into the valley to bivouac, Allnutt made the second of his twice-daily reports to 43 Column. He was pleased to learn that a drop site had been selected. It was just before the last hill to be climbed. Unfortunately, a bad night followed and the Recce Platoon floundered in mud the following morning. The chaungs had flooded. One slip could mean death, with the victim pinned to the stream bed by the sheer weight of his pack. Some men died in this manner and even mules were washed away.

They turned east, moved out of the deep mud at the banks and waded in the river shallows. The rain stopped, the sun came out and conditions became unbearably steamy. His men were exhausted but Allnutt was determined to reach the rendezvous before nightfall. They arrived in the early afternoon, only to learn that bad weather had delayed the drop. Several Columns were in the vicinity, awaiting re-supply.

The Platoon had rations only for that day. They knew it was useless to attempt to live off the land. Allnutt never saw game in the jungle, although he had discovered that banana tree hearts are edible when boiled with soup powder; but that was it.

They then spent a miserable four days waiting their turn. Some of the time was spent clearing a light aircraft strip, for evacuating sick and wounded. Dysentery,

malaria and jungle sores took their toll, particularly among the Europeans. The subdued group of sick and wounded waiting by the strip continued to grow. Peter Allnutt:

'Some died but they were soon replaced by gaunt, ragged men emerging from the jungle, having dropped out from Columns days before. If a man could not march, there was nothing you could do for him. He simply had to drop out and hope for the best. Sometimes he would be found by the Japs. Or he would be found by the Burmese and hidden until more British troops passed that way again. Our Columns collected quite a number of men left behind from Wingate's first expedition. They had recovered and had lived with local villagers until British Columns were in the vicinity once again.'

With a successful drop behind them, 43 Column's Recce Platoon continued. The going was awful, with flooded chaungs now waist-deep torrents. One small Burmese, knocked off his feet, was saved by a grab from a quick-thinking African. There was a constant drizzle, with the cloud base virtually sitting on their heads.

Standing on the highest ridge, Allnutt looked across the valley to the river that debouched into Indawgyi Lake. Deep in the teak forest, the leeches had tortured them throughout the night. In the morning Allnutt was cheered by the sight of a group of Burmese carrying fish. Desperate for anything to supplement K-rations, the men soon changed their minds when the stink of rotting fish got into their nostrils.

Notes

1. Rooney. D. (1997), *Mad Mike*, 94–96
2. Towill, B. (2000), *A Chindit's Chronicle*, 89–90
3. Baty, J. A. (1979), *Surgeon in the Jungle War*, 88
4. Towill, B. (2000), 87
5. Ibid, 93
6. Larson, G. A. (2008), *Aerial Assault into Burma*, 192
7. Calvert, M. (1974), *Chindits: Long Range Penetration*, 114
8. Rooney, D. (2000), *Wingate and the Chindits: Redressing the Balance*, 186–187
9. Allen, L. (1986), *Burma: The Longest War 1941–45*, 367–368
10. Slim, Field Marshal Viscount (1999), *Defeat into Victory*, 275
11. Calvert, M. (1974), 116–118
12. Ibid, 124–125
13. Rooney, D. (2000), 154
14. Ibid, 131
15. Rhodes James, R. (1981), *Chindit*, 130–132
16. Mackay, Rev. Donald, 1st Cameronians, 'A Padre with the Chindits', *Dekho*, Autumn 2000, 20–25
17. Towill, B. (2000), 88
18. Miller, W.H., 2nd King's Own, *A Chaplain with the Chindits*, Imperial War Museum, 80/49/1
19. Graves-Morris, Lieutenant-Colonel P. H., unpublished MS (via Bill Smith and Corinne Simons)
20. Dobney, Major R.P.J. 'Paddy', unpublished MS, July 1981 (via Bill Smith and Corinne Simons)
21. Rooney, D. (2000), 173

ISOLATED AND OVERWHELMED

22–26 May 1944

'Some people were in a shocking state. Outside, I saw a Dakota make a low pass, dropping supplies. I saw the guy at the aircraft door. I was gripped by the thought that this wasn't going right. I said to myself: "If this is going bad, I want to be with my mates".'

Peter Heppell, 82 Column, 1st King's (Liverpool)

A BRIEF LULL in the fighting at Blackpool ended on 22 May, when the airstrip working parties came under fire. A large Japanese patrol was driven off, with 50 enemy killed. They returned in strength the following morning. Major elements of the Japanese 53rd Division reached Blackpool, bringing up anti-aircraft guns, field artillery and the much hated 150 mm mortar.[1] Blackpool's garrison now faced an all-out assault by 128th Regiment and 14 Brigade, 77 Brigade and the Nigerians were unable to get close enough to help.[2] 111 Brigade Commander Jack Masters still hoped 14 Brigade, at least, would be able to intervene.[3]

The King's Own had suffered severely in the Blackpool defensive position known as 'The Deep'. Having recovered, to some degree, following their relief, they took up a semi-floater role around 'Parachute Ridge' and adjacent features. Their job was to challenge Japanese units gathering to attack the Block. Richard Rhodes James, 111 Brigade HQ Cypher Officer: 'It was a very tricky assignment, especially in the rather involved topography of the area. It was something entirely new for us and the experiment was not an unqualified success. Even now we were still learning, but I am sure that the presence of that Battalion altered the enemy's plans appreciably.'[4]

The distribution of the Block's forces left the perimeter's southern sector lightly defended. It was assumed (wrongly, as it happened) that the enemy would be unlikely to attack up the steep slope from the airstrip. The Gurkhas manning the southern sector wanted to reinforce their weapons pits and improve head cover, but it was too risky to bring in heavy timbers through the forest of booby traps now rigged within the Dannert wire. The booby traps included 'Pineapple' fragmenta-

tion bombs, usually lashed to a tree at waist height, with a black, almost invisible trip-wire.[5]

Blackpool's guns offered no counter-battery fire as the Japanese guns could not be located. Richard Rhodes James described the growing concern as more mass attacks were thrown back:

The Gurkhas stood firm and fired back until the wire was strewn with bodies. The stream from which we drew our water was now in enemy hands but we found water elsewhere within the perimeter. Night after night the bombardment continued and Masters began to get anxious. How long could the troops hold out? They were in the last stages of exhaustion and now the enemy was closing in against the wire on every side ... It was our mortars, more than anything else, that kept the enemy back. All night they fired until their barrels steamed, pouring a continuous stream of bombs into the enemy as he formed up.[6]

The Japanese shelling grew in intensity. The enemy's anti-aircraft guns effectively closed the Dakota strip. Drops became far more dangerous, the Block's supplies dwindled and the wounded and sick could no longer be flown out. Lieutenant-Colonel 'Doc' Whyte, RAMC, struggled to cope with the constant stream of wounded. The Main Dressing Station received two direct hits from Japanese shells. The attacks became heavier and more determined and an assault across the airstrip forced the British Gunners to abandon the Bofors.

Peter Heppell, an NCO with the King's 82 Column, was wounded. The Sappers were on top of a ridge, looking down on the attacking Japanese and under mortar fire:

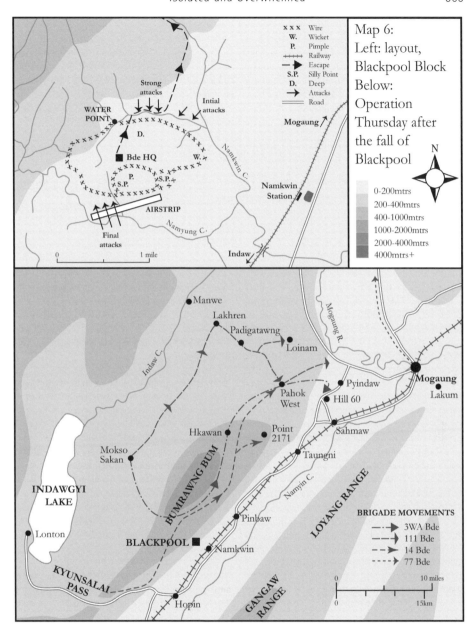

Map 6:
Left: layout, Blackpool Block
Below: Operation Thursday after the fall of Blackpool

'There was an almighty explosion from a mortar bomb. I was thrown back on the bank, with shrapnel in the left leg. The metal is still there. I felt relieved that the fragments had missed the three primed grenades in my pocket. I put a field dressing on my leg and hobbled towards the First Aid Post. I had just one thought in my mind: "The only way to get out of here is to walk." The most important thing was to avoid a leg or foot injury.

'Looking round, inside the Post, I saw that my problem was superficial. Some people were in a shocking state. Outside, I saw a Dakota make a low pass, dropping supplies. I saw the guy at the aircraft door. I was gripped by the thought that this wasn't going right. I said to myself: "If this is going bad, I want to be with my mates".'

Vickers gunner Frank Anderson, with the King's other Column, 81, also realised that things were going badly:

'Once we arrived at Blackpool we were, in effect, locked into the perimeter by strong Japanese pressure. We had nearly three weeks of fighting at Blackpool and things were very rough. We made widespread use of sharpened bamboo pangis, to help keep the Japanese out of our positions.

'A lot of men were killed by high velocity guns, mortar bombs and in hand-to-hand fighting. Around 200 of our men were killed in action at Blackpool. I saw a lot. I was detailed for many burial parties. The bodies were buried in shallow graves.'

Ronald Swann, RA, was Gun Position Officer with U Troop's 25 Pounders. He worried about the sharp decline in ammunition stocks as Monsoon weather and Japanese guns put a stop to the air drops:

'By 23 May, the day I was promoted to Captain, things became very tight indeed. We were virtually out of ammunition and food. What shells we had in the last day or two were dropped, four shells per metal case – some without statichutes as the planes were flying too low in the Monsoon conditions.'

The shelling was not entirely one-sided. The 25 Pounders continued in action. At 11.00 on 22 May No. 1 gun engaged a pinpoint target, a train towed by a motor vehicle. This received 55 HE rounds and was destroyed. Less than three hours later the guns engaged a convoy of six trucks, laden with troops and equipment and making for Kyagigon. They received 40 rounds of HE. Another worthwhile target soon appeared – a party of 50 Japanese and two heavy vehicles, towing what

appeared to be 105 mm guns. One gun unit was hit and the other retreated, with 46 HE rounds fired.

Masters imposed restrictions on 25 Pounder ammunition expenditure that evening. During 22 May U Troop's guns had fired nearly 200 rounds of HE. Nevertheless, during the night of 22/23 May the 25 Pounders fired on a convoy of 30 trucks moving towards Kyagigon. They received 28 HE rounds.

U Troop's War Diary then records the intensification of incoming artillery fire during the afternoon of 23 May. The Japanese now had at least two 105 mm guns, four 70 mm guns and heavy mortars.[7]

Corporal Fred Holliday, with the King's 82 Column, also worried about ammunition shortages:

'I don't remember feeling really hungry – I was probably too afraid. Conditions were appalling. As soon as you dug a slit trench it filled with water. I saw Masters occasionally. He'd walk around with a carbine on his shoulder and a couple of grenades on his chest. He certainly looked the part, but he had a lot to contend with. Firstly, he had chosen the site. He also knew that the weather wouldn't improve and that air supply was down to a trickle. As for me, I really began to doubt that we would get out alive.'

Some officers, including Bill Towill, disliked Masters (although his opinion may have been influenced by subsequent events). He described Masters as 'a far from happy choice' as Brigade Commander.

The heavy Japanese attacks resulting in the loss of the Bofors were launched on 23 May. Air supply broke down and Blackpool's ammunition stocks were not replenished. Rhodes James saw ammunition stocks fall to an all-time low: '... all day long the mortars continued to fire, until the stock of bombs diminished to a bare minimum. And now the enemy was attacking by day, bombarding, probing and wearing us out 24 hours a day.'

The aircraft returned for one last co-ordinated attempt: 'The dropping zone had now shrunk to a very small area, which made a difficult target for the Dakotas. They started their run-in from the west, coming in off the hills ... The Japs opened up with everything they had: small arms, anti-aircraft cannon and heavy stuff. The planes were a sitting target while they steadied for the drop and, below, we watched them anxiously.'[8]

Bill Towill also witnessed this final attempt to supply the beleaguered garrison:

'From the west three Dakotas came in low and flying abreast, holding their formation despite heavy AA fire. Passing just over us, the thunder of their engines *mingling with the yammering of the guns, they made a drop of supplies, but one of them was shot down and, sadly, most of the drop fell outside our perimeter and into enemy hands.'*

Watching the aircraft brought a lump to Towill's throat: 'By the time everything had been collected and distributed, we had just one meal per man and ammunition only for another 24 hours. We knew there was no possibility whatsoever of our receiving any more supplies.'[9]

Rhodes James watched as most chutes fell beyond the perimeter: 'They gave it out that there was no hope of getting any more. That day's supply drop had failed and further attempts would have no greater chance of success. Our casualties were mounting steadily and we had nowhere to take them ... The most serious question of all was how we were to get out, as it became increasingly obvious that we must either get out or perish.'[8]

The main Japanese attack on 23 May, made in Battalion strength, began at 18.00 and hit the relatively weak southern perimeter. The Japanese were beaten back but the pressure was such that every man was called back inside the perimeter. The defenders had consumed much of their remaining ammunition, and replenishment drops planned for the night of 23/24 May were aborted, due to the fierce enemy anti-aircraft fire.

23 May had been discouraging. The fighting began at 06.00, when elements of the King's 81 Column ran into a Japanese force and fought a three-hour engagement. The enemy continued to advance and 81 Column's floater Platoon was ordered to withdraw to the hill known as 'Whitehead'. 111 Brigade Commander Jack Masters had another 81 Column patrol positioned on the 'Greenoch' feature and a patrol of the Cameronians' 26 Column outside the perimeter in positions southwest of 'Pimple'. The enemy progressed and a Japanese Company dug in near 'Whitehead', covered by a second Company, machine guns and artillery.

During the afternoon the Japanese captured 'Pimple', which commanded the airstrip. Their attempts to push on to OP Hill failed, but the Japanese on 'Pimple' brought the features 'Point' and 'Extra Cover' under heavy mortar and machine gun fire. At 13.00 the attackers captured a mortar position between these features but a counter-attack pushed them back. At 16.00 Masters ordered an attack to clear 'Pimple' and 26 Column elements took the feature. Subsequently, however, the heavy shellfire forced them to withdraw.

By 17.00 the Japanese had advanced east along the ridge line, occupying 'Greenoch'. It was this that prompted Masters to call in all units still outside the perimeter. Their return was difficult. Units still outside

the wire included patrols from the King's Own's 41 Column, positioned to the north and east. They had failed in their attempt to capture 'Parachute Ridge' and were brought back in by Lieutenant-Colonel Thompson. The King's patrols were also called back.

Things deteriorated rapidly during the night. Japanese probing attacks on the western perimeter were pushed back but the enemy established numerous mortar and machine gun positions. These brought 'Fine Leg' and 'Square Leg' under sustained fire throughout 24 May. The defences continued to crumble.

Masters' report on Blackpool's fall clearly conveys the methodical way in which the Japanese set about breaking into and demolishing the defences. The entire Block was under incessant shelling from 07.00 on 24 May. According to Masters some 600 shells were fired into Blackpool during that day.

The Japanese Commander, Takeda, then ordered more attacks on the southern perimeter. Bill Towill: 'The night of 24 May was the very worst we'd experienced. All around the perimeter the enemy came at us again and again remorselessly and relentlessly, taking all the devastating fire we poured at them and still coming back for more. We were taking heavy casualties, but their casualties must have been quite horrendous.'[10]

Some of the fighting was desperate. Captain Whitehead's patrol had been relieved on the feature given his name during the evening of 23 May but then found they could not withdraw. They fought on until 17.00 the following day, completely surrounded, until the ammunition ran out. By a stroke of incredible good fortune, at that very moment a parachute container of ammunition – from a last-ditch drop by a single aircraft – drifted down and landed at their feet. The men continued to resist until dark. The 12 survivors of the 35-strong patrol then slipped through the Japanese positions, making for 'Basha Ridge'.

U Troop's 25 Pounders remained in action. The Troop Log records that two Japanese 70 mm guns were spotted on the edge of a wood, 300 yards from the OP south of 'Pimple'. They were engaged by 3 in. mortars and both were destroyed.

During that last night Masters ordered the positions held by the Cameronians' 90 Column, on the southern perimeter, to be reinforced. Attacks on the western perimeter had been beaten back and working parties were now attempting to repair the defences. Their efforts were hampered by lack of wire and booby traps. At 05.00 the Japanese seized 'Silly Point' by attacking from 'Pimple'. The Gurkhas at 'Silly Point', according to Masters' report, abandoned their positions. He was far more circumspect about the loss of 'Silly Point', however, in his compelling account of Blackpool's fall in *The Road Past*

Low pass: a Dakota running in over Chindit positions at Blackpool. (Captain Michael Williams, King's Own, via Ronald Swann)

Mandalay: 'I learned that the Japanese had got inside the perimeter, overrunning a post held by 3rd/9th Gurkhas. How it happened, no-one knew.'

The enemy advanced rapidly east and south as the defences progressively collapsed before them. A counterattack stalled around 400 yards north of 'Silly Point', with the attackers – led by Lieutenant-Colonel Scott and Lieutenant-Colonel Thompson – under intense machine gun, mortar and artillery fire.

The end approached. Masters' report stated: 'Enemy artillery, which was extremely well handled, continued to cause severe casualties.' The attackers held on to 'Silly Point', overran 'Point' and advanced on 'Cover' and 'Extra Cover', while keeping 'Fine Leg' and 'Keeper' under heavy fire. Indeed, the entire 'Keeper'–'Umpire' ridge now received a deluge of shells.

Masters' charge that the Gurkhas abandoned 'Silly Point' still rankles. Bill Smyly, 3rd/9th Gurkhas' Animal Transport Officer, offers his view on the loss of 'Silly Point':

'We were under very heavy attack and a report went out that we were overrun. Colonel Scott put together an ad hoc group of the King's and came to back us up. Sadly, some of my men thought they were being relieved and retired. They had been under attack most of the night and it was a reasonable idea. I suppose I was too interested in the battle to see them go.'

Others have more forceful views. According to the 3rd/9th Gurkhas' Adjutant, Bill Towill, Masters' allegation was 'totally untrue':

'The facts are that, to strengthen and back up the Cameronians, Jack Passmore and his D Company held that position. After some heavy fighting, the Cameronians received the order to withdraw and did so, but without telling Passmore, who was left with his men alone to defend the position. When eventually he did withdraw he was among the very last to do so. He had been wounded five times but still grimly held on and his heroism was recognised by the award of the MC. It shows the paucity of Masters' character that he could make such a fearfully devastating accusation against our Battalion without checking his facts.'

The 3rd/9th Gurkhas War Diary sheds little light on the controversy. The entries for 24 May and 25 May read:

24 May: Heavier shelling continued throughout the day and small enemy attacks had to be beaten off. Night attacks became heavier, especially on features in the area of Silly Point held by our composite HQ Defence Platoon. Rain and mud and the difficult [sic] of internal communications were two more very potent enemies we had to contend with. A supply drop at 19.00 hrs was especially welcomed,

as everyone was extremely short. Half these, however, landed in Jap-occupied area.

25 May: Very heavy and continuous shelling and mortar fire continued all through the night and morning. LMG and snipers created some casualties. Silly Point was evacuated at dawn under extremely heavy enemy pressure. Lieutenant Smyly distinguished himself in this action by closing with the enemy and doing considerable damage with hand grenades.

The King's Own War Diary gives a remarkably terse account of Blackpool's fall: '05.00. Under cover of heavy artillery fire, enemy attacks Block and penetrate our defences. Lieutenant F.L.O. Milnes is wounded. Lieutenant-Colonel A.W. Thompson, MC, is wounded while leading a counterattack.'

During those grim early morning hours 111 Brigade's Commander realised that his only hope of restoring the situation was a sweep clearing the entire southern perimeter. Masters also knew this would have no chance of success. Evacuation was now inevitable.

Bill Smyly was still fully engrossed in the fighting around 'Silly Point':

'In front of me one of the King's men was killed by his own grenade. He had a discharger cup on his rifle. He fired the grenade but it failed to clear a tree-top and slid back down the branches towards us. He ran to pick it up just as it went off in his hand. The man looked dazed, his hand in shreds. I shouted to him – nothing sensible, just an encouraging "Well done! Well done!" He came shambling towards me, climbed down into the trench and sat down on an ammunition box. There was a sort of rattling breath as he died with his eyes open, sitting on the box holding the rest of our grenades.

'Other men climbed out of the trench. We went on firing for perhaps 20 minutes. Colonel Scott then got the news that the Block was being evacuated and we withdrew. Everyone vanished pretty fast. There was no enemy in front when I left and I was with the last to go. There were some trenches in front of us and I wanted to be sure these were clear of Japanese before we attempted to leave. These were covered trenches but I managed to put a grenade in each one. I had a horror of covered trenches – you can't tell what's inside.'

Smyly received a Mention in Despatches.

The main Japanese force was positioned in a half circle around the Block. They kept up the pressure throughout 24 May and had forced the defenders to further deplete their already low ammunition stocks during the night of 24/25 May. The end came when the attackers smashed through the perimeter, consolidated on a small feature and then took the surrounding features, supported by a blizzard of artillery, mortar and automatic fire. The garrison's determined counterattacks failed, with heavy losses. The defenders noted that the Japanese had no qualms about shelling their own troops whenever a captured feature was in danger of being retaken.

Masters knew it was impossible to keep the Japanese at bay – even Brigade HQ was told 'Stand to!' Richard Rhodes James: 'Having failed to eject the Japs, without food and with sufficient ammunition only for another 12 hours' fighting and with no prospect of getting any more, with a large number of casualties and with no means of evacuating them, and with utterly exhausted troops, Jack Masters gave the order to withdraw.'[11]

The guns were under immediate threat. U Troop's War Diary records that as early as 07.00 on 25 May No. 4 gun pit was evacuated, its crew ordered to bring sights and firing mechanism to the Command Post. Within 30 minutes the heavy Japanese attack on 'OP Hill' broke through, 'Silly Point' was occupied and Lieutenant Large ordered 'temporary evacuation' of the entire gun position. The situation was very confused. During the move to Brigade HQ, U Troop's men came under shell, mortar and small arms fire. On arrival they had three men missing and another died of wounds. Captain Swann was wounded, together with 14 ORs. Ronald Swann remembers nothing orderly about the evacuation:

'I had every reason to be grateful that I had learnt some Urdu at OCTU. Gurkhas suddenly came over the hill in front of the gun position and one said to me: "Dushman hai, Sahib! Dushman hai!" ("the enemy is here"). In fact, an English Sergeant had just received instructions that Masters was closing the Block and that the troops were to withdraw. This came as a complete surprise to us, as we were still firing.

'Anyway, I confirmed the order to evacuate. We had no time to spike the guns. We just took the dial sights, clinometers, telescopes and firing pins as the Japanese opened a fierce mortar barrage on the centre of the Block. One or more of the guns might have been damaged by enemy fire at that point, but my memory is uncertain. The intelligence summary states that one of the guns was hit and suffered damage to tyres.

'Later, while in hospital, I saw Masters and told him no-one had warned us, despite my Command Post having a serviceable wireless. He said: "We just hadn't time to notify everybody." I thought this was a terrible admission.'

The four 25 Pounders were lost but their performance at Blackpool showed a handsome profit, as documented in the Troop Log. Ronald Swann:

'A good heavy mortar would have sufficed for the railway station, but we also shelled the Japanese at Pinbaw, hit an ammunition train, shot up lorries and troops massing for attack and destroyed road and rail bridges to the north and south of Namkwin railway station.'

Hundreds of men now started the long, difficult hill climb away from Blackpool as it was overrun. They soon came under fire from the much loathed 150 mm mortar. One of Ronald Swann's Gunners, Sammy Parsonage, was hit by shrapnel as a mortar bomb exploded:

'He gasped: "They've got me! They've got me, Mr Swann." I'm almost certain that what killed this poor chap would have killed me but for the fact that his body acted as a shield. Shrapnel must have come over the top of Sammy's body and it would have gone straight through my skull, but for the fact that I was wearing a steel helmet. As it was, the helmet had a quarter inch dent in it. Some fragments were shaved off the rim and caught my eyes. I carried on marching but could see only by looking up. Both eyes had haemorrhaged. The sight in the right eye improved a little after a few hours.'

Swann had a fragment lodged in the left temple. In addition, a 4 mm x 1 mm fragment penetrated the left eyelid. Travelling downwards, it lacerated the cornea and lens, coming to rest in the anterior fossa, 1½ in. below the left orbit. A large fragment pierced the right eyebrow, traversed the right orbit, bruising the globe of the eye and causing retinal and choroidal tears, with internal haemorrhages.

At 08.00 Jack Masters ordered the withdrawal of all sick and Brigade HQ. According to his report on the Block's fall, written three days later, the remains of the Cameronians' 90 Column and Field Artillery were then told to withdraw, although, in the latter case, this is disputed (and rather conflicts with Masters' subsequent response to Swann). Masters' report sketches out his 'plan' for withdrawal, although the men interviewed by the author had no sense of a plan being implemented. In any event, 90 Column was to leave first and closely picket the path near the Water Point for 600 yards. 'Basha Ridge' was already held as the second layback, with 41 Column elements in place as third layback. Subsequently, the wounded, sick, Brigade HQ and elements of other Columns would withdraw through them.

By 08.30 Masters had put Major Larpent in charge of the rearguard. The withdrawal had two phases: the first, to begin within 15 minutes, would involve positions on 'Keeper', 'Fine Leg' and 'Pavilion', followed by the remainder of the garrison, commencing at 08.55. Masters noted: 'This plan was carried out in the face of fierce enemy fire of all calibres.'

The nightmare of Blackpool's final days left an indelible impression on men's minds. Captain Miller, the King's Own Chaplain:

For three days the battle surged to and fro. At times it seemed to us that all hell was let loose – the inferno, the racket, the bloody death, the stern look on men's faces, the stench, the mud – who can forget such things?

In the early morning of 25 May Miller knew the end had come. When Masters ordered the evacuation, he and his Batman, Cook, got their kit together. Then the shell landed: 'A blinding flash, followed by a deafening explosion and our trench was filled with hundreds of flying, red-hot fragments of shrapnel.' The Chaplain felt blood trickle down his face. Fortunately, he'd just been scratched. Moving out, Miller heard a man in deep distress:

Climbing down, I found a young Cameronian who had caught the fearful blast ... for both an arm and a leg were practically severed from his body. The curious thing was that there seemed to be very little loss of blood. He was alive and calling desperately for a friend and for his mother. I tried to ease him but it was impossible to move him. A doctor coming down the path drugged him with morphia. He must have died shortly afterwards.[12]

With the decision now taken, the question was whether it was still possible to escape. Rooney wrote that the remains of 111 Brigade, 'men who had reached the limit of hunger and physical and nervous exhaustion, began a slow and painful withdrawal from Blackpool towards Mokso Sakan, which they had left just 17 days before.'[3] Mokso Sakan, east of Indawgyi Lake, was about 18 miles away.

According to Bill Towill, a gap in the Japanese encirclement had been discovered. There was still a way out through 'The Deep'. All heavy equipment and most of the mules were left behind.[13] The sheer numbers of wounded presented a serious problem. Towill described how the decision was taken to leave no-one alive for the Japanese:

Brief moments of comfort: tending the wounded. (Trustees of the Imperial War Museum)

'Those who had a reasonable chance of survival we took with us. There were about 60 severely wounded, on stretchers or pony-back, and a hundred walking wounded. Anyone who could possibly hobble along just had to do so. But some were in extremis, *were either already dying or very close to the end and would not be able to survive the long and hard haul over the mountains to Mokso Sakan.*

'It was quite unthinkable that these should be left for the Japs, who would have slaughtered them brutally, going out of their way to inflict the maximum suffering and humiliation. They were quite implacable, without a shred of compassion or humanity, and we knew of previous occasions when they had overrun our hospitals, butchering staff and doctors as well as sick and wounded. What could not be avoided had to be done and these desperately ill men, about 18 of them, were put out of their misery with a shot to the head, before the survivors left the Regimental Aid Post for the last time.'

Jack Masters:

A doctor spoke to me – 'Will you come with me Sir?' I followed him down the path. It was clear of moving men. The whole Block was clear, except for a part of

26 Column. A little way down the path, we came to 40 or 50 ragged men, many slightly wounded, who had carried stretchers and improvised blanket litters from the Main Dressing Station as far as this. Here they had set down their burdens and now waited, huddled in the streaming bamboo, above and below the path. I noticed at once that none of them looked at me as I stopped among them with the doctor.

The stretchers lay in the path itself and in each stretcher lay a soldier of 111 Brigade. The first man was quite naked and a shell had removed the entire contents of his stomach. Between his chest and pelvis there was a bloody hollow, behind it his spine. Another had no legs and no hips, his trunk ending just below the waist. A third had no left arm, shoulder or breast, all torn away in one piece. A fourth had no face and whitish liquid was trickling out of his head into the mud. A fifth seemed to have been torn in pieces by a mad giant and his lips bubbled gently. Nineteen men lay there. A few conscious. At least their eyes moved, but without light in them.

The doctor said: 'I've got another 30 on ahead, who can be saved if we can carry them.' The rain clattered so loud on the bamboo that I could hardly hear what he said: 'These men have no chance. They're full of morphia. Most of them have bullet and splinter wounds beside what you can see. Not one chance at all, Sir, I give you my word of honour. Look, this man's died already, and that one. None can last another two hours, at the outside.'[14]

Masters told the doctor: 'Very well. I don't want them to see any Japanese.' The Brigade Commander was then told that there was very little morphia left. He told the doctor: 'Give it to those whose eyes are open.' He heard the shots as he went back up the ridge.

Blackpool's last hours were a torment of heavy rain, mud, shelling and the constant explosion of mortar rounds, made worse by uncertainty, confusion and a rising sense of being trapped, with no way out. Cypher Operator Norman Campbell, with the Cameronians' 90 Column, describes how he became aware of the evacuation:

'We had occupied Blackpool Block for 17 days and on the eighteenth day I was sent to Brigade HQ with a message. Expecting to return to my position I took only my carbine and four filled magazines in my pockets. Message delivered, I was told not to return as the Block was being evacuated. I was ordered to help carry a wounded man on a stretcher. I took the front and we slithered and slid down the muddy track. At one point I began to lose my grip and called for a halt.

'That pause kept us alive. A mortar round almost immediately fell a few yards ahead and killed a West African soldier. It blew him to pieces. The boots remained, with his feet inside. His head was close by, on the track. I had his blood on my face. I remember thinking how big a human head looks when detached from the body.'

Frantic efforts were made to find more stretcher-bearers. All the fit men of U Troop – the 25 Pounder crews – were mobilised to help carry wounded. Life or death was a roll of the dice as the men left the Block. Bill Towill and the 3rd/9th Gurkhas received no briefing:

'We were just told to leave and we were among the very last to do so. I found myself marching, just behind the Colonel, down a shallow, jungle-covered nullah. To my left, just below the height of my shoulder, the jungle gave way to a flat, open clearing – perhaps a hundred yards or more wide – before, on the far side, the jungle-covered slopes took over once more. Across that clearing, right out in the open, many of our men were marching in extended order. I remember vaguely thinking that, with the enemy all around us and so close at hand, this was unwise. Why had they not followed the usual infantry practice of making use of all available cover?

'Suddenly, all hell broke loose! In what was obviously a carefully coordinated operation, several enemy machine guns and a number of mortars simultaneously opened fire from the ridge behind us, bringing down a devastating volume of fire on the men crossing the clearing. In a trice, what had been a peaceful scene was turned into one of carnage, with men hit and others lying still in death.

'About 30 yards out, in the open, we could see our Cypher Sergeant and the Colonel and I dashed out to give aid. Ignoring his call – "Leave me, Sir, I'm done for!" – we each looped one of his arms around our neck and dragged him back to safety, under intense fire but, amazingly, without getting hit ourselves. He had been badly wounded in the groin. Once back in cover, our men readily made an improvised stretcher for him, using bamboo and a groundsheet. Months later, back in camp, I came across him hobbling around, delighted that we had not left him to his fate.'

Blackpool's fall was sudden, traumatic and bloody. Each death would become a family tragedy. 81 Column Vickers gunner Frank Anderson:

'When we had to go we left several wounded behind. They were just lying there, on the ground. They included my friend, George Charnock. George was a nice fellow – we got on well together. He was in our Mortar Platoon. He had been bayoneted and was dying when I left his side. I got a letter from his parents, who knew I had been with him. I couldn't go and see them and I couldn't even bring myself to reply. I knew I would break down if I visited them. I just couldn't face it.'

Mrs Charnock sent her letter to Frank Anderson in response to a brief note from him. The letter, posted in Manchester on 5 September 1945, is still in Anderson's possession. It is short and extremely poignant. Typically, it raises the possibility that George Charnock could have survived as a prisoner. It asked Frank to get in touch with the MO and ask whether he stayed with George or had to leave him. The letter adds: 'I know George was brave. I have a son to be proud of. I see George as plain as anything in my mind every night and he looks so peaceful.'

The King's survivors included 82 Column NCO Peter Heppell. He struggled to keep moving, having been wounded in the leg. This caused his family terrible anguish:

'Later, unbeknown to me, I was reported wounded and missing. My family was informed and I was only able to reassure them some time later. They suffered great distress. I remained lucky during Blackpool's evacuation. We were told to leave our big packs and take as little as possible. We began to advance along the long track to the perimeter. Some men had been left on stretchers. They pleaded with us as we walked past. Beyond the outer perimeter the open ground we needed to cross was under fire. One of our men was killed while carrying a box of K-rations on his shoulders. We got mixed up and I found myself with the MO's party. That's how I got involved in carrying stretchers. I also carried several rifles.

'At the top I looked for my Section but went on alone. I came across an RAF Sergeant to one side of the track. He had a wounded foot and he was crawling. He muttered that I should go on. I told him that the MO's party was coming up and left him to be in their care. Still carrying several rifles I caught up with the Column. I was challenged for the night's password and didn't have a clue. I found the Sapper section on top of a hill, sitting in constant drizzle.'

Some men found an iron resolution to live. The RAF Sergeant seen by Heppell was not the only man crawling on the track. 46 Column Recce Platoon Commander Captain Neville Hogan:

'At one point I heard screaming – the incoming Japanese were bayonetting our wounded on the other side of some bashas. I saw remarkable things. One King's Own Sergeant Major, CSM Robson, MM, was hit in the ankle. He was determined to live but refused to be helped. He took off his boots and socks, wore them on his hands and then moved off on his bum. He survived Blackpool.

'I was close to Colonel Thompson when he was shot. I think he was hit in the collarbone. I helped carry him out on a stretcher. My Orderly was with the stretcher party. He only knew one hymn: "Nearer my God to Thee". He could sing, hum and whistle it. We climbed ever higher. At one point, on his stretcher, the Colonel asked my Orderly to be quiet, on the grounds that we were now 4,600 ft high and it would be difficult to be nearer to God.'

90 Column's Norman Campbell also carried a stretcher during the escape. By the time he was relieved of stretcher duty his party had come down off the hills. They were on the flat, facing half a mile of open ground virtually devoid of cover. The hilly, well wooded ground opposite seemed a long way away:

'There was no pause. We moved as quickly as we could, with repeated "splats" as bullets hit the wet ground.

That didn't worry us too much. We didn't think much of Japanese marksmanship. Then they started shelling. The shells exploded behind us, but got nearer each time. We hurried on towards the treeline. We then found a series of abandoned Japanese slit trenches. Had these been occupied, every Chindit at Blackpool would have been killed or captured. A dozen Japs and a few machine guns would have finished us. As it was, we escaped in a sort of Burmese Dunkirk, but Eddie Walsh was among the many who didn't get out. I believe he was lost during the evacuation.'

Bill Smyly's group, unlike Bill Towill's party, did not come under fire as they left the Block:

'I came across eight men attempting to carry a man on a stretcher. The ground was thick with mud and they were slipping and sliding all over the place. I watched as the wounded man tumbled out and fell heavily to the ground. He was screaming, not loud but in agony, in a way I can't describe. His arm had been blown off and the top of his shoulder gone. There was another officer there. I suppose we should have told the men to move on, or what to do, but it didn't work like that. What actually happened is easier to understand than to explain in words.

'In war, accident or emergency, it is physically difficult NOT to do anything for an injured person and to "walk by on the other side". They have a claim on you. However, with the threat of Japanese behind and no clear instructions ahead and no place to take him to, the men at the ends of the stretcher had a great desire for someone else to take over. Here were two officers and the men around the stretcher melted away. The casualty was ours. Well, you can't just leave him! I took the back end of this heavy stretcher and the other officer took the front and we carried him down to the bottom of the hill. Here we put him down.

'The wounded man was a Scotsman. He was in deep shock and trauma, probably feeling little pain. I knelt at the head of the stretcher and spoke to him. I asked him where he was from and said he would soon be back there. He was on his stretcher, looking up at the sky. I was at his head, kneeling to talk to him. I shot him in the middle of the forehead. It was the way we shot the mules. I closed his eyes.'

The author asked Smyly whether he had killed a man before:

'Well, there was that Japanese officer with the sword. I think I got him and I fired a lot of rounds at shadowy figures on the hill.'

The author then asked whether, in the general confusion and danger of Japanese pursuit, it was a question of choosing between one life saved — possibly — at the risk of placing at least four more in jeopardy?

'No. You may say that and it may be true, but if I said that I would be making excuses. The fact is that what I did was part of General Orders. I didn't have orders to kill but General Orders made the notion possible and, at that moment, I think I felt there was nothing else to do. I couldn't, at that time, just stand up and walk away. The Japanese were regarded as merciless and not prepared to accept the wounded, who would most likely be the target of atrocities. In the first show it was general policy that wounded were left behind. Here, it had been decided not to leave our seriously wounded to fall into Japanese hands.

'I'm not trying to blame anyone else but I think the decision was wrong. This is something I have always regretted. If our positions had been reversed, I would not have wanted a young officer to make that kind of decision for me. I am also sure that those horror stories about the Japanese were exaggerated. Yes, there was a chance that the man could have been taken and tortured, but I doubt it. We now know that the Japanese did take prisoners. He might have had a chance.'

In a note to the author concerning the fate of the gravely wounded, Bill Smyly added:

'Walking out of Blackpool past the stretchers of people we were leaving behind was probably the most harrowing memory any of us can remember and I don't suppose anyone wants to talk about it. I had never spoken of it except to another officer who had the same experience, but when you asked the question there wasn't any way around. Maybe it was time to tell.

'What I now guess is that Wingate himself had a similar experience in Ethiopia. That was when he got the idea of LRP. His tactic with us, I think, was to raise the shocking possibility so that it would be present in our minds as an option if the situation should arise. You will find some accounts that Medical Officers were asked to kill off the seriously wounded who had been taken to the First Aid Post. I don't believe it. In each case, the decision must have been individual — not general. But the possibility was in one's mind when faced with impossible alternatives. An officer who can't make up his mind is no longer an officer and, of course, that could be an option too. Just collapse. Faced with two impossible alternatives, I suppose one's training slants one towards one option or the other.

'When he met Roosevelt in America, Wingate's first and most important request was for light planes to pick up the wounded and I don't think he was concerned only with saving their lives. He would have been much more concerned with the mental well-being of his whole Force. When you see a man wounded, the urge to do something is overwhelming. Abandoning him is an offence to one's nature.'

To this day Bill Smyly wonders how they got out of the Block:

'It was a miracle. Perhaps the Japanese didn't want to chase us too closely. They may have lost quite a number themselves. I don't know how many there were; they came after us with little rising sun flags. The way through the tall grass was lined with abandoned stretchers — the wounded looking up at us, expressionless, as we walked past and abandoned them. You could see the flags behind you, coming through the grass. Thinking of it now, those in pursuit were more like dogs driving sheep than victors with their blood up and out for slaughter.

'I don't think anyone has ever explained how we got out so lightly. We made our way through tall elephant grass, on flat ground, with the little Japanese flags above the grass, about 60 yards back. They kept their distance. Then we had to climb the open base of the foothills and they let us go. Not a shot. I don't remember any firing. Why didn't they fire on us? Getting out was a kind of miracle. Once we were in the hills and the trees again, the Japanese didn't follow.'

Many men achieved wonderful things on this day. The 3rd/9th Gurkhas' War Diary, for example, records the resolution of the wounded and their comrades. It remembers Rifleman Jagat Bahadur of D Company, who carried Rifleman Moti Bahadur on his back for over three miles.

U Troop's war diary for 25 May includes a crisp entry for 16.00: 'Reached night RV 92C 109235. Rations exhausted.'

The escape from Blackpool required a gruelling climb of over 3,000 ft, an effort beyond the capabilities of some men. Writing of his departure from the Block, Richard Rhodes James said:

There came a parting of the tracks, one leading through some tall grass to the left of a cluster of bashas, the other going across the paddy to the right of the bashas. Not knowing where I was going I turned left. This was the most fortunate decision of my life. Few of those who turned right survived that day. And so we kept going. From the paddy the track went up a slope so steep that we had to crouch on our hands and knees. The peculiarly oppressive heat of that day, combined with the accumulated weariness of weeks of fighting, reduced us almost to helplessness, and that short slope cost us a lot … Finally, at the top of the slope, the path levelled off into the jungle and there was silence. The noise of war floated away and we were at peace. We had escaped the inferno and it was now just a terrible dream.

Rhodes James was among the many asking themselves why the Japanese had allowed them to escape:

By all the rules of war we were doomed, surrounded by an enemy 2,000 strong, who were fresh and determined. For two weeks we had beaten them off and could fight no more, defeated by our own system of war. When our fighters and bombers failed to turn up the enemy emerged and was free to roam at large. When the weather broke and the supply planes could only come by day, our days were numbered … We were faced with the alternatives, either to break out into the valley or escape into the hills and the peaceful seclusion of the Indawgyi Lake. To attempt the first would have been suicidal and the second could easily be countered. There was one main path out of the hills, which we took, a Brigade in single file, and the enemy allowed us to escape along that track, albeit at a cost. Perhaps it was a miracle; these things do happen and it would be rash to assume that the hand of God was not with us that day.[15]

'Why did the Japs not attempt to follow us up? Having let us escape they might yet have caught us on the long trail up the mountain. We were entirely defenceless, having so many wounded to attend to that we had few men to fight, and those who were not on the stretchers were in no mood for anything except the steady plod to freedom. The enemy, if he had wished and so decided, could have wiped the Brigade off the map.[16]

The march to the Mokso concentration area involved immense suffering. Rhodes James: 'Rations were almost non-existent and a collection was taken to provide for the wounded. Meals had to be reckoned, not in cartons, but in single biscuits and half-tins.'[17]

The Gurkhas at the lake brought supplies to the top of the pass, together with medical stores and parties of stretcher-bearers. Meanwhile, the survivors continued the terrible climb. 'Some walked who should never

have left a stretcher, bandaged and with expressions of terrible resignation on their faces. One RAF Sergeant, I remember, who had been badly wounded in the head, tottered up the path with eyes that pierced you through with their pain. This man died walking halfway to deliverance on that rain-drenched mountainside.'[17]

Blackpool's survivors may have been fewer without a determined rearguard. Private Jim Unsworth, with the King's Own's 46 Column:

'My Platoon was the last to leave our part of Blackpool's perimeter. We were the rearguard – 10 men under Major Openshaw. There was a Japanese quick-firing gun on a small overlooking hill. Openshaw was told to take his 10 men and silence that gun. We went up the hill and found a good position. I was told to go back and report. I was about to leave when heavy firing broke out. Our lads were giving them something. Suddenly, I heard a Japanese bugle sound the charge and all hell broke loose. Then it went quiet and the Major told me to go further up the hill and take a look. I had almost reached the top when I began to hear voices around me. I sat under cover and listened to the Japanese. I had the strong feeling that a large force was close by. They made enough noise for a Battalion. I returned along the narrow track, to find only two men still with the Major. I told Openshaw that we had to get out. The Block had gone.

'We began the steep climb away from Blackpool. Luckily, the Japs were very slow on the uptake. If they had followed, they would have killed us all. I had had no food for a long time – many days. Strangely, you get used to not eating. We struggled up that jungle hill and eventually reached the top during the late afternoon. I was helping a chap who had been wounded in the side.'

Jim Unsworth handed over his charge at an Aid Post. Blackpool's survivors made contact with the West Africans near the top. They found the going a little easier nearer the summit, thanks to the Nigerians' efforts to cut steps into a steep, muddy slope. Unsworth had his first meal for a long time. He was given just one K-ration packet:

'I didn't think we'd get away with it, as we were the last two of the rearguard and my companion had been hit. To this day, I don't know who he was but, wounded or not, he still had his pack and rifle. I sat in that Aid Post all night, trying to shelter from the heavy rain. At first light I then set off for the very top.

'Openshaw and the rest of the rearguard were already descending the hill. They stayed in an area of level ground that next night. When I arrived, Openshaw

told me there was no food but he had ordered a mule to be killed. I couldn't chew the meat. During the following day we continued down and eventually entered Mogaung valley. When we stopped that night, our Medical Officer told us to take off our boots and wash our feet, ready for inspection. I remember him reaching me and saying: "What nice little feet you have! Have you had any problems?" I said I'd had a few blisters but, otherwise, they were OK.

'We progressed along the valley and stopped for the night near the halfway point. There was thick jungle to either side of the dirt track. I walked off the track to relieve myself and got a fright. There were bodies all over the place ... just skeletons. Row after row. They must have been Japanese.'

The tensions of the past few days began to surface. Jim Unsworth had an uncharacteristic row during the march:

'We were going up a steep hill. The going was very wet and boggy. I saw a man lose his temper with a mule. He began raining blows on it with his rifle butt. I said I would do the same to him unless he stopped. Then an officer came up and warned me that he'd put me on a charge if I didn't let it go. I had grown very fond of the mules. Many survived Blackpool, as they were moved into safe harbour before the heavy battles began.'

Unsworth had a second brush with authority on the march. Even today, 65 years on, there is a hint of resentment at a long-standing injustice:

'We were high in the hills when we stopped for a 10-minute halt. There was a small waterfall close by and I walked over to fill my bottle. Later that day, in night harbour, the Column Commander sent for me and another lad. We were told we had disobeyed orders by getting water. He asked: "How do you plead?" I said I had filled the water bottle but that I had understood that we should take every opportunity to do so. The officer ignored that and asked: "Will you take my punishment?" I then received five days' Royal Warrant – loss of five days' pay, including my wife's money. He left us with a parting comment: "Do it again and you'll get more!"

The Brigade rearguard also included elements of the King's 82 Column. When the time came to leave, Corporal Fred Holliday's Section passed the Main Dressing Station, where the seriously wounded would remain. It was a traumatic leave-taking:

'We followed each other blindly. It wasn't quite "every man for himself", but it was fairly close to that. Where men were leaving without officers or NCOs, discipline was a problem. We were lucky as we reached a rendezvous established by Scottie. It was then a case of onwards and upwards. It took four or five days to get up into the hills and reach safety. Linking up with the Nigerians gave us a real boost, after crossing that terrible country.

'Along the way we heard rumours that the seriously wounded and dying at Blackpool had been shot. We didn't believe this and were really shocked when Captain Woodburn confirmed this had happened. I kept marching towards Mokso but I was really done for. I'd had enough. All things considered, my health had held up well. When we finally reached Mokso, we had a wonderful mug of tea. I was surprised to find that many men had dumped even their essential equipment – including mess tins.'

Bill Towill and the Gurkhas took up a rearguard ambush position. They were to protect the Brigade rendezvous, about three miles along the Namkwin Chaung – now in spate and flowing fast and deep:

'I lay with my men, just inside the edge of the jungle and keyed up for the arrival of the Japs, tense in the sudden silence. There was no sound whatsoever, apart from the rushing water of the river and the incessant rain on the foliage above our heads. After all the fury and pandemonium of the last few days, it was difficult to get used to the stillness. We were very hungry, having had no food for the last couple of days and no prospect of any, since all that we'd had had been given to the wounded. We were cold, chilled through and through by the ceaseless rain. We were plastered head to foot in mud and utterly exhausted, but we were ALIVE and reasonably fit, when so many of our comrades were now dead.

'The Japs did not put in an appearance so, after a couple of hours – time enough for our men and all the stragglers to get clean away – we eased ourselves out of our positions and followed where our men had gone. Not long after, the track left the chaung and began climbing the hillside in the direction of Nawku. We bumped the end of our survivors and found that they had bivouacked for the night. They had no food, but Steve Smele had a mug of hot water, which he kindly shared with me. The rain was still teeming down. It was very cold and we sat on the ground, in the mud, back to back, with a blanket over our heads to give a little protection and induce a little heat and prayed for dawn.

'The next day we continued over the mountain range to Mokso Sakan and Indawgyi Lake. The going was really tough. We were up to the top of our boots in mud most of the time and it was exceedingly difficult to keep your footing. We struggled on with the sweat dripping steadily from the tips of our noses, grabbing at branches to support and help us up.'

Donald Mackay, the Cameronians' Padre, described the evacuation of Blackpool as 'not easily forgotten'. There were many heroes among the wounded: 'Men walking in constant agony, with severe chest wounds, broken arms, wounded legs and feet. On and on they went, in the pouring rain, and on we herded them – for it was all we could do – on to the mountain where safety lay.

During the second night of this struggle to safety it rained very heavily as night fell. Mackay wrote: 'There was a tropical thunderstorm, followed by heavy rain all night long. Sleep was impossible and my Batman and I sat huddled together beneath a torn gas cape, shivering and groaning occasionally to release our feelings.' A makeshift Field Dressing Station had been set up in a nearby ravine:

> At first light I staggered thankfully to my feet and looked down the slopes to the rocky platform on which the FDS was perched. The rain was still pouring down pitilessly. The frail bashas had all collapsed. Among the wreckage, half-covered by leaves and sodden blankets, muddy and motionless, lay the wounded. Fires and a hot meal were impossible. We drove them into motion.[18]

When Masters realised Blackpool was about to be overrun, he gave the order for withdrawal without official approval, but he had been given some discretion to act independently in extreme circumstances. He exercised that freedom, hoping that approval of his decision would be forthcoming.

Ironically, Lentaigne visited Stilwell's HQ at 09.00 on 25 May, just one hour after Masters gave the order to evacuate Blackpool. Unaware of the turn of events, Lentaigne sought Stilwell's permission to give Masters more flexibility – a green light to withdraw 'if, in his judgement, lack of ammunition and supplies made it likely that the garrison would be overrun.'

Initially, Lentaigne had to content himself with Boatner, Stilwell's Chief of Staff. Boatner took Lentaigne's proposal to Stilwell and returned half an hour later with a 'questionnaire'. Stilwell didn't bother to greet the Special Force Commander in person!

This charade continued for hours. Replies to the now irrelevant questionnaire were typed and Boatner took them to Stilwell. Lentaigne did not get to see Stilwell until 13.15; they talked for 45 minutes. Stilwell said he needed half an hour to make up his mind, adding that he wanted to know what 111 Brigade would be doing to continue to block Japanese lines of communication if Blackpool was abandoned. Lentaigne asked for a decision by 14.30. In the event, permission was given grudgingly, only after more discussion, at just before 16.00. Stilwell stressed that permission was given only with great reluctance. He then took the opportunity to imply that 111 Brigade and other Chindit formations had under-performed. Even 77 Brigade was included in this accusation. By the time Stilwell relented, the Japanese had already taken Blackpool. The garrison's survivors were attempting to escape with their lives, having been forced to shoot the wounded who could not be moved. One British veteran told the author, with the utmost sincerity, that he would have welcomed an opportunity to shoot Stilwell.

The West Africans made a tremendous contribution by improving the track in the final stages to Mokso and in receiving and assisting Blackpool's traumatised survivors. Lieutenant Larry Gaines of 6 NR's 66 Column remembers that 8 Platoon set up a block to prevent any Japanese advance on the pass, while 6 and 7 Platoons worked on revetting and building steps, to allow men and mules to negotiate the final stretch of track to Mokso:

'Jap artillery could be heard shelling the Block and the going got worse. Virtually every yard of track had to be revetted and mule loads were manhandled up the steepest sections. Masters was informed of our Column's difficulties and slow progress. We were virtually out of rations and two Platoons went to Nawku Pass, to block the tracks from the south and take a major supply drop.'

The first survivors began to reach 66 Column after a punishing forced march from Blackpool. This was a patrol led by Major Reece of the King's Own's 41 Column. Intelligence Officer Lieutenant Bill Cornish noted: 'It consisted of two British officers, 10 British ORs, one Gurkha and one African. They were in a bad state of exhaustion and some were wounded. Major Reece reported that the Block had fallen and that he had been sent on ahead to warn us. Not long after, the rest of the garrison began to come through. They were a pitiful sight, ragged, tired, dazed, they staggered up the track. The worst cases followed at the end. Two Platoons of Gurkhas protected their rear. The force consisted of the remnants of the following Columns: 48, 41, 46,

81, 82, 90 and 93. They bivouacked up the track to the west of the Column. There was not much we could do for them except carry the stretcher cases, for we had no food to give them. That night our QQ [request for an air drop] was accepted for 08.00 on the 27th.'

The surviving Gunners of U Troop reached Mokso Sakan at 13.00 on 28 May. Over the next few days the Troop's 14 wounded and five sick were evacuated by light aircraft and flying boat from the 'Plymouth' base established on the shore of Indawgyi Lake. Ronald Swann, wounded in the head and eyes, was flown out by light aircraft on 30 May.

Masters' report to Lentaigne is dated 28 May 1944. It reads: 'My casualties 08.00 24 May to 08.00 25 May were, I estimate, 120 killed, 60 wounded, 30 missing. Japs about 350 killed.' With the shock of the collapse still raw in his mind, he then blamed the Gurkhas:

I much regret I was unable to carry out your orders to hold Blackpool until further orders. My failure was due in the instance to the desertion of Silly Point by its garrison, but I feel that its fall could not have been long delayed, in view of:

1. No floaters
2. No food
3. No ammunition
4. No D A S
5. Considerable casualties and no replacements.

He added: 'I wish to bring to your notice the fact that all comds, offrs and British tps under my comd behaved with the most superb heroism it has been my privilege to witness. Since then, the courage and endurance and cheerfulness of these men, particularly the wounded, has been beyond all praise.'

The agony of Blackpool's fall remains raw in many minds, over six decades later. Bill Towill made a bitter observation: 'The strong, wide-ranging and most effective Commando forces deployed at the White City, or their equivalent, were totally absent and we were to be left by our General, who had not even visited us, or the other two Brigades, to sink or swim on our own.'[19]

Rooney commented: 'It is true Masters suffered with his men and, afterwards, his descriptive ability told their story to the world, but at no stage did he admit that his decision where to site Blackpool was a blunder.'[20]

77 Brigade Commander Michael Calvert's views on Blackpool's fall may have been coloured by his dismay at being ordered to close White City: 'In the light of events it seems certain that it would have been best to have held White City, which was established and not near the fighting front, with the aid of all the Chindit

Brigades, rather than try to establish a new Block in the face of the enemy.'[1] This observation, of course, does not address the point that the Japanese were circumventing White City, so reducing its effectiveness. It also largely implies the sacrifice of Chindit mobility.

Calvert, in many ways the ultimate Chindit fighting commander, went on to pay a heartfelt compliment to 111 Brigade: 'Masters and his garrison did magnificently under appalling conditions. It was to Masters' credit that he held out so long. The [Japanese] 53rd Division lost over 500 casualties.'[1]

According to Calvert, Masters 'showed a great example by his rapid march to install the Block, arriving there first with his Brigade HQ and then gathering the rest of his Battalions around him.' Calvert also had views on the siting of Blackpool:

111 Brigade had not the advantage that we had had of rehearsing our installation of White City before we flew in ... We had been fortunate in that the Japs attacked White City with too few and too early, in their overweening belief in themselves. Jack Masters was attacked strongly almost as soon as he had arrived. He had been given the task of forming a Block between certain limits, whereas I had been able to choose, in my reconnaissance from the air, practically any place between Hopin and Indaw.[21]

Equally, Calvert had no doubt that Blackpool was too close to the enemy's front:

It will always pay greater dividends if the penetrating force cuts the enemy's communications many miles behind the enemy's own reserves. He must then either move his reserves away from the main battle, to free his communication, or draw troops from elsewhere, both of which can be easily resisted.[22]

On 26 May, the day following Blackpool's fall, Stilwell's anger at its loss was probably aggravated by other unfortunate developments. The Japanese had reinforced Myitkyina and ejected the Marauders and Chinese from the town's western district. Merrill's Marauders were spent. Stilwell needed fresh, experienced infantry, but he ignored the British 36th Division, available to fly into Myitkyina airfield. He preferred to put together a scratch American force with little or no infantry fighting experience.

Rooney described this as a 'disgraceful decision', adding: 'Had Myitkyina been captured as soon as the airfield fell – as it so easily could have been – many of the traumas and sufferings of 77 Brigade, 111 Brigade and Morris Force would have been prevented.'[23]

Chiang Kai-shek pulled the strings behind Stilwell's back. Chinese divisional commanders were told to go slow until the outcome of the Kohima struggle became known. Chinese Divisions in the Salween sector were inactive due to the threat of a Japanese offensive in Central China. Chinese inactivity greatly reduced potential returns from Chindit operations against the lines of communication serving 18th and 56th Divisions. Takeda's 18th Division, with orders to hold Kamaing, was reinforced by two Battalions from 56th Division (Salween) and two more from Indaw (available following White City's closure). By mid-May Chiang Kai-shek gave the go-ahead for an advance south. This was the background to the wasted opportunities when Myitkyina airfield was captured.[24]

It was also the backdrop to the subsequent sufferings of Morris Force, which had successfully disrupted movements on the Bhamo–Myitkyina road. Stilwell held back the Marauders to give the Chinese a chance to take Myitkyina before it was reinforced. When they failed the consequences included an urgent order, on 24 May, for Morris Force to take Waingmaw, on the Irrawaddy's east bank, opposite Myitkyina. Stilwell had refused a Morris Force offer to take this town five days earlier. Now, once again, it was too late.[25]

Boatner told Brigadier 'Jumbo' Morris that there were 'practically no Japanese' at Waingmaw and at Maingna, to the north. In the event, Morris Force's 40 and 49 Columns ran into strong Japanese defences at Waingmaw. They inflicted heavy casualties on the enemy, but persistent flanking moves forced them to withdraw. Boatner ordered another attack that night. 40 Column was thrown back into the fight but gave ground in a counter-attack. This left another Column's flank exposed to a series of fanatical attacks. Morris ordered a light aircraft strip to be cleared, to fly out the wounded. The Brigadier then crossed the river to meet Boatner. Typically, Boatner claimed that Morris Force lacked courage. Morris responded with an offer to cross the river and assault Myitkyina. Once again, sensitivities concerning the Chinese led to this offer being refused.

Savage fighting was to follow in June for the Morris Force Columns. The southern route to Waingmaw was blocked. Morris then considered attacking Maingna, following yet another Stilwell 'attack at all costs' signal. 94 Column approached Maingna and killed some 90 Japanese in Houla village on 11 June, but were then attacked in turn by Japanese from Maingna.

The Gurkhas had few officers left, yet put in another attack on Maingna. 40 Column reached the town centre, where they were joined by another Column and were eventually fought to a standstill. The Gurkhas consumed over 950 3 in. mortar rounds in just 24 hours.

At the beginning of June Boatner – true to form – blamed Morris for the Chinese failure to capture Myitkyina, alleging that this was due to the Chindit failure to take Maingna. Stilwell removed Boatner and his successor, Brigadier-General Wassels, ordered Morris not to re-enter Maingna.[26]

———————

As for 14 Brigade, the York and Lancaster's 65 Column reached Nammun on 23 May, undetected by the enemy. They moved into a derelict Japanese camp, consisting of a group of bashas. Nammun's Headman sold them a skinny bullock but, somehow, the animal escaped before it could be slaughtered. The Column remained meatless but successfully traded statichute cloth for rice.

65 and sister Column 84 had been earmarked for the floater role around Blackpool. In heavy Monsoon rain and with thick mud underfoot, they advanced along the Indawgyi valley's swampy tracks, then climbed the steep hills towards the Block. They knew every hour was precious. As the men struggled up the muddy hillsides, they suddenly received news that it was all too late – Blackpool had fallen.

They turned back and headed for the Kyunsalai Pass area. The Japanese wanted the pass to reinforce Kamaing against the advancing Chinese. The Chindits wanted the pass to prevent the Japanese securing the Indawgyi Lake area and threatening the evacuation of wounded and sick. 84 Column was to block the Zigon track, east of the pass. 65 Column was told to move to the south-eastern area of the lake. The Japanese called up reinforcements from Hopin and 74 Column, in turn, was reinforced by 3(WA) Brigade elements. The pass was heavily booby-trapped and the surrounding hills occupied. Concentrating forces in such terrain, with the Monsoon now in full swing, proved no easy matter.

The men of 84 Column staggered in deep mud and forded a long succession of swollen streams, now waist-deep. The rain was so heavy that it was impossible to cook food. A waxed K-ration carton gave just enough flame to yield a hot drink. The sick were in dire straits and animals began losing condition at an alarming rate. Clusters of leeches adhered to legs and underbellies.[27]

84 Column Administrative Officer Paddy Dobney remembered one particularly horrific night storm:

> The lightning was so intense the jungle was illuminated for long seconds at a time, so that it was possible to see the nearest soldiers sitting on their packs, their groundsheets over their heads, looking in the electric flashes like so many giant mushrooms in the forest. In the flashes the mules could be seen standing (they never lie down), heads down in

abject misery as water bounced and poured off their shaggy coats ...

Movement was unthinkable; to try to walk five paces would have been impossible, for one would have been knocked to the ground and nigh drowned. The temperature dropped and we shivered in misery. Through it all, our exhausted, sick men, some with raging temperatures from malaria, somehow survived the night.[28]

The rain eased after 12 hours of cloudburst conditions. Much of 84 Column's equipment, stores and weapons had been swept away and scattered in the deluge. The men searched for their missing kit before resuming the march. In due course they reached the village they had left just four days previously. One track led to the pass, where the Leicesters had won the race to the summit, and 84 Column's Battle Group climbed to the hilltop five miles distant. Dobney's party stayed near the village, to arrange supply drops and bring up supplies. Meanwhile, 65 Column headed towards the lake, to help prepare a reception area for wounded and sick.

Paddy Dobney moved his heavily laden mules forward the next day. They entered the pass 'block' — a network of defences manned by units from six Columns. They were still digging in as Japanese pressure increased. Dobney got Lieutenant-Colonel Graves-Morris' permission to visit Company Commander Peter Vasey. His men had repulsed continuous attacks in a very isolated position forward of the main defences. Their trenches were very shallow, dug only with machetes, mess tins and bare hands. Picks and shovels had been requested for the next supply drop. After a chat, Dobney began reading a four-month-old *Daily Mirror* when mortar bombs suddenly began to fall. The three regular occupants of the trench filled it completely. Dobney felt vaguely embarrassed as he flung himself full length on top of Vasey.

The Japanese attacks intensified. Dobney heard the Leicesters' Colonel call for one of his fighting Platoons to move up the hill and challenge the Japanese, who could be seen moving down. It seemed a good time for the mules to leave and make the five-mile return trip. Dobney found Philip Graves-Morris, carbine over his shoulder, and told him he was leaving and would return with more supplies. When they reached the water point to the rear of the block, firing broke out down the track. The Japanese had worked their way around the back and had cut the incoming track. Dobney was worried. Darkness was fast approaching and he had to get back, to load more supplies for the next morning's trip. Then

someone said the way was clear. The Japanese were still there, however, and opened fire on Dobney's men and animals at only 40 yards range:

> There was only one thing to do – move quickly. Shouting to those just behind me to double, I broke into a trot. The soldiers needed no urging and, for once, the mules, free from their loads and sensing they were heading home, joined in the spirit of the affair and we thundered down the track in great style.[28]

There was plenty of firing but Japanese marksmanship against this dream target was atrocious. Everyone, human and animal, came through unscathed. Animal Transport Officer Frank Luxa was ready for Dobney when he arrived. Luxa then asked to take the convoy up in the morning. Dobney agreed but warned him to come off the track where the enemy were positioned, but Luxa ran into the Japanese – who had remained on the track – and took casualties as they moved into the chaung. Luxa received a bullet wound in the thigh. It had passed straight through and he made a good recovery after resting the leg for a couple of days.

Lieutenant Ronald Bower, MO with the Bedfordshire and Hertfordshire's 16 Column, was based at Nammun. He described the conditions around the pass as 'rather like trench warfare'. He saw many cases of trenchfoot, jungle sores and 'mud rash'. Bower ran an improvised 'hospital' dealing with around 20 wounded and sick at a time. Most were men with malaria, typhus, oedema of the legs and jungle sores. New cases arrived from the fighting area every day.[29]

Lieutenant Bower may have been short of many things but he would not run out of quinine. The Battalion had captured one of the largest dumps destroyed by any Special Force unit during the campaign. This dump had a very extensive medical store and the haul included a hoard of three-quarters of a million quinine tablets.

With Blackpool gone, Brigadier Calvert's 77 Brigade now faced the daunting task of taking Mogaung. On 21 May the Gurkhas had reported 4,000 Japanese in heavily fortified positions around Mogaung. To make matters even worse, Blackpool's loss allowed 53rd Division elements to further reinforce the town. On 27 May Lentaigne, stung to some extent by Stilwell's verbal abuse following Blackpool's fall, ordered Calvert to take Mogaung regardless of the scale of opposition.[30]

Notes

1. Calvert, M. (1974), *Chindits: Long Range Penetration*, 118
2. Allen, L. (1986), *Burma: The Longest War 1941–45*, 360
3. Rooney, D. (2000), *Wingate and the Chindits: Redressing the Balance*, 141–142
4. Rhodes James, R. (1981), *Chindit*, 138
5. Towill, B. (2000), *A Chindit's Chronicle*, 91–92
6. Rhodes James, R. (1981), 139
7. War Diary, U Troop, 160th Jungle Field Regiment
8. Rhodes James, R. (1981), 140–141
9. Towill, B. (2000), 93
10. Ibid, 94–95
11. Rhodes James, R. (1981), 142
12. Miller, W. H., 2nd King's Own, *A Chaplain with the Chindits*, Imperial War Museum, 80/49/1
13. Towill, B. (2000), 97–99
14. Masters, J. (1961), *The Road Past Mandalay*, 258–259
15. Rhodes James, R. (1981), 144–146
16. Ibid, 148–149
17. Ibid, 147
18. Mackay, Rev. Donald, 1st Cameronians, 'A Padre with the Chindits', *Dekho*, Autumn 2000, 20–25
19. Towill, B. (2000), 90
20. Rooney, D. (2000), 137
21. Calvert, M. (1973), *Prisoners of Hope*, 160
22. Ibid, 164
23. Rooney, D. (2000), 187
24. Calvert, M. (1974), 121–122
25. Ibid, 124–126
26. Ibid, 126–127
27. Graves-Morris, Lieutenant-Colonel P.H, unpublished MS (via Bill Smith and Corinne Simons)
28. Dobney, Major R.P.J. 'Paddy', unpublished MS, July 1981 (via Bill Smith and Corinne Simons)
29. Bower, Lieutenant Ronald James, RAMC, memoir, Imperial War Museum, 80/49/1
30. Rooney, D. (1997), *Mad Mike*, 94–96

22

MOKSO SAKAN – THE RALLYING POINT

27 May–1 June 1944

'What really helped me was the strong inner belief that I would get out. I knew I was lucky. I had a strong constitution, despite the malaria and weight loss.'

Frank Anderson, 81 Column, 1st King's (Liverpool)

ON 28 May, as 111 Brigade's Jack Masters prepared his initial report to Special Force Commander Joe Lentaigne on Blackpool's fall, his sorely tried command continued the trek to Mokso Sakan. The plan was to withdraw around Indawgyi Lake's southern shore, with 14 Brigade holding the Kyunsalai Pass, 6 NR's 66 Column holding the Nawku Pass and 39 Column making for Lepon, to seal the tracks from Mokso to the pass. 111 Brigade would then pass through Lepon to Lonton, to be joined subsequently by 66 Column, with 39 Column bringing up the rear. The wounded and sick would be evacuated by Sunderland flying boat from Indawgyi Lake or by light aircraft operating from Mokso's strip.

These plans were implemented. 66 Column secured the Nawku Pass and patrolled the surrounding tracks. 39 Column covered the hill tracks from Mokso to the Kyunsalai Pass and 14 Brigade held the pass itself against the Japanese. Masters, however, expected that things would get worse. There were already around 350 wounded and sick requiring evacuation. Their numbers increased at an alarming rate after two weeks of Monsoon rain and little or no food. The men were also short of arms and ammunition; many heavier weapons had been left behind due to a shortage of mules. Morale had reached a low ebb.

Nevertheless, the Chindits remained aggressive. On 27 May, 77 Brigade blew the railway in three places north of Taungni. 14 Brigade patrolled vigorously, tightening its grip on the Kyunsalai Pass. Yet, Stilwell, as always, was dissatisfied. On 26 May he queried Morris Force's failure to reach Waingmaw, opposite Myitkyina. Lentaigne attempted to explain that they had been caught on the wrong (south) side of the Namtabet River. Stilwell then complained about the 'slow progress'

of 3rd/9th Gurkhas' recce of Mogaung. He ordered 77 Brigade (less 81 and 82 Columns, now with 111 Brigade) to advance and take the town.

───※───

Masters had the foresight to establish a safe haven for 111 Brigade – an area where the Columns could rally and recuperate. 30 Column (3rd/4th Gurkhas) had remained at Mokso Sakan, just over four miles from Indawgyi Lake. Most of the mules stayed with them. Experience at White City was still fresh in everyone's mind: shelling had killed a large number of mules.[1]

According to Slim, Blackpool had succeeded in 'cutting the enemy's main line of communication at a critical time.'[2] Yet wider political and strategic issues, at the Stilwell/Lentaigne level, were of no interest to thousands of men still locked into personal battles for survival.

Captain Miller, the King's Own Chaplain, was lucky to escape Blackpool, having been wounded. He and his Batman, Cook, had carried a stretcher on the steep, muddy path out of the Block. They reached open ground at the foot of the hill and crossed this area under fire. They arrived at the chaung, where efforts were made to organise parties for the long climb to safety.

During the march to Mokso Sakan the Senior Medical Officer asked Miller to establish a 'Rest House'. They drew water from a stream, built a fire and brewed tea for the steady stream of wounded passing by. Miller and his helpers manned the Rest House for three days.[3]

The men on the track to Mokso included Cameronian Norman Campbell. Somehow, he and a dozen others from 90 Column became separated from the main body after leaving the Block. They struggled on alone for five days: 'All I had was my carbine and four magazines, but not a crumb of food. The others were in much the same state.'

Many men were already in very poor condition due to weeks on a near starvation diet. Blackpool's survivors were weak and debilitated; most were ill and traumatised by their experiences. Heat exhaustion could be deadly in these circumstances. Any sudden chilling of the body, as a result of resting in wet clothing during a cool night, was especially dangerous.

Lieutenant Denis Arnold, MC, Platoon Commander with 7 NR's 29 Column, was among those suffering extreme hunger:

'The jungle was unfriendly from a food point of view. At one stage I attempted to eat a kind of root and the results were severe. K-rations were generally satisfactory but lacked bulk. There were not enough free drops of onions and potatoes. We craved vegetables. Some willingly traded the pork loaf in the K-rations for fresh vegetables.'

It was remarkable how individuals fared so differently on the same meagre rations. Denis Arnold lost a great deal of weight yet his close friend, Bob Walsh, seemed almost to thrive on that hard diet.

Norman Campbell's health was good, given the circumstances. He had no malaria and was free of dysentery. He had a sweat rash and two unpleasant jungle sores on his legs caused by cuts from his Dah, made when the big knife slipped while cutting bamboo. His greatest discomfort was prickly heat. The hunger grew steadily worse and he began to fantasise about food:

'I disliked K-ration cheese and deposited around 12 tins in a slot cut into the wall of my slit trench at Blackpool. I thought about that cheese many times over during the march. I was like a car with a duff battery that would no longer hold a charge. Fortunately, water wasn't a problem. We took water from fast-running streams. As a general rule, if a stream ran quickly, the water was probably safe to drink. I never bothered with purifying tablets, but I had one nasty surprise. I was wading along a swift-running stream, against the current. I took a drink, rounded a sharp bend and saw a dead horse, half-submerged and just ahead of me.'

Crossing flooded chaungs posed obvious risks, but there were other, background dangers such as the risk of leptospirosis – caused when floodwaters wash urine from rat-holes in the banks.[4]

The animals were also starving. Many men greatly admired the mules' ability to carry on. Bill Towill:

On hardly any feed at all and just what we could forage from the jungle, they kept on and on, valiant and stout-hearted to the end. Occasionally, you would see them in a 'light-hearted' mood, cantering away, bucking as they went, scattering their loads in all directions and dragging their cursing Muleteers around on the end of their bridles as if they were no weight at all.[5]

Starving men began to long for despised K-rations: 'There were times when we starved for days on end and then longed for our hated rations again.'[6] Towill records a bizarre incident:

I recall one day when our general discomfort was increased by an attack from hornets. I took a swipe at one ... it rewarded me by stinging me between the eyes. The poison it injected must have been of a particularly virulent kind ... my face and eyes were so badly swollen that I could hardly see.[7]

Shrapnel had done more permanent damage to Captain Ronald Swann's eyes. He left the Block with his Gunners in the early morning of 25 May, helped along by one of the Sergeants as, at this time, he had only partial sight in the right eye. They marched continuously towards Mokso for 15 hours, with breaks every two hours. They halted for the night at 20.30 and the MO gave Swann cocaine in both wounded eyes, together with two Sulpha tablets. The following day they marched continuously for 10 hours. On 27 May they reached Mokso at 16.00, at 3,700 ft., continued on and reached Mokso Sakan at 13.00 the next day. Ronald Swann:

'We would never have got up that final hill without help from the West Africans. They revetted the upper slopes and put in bamboo treads, which stopped us slipping back in the mud. We were extremely hungry but when I met the Africans they were no better off. In fact, I gave away half of what little food I still had from my emergency rations.

'Eventually, we reached the hill crest at Mokso, overlooking Indawgyi Lake. On that hilltop we took a free drop of bullock carcasses and we roasted the meat, barbecue fashion. After that feed, we went down to Mokso Sakan, on the lake edge. I was classified as a priority for evacuation, due to the state of my eyes.'

Ronald Swann was flown out from the light plane strip at noon on 31 May:

'The L.5 could take two walking wounded and a stretcher case, or two stretcher cases. I couldn't see

much and the American pilot chatted continuously as we flew over the hills. His repeated comment "Japs are down there" was less than comforting. We assumed light gun or machine gun fire would hit us but we landed unscathed at Shadazup's 156 American General Clearing Hospital an hour later.'

Swann was seen by Major H.J. Scheie, an American surgeon, and received immediate treatment to the right eye.

Many men were in desperate straits as they approached Mokso. Bill Towill's group reached safety at the top of the peak and then headed down to Mokso Sakan:

> We had been without rations for five or six days and were literally starving. Our men employed their jungle lore to gather edible roots and bamboo shoots. We butchered one of our mules but, even in death, the poor animal proved recalcitrant! Our teeth literally bounced off the meat and we might just as well have been eating the sole of an old rubber boot.[8]

Norman Campbell struggled on the final leg to Mokso:

'Each day my strength ebbed away a little quicker on the march. Luckily, we found the main body again on the sixth day. We stood there, stark naked, and dried our clothes by a fire of sodden bamboo. I reported to Captain McLean. Typically, when he found I had nothing other than a carbine, he cut his own blanket in two and gave me half. He also gave me some of his very small store of food.

'Morale was as good as could be expected. As the march continued, we had reached the point of having absolutely nothing to eat. One of the mules paid the price. My mucker, Frank Hunt, had been a butcher. He got on with the job of skinning and jointing the sacrifice. I got some liver and an unidentifiable chunk of meat. It helped keep body and soul together, but I never ate mule again.'

82 Column NCO Peter Heppell, at the outer limits of endurance, also found himself eating mule:

'I don't know whether it was the cold or the aftershock, but I was shivering all over. We had very little to eat but made a fire for tea. Some men cut banana leaves and we huddled together in the mud, under the leaves. They put me in the centre, to try to stop that awful attack of trembling. I must have slept eventually. The morning was cold and miserable; we collected water from the hollow where our cooking fire had been and used it to make cha.

'Even at that point I never doubted I would get out, but there are long blanks in my memory. Others have since told me that they experienced similar blank episodes. I think you are too busy to worry in such extreme situations. All you care about is putting one foot in front of the other. We arrived at Mokso Sakan and did our best to recuperate. We had little food and it was decided to kill a mule. I had mule stew – it was horrible, like meaty leather. For a vegetable, I cut chunks from the centre of banana trees. They looked and tasted rather like rhubarb.'

Bill Smyly offers another vivid account of the trek to Mokso:

'Much has faded in 65 years but some things stand out. We had wounded with us. We had lost a lot of our mules in the shelling and some loads had to be jettisoned to let wounded ride bareback. When men fell, their weapons were abandoned. I picked up a Tommy gun, which I carried for the rest of the campaign.

'The trail of men was strung out over the hills. There was the regular Chindit headache when walking single file: men and mules had to queue up before each obstacle while those ahead got over it and, then, when each man and his reluctant mule had negotiated the obstruction, they had to race to catch up. The people leading the Column showed little mercy. They took their regular marching halt of 10 minutes in the hour, while those at the back spent their whole day either queuing or racing to catch up.

'I was Column Marshal, which didn't mean very much, but I thought it my job to do something about this problem. All Animal Transport Officers had to patrol the Column, getting up to the front when they could and then standing to watch it all go by. One of my tricks, when I sensed a particularly long hold up, was to order a group in the standing queue to fall out and sit. I would give one man a cigarette and say: "We won't move till you get to the end of that."

'There is a friendly way of smoking in India. You grip the fag, or "birri", between the third and fourth fingers and suck through the fist. This, for those who are used to it, mixes smoke with air, as in a hookah. And, as with a hookah, you take your puff and pass it on. So, four or five soldiers would squat down together and set to work on my cigarette. Then we would move on.

'On one occasion Jim Blaker's C Company came storming through. Blaker didn't see me and thought my men were malingering. Well, that was one thing he couldn't stand and he shouted at them as they sucked away, obediently obeying orders and trying to get through "Smyly's obligatory rest period". I interrupted

Lifesaver: the seats used occasionally for carrying wounded or sick unable to walk. Few mules were available during the withdrawal from Blackpool. (Bill Smith)

quickly and deflected his wrath on me, but Jim Blaker wasn't a man one argued with. It was a general rule in the Army that "if you can't explain in three words, best not try." I didn't but I think he got the message. He was always very nice to me after that.'

Most Chindits fighting exhaustion, starvation and disease were in no doubt about the debt they owed the West Africans. Lieutenant Peter Allnutt, with 12 NR's 43 Column:

'It is estimated that, but for this timely help, half of those who got out of Blackpool would have died trying to get back over the mountains.'

Over six decades later, many Blackpool survivors find warm words for the Nigerians waiting for them at Mokso. Neville Hogan, Recce Platoon Commander with the King's Own's 46 Column:

'Thank God for the West Africans and the steps they cut into the top of that steep, muddy hillside. At the same time, the steps were huge and many of my men were just 5 ft tall. We had to pull each other up the revetments. At the end of it all, on reaching Mokso Sakan, a service was held on 29 May by Rev. John Matthew, a Karen. The sermon had an appropriate theme: "If God be with us, who is against us?"'

Hogan's health had held up well. He started out fit and strong, with a reputation for sleeping like a log:

'One night I heard my Orderly mutter to someone next to him: 'My Thakin (officer) – he can sleep through anything and he is always hungry.' As the campaign continued after Blackpool, however, I developed typhus, malaria and pneumonia.'

Yet Neville Hogan never lost his manners. On entering a village he knew to be free of Japanese, he walked into a hut and found rice in an earthenware pot hanging from the ceiling, safe from the rats. He took the rice and left a gold sovereign in the pot, by way of payment.

As Blackpool's survivors continued to reach Mokso Sakan, the meagre food supplies available were distributed. After provision for the wounded, each man received two K-ration meals.[9]

By 30 May work was progressing to establish flying boat bases, to evacuate wounded and sick from Indawgyi Lake. There were two bases: 'Dawlish', in the north, and 'Plymouth' in the south. The plan to use Sunderland flying boats had been prepared during the first week of May, as a contingency should the Monsoon break before ground contact with the Chinese was established. There was no area near the lake suitable for a Dakota strip. On 31 May 111 Brigade was given the task of protecting the northern half of Indawgyi Lake until all casualties were cleared. 14 Brigade had similar responsibilities for the southern sector of the lake, together with orders to undertake limited offensive action in the Mogaung valley.

The Blackpool survivors were reorganised at Mokso Sakan. The King's 81 and 82 Columns became a

Sending a QQ: a King's Own Wireless Operator at work, requesting a supply drop. (Trustees of the Imperial War Museum)

composite 81 Column. The King's Own's 41 and 46 Columns became a composite 41 Column. The Cameronians 26 and 90 Columns became a composite 26 Column. A very large supply drop was requested, not only for desperately needed food but also to refit and replace the heavy weapons lost at Blackpool and during the subsequent march to Mokso.

Bill Smyly and the 3rd/9th Gurkhas were cheered by a curious incident at the end of their struggle to Mokso:

'As we came into the rest area, where the whole Brigade was to take a supply drop, there was a familiar sound. The Cameronians were ahead of us and it sounded like pipes. I thought one of the Jocks must have brought his bagpipes. It turned out to be a Sikh Havildar playing us in. We didn't have any Sikh units with us but he may have been a dresser in the Indian Army Veterinary Service. There he was, all smiles, with his tidy beard and his chanter. When the badly mauled Cameronians reached the rest area he 'played them in'. It was an inspired gesture. Smiles and shouts from the Jocks! A very happy end to a long day.'

The eagerly awaited supplies were dropped to the Brigade. The Cameronians reaching Mokso Sakan included Norman Campbell. Captain McLean's Batman had flown out sick and Campbell was asked to take his place:

'I would not have accepted this but for the fact that Captain McLean had been so decent to me. I was happy to do that for him. Many weeks later, when I got back to India, I found he had left me a note of thanks and 150 Rupees. That was typical. He was a thorough gentleman. I did the cooking for both and, on one occasion, we enjoyed a memorable meal of chicken – purchased from a Burmese villager – and captured Japanese rice.'

Patrolling around Indawgyi Lake was difficult and dangerous for men in such a poor state. Bill Towill:

'We were enveloped in mud. You would be struggling along with a very heavy pack on your back and with mud and water halfway up to your knees, when your leading foot would enter a void and you would go face down in the mud and have, with a great struggle, to pull yourself to your feet again. You had stepped into a hole made by the foot of an elephant as the animals passed that way! If we went up the hillside a little, we could often see them away in the distance.

'On one occasion I was sent out with a very small patrol, just four of us, to make contact with our forces on the other side of the lake. This meant going to the northern edge of the lake and crossing the river running into it. This proved very difficult, as we immediately

entered a vast area of 12 ft high elephant grass. We had to use the trails made by animals. With the sun totally obscured, there was nothing to help us navigate but, eventually, we made it to the river. We found a boat and paddled across, driving before us a huge fish. One of my quick-witted Gurkhas whipped out his bayonet and skewered it. Our task completed, we started back but had to bivouac overnight. This caused great alarm at HQ and they were getting together a strong fighting patrol to come out and look for us.

'At about this time I noticed that some British troops were dying. They weren't wounded or suffering from any illness, so this was very puzzling. I asked our MO what the trouble was. He said the men had suffered more than they could take and, so to speak, had "turned their faces to the wall" and given up on life. This is some measure of what we had endured, for, surely, life is one of the most precious things we struggle to preserve. For months we carried on with no prospect of relief, when relief had been promised after three months. Clearly, in such conditions, psychological health is just as important as physical health – the determination to win through to the end, come what may.'

The rest at Mokso Sakan was all too brief. The Cameronians of 90 Column resumed their march, setting off up the valley to Lakhren. Some men, including Norman Campbell, benefited from the successful supply drops:

'We received American jungle hammocks. What a joy! It was sheer luxury to lie in your hammock, with the rain pelting on the canopy and not a drop reaching you. The mosquito netting zipped up and we listened to the frustrated mozzies trying unsuccessfully to get at us. I had a few good nights' sleep.'

On the quality of the drops, 111 Brigade's Richard Rhodes James wrote: 'A supply drop was always judged by the "chucking out" and the criterion was how many chutes landed in the dropping zone in one run. The first American planes to arrive impressed us considerably in this respect, delivering some very "tight sticks"[10] Meanwhile, some men were still surviving on mule: 'The broth ... was delicious.'[11]

On the night of 31 May/1 June the men of 7 NR's 29 Column were operating in the Kyunsalai Pass area. They were encouraged by a successful action that killed 23 out of a party of 30 Japanese signallers. A patrol followed a telephone wire and surprised the enemy. Lieutenant Denis Arnold was decorated for an act of cold-blooded bravery. The events that led to the award

of the Military Cross began when he was summoned by Column Commander Charles Carfrae:

'There was always a slight feeling of apprehension whenever you were sent for by the Column Commander. The conditions in the pass were unpleasant and constant heavy rain turned the track into a quagmire. We sent patrols to look for a Japanese presence in the area. Charles told me to take a fighting patrol up a steep hill, of about 4,000 ft, overlooking Nammun. We set off on the track towards the pass, with dense jungle to either side. My job was to follow a Japanese telephone wire, discovered earlier.

'I was some way in front of the Platoon, following a slope, and had almost reached the top when I realised that just three or four yards away was a slit trench accommodating four Japanese and a machine gun. I stopped and realised that all four were asleep.'

In an account (*Some Recollections of my Army Service*, Imperial War Museum, 99/21/1), Arnold described what happened next:

In essence, I made a simple plan, split the Platoon in half, one side (left) under Sgt. Umoru Numan, the other (right) under European Sgt. R. Keevil. Both NCOs were splendid, brave men, soldierly and willing. It seemed at the time that the best way to start the attack was for me to advance up the hill again, with the flank parties more or less in line with me, and hoping to find the Japanese once more asleep. I would then proceed to shoot the occupants in the slit trench, which, of course, would be the signal for an all-out attack from the flanks.

Over 60 years later, Arnold told the author:

'I then turned round, walked straight back, shot all four Japanese and threw a grenade into the trench. For some reason I felt no fear. In fact, I felt no apprehension at all.'

The Platoon then took the Japanese position on the crest. Arnold's bravery was recognised with an immediate MC.

On 1 June Morris Force attacked Waingmaw, as ordered by Stilwell. They forced some Japanese bunkers and beat off counterattacks, but withdrew when their ammunition ran low. Meanwhile, in the Kyunsalai Pass, 14 Brigade and the West Africans continued to cooperate. Captain Dick Stuckey, Staff Officer with 12 NR's 43 Column, changed roles when Rifle Company Commander 'Mac' MacKenzie was wounded. Stuckey took over:

'At one stage I accompanied Lieutenant-Colonel Pat Hughes on a visit to Tom Brodie, commanding 14 Brigade. They were protecting the evacuation of sick and wounded from Indawgyi Lake by holding the Kyunsalai Pass. Brodie said things were going well. His men were keeping the Japs out of the pass but they couldn't shift one particular Jap Platoon, who were determined to die for their Emperor. Their positions had been mortared and bombed from the air but nothing could persuade them to leave. Hughes offered to help and Lieutenant Hayden was briefed. His Platoon attacked the hill and the Japanese soon took flight. Thinking about this afterwards, I suspect the Japanese were surprised and alarmed at their first encounter with black soldiers. They took to their heels when confronted with the unexpected.'

The York and Lancaster Columns, 65 and 84, were among the exhausted defenders of the pass. Their intended role as floaters at Blackpool had been overtaken by events. When the Block fell, they were ordered to turn about and make for the pass. They now found the going even harder as the numerous chaungs had swollen into torrents. Then, during the night of 27 May, 65 Column's night bivouac was flooded out by a tidal wave of water. Battalion Commander Philip Graves-Morris: 'The men spent a miserable night soaked to the skin, sitting on their kit on the highest level ground, swathed in their dripping groundsheets.'[12] On reaching the pass 84 Column contributed to its defence, while 65 Column made for Lonton, on the lake's western shore, to help prepare for Sunderland operations. Nammun's Dakota strip was now waterlogged and unserviceable.

84 Column occupied positions at the pass on 28 May, while the 'soft skin' elements made for Nammun to collect rations. Every spare pony was sent to Mokso Sakan to help carry wounded stragglers still coming in from Blackpool. On arriving at Mamonkai, 65 Column began work on 'Plymouth', the southerly lakeside evacuation base. 84 Column elements blocked the Zigon track east of the Kyunsalai Pass. A Japanese patrol set off a booby trap and the Chindit positions came under shell and mortar fire, followed by three attacks. All were beaten back with fire from four Brens and a Vickers. The Column took several casualties – lack of tools had made it difficult to dig in.

Rations arrived from Nammun, brought up by escorted mule convoy. The water point was a stream a mile behind the block on the track. Japanese snipers forced the convoys to 'run the gauntlet' as they passed the water point, moving at the double round what became known as 'sniper's corner'. There was persistent Japanese sniping during the fighting in and around the pass.

Defences in the pass were reorganised on 31 May, to improve the chances of holding a major assault. Small parties of Japanese continued to probe the Chindit positions. During the following day 84 Column's ration party was ambushed, pinned down for two hours by automatic fire. Subsequently, all ration convoys moved only at night.

The Japanese continued to probe for weaknesses in 84 Column's defences. On the left flank an attack on 5 Platoon was thrown back and further attacks were also repulsed. Fires were banned due to the close proximity of the enemy. It was then decided that 65 Column should relieve 84. That Column's Battle Group had fought in trenches for five days and nights. Knowing they were about to be relieved, Paddy Dobney made a second visit to the pass. He was glad to see that their slit trenches had been deepened. These men were at the end of their tether and one individual was caught asleep with the nearest Japanese just 50 yards away. He agreed to be flogged.[13]

14 Brigade's HQ was at Nammun. Everyone understood the importance of holding the Kyunsalai Pass, the lifeline for Blackpool's wounded and sick, now making for Indawgyi Lake. The Japanese tried to squeeze the Chindits out of the pass but failed, paying a heavy price. The York and Lancaster defenders were tired and desperate for relief. 12 NR's Columns, 12 and 43, now took their turn. Lieutenant Peter Allnutt, with 43 Column's Recce Platoon, made the most of two days' rest near Nammun. His Platoon seized the opportunity to bathe in the clear, swift-running river. Allnutt is among those who remember their introduction to American jungle hammocks with great affection:

'Those hammocks were magnificent. For the first time we slept dry and clear of the ground. Without them, I doubt whether we could have survived the rest of the campaign. Many lives would have been saved if we had been given hammocks early on.'

Peter Allnutt reported to 14 Brigade Commander Tom Brodie. On their third day in the area they moved into Nammun village and assumed responsibility for defending a section of the pass. As Allnutt's Platoon took up their positions, the rain fell in a solid sheet and the 'road' became a stream:

*'We crossed a bamboo bridge at the foot of the pass. One member of a bedraggled group of British troops at the bridge described what awaited us: "Its f****** awful. There's Japs all around you. You can't move anywhere without one of the little bastards having a pot at you. 'Ave to keep your 'ead down all the time. And the bloody*

foxholes are full of water. Every hour or so they open up with mortars. Yesterday they had snipers overlooking the water point and got a couple of our boys. I'm glad to be out of it and I don't envy you, chum! Still, all the best!" He grinned and trudged on through the rain. "Cheerful sod!," I thought.'

Peter Allnutt didn't like the look of things. The upslope 'road' looked particularly uninviting. To one side, a precipitous, bush-covered bank disappeared into low cloud ahead. On the left was a drop of several hundred feet into a rocky valley, with a mountain torrent at the bottom. They knew there were snipers at the water point ahead.

Allnutt decided to await 43 Column's main body. On arrival, Pat Hughes ordered half a Rifle Platoon to flush out and kill the snipers. They cleared the area with the bayonet and the men then relieved British troops on the perimeter. The Recce Platoon joined HQ at the centre, held in readiness for more patrolling. The Command Post was close to the ridge and defence positions ran for around 400 yards north and south. The entire area was covered in dense jungle offering just 20 yards' visibility at best. In these conditions each defence position was isolated and the Japanese could infiltrate with ease, but it was virtually impossible for them to mount a full-scale attack. Yet this terrain was a paradise for the snipers. Nevertheless, the Africans began well, flushing out a number of Japanese infiltrators.

On 27 May, 77 Brigade Commander Michael Calvert received orders to take Mogaung. He was pressed to fix a date for its capture and offered 5 June in response. On 31 May Claude Rome progressed with the 3rd/6th Gurkhas and took Lakum, in the hills just three miles from Mogaung. The town was weakly garrisoned at that point, but small parties of Japanese troops were dug in. They had orders to slow the Chindit advance, buying time to stiffen the defences.[14]

Captain Norman Durant, MC, commanded the Machine Gun Platoon of the South Staffords' 80 Column. He described the difficulty of advancing against small, determined parties of Japanese hidden in thick cover with their automatic weapons. Durant was seen as the solution. He was repeatedly ordered to bring up the Vickers guns and spray the jungle. This would be followed by a shower of grenades and a prompt attack by a Rifle Platoon.[15]

On 30 May Boatner took over the assault on Myitkyina. It failed badly, with substantial Chindit losses, suffered by the Gurkhas of 49 and 94 Columns (9 GR) and 40 Column (4 GR). Morris Force remained around Maingna, too weak to punch through.[16]

Men had to dig deep to find the will to carry on. Frank Anderson, a Vickers gunner with the King's 81 Column:

'By this time I had malaria and had lost around three stone in weight. My feet were good and I could still march, but I was weak and quite fatalistic by this stage. I didn't really care whether I lived or died. Yet my body always seemed to find a little bit more, to keep me going. What really helped me was the strong inner belief that I would get out. I knew I was lucky. I had a strong constitution, despite the malaria and weight loss.'

Some men, however, had seen too much. One officer with 111 Brigade was ordered back to a village following an ambush on a Column taking a supply drop. He found one decapitated prisoner, his head stuck on a pole. He was then ordered back, to search for and recover other British dead from this village.[17]

Bill Smyly and the 3rd/9th Gurkhas had only a short breather at Mokso Sakan:

'We spent two nights at Mokso Sakan and, on the third day, marched north towards Mogaung, passing through the beautiful marshland forest bordering Indawgyi Lake. The Cameronians were ahead of us and their engineers had prepared the way. At one point, one of their mules had got stuck. They had laid a bamboo walkway across a stretch of marsh. This supported boots, at a pinch, but not hooves. Muleteers ran at this crossing and the mules plunged after them, through the mud at the side of the walkway. I suppose one mule went too slowly, forcing the animal behind to halt. This second animal then sank into the mud.

'A cow's cloven hoof in mud spreads as it presses down and draws together, to come out smoothly, as it is pulled up. The hoof of the horse or mule looks and acts like a plunger. The deeper it goes, the harder it is to extract. Along the way we came across this Cameronian mule in deep mud. I stayed with her and the group of Jocks who were helping. I climbed into the mud, cut the girth with my kukri and pushed the load and saddle off, into the mud on the other side. There was a D-ring on the halter to which we attached a rope and made a tug-o-war team. Pulled from the front and urged on from behind, this poor animal tried to buck and plunge and then visibly gave up. There was no more spirit in her. She was sunk up to her belly and her eyes were staring. I shot her there. Perhaps the mud into which she slowly sank has preserved her, so she will be there still, like the mummified bodies of our Celtic ancestors in Cornwall and Connemara, preserved in an ancient bog. We hurried on to rejoin the rest.'

Smyly has vivid memories of the night that followed:

'It illustrated so much about life in the jungle for the British, so far from home, the Gurkhas from much nearer, the Burmese whose relatives lived in these hills and, of course, the undeserved comfort in which a British officer lived when serving with the Gurkhas. Evening comes suddenly in the tropics. At 5.30 it is full day and at 6 or ten past it is dark. In the forest it is pitch dark. The Column halted at about 5.30 and I thought it might be too late for the Cameronians, with their remaining mules, to press on and rejoin their unit. I suggested they stay with us for the night and catch up in the morning. The day had been long and exhausting and what was more natural than to light up a cigarette and brew tea? But by the time these men had had their tea and something to eat it was pitch dark. They had still to water their mules and find a place to sleep. To sleep in the open we all had our own tricks but the usual drill, at least in the dry season, was to find a smooth piece of ground, dig a little dent in it for your hip and lace yourself and your blanket into a groundsheet. Some people used their packs as a pillow and some used a boot. I slept with one boot on and one under my head.

'This was the busiest time of the day for the Gurkhas. Some led mules to water. The rest fanned out in the forest to collect bamboo. We were no longer afraid of being observed by Japanese aircraft and I ordered Mule Lines. In the Monsoon, these were quicker and easier to make than individual billets.

'From the forest the men came back dragging different kinds of bamboo and, when they could find it, a roofing material called "Attap". When there was no Attap and no banana leaves (which were almost as good), we used groundsheets. Slim, strong stakes were driven into the ground for uprights. Long, heavy poles were lashed on crossways to hold up the floor and roof and a curiously light bamboo, which might be quite long and wide but had a thin wall, was split open to make the floorboards of the long bunk bed. Mule Lines consisted of a post and rail fence and, near it, a long, roofed bed for 30 or more men. The gap between was filled with bamboo leaves as fodder. When it was done the mules were tethered one side of the fence, with fodder in front to chew during the night. The men had a sleeping floor 18 in. or more off the ground and either a thatched roof or groundsheets overhead. Men and mules were quite close to each other all night – which was probably a comfort for both.'

Bill Smyly slept in style that night:

'My Orderly excelled himself. I did not allow him to cook for me, as Gurkhas did not do well on K-rations. He may have felt slighted and wanted to prove himself. Anyway, that night he made me a pavilion. The bed was about 5 ft long and 4 ft wide, roofed, and he had cut lengths of parachute cord to smoulder in the night and keep away mosquitoes. Before this house was a small fire with a bamboo kettle bubbling away in the middle of it. This "kettle" was a watertight section of bamboo, filled with water and propped up on two sticks with one end in the fire. The water will boil away and protect its holder till there is no water left. Near these quarters, in and around a clump of bamboo, bamboo shoots were bursting from the ground. You could have fed an army! My meal that night was a single spear of bamboo shoot as thick as my leg, cooked with a whole can of American processed cheese. The cheese, of course, was Kraft.'

After supper came the ritual of 'visiting time'. The officers circulated, for a smoke and a chat:

'An interesting party was going on nearby, where the Burma Rifles were having supper. These men had saved their K-rations to give away in local villages (for some of them, their own villages) and, in exchange, came back with rice and home-cooked food. Each man brought to the picnic a different dish and the rice was cooked together. It was like a feast. Each man had prepared something different. Apparently, they were Christian; the meal began with Grace.

'We were in the clothes we had worn all day, but these men had bathed at the water point as soon as the Column halted. They had brilliantine on their hair and their trousers, washed and hanging upon trees, were exchanged for colourful lungis. These Shans, Karens and Kachins dressed for dinner! Truly, they were the aristocrats of the forest.

'Around us a hundred little fires glimmered and there was the murmur of evening talk and laughter. This faded as the fires dimmed and went out. But this was the Monsoon and a rainstorm began at about 2 am. In my faintly illuminated pavilion I lay, shirtless, and listened to the storm pounding on the roof. A light spray came in – cool and pleasing. I was in luxury. Around me, the little red ends of smouldering parachute cord made a pleasant smell that kept away mosquitoes. The Gurkhas, of course, were in their long house. Of the Burma Rifles I had no idea. But, for the British, the night was a different story. The flattish ground on which our Cameronians settled became a stream. They were washed out of their cocoons. Groundsheets and blankets were soaked. They were dripping and on their feet in the middle of the night when Gurkhas called out

"Tommy!" or, for the exceptionally well-informed, "Here, Jock!" and moved over to give them room in or under the Mule Lines' enormous bed.'

Bill Smyly's keen eye noticed the differences in eating habits:

'When the Burrifs sat down to supper, 9 or 10 men would prepare, at different fires, various dishes for a shared feast. We looked on in awe. Gurkhas, who were technically Hindu with caste restrictions, ate on their own and, like British soldiers, not very well. British officers were, of course, very "low caste" and kept clear of the men when they were eating.

'The Gurkhas were jungle-wise and supplemented their diet in the forest. One of my men could smoke out lethally dangerous wild bees. I was once given a piece of wild honeycomb — much like the food John the Baptist ate with his locusts. The wax comb itself is delicious and filling, the honey sweet and the little fat grubs rather like cream cheese. There is no way, as far as I know, to separate these out and the men didn't try. Eaten together, it was sweet, filling and creamy.

'When Gurkhas picked the curling tops of bracken, they melted in the mouth. When I picked what looked like the same thing the men laughed. The little shoots I put in my mouth tasted like straw. On another occasion they gave me the fat, red petals of a jungle flower which, when fried, tasted like liver.

'British soldiers had the hardest life of all. The different units had various terms for the break in which they could light fires and cook: "brew-up", "mash down", or "crash". The results were similar: stew up what you have in your mess tin — biscuits, milk powder, sugar and spam — mash it together and feed before it gets too dark.'

When they reached the end of this march north and entered more open country, Bill Smyly was ordered to deliver a sealed message to 111 Brigade Commander Jack Masters:

'I have no idea what it was but it may have contained citations. It had been sent by me in case Masters wanted to question me about "Silly Point". In the event he didn't mention this. I assumed Harper sent me because I was Animal Transport Officer and he knew I would enjoy the ride. I took Charlie and we rode 60 miles in one day. During the course of this ride my marvellous pony had to swim two deep and fast-flowing rivers.'

While the trauma of Blackpool's fall is still deeply etched in many minds over 60 years later, feelings were strong

at the time. In hospital in Poona a couple of months later, 43 Column's Peter Allnutt wrote: 'It was a great error to have tried to establish this Block. Wingate would certainly have never done it. As it was, Special Force paid dearly in men's lives for this unfortunate decision.'

Many later assessments condemn the Blackpool venture. In his foreword to Richard Rhodes James' book, *Chindit*, 16 Brigade Commander Bernard Fergusson was emphatic:

> It was a major mistake to try to repeat the brilliant exploit of Brigadier Michael Calvert's 77 Brigade. A few weeks earlier he had virtually garrotted the northward Japanese lines of communication by establishing his Block across their road and railway at White City, near Mawlu. He speedily made it impregnable before an adequate force could be built up to dislodge him and 'dislodged' he never was: he held it triumphantly against several times his strength for two months and only moved out, at a moment of his own choosing, so as to adjust to the changed strategy of the campaign. It was an error of judgement at a higher level to think that such a *coup* could be repeated: the Japanese were the last soldiers in the world to be caught out that way twice within two months and 100 miles. Hence the foredoomed catastrophe at Blackpool.[18]

Regarding the performance of the Brigades attempting to help 111 Brigade, 29 Column Commander Charles Carfrae made the critical point: 'Three Chindit Brigades had been ordered by General Lentaigne ... to assist Blackpool or, at the very least, to show some sort of presence or threat. All failed because of the Monsoon.'[19]

Such matters were of no consequence to the debilitated men of 12 NR's 43 Column. They had suffered three weeks of cold, hunger, rain and constant skirmishing with a determined enemy around the Kyunsalai Pass. Supply drops at Nammun were often cancelled due to low Monsoon cloud, hanging down just above the trees. The sorties flown frequently dropped stores beyond reach, into the swampy lake margins. The Japanese gave up trying to seize the pass and now contented themselves with constant sniping – inaccurate but hard on the nerves.

The men loathed the rain, mud and leeches more than the Japanese. Foxholes and trenches were permanently flooded. Every track was ankle-deep in glutinous mud and men's boots rotted away. The slightest scratch soon went septic, then developed into a jungle sore.

Peter Allnutt and his Recce Platoon preferred to keep moving. Their patrols down the slopes, towards the railway corridor, were uneventful but arduous. Meanwhile, the Sunderland flying boats were about to begin their shuttle flights to the lake, to evacuate wounded and sick. When these operations eventually ceased, the pass was abandoned. Sappers attempted to block it with explosive charges.

Notes

1. Rhodes James, R. (1981), *Chindit*, 120
2. Slim, Field Marshal Viscount (1999), *Defeat into Victory*, 277
3. Miller, W.H., Chaplain, 2nd King's Own, *A Chaplain with the Chindits*, Imperial War Museum, 80/49/1
4. Cross, J.P. (1989), *Jungle Warfare*, 39
5. Towill, B. (2000), *A Chindit's Chronicle*, 74
6. Ibid, 70–71
7. Ibid, 107–108
8. Ibid, 103
9. Rhodes James, R. (1981), 148–149
10. Ibid, 157–158
11. Ibid, 156
12. Graves-Morris, Lieutenant-Colonel P.H., unpublished MS (via Bill Smith annd Corinne Simons)
13. Dobney, Major R.P.J. 'Paddy', unpublished MS, July 1981 (via Bill Smith annd Corinne Simons)
14. Calvert, M. (1974), *Chindits: Long Range Penetration*, 135
15. Durant, Captain Norman, MC, 80 Column (1st South Staffords), memoir, Imperial War Museum, 80/49/1
16. Rooney, D. (2000), *Wingate and the Chindits: Redressing the Balance*, 155–156
17. Telephone conversation with the author, 2009
18. Rhodes James, R. (1981), 2
19. Carfrae, C. (1985), *Chindit Column*, 147

23

SAVING THE WOUNDED AND SICK

2–9 June 1944

'Having rested and refitted, we got the shock of our lives. Instead of being flown out, we were told we were to form part of the eastern arm of the attack on strongly held Mogaung. It would be over two months before Stilwell would let us out.'

Captain Larry Gaines, 66 Column, 6th Nigeria Regiment

INDAWGYI LAKE is around 15 miles long and five miles across at the widest. A light aircraft strip had been established at Mokso Sakan – flying casualties to Shadazup, for transit by Dakota to hospital in India – but the area was too waterlogged for C-47 operations. The supplies position at Mokso Sakan began to improve during the first few days of June, but the numbers of sick requiring evacuation grew at a frightening rate.[1]

The idea of operating Sunderland flying boats from Indawgyi Lake is attributed to 111 Brigade Senior RAF Officer 'Chesty' Jennings, a former Navigator on Sunderlands. These flights would save hundreds of wounded and sick. Brigade MO 'Doc' Whyte and the regimental MOs did what they could until the men could be flown out.

A service of thanksgiving for deliverance was held when Blackpool's ragged garrison reached Mokso Sakan. The multitude of wounded and sick dominated all concerns. 111 Brigade's Richard Rhodes James wrote: 'Doc Whyte would announce periodically the passing away of another wounded man but, as the worst cases were taken out, the announcements became mercifully less frequent.'[2]

Many Blackpool survivors harboured bitter feelings about their experiences. Rhodes James: 'I talked to men at base afterwards and they said that, from the beginning, there was a feeling that Blackpool was doomed.'[3]

Two Sunderlands were earmarked for the Indawgyi Lake sorties. These 230 Squadron aircraft operated from a base in Ceylon. They withdrew from anti-submarine patrols and flew to the Brahmaputra river in northern Assam. They would make 13 successful sorties to the Indawgyi Lake.[4]

Many lives now hinged on prompt evacuation. Months of marching, hard jungle living and savage fighting had ravaged 111 Brigade and the rest of Special Force. Yet only the seriously wounded and gravely ill were evacuated. Long weeks of further suffering awaited the rest. Richard Rhodes James observed: 'From now on, life became a tale of discomfort and disease, of hardships borne often not to further a military operation but merely to survive, in a sea of mud and rain.'[5]

Accounts differ on the date Sunderland operations commenced. According to Rooney, the first Sunderland flights took place on 3 June.[6] The post-campaign *Report on Operations* states that the first flight was on 2 June, evacuating 31 casualties. The two flying boats were soon dubbed 'Gert and Daisy' (after the comic characters played by Elsie and Doris Waters). Each could take around 40 wounded and sick per trip, yet they failed to keep pace with the alarming increase in numbers of sick. At one point 'Daisy' was damaged and 'Gert' continued alone.

When 14 Brigade's Columns arrived at Indawgyi Lake, a Buddhist monastery at the northern end was taken over as a field hospital. Sapper Eric Sugden, with the Bedfordshire and Hertfordshire's 61 Column:

'It was a typical Burmese building, with a teak frame and a single storey raised above ground and open underneath, except at the back — where a short bridge connected to a smaller building which served as the latrine. This was enclosed down to ground level. In the floor there were two small trapdoors. If the doors were opened all one could see was a sea of wriggling maggots.'

To save time, casualties were carried down to the lake shore from the makeshift hospital whenever a

Straight to hospital: wounded and sick flown out from Indawgyi Lake by Sunderland flying boat are ferried ashore on the Brahmaputra river. (Walter Longstaff)

Sunderland was due. York and Lancaster Commander Philip Graves-Morris later wrote: 'It was distressing to see these disappointed and dying men carried back again in the evening, when aircraft failed to arrive.'[7]

Malaria cases spiralled after Blackpool and the sudden release of tension on reaching Mokso Sakan. According to Rooney, Doc Whyte informed 111 Brigade Commander Jack Masters that the majority of his men were on the threshold of death from exhaustion, undernourishment, exposure and strain: 'Men just died from a cold, a cut finger, or from the least physical exertion.'[8]

The first half dozen Sunderland sorties flew out around 240 wounded and sick but the numbers waiting never seemed to diminish. According to Lieutenant Larry Gaines, of 6 NR's 66 Column, the Sunderlands were weight-restricted due to their difficulties in clearing the surrounding hills with a heavy payload. The pace of evacuation slowed and Mokso's light aircraft strip became waterlogged and could no longer be used. During early June the numbers requiring evacuation at 'Dawlish' remained at between 250 and 350.

The men became very close in adversity and helped each other. Eric Sugden of 61 Column: 'Everyone had a mucker. Mac was mine. He was a solicitor's clerk from Birmingham and a very affable sort of bloke. We were together all the time in Burma.'

The fighting at this time was often small-scale and hand-to-hand. After one skirmish on 2 June, for example, a Japanese officer attempted to escape on a raft on a chaung. He was pursued by another raft, manned by an officer and an NCO of 61 Column, cornered and dispatched with a knife.

Sugden was troubled by leeches as the Monsoon continued:

'The bottom of my trousers became soaked with blood. They stayed that way as there was no change of clothing. The condition of our feet began to deteriorate. I developed athlete's foot and one of the infantry First-Aiders applied zinc ointment and bandaged each toe separately. It soon cleared up completely.'

Paddy Dobney, with the York and Lancaster's 84 Column, noticed the sharp rise in numbers of sick as long-distance patrols were sent out to check for the presence of Japanese at various villages. Severe cases of malaria and typhus filled the makeshift hospital. The small cemetery expanded as men passed beyond help and died. Major

Downward, leading sister Column 65, contracted typhus but refused to be evacuated and eventually fell into a coma. He was flown out by a light aircraft at Nammun.[9]

NCO Peter Heppell, with the King's 82 Column, had been told he would be evacuated from Indawgyi Lake. He was present when Major Dick Gaitley, his Column Commander, departed in the aftermath of their dispersal in a night engagement three weeks earlier: 'I saw Gaitley and his Batman fly out. Gaitley just walked past, looking straight ahead and without giving an acknowledgement. His Batman gave a smile as he passed.'

Heppell was put in charge of a hut. He was not impressed by the method of selecting the wounded and sick for evacuation. This was controlled by the MO and Senior RAF Officer Chesty Jennings:

'It seemed to me that they had the wrong approach. The men were inspected at parades held outside each basha. I got the impression that those who limped the most were flown out. Naturally, there was a temptation to "improve your chances". There were an awful lot of heavily bandaged legs around and I can't say I blame them! Morale was very low. In contrast to many in better condition, my counterpart in 81 Column couldn't walk. He stayed inside his basha and died.'

During a lull in the fighting following Blackpool's fall, Captain Neville Hogan, Recce Platoon Commander with the King's Own's 46 Column, together with other Platoon members, took shelter under a basha that had fallen on its eaves:

'We crawled under it and settled down to sleep. During the night I was bitten by Bandicoots, large rat-like animals with powerful fangs. I was bitten five times – the first three woke me up and I really felt the last two. These bites turned into pus-filled boils. I developed a high temperature and then went down with typhus.'

Hogan was among those evacuated from Indawgyi Lake:

'I remember entering the Sunderland and being greeted with the words: "Welcome on board." The crew used nautical terms! I was semi-conscious during the flight, but an extremely heavy landing on the Brahmaputra certainly woke me up. In hospital we were given M&B 693, a precursor to penicillin. There were five men in my small ward and the other four died.'

Sunderland 'traffic' was not entirely one-way. Opportunities were taken to fly in officer replacements and others who, for a variety of reasons, did not enter Burma earlier. Lieutenant (later, Major) Denis Arnold, of 29 Column, recalls a Sunderland bringing in Major I.F.R. Ramsey, who had been wounded by a grenade during training. Another flying boat delivered Captain Philip Banfield of 6 NR's 39 Column, who had received a bullet through the shoulder in an attack on Japanese positions around White City. He rejoined his Column. Both Ramsey, a regular officer, and Banfield, wrote Arnold, had 'excellent soldierly qualities'.

The men of 77 Brigade were locked into hard fighting during their advance on Mogaung. There was much more to come. Brigadier Calvert's stores request for the main attack included 5,000 rounds of 3 in. mortar ammunition, but expenditure was much higher.[10] On 3 June they captured Lakum and a detachment seized Japanese positions at Tapaw Ferry. A group of parachutists dropped with river crossing equipment, giving this forward unit the option of crossing the Mogaung River or establishing an evacuation route to Myitkyina, if required. In the 5–8 June period, the Brigade took Pinhmi, despite stiff resistance, capturing dumps, two hospitals and 200 wagon-loads of ammunition. They also secured a bridgehead over the Wettauk Chaung. Casualties were heavy on both sides.

Captain Norman Durant, MC, of the South Staffords' 80 Column, remembered the delight of discovering British rations captured at Rangoon: 'We had a series of large meals of steak and kidney pudding, meat and vegetable stew, beans, etc., and felt very much stronger for it.'[11]

14 Brigade now had orders to protect both flying boat bases on the lake. On 2 June the York and Lancaster's 84 Column still manned the main block in the pass. They were relieved the next day by sister Column 65. A patrol then found that the Japanese had left their positions. 84 Column spent the night in the former Japanese camp at Nammun, taking delight in a new issue of kit and access to long-denied 'goodies', including tinned fruit.

The Padre held a memorial service for those who died defending the pass. The wounded were carried on improvised stretchers the four miles to Nammun's Casualty Clearing Station. They travelled on by bullock cart to Indawgyi Lake's eastern bank, from where they were ferried by open boats to 'Plymouth', the southerly evacuation base at Mamonkai.

Lieutenant-Colonel Graves Morris recorded the first flying boat as arriving on 4 June: 'The crew, in their starched drill uniforms, with their clean-shaven faces and tidy hair, caused much merriment to the bedraggled, bearded, laggard spectators who watched their arrival.'[7]

Arrangements protecting the evacuation bases included two Platoons positioned to block tracks north of Lonton. In addition, a Recce Platoon was ready to warn of any Japanese infiltration across the hills from the north-west. According to Graves-Morris, the final evacuation flight from Plymouth was on 8 June. Meanwhile, the death rate from disease – especially scrub typhus – continued to rise, with daily burials at Mamonkai's small cemetery.[7]

There was still a severe shortage of food. 82 Column's Peter Heppell remembers breaking the rules:

'When the flying boats came in, they were laden with K-rations. Someone got hold of a box and put it to one side in the reeds. I dished out some of the meal packs in my hut. Then the MO arrived for a snap inspection. They turned over our basha and found the empty packets. I just said the rations had arrived yesterday. It didn't seem so bad at the time but, of course, putting rations aside was a criminal offence.'

Paddy Dobney was at the lakeside. 84 Column was helping to protect and operate one of the flying boat bases. They found relief from hunger and the now nauseating K-rations by dining off lake fish three times daily:

'All we could do was boil the fish and they were full of bones and almost tasteless. So, after five days, I welcomed a sudden change when Heney produced some fried fish. I knew we had neither butter nor margarine and wondered how he had managed this culinary miracle. I was only slightly deterred when Heney told me he had used dubbin.'

Despite the savagery of war in Burma, many Chindits retained their natural reluctance to kill an animal. 61 Column's Eric Sugden:

'One day the RAMC Sergeant handed me a live chicken and told me to cook it, feed two men and offer the broth to a third. I'm afraid that I killed the bird with my machete, drew and plucked it and then cut it into joints. I boiled it up in mess tins but had great difficulty persuading the men to eat it.'

———◆———

Chinese forces maintained their leisurely advance. They occupied a village 15 miles north of Mogaung on 3 June. They had orders to push on to Mogaung and could have reached the town in just two or three days, but didn't arrive until 18 June. However, the Chinese had been fighting the Japanese for over a decade and had stayed in the war that long only by adopting a prudent style of combat.

In sharp contrast, 77 Brigade progressed methodically along the Pinhmi-Mogaung road, overcoming strong enemy defences. The South Staffords' 38 and 80 Columns secured Ywathitgale, were pushed out in a counterattack but recaptured it in fierce hand-to-hand fighting. The Japanese regained Mohaung as the fighting grew more intense, drawing in the Lancashire Fusiliers' 20 and 50 Columns and the 3rd/6th Gurkhas. Calvert's Brigade reached wired positions around Natgyigon and were shelled. The Japanese held on to Mohaung and both sides suffered heavy casualties.

Meanwhile, evacuation of the wounded and sick continued at the lake. One man who was relatively fit and free of wounds passed up a chance to get out. Corporal Fred Holliday, of the King's 82 Column, decided to stay despite his lack of enthusiasm for Mokso Sakan:

'That place was full of vicious mosquitoes and leeches. We were there for a couple of weeks and we watched the Sunderlands evacuating casualties. Somehow the idea took hold that we would be next – that we would be flown out after the casualties. We were mistaken.

'It was at this time that Captain Woodburn approached me. He said he had spoken to Scottie and it had been decided to fly me out to attend an OCTU. He said Chindit-style fighting would carry on in southern Burma and across the Salween. This would require officers with real experience. I replied: "But I'm only a Corporal." He responded by pointing out that other NCOs had been selected. I was given the choice and I decided to stay with the Column. I couldn't leave at that time, with the men knowing I was being flown out unwounded and still relatively fit. I told Captain Woodburn I wouldn't be able to face my pals. He said he understood.'

Captain John Riggs, leading the Recce Platoon of the Bedfordshire and Hertfordshire's 16 Column, participated in the defence of the area around Mokso Sakan. They operated north-west of the lake:

'As usual, we tuned into the midday "Force Reuter", a global Morse news broadcast from London providing a very brief bulletin on the war situation. We caught the phrase "landing in force on the north French coast". It was 6 June 1944. Had D-Day arrived in North West Europe? We were anxious to learn if our forces had succeeded in securing a toehold on the French coast. As far as I was concerned, the war in Burma was on hold until we had the answer. If they had failed, the war might have been prolonged for years.'

Night bivouac: 16 Column officers gather for the briefing and announcement of the next 24-hour rendezvous. Pictured (left to right) are: unknown; Recce Platoon Commander Captain John Riggs; Rifle Platoon Commander Lieutenant Mike Colson (bare back); 16 Column Commander Pat Eason (bearded, face turned towards camera); Platoon Commander Captain Ian Ross, MC (seated, face visible); Platoon Commander Lieutenant Bill Ray (standing); Mortar Platoon Commander Lieutenant Graham Humphrey (standing); and, sitting: Platoon Commanders Lieutenant George McKnight and Lieutenant 'Cabby' Day; (?) Gilbert; Lieutenant John Mathias, Animal Transport Officer; and RSM 'Froggie' French. Lieutenant-Colonel Eason, ex-Royal Scots, later developed scrub typhus, was evacuated but died later in an Indian hospital. (John Riggs)

Good company: 'General' Lee Turner (left) led 61 Column's Sapper Detachment. Pictured centre is Major John Barrow, DSO, 61 Column's Commander. He was only 27 when he came out of Burma. Later, he took command of the 1st Bedfordshire and Hertfordshire Regiment. On the right is Captain John Riggs, 16 Column's Recce Platoon Commander. (John Riggs)

Riggs dealt with a medical crisis during this patrol:

'One member of my Platoon, a big man, developed a high fever which I assumed was malaria or scrub typhus. All officers carried syringes and phials of quinine. Intravenous quinine sorted out even a bad case of malaria very quickly. This was the only time I administered intravenous quinine. I found it very difficult to find a vein. It was important to get it right, otherwise I would have made a terrible mess of his arm. I was anxious to remain mobile because there may have been Japanese in the area. There was no time to hang around. The results of the quinine shot were quite amazing. The man was up on his feet within 20 minutes. He could march, although his pack went on a mule. I was relieved. I had never been so close to leaving someone behind.'

Meanwhile, preparations went ahead to speed up the evacuation from the lake. The new plan was to bring out the wounded and sick by boat. Casualties were to be taken upstream to Kamaing, a distance of around 50 miles, and then upriver to Dakota strips (when the route was finally cleared of Japanese).

A large drop delivered 'Ranger' rubber boats and 22 hp outboard motors. An engineering team then built the 'Chindit Navy' – a fleet of large, powered rafts each capable of taking 40 men. These vessels were known as 'Dreadnoughts' and given names such as 'Renown' and 'Ark Royal'. Engineers and technicians parachuted in to help build the big rafts, each consisting of five Ranger boats lashed together, with a bamboo superstructure and two outboards.

Some 200 men were taken by rafts to Kamaing, then ferried out by light aircraft to Warazup – where they boarded Dakotas for India. Over the next two months, more than 1,000 wounded and sick were transported by the Chindit Navy to evacuation airstrips.[12] The Plymouth base was shut down in due course and all wounded and sick moved to Dawlish, the northern lakeside base with a hospital area built by Gurkhas. The river evacuations to Kamaing departed from Dawlish.

In due course John Riggs' Recce Platoon was ordered to rejoin the main body of 16 Column. By that time Riggs had a problem. An abscess had formed on the small of his back. It was in an unfortunate place – just where the bottom of his heavy pack sat. The abscess continued to swell, reached the size of a tennis ball and showed no sign of abating. The Column MO could do nothing with it. Riggs would have to be evacuated:

'I felt this was an over-reaction and we quarrelled. Our Column Commander settled things. He ordered me out.

Years later I learned that the MO had told him that, without treatment, I would be dead from septicaemia within the week. Many men had jungle sores and similar problems due to general debility. We existed on 1,100–1,200 calories daily for many weeks, when the very minimum should have been 2,500 calories.'

John Riggs may have been ordered out on medical grounds, but getting out was another matter:

'The Sunderlands were so overloaded with wounded and sick that they could scarcely get off the water with engines racing at full power. I lost my chance, being the next one in when they shut the fuselage door in my face.

'I ended up on one of the Dreadnoughts, on a voyage north-east from the lake, along the river to Kamaing and the Americans. This took about three days – long enough for some of our group of wounded and sick to die. From a normal weight of about 10 stone I had lost a couple of stone over a period of just over three months. When we reached Kamaing we were taken in fast, small boats to Shadazup, where Lentaigne had his headquarters.

'An American doctor, Frank Mainella from New York, operated on me. He sprayed my skin with local anaesthetic, pierced the abscess with sharp scissors and then opened them up to drain it. He pushed vaseline gauze into the wound to keep it draining. A photo taken a few minutes afterwards shows me looking gaunt and bearded but happy with the outcome, even though the anaesthetic was none too effective.'

Riggs made contact with one of Lentaigne's staff officers who had been with his Battalion at Tobruk:

'I was ushered into Lentaigne's presence. He put a few questions and then asked me if I wanted to go in again. I said: "Yes, of course." Lentaigne then looked at me and said: "Well, you can't do that." Instead, I was flown by light aircraft to Ledo and then on to hospital in Assam. That was it – the last of Burma for me, until a return visit in 2006!'

Now back in India, John Riggs' admission to hospital began in a large reception marquee. A tough-looking Nursing Sister ordered him to remove all clothing and drop it into the large paper bag provided, ready to be burnt. He was rather reluctant to follow instructions, but her stern manner allowed no resistance. He was then ordered into a nearby tin bath, gasping as it contained barely diluted disinfectant:

'Perhaps the bath helped the abscess to heal more quickly. I wasn't lousy but she had decided that Chindits needed de-bugging. I was in a ward for a few days, surrounded by men wounded in battle, including my Sapper Officer. Here I was, with the remains of an abscess! I felt awkward in their company. As soon as possible I joined the Battalion's rear headquarters. Again I was told I could not return to 16 Column.

'Brigade base was now in Bangalore, weeks away by train. A Black Watch friend got me out of this fix. He promised to find me a seat on an aircraft. He turned me into a courier, handing over a "Highly Secret" packet required at Bangalore as soon as possible. I flew to Calcutta and changed planes twice en route. As instructed, I handed over the packet to a Brigade Staff Officer, who promptly threw it back at me. That large, sealed envelope was packed with waste paper!'

82 Column's Peter Heppell also left Indawgyi Lake by river. He was put in charge of a modest boat, consisting of two native canoes lashed together and fitted with an outboard:

'During the journey the outboard's shearpin went and I fixed it with a nail. I had six other sick and wounded with me. In the Monsoon the Kamaing River runs very fast. If that nail had gone I had nothing to replace it. Anyway, we reached Kamaing in two days and continued on by boat, making for the American airbase.

'That river was full of sandbanks. We grounded many times. I would get out and push us free. We spent one night on a sandbank – at the time it seemed the safest thing to do. I had scrounged an American jungle hammock but my companions had nothing, so I felt unable to use it. I was deeply touched when one of the blokes, a King's Corporal, said: 'Look. You've done your job today. Go and get your head down – we'll look after things.' It was such a wonderful gesture by an ordinary chap.'

A great relief: John Riggs shortly after having a large abscess drained by American doctor Frank Mainella. (John Riggs)

When at Mokso Sakan, 111 Brigade's battered Columns were re-equipped, merged into 'Brigade Columns' and readied for more weeks of campaigning. When Captain Miller, the King's Own Chaplain, saw a new consignment of mortars arrive, he had no doubt about what was to follow. Brief religious services were held at Mokso Sakan and Lakhren:

> They were moderately well attended. Contrary to some popular notions ... I did not notice any waves of enthusiasm for religion, though I believe that, in the depths of his heart, the soldier who served in the jungle had a faith, however weak or ill-informed, in God and his care and providence.

Many men guessed they would be staying in and would see more fighting. Vickers Platoon Commander Lieutenant Larry Gaines, with 6 NR's 66 Column, was briefed to help continue to hold Nawku Pass until relieved by 14 Brigade, then to join sister Column 39 and make for Lakhren. On 8 June 111 Brigade was ordered to move on Mogaung from the west. Corporal Fred Holliday's unit, the King's 82 Column, would take part in the Mogaung attack. Having passed up the chance to fly out to begin officer training, he now faced an uncertain future:

'Having rested and refitted, we got the shock of our lives. Instead of being flown out, we were to form part of the eastern arm of the attack on strongly held Mogaung. It would be over two months before Stilwell would let us out.'

Lieutenant Denis Arnold, with 7 NR's 29 Column, continued in the thick of it, seeing plenty of action. On one occasion, Arnold, out in front again, descended the steep bank of a dry chaung. When he climbed the other side he found himself looking at a large party of Japanese engaged in their ablutions: 'I let loose a few rounds and went back. We then let fly with rifle grenades, breaking up the party'. Denis Arnold's health then began to deteriorate:

'I had malaria most of the time, together with dysentery and prickly heat. Eventually, my discomfort was completed by the onset of scrub typhus and several days with a temperature of up to 107 deg. Scrub typhus brought some men so low that they shot themselves.

'We were also very short of food, but I couldn't eat much anyway. We had liberated some rice after a successful ambush near Blackpool, close to the pass. One of the trucks hit was carrying rice. We dished it out but I found I couldn't eat it without salt and we had none at that stage.

'Our Africans were adventurous eaters. In one area, near the Indawgyi Lake, there was a sandy cliff covered in the nests of small birds. I watched as some African soldiers let themselves down using rifle slings and collected the hapless birds. They then boiled and ate them with rice.

'By this time food was so short that dead mules were eaten. The meat was almost inedible, but the broth helped keep us alive. The most edible portion of a mule is the liver. I remember being presented with a chunk of liver on one occasion.

'If all this sounds unpleasant, the Monsoon made things much worse. We advanced on Mogaung in Monsoon conditions. At one point we stopped in a dry chaung. The chaung bed had a raised area in the middle. At that time I had a pounding malarial headache. I sat nursing my head, with my cape draped over to give some protection against the torrential rain. I fell asleep eventually and, when I came to, I was sitting on an "island" in the middle of the now flooded chaung.'

The build-up for the Mogaung attack continued during the first week of June. The South Staffords linked up with the 3rd/6th Gurkhas on 1 June. 77 Brigade Commander Michael Calvert and the Lancashire Fusiliers reached the rest of the Brigade the next day. At Lakum, just south-west of Mogaung, they came under shell fire from the town.[12] Calvert called up Mustang air strikes against Japanese gun positions.[13]

Calvert faced problems when planning and executing the assault. The difficulties were aggravated by the topography and Monsoon floods. Mogaung is sited in

a loop formed by the Mogaung river and the Namyin chaung. The area between hills and town was heavily flooded. The attack had to use the road from Tapaw Ferry to Pinhmi.

Calvert built up supplies, arranged for the wounded to be flown out and called up more air strikes to hit known Japanese strongpoints. He also requested heavier mortars with the necessary range to reach enemy gun positions.[14]

The main phase opened with the capture of Tapaw Ferry. The South Staffords followed up, taking the high ground above Pinhmi. This brought them within 4,000 yards of the town and the railway bridge across the river. On 6 June the South Staffords progressed down to the Wettauk Chaung and captured ammunition dumps. During the night the Lancashire Fusiliers passed through and prepared to attack Pinhmi bridge, across the Wettauk Chaung, at dawn. They were late and machine gun fire inflicted heavy casualties, forcing a withdrawal. A second attempt was also repulsed. Major Monteith was among those killed in action. According to Calvert 'the difficulty was that the road leading to the 150 ft bridge was in clear view of the Japs, who had burrowed into the embankment on the other side'.[15]

Calvert needed another way in and the 3rd/6th Gurkhas found a ford across the Wettauk Chaung and took Mohaung village. The South Staffords then took the adjacent village of Ywathitgale and established a strong block on the Pinhmi-Mogaung road. The Gurkhas began clearing the Japanese from Pinhmi Bridge. The fighting cost 77 Brigade another 130 casualties.

Calvert received information about Mogaung's defences from a small group of prisoners. One willed himself to die, although being forcibly fed; another killed himself by eating his blanket.[16]

Many wounded evacuated to hospitals in India were attempting to come to terms with their injuries. They included Captain Ronald Swann, RA, wounded in the head and eyes as Blackpool was overwhelmed. Swann was sent to the 44th Indian General Hospital, Ledo, and then transferred to the nearby 20th American General Hospital. It was time for him to confront his wounds. He was in the very capable hands of Major H.J. Scheie, an American surgeon specialising in eye injuries:

'I was in hospital for a month. Scheie tried to remove the shrapnel in my left eye, which had penetrated the cornea and the front part of the eye. The Sulphadiazine tablets I had been given were not powerful enough, however, to overcome the inflammation. My surgeon was blunt in his assessment: "Well, it's not going to work in conjunction with your right eye and I'm worried that

the inflammation in that eye will spread to the other." I didn't know what to say and could only comment: "You're the only person who knows the answer. You're the professional".

Ronald Swann's left eye had to be removed. Scheie performed the enucleation. His skills as a surgeon were matched by his understanding of psychology. It wasn't until a week before Swann was due to be discharged that he gave him chapter and verse on the other eye and the head wounds:

'He said: "You've got an injury in your right eye. It's shrapnel. You had three pieces of shrapnel in the head: one in your left temple, one which came down through your left eye and one which went round the orbit of the right eye but didn't do anything other than press it, as a balloon would be squeezed. Another millimetre and you would have lost that eye. As it is, all it's done is cause an extra loss of sight in the nasal field. You'll have to get used to it, of course, but your sight in that eye will be perfectly alright." He was correct. The vision in my right eye is fine and has been OK ever since. A

piece of shrapnel around 5mm in diameter sits on the right cheekbone.'

Ronald Swann had a distinguished visitor while at the American Hospital. He was surprised when Noel Coward walked into the ward:

'I was told later that we shared the same birthday. He was visiting under the auspices of ENSA. He had a chat with me as I was the only British officer in the hospital. One of his comments gave some comfort when he said: "Ah! My dressmaker, Molyneux, had only one eye".'

Swann was bemused by an American nurse's frosty attitude towards him. He was blindfolded at the time, due to the eye injuries, but her cold voice made him uncomfortable. He was being fed one day by a kindly American Colonel, who was a patient in the ward, when he happened to mention the unfriendly 'Sister'. The Colonel laughed and explained that 'Sister' was a disparaging term in the US, often used for 'ladies of easy virtue'. Swann was horrified and apologised at the first opportunity. The two got on very well thereafter.

Notes

1. Rhodes James, R. (1981), *Chindit*, 159–161
2. Ibid, 154–155
3. Ibid, 151
4. Nesbit, R. C. (2009), *The Battle for Burma*, 155
5. Rhodes James, R. (1981), 153
6. Rooney, D. (2000), *Wingate and the Chindits: Redressing the Balance*, 168
7. Graves-Morris, Lieutenant-Colonel P.H., unpublished MS (via Bill Smith and Corinne Simons)
8. Rooney, D. (2000), 142–143
9. Dobney, Major R. P. J. 'Paddy', unpublished MS, July 1981 (via Bill Smith and Corinne Simons)
10. Calvert, M. (1973), *Prisoners of Hope*, 178
11. Durrant, Captain Norman, MC, 80 Column (1st South Staffords), memoir, Imperial War Museum, 80/49/1
12. Calvert, M. (1974), *Chindits: Long Range Penetration*, 132–137
13. Calvert, M. (1973), *Prisoners of Hope*, 187
14. Rooney. D. (1997), *Mad Mike*, 98–99
15. Calvert, M. (1973), 203
16. Ibid, 197–198

24

CALVERT CONTINUES

10–22 June 1944

'The fire was murderous. I was hit in the left arm. The round struck my elbow, travelled through my forearm and emerged at the wrist. They took me into a bamboo basha and a surgeon put me to sleep.'

Corporal Jesse Dunn, Commando Platoon, 80 Column (1st South Staffords)

THE FINAL, costly phase of the 1944 Chindit campaign unfolded. 77 Brigade would assault Mogaung from south and east, with the Chinese 38th Division attacking from north and west. 111 Brigade was to move north-east and operate in the Pahok-Sahmaw area, destroying dumps and blocking enemy movements. 14 Brigade had held the Kyunsalai Pass, protected the evacuation at Indawgyi Lake and disrupted road and rail communications. This Brigade was to capture Taungni.[1] Morris Force had attacked Maingna but stalled after some initial success. Forward elements were withdrawn and 49 and 94 Columns (4th/9th Gurkhas) were merged into a composite 49 Column.

With the enemy failure at Imphal/Kohima, Slim wrote that the Japanese, at this stage, were 'now plainly reduced to fighting merely a delaying campaign in North Burma'.[2] Yet some Chindits were openly bitter about fighting on in Burma during the Monsoon. These feelings were matched by the short tempers of commanders. Stilwell was vitriolic in equal measure towards British, American and Chinese units. He accused the Chindits of abandoning Blackpool prematurely, so allowing the Japanese to reinforce the Kamaing/Myitkyina sector. In turn, Lentaigne claimed that Stilwell had refused him time to evacuate the sick. In late May Stilwell asked SEAC's Supreme Commander, Mountbatten, to withdraw Special Force. Slim was left to adjudicate. He said the Chindits should be allowed to reorganise and fly out their sick. They would then stay in for a short period, until Myitkyina fell – hopefully by mid-June. This proved over-optimistic.[2]

Given the poor state of Special Force, there was little prospect of achieving much more in Monsoon conditions. Slim had the grace to admit this:

It would have been wiser to take the whole of the Chindits out then; they had shot their bolt. So, too, had the Marauders, who a little later packed in completely. Both forces, Chindits and Marauders, had been subjected to intense strain, both had unwisely been promised that their ordeal would be short, and both were asked to do more than was possible.[2]

———◆———

111 Brigade had been stretched beyond its fighting capabilities. Following Blackpool's fall, the men were allowed only a short pause for re-equipment and the evacuation of wounded and sick. They were soon ordered north, to the hills east of Lakhren and west of Mogaung. It was difficult to get going again. They were now much weaker and had grown unused to their heavy packs. Richard Rhodes James: 'We seemed to be starting all over again, learning the hard corners and the ill-fitting straps and the wet socks which were to become the bane of our lives.'

Conditions were appalling on the three-day march to Lakhren. The idea was to reach this deserted village and then decide on the best approach to Mogaung. The mud was deep and men and animals sank into the ooze. Lakhren was in a waterlogged area north-east of the lake. Rhodes James added: 'Mosquitoes seemed to thrive in the low-lying swamps and they made much of us.'[3]

The Bedfordshire and Hertfordshire Columns of 14 Brigade were to secure the area immediately north of Indawgyi Lake. Meanwhile, 111 Brigade patrols moving towards Mogaung found the area alive with Japanese.

111 Brigade was expected to support 77 Brigade's attack on Mogaung. They would push from the west as 77 Brigade advanced from the south-east. 111 Brigade's

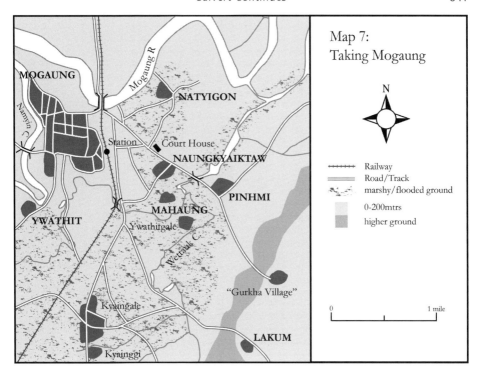

Map 7:
Taking Mogaung

Columns set out from Lakhren. Many men were now so weak that they were soon forced to return to the village. Richard Rhodes James:

> Between the hills and the town of Mogaung lay 10 miles of open country. To a Regular force this would have been a fairly easy proposition, but for us it was impossible. Our only artillery pieces were mortars which could fire a maximum of 3,000 yards and the only other weapons of offence were our Vickers machine guns. To expose ourselves on that stretch of flat country would have been to invite annihilation.

The area crawled with Japanese. 111 Brigade's Columns were short of ammunition and had no ability to advance or hold ground:

> Problem number one had already cropped up: namely, that a mobile Column could not carry ammunition for more than a few hours' fighting. The answer to this is either to sit down in a Block with continuous air supply or to desist from making any but lightning attacks.[4]

Patrols entering this open country were soon in action. They had no choice but to confine their activities to patrolling the lower hill slopes. There was cold comfort when they discovered that enemy soldiers were in even worse condition. In many cases sick or wounded Japanese soldiers were abandoned and these individuals were often prepared to sell their lives dearly.

According to Bill Towill, Lakhren was not deserted, but the Japanese in the village were surprised and soon dispersed. There was also a sharp but brief fight to take Manwe, a ferry station on the Indaw Chaung north-west of Lakhren. The intention was to block any Japanese move south.[5]

Some of Calvert's men ran out of luck before the last push on Mogaung. Private Horace Howkins, with the South Staffords' 80 Column, suffered successive bouts of malaria and dysentery after White City closed. When the Monsoon broke, they moved towards Mogaung:

> *'We went into a village that turned out to be occupied. One Jap threw a grenade at me. I was hit by shrapnel in the arms and legs and, this time, some wounds were severe. They patched me up but I had to come out. I was picked up by light plane and eventually arrived in India, where I spent a few weeks in hospital.'*

RAF driver Ray 'Lofty' Newport was impressed with the efficiency of the evacuation flights:

'I helped with some of the medical flights. When our aircraft landed, the wounded were ready for us and ambulances were waiting at dispersal when we returned. We had firm instructions never to remove or interfere with emergency dressings during the flight. Some wounded were in a very bad state. I remember one man covered in bandages, but I know he survived as I met him after the war.'

80 Column's Corporal Jesse Dunn remained relatively fit when they left White City:

'I took care of myself. I always used water purifying tablets (and left the water for half an hour before drinking) and I took my Mepacrine. I was free of dysentery, although no-one had anything solid to pass. Other things were mere annoyances. I found leeches all over me and prickly heat was distracting. My boots were full of blood when the leeches burst. However, my new boots had softened up. I received a new pair after a drop. I put them on and slept with my feet in a stream, to soften the leather.'

The South Staffords fought several engagements on the way to Mogaung. Jesse Dunn was with 80 Column's Commando Platoon:

'Our Engineers destroyed a large supply dump. We covered them as they laid charges. We were too close when they went up and were showered with debris. One chap suddenly started to yell. We couldn't see what his problem was – until we discovered that a big chunk had landed on him and had broken his neck.'

Jesse Dunn was wounded during fighting near Mogaung. As the South Staffords neared the town, Calvert gave them the job of securing the Brigade's right flank, by clearing ground between Mogaung road and the river:

'This followed the job of clearing a ridge of hills. At that stage we were really hungry, having been out of rations for some days. Anyway, we took a drop and prepared to clear open paddy leading into Mogaung.'

The open ground could not be crossed in daylight:

'We crossed by night and lay along the railway. The next morning, 21 June, we went into Mogaung.'

Lighting up: a Bedfordshire and Hertfordshire Column stops for a midday break in the Lakhren Hills. It was not always possible to find convenient flat ground. In many instances the Columns made the best of sloping ground, in heavy undergrowth. (John Riggs)

They had to take strong Japanese positions, including concrete bunkers and the fighting reached new heights of ferocity. Jesse Dunn:

'The fire was murderous. I was hit in the left arm. The round struck my elbow, travelled through my forearm and emerged at the wrist. They took me into a bamboo basha and a surgeon put me to sleep.'

Dunn's war was over. When he came to, the surgeon had a few words with him: 'He said: "I've set your arm at right angles, as that will be of more use to you." He was absolutely right.' This young doctor's decision limited the degree of disability. The bullet had shattered Dunn's left elbow. Over 60 years later, his left forearm remained at 90 degrees but he had full use of the hand and fingers. Surgical skill and the passage of time reduced the impact of a potentially crippling injury.

Dunn waited patiently in the basha. Chinese soldiers were just arriving as he was readied for evacuation. He was squeezed into a light aircraft, with the pilot's head fitting snugly between his knees. The L.5 took off successfully, across rafts of matting laid across the worst areas of sodden paddy.

The casualty evacuation flights by Sunderland flying boat drew to a close in the second week of June. The York and Lancaster's 84 Column left the 'Plymouth' lakeside evacuation base on 10 June. They went north to take over positions from two West African Columns in the Wabaw Bum area. They climbed from 176 ft to 3,500 ft with no flat rest areas. The difficult terrain led to an unusual request for the next drop. The West Africans had bribed two Mahouts and had used their elephants to help bring up supplies. The Mahouts refused money and would only work for opium. York and Lancaster Battalion Commander Philip Graves-Morris:

> This had to be obtained as a special item in the supply drop. A small piece, about half the size of a little fingernail, would be sufficient to keep them going for three days. When the supply failed, the subterfuge of giving them half a morphia tablet seemed to work.

Yet, the problem of supplying 84 Column from the 'soft skin' base was never solved. The Wabaw Bum ridge was largely free of mosquitoes but there were leeches in profusion. Rations were scarce. Four days' K-rations had to last seven days. Men began adding leaves from trees to their tea and soup. Supplies from Nammun did not reach the Column until 17 June.

The Japanese were in the valley below the Wabaw Bum and 84 Column had to prevent them disrupting the evacuation of 111 Brigade's wounded and sick from 'Dawlish', the northern lakeside base. The two Platoons led by Lieutenant McMellan and Lieutenant Vincent organised fighting patrols. These young officers were unhappy with a purely defensive role. McMellan paid for his aggressive attitude. He was wounded in the arm by a Japanese sentry guarding the gate of a village. He set a trap for the enemy but became frustrated when they refused to walk into his ambush. He returned to the village the next day and on this occasion received a severe wound to his left hand – probably inflicted by the same sentry.

The York and Lancaster sister Column, 65, had held on to the Kyunsalai Pass. The final days of occupation were difficult. When the Japanese pulled back from the perimeter, the Chindits took the opportunity to stiffen their defences with Dannert wire rigged with explosive charges capable of remote detonation. Lieutenant-Colonel Graves-Morris remembered the stench: 'Incessant rain washed away the loose earth covering the hastily buried bodies of the casualties of 84 Column. Their exposure had a macabre and depressing effect on the new occupants.'[6]

65 Column entered a downward spiral. All ranks now had acute diarrhoea (some with dysentery) and they were emaciated. Patrolling acted as a stimulus, keeping men going who might otherwise have succumbed. The Japanese refused to challenge their strengthened perimeter. 65 Column's Commander, Major Downward, developed typhus and was evacuated by light plane from Nammun. Major Bruce succeeded him.

Paddy Dobney, 84 Column's Administrative Officer, described the hard climb to relieve the West Africans holding smaller passes north of the main Brigade area:

> It took us all one hot, steamy day to march back round the bottom of the lake, past Nammun once more, and struggle a further three miles up the eastern side of the lake. The Battle Group toiled up the hillside, to stake its claim along the ridge top, where it could oppose any Japanese attempt to turn the Brigade's flank and threaten the evacuation of 111 Brigade's casualties further up the lake valley.[7]

Dobney, with the soft skin elements stationed around a few huts at the bottom of the hill, had to supply the men on the ridge. The supplies had to be moved up the hillside's steep, narrow tracks. He put the two elephants to work, as many of the mules had lost condition and were showing signs of sickness. He was helping to load K-rations into one of the elephant's baskets when he grazed his hand on the bamboo. He ignored the small cut but had cause to regret this later. He led the supply party up to the ridge and received a warm welcome from men who had been on half rations for some days. On the way back Dobney noticed that his hand was swollen. The small cut had become infected. Another supply drop took place 48 hours later. By then Dobney's hand was swollen, painful and heavily bandaged. He was unable to use his fingers.

There was no escape from the limitations of flesh and blood. The Chindits were worn out. Disease, exhaustion, malnutrition and the Monsoon, together with the actions of senior commanders blind to Wingate's original intent, conspired to destroy Special Force. There was growing anger among men who recalled Orde Wingate's pledge that they would stay in for no longer than three months. Charles Carfrae, commanding 7 NR's 29 Column, summed it up:

> Wingate, a hard man indeed, aware from his own 1943 experiences of the strain, undernourishment

and exhaustion bound to dog its steps, however little actual fighting it might become involved in, had intended that no Chindit Column should remain in Burma for longer than 12 weeks at a stretch. But Wingate was dead.[8]

111 Brigade went beyond the three months and was overwhelmed by the numbers of sick. King's Own elements were ordered to guard them at Padigatawng village. Meanwhile, the casualty situation at Indawgyi Lake reached crisis point, despite the efforts of the Sunderlands. Over 500 casualties had been flown out in a fortnight, but the prospects for those remaining looked bleak. A blunt message from the lakeside warned: 'Situation critical. Men dying daily and morale at very low ebb. Unless medical supplies and food dropped immediately there will be more deaths and complete collapse in morale.'

The men at the lakeside were suffering from malaria, dysentery, jaundice and a host of other conditions. For much of the time there was no food, bar the small, bony lake fish. Those still relatively fit now suffered as their feet were attacked by the mud. Richard Rhodes James:

> It was impossible to keep the mud out of one's boots and it would work its way into the socks by constant pressure. After that, there was no hope; the continuous rubbing of the mud against the soft, wet skin reduced it to the state of raw pulp. I have never seen human feet reach such a state. They looked like raw steak, rubbed bare of all protective covering until the red flesh below was showing. How men walked with feet like this I do not know.[9]

Rhodes James added: 'Sick men had been dissuaded from going down to the flying boats by the hope that the whole Brigade would soon be going out; when they returned to the Column it was to pick up their packs for another job. There was a story in the 14th Army newspaper that we were "the toughest of the bunch." It was ludicrously different from how we felt. It was a very bad moment.'[10]

The author's father, Jack Redding of the King's Own, kept a neatly folded cutting of this story, preserved out of pride or, possibly, scorn. The story appeared just after Special Force came out, in the *SEAC Newspaper* edition of Saturday 2 September 1944. By-lined a 'Fourteenth Army Observer' it carried a strapline offering unconscious humour: 'Full story of Lentaigne's ghost force.'

The Chinese capture of Kamaing on 16 June opened up a land link for the evacuation of Chindit casualties. Engineers had built the fleet of 10 large 'Dreadnought' rafts. Each consisted of several small boats lashed

together with a deck platform and outboard motors. A 'Dreadnought' could take up to 40 men per trip. Around 400 casualties were to be evacuated by the 'Chindit Navy' from Indawgyi Lake, heading north through a labyrinth of waterways to the Mogaung river at Kamaing. The powered rafts were then used to ferry trucks across the river for 36th Division, now advancing to relieve the Chindits.[11]

14 Brigade's Columns moved further north as flying boat operations ceased and the rafts evacuated the remaining casualties. The Japanese were no longer attempting to force the passes. The Kyunsalai Pass was abandoned on 21 June. York and Lancaster Chindits took their leave of the Wabaw Bum that day, having heavily booby-trapped an area of the Kyunsalai Pass. 14 Brigade was to push northwards, along the western flank of railway valley, towards Mogaung. The men of the York and Lancaster's 84 and 65 Columns continued to decline in the steamy swamps. Dysentery was rife. Animals collapsed and were shot where they dropped.

Morris Force had run into trouble at Maingna. Forward elements were attacked by a reinforced enemy and came under artillery fire from the Irrawaddy's west bank. During the night of 20/21 June they were forced to withdraw to the north end of the village, where fighting continued throughout the next day. Meanwhile, Dah Force (excluding those elements retained by Morris Force for further operations) was evacuated.

Meanwhile, the York and Lancaster's 84 Column took 'three fearsome days' to advance just 12 miles along the lake edge to Mokso. This track had been much used by other Columns and was in a terrible state. Much the same could be said of Paddy Dobney's infected hand:

> The whole of my hand was now very swollen and discharging and throbbed with pain. The straps of my heavy pack cut more cruelly than ever into my shoulder, making my hand even more painful. I could not use my fingers, which made life especially miserable, restricting my activities at the evening cooking fire and making it impossible to manage bootlaces and the buckles and straps of my equipment. Nor did it help matters when I had to dash suddenly into the bushes with calls that couldn't be denied. The newly issued jungle hammocks were the sole saving grace in a long succession of extremely uncomfortable nights.

The end of this trek, during the morning of 25 June, offered no reward. Mokso was a cheerless anticlimax – just four huts in a sea of mud and detritus. Black clouds of flies hung over everything. Dobney described it as 'widely regarded as top of the fly league.' 65 Column had arrived

Gathering intelligence: 61 Column's Recce Platoon meet the villagers. In the centre, with the cigarette on, is Platoon Commander 'Tubby' Baker. The usual questions were 'Japan Lu shi-de?' (Are there any Japanese about?) and 'Have you got anything to eat?' (John Riggs)

at this filthy site the evening before. The only good thing about Mokso was a brief improvement in rations. The men needed fuel, as they now faced an awful climb into the mountains. This ordeal was eased somewhat by an enterprising Brigade Liaison Officer who had worked in Burma before the war. He found a new way up and both Columns made it to the top in 10 hours.

Many new cases of malaria and typhus appeared and rations were being consumed rapidly in an area devoid of drop zones. 14 Brigade's Commander, Brigadier Brodie, took action. He issued new orders recognising these extreme circumstances. His Columns were still expected to descend, harass the Japanese along the railway and support 77 Brigade in its attack on Mogaung. They now spent two days moving east, hacking through virtually impenetrable jungle.

Brodie organised his Columns into 'Light Battle Groups', free of heavy weapons, wounded and sick. Paddy Dobney was ordered to take the York and Lancaster casualties back down the mountain, reversing the painful ascent. When the casualties were handed over, Dobney's party would then head north, up the lake valley, re-cross the mountains and rejoin the main body. Dobney had been deeply disturbed by his last visit to the Battalion's sick. Many were lying in the mud. They asked

the same question, time and again: 'Do you think we'll get out, Sir?'

Dobney felt disheartened at this stage:

My hand was still giving me hell, my guts turned to water six times a day and I was plagued with a sort of jaundice, with its accompanying sickness, but at least I was able to march. What could I answer these men, many of whom could scarcely put one foot in front of another, when I knew we had a fearsome 20-mile march, much of it through swamps, to reach Lakhren, our next hope for evacuation? Our mules were starving for want of grain. I realised that if they were to reach Lakhren we would have to take a supply drop somewhere, somehow, just for them.[7]

Dobney then had a stroke of luck. Private Clixby staggered into the bivouac. He had been unable to keep up with the Recce Platoon and he now warned Dobney about the appalling state of the track to Lakhren. He also told him that there was only one possible drop site and that this would take three or four days to reach.

On 12 June 7 NR Commander Peter Vaughan felt relieved to get going. They had been kicking their heels

Making the effort: 61 Column's 'Skipper' Franklin pulls a comb through his matted hair. Unusually, Franklin has also had a shave. His nickname referred to his past service in the Merchant Navy. (John Riggs)

at Nammun since Blackpool's fall over two weeks earlier. Brigadier Gillmore's replacement, Ricketts, had proposed staying at Nammun throughout the Monsoon. Vaughan and 29 Column Commander Charles Carfrae argued forcefully against this plan.

Rooney wrote: 'This inactivity, when two Brigades were less than 40 miles from Mogaung, where the dangerously depleted 77 Brigade was in urgent need of support, is another indictment of Lentaigne's leadership.'[12]

The men of 6 NR's 66 Column were also on the move, leaving Nawku Pass on 17 June by a track along the forest boundary to Padigatawng. The going was appalling. They cut their way through bamboo thickets and built miles of track up and down steep inclines in constant, torrential Monsoon rain. The going got progressively worse and 66 Column now had just one day's rations in hand, with little chance of finding a drop site. They abandoned the forest boundary and moved down

into the Indaw Chaung valley, making for Padigatawng via Lakhren.

Savage fighting had continued around Mogaung. Michael Calvert's Brigade suffered more casualties with each passing day. On 10 June Calvert's men had taken Pinhmi bridge, on Mogaung's outskirts. Mahaung had been taken the previous day and was now held by the Lancashire Fusiliers. The fighting for the bridge cost another 130 casualties. On 11 June a Platoon of Lancashire Fusiliers used grenades to clear foxholes and capture Mogaung's Court House. The South Staffords worked along the right flank, to clear the bank of the Mogaung river. Led by Archie Wavell, the Viceroy's son, they put in two attacks but were stalled by machine gun fire. They dug in and the Gurkhas went through them in the morning to deal with the Japanese.

77 Brigade was now fighting for Mogaung town. The railway station and road bridge were just 800 yards away, but across open paddy. The only area still held by the enemy east of the railway was Naungkyaiktaw village.[13]

Two days later, on 13 June, the three Battalion Commanders told Calvert that they were reduced to a Company each through sickness, battle casualties and sheer exhaustion. Meanwhile, Japanese reinforcements had reached Mogaung. Two additional Japanese Battalions entered the town during 10–12 June.[14] These concentrations were punished by Mustang air strikes. Japanese weapons pits were marked by smoke and the bombs fell just 150 yards from the Chindits' positions.

The Brigade's attacking strength on 13 June totalled only 550 men, from an original strength of around 2,000. There were now 250 battle casualties clustered around Brigade HQ, awaiting evacuation, and half were stretcher cases. Calvert was as determined as ever but he faced severe handicaps. Trenchfoot was rife in the flooded conditions. Calvert told Lentaigne that he could not hold indefinitely in such a low-lying area. He was cleared to pull back into the hills, provided Pinhmi bridge and Tapaw Ferry continued to be held, to await the arrival of the Chinese.

The few replacement officers flown in by light aircraft were usually killed or wounded within two or three days. At one point several British Sergeants approached Calvert and proposed that they should lead the Platoons, rather than see more 'green' Lieutenants die. Calvert accepted this idea.

On 15 June Calvert bowed to the inevitable and ordered a general withdrawal to the Pinhmi area for rest, although fighting soon resumed. On 18 June there was a successful attack on enemy units in and around Naungkyaiktaw. Over 100 Japanese were killed, but the Chindits suffered another 50 casualties. Elements of the

Chinese 114th Regiment then arrived on the north bank and were told to secure the left flank. Calvert knew he had to get on with it, as his depleted force continued to shrink due to sickness and shelling. He would make one last, all-out effort on 24 June.

On 20 June 111 Brigade joined what became a near three-week battle to take a commanding height across railway valley. Point 2171 was a spur above Taungni, overlooking the Mogaung river. This vicious struggle drew in the 3rd/4th Gurkhas, 3rd/9th Gurkhas, King's Own and Cameronians, together with the 7th Leicesters from 14 Brigade. The Gurkhas and King's Own led the advance. Rooney:

Against a murderous fire the 3rd/9th Gurkhas went forward. Major Blaker, who had been outstanding during the whole campaign, led the final assault and was mown down by bullets, but such was his leadership that his death raised his Gurkhas to a wild, unstoppable charge which drove the Japanese off the peak.[15]

Blaker was awarded a posthumous VC. Conditions at the top of Point 2171 were appalling. The shallow soil made it difficult to dig in securely. It was also difficult to bury the dead. There was great bitterness when the victors were ordered to pull back.[15] The Japanese returned to Point 2171 in early July.

Notes

1. Calvert, M. (1974), *Chindits: Long Range Penetration*, 132
2. Slim, Field Marshal Viscount (1999) *Defeat into Victory*, 277–280
3. Rhodes James, R. (1981), *Chindit*, 164–166
4. Ibid, 169–173
5. Towill, B. (2000), *A Chindit's Chronicle*, 108–111
6. Graves-Morris, Lieutenant-Colonel P.H., unpublished MS (via Bill Smith and Corinne Simons)
7. Dobney, Major R.P.J. 'Paddy', unpublished MS, July 1981 (via Bill Smith and Corinne Simons)
8. Carfrae, C. (1985), *Chindit Column*, 154–155
9. Rhodes James, R. (1981), 177–178
10. Ibid, 163
11. Gerrard, F. (2000), *Wingate's Chindits*, unpublished MS (via Bill Smith)
12. Rooney, D. (2000), *Wingate and the Chindits: Redressing the Balance*, 174
13. Calvert, M. (1974), 137–143
14. Rooney, D. (1997), *Mad Mike*, 99
15. Rooney, D. (2000), 143–144

25

TAKING MOGAUNG

23–27 June 1944

'There were many heavily fortified bunkers, but by this time the Japanese seemed to lose heart. ... When we got into Mogaung it was littered with dead Japanese.'

Ian Niven, 20 Column, 1st Lancashire Fusiliers

IT TOOK bitter fighting to position 77 Brigade's combat groups for the final push against Mogaung. 20 Column's Ian Niven knew only too well what this long struggle had already cost: 'We fought one hell of a battle at Pinhmi, charging that bridge over the Wettauk Chaung.'

On 3 June Brigadier Calvert had stood on a high ridge. He examined Mogaung through field glasses. The town was just two miles away. It would be difficult to take but Calvert drew comfort from the news that the Lancashire Fusiliers' two Commando Platoons had captured the Tapaw Ferry on the Mogaung river. His Brigade now had a way out if things went wrong. To the west, the Wettauk and Namyin chaungs were flooded. To the north was the Mogaung river and its damaged rail bridge. Mogaung could be attacked from the south, along the railway from Loilaw to Ywathit, but this was too obvious. Calvert decided to assault from the south-east and cross the Wettauk Chaung by the Pinhmi bridge. The Lancashire Fusiliers took Pinhmi village and now waited to attack the bridge.[1]

Pinhmi village consisted of half a dozen huts, swarming with flies, alongside the Mogaung river. Taking Pinhmi was the next step in penetrating Mogaung's defences. The stress of long weeks of jungle combat, with no quarter shown, surfaced when a sick Japanese was taken prisoner. The soldier was suffering from malaria. He was being badly kicked and beaten when an officer intervened and saved him. He bent down and gave the stricken man water from his own bottle.[2]

The Japanese defenders at the bridge were in strong, concealed positions ranged along a 15 ft high embankment. The attackers had to advance along an elevated road, with a flooded ditch to one side and thick jungle

to the other. The ditch was overgrown and the water too deep to provide cover. Calvert arrived at the scene and ordered two Platoons to attack straight down the road, rush the bridge and knock out the bunkers. The Lancashire Fusiliers fixed bayonets and charged. The Japanese machine gunners waited until they reached the bridge before opening fire from the bunkers. The attackers lost heavily and withdrew to Pinhmi village, having failed to get close enough to the bunkers to throw grenades.

The Company Commander who had given water to the Japanese prisoner set out the following morning to find a way to get behind the bunkers. He was shot in the spine by a Japanese sniper. Captain Jeffrey, 50 Column's Administrative Officer, sent a Runner to find the Father, having remembered that the dying man was a Catholic.

Pinhmi bridge was the scene of desperate fighting. An air strike hit the Japanese bunkers. One bomb then fell into the Lancashire Fusiliers' positions and caused a dozen casualties. The 130 Chindit dead and wounded in this fighting included Major David Monteith.[1] The Gurkhas forded the chaung south of the bridge and drove out the Japanese defenders by attacking their rear. Ian Niven was shocked by the loss of Monteith: 'He was an outstanding man and I was upset.' Captain Jeffrey assisted a man badly injured by the Mustang's bomb:

I remember helping to carry one young soldier with a great gash in his stomach to the RAP, where our Doctor was working, stripped to the waist, grim and terribly deliberate. The boy was babbling and crying and one of his mates was gripping his shoulder and trying to comfort him. The Doctor bent over him

The desperate struggle: a mortar team in action during the final assault. (Trustees of the Imperial War Museum)

and looked at me and shook his head: 'Not a chance', he said. 'Keep him under morphia till he goes'. Then he turned to the next case.[2]

The Lancashire Fusiliers' Columns, 20 and 50, fought as a Battalion around Mogaung. Captain Jeffrey:

> We had two main weaknesses. In the first place we had far too few Riflemen, on whom the main burden of battle must fall. The capture of a fortified town such as Mogaung involved constant patrolling, raids and probing attacks, as well as the assault itself. Equally serious was our lack of weapons of heavier calibre than a 3 in. mortar, which was admirable enough for breaking up enemy groups in the open and neutralising areas of jungle, but ineffective against sandbagged bunkers or pillboxes.[3]

Every yard was contested as they gradually penetrated Mogaung's outer defences. Small groups of Japanese fought to the death to slow them up. This fanatical opposition occasionally drove men beyond breaking point. They then went berserk. Captain Jeffrey:

> A Bren gunner in the leading Rifle Section lost his temper and pushed straight up the hill, firing from the hip and screaming curses at the Japanese. He was an ordinary soldier who had never been noticed much before. But there is no knowing who in battle will go mad suddenly and leave everyone gasping at his recklessness.[4]

The Lancashire Fusiliers continued their costly, stop-start advance. They often halted to overcome fresh resistance before pressing on under constant sniper fire. They eventually reached South Lakum, where Brigade HQ and the South Staffords were bivouacked. They were less than three miles from Mogaung.

Even the naturally aggressive Michael Calvert found it difficult to commit his decimated force for an all-out attack on Mogaung.[5] Meanwhile, Captain Jeffrey and other 50 Column officers were annoyed by 'irritating

Expecting trouble: a 61 Column position on the edge of a village in the Mogaung area, overlooking a damaged bridge. (John Riggs)

messages assuring us that Mogaung was only lightly held and that we need have no anxiety about capturing it at once. Our own intelligence, based on villagers' reports, advised us that it was held by about a Battalion strength.'[3] In fact, the Japanese garrison had been reinforced and was now much larger.

Calvert's force launched their main attack on Mogaung at 0300 on 24 June. It opened with a heavy air strike and a fierce mortar barrage of over 1,000 rounds.[5] The line of the main road, from the rail bridge to the railway station, was secured with the help of over 50 air strike sorties. In addition, the Chinese took Ywathit and pushed towards the Namyin bridge.

Chindits were not trained or equipped for attacks on fortified centres such as Mogaung. There are those who believe that the use of Chindits in this way amounted to cold-blooded murder on the part of the much-loathed Stilwell.

Philip Graves-Morris, the York and Lancaster's Battalion Commander, wrote:

> Each Column was trained to be capable of moving over long distances hidden from the enemy, then quick sharp-hitting by its one large Rifle Company, supported by mortars and machine guns, with its Commando Platoon capable of extensive demoli-

tions. The Columns were NOT designed, nor trained, for the more conventional types of warfare, for they were not capable of long, set-piece attacks, withdrawals or pursuits of an enemy.

By the third week in June, Graves-Morris became alarmed at the poor condition of the men:

> The men's stomachs were already revolting against the concentrated K-rations which had now been consumed continually for 10 weeks. We had not had a proper meal since leaving India, where our cooks served us a last frantic stew as we emplaned on the airstrip. The only meat we had eaten was when, at the end of April, we had shot one of our two bullocks. We had little nourishment from that – he had been as lean as ourselves.[6]

The York and Lancaster Columns enjoyed only a brief improvement in rations at Mokso, as they prepared to cross the hills to the east and operate in railway valley, in support of the 77 Brigade/Chinese attacks on Mogaung. Graves-Morris noted the short-lived increase in drops of tinned foods, together with their first bread in six weeks. A slice of tinned peach ranked as 'the most precious luxury'.

The key positions at Mogaung included the embankment in the area of the rail bridge over the Mogaung river and Natyigon village. The plan called for the Gurkhas to advance on the right and the South Staffords on the left. Captain Michael Allmand, of 3rd/6th Gurkhas, was killed in the fighting for the bridge and was awarded a posthumous VC. His men sought cover when the enemy opened an intense fire, but Allmand charged the enemy alone. Two days later he led another attack in the face of machine gun fire. His superb courage was again evident when the rail bridge attack went in on 23 June; he single-handedly charged a machine gun nest for the last time. Remarkably, the Regiment also gained a second VC – on the same day in the same action! It was awarded to Rifleman Tul Bahadur Pun. Bill Towill:

'He set out to attack a strongpoint. He started off with two comrades, who were both shot down. He continued alone. He had to cross 30 yards of the most difficult terrain, blocked by shell holes and fallen trees and, silhouetted against the first light of dawn, he presented a first class target to the enemy. Yet he got to the enemy strongpoint, killed three of the defenders and put the five others to flight. A single Gurkha Rifleman caused five of the bravest soldiers in the world to turn on their heels and run!'

Bladet's flamethrowers were turned on the enemy bunkers and linked craters from the heavy air strikes gave the attackers some measure of cover. Nevertheless, an undetected Japanese strongpoint inflicted heavy casualties on the advancing South Staffords.[7]

Calvert soon discovered that the South Staffords' left flank was exposed. A Chinese claim to have taken the railway station proved false. Surviving elements of the Lancashire Fusiliers joined a fresh attack on the station strongpoint. Several hours of heavy fighting cost the Brigade around 160 casualties. The attackers dug in where they were, pinned down by intense fire. Calvert then gathered his last reserves: his headquarters and animal transport personnel. Both Calvert and Colonel Scott of the King's were firm believers in the principle that every Chindit was a fighting soldier. 50 Column's Captain Jeffery:

I had thought of Mogaung as a town, but it was, in fact, little more than a large village consisting of bamboo huts raised three or four feet off the ground on stilts. There was, however, one red-brick building – at the railway station, on the north-east corner – which we guessed rightly the Japanese would make a strongpoint in their defensive system.[2]

During the approach to the town the Lancashire Fusiliers attacked a succession of small villages, including Naungkyaiktaw – just 100 yards by 200 yards. Flamethrowers could not be used as they illuminated advancing troops. They had to kill every Japanese in every foxhole and trench, mostly with grenades. Now the brick-built station building was just 300 yards away. The South Staffords took the building and the Lancashire Fusiliers came up, ready to exploit a breakthrough. Heavy fighting continued on 26 June.

Signaller Ian Niven was serving as a Rifleman with 20 Column when 77 Brigade finally bludgeoned its way into Mogaung:

'There were many heavily fortified bunkers, but by this time the Japanese seemed to lose heart. They began to retreat into the town and beyond. When we got into Mogaung it was littered with dead Japanese. It was only then that I saw my first Chinese warrior! I went into the railway station and took some souvenirs – tickets from Mogaung to Myitkyina. I still have them today.'

Calvert's Brigade encircled the town's eastern perimeter and the Chinese pushed from the south. The Gurkhas reached the Namyin Chaung, on the town's western perimeter. Most Japanese had been killed or had withdrawn and Mogaung was finally cleared on 30 June.[8] Calvert's much diminished force had lacked the strength to sweep through the town; final pockets of resistance were crushed piecemeal. 77 Brigade's success, in the face of so many difficulties, owed much to the sheer determination of Calvert's men and the close support flown by 5320 Wing of Northern Air Sector. Now the Chindits handed over their positions to the Chinese 38th Division and moved into the hills east of Pinhmi. Four weeks earlier, when the Mogaung struggle began, Calvert had some 2,000 men. 77 Brigade had since suffered over 1,000 battle casualties and now had 150 seriously sick. In the aftermath Calvert became deeply disturbed. Rooney wrote:

There were over 250 killed, over 500 seriously wounded and many more men who ... just lay down and died now the pressure was off. Calvert was haunted by the thought that his loyalty to Wingate had made him ask too much of his Brigade, that he and 77 Brigade had been the willing horse whom others had relied on, with the result that over one-third of his Brigade had been killed or wounded.[9]

Calvert's mood was not improved when the BBC announced that Chinese-American forces had taken Mogaung. He responded with his now famous signal

Mopping up: Michael Calvert (left), outside Mogaung's severely damaged brick building. Standing with him is the 3rd/6th Gurkhas' Major Shaw, with Major Lumley on the right. (Trustees of the Imperial War Museum)

to Stilwell: 'The Chinese-American forces having taken Mogaung, 77th Indian Infantry Brigade is proceeding to take Umbrage.'[7] This is said to have prompted Stilwell's staff to search in vain for 'Umbrage' on the map.

As 77 Brigade attacked Mogaung, 111 Brigade engaged Japanese units forced south by Chinese pressure in the north-east. In addition, 14 Brigade and 3(WA) Brigade were operating in the railway valley and to the north.[10]

6 NR's 39 and 66 Columns struggled with a difficult descent into the Indaw Chaung valley. They were heading for Lakhren and on to Padigantawng. Having been out of rations for two days, they had to reach the valley floor as a coherent force and take a supply drop. On 25 June two aircraft dropped two days' rations for both Columns. They moved off that morning and soon encountered the tail of 12 NR's 43 Column, also making for Lakhren.

According to Richard Rhodes James, when 111 Brigade Columns heard Mogaung had been taken, many felt there was no longer any reason for stay-

ing in: 'We had ceased to be operationally capable of anything of significance and in a short time would become a shambles.'

Some 111 Brigade elements had to rest at Lakhren due to their poor state. Rhodes James: 'Mogaung was clear, the road to Myitkyina was open and we continued to wander around the hills, watching the rain beat down against the mountainside and turn the paths into quagmires. We watched our feet rot and felt the leeches digging into our flesh.'[11]

6 NR's Columns continued towards Lakhren. The going was awful and men and animals struggled in the mire. Mule loads were manhandled across bogs. Paddy Dobney, now in charge of the York and Lancaster sick, left a powerful account of his march from Mokso. He described it as the worst experience of his life:

> We moved off in pouring rain across the mud-covered landscape, myself leading, trying to pick the shallowest mud path across this horror stretch. We set off some 300 strong, of whom about 200 were

very sick; some of them were soon to die. The first of these, a young Lance-Corporal, occurred almost before the tail of our Column had cleared Mokso.

The Column MO, 'Doc' Arkle, did his best. Dobney wrote that Arkle had the job of 'hustling along men already past marching and, in some cases, past caring'. The presence of an overwhelming number of sick turned this trek into a nightmare:

> We had few mules or ponies to spare to carry the worst sick cases ... if we travelled at the speed of the slowest marcher we would have travelled nowhere. Another delicate factor was to try to establish which were the sickest cases deserving most care and attention and minimum duties. Hearts had to be hardened and everyone, except those obviously near death, was pushed and chivvied.

Private Clixby, the member of the Recce Platoon who warned about the state of the Lakhren track, also told of an atrocious stretch of swamp barring the way to the only site suitable for a supply drop. They tried to march around it but failed. They ran into a barrier 200 yards wide, covered in 4–5 ft high elephant grass. Paddy Dobney:

The leading men and I plunged into warm, muddy water, to sink nearly to our waists. Our feet held in the mud and undergrowth. We then found that by beating down the elephant grass we could create a sort of squelchy footpath and, by moving quickly, prevent our feet from sinking too deeply. About 25 of us gained the far bank. Here, we all stripped off down to our underpants and boots. We left a small guard on our equipment and arms and plunged back into the swamp to organise the crossing.

All relatively fit men were ordered to cross, strip down and return to help the sick and the mules across. Each mule required an escort of six men, to stop it sinking:

> The soldiers were wonderful that day, somehow finding some hidden energy as they crossed and recrossed that horror stretch. And the more times crossed, the wider into the elephant grass we had to go, making the crossing longer each time.[12]

It was impossible to complete the crossing before dark, so the men spent the night in two groups. The tail struggled over in the morning. Doc Arkle took Paddy Dobney aside and told him that a Corporal had collapsed and died. He had been buried beside the muddy

Making sure: Chindits check Japanese dead outside Mogaung's brick building. (Trustees of the Imperial War Museum)

track. A single Dakota then made a drop and the animals had their first proper feed for two weeks. Yet morale continued to decline as each day brought more deaths. Dobney told a Lance-Corporal to take his mule and go back for a straggler. Nothing more was seen of man, mule or straggler. A brief search, just before dark, proved fruitless. Later, a second, more extensive search also revealed nothing. They had disappeared. Another man died during the night. The Column stood bareheaded in the rain as the body, wrapped in a blanket, was lowered into a hastily dug grave marked by a bamboo cross. Six months later, Graves Commission teams – helped by volunteers from all Chindit columns – scoured the jungle tracks and collected remains for reburial.

Dobney reached his personal nadir. He stood by at dawn as the Column set out in the pouring rain. He wanted to observe the state of the entire Column. All the worst cases were at the front, the idea being that they would be encouraged by the others and stay within the Column as they lagged. Suddenly, Dobney was racked with dysentery:

I had not gone 20 paces when my guts gripped me in a violent call, giving me scarcely time to wriggle out of my big pack and all my other equipment and sink down panting as the scalding flux ripped from me. I had already had two calls since dawn but this was the worst.

This was repeated twice over the next half-mile:

Dear God, where did it all come from? Would it ever stop flowing from me? The last time I was so weak and exhausted I could hardly get to my feet again. My hand was throbbing and the bandage was hanging in sloppy folds, trailing in mud when I squatted.[12]

Paddy Dobney neared the point of no return. He was staggering from side to side of the track as the Column's tail came into view. Buoyed up, he found the strength to return to the head of the Column: 'Never again would I come so near to letting go.'

————•◄►•————

Many men faced the most severe test of their lives during the fighting around and inside Mogaung. Private Jack Hutchin of the South Staffords' 80 Column, however, confronted every Chindit's worst fear immediately afterwards:

'Until we left White City my health was quite good, all things considered. During the final phase of the march

to Mogaung, however, I was racked with malaria. I had eight successive bouts of fever. I had also been wounded in the neck. I was hit by shrapnel from a mortar round. It happened when our Rifle Platoon was told to join in a Company-strength attack to clear some Japanese attempting to block our way to Mogaung.

'Three of us were in front of the others, in an area of low scrub leading to a position we knew as "Gurkha Village" – south-east of Pinhmi, on a track leading into Mogaung. It was full of Japanese. I remember a Bren suddenly going into action on my left. Then the mortar round exploded and we pulled back. The Captain told me later that our Platoon was positioned to cover the withdrawal of the Company and that the three of us were covering the withdrawal of the Platoon. It would have been nice to have been told beforehand!

'Shortly after being wounded, I was in a position where I could see the Japanese ahead. They were well dug-in. I had a good friend, Bryn Coulson from Newport. He was a soldier's soldier and a fine man. Bryn took out one of the Japanese but stuck his head up once too often. He was hit by an explosive bullet. It struck the side of his head and, luckily for him, went on to explode in his pack. He was covered in blood and it looked very bad. I thought the entire side of his face had gone, but he was still alive. It took four days to carry him to a light aircraft strip. He was evacuated to hospital and later recovered. Bryn has gone now, but I still ring his wife every Sunday morning.

'I got my wound cleaned up. It was a fairly open gash. They took maggots from under the saddle of a mule and bound them into the wound, to stop the onset of infection. The wound didn't weaken me. It was more a combination of factors: hunger, exhaustion, the wound and the constant bouts of malaria, together with the extra heavy going as we pushed on to Mogaung. That track was a mudbath. Our legs sank well past the ankles. Nevertheless, I reached Mogaung and took part in the hard fighting there. When we marched away from Mogaung I was in a state of delirium.

'I vaguely remember we came across a group of Chindits from the first expedition, Longcloth. They had survived by "going native". Meanwhile, the Chinese were also advancing, but on higher ground. I have no idea why we didn't join them, but we stayed in the mud. It was now knee-deep in places.

'There came a point when I could go no further. I sat on a bank, near a tree. I was given an extra water bottle, a spare clip and one K-ration meal. Nothing much was said. No regrets were expressed. I looked at my legs and they were covered in deep jungle sores. My will had gone. That was that. I was finished and would never see my home again.

'I don't remember much else. I must have lost consciousness. I do remember waking to find myself surrounded by soldiers. I thought they were Japanese but had the wit to realise that I'd be dead if that had been the case. They were Chinese and, in my demented state, there seemed to be hundreds of them. One looked down from the bank and started to laugh. He may have been trying to encourage me but I was overcome with fury. I got up, found my rifle and struck him hard on the side of the neck with the butt. I have no recollection of what happened immediately afterwards, but I had found a spark. I began marching and caught up with the tail of the Column three days later. There was the white horse and Major Wilson. I knew then that I would survive.'

Hutchin continued to march with 80 Column:

'I carried on but was out of my mind. Determination and hate had vanished. I was drained of all emotion. I didn't care about anything, beyond the need to keep marching. We arrived at the American base at Shadazup two days later.

'No-one knew who we were. I was so hungry that I stole food at Shadazup. My weight had fallen to eight stone four pounds. I lifted the Mess tent flap and saw a large table. A man was slicing bread, piling the crusts at my end. I grabbed a handful. He saw me and immediately offered an entire loaf. I was one of 80 men who marched out.'

Notes

1. Chinnery, P.D. (2002), *March or Die*, 210–211
2. Jeffrey, W.F. (1950), *Sunbeams Like Swords*, 138–146
3. Ibid, 127–128
4. Ibid, 129–133
5. Rooney. D. (1997), *Mad Mike*, 98–104
6. Lieutenant-Colonel P.H. Graves-Morris, unpublished MS (via Bill Smith and Corinne Simons)
7. Calvert, M. (1974), *Chindits: Long Range Penetration*, 143–147
8. Jeffrey, W.F. (1950), *Sunbeams Like Swords*, 157–163
9. Rooney. D. (1997), 105
10. Towill, B. (2000), *A Chindit's Chronicle*, 117–118
11. Rhodes James, R. (1981), *Chindit*, 180–181
12. Dobney, Major R.P.J. 'Paddy', unpublished MS, July 1981 (via Bill Smith and Corinne Simons)

26

NEW OBJECTIVES

28 June–6 July 1944

'The youngest of the British fared worst; men in their early twenties proved to be sprinters rather than marathon runners.'

Charles Carfrae, 29 Column Commander, 7th Nigeria Regiment

ON 30 June, 77 Brigade was instructed to stay put, pending evacuation. The three other Special Force Brigades still in Burma were expected to do more. 3(WA), 14 and 111 Brigades received fresh orders. 14 Brigade was to attack enemy units in the Pinlon-Pinbaw area (its soft skin elements moving to Pahok). The Nigerians were to concentrate for an attack on Pyindaw, planned for 8 July. On the same day 111 Brigade units were to attack an occupied village, while Morris Force was confined to offensive patrolling. There were probing attacks against Maingna on 6/7 July and the Japanese were reported to be heavily reinforced. Meanwhile, Sunderland flights, evacuating the casualties remaining at Indawgyi Lake, resumed after a two-week break due to poor weather and aircraft unserviceability.

As the York and Lancaster's 84 Column struggled across the hills to railway valley they followed a new route found by Brigade Intelligence Officer Major George Carne, who was a Forestry Officer in Burma. This involved a steep 3,500 ft climb, but on virgin ground. They reached the top during the morning and sister Column 65 followed on. The 84 Column Recce Platoon, commanded by Lieutenant Liddy, had gone ahead to explore the route to Lakhren.

On reaching the top of Point 3551 the Battalion found it difficult to descend on the other side. The going was slippery and precipitous and 'slashers' were required to cut a way. It was utterly exhausting work, with progress down to a mile a day. Something had to be done. It was decided to retain only minimum mules with the Battle Groups (each now just over 100 strong), in the hope they would get through to railway valley. The soft skin elements and sick, led by Major Paddy

Dobney, were to be taken to Lakhren and Mokso Sakan. Dobney's group would then recross the hills, to rejoin the Battle Groups.[1]

On reaching Lakhren, Dobney's party was in a bad way. Gritty mud had opened up sores and turned them into running ulcers. Doc Arkle evacuated as many sick as possible by river. Paddy Dobney: 'Such was the weakened state of everyone and so vicious was the local strain of malaria and typhus that a man could be mobile one day and dead 48 hours later.'[2]

According to York and Lancaster Battalion Commander Philip Graves-Morris, 'Freedrop', the foal born in April, died of exhaustion on 2 July. In its first few weeks of life the Battalion mascot had travelled on its mother's back. The mare also lost condition and had to be destroyed. One veteran recalls that the foal was shot much earlier on, 'as an act of mercy'.

Later, in mid-July, Paddy Dobney and the York and Lancaster soft skin elements attempted to rejoin the Battle Groups. Dobney had led some 300 men and 80 animals. Having handed over a large number of sick at Lakhren on 14 July, he and his group would struggle to re-cross the hills and link up with the rest of the Battalion. Discipline in 'Dobforce' was harsh of necessity. On the trek to Lakhren, a sick man had to have a temperature of 104 deg. to be carried by one of the four remaining ponies and the elephants still accompanying them. The surviving animals were saved by an emergency drop of grain at the edge of the swamp. The MO's bandages had been laid out in the elephant grass to provide a marker. The track towards Taungni held more horrors. The men were forced to negotiate near vertical inclines and cross scores of swollen streams. Fallen trees held them up. Dobney's boots dis-

A few minutes peace: 'General' Lee Turner catches some sleep, his rifle within easy reach. Most officers carried rifles or carbines and avoided sidearms (which made them targets for snipers). (John Riggs)

integrated, the uppers breaking away from the soles. He had to bind them up with string. This track was littered with debris and dead mules, marking the earlier passage of other Columns. Dobney saw the relatively fit men 'adopt' those now past helping themselves. They made them bamboo beds and brewed tea for them. It took four terrible days to re-cross these hills.

Elsewhere in 14 Brigade, Sapper Eric Sugden of the Bedfordshire and Hertfordshire's 61 Column had been doing well until mid-June. His eyes then went yellow as he went down with jaundice. Sugden was one of the first to fly out from Indawgyi Lake when the Sunderlands returned:

'I vomited and couldn't keep anything down. The MO told me to try to eat. I joined the growing band of "sickies" beside the lake. On 30 June, having ploughed through a stretch of flooded paddy, I was ferried out on a raft and boarded a Sunderland flying boat. All kit was taken from us, to save weight. We left with just the clothes we wore. I was sent into the upper gun turret as I was one of the very few able to climb stairs. Years later, flying on the upper deck of a 747, I recalled my climb into that turret.'

On 30 June SEAC Supreme Commander Lord Louis Mountbatten, accompanied by Special Force Commander Joe Lentaigne, visited Stilwell's headquarters. They wanted to agree arrangements for withdrawing Special Force. Stilwell opposed this but Lentaigne pointed out that 77 and 111 Brigades each had only 350 men capable of fighting. Stilwell challenged the figures. It was decided that both Brigades (including Morris Force) would remain in until Taungni was taken. There was to be a joint Anglo-American medical inspection of the Chindits. Having gone along with this demand, widely regarded as a gross insult, Lentaigne left in the belief that two Chindit Brigades and his HQ had been cleared for evacuation – 77 Brigade immediately and 111 Brigade after advancing with the Chinese 38th Division to the Pahok–Sahmaw area. Stilwell, of course, had a very different view. As far as he was concerned, 77 and 111 Brigades remained under his firm control. The Chindits would go nowhere until he was ready.[3]

111 Brigade received orders for another operation, to support the West African advance along railway valley. The immediate target was a village north of Taungni. The wounded and unfit were to be spared this final ordeal. Meanwhile, Jack Masters and his officers worried

Advanced years: Roger Curry was the oldest man in 12 NR's 43 Column, at 39! He was Administrative Officer, in charge of supply drops and distribution. Curry is remembered by Dick Stuckey as 'the epitome of the English Gentleman ... a gallant soldier of the old pre-war school.' The effects of war in Burma can be seen on his emaciated frame. (Peter Allnutt)

marathon runners. Fresh, they would be capable of considerable exertion, able to march farther and more quickly than men rather older, but, having had few years in which to build up stamina, suffered more from lack of sleep, shelter and food. While these young Platoon Commanders and white Sergeants, burning themselves out, fell ready victims to fever or other ills, mature men from their late twenties up to about 35 years old had a good chance of finishing the course if not cut down in action or by typhus: their stamina had reached its peak and hardships bore upon them less heavily. Very few in their forties took part in the Chindit campaign. The unrelenting physical effort wrung from ageing muscles was too much for all but the strongest ...

Supply drops became hopelessly irregular; for three or four days in succession we subsisted on herbs, boiled to make a thin and tasteless soup. Any man who had saved a biscuit or morsel of cheese from the last ration drop would shrink out of sight to eat it, unable to withstand the involuntary gaze of less provident comrades.[5]

Another West African Battalion, 6 NR, reached Pahok a few days later. 66 Column had arrived at Lakhren on 28 June. Lieutenant Bill Cornish noted: 'All ranks were very exhausted and there were many cases of footrot owing to the constant exposure of the feet to water.' Lieutenant Larry Gaines, a 66 Column Platoon Commander, remembers some of the sick being flown out from Lakhren's light aircraft strip. The men spent three days resting, reorganising and eating. The Monsoon caused much of their personal equipment to rot. They were especially short of mule girths, which rotted quickly in the Monsoon rain and fell apart. Webbing was at a premium. Some replacement webbing was dropped but not nearly enough to meet demand.

On 1 July, 66 and 39 Columns left Lakhren and set out for the Brigade RV at Pahok, via Padigantawng. 12 NR's 43 Column was ahead, with a three-hour start. Consequently, 43 Column dictated 66 Column's speed; both found it heavy going in the thick red mud. The men passed what was left of the Cameronians' 90 Column. Lieutenant Cornish noted: 'They had suffered such heavy casualties that they were in no condition to fight.'

On 4 July, 66 Column reached Padigantawng. Some men with bad footrot could go no further and joined the concentration of casualties and sick at this village. The others, on their last legs, pushed on to Pahok, where the Brigade had established a perimeter.

Meanwhile, Paddy Dobney, with 14 Brigade's 84 Column, had an unusual 25th birthday present. He had his first solid bowel movement for two months and

about their vulnerability immediately after taking the village (assuming the attack met with success). They would have to move quickly to defend their positions. This would require a well timed drop of picks, shovels and wire. Underlying their concerns was the fear of a repeat of Blackpool's horrors.[4]

By now 77 and 111 Brigades were in a terrible state. 3(WA) Brigade and 14 Brigade were not much better. Charles Carfrae's 29 Column (7 NR) reached the 3(WA) Brigade rendezvous at Pahok on 2 July, several days before the other Battalions. Pahok amounted to just four deserted huts, around 14 miles west of recently captured Mogaung. Sister Column 35 skirmished with the Japanese on the way to the RV.[5] Carfrae's men endured much:

The youngest of the British fared worst; men in their early twenties proved to be sprinters rather than

regarded this as a good omen: 'Alas, it was a flash in the pan – or, rather, the mud – for next day it was business as usual and remained so for the rest of the campaign.'[2]

Later in July 'Dobforce' neared its rendezvous with the York and Lancaster Battle Groups. On entering a clearing recently occupied by a West African Column they came upon piles of abandoned new equipment. Dobney was delighted to remove his ruined boots and put on a well-fitting new pair.

During one wet, miserable breakfast halt, Captain Ken Griffin's Batman, Private Green, was attempting to warm some water for coffee. A tall, bearded figure passed by, slipped in the mud opposite Green and upset the mess tin. The Batman was too exhausted to get up, contenting himself with the comment: 'Ee! F****** clumsy bastard!' Tom Brodie then offered profuse apologies, handing over his own water bottle in compensation. Obviously, Green had no idea he was addressing the Brigadier, who looked like any other Column member by that stage. Brodie took it in good part.

As Paddy Dobney drew closer to the main body he realised his party was not alone in its distress. They came upon a young officer dying on the track. An Orderly had stayed back to tend him. They then reached a staging post for 14 Brigade wounded and sick and bivouacked beside them for the night. Just before they reached this

bivouac Dobney spotted a slight movement in a mound of mud. It was a human body and it was alive: '"Come on!" I said. "Let's get you back on the track." "Just leave me be, Sorr. Just let me die." At least I knew then which Column he belonged to.'[2]

Dobney and a Muleteer struggled with the man: 'He was so encased in mud that his weight was nearly doubled and we couldn't get a grip on him anywhere.' Eventually, they slung him across a mule. They had to cut off his mud-caked trousers. He lay on the animal's back, inert: 'His head and arms hung down one side and his bare legs the other, his shirt tails hung over his head, with his bare bottom pointing skywards. In this undignified manner we trudged into the staging post, where I was happy to find one of the Jock's officers and hand over my miserable charge.'[2]

Paddy Dobney set off the next morning to locate the Battle Groups. He found them preparing for their last fight with the Japanese. Dobney was ordered to bring up his party in two days. Just before he left, he saw a man commit suicide:

A rifle muzzle placed in the mouth, a quick jab on the trigger and another poor wretch was past the reach of any more jungle, rain and Japanese. In the bivouac that morning a Subaltern from another

The strain shows: 12 NR Chindits towards the end. From left to right: 'Dapper' Brown, Captain 'Flash' Pearson, Lieutenant Tommy Jones and Lieutenant 'Ting' Bell. (Peter Allnutt)

Column had rolled on a grenade and blown himself to oblivion. Also one of the Brigade HQ officers had lost his reason and had been flown out.[2]

On rejoining his group Dobney was saddened to learn that Private Mossman had died. Mossman was a cockney. Only a few days before he had been helping another sick man stay alive. Doc Arkle told Dobney: 'Just before he died he asked me to give you this.' The MO held out his hand and in it were three silver Rupees – the coins Mossman and everyone else had been given before leaving India: 'Without a word I took the coins and hurried outside.'

Paddy Dobney's mood was not improved when Heney told him that, in his absence, he had cleared out his pack and thrown away a mouldy half-slice of bread. In his reduced state, Dobney exploded with rage in front of his unfortunate Batman. To make matters worse, Corporal Ripley told him that an officer was required to perform the burial of a young officer at the camp up the hill. Dobney couldn't persuade himself to make the climb. The other officers were as bad or even worse than him. Ripley, for some reason, was still astonishingly fit. Dobney handed over a prayer book and ordered him to officiate. Ripley was startled but set off up the hill. Dobney regretted this for the rest of his life.

Yet, as his group approached the Battle Group RV Dobney discovered that he still had his sense of humour. He was stopped suddenly on the track by RSM Hemmings, a new pair of jungle green trousers over his arm.

Dobney had recently taken to wearing a towel 'kilt', so freeing himself from wet, mud-caked trousers. The RSM said: 'Beg your pardon, Sir, but I have express instructions from the Colonel that I am not to allow you near him without your trousers on.'

The Adjutant later told Dobney that he had been the subject of a 'missing, believed lost' casualty signal: 'Fortunately, Rear Base sat on the signal for a couple of days in case I turned up, thus saving my parents the worry of a War Office telegram.'

Suddenly, the drops included what, at that time, seemed unbelievable luxuries – bread, jam, tinned meat, rich steak and kidney and tinned fruit. The doctors warned against over-indulgence but many men succumbed to temptation. They were soon rolling on the ground in agony, clutching their stomachs.

The Brigade was to be relieved by 36th Division. Dobney was ordered to prepare a staging post near Pahok. While sitting in a small hut with some Americans, being plagued by flies, Dobney saw his first aerosol can of fly killer. He was most impressed.

Notes

1. Graves-Morris, Lieutenant-Colonel P.H., unpublished MS (via Bill Smith and Corinne Simons)
2. Dobney, Major R.P.J. 'Paddy', unpublished MS, July 1981 (via Bill Smith and Corinne Simons)
3. Calvert, M. (1974), *Chindits: Long Range Penetration*, 149
4. Rhodes James, R. (1981), *Chindit*, 182–183
5. Carfrae, C. (1985), *Chindit Column*, 164–169

27

POINT 2171 AND HILL 60

7–18 July 1944

'Our Medical Officers spared no efforts to alleviate the state of the sick and dying, but in many cases they were past medical aid.'

Lieutenant-Colonel Philip Graves-Morris, Battalion Commander, 2nd York and Lancaster Regiment.

WITH MOGAUNG taken, Stilwell now expected more from the Chindits. Elements of the Japanese 18th and 53rd Divisions, retreating from Mogaung and Kamaing, established new strongpoints west of the Namyin river, including positions at Sahmaw and Taungni. They sought to block the Chinese advance south. The key defensive features included 'Point 2171' and 'Hill 60', west and north of Sahmaw.[1]

Efforts intensified to evacuate the wounded and growing numbers of sick. L.1 light aircraft equipped with floats joined the Sunderlands flying out casualties from Indawgyi Lake. On 7 July a small unit parachuted in near Lakhren. This 30-strong team included power boat specialists, briefed to speed up evacuation by 'Dreadnought' rafts.

The withdrawal of the depleted Chindit Brigades hinged on the progress of the relieving force, 36th Division. On 7 July Brigadier Calvert was given the choice of awaiting 36th Division's arrival and flying out from Myitkyina or immediately marching his 77 Brigade survivors to Warazup. Wisely, he took the latter option and began marching north that very day.

14 Brigade continued its campaign of small-scale but successful actions, including the capture of Hkawan on 10 July. 3(WA) Columns pushed on, with orders to take Pyindaw and make contact with Chinese forces to the north. The West Africans attacked Pyindaw at dawn on 11 July. After a brief battle they discovered they were fighting the Chinese.

From 8–18 July, 111 Brigade took part in hard fighting around Point 2171. The struggle for possession of this commanding feature began on 20 June. Following the opening skirmishes, the 3rd/9th Gurkhas attacked

Point 2171, where a Company of Japanese had established machine gun nests. They took the hill and killed 50 of the defenders. Enemy artillery then opened up, heralding a series of counterattacks. The fighting on and around Point 2171 was handicapped by patchy air support, due to poor weather and the reorganisation of USAAF command structures and priorities.

Point 2171 was 111 Brigade's last major objective. This high feature overlooked railway valley to the east and dominated the approaches to Taungni.[2] The notation '2171' referred to its height in feet.

30 Column (3rd/4th Gurkhas) had pushed enemy outposts back towards the summit. Bill Towill was up early on the morning of 9 July. 3rd/9th Gurkhas were about to storm the summit:

'We were to put in a two Company attack. John Thorpe's B Company would follow the track on the right. This scarcely warranted the name "track" because in places you had to go up on your hands and knees. Jimmy Blaker's C Company would do a left hook through pathless jungle. I was ordered to precede these attacks by taking out a dawn patrol.

'Before we left I went to Jimmy to see whether he had any special orders for me. It was dark and he was eating a K-ration hash of biscuits and cheese by the light of a special torch he had captured on one of his forays. It had a lever which you squeezed into the body and this actuated a dynamo which gave you light for a few seconds. He had no orders for me, so we chatted briefly, wished each other good luck and went our separate ways. I had no idea this was to be the last time we would see each other.'

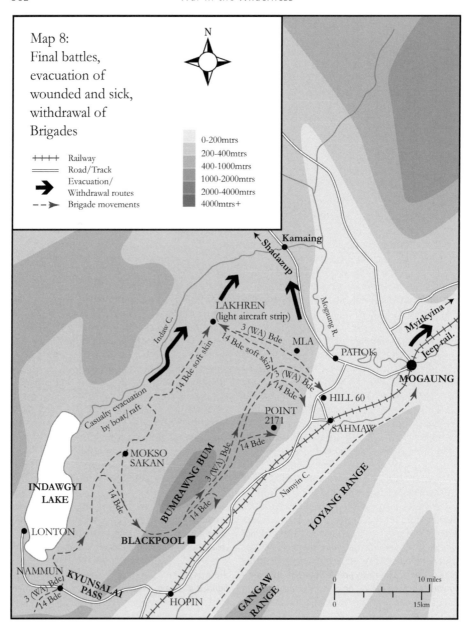

Map 8:
Final battles,
evacuation of
wounded and sick,
withdrawal of
Brigades

Towill then visited John Thorpe, the other Company Commander:

'It was decided that I would clear the path as far as I could for him. We made our way with great caution up the path. After we'd gone quite a long way we rounded a bend and there, in the dim light, just to one side of the path, was a Jap squatting behind a machine gun on a tripod. It was pointed straight at me! I leapt back into the jungle, took a careful look and saw that the Jap was dead, his arms hanging loosely by his sides and his head on his chest. Instead of falling sideways, he had remained squatting behind the machine gun.

'I decided I had done enough to give John a good start, so I went back and reported to him. His Company set off at a good pace and bumped the enemy just beyond where I had stopped. Looking back, I fear my patrol was counter-productive. It enabled B Company to reach the enemy long before C Company did.'

Bill Smyly, also with 3rd/9th Gurkhas, remembered this assault's 'co-ordination problem':

'B Company, on one side, bumped the Japanese outposts too soon. On hearing the firing, C Company speeded up and had almost reached the top when they encountered heavy machine gun fire. Blaker, who had won the MC in the Arakan fighting 12 months earlier, called for his men to charge. Blaker was fatally wounded but not killed instantly. From the same gun, Lieutenant Sweetman had the crown of his Gurkha hat shot away but escaped with his head.'

Bill Towill describes this determined attack in more detail:

'B Company put in a two Platoon attack, Yem Bahadur's on the left and Jemadar Kesh Bahadur Khattri IDSM (who was to receive the MC for his bravery on that day) on the right. With great heroism they secured the leading edge of the enemy position but Yem Bahadur's leg was shattered above the knee by a machine gun bullet. He was brought down on a stretcher, wallowing in his own blood. As they came to an abrupt halt before the Colonel and me, I saw a great gush of blood spill out over the front edge of the stretcher. But he wasn't concerned about his wound – only that he had been cut down before being able to get among the enemy with his kukri. He virtually ordered the Colonel to carry on with the attack!'

As for C Company:

'Leading from the front as usual, Jimmy, after some difficult navigating through the dense jungle, bumped the enemy and came under intense machine gun fire. Realising that this would cause heavy casualties among his men, he leapt to his feet and charged the main gun single-handedly, cheering his men on. Sadly, his luck ran out. He was mortally wounded by a burst of fire which struck him in the abdomen, slamming him back against a tree. As he slid down, he continued to cheer his men on as they charged and took the position. His second in command, Sweetman, went to comfort him but was told to go out to the right flank, to check that the men had linked up with B Company. Sweetman hesitated, since it would obviously be a great comfort to have his friend with him during his dying minutes, but Jimmy, putting the safety of his men first, added – "That's an order!" It was the last he was to give. His great heroism was recognised by the award of the Victoria Cross.'

Some 111 Brigade elements had remained at Lakhren. Cypher Operator Norman Campbell, with the Cameronians' 90 Column, celebrated his 21st birthday in these depressing surroundings on 13 July 1944. He fashioned a stove from two Army biscuit tins. He filled the bottom one with soil and poured in some petrol from the battery-charger's supply. The second tin served as an oven. He baked meat pies and apple pies and invited friends to dinner. He had made a reasonable pastry by crushing hard-tack biscuits into a flour, in a square of parachute cloth. The pies were washed down with a rum and water mix: 'Our Captain enjoyed a few pies but I didn't push my luck by offering him a drink, as the rum had been "liberated" from the officers' stock.'

While at Lakhren Campbell witnessed the demise of a Burmese who came into the camp demanding weapons to fight the Japanese. He was promptly denounced as a collaborator by a fellow Burmese:

'He was taken away by a Sergeant who had been handed a Thompson sub-machine gun by an officer with the words: "Try this. I've never used it." We heard a burst of fire. The Sergeant then returned and gave the weapon back with the words: "It works".'

111 Brigade's HQ was located at Padigatawng, a short distance over the hills from Lakhren. Yet this proved too much for many. The King's Own now managed only two to four miles a day. By this time the King's Own Chaplain, W.H. Miller, was very ill. He boarded one of the Dreadnought rafts leaving Kamaing and reached Warazup. He was flown out from Shadazup airstrip.

14 Brigade's York and Lancaster Columns fought their last battles during the second week of July. 84 Column's grossly reduced Battle Group now totalled only 112 all ranks. Nevertheless, they set off on 7 July to attack an enemy post near Sawnghka. The Japanese fled, managing to escape without casualties. The Battle Group found the village unoccupied. They then met up with two Platoons of Leicesters, responsible for a 'stop' on the track between Sawnghka and the supply drop area organised by their Battalion.[3]

The conditions were atrocious. Lieutenant-Colonel Graves-Morris, the York and Lancaster's Battalion Commander, described the ghastly monotony of incessant rain, which fell 'in a thundery, merciless deluge':

Men and animals were never dry. They marched and fought in mud and rain, ate and slept in mud and rain, and fell and died in mud and rain. Rain, hour after hour, day after day, beating its ceaseless tattoo on the ground and the trees, on men's bodies and on men's minds.

Our Medical Officers spared no efforts to alleviate the state of the sick and dying, but in many cases they were past medical aid. There appeared to be no antidote for typhus, Mepacrine scarcely subdued malaria and if they had had a cure for dysentery and rampant diarrhoea, they would have used it on themselves. Their total medical equipment was in two panniers – one mule load. They would set up a RAP in the rear of a battle and, in the rain and mud, would attend casualties on a makeshift bamboo table under a groundsheet for shelter. There, water was often in short supply and sterilisation probably done in a mess tin. Yet they patched up so many men to enable them to survive the long 'wait and carry' to a light plane for evacuation. They were also dentists. Despite wholesale dental attention while in India, the odd case of toothache was inevitable. The unfortunate one would report to the MO at evening bivouac, be made to lie on the ground, given a shot of pentathol in the arm, and the MO did his worst. The total dental equipment was two instruments – two different types of extractors. They either fitted or they did not.

On 9 July the York and Lancaster's 65 Column moved near Hkawan. The following day 84 Column moved back to Lower Sawnghka and a recce patrol went forward to find an approach for an attack on Pinlon, near Point 1497. The country was very open east of Sawnghka, with little cover available. They skirmished with Japanese patrols and evaded a night ambush without casualties.

Once again the York and Lancaster's Battle Groups became severely burdened with growing numbers of wounded and sick. By now the mobility of all Chindit columns was much impaired. Many men had problems with soft, swollen feet. Men who removed their boots often couldn't get them on again. They then continued in socks, with puttees wrapped around their feet. A virulent form of prickly heat attacked them. Their bodies were spotted with boils and jungle sores. Graves-Morris:

Some of these, as big as teacups, refused to respond to treatment. They spread with alarming rapidity and attracted a black ring of flies if exposed for any length of time. Due to lack of condition, the men's normal bodily resistance to skin sores was at a low ebb and made them easy targets for infection.[3]

84 Column had deployed to defend 14 Brigade's supply drop area as 65 Column headed north from the Hkawan area. They fought several successful engagements despite the frequent failure of automatic weapons and grenades. There was no oil to keep weapons fit for combat. When the Brens failed, the men took needless casualties.

84 Column's Battle Group reorganised the defences around the supply drop area and took the opportunity to refit and 'feast' on the dump of K-rations. On 18 July the two Columns reunited and planned an attack on the village of Ngausharawng. A fighting group of 13 and 15 Platoons (65 Column) left Hkawan to set up a block on the Hkawan-Ngausharawng track. The enemy was to be denied the high ground on the village approaches. The Japanese already on the ridge were driven off in a frontal attack. They made two attempts to retake the ridge but were beaten back. Private Ned Spark stood up at one point and fired his Bren from the shoulder.

Before the 3rd/9th Gurkhas assaulted Point 2171, ATO Bill Smyly had visited the Chinese, taking his favourite pony, 'Charlie':

'They came from North China. I met men from Shantung Province (where I had grown up, in the walled city of Tsinan) and heard their familiar dialect once again. Unlike our soldiers, who had been in the Army maybe two or three years, like myself, these men had been soldiering and at war for the past 11 years.'

The Chinese forces under General Stilwell were well supplied the most part but supplemented rations by contact with local villages and hunting and foraging in the jungle. The Chinese had built their own village, complete with barracks and the usual pigs and chickens underfoot. Building work was still under way:

A painful moment: York and Lancaster Sick Parade in the jungle. 'Stinker' has his boil dressed. (Walter Longstaff)

'Their Commander, dressed only in vest and pants, lived in a two-storey basha. We went up the ladder to the room above and sat on the floor. I was in the company of the Commander and his immediate circle as the evening meal was served: rice with accompanying dishes, meat and vegetables.

'One dish seemed to arouse both amusement and embarrassment. When it was offered I helped myself and said, "Very good!" There were giggles. Someone said, "Monkey" and the others laughed. Oddly enough, in all my time in Burma over two years I do not recall seeing a monkey. But there were plenty of dead Japanese. This did not occur to me till later. I can't remember anything very special about the meat.'

On 9 July the Gurkhas had around an hour to dig in on the summit of Point 2171 before the Japanese counter-attacked. Bill Smyly:

'Nearly all the explosions I saw were Japanese stick grenades, which detonate on impact. My Orderly and I shared a slit trench. The area was littered with unexploded stick bombs. I lay on a kind of earth couch just below ground level. My Orderly passed earth up to me and I threw it out. He was in the deeper part and going deeper. He was a perfectionist; it was a most beautiful slit trench.'

Bill Towill was also on the hilltop:

'I found it chilling to discover that in front of one of the enemy weapon pits the trees had been cut down by machine gun fire, such was its intensity. We held the hilltop for a couple of days before being relieved by another Battalion, whom we, in turn, relieved a few days later. During that time the Japs put in fruitless attacks which followed the same pattern. They came up the steep slope from railway valley, attacking fiercely under an intense shower of mortar bombs and shells. After about half an hour there would be a lull, followed by a brief resumption of the attack, under cover of which they removed their dead and wounded.

'At either side of the slope we had Vickers machine guns, which caught the enemy in enfilade as they came up the slope. During one attack a Gurkha dashed up to me to report that one of the Vickers had jammed fast. There was a spare Vickers just in front of my slit trench. I jumped out, picked it up, cradling it in my arms. With its tripod it was a very unwieldy burden and very heavy, too – probably well over a hundredweight. I got it into action. Mortar bombs and shells were falling so thickly that it really was miraculous that I wasn't hit.

'As we came under machine gun fire I could see bullets striking the trees just above my head. The bravery of my Gurkha Orderly, Gupta Bahadur, resulted in the award of the Military Medal. He was a Bren gunner during the battle. He was a loveable little chap, totally devoted to me and a very fine soldier. I can still remember his Regimental Number: 10205. This is no

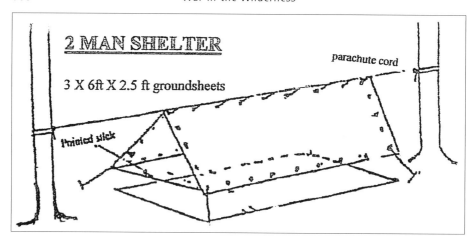

Jungle shelter: American zip-up jungle hammocks were a revelation to the Chindits, who were accustomed to making do. This sketch shows how a groundsheet was used to give some protection from Monsoon rain. (Fred Gerrard, via Bill Smith)

great feat of memory. Gurkha names were so similar that men always called themselves by the last couple of numbers.'

Bill Smyly picked up a stick grenade as a souvenir:

'I took it in my pack, all the way back to Dehra Dun. I presented it to the Mess Secretary, thinking that he might like to keep it in the Mess as a trophy. The poor man was deeply shocked and told me, a few hours later, that he had called in an explosives expert to detonate it. It had made "a nice big bang".'

The 3rd/9th Gurkhas were relieved on 11 July by the King's and 30 Column. Bill Towill's luck continued to hold:

'I had another remarkable escape. We were resting at the foot of the hill. I was ordered to take a patrol along Point 2171's left flank. I gathered together a scratch Section of men from HQ who were not used to patrolling and, since they seemed rather edgy, I decided to give them some confidence by going point – that is, at the very front and the most dangerous position in the patrol. We came to a narrow stream and crossed it. Ahead of us, steadily climbing upwards, was a very narrow trail hemmed in by thick jungle and going straight for about 400 yards before turning off to the right. I took a very careful look and moved off. I had gone about halfway when suddenly, from my left front, a sniper fired at me and missed. He reloaded in a flash and fired again. Once again, he missed as I leapt to my left into the undergrowth.

'I shall never forget the sound of his rifle bolt flashing back and forth as he ejected the spent cartridge case and rammed a new round into the breech for his second shot. It was so loud and clear – just as if I had been standing immediately behind him on a rifle range. He was not yards but only a few feet away. So, why did he miss me, not once, but twice? Somehow, I managed to get away with it. Someone up there was looking after me!'

The accumulation of casualties around Point 2171 caused problems. The King's Own reported that the Japanese were moving to cut them off and prevent the evacuation of wounded. On the summit of Point 2171 reliefs became more frequent. Around 150 wounded were concentrated at the Brigade's jungle hospital.

14 Brigade was expected but had not arrived when the casualty situation became critical. 111 Brigade lacked the strength to hold Point 2171 and provide protective escorts for parties of wounded and sick. The trauma of Blackpool still haunted them. Richard Rhodes James: 'At Blackpool some of the wounded had been left and we still felt the guilt. While there was still a chance to get them out, that chance must be taken.' The decision was made. Permission was given to pull out and head north to Mla, prior to marching out:

In our present state we could not afford to risk an encounter with the enemy and must pick our way carefully down circuitous, unfrequented paths until we were once more safe behind our own rather thin lines. There was no line as such, only a series of isolated positions manned by troops who had had enough.[4]

Corporal Fred Holliday, with 10 Platoon of the King's 82 Column, described the fighting around Point 2171:

'It was another terrible battle. It was also a very confusing time. Depleted groups were being merged and unit commands were changing on a daily basis. Our Platoon Officer, Lieutenant Thomas, was killed. I remember sitting in a group with him, around a bivouac fire, swapping stories along the lines of "where one would like to be now."

'Lieutenant Thomas, a Welshman, always wanted to be at Townhill, looking down over Swansea Bay. My wife comes from that part of the world. I often think of Thomas when I look out over Swansea Bay.'

When the Kyunsalai Pass was abandoned, some West African elements headed away from the Indawgyi Lake area and turned north-east towards Pahok. The intention was to move further east towards Pyindaw, then swing south-west for an attack on the Hill 60 feature.

At first the Nigerians negotiated the eastern margins of the lake, between the swamps and the mountainous terrain separating them from the railway corridor. Good progress was made, despite clouds of highly aggressive mosquitoes. Things changed on the second day, however, when the track disappeared into a black bog. A soft, deep ooze lay beneath evil-smelling water up to three feet deep. The Chindits' heavy packs pushed their feet into the bottom slime and the men cut long sticks to probe their way forward. Lieutenant Peter Allnutt was with 12 NR's 43 Column:

'Mosquitoes collected in black masses on my shoulders and bit through my battledress. A particularly vicious type of fly, with a bite like the prick of a needle, added to our pleasures.'

They plodded on as there was nowhere to stop. Allnutt suddenly noticed that the wireless mule was in trouble. It stumbled and fell over in two feet of water. The carrying boxes were unhooked and carried to the nearest tuft of reeds. The mule was coaxed to its feet, reloaded and persuaded to move – until it fell again. This painful process was repeated in the stinking mud and water. The mule fell 12 times that day. The heat and humidity reached unbearable levels and everyone had had enough by 2pm. Luckily, they came across an island in the swamp and spent the next two hours resting. Things looked up that afternoon, when they saw a Dakota dropping supplies in the distance. That meant dry ground ahead. Shortly afterwards they passed the sister Column in bivouac. Peter Allnutt:

'It had been an appalling day. Not a breath of wind cooled our sweaty, mud-stained faces. It was probably the worst of many grim marches. We set double guard that night, as 12 Column had reported a force of 100 Japs with elephants in the area, trying to rejoin their forces in the railway corridor.'

43 Column's Recce Platoon rested for a day or so, awaiting a drop. They set out again in good spirits, with five days' rations up. Within two hours, however, they were back in the filthy, mosquito-ridden morass, broken only by deserted Japanese positions on small 'islands' in the swamp. During the last hour of daylight they reached a drier area with few trees. They came across a number of Japanese and African dead – one of 6 NR's Columns had been surprised during a supply drop. The men were bitten by mosquitoes throughout the night. Peter Allnutt:

'I learned subsequently that we were in Burma's worst Blackwater Fever area. No European would visit it if he could avoid it. Dawn began with a mass attack by sandflies. They drove us crazy. I defended myself by damping my towel and winding it round my head and face. The others followed suit and we soon looked like a group of walking mummies.'

Weary from lack of sleep and puffy with insect bites, the Platoon left the lake basin behind, entered forest and reached the Brigade RV that evening. 43 Column's main body came in the next morning. They spent the next three days resting up and preparing for the trek across the mountains. Those too ill to face this were evacuated to Kamaing.

The Recce Platoon marched east into the mountains, climbing steeply in torrential rain, with up to 18 inches of glue-like mud underfoot. The mules had been left with the main body yet it took until early afternoon to climb the first, 2,000 ft summit. They paused, shrouded in Monsoon cloud, then encountered a group of 111 Brigade wounded who warned that the going ahead was even worse.

Later, they bivouacked where they stood, on a 45-degree slope. The following morning brought fresh challenges. One 3,400 ft climb took six hours, pushing up against the track's deep slime. Panting at the top, Peter Allnutt watched the rest come in, only to find that Sergeant Radcliffe was missing. He appeared a little later, caked in mud. Having slipped, he fell onto his face and was propelled downslope for several hundred feet by muddy lubricant and the weight of his pack.

During the afternoon the track disappeared into a mountain torrent, allowing Radcliffe to clean himself.

They stayed in the shallows and pushed through the strong current, but the water became waist high and continued to rise. They emerged, exhausted, after half a mile and stood on a slope leading to the highest point they were to cross. 111 Brigade HQ was established at the top.

This location was useless for supply drops, being permanently enveloped in cloud. 43 Column took its next drop in the foothills below, closer to the railway corridor. At one point they moved off the track to let an exhausted 111 Brigade Platoon pass. One of their Bren gunners lost his footing in the slurry and fell on his face in front of Peter Allnutt:

*'I heard him shout: "I'd f****** well like to see that f****** Stilwell here. I'd wipe his f****** face in it!" We all felt that way. Keeping us in longer than three months, in Monsoon conditions, halved our strength due to disease and battle casualties.'*

They neared 3(WA) Brigade HQ at the small mountain village of Pahok, where the Columns were concentrating for supply drops. The Japanese soon attacked them but a 7 NR Column threw them back, inflicting heavy casualties. Allnutt noticed a peculiarity of warfare in the unusually dense bamboo thickets:

'These magnified noise and an attack sounded much closer than it really was. Rifle shots would echo, so that it was impossible to tell from which direction they had been fired. One bullet sounded like a dozen. Automatic fire close by sounded quite terrifying and was enough to put fear in the stoutest hearts.'

Peter Allnutt lost his right-hand-man at Pahok. Allnutt had been out on patrol when Sergeant Radcliffe was told to accompany an inexperienced Subaltern on a recce. Radcliffe was wounded and evacuated from Indawgyi Lake with a chip out of his arm and a bullet in the calf.

43 Column prepared to attack Mla village, believed to be the base of the Japanese force that had attacked 7 NR. They would then break out into the railway corridor. There were good targets to attack. The men could hear Japanese trucks on the road, retreating from Mogaung.

Once again, Allnutt's small group took the lead and they soon exchanged fire with Mla's outposts. The evening brought a reminder of the hazards of close combat in thick jungle. Groups of men in bivouac were awaiting news of the attack on Mla. There was a sudden burst of automatic fire. A jumpy sentry fired into the bushes, not knowing that the track turned at 180° and

that he was firing into the next group. The only casualty was a slightly wounded wireless mule.

As the rest of 3(WA) Brigade advanced on Pyindaw, 12 NR was held up at Mla for two days. The main defences consisted of a wired block at a track junction, with hills covering both flanks. The jungle was dry, thick and very noisy, ruling out movement by stealth. The Japanese refused to budge, frontal assaults were costly and heavy mortaring had no effect. During the first evening Allnutt was told by Lieutenant-Colonel Pat Hughes to go out at dawn and check that the village was still occupied. He was given the services of an elderly Chinese guide who hated the Japanese, having been strung up and flogged by them.

A few hours later, in the dim early morning light, Peter Allnutt prepared to move out. This small group consisted of Allnutt, the Chinese guide, a Burrif interpreter and seven others. They edged forwards, clambering over fresh mortar craters until just 10 yards from the Mla track. Moving ahead on his stomach, Allnutt got to within 20 yards of the block's wire. The Japanese positions appeared empty. Looking back along the track he could see two corpses and what looked like a Bren. Feeling extremely vulnerable, he stepped onto the track and thus confirmed that the Japanese had gone. Captain Dick Stuckey's patrol also reported no Japanese. Allnutt, meanwhile, had a new Recce Platoon member. His Chinese guide had asked to stay: 'We made him an honorary member of the Battalion. He became a great favourite with the men.'

The West Africans concentrated for their attack on Hill 60, midway between Sahmaw and Pyindaw, to the north. This strongpoint had to be overcome if the Japanese were to be pushed back along the railway corridor. The Chindits fought hard for Hill 60 until 16 July, but failed to take the feature. It finally fell to a much larger 36th Division force.

On the approaches 6 NR's 66 Column skirmished repeatedly with Japanese detachments. On 11 July a patrol explored two roads in the area, one leading to Pyindaw village. A 66 Column block was then attacked by the Japanese. The key objective, however, was Hill 60, at the junction of the Pyindaw–Nampadawng road and the Sahmaw road. The assault opened on 13 July; 43 Column attacked the hill from the east but was repulsed.

During the previous day, Lieutenant Allnutt was ordered to recce Hill 60. He found the area between road, railway and hill littered with wrecked trucks and mule skeletons. It was also honeycombed with abandoned foxholes, which would save the West Africans the trouble of digging their own. Hill 60 was a low,

A grim sight: Hill 60's bare summit. It was covered with trees and shrubs when first attacked. It was then stripped bare by close support bombing. (Peter Allnutt)

lozenge-shaped feature no more than 50 ft high, running east-west for several hundred yards. The Japanese were firmly entrenched. Chinese forces had been held up by a similar feature – the two hills dominating the surrounding area.

Hill 60 itself was occupied by several hundred Japanese troops, squatting in a network of deep trenches and dugouts. Allnutt took his patrol to the very edge of the Japanese positions. He was concerned about the dense brush covering the approaches. This would make the following day's assault difficult and there was open ground to the west, ruling out any flanking move from that direction. On the other hand, it should be possible to crawl right up to the Japanese trenches unseen.

The next morning, 13 July, Allnutt watched Dick Stuckey's Company leave the edge of the scrub and enter the brush on Hill 60. The lead Platoon was slowly crawling uphill when the Japanese woke up. A long burst of automatic fire, from the eastern end of the hill, brought the defenders to life. There was automatic and rifle fire and showers of grenades. The attackers were pinned down, with the forward units just 15 yards from the Japanese and unable to move.

Allnutt used his carbine from a range of 80 yards. Firing over the heads of the men trapped in the dense brush, he hit several Japanese. He tried three times for an officer who repeatedly showed himself while using binoculars. Earlier heavy bombing had failed to shift the entrenched Japanese. Dick Stuckey:

'Hill 60 had been well and truly blasted. It was virtually bare and offered little cover. When I got closer to the hill I found myself in a quandary. The advance through the secondary scrub had taken much longer than expected. The Japanese were raking the area with fire and I had lost one of my Platoon Commanders and several men. What now? Fix bayonets and charge with my four Platoons?'

During the afternoon Stuckey's men made a fresh attempt to take Hill 60. According to Peter Allnutt, they simply stood up and made for the Japanese trenches. Once again they met with heavy automatic fire and it was obvious that the attack would fail. 6 NR tried from the west, also without success and a promised air strike failed to materialise. Hill 60 would not be taken without air and artillery support. Dick Stuckey remembers the loss of an outstanding man:

'I had an excellent CSM, Bukar Mau. We were kneeling down, in conference, when Bukar Mau wanted a better look at the surrounding ground. He stood up and got a sniper's bullet. I saw his brains spill from the back of his head. I was relieved to receive orders from Pat Hughes to pull back. We would have taken heavy losses without support. American-led Chinese forces then began shelling Hill 60. One shell fell short and killed two of our officers – Captain Bill Briggs and the recently married Bob Heap – together with three Nigerian soldiers.'

Killed in action: Sergeant Matthews (left), of 12 NR's 43 Column, was killed when Dick Stuckey and his men first attacked Hill 60. He had taken over a Platoon when the Subaltern was evacuated sick. He is pictured with Sergeant Baldwin. (Peter Allnutt)

A new attack on Hill 60 by 66 Column had made good progress but the Japanese rallied and reoccupied their positions. The attacking Company withdrew under heavy artillery and mortar fire and there were numerous casualties from machine guns as they crossed open ground.

During the next day 66 Column rested just west of the road. On 15 July their night flanking attack on Hill 60 was inconclusive. They were attacked in turn during the late evening of 17 July but drove off the Japanese with machine gun fire. On 18 July the Column withdrew east of the road and watched Mustangs attack the Japanese positions. The situation on and around Hill 60 had reached stalemate.

Allnutt spent the next few weeks leading a sniper patrol. They took a steady toll of Hill 60's defenders. The Chinese became a nuisance as they often pillaged Chindit supply drops. On one occasion tempers flared and Chinese pilferers were dispersed by Sten gun fire.

A medical inspection of 111 Brigade's survivors took place at an American Field Hospital now established at Mla, the village below Pahok. The results revealed the full cost of using already exhausted and sick Chindits as assault troops in Monsoon conditions. The Commander of 77 Brigade, Michael Calvert, wrote: 'All ranks, both British and Gurkha, were physically and mentally worn out and had lost an average of two to three stone. Most men had had three or more attacks of malaria and some over seven, but had remained fighting with their units. The incidence of death from cerebral malaria and typhus was rising.[5]

When the shocking results of the medical assessment became known, the criterion for being 'fit' was changed, from the capacity to continue for an additional two months to just one month. Wingate must have turned in his grave. Richard Rhodes James: 'Perhaps they wanted better figures. If so, they were disappointed. We stuck to our figures and repeated them.'[6] Bill Towill provided a disturbing description of the depths to which 111 Brigade's men had plunged:

The will to survive must surely be one of the most, if not, in fact, *the* most fundamental and compelling of all the drives in the human personality. Any normal man will do almost anything just to survive, just to keep on living. How fearful, therefore, must be the pressures brought to bear on the human spirit, to make it relinquish the will to live and, instead, just to lie down and die. Yet these were, in fact, the immense pressures which, over the last four months and more, had been brought to bear on us. I found it a very sobering, indeed frightening, thought that some men, having survived the assault of wounds and disease, had yet succumbed to the psychological assault and, what is more, had done so when relief was almost in sight.[7]

York and Lancaster Chindit Fred Gerrard had no doubt about the fundamental cause of the catastrophic collapse in health: months living on what was intended to be an emergency ration for just a few days, aggravated by the effects of the Monsoon:

> By June the condition of all Brigades was on a downward spiral, as forecast by Wingate when he set the recommended 90-day limit. It was known that those on K-rations were receiving a daily deficit of 800 calories – 72,000 over 90 days. Those Columns employed in a mobile role, having to carry their 50/70 pound loads over hills that seemed to go up forever and had to make their meagre five days' rations last 6–8 days (or more) when a suitable drop site could not be found, had an even greater deficit. Add to this the aversion of some to certain parts of the K-ration, by four months most Chindits had lost three stone in weight, were invariably lethargic and became susceptible to many ailments. The Monsoon was an addition to the equation.[8]

Following the doctors' examinations only 118 out of 2,200 men of 111 Brigade were found to be 'fit' for duty: seven British officers, 21 ORs and 90 Gurkhas. 111 Brigade's Commander put the correct figure at 119, including himself. The King's Own War Diary states that the medical inspection at Mla had found just one officer and 10 British ORs fit to continue (from an original strength of over 900). Special Force Commander Joe Lentaigne told Stilwell that 111 Brigade was being withdrawn on his own decision, regardless of consequences. Over 2,000 unfit survivors were withdrawn to Kamaing and the remaining 119 were formally released around 10 days later. They included Corporal Fred Holliday of the King's 82 Column, who had taken part in the Point 2171 fighting:

Battle over: Hill 60 was secured eventually. Pictured afterwards are (left to right): Ian Gunn (described by Dick Stuckey as 'a natural soldier'), Peter Allnutt and Tommy Jones. (Peter Allnutt)

Survivors: the remaining Europeans with the Nigerians at Hill 60, gathered by a large bomb crater. According to Dick Stuckey, Brigadier Ricketts took this opportunity to deliver a pep-talk. (Peter Allnutt)

'We marched to Mogaung, boarded the Jeep railway to Myitkyina and were flown out. I was one of the lucky ones. I wasn't wounded. I had plenty of jungle sores, however, and "duck feet" – trenchfoot. Things changed as soon as we got out. I went down immediately with malaria and hepatitis.'

Allen wrote of 111 Brigade: 'They had fought long past the prescribed period set by Wingate, long past the limits of endurance and even in their final hours had shown gallantry of the highest kind, as when 3rd/9th Gurkhas assaulted Point 2171.'[1]

Efforts continued to bring out the survivors. Lentaigne had conferred with Brigadier Morris on 14 July. Shortly afterwards the Gurkhas were flown out, having suffered over 50 per cent casualties (70 per cent losses among the original strength of British officers). At the time of this meeting Morris Force had an effective strength of around three Platoons. Stilwell still refused to agree to their evacuation. Nevertheless, they were taken out a few days later, relieved by 72 Brigade of 36th Division.[9]

Notes

1. Allen, L. (1986), *Burma: The Longest War 1941–45*, 374–379
2. Rhodes James, R. (1981), *Chindit*, 184–187
3. Graves-Morris, Lieutenant-Colonel P.H., unpublished MS (via Bill Smith and Corinne Simons)
4. Rhodes James, R. (1981), 189–192
5. Calvert, M. (1974), *Chindits: Long Range Penetration*, 149
6. Rhodes James, R. (1981), 195
7. Towill, B. (2000), *A Chindit's Chronicle*, 118–119
8. Gerrard, F. unpublished MS, October 2000 (via Bill Smith)
9. Rooney, D. (2000), *Wingate and the Chindits: Redressing the Balance*, 156

28

COMING BACK FROM HELL

19 July–29 August 1944

'We pleaded with him to accept evacuation. He said he had walked in and he was going to walk out. And walk out he did, straight into hospital — where he died.'

Norman Campbell, 90 Column, 1st Cameronians

ARRANGEMENTS FOR evacuating Special Force were accelerated. In his final insult to the Chindits, the American General Stilwell ordered the hundred or so men of 111 Brigade still capable of functioning to guard Chinese gun positions near Pahok. Over 2,000 wounded, sick and exhausted survivors of 111 Brigade arrived at Mogaung on 27 July. The evacuation of Morris Force also began; they had left Myitkyina by 29 July. 111 Brigade (less Stilwell's '111 Company') had left Myitkyina by 1 August. 77 Brigade flew out from Warazup.

With Myitkyina town finally secured on 3 August, the Ledo Road's construction continued. This project cost US$137 million, a vast sum at that time.[1] The Ledo Road was extended past Kamaing to Myitkyina. Eventually, it joined the old Burma Road leading into China and, eventually, Chungking.[2]

The decision to hasten the evacuation of the Chindits came after Lentaigne complained to Mountbatten, on 23 July, that Stilwell remained determined to keep them fighting. Lentaigne added that little was being done to bring up 36th Division to relieve the Chindits, despite the fact that so many lives now hinged on immediate evacuation and hospitalisation. SEAC's Supreme Commander had had enough. Mountbatten ordered Stilwell to immediately evacuate all unfit men.[3] Units involved in this large-scale operation included the 803rd Medical Air Evacuation Transport Squadron, based at Chabua, India. They evacuated thousands, including Chindits, Gurkhas, Chinese and Kachins.[4]

14 and 3(WA) Brigades remained operational and faced fresh demands from Lentaigne and Stilwell. 3(WA) was to cooperate with 36th Division's 72 Brigade, which was to attack Nampadaung. The West Africans took over positions captured by 72 Brigade. 14 Brigade cov-ered 72 Brigade's flank by seizing high ground around Labu, Padaung and Sizguhtawng, with its main attacks set for 5 August. In addition, 14 Brigade was expected to occupy Point 2171 (the Japanese were back in residence) and the Taungni Bum.

The last weeks of Operation *Thursday* unfolded. 14 Brigade's 74 Column (7th Leicesters) was to take Taungni Bum. The York and Lancaster Columns, 84 and 65, were to take and hold the area around Point 1497, north-west of Labu, with the Black Watch's 42 and 73 Columns passing through to take Brigade objectives. The Bedfordshire and Hertfordshire's 16 and 61 Columns returned to Point 2171. On 4 August 12 Mitchell bombers struck Japanese positions around Hill 60, which fell the next day. Point 1497 fell on 6 August, Taungni Bum on 8 August and Point 2171 shortly afterwards.

Merrill's Marauders withdrew on 10 August. Eventually, they reformed as 75th Infantry Regiment, with the Battle Honour 'Myitkyina'. The capture of Mogaung and Myitkyina was instrumental in breaking the Japanese grip on North Burma. With the availability of Myitkyina airfield, the tonnage flown over 'The Hump' to the Chinese trebled within a couple of months.

The West Africans took over positions captured by 72 Brigade on 5/6 August. Two days later patrols reported that Sahmaw had been abandoned by the Japanese. During the third week of August preparations were under way for the handover as 36th Division continued south. The remaining Special Force Brigades left their operational positions immediately prior to evacuation. The West Africans flew out from Myitkyina on 17/18 August, followed by 14 Brigade during 21–26 August. The last of the Chindits left Myitkyina on August 27. It was over.

Captain Bill Towill of 3rd/9th Gurkhas was one of the very few 111 Brigade Chindits passed 'fit' at Mla: 'Yet when I got to India I ended up in hospital for five weeks, with a fever which would not respond to treatment and which, so far as I know, was never diagnosed. I believe tests established that my leukocyte (white cell) blood count was very low.'[5]

When 3rd/9th Gurkhas arrived at Mogaung on 28 July, there were two Jeep trains to Myitkyina leaving daily, at around 13.00 and 18.00. Each carried up to 400 men. The 3rd/9th Gurkhas had to wait. They left on the afternoon of 30 July, making the two-and-a-half hours rail journey to Myitkyina. They then had a hard march of one-and-a-half hours through swampy country to reach the airstrip. On the way, they could hear the battle for control of Myitkyina town still under way.

Those too weak or otherwise unable to march to Mogaung and board the Jeep trains to Myitkyina were flown out by light aircraft. After the medical inspection, Lentaigne put in an appearance at Mla. According to Richard Rhodes James, he got a 'not very friendly reception' from British troops.[6]

Those with harrowing memories of their last days in Burma include Cameronian Norman Campbell. American-led forces finally took Myitkyina town 78 days after Stilwell first claimed it had been captured.[7] 90 Column was ordered to help take the town; the Cameronians knew they were being abused. Norman Campbell:

'Wingate would never have kept us in, had he been alive. We stayed in and suffered needless loss. As we were always sweating, large yellow blisters began to form under our arms, round the waist and in the groin, smelling horribly when they burst. It was as though we were rotting away. All our medics had to treat them with was talcum powder and not my favourite brand at that – "Old Spice".'

This Column's first contact with the Chinese almost resulted in disaster. They were taken for Japanese. Bill Smyly was not alone in being impressed with Chinese 'home comforts'. These troops had built long bamboo bashas, fully lined with white parachute cloth. Norman Campbell: 'It looked as if they had been there for some time and were having a more comfortable time than we were.'

The Cameronians' two Columns, 90 and 26, barely mustered a Company between them. Brigade HQ was warned repeatedly about the collapse in health. Norman Campbell:

'Men were still going down, totally worn out or sick, and the worst cases were being carried on two elephants we

had enlisted. These were wonderful creatures. They kept going through the deepest mud, walking non-stop all day long. They must have saved a few lives.'

Private Jim Unsworth, of the King's Own's 46 Column, didn't think much of Mogaung when he arrived for evacuation:

'Signs of the recent fighting were all around. Everything was in ruins and steam locomotives and trains had been blown up. We settled down and spent our sixth night without food. During the next morning Major Openshaw told us to board flat wagons pulled by a converted Jeep. This would take us to Myitkyina, where we would be flown out.

'Before we left the Major asked me to look for the canteen. This was in a large canvas tent. I shouted: "Anyone in?" A Yank appeared and said: "You just come in? What do you want?" I told him that, for starters, I wanted a bucket of tea for 10 men. It is hard to describe how good that tea tasted. This Yank had tins of "Ideal" condensed milk! He then asked whether we wanted something to eat. "What about a bacon sandwich?" I had come to think that K-rations were the only food left in the world. I couldn't believe this. He opened a huge tin of bacon and began sawing off slices of good bread. Openshaw couldn't believe it either, when I gave him his bacon sandwich. We made the most of it, as we didn't get anything else to eat. During these long months of hardship, the one thing I really craved was a good sandwich made with fresh white bread. We did have bread dropped occasionally, but it was always eaten through with maggots. I do remember, however, being dropped a very welcome seven-pound tin of stewed apple. That was great. We dipped into it with our spoons for a very long time.'

When Jim Unsworth flew out from Myitkyina he was bone weary and emaciated, weighing just six stone.

Still marching with 90 Column, Norman Campbell nursed an obsession. He was determined to finish on his feet. Another Chindit, Rifleman Dougie Walker, felt the same, despite being ravaged by malaria and jaundice:

'We pleaded with him to accept evacuation. He said he had walked in and he was going to walk out. And walk out he did, straight into hospital – where he died. We'd had four-and-a-half months of it by then and were absolutely buggered.'

90 Column's survivors were told to make for the American airfield at Warazup. They would have to march through thick mud, in torrential rain, across

Trophy of war: members of 20 Column's Commando Platoon with a flag taken after the Tapaw Ferry battle, prior to Mogaung's capture. Fusilier Harold Shippey, of Hull, East Yorkshire, is standing on the right. (Harold Shippey, via Ian Niven)

Safe at Tinsukia: Officers of 6 NR's 66 Column at the Reception Centre, at the end of Operation *Thursday*. From left to right (top): Captains Dunkley, Walsh and Bennion, Lieutenant Kealty and Captain Cornish. From left to right (middle): Major Mackenzie, Lieutenant-Colonel Upjohn and Majors Griffin and Crews. Front: Lieutenant Farrant. (Larry Gaines)

the usual appalling terrain to reach salvation. Norman Campbell:

'Somehow these problems didn't seem to matter quite so much. We had food, those wonderful jungle hammocks and, above all, we were safe. That was a huge weight off my mind. No-one regretted the prospect of leaving Burma! We now had some luxuries, including tinned fruit and bread. I tried and failed to eat a thick slice. Our stomachs had shrunk so much that we couldn't handle any sort of bulk.'

Campbell took a liberty on the morning of that last march. He stowed away Captain McLean's hammock, together with his own, on the two elephants. Unfortunately, the elephants failed to turn up at the night bivouac. Campbell didn't know how to explain things to his Captain. Happily, the elephants put in a timely appearance and he was spared embarrassment.

Ian Niven faced the toughest march of his life. The 20 Column Lancashire Fusilier stood in the wreckage of Mogaung:

'I looked around at the devastation. I was completely knackered. I asked myself all the obvious questions: "What happens next? Will I live?" After the battle I became so ill I could hardly walk. We were then told to make for Shadazup. Somehow I made that march. I said to myself: "If you can get there, you can live." I was determined to see my mother again.'

This extraordinarily fit young man had become a physical wreck: 'My fitness had gone completely. I had weighed 10 stone five pounds. I now weighed seven stone seven pounds. This was recorded on my arrival at the field hospital.'

Captain Jeffrey was Administrative Officer with the Lancashire Fusiliers' sister Column, 50. He wrote of that final march:

We were suffering from the dark and complex aftermath of fear, with its associations of uneasiness and self-examination. We began to think and remember. I know that, for the first time since I landed at Broadway, I began to dream violently at night.'[8]

Ian Niven has only faint recollections of flying out:

'I remember being in the Dakota, standing up and holding on to the statichute line running along the fuselage roof. I stared down at the thick jungle below, swaying at the open hatch. Then the plane lurched suddenly and someone grabbed me. Perhaps I passed out.'

Peter Heppell of the King's 82 Column had a leg wound and went on to develop a massive jungle sore on the same limb:

'When we reached Warazup I reported to the American medic. He cleaned up my leg and applied the latest thing — sulphanamide. Within a week that deep sore had cleared up. I boarded a Dakota, bound for India with other sick and wounded. When we landed I saw some ex-prisoners of war. They looked even worse than we did.'

On 12 August, 6 NR's 66 Column received orders to evacuate via Mogaung and Myitkyina. They arrived at Mogaung the following day. Their eventual destination was Tinsukia Reception Centre in Assam. Lieutenant Larry Gaines, however, was one of three officers too ill to move from Pahok. Gaines took a turn for the worse:

'My health had deteriorated gradually but, by this time, I was in a terrible state. I went down with typhus and that was my worst experience. Naturally, everyone got a bit low towards the end. We all had severe runs and felt very ill. I remember looking down at what I had "done". The stool was a green liquid and it was bubbling! Within a few days extra medical supplies were dropped, together with more American jungle hammocks. Two doctors parachuted in and gave many men intravenous drips, which rapidly improved their state. A saline drip rehydrated me.'

Until then Gaines had doubted his ability to pull through. Now he could walk to the holding area. He went by boat along the Mogaung river and joined around 40 others at a riverside halt. He was still in a bad way and the rest of the trip is lost to his memory. He flew out to Tinsukia Reception Centre and finally entered hospital in Poona. At that point malaria added to the miseries of typhus and dysentery.

Lieutenant Denis Arnold, MC, had been ill for some time. The 29 Column Platoon Commander went down with malaria before reaching the Indawgyi Lake area. He continued marching with his Column towards Pahok but then fell seriously ill:

'Scrub typhus was diagnosed. I had a very high temperature and a severe headache – there was no chance of continuing. The rain poured down on men just sitting on the ground. Very many gave up. I was lucky. My American jungle hammock was a lifesaver and I also had some morphine, which eased the persistent, violent headache and a temperature of up to 106 deg. I was carried on an improvised stretcher towards Pahok East. I then travelled on the Mogaung Jeep train to Myitkyina and arrived at an American hospital.'

Denis Arnold was flown to a hospital in the Hukawng Valley and, finally, to another hospital at Secunderabad. He remained in hospital for just over a month. He rejoined his Battalion near Poona in early October, still suffering from malaria, but avoided another stay in hospital by taking leave in the Hills.

12 NR's 43 Column occupied Hill 60 for several days following its capture by 36th Division (which had attacked with two Battalions, rather than one or two Companies). Lieutenant Peter Allnutt looked at the tired, thin men around him. It was 15 August:

'We were at less than half our original strength. I shall never forget that last march north to Mogaung. It was a blistering, humid day. What water we had was soon exhausted. Men started falling out. By now there were less than 20 Europeans left with our Column but, somehow, we kept on our feet. It was a nightmare that lasted until nightfall, when we went into bivouac at Mogaung, a battered town of mud, ruins and the litter of war.'

They reached Myitkyina by Jeep railway and flew out to Assam. The ordeal finally caught up with Peter Allnutt. He was one of many who immediately developed jaundice, requiring some weeks in hospital. Captain Dick Stuckey, meanwhile, grew steadily weaker:

'I'd lost a couple of stone in weight. We were all extremely debilitated and the march to Mogaung railhead was very difficult. One African soldier stopped and died of exhaustion right in front of me. It was very sad. He had come through so much. At Myitkyina I remember the Jeep refused to start. It couldn't get sufficient traction. Around 20 of us jumped down from the wagons and pushed the Jeep, to set it rolling. At that point most of us had yellow jaundice. I certainly did!'

14 Brigade was in no better shape. Flight Lieutenant Walter Longstaff, RAF Officer with the York and Lancaster's 65 Column: 'The men were scarcely

Time to go: this Chindit lost his bush hat and used his small pack as protection from the sun. (Trustees of the Imperial War Museum)

recognisable as combat troops when they finally got out in August.' The sister Column, 84, reached Pahok, then left at midnight on the final march to Mogaung and the Jeep railway. Before emplaning at Myitkyina, Column Administrative Officer Paddy Dobney watched Private Clixby wolf down a tin of oily fish. During the bumpy flight to safety Clixby went a funny colour, got to his feet, shouted a single word – 'Sardines!' – and let the lot go.

Paddy Dobney had looked after his Battalion's soft skin elements and had helped bring many sick and wounded to safety. He had rejoined Battalion HQ after a four-week absence, as they prepared for their final action. The assault on Point 1497 was planned for 5 August. There was much scepticism when they were told this would be their last fight.

On 4 August a patrol had found that Japanese forward outposts were unoccupied and the attack's timing was advanced. Two Platoons of 65 Column went forward to occupy the first ridge. Meanwhile, two Platoons of 84 Column set out on a 10-mile encircling march, to attack Point 1497 along the ridge from the south. It was slow going. They bivouacked for the night and moved off at first light on 5 August. After an hour they came under fire and two men died attempting to clear the

opposition and recover the wounded. The problem was 200 yards of open ground immediately in front of the Japanese machine guns. An air strike was requested. This finally appeared at 11.00 the following morning; another attack went in and the men found that the Japanese had withdrawn east.

At this point, the Black Watch passed through the Battalion and captured Labu after some hard fighting during the evening of 7 August. The Japanese had been driven from the hills west of the railway and the incoming 36th Division's right flank was secured. At this stage many York and Lancaster Chindits could no longer eat. Philip Graves-Morris' Columns had subsisted on K-rations for 20 weeks, '... with the result that stomachs finally revolted and the mere sight of a K-ration packet brought intense nausea.' Drops then delivered a wide variety of foods but it was too late: shrunken stomachs rejected any attempt to eat 'luxury' items.

The York and Lancaster Columns were the last to leave the hills. In the heat they marched down to the main road, through 36th Division's positions, and reached Pahok on 23 August. The final 12 miles north to Mogaung were covered the following day. Battalion Commander Graves-Morris: 'It was a sorry sight to see these Columns of diseased and dying men dragging themselves along or being helped by their less sick comrades.' An Army photographer said he had to take photographs, 'for nobody would believe it, without the evidence.'[9]

It has been suggested that this evidence was suppressed. Certainly, the author failed to find the photographs. Fred Gerrard, a veteran of 84 Column who died in 2008, claimed that the men of Special Force were segregated from other troops due to their extremely emaciated condition. He added: 'I have yet to see a photo of the remnants of a Column coming out.'[10]

The last of the York and Lancaster Chindits left Burma on 26 August, flying from Myitkyina to Tinsukia. Of the Battalion's 900 all ranks who had flown into Aberdeen on 2/3 April, only 18 officers and 380 ORs made that last march to Mogaung and safety. Of the 398, only 12 escaped hospitalisation back in India. They lost 29 killed in action (including five officers), 107 wounded (including seven officers, three of whom were wounded twice) and another 58 ORs died of sickness and exhaustion. A total of 15 officers and 315 ORs were evacuated sick.

Early in 1945 the Imperial War Graves Commission (later, the Commonwealth War Graves Commission) organised the recovery of remains in North Burma. Volunteers from the Columns trekked once more into the Burmese jungle. They had records giving the locations of graves. Philip Graves-Morris: 'From battle sites, from the small cemetery we built at "Plymouth", where our sick and casualties had died while awaiting the flying boats, and from lonely graves beside jungle tracks and swamp, wherever they could still be found, the remains of our dead were removed. They now lie in the military cemetery at Mogaung.'⁹

Following the successful campaign around Imphal and Kohima, the detached 23 Brigade pulled out. Captain Tony Wailes, with 60 Column (60th Field Regiment, RA), had marched in across the Naga Hills and returned through Ukhrul and Imphal:

'I covered around 400 miles and climbed 'hills' up to 8,500 ft high. In all, I climbed over 70,000 ft and I am still trying to forget the experience! I remember one particularly uncomfortable, wet night, sitting in water with a sodden blanket round me. When we pushed on at dawn the first "person" we met was a Jap skeleton, fully dressed and lying on a stretcher in the mud.'

They kept moving east, making their way to safety. The Column took a supply drop and climbed to 8,000 ft. They were close to the retreating enemy and enjoyed a warm welcome from villagers delighted to see the backs of the Japanese. One particularly difficult climb was made at night. Phosphorescent sticks were placed on backs, to allow the Column Snake to progress in the darkness. Tony Wailes:

'Halfway up I put my hand on my shin to see what was biting, only to feel, through my slacks, the swollen bodies of two very large leeches. I stopped and persuaded them to leave go with a cigarette. I bled profusely for some time but I think the loss of blood did me good!'

60 Column, now operating as two units, was astride a Japanese main line of communication to the Chindwin. Several Japanese were killed in skirmishes. The journey to Ukhrul gave the Column an excellent view of the motor road. They watched RAF aircraft bomb and strafe a Japanese-held village. A convoy of over 20 trucks then left this well defended area. Later, they were told they had seen a Japanese Divisional HQ pulling out. In a letter home Tony Wailes wrote:

> After our next move we set up a permanent ambush on the road and literally set up a shooting gallery. The Japs who came back along that way were all dead beat and had one rifle to about three men. Still, we had learnt never to trust a Jap and no prisoners arrived. Just a pile of corpses, down the mountain, marked the spot.

Yet his Platoon did take a prisoner. He emerged from a deserted village, with his hands in the air, and turned out to be a lawyer from Tokyo. He spoke a little English,

Back to civilisation: the survivors of the Queen's 22 Column were evacuated in May. Platoon Commander Gordon Hughes is in the middle of this group. (Barbara Bennett)

read quite well and was amazed at the content of the *SEAC Newspaper*. The Platoon guarded him and a party of 10 coolies who had been working for the Japanese. The Japanese prisoner attached himself to Wailes:

'He spent a lot of time bowing and scraping. I was never allowed to bury my own empty ration tins and I made him carry much more than most of us.'

23 Brigade's four Battalions had been successful, ambushing the Japanese, disrupting communications and destroying supplies during the April–July period. They killed, wounded and captured over 800 Japanese, for the loss of 74 killed and 88 wounded. The sick, as always, far outnumbered battle casualties.

When 60 Column arrived at Ukhrul, they had a chance to clean up before proceeding to Imphal. In his letter home, Tony Wailes described his first view of the Imphal Plain: 'After a stiff climb we came over a ridge to see this magnificent sight in front of us: miles and miles of green Paddy fields stretching out in front of us, with a thin thread running through its midst – the Imphal Road – and, better still, 16 trucks waiting to convey us to the city itself.'

Lieutenant Andrew Sutherland, also with 60 Column, had had dysentery for four months. He was now suffering from blackouts. The MO ordered him to lead 47 unfit from both 60 and 68 Columns to Jessami, three days away. Most of the sick had little appetite, but Sutherland had developed an intense craving for tinned tomatoes. After three weeks on the track, now heading towards Kohima, they were met by Jeep ambulances for the last stretch. Kohima was in ruins; the hospital had been patched up but the walls were full of bullet holes.

23 Brigade had suffered badly. One Battalion, the 2nd Duke of Wellington's, dwindled to half strength and eventually merged into one Column. 76 Column RAF Officer W.A. Wilcox was evacuated. Later, he wrote: 'I talked to many who saw them come out into Imphal, weak, tired, but victorious. They spoke of seeing skeletons.'[11]

As for the men of Special Force, their condition was no better. Fred Gerrard, with a York and Lancaster Column, was near Myitkyina airstrip and uncertain of the date. He thought it was about 21 August: 'When asked the way to the airfield an American's jaw dropped. It was probably the first time he had seen a skeleton move and speak.'[10]

Some men have clear memories of their return to India, but many remember little more than an intense feeling of relief. Frank Anderson of the King's 81 Column:

'When we got to Dehra Dun I remember being left to sleep for a very long time. I didn't need to go to hospital, but it was difficult to eat properly for a while.'

Most men were taken to well organised reception centres. They were overwhelmed by the luxurious facilities, including hot baths and made-up beds with blankets and mosquito nets. 84 Column's Paddy Dobney remembered how everything seemed so clean. A pile of gifts had been left on each bed – a toothbrush, comb, a chocolate bar, writing paper, envelopes and a pencil: 'They were a bridge from the life just left to a normal world.' The York and Lancaster's Rear Base party, two officers and 20 men, had organised this welcome. They had purchased the gifts themselves. Dobney was touched when he found they had included his Shoulder Crowns: 'I had been a Major for exactly two months and I could now wear my new rank.'

Jim Unsworth was among the 111 Brigade arrivals at Myitkyina. He was now a six stone skeleton:

'My health was still quite good but I had malaria. I was filthy. During my entire time in Burma I can only remember washing in a river on one occasion. It felt marvellous to be safe.'

A Sergeant told them to dump their clothes and enter the first tent. Jim Unsworth:

'He handed out towels, soap and shaving kit. Showers had been rigged up. We scrubbed ourselves and went to another tent for a haircut and shave, then on to another for new clothes and boots. There was one last marquee to visit. We went inside and saw a huge meal: fresh fruit, pineapples, mashed potato and meat. No-one ate the food. We just had some tea. The MO said it was understandable, as our stomachs had shrunk so much, but I do remember having a bit of breakfast the next morning. During the next day we were promised a film show, but this was a disappointment – an Indian production on the dangers of malaria!'

Bill Smyly recalls the psychological challenge:

'I remember the day we handed over the mules. From force of habit we still sheltered in the jungle, safe under the canopy. Suddenly, we saw British troops marching in threes down an open road. It was unbelievable. We were reluctant to leave forest cover and we slowly emerged in dribs and drabs. They had come to pick up our animals. I said goodbye to Charlie.'

According to the *Report on Operations Carried out by Special Force* (October 1943 to September 1944), the six Brigades (including 23 Brigade) began operations with 547 horses and 3,135 mules. The casualty rate was 50 per cent for horses (273) and 37 per cent for mules (1,169).

From Myitkyina airstrip Bill Smyly and his Gurkhas flew over the hills and eventually reached a reception centre in Assam:

'We undressed and left our weapons, clothes and packs with the decontamination unit. We passed through a sort of Belsen bath routine. The naked men were given cloths and soap and passed through showers to shampoo and scrub. All clothing was burnt. I suppose they were afraid of lice. We did have lice in the first show. We picked up lice in the villages, but I don't remember any lice in the second campaign.'

Some men arrived in India on the edge of death. Lancashire Fusilier Ian Niven had passed out during his evacuation flight:

'I woke up on a "slab" in a tented field hospital. I was laid out, stark naked, with people throwing buckets of ice over me. As I came to I had the sensation that I was flying to Heaven, moving through white clouds. Later, I discovered they had more or less given me up for dead. My temperature had gone way over the top; I think it reached 108 deg. Higher than that and it's curtains.'

The doctors decided Niven was suffering from amoebic dysentery, which attacks the liver. When Niven began to recover he discovered that his closest pal, 'Chindit Alf', had also survived. He was among those who had completed more service abroad than the younger men and so became eligible for repatriation. Niven was less fortunate; he was shunted from hospital to hospital, from Dehra Dun to Delhi: 'I spent about six months in hospital. At this point I didn't much care. I'd had it – no longer any good for combat. My fitness was downgraded.'

Some men came out angry, including Jack Hutchin of the South Staffords – so starved that he attempted to steal bread at Shadazup:

'Sores on my legs were the size of a 10p piece. I also had bad prickly heat, as the pack had chaffed my back red raw. I was suffering from malnutrition and dehydration. Consequently, I remember very little of Shadazup, beyond trying to steal the bread and a church service. I was brought up in the strict Irish Roman Catholic tradition. I went to Mass and Holy Communion every Sunday. The Padre described his service at Shadazup as a "Thanksgiving". That was too much for me – I couldn't stand there and listen to him. I had lost my faith. All I

had left was my fists and my anger. My next memory is of waking up in an Indian hospital, where I spent the next few weeks.

'I perked up when I received a personal invitation to the Viceroy's Lodge at Simla, for rest and recuperation. This was an invitation from Archie Wavell's father, the great man himself! Perhaps it recognised the role I played in helping Archie. Looking back, Archie was no obvious Chindit: he lacked that streak of utter determination. He had more of an ascetic mind. We focused on the first priority, beating the Japanese, but Archie had a feel for the finer things of life and he was not afraid to speak of them. In fact, I swapped my one book with him. Archie got The Rubaiyat of Omar Khayyam *and I got* The Complete Works of William Shakespeare. *Unfortunately, there was no room for finer things in our war. If you are supposed to be hard, you must be hard!*

'Archie was wounded on 6 June 1944 – D-Day in Europe. A Major had been killed, then Archie was hit. He was struck by an explosive bullet of the type much favoured by the Japanese. It mangled his left hand and lower arm. This happened on the heights above Mogaung; we were close enough to have the Pagoda in full view. I held Archie's upper arm as the doctor cut off his lower arm.'

Later, there was gossip that a flight had been laid on to evacuate the Viceroy's son, but that Archie had put one of his own men on the flight, in his place. The aircraft was met by Wavell, who was furious and sent a sharp signal ordering all concerned to ensure that Archie was on the next flight.

South Staffords Platoon Commander Norman Durant, MC, remembers the torture of his last couple of days in Burma, making for Shadazup airstrip: 'I was sick with jaundice and had a temperature of 102 deg.' He remembered the clouds of tiny stinging insects attacking the men. They 'gave a sharp, burning sting … on two mornings we woke to be bitten all over the hands, face and ears by these, until one felt quite hysterical and scratched and swore in impotent rage and despair.'

Norman Campbell was among the Cameronians at Warazup. He was impressed with American facilities:

'If you have to go to war, do it American style. These lads had just about every comfort known to man: beds, waterproof tents, Coke (the drinking sort), ice cream, a PX, a canteen, radios and a mobile cinema.'

Within a day or two the Cameronians reached Tinsukia Reception Centre. Campbell had his first hot water wash in nearly six months: 'The hot water released all

At the point of liberation: Rangoon Gaol from the air, with the words on the roof: 'British here.' An RAF prisoner climbed onto the roof and laid out this message. (Ted McArdle)

the accumulated muck in my pores and it ran down me in grimy rivulets.' Now clean and wearing fresh clothes, Campbell's next priority was to spend the 150 Rupees accumulated but not spent buying food in Burmese villages. It was soon gone, before the Army had the chance to demand its return. One encounter at Tinsukia is frozen in Campbell's memory. He went up to an Indian WI tea wagon. Two ladies were laughing and chatting as he approached:

'One turned to serve me and I saw the smile leave her face. She looked at me with disbelief and sympathy, the pity written all over her face. I had lost a lot of weight. I was gaunt and my ribs were showing. I was as yellow as a canary through taking Mepacrine. I will always remember that look.'

Many men came out exhausted yet still standing, but quickly succumbed to disease when released from tension. Bill Towill remembers the stark contrast between the Chindits and 36th Division: 'They looked so smart and well turned out, very different from us, a bunch of ragged, starving ruffians, but perhaps we could be proud of having achieved something.'

Many 23 Brigade elements concentrated at Kohima. Most went by truck to Dimapur and boarded hospital trains. Their destination was No. 3 Indian Base General Hospital, Bihar Province. Lieutenant Andrew Sutherland of 60 Column had malarial fever: 'A hospital examination showed that I now weighed nine stone 12 pounds – about 60 pounds lighter than I had been five months before and the same as I had weighed when I was only 13 years old.'

His diet now consisted of minced boiled liver and mashed bananas, supplemented by M&B sulfa drugs and enemas. He spent five months in hospital. During this period he became 'scribe' to Lieutenant-Colonel Thompson, the King's Own's CO, who had been hit in the right shoulder and was unable to write his own letters home.

The author's father, Private Jack Redding of the King's Own, remembered little of coming out, other than that the last leg was by truck. They had landed at Dinjan and were driven to Tinsukia Reception Centre. Jack Redding had lost around three stone from an already wiry frame. On recovering and after leave, he was offered the choice of becoming a driver or transferring to the Catering Corps. This was not a difficult decision, as he had starved for five months. He was posted to a Catering Corps unit and was content to spend a peaceful, well fed six months cooking breakfast for troops. At this time he developed a habit which stayed with him for the rest of his life. He began each day with a small cooked breakfast: one rasher of bacon and some fried tomatoes.

Jesse Dunn of the South Staffords had been seriously wounded in the arm and spent nearly two months in hospital. When no longer a bed patient he received a dinner invitation from Captain Butler of the Lancashire Fusiliers:

'Butler greeted me with the words: "I've got your sword!" During the White City fighting, when Colonel Richards was wounded, I recovered a sword from the battlefield. They had my name engraved on it.'

Sapper Eric Sugden, with the Bedfordshire and Hertfordshire's 61 Column, had been flown out some weeks earlier by Sunderland. The aircraft landed on the Brahmaputra at Dibrugarh and he went into No. 49 Indian General Hospital, transferring two days later to No. 13 Indian Malarial Field Treatment Unit. On 7 July he was put on Ambulance Train No. 19 for the overnight journey to Gauhati, then to No. 52 Indian General Hospital. On 9 July he had time to draw breath, following an ambulance journey to No. 25 Indian Convalescence Depot at Shillong.

The Europeans of 6 NR's 66 Column, resting at Tinsukia Reception Centre, were now clean shaven. Only 10 were in reasonably good shape. Lieutenant Larry Gaines was among those sent to a large military hospital in Poona, where they occupied two wards: 'It was just like Heaven, with clean sheets, soft bed, kind nurses, etc.' On the day Gaines was to be discharged, he went down with jaundice and stayed another month. He was in hospital for 10 weeks in all. He then had a month's leave and went to Ootacamund, the hill station in the Nilgiri Hills known as 'Snooty Ooty.'

Captain Dick Stuckey of 12 NR's 43 Column was also in hospital near Poona, under the care of Matron McGeary:

'I found I couldn't eat much. With our shrunken stomachs a light diet was essential. We made a potentially fatal mistake at Myitkyina, when several of

Communal living in Rangoon Gaol: this room housed 10 prisoners along each side. The 'beds' are packing cases, with boards over. Ted McArdle: 'The flies were the worst torment. When we were given Japanese tea we put some out for the flies.' (Ted McArdle)

Free but still in prison: Ted McArdle (far right, seated) pictured on liberation, very weak from the effects of beri beri. (Ted McArdle)

us went for a "blow-out" at a local restaurant. We had a substantial rice curry and were very ill as a result.'

Dick Stuckey never doubted he would get out:

'When we took casualties I simply thought: "Bad luck. He's gone. It can't happen to me." We had a very schoolboyish outlook. I never felt real fear, but I did develop a strong sense of self-preservation. I don't think the experience changed me, but the role of Rifle Company Commander did encourage a mature view.'

Neville Hogan had led a King's Own Recce Platoon. He was flown out by Sunderland and was still in hospital in late July:

'Much later in life – at the Imperial War Museum in 1995 – I met Vera Lynn and told her that she had kissed me on 25 July 1944, at a Field Hospital at Dibrugarh, Assam. She said: "How can you be so precise?" I answered: "Well, you visited that hospital in India on 25 July and kissed my forehead. That was the day after my 21st birthday".'

As Operation *Thursday's* survivors returned to India, many others remained in Japanese captivity and they

were all sick and starving. Philip Stibbe had been a prisoner for nearly 17 months. He survived captivity and later wrote:

The human mind and body can accustom themselves to almost anything if there is no alternative. Conditions were bad but, once we had adjusted ourselves and lowered our standards accordingly, we became quite used to doing without certain things which we had always looked upon as essential.

After a time we became hardened and even callous about the everyday sight of suffering and death. Some of us even laid bets as to who would be the next to die. Perhaps this was heartless but it was preferable to the utter misery and total despair which could so easily have overwhelmed us. Everything possible was done to save the lives of the sick but it was worse than useless to grieve over the inevitable.[12]

The prisoners had three constant fears: being struck down by disease, being hit by Allied bombs (a number of which fell on Rangoon Gaol) and the possibility that the Japanese might decide to kill everyone when faced with defeat.

Beri-beri, due to lack of Vitamin B, was a much feared disease. Philip Stibbe:

Our only real source of supply for this vitamin was the repulsive rice bran gruel ... often even the bran proved insufficient and it was pathetic to see some of the fittest men suddenly develop beri-beri, knowing that nothing could be done for them. A few did manage to keep it in check by eating huge quantities of bran but in most cases nothing seemed to stop it. The disease seemed to attack men in two ways: some of them developed chronic diarrhoea and grew thinner and thinner until they died. Others swelled up to an enormous size, starting at the feet and working upwards until their faces were nearly twice the normal width. This swelling was caused by quantities of fluid under the skin and it was ghastly to see men becoming more and more inflated with water until they could hardly breathe and, finally, their hearts stopped beating. We knew that anybody might develop the disease at any time.[12]

Notes

1. Nesbit, R.C. (2009), *The Battle for Burma*, 157
2. Rooney, D. (2000), *Wingate and the Chindits: Redressing the Balance*, 188-189
3. Calvert, M. (1974), *Chindits: Long Range Penetration*, 149-157
4. Larson, G. A. (2008), *Aerial Assault into Burma*, 123
5. Towill, B. (2000), *A Chindit's Chronicle*, 140-141
6. Rhodes James, R. (1981), *Chindit*, 197-198
7. Calvert, M. (1974), 127
8. Jeffrey, W.F. (1950), *Sunbeams Like Swords*, 168
9. Graves-Morris, Lieutenant-Colonel P.H., unpublished MS (via Bill Smith and Corinne Simons)
10. Gerrard, F.E., *Wingate's Chindits*, unpublished MS, October 2000 (via Bill Smith)
11. Wilcox, W.A. (1945), *Chindit Column 76*, 136
12. Stibbe, P. (1995), *Return via Rangoon*, 163-174

29

AFTERMATH

PLANS FOR more Chindit operations were abandoned and Special Force was disbanded in early 1945. In a letter to Michael Calvert, Mountbatten wrote: 'It was the most distasteful job in my career to agree to your disbandment. I only agreed because by that time the whole Army was Chindit-minded.'[1]

This observation was accurate, at least to some degree. Conventional Army formations now fought the Japanese in a more flexible manner. The Chindits, however, paid a heavy price for demonstrating a new style of warfare. Special Force Chindits and the men of the 1943 expedition endured such prolonged suffering and stress that many survivors were hospitalised and required convalescence. Some were no longer fit for a fighting role.

It proved to be impossible to obtain sufficient British replacements to re-form the Chindits as a six-Brigade force. What remained of Special Force came to be seen as one of the very few reservoirs of soldiers with combat experience available in the Far East.

Most survivors had the instinctive feeling that something bordering on the unique had been achieved. They had fought together at the outer extremities of human endurance. There was a cachet to being a Chindit. The very word produced mixed emotions, a blend of awe and something approaching pity. 16 Brigade was proud of its almost impossible march into Burma and the valiant struggles around Indaw. 111 Brigade remembered the heroism and trauma of the unequal struggle at Blackpool. 77 Brigade found glory at White City and a near Pyrrhic victory at Mogaung. There were also the achievements of Morris Force, along the Bhamo road, and of 14 Brigade and 3(WA) Brigade after Blackpool fell and, of course, of 23 Brigade around Kohima.

Chindit Battalion Commander Philip Graves-Morris:

This was warfare made possible by science and technology but fought at the most primitive level, with no acknowledgement of Western concepts of 'civilised' warfare. With the Monsoon rains the Chindits starved as air-dropped supplies dwindled. Eventually, fewer than five per cent of the surviving force were judged on medical assessment to be fit to continue operations.[2]

During their rest and recovery, the Chindits found that recent hardships offered no immunity against the routines of Army discipline. The Chindit shoulder flash marked a man as a member of an elite force, yet notices at Dehra Dun reminded the survivors of the need to salute.[3] Dehra Dun was not behind enemy lines in Burma!

A 15 June 1945 report by Lieutenant-Colonel J.N. Morris, RAMC, The *Report on the health of 401 Chindits*, states:

These men came from all parts of Britain, belonged to different formations and presented manifold disorders, but they tended to conform to a clinical pattern and the group spirit was strong among them. What we learned to call 'the Chindit Syndrome' soon emerged – the frequent association of long hair and long dirty nails; superior intelligence, morale and manners; fatigue and hunger, pallor and loss of weight, skin sepsis, diarrhoea and malaria. ... I think it may safely be said that each patient had two or three conditions requiring hospital treatment.[4]

Japanese officers hand over their swords at a ceremony in Rangoon. (Jim Unsworth)

Some of the fitter Chindit survivors took leave almost immediately. Many more required hospitalisation and convalescence. Jack Redding enjoyed leave in the foothills of Kanchenjunga (the third highest mountain in the world), where he took to riding in the fresh mountain air. Another member of 111 Brigade, Bill Smyly, had an inauspicious start to his leave, much resenting the way he was 'kitted out':

'The clothes we got were terrible. The men behind the counters just threw things at you. They didn't even look at you for size. I was given an enormous bush shirt and trousers that were also far too big. No belt! White issue braces were supposed to hold things up. I couldn't wear the shirt over the braces or the braces over the shirt. It was unbelievable — the British Army at its bloody-minded worst. Everything was ill-fitting and I had no money to buy anything. I went to Calcutta dressed like that. Gone with the Wind was showing and I was so embarrassed by my appearance that I went to the cinema after lunch and sat through this marvellous three-hour film twice, coming out only after dark.'

The Bedfordshire and Hertfordshire Chindits slowly reassembled at Bangalore. Captain John Riggs set out on a month's leave:

'I wanted to see Kashmir but it would have taken well over two weeks to get there by train. I settled for somewhere closer, high up in the Nilgiri Hills above Bangalore. Our party of four took a bungalow and, initially, we did little more than eat, sleep and maybe drink too much.

'There were many Indian Army families in the area and the wives looked after us. We began by eating many times a day. We could manage only a little food at first, as our stomachs had shrunk, but we would be hungry again just an hour or so later. The climate was cool and invigorating. I recall that our CO met and married a widow there. Her first husband had been killed in the Western Desert. When she suggested going for a walk, he replied: "I have just walked 800 miles!"'

Corporal Ted Treadwell of the Leicesters made a bad choice:

'It was a waste of money. I should have gone to Darjeeling. The place I ended up in was full of beggars. I took £200 back pay with me and blew the lot. What a waste! When I got back to the Regiment they asked me to carry on for another six months. I would be made up to full Sergeant, with three months' back pay, if I looked

A few words from Wavell: the Viceroy with Lancashire Fusiliers' RSM 'Kitna' Price. Ian Niven remembers Price as a hard man: 'He must have been a model for the "typical" bastard RSM!' In a letter to the author, Niven adds: 'I found ex-Chindit NCOs very tolerant and understanding, except our RSM Price. His nickname "Kitna" comes from the Urdu for "too much". (Ian Niven)

after new recruits coming out from England. I preferred the boat home. After all, I had been away for five years!'

When Bill Williams rejoined the South Staffords at a hill station, he went in search of his missing Japanese sword. He was delighted when an American returned it to him, having looked after it during Williams' stay in hospital. He still has that sword, recovered from the scene of battle on Pagoda Hill over 60 years earlier.

Medical Orderly Percy Stopher, who had been attached to 23 Brigade, had no plans to be prudent during leave. He and seven others drew their back pay and borrowed more. They went on leave with the huge sum of £1,400 (over £5,000 each in today's money): 'We dressed in civvies and sunglasses, playing tourists. We had a smashing time. When we returned we had just £32 between us!' (The average house price in Britain in 1944 was £500.)

In mid-September 1944 Corporal Jim Welland, who had fought at Kohima, heard that Vera Lynn was about to visit:

This was hard to believe as things were still pretty dangerous, with the occasional sniper. However, she did show up. What a lovely young lady, with a beautiful voice. She was like an angel. I was lucky – I got a space almost at the front. I stood there and thought of home instantly.

A few days earlier a Japanese soldier had wandered into my position. He looked lost, but I shot him before he realised where he was. He fell to the ground dead. His helmet came off and rolled towards me. I picked it up, still warm from his head, and a neatly folded Japanese flag fell out, a nice souvenir. I thought to take it home. Yet Vera Lynn had had the courage to entertain us in the front line, so I gave this flag to her.[5]

Bill Smyly's return from Calcutta to Dehra Dun was as pleasant as his joyful experience in 1943:

'I had a first class carriage every night on those wonderful Indian trains. To spin out my journey and see India I got

off the train at its first stop every morning and boarded the last train each night. I wandered all over North India, in the general direction of Dehra Dun, and finally arrived in time for breakfast in the Mess of the 2nd King Edward VII's Own Gurkhas – the "Sirmoor Rifles" – and then up to Colonel Fell's office, to ask if there were any jobs going. He offered a place with Force 136 (another Special Force), but which appeared to be winding down, and another from Mike Calvert to command his "Assault Company". In any other Brigade this would have been known as the Brigade HQ Defence Company.

'I had been with the Chindits from the start and I chose to stay with them. Wrong choice! They were wound up even earlier, I think, than Force 136. Anyway, I chose the Assault Company and was attached to the 3rd/6th Gurkhas a month or two before the Chindits were disbanded. They found themselves lumbered with an extra officer they didn't know what to do with. Instead of the Assault Company I was given "Admin Company", with 60 or so auxiliaries who looked after such un-Chindit things as the cookhouse, the Durzi (the tailor's shop), sweepers, cleaners and Mess orderlies. I nearly caused a riot when I made my whole Company come on parade for half an hour in order to count them, delaying breakfast by 10 minutes. We were back in Burma when the atomic bombs were dropped. No-one believed the first newspaper reports. We had to think again when Japan surrendered.'

Glad to be out: a snapshot sent home by the author's father, Private Jack Redding, 2nd King's Own.

Having played a full part in both Chindit operations, Bill Smyly still hungered for adventure. His Battalion went by sea to Siam (Thailand) and was there when the young King returned to Bangkok from Switzerland, where he had spent the war:

'We then returned to the 6th Gurkhas' Regimental Centre at Abbottabad, on the borders of Kashmir. When a vacancy was advertised for an Animal Transport Officer with the 5th/1st Gurkhas on the North West Frontier, I jumped at it and stayed almost till demobilisation, returning to Abbottabad for a few weeks and then Lahore, Bombay and the troopship back to Britain.'

14 Brigade's Lieutenant Dick Hilder returned from Burma and was posted to Bangalore:

'14 Brigade was "Indianised". I became Camp Commander at Secunderabad, where the 26th Hussars had been broken up. In 1943 we were promised we would return to the Armoured Corps when the Chindit operation was over. Our problem was how to arrange a posting to Poona Depot for our close friends, who all

Happy Christmas! Greetings from India – a note sent by the author's father to his mother and sister at the end of 1944.

Peace returns: Walter Longstaff, former RAF Officer with the York and Lancaster's 65 Column (far right), with friends at 63 Maintenance Unit, Carluke, in 1946. (Walter Longstaff)

happened to be ex-26th Hussars. Tom Brodie had gone sick at that point and we managed to fix things. We had a party – one hell of a piss-up. The postings to Poona were slipped into a bundle of other documents when minds were distracted. Accordingly, we all finished up at Poona.'

Hilder soon had a new tank. He was posted to the 3rd Carabiniers, who had confronted the Japanese at Imphal and were now taking part in the drive toward Rangoon: 'Over 100 former Hussars went to the 3rd Carabiniers. We had General Lee tanks, good machines with side-mounted 75 mm guns. We joined the push to Rangoon.' Hilder now commanded 4 Troop, B Sqn:

'I hadn't seen the inside of a tank for two years and felt rather unsure, but it's a bit like riding a bike. Once you learn, that's it. I had an excellent crew. They had been introduced with the comment: "Just tell them where the target is and they'll hit it".'

Some men found it difficult to shake off disease, especially malaria. Even the relatively fit, like Flight Lieutenant John Knowles, felt drained:

'We had no energy reserves. I remember we came to a small village and saw the most gorgeous young Burmese girl. One man said: "Isn't she lovely?" We all

agreed. With only one exception (and I think he was a liar), we had no lustful feelings. We became pure through sheer exhaustion. It took me around a month to recover. My libido returned with my weight gain from a skeletal 126 pounds back up to its then normal 165 pounds.'

Malaria had the habit of revisiting the sufferer. Knowles had his first bout on the march, took quinine and simply walked it off. When he came out he escaped immediate hospitalisation but malaria dogged him for months. He was struck down by fever during his first leave and entered hospital at New Delhi. He had several bouts in quick succession, bouncing like a yo-yo between hospital and various hill stations. Life followed a pattern: two weeks in hospital, three weeks on sick leave. He celebrated his 21st birthday in Naini Tal on sick leave, between attacks of malaria. He never returned to the Queen's, beyond a short visit to pick up his kit. The RCAF caught up with him in November 1944 and he returned to England.

Cameronian Norman Campbell also struggled with malarial fever. The Battalion went on leave, Company by Company, to hill stations including Naini Tal and Simla. As soon as Campbell recovered, another bout would put him back in hospital. On returning to Dehra Dun he spent most of February and March 1945 in a hospital bed.

The Ledo Road opened on 27 January 1945, having taken over two years to build. It ran for 483 miles, from the Ledo railhead, through the Patkai Range passes and the Upper Chindwin, to connect with the town of Wanting — in an area of the Burma Road not occupied by the Japanese.[6] With Myitkyina finally secured on 3 August, the petrol pipelines were extended to this strategic town.[7]

The Chindits and Marauders helped make this possible, but the value of Special Force's contribution was controversial from the first.

In the post-war years Slim was dismissive, concluding that Chindits and other special forces 'did not give, militarily, a worthwhile return for the resources in men, material and time that they absorbed.' They 'skimmed the cream' and, in doing so, reduced the overall quality of the Army. They encouraged the belief that 'certain of the normal operations of war were so difficult that only specially equipped *corps d'élite* could be expected to undertake them.' He added:

> Armies do not win wars by means of a few bodies of super-soldiers but by the average quality of their standard units. Commanders who have used these

special forces have found, as we did in Burma, that they have another grave disadvantage – they can be employed actively for only restricted periods.[8]

Many Chindits, of course, would argue that their period of service was not restricted enough! Slim's comments about 'super soldiers' can be discounted, given the background of a large proportion of Special Force and the Chindits of 1943. Nevertheless, his remarks sum up one influential school of thought about the Chindits' contribution to victory in Burma.

New perspectives develop, however, with the passage of the years. Orde Wingate's vision of mobile warfare by light forces, supported from the air, has had a profound impact on modern military thinking. Capabilities have been further transformed by the availability of heavy helicopters and armed helicopter support. Michael Calvert wrote: 'Highly mobile units, travelling light and supplied by air, are now widely used in the armies of the West as a whole and are, in fact, the very basis of the modern British Army. These were the methods Wingate pioneered in Burma with the Chindits.'[9]

In this, Wingate may be said to have answered his critics.

What, exactly, did the Chindits of 1944 achieve? Special Force was broadly equivalent to two Light Divisions. In assessing its achievements, it makes sense to first consider the enemy. The hard-fighting Japanese had an immense capacity to tie-up Allied forces. Three Japanese Divisions had engaged seven-and-a-half to nine British/Indian Divisions at Imphal/Kohima. One crack Japanese Division, the 18th, resisted three and,

later, five Chinese Divisions and one American Brigade in the Hukawng Valley and a single Japanese Division confronted 12 Chinese Divisions on the Salween.

The Chindits cut communications and destroyed supply dumps of all five enemy Divisions. They largely destroyed a Japanese force of 10 Battalions – approximately Divisional strength – and subsequently took on the 53rd Division. According to 15th Army Commander Mutaguchi, just one Regiment of 53rd Division 'might well have ensured success' on the Imphal front.

Calvert wrote: 'Probably the greatest of the Chindits' achievements was to prevent the Japanese using their magnificent position on interior lines of communication to achieve numerical superiority at each thrust over the mountains and defeating each Allied force in detail, one by one.'[7]

Sir Robert Thompson, who took part in both Chindit operations, reflected on Wingate's originality:

In strategic concepts and ideas, Wingate was ahead of his time. No-one else would have thought of establishing and maintaining Strongholds with airstrips in Japanese-held territory. The reconquest of Burma was itself General Wingate's greatest memorial. No planner and no General had ever considered retaking Burma from north to south.[10]

The Chindit operations *were* expensive. The factors of climate, wilderness, starvation, disease, Monsoon and a remorseless enemy made for heavy casualties. Many Chindits died due to a change in role, from Long Range Penetration (for which they had been trained) to front-

Ready to go: York and Lancaster NCO Reg Smith's paperwork, required to board a troopship for the return to Britain. (Bill Smith)

line assault troops. They had not been trained and most importantly, not equipped with heavy weapons for the latter role. Chindit casualties (excluding all sick) from 16 May 1944, the onset of the Monsoon, to 19 August totalled 3,628 killed, wounded or missing.[7]

The 1944 Chindit campaign could not have been fought without 1st Air Commando. The P.51 Mustangs flew 1,482 combat missions and lost five aircraft. The B.25 bombers flew 422 strikes and lost one aircraft (in a crash landing). There was also the aircraft lost when Wingate died. Light aircraft flew 7,500 missions and evacuated 2,200 men. The Light Plane Force lost 40 L.1 and L.5 aircraft and five pilots.[11] There were also the C-47 and glider losses during the initial landings and subsequent operations.

The author's father, Jack Redding, was propelled by war from the suburbs of South East London to India, Ceylon and Burma. He was not alone in finding the return to 'normality' difficult to manage. He had been away for four years and four months. After a short leave, he was told to report to the 'Yorkshire Grey', a large public house at Eltham taken over by the Army. He expected to be demobbed and was shocked to learn that, instead, he was to be posted to Palestine. This was too much. He refused to accept the posting and argued his case so strongly that he was demobbed and entered into the 'Z Reserve'. He never forgave the Army for this episode and sent back his medals in protest. It took over 50 years for these feelings to subside.

The Army had not finished with Lou Lake of the 2nd Leicesters. He returned to Britain in late 1944:

'After leave I was posted to Belgium and then on to Germany with 2nd Army. During the Rhine Crossing my unit laid aluminium strips, to reinforce the river banks for Montgomery's set-piece crossing.'

Lake saw the destruction in German towns:

'Goch, in particular, was virtually flattened. I suppose they got what they deserved, given what they had done to refugees, the Jews and the populations of occupied countries. Yet, today, it all seems so pointless.'

Some men in the Far East with no immediate expectation of repatriation were lucky enough to get home leave. Gordon Hughes of the Queen's had the amazing good fortune to be selected for 'LIAP' (Leave in addition to Python), this strange term referring to repatriation. LIAP was a ticket to Britain and there was room for just two officers and 10 men from the entire Battalion. During his four weeks in England, Hughes married

his fiancée. He returned to Bombay and rejoined the Queen's at Ranchi in April 1945.

Tony Howard, also with the Queen's, was in remarkably good condition on his return to India, although he wore a bandage over one eye, injured by a twig springing back. He stayed free of malaria and dysentery but had lost a great deal of weight:

'I found K-rations boring and very salty. I've still got one of the tins, after 65 years! Occasionally, we were given "Indian Dehydrated Potatoes", but they never reconstituted properly and tasted like rubber. Yet I did have a couple of lucky days. On one occasion I saw an egg on the side of the track. God knows why no-one else saw it. Anyway, I picked it up and cooked it with rice at the first opportunity. It was wonderful. I felt it had saved my life. On another day we passed a village and I spotted some small yellow tomatoes at the side of the track. I had those, too.'

As men recovered they began training for future operations. In early September 1944 Tony Howard was training near Mangalore:

'There were new faces everywhere. Everything had changed. Even the rifles had gone. We now had American carbines. I was having a good time. Life here felt like a holiday after Burma. We were allowed to go out hunting – shooting at anything that moved, although I never hit anything.'

Tony Howard and Signaller George Hill were reunited with 21 Column. When 16 Brigade broke up they were posted out on New Year's Day 1945, to 23 Brigade. When Special Force disbanded George Hill began training for Operation *Zipper* and the recapture of Singapore. Tony Howard parted company with Hill at Bangalore. Howard was posted to a communications unit at Ranchi, then returned to the UK and was demobbed:

'I had thought of staying in but concluded that seven years in the Army was enough.'

On his return to the Queen's, Gordon Hughes was touched when his Colonel, on behalf of all officers, presented him with a silver cigarette box as a wedding present. At the end of May 1945 the Battalion moved to Poona, but Hughes was posted to the main Signals Centre near Madras. When the Japanese surrendered in August, the Queen's expected to be sent to Japan on occupation duties but, in the event, they stayed in India to help deal with growing unrest. By now Hughes was a Major and 2i/c of the Battalion. In September 1945

Great to be alive: Frank Anderson of the King's 81 Column.
(Frank Anderson)

When he had recovered Heppell rejoined his RE Company and began training for the liberation of Rangoon. When the city was occupied he became Orderly Corporal, a job he much disliked. His unit helped clear wreckage and repair buildings in the city.

The three West African Battalions moved to Jhansi after a short rest at Tinsukia, then joined the other Chindit units training for future operations. Later, they moved to southern India to train on more conventional lines. Lieutenant Larry Gaines sought a posting to a British unit and transferred to the 12th Sherwood Foresters, then part of a training Division based west of Ranchi. He was not impressed:

'Few of the other officers had been on active service. There was no sense of unity and comradeship.'

Following the Japanese surrender, Gaines was promoted to Captain and posted to Brigade HQ. He heard that some Sherwood Foresters POWs were recovering in Ranchi Hospital. Being a Forester himself, he visited the hospital, walked into the ward and was greeted with the cry: 'Good God! It's Larry Gaines.' The Foresters were from his former unit, way back in 1941. It was an emotional moment: Gaines was their first link with home.

The HQ CO was a highly respected Chindit leader, Brigadier Scott, a Column Commander in 1943 and a Battalion Commander in 1944. Larry Gaines:

they were called out in full Battle Order to help quell disturbances in Bombay. British and Gurkha units had received training in 'Aid to the Civil Power'.

These events delayed Gordon Hughes' repatriation. In February 1946 the Battalion was suppressing riots in Bombay once again but, by this time, Hughes had been back in Britain for several months. He was demobbed, receiving a £100 gratuity and a 'demob suit', and was reunited with his young wife.

Fred Holliday of the King's also became familiar with riot control:

'I went to OCTU and life took a different turn. I trained for six months and, by the time I had finished, the atomic bombs were dropped and it was all over. I was posted to The Buffs and ended up in Singapore and Java. Our forces had to deal with civil unrest in Java.'

Another King's Chindit, Peter Heppell, kept a souvenir of his long, hard months in the Burmese jungle. The reception process required the destruction of all heavily soiled clothing and personal equipment, but Heppell refused to give up his treasured jungle hammock:

'I remember the train that took us across India. It had a huge Chindit badge mounted at the front of the locomotive. I also remember the ladies turning out with tea at the stations.'

A chance to relax: Larry Gaines of 6 NR pictured in April 1946.
(Larry Gaines)

'I was at his HQ for only a short time when it was disbanded. My next posting – the last before demob – was to the South Staffords. The CO, another former Chindit, was pleased to have me on board as most of his officers were newly commissioned and the troops were fresh from the UK.'

Some men were stalked by malaria. They included Jim Unsworth of the King's Own. Starved for months, he took his opportunity to stay close to food:

'I was sent to Dehra Dun and went into hospital to fight the malaria. On recovering, I went to Kitchener Barracks at Cawnpore, where I became a cook. On arrival, the Quartermaster asked: "Are any of you cooks?" There was no response. He then said: "Have any of you got any idea of cooking?" I said yes, having spent some time working in a hotel, alongside the pastry cook, after leaving school.

'I was led into the cookhouse and told that the barracks had no cooks but there were 20 men who wanted to learn! I asked the Quartermaster: "Who's going to learn them?" He replied: "I don't know. They've just arrived from England." I told him I'd manage on my own and got on with it. I found plenty of supplies, including huge tins of Maconochie's meat and veg. I made some pastry and used the contents of the tins to make Cornish pasties, served with onion gravy, followed by tinned fruit. The Captain turned up to inspect the cookhouse. He had a look at a tray of newly baked Cornish pasties, bit off one end and said just one word: "Lovely!" Before I knew it he was trying to persuade me to cook for the Officers' Mess, but I wanted to stay with the lads. Then, a couple of days later, I had a similar invitation from the Sergeants' Mess. This was more attractive. There were only eight of them and they paid Mess fees. This meant I could buy everything I wanted from the NAAFI.

'While at Cawnpore I was offered three stripes, on an undertaking that I would serve another six months. I declined. That was the second time I refused promotion. On the first occasion I was in a slit trench at Blackpool. Lieutenant Littlewood sent the Sergeant-Major to me with a question: Would I take Lance-Corporal? If he had offered Sergeant, I might have said yes at that point.'

Lieutenant Andrew Sutherland struggled to recover from jungle service with 23 Brigade. He rejoined his Regiment at Jhansi just before Christmas 1944, but was soon in hospital with another bout of malaria. On recovering he was posted to a Special Force training unit, but this was soon broken up. Sutherland went to Ranchi and 50th RA Reserve Regiment, becoming Jungle Training Officer. On Victory over Japan (VJ) Day, 15 August 1945, Sutherland entered hospital yet again, this time with jaundice. He stayed for 10 weeks before convalescing near Darjeeling.

Some men went to Japan when the war ended. They included John Pearson, formerly 111 Brigade's RAF Signals Officer. With Operation *Thursday* over, Pearson reported to Air HQ, Delhi. He was posted to a Tactical Support Wing flying Spitfires and Hurricanes during the main advance from Imphal. The pilots flew in support of IV Corps, jumping south from strip to strip every few weeks. Pearson returned to India for Operation *Zipper* in July 1945; he was still training when the atomic bombs were dropped and the war ended:

'We went to Japan and landed at Kure naval base, 30 miles east of flattened Hiroshima. The British Commonwealth airbase was a similar distance to the west of that devastated city. Five months after the bomb dropped we had our first look at Hiroshima. We visited the port to supervise the landing of stores. We drove through the city centre and took the opportunity to walk around. We came across a factory which had produced preserved foods in jars. There were solid blocks of half-melted jars on the floor, welded together in an atomic furnace. It was several months before anyone mentioned the dangers of radiation exposure. Japan took some getting used to. We went about unarmed, surrounded by crowds of Japanese.'

Some men faced a new challenge, having been 'volunteered' for jump training. Many were South Staffords. The Regulars were repatriated after six years overseas. The rest, including Sergeant Les Grainger, began jungle training once again. Grainger had been injured and missed Operation *Thursday*. His second chance vanished when the Chindits were disbanded:

'We had the choice of transferring to other infantry units or reforming as a Parachute Battalion. When Brigadier Eric Down visited us, to call for volunteers for paratroop training, he went about it the wrong way. He asked for volunteers and there were no takers. The Staffords' officers put him right. He came before us once again and said that we were to become paratroopers, unless we wanted to opt out. That was that – few opted out. Our unit was then broken up. Some men were absorbed into other units and others went to Rawalpindi for jump training.

'The reaction to parachuting was mixed. A few men refused to jump. Others were so enthusiastic that you had the impression that they would jump with an umbrella. I enjoyed it, making seven jumps in all –

including one in the dark. I never came to any harm, although broken ankles were an occupational hazard.'

They were still training for an attack on Singapore when the atomic bombs brought the war to an end. Les Grainger:

'It was fortunate that we didn't go in. When the sea landings eventually took place after the surrender, the vehicles got bogged down in soft sand on the beach. We would have been on our own.'

At that point Grainger was a Quartermaster Sergeant. He still had a taste for excitement and volunteered for a planned drop over a POW camp in Burma: 'When I went to see the Company Commander, he explained that everyone – including him – had also volunteered!' These plans were known to Jack Hutchin of the South Staffords. He had been passed fit for duty and posted to Rawalpindi for paratroop training:

'I had heard a rumour that Chindit paratroopers were to be dropped into Burma to free a remote camp full of Allied POWs. I didn't believe a word of it. I did a few jumps but that was enough, after what I had been through.'

Hutchin was given an unusual new job. He was posted to 60 Company, 'D Force', specialists in psychological warfare:

'I joined a Major and several others on a mission to Batavia, Java, as the war in the Far East ended. When we arrived, we found the Japanese garrison lined up on the quayside. They surrendered Batavia to us – a small force of men with 12 Jeeps and 'SONIC' trailers equipped with loudspeakers. We moved inland and spread the word to Japanese forces that the war was over.'

———◆———

Controversy over the relative performance of Special Force Brigades grew in the immediate aftermath of Operation *Thursday*. They have continued ever since. Rooney: '77 Brigade under Calvert were devoted to Wingate and his ideas, while 111 Brigade under Lentaigne and Masters were strongly anti-Wingate.' According to Rooney, when Calvert invited Masters to visit White City and examine its defences, Lentaigne 'forbade Masters to go in, saying that 111 Brigade would show that they were better than Wingate's favourite Brigade.'[12]

Rooney added that there had been 'bitter criticism from Masters of 14 Brigade's failure to help at Blackpool.

A peaceful ride: Jack Hutchin of the South Staffords. This photograph was taken in Singapore during September 1946. (Jack Hutchin)

14 Brigade sat between the extremes represented by 77 and 111 Brigades. Its Commander, Brodie, had accepted the Chindit challenge and got on with it.' Criticism over inactivity during the Kyunsalai Pass period was answered by 14 Brigade's strong battle performance towards the end of the campaign: 'If there has been criticism that it marched about aimlessly, this criticism should be directed, not at Brodie, but at Lentaigne for his remote and ineffective direction of 14 Brigade and, indeed, of all the other Brigades in that part of the final Chindit campaign.'[12]

Turning to 3(WA) Brigade's three Battalions, Rooney noted that they were relatively untested and for this reason were deployed in garrison roles.[13] The Nigerians fought well. Not surprisingly, perhaps, 111 Brigade has attracted the most controversy. Rooney commented: 'In spite of their appalling suffering at Blackpool, 111 Brigade achieved little. ... When 111 Brigade did get into serious action, they were tactically and mentally unprepared for it.'[14] Rooney pins the blame on those at the top:

All smiles: Ian Niven (right) back in India and now Orderly Room Colour Sergeant. He is pictured in late 1945 with Sergeant Bill Tideswell outside the Lancashire Fusiliers' Orderly Room, Lucknow. (Ian Niven)

111 Brigade sustained heavy casualties and suffered atrocious conditions but, although they inflicted heavy casualties on a Japanese Regiment from 53rd Division, they had no obvious achievement to their credit. Critics of Long Range Penetration have said, unjustly, that 111, 14 and 3(WA) Brigades achieved no striking success. Such criticism does not invalidate Wingate's conception of Long Range Penetration: rather, it highlights the disasters caused to a large number of highly trained and brave men because, at the top, Slim did not support the idea of LRP and condemned the Chindits to be used as normal infantry under the control of Stilwell. At the next level, Lentaigne, who openly derided Wingate's ideas but had nothing to put in their place, weakly went along with Slim's arrangements.[15]

The Chindits blocked the Indaw–Myitkyina railway and road and disrupted 18th Division's supply routes and those of 31st Division attacking at Kohima. The Bhamo–

Myitkyina road then became more significant. This was attacked by Morris Force and Dah Force, disrupting supplies to both 18th Division and a Division on the Salween front. Rooney:

> Morris Force and Dah Force illustrate both the possibilities and problems of Chindit-style operations. They had their successes and their failures and then, like most of the Chindits, they ended up in the Myitkyina–Mogaung area under the murderous influence of Stilwell and Boatner, neither of whom had any idea how best to use the lightly armed Chindits in their proper roles.[16]

As for 16 Brigade, Philip Sharpe of 45 Recce maintained that the odds were stacked against Fergusson in his attempt to take Indaw, due to the exhaustion caused by the 'long, life-sapping march' into Burma. As to why 16 Brigade was required to march in, Sharpe rejects the 'surprise argument', pointing out that a huge air landing behind the lines is a much bigger surprise. He also rejects the 'lack of aircraft argument', as 16 Brigade had to be supplied by air weeks before the Operation *Thursday* landings began: 'If the alternative option had been taken to fly the Brigade into Burma, surely it would have been more successful and profitable all round.' As for failure at Indaw, he added: 'If Aberdeen had been ready even two weeks earlier, then both 14 and 16 Brigades could have made a combined direct assault. Indaw was virtually undefended until a few days before our eventual attack.'

Sharpe is scathing in his verdict: 'Overall, my considered opinion is that the march by the 16th Infantry Brigade was a contrived publicity stunt and an absurd act of showmanship by General Wingate.' This criticism may have some justification, but the most likely main reason for requiring 16 Brigade to march in was the need for an early start – four weeks before the fly-in. This can be interpreted as Wingate's insurance against the last-minute cancellation of Operation *Thursday*.

The Chindits, of course, have staunch champions. Sir Robert Thompson (in one of his more moderate observations) wrote: 'I am quite sure that history will accept that the counterstroke of landing the Chindits in Northern Burma was a, if not the, major factor in saving Imphal.'[17]

Naturally, critics will argue, correctly, that the Japanese at Imphal and elsewhere were broken by large-scale conventional forces. Yet, as Allen wrote: 'They miss the point. What the Press and world opinion made of Wingate's initial exploits infused a new spirit into the affairs of Burma.'[18]

Many Chindits remained prisoners of the Japanese when Special Force came out of Burma. Their sole concern was to stay alive long enough to be freed. Ted McArdle of the King's spent just over 12 months in Rangoon Gaol, from April 1944 to May the following year. His friend, Matty Ashton, was also in the Gaol and they saw each other occasionally. The fittest men went outside on working parties, but McArdle was too ill to accompany them. Those remaining behind were left to their own devices:

'We passed the days walking up and down and playing "games". One game involved seeing how many flies we could catch. There wasn't much else to do. Some men lived like that for three years!'

Captain Alec Gibson was with Calvert's 3 Column during Operation *Longcloth*. His family had been told

Rangoon staple: Ted McArdle and fellow POWs with the rice ration. He recalled being asked to re-stage this just after the liberation, for the benefit of an American photographer. (Ted McArdle)

that he had probably drowned attempting to cross the Irrawaddy:

'They had no idea I was alive. For the next two-and-a-half years they thought I was dead. With the German bombing back home I had no idea whether I still had a family. That period as a POW seemed an eternity. Yet it is surprising how one adapts. It may have been more difficult, psychologically, for the poor devils captured when Singapore fell. They were surrendered and never had the chance to put up a fight. In Rangoon Gaol we got into a routine and lived from day to day.'

Each day began at dawn with 'Tenko' – roll call – followed by a brief breakfast. All officers were required to work. Alec Gibson:

'Most of us went on working parties. We worked in the docks, unloading stores, or filled up bomb craters and dug up unexploded bombs. Some dug underground shelters for the Japanese. Each working party consisted of a British officer, a number of men and two or three Jap guards. Some were officers only. Some parties were put to work inside the Gaol. Those going outside took supplies for a lunch break and returned at dusk. We had one rest day a week.

'Everyone did their best to do as little as possible or to sabotage the work. We had to be careful. If the Japs suspected anything they beat up the men concerned and the officer in charge. I was in charge when we were unloading rice from barges and stacking it in a warehouse. We cut holes in the bottom of the sacks and the rice began to leak out. When the guards became suspicious I went over and complained that the sacks were no good.

'On another occasion we were unloading artillery ammunition from a ship and got all the shells ashore safely, but a large case of fuses managed to fall into the water despite our "desperate efforts" to save it. Any such success was a great boost to morale. We were accomplished thieves and brought back all sorts of goods and food, hidden in bamboo poles or elsewhere. We also obtained local newspapers, printed in English, which gave us a rough idea of what was happening in the outside world.'

Philip Stibbe also described life in Rangoon Gaol:

It is difficult to convey any idea of the atmosphere in which we lived. Normally, it was far from gloomy. We were all completely accustomed to the life; the craving for sugar and fats had long disappeared and our stomachs were fully acclimatised to our monotonous diet. The primitive sanitary arrangements, the constant bowing to the Japs, the rats and mice and smaller vermin which crawled over us in the night, the complete lack of privacy, the prevalence of scabies and the sight of men covered from head to foot with ringworm – all these and many other things which normally were now a routine part of our lives and passed unnoticed.[19]

Ted McArdle endured the more disgusting aspects of captivity in such conditions:

'Dysentery was rife. The toilet was just a pit: a hole in the floor with a plank across it. I remember passing a stomach worm at some point. When we were liberated I weighed less than eight stone. I could not have survived another year but I always thought I would get out. I was very religious at that time and my faith sustained me.'

McArdle witnessed no executions but saw many men die from lack of the most basic medicines. It was the casual nature of daily cruelties which left deep scars. As the day of reckoning approached, the Japanese marched the fittest away, leaving the sick and dying to fend for themselves:

'I'd lost a lot of weight and had beri-beri. There are two types. I had "wet" beri-beri and this makes your legs and face swell up. My legs were badly affected and I found it difficult to walk.'

The prisoners knew liberation was at hand as they received scraps of news from the Burmese when they went out on working parties. By early 1945 they were aware that Allied Forces were making progress in their push from the north. Alec Gibson:

'On 25 April 1945, the Japanese ordered us to prepare to leave Rangoon. Around half the prisoners, about 400 in all, were judged fit enough to march. The rest were left behind.'

Those who could march went north and were abandoned by their guards when they bumped a detachment of British troops:

'We marched north-east and were left at a small village as our forces were very close. The Japanese senior officer told us we were free and he hoped he would soon meet us in combat again! After they left, Allied aircraft bombed and strafed the village. We had only

minor injuries, with the tragic exception of our Senior British Officer, Brigadier Hobson, who was killed by a cannon shell.

'When night fell an American teamed up with a Burmese, dressed as natives and set out to find our troops. We soon had friendly company and were truly free. Our problem at this time was not lack of food but too much of it! We found it very difficult to keep it down. I weighed just six and a half stone at that point. Our liberators prepared a huge meal for us and we couldn't resist, but our stomachs couldn't take it. We became violently sick. I was to spend many weeks in hospital, or rather, four hospitals.'

The first friendly face Ted McArdle saw at liberation was a British sailor. He came into the prison armed and looking for Japanese:

'One of the prisoners left behind borrowed a sampan and went downriver, eventually reaching a British warship standing off the port. He warned them that Rangoon Gaol still housed many British POWs. Their lives would be at risk if the ships bombarded the city.

'We left the prison, marched to the docks and boarded a hospital ship for India. We had to take solid food very gradually and started to build ourselves up with nourishing soups. My feelings were a mix of relief and disbelief. Was this really happening? Later, I had the option of flying back to Britain or going home by ship. I chose the ship, the Queen of Bermuda. I thought it would give me more time to recover.'

Alec Gibson witnessed many brutal acts by the Japanese:

'I felt real hatred towards our guards. We would have cheerfully killed them all, if we had been given the chance. I have no idea whether any were brought to justice after the war. This feeling of hatred came not only from our own suffering, but for all those completely unnecessary deaths, due to lack of medicines and

The will to live: a couple of prisoners in Rangoon Gaol survived amputations without anaesthetic. (Ted McArdle)

decent food. God knows how our doctors coped. They had nothing. They even managed to perform two successful amputations under those terrible conditions.

'A strong desire to live kept me going. The will to live was critical. I remember talking with an Australian Flight Sergeant towards the end of 1944. He told me: "If our troops can get here by Christmas, I will be alright." Well, they didn't arrive for another five months and he died two days after Christmas Day. He just lost the will to live.'

When Alec Gibson returned to India he was warned not to speak openly about his experiences, due to the risk of retaliation against POWs yet to be freed. He regained a modest level of fitness on double rations and returned to Britain, arriving in June 1945. He had written to his family – the first news of his survival as a POW. He did not hear from them. He had moved around so much in India that his mail never caught up with him:

'I had three months' POW leave and met my future wife, Kathleen. We became engaged. I was still far from fit at that point. Despite extra food and much effort, I found it very difficult to put on weight and felt lethargic most of the time. Yet I still had that fantastic feeling of being free at last.

'As an officer commissioned in the Indian Army, I was posted back to India. In one sense I was pleased to return. There was no rationing for an Indian Army Officer. We lived in relative luxury. When I finally reached Regimental HQ at Quetta, they didn't know what to do with me. I was then posted to Rangoon, of all places! I told the CO straight: "You've got a bloody cheek. I can't understand how you could have the gall to ask me to go there!" The posting was changed and I went to Delhi.'

The file of 'Narratives' used in the preparation of the *Official History of the War Against Japan*, Volume III (*National Archives, CAB 101/202*), includes documents reviewing the various possibilities considered for the deployment of Special Force for a third Chindit operation. Efforts to reconstitute Special Force and plan for fresh operations continued until late 1944. From the beginning of 1945, however, these plans were shelved and Special Force elements were steadily distributed among other units. In particular, the idea took hold of forming a new Parachute Brigade from the Chindits.

The planning for a new Chindit operation began in May 1944, with Operation *Thursday* still some months from completion. Clearly, the air landing of four Brigades for Operation *Thursday* was uppermost in the planners' minds, as the focus was on use of the

Chindits to assist the landing of main forces in enemy territory, either by seizing airstrips or by attacking beach defences from the rear and delaying the concentration of enemy troops.

Yet doubts remained about the value of Chindit-type operations. Mountbatten raised the issue of the future deployment of Special Force in July 1944. The considered view was that it would take five months to be ready for a new Chindit operation and that a Special Force of six Brigades would require 7,000 British reinforcements. This was unrealistic and thinking then focused on a Special Force of four Brigades: 16 Brigade all-British and 23, 77 and 111 as mixed Brigades. This goal was also found to be beyond reach. By October 1944 Special Force had been reduced to three Brigades. As demands for manpower grew more intense, Special Force came to be regarded as a SEAC manpower reserve. Between July and December 1944 four different plans were put forward for the deployment of Special Force and none were implemented. The rapid progress of 14th Army made plans for Special Force out of date before they could go ahead. This probably contributed to the continued fragmentation of Special Force and its eventual disbandment.

Special Force Commander Lentaigne received a letter from General Claude Auchinleck, C-in-C India, concerning the decision to break up Special Force. He wrote:

> I am anxious that you and all ranks of the Force should realise that this decision was only made after very careful consideration by the Prime Minister, War Office, the Allied Supreme Commander and myself. The reason for the decision was that Special Force had achieved the object for which it was created and the need for the special type of operation for which it was expert has ceased to exist. On the other hand the need of the Allied Supreme Commander for other types of troops was growing daily and becoming daily increasingly urgent. The best source from which such troops could be made quickly available was Special Force.

He added that he hoped the Chindits would console themselves 'with the thought that they have once belonged to this splendid formation...'

In Lentaigne's letter to his Command, he said:

> I am certain all ranks of this Force will appreciate the reasons behind the orders that have been given and will accept them without resentment. Let each of us remember that we are still Chindits. Be proud of this in yourselves, but do not be arrogant and, above all, critical of others. It is better for people to

find out that you are a Chindit rather than for you to tell them.

The 17 June 1946 edition of the *Daily Sketch* carried a story headed: 'Chindit flag on Admiralty Arch':

High over the Admiralty Arch, Trafalgar Square, above the flags of the Allied Nations, flew a banner with a strange device yesterday. It was the standard of the Chindits. But no-one at the Admiralty could tell how it got there. I did find out, however, that on Saturday night the Chindits held their first reunion dinner somewhere in the West End. They say it was quite a festive affair.

Notes

1. Calvert, M. (1996), *Fighting Mad*, 183
2. Graves-Morris, Lieutenant-Colonel P.H., unpublished MS (via Bill Smith and Corinne Simons)
3. Thompson, Sir Robert (1989), *Make for the Hills*, 62
4. Fergusson, B. (1946), *The Wild Green Earth*, 283
5. Welland, R.W.J., memoir, 29 July 2009 (via Bill Smith)
6. Nesbit, R.C. (2009), *The Battle for Burma*, 217
7. Calvert, M. (1974), *Chindits: Long Range Penetration*, 157–159
8. Slim, Field Marshal Viscount (1999), *Defeat into Victory*, 546–547
9. Calvert, M. (1996), 9–10
10. Thompson, Sir Robert (1989), 72
11. Larson, G. A. (2008), *Aerial Assault into Burma*, 199
12. Rooney, D. (2000), *Wingate and the Chindits: Redressing the Balance*, 170
13. Ibid, 171–173
14. Ibid, 132–133
15. Ibid, 143–144
16. Ibid, 145–148
17. Thompson, Sir Robert (1989), 76
18. Allen, L. (1986), *Burma: The Longest War 1941–45*, 118
19. Stibbe, P. (1995), *Return via Rangoon*, 197

30

REMEMBERING

CHINDIT VETERANS retain the wry sense of humour that sustained them so long ago. Former Lancashire Fusilier Ian Niven summed up his feelings about Burma:

'If I ever forget Broadway, Mawlu, White City, Mogaung and Shadazup, I'll know I am for the knacker's yard.'

During 1944 a remarkable book was published, giving a 'humorous' view of Chindit warfare. *Jungle, Jungle, Little Chindit*, by Major Patrick Boyle of the Cameronians and Major John Musgrove-Wood of The Burma Rifles, defies description. The book opens with a short foreword by Lentaigne, then still commanding Special Force. It is written in the contemporary vein and some of its content will surprise the modern reader. The wonder of it is that, after such horrific experiences, the authors could even contemplate such a book. One offering, entitled 'Lullaby of Broadway', is sung to the tune of 'Bring back my Bonny to me'. The chorus goes: 'Send down — oh, send down – oh, send down a light plane for me.' Presumably, Musgrove-Wood would have welcomed the arrival of light planes during Operation *Longcloth*, when he led a dispersal group on the long walk north to Fort Hertz and safety.

Most men took a far more serious view of their experiences in Burma and were reluctant to talk about it. The author's father never had a lengthy conversation about his experiences with the King's Own. There were only occasional asides. His reticence was understood and accepted within the family. John Simon, a 16 Brigade Bren gunner over 60 years ago, had this to say:

'Family members ask me about the war on occasion. I never make a big thing of it. Looking back, I remember that feeling of not knowing where we were going. I remember taking in the sheer size of the Chindwin river. I remember the short guy who led our Platoon during a river crossing. One moment he was there and the next he disappeared. He had walked into a deep hole in the riverbed.'

Looking back across the years, John Knowles, an RAF Officer with the Queen's, has no regrets: 'I was happy to have had that experience but I wouldn't do it again. I treasure the warmth of the comradeship.'

Knowles returned to the UK in January 1945 and became an Intelligence Officer with No. 6 Group, Bomber Command's Canadian Group. He was asked to prepare a lecture on his Chindit experiences for aircrew expecting to serve in the Far East after Germany's defeat. His lecture notes were rejected as 'too grim, too appalling.'

As a Medical Orderly in Burma, George Fulton saw terrible things: 'I've made a determined effort to forget them. I have spoken to other Burma Star Association veterans. Most have tried to obliterate these memories.'

Alec Gibson, captured during Wingate's first expedition, never talked about his Chindit and POW experiences. It was a closed book, even to his wife and family. This changed completely in 1985, on a Royal British Legion visit to Burma by war widows and veterans:

'At least half of our party were war widows. We visited a small cemetery in Rangoon. It was our POW cemetery. When established, it was just a small grass field. I saw one widow in obvious distress, standing beside a grave. I walked over and noticed that her lapel badge didn't

match the name on the grave. She explained that she had remarried. She was standing before the grave of her young first husband, who had died 40 years before.

'She went on to explain that her husband had worked on the "Railway of Death". I told her, gently, that this was unlikely, as that infamous railway was in Thailand. It soon became clear that she knew absolutely nothing about what had happened to her husband. I went to bed that night close to tears myself. I was horrified. Widows and children hadn't a clue about what had really happened to their loved ones. The only people who could tell them were people like me – the survivors. Suddenly, my refusal to talk about the war seemed selfish. After that trip I got in touch with the War Widows' Association and wrote an article for the Association's journal. From that moment on, I have been completely open and I am always happy to talk about things.

'Looking back, I now see how my service with the Chindits and, in particular, my time as a POW influenced the rest of my life. It had a profound impact on my outlook. These experiences gave me a greater ability to accept things in life, particularly the setbacks.'

Many men found Chindit warfare a life-changing experience. Jack Hutchin of the South Staffords came close to dying. Afterwards, during quiet days at Simla, he gathered his thoughts:

'I knew the futility of war. I hated it. Nobody really cared when I got back. Later, I brought up my children to have a non-combatant's view of life. Burma changed me in other ways. I had a poor upbringing in a family with genteel pretences. When I joined up, I had no idea that most people lived their lives differently. I remember Lance-Corporal Cook. When we came out of Burma, I wrote his letters home. He couldn't write!'

Major Bill Williams was in Hutchin's Column. Afterwards, he spent little time talking about Burma:

'My family showed interest but I don't believe in re-fighting old battles. That said, I think about Burma a lot and I have been involved in the Chindits Old Comrades' Association since its formation. Whenever I think of Burma I see White City before me. I find memory a kind thing. It erases painful events and focuses on comradeship – the friendship.'

Many men set aside Burma as a closed chapter. Major Denis Arnold, MC, a Platoon Commander with the Nigerians in 1944: 'I have few painful memories. Generally, I went on to lead a positive and happy life.'

Comradeship: former 16 Brigade HQ Column Bren gunner John Simon (right), pictured with Les Martindale during a reunion at the Albert Hall in the late 1960s. (John Simon)

Some men buried their memories. The author's father, Jack Redding, made an occasional wry comment about walking a thousand miles in the jungle, when, later in life, he took a wrong turning in the car. Sometimes he would tell his son, good-humouredly: 'You'd be no good in the jungle!' – an observation with the ring of truth.

Burma gave men fresh perspectives. Philip Stibbe wrote of a change in attitude after two years as a Japanese prisoner: 'When we returned to England at the end of the war, we found it difficult to understand why people worried if they could not find a bed for the night or couldn't put milk in their tea; it seemed strange to us to complain so much about the shortages.'

A high proportion of Chindit POWs died in Rangoon Gaol. Philip Stibbe notes that over 200 captured Chindits from both expeditions were held there and more than half died of wounds, disease and malnutrition: 'Nearly always they died peacefully, usually in their sleep. In almost every case, towards the end, they seemed to lose the will to live and to become quite content to go; once this happened we knew nothing more could be done.'[1]

Some men changed at the day-to-day level. Eric Sugden of the Bedfordshire and Hertfordshire's 61 Column:

In discussion: former Medical Orderly George Fulton, watched by wife Jean, in conversation with HRH The Duke of Edinburgh at High Tea in Aberdeen's Beach Ballroom in July 2005. (George Fulton)

'Chindit service changed my values. Certainly, it gave me a permanent and deep appreciation of good, straightforward food. Even today, I enjoy my food in a different way having been in that Column.'

Special Force was multiracial, with the Burrifs – the Karens and Kachins – providing essential jungle expertise. Bill Smyly described them as 'the princes of the jungle'. John Riggs, Recce Platoon Commander with 16 Column, could draw on the knowledge of his Platoon's Burrif team. He remembers the challenge of living and fighting in the Burmese jungle:

I am sometimes asked if I was frightened. I was never involved in a pitched battle with the Japanese, as we were with the Germans and Italians in North Africa three years before. The Recce Platoon's job was to see but not become involved. I was too tired and too busy keeping the Platoon going to be frightened. Burma became even more difficult after the Monsoon broke. There were always problems finding suitable places for the Column to cross a river or take a supply drop. Torrents of Monsoon flood water poured out of the Himalayas. The few suitable crossing places were always potential ambush sites.

'Late one evening, when looking for a crossing along the bed of a dry chaung, my Burrif NCO put a hand on my shoulder and pointed. I thought he had spotted Japs and I froze. He whispered: "Yes. Look! Look!" I did look — very hard — but could see nothing. Then I saw a pair of unblinking eyes staring at me from the river bed. It was a large lizard. My companion muttered, "Good to eat." He hit it on the head with his kukri, tied it to his rifle and put it over his shoulder. When we got back I asked for special permission to light a fire at night. My NCO got his fire and boiled up chunks of lizard enhanced with soup powder. We were always hungry and if he said it was edible I was happy to join him. It had the texture of very rubbery squid, but was better than nothing. "Calamari à la Burma"!'

Many British soldiers never lost their deep loathing of the Burmese jungle. George Hill, with the Queen's 21 Column:

> Why was this part of the world so malevolent and what caused it to be so? As far as we were concerned, every damn thing! The heat and humidity. The sweat, the rain, or its absence — too much water (if only from above) or too little — the mud or the dust, the jungle, the sometimes almost impenetrable undergrowth, the mountains, the precipices, the murderous slopes, the insects and the disease, in almost any permutation. One must also not forget, of course, those bloody packs!

Warm memories of Burma focus on comradeship at a depth usually denied men living in normal circumstances. Memories are often tinged with the sense of profound loss.

Platoon Commander Denis Arnold may hold the distinction of being the first combat soldier to be evacuated by a helicopter. He was certainly one of the very first to arrive at a hospital by helicopter. At that point he weighed less than seven stone:

A profound impact: Alec Gibson survived service as a Chindit and as a prisoner of the Japanese. (Alec Gibson)

'At one point during the fighting one of my Gunners looked very dejected. He'd stepped on his pipe and broken it. I can still see the look of delight on his face when I handed over mine, which was almost new. Instant happiness!'

21 Column's George Hill left Burma far behind and got on with life. His attitude changed in 1989, when in hospital with a serious condition. He recovered and got talking to another patient who was Secretary of a Burma Star Association branch. Hill rejoined the Chindits Old Comrades' Association: 'Having reached the stage of "reflection" — advancing years and retreating health — the dim and distant past suddenly seemed a matter of some importance, regardless of the unpleasant circumstances at the time.'

After nearly 57 years George Hill took the initiative and contacted Tony Howard, his former Corporal (or, rather, Acting Sergeant). George Hill died in 2003 and is remembered with great affection by Howard. The past had also surfaced in Tony Howard's mind. He was a member of a rambling club and was asked, at one point, to give a talk about the Chindits:

'It took me three months to get over it, much of that time at No. 132 Indian General Hospital. When the Japanese surrendered we began organising the repatriation of our African troops. I was back in West Africa by March 1946, as a Major and Company Commander. I remember, with great sadness, the loss of our CSM, Adamu Hadajah. He suffered all the privations of Burma, had survived and then returned to India. He made the voyage to Lagos, via Suez, only to die shortly after his return from amoebic dysentery. He kept his troubles to himself. I had no idea he was at risk. He was such a good man and it was dreadful that we should lose him after all that.'

Another 3(WA) Brigade veteran, Larry Gaines, adds:

'One thing that still strikes me today is the remarkable closeness between Chindit officers and their men. Everyone, from the CO down, carried their arms, equipment and rations. I am proud of my service as a Chindit. People who know me are very conscious that I was a Chindit.'

Some remember moments which touched them. Ronald Swann was with the guns at Blackpool:

With the guns at Blackpool: Ronald Swann returned after more than 60 years and found his old Command Post. (Ian Swann)

'It was a two-hour meeting and it took nearly all that time to describe the set-up and working of the Column. It went down well. I was proud to have been a Chindit. It was the highlight of my life. Fortunately, I had missed that part of the campaign when Special Force was put under Stilwell and had such a terrible time. Our march in was very tough but we knew how to cope. Compared to 77 Brigade, 16 Brigade was lucky. We were also lucky as Signallers, as we were sheltered from much of the fighting.

'That said, I remember what happened when RAF Officer Gillies located and organised the bombing of those Japanese supply dumps. Our Column was sent to occupy the area. The Japs were expected to attack and all HQ personnel, including Signallers, were ordered to fix bayonets. It was difficult to take that seriously. It wasn't the sort of thing the Royal Corps of Signals usually did! We Signallers thought it was a huge joke. We couldn't stifle some rather self-conscious laughter.'

Before he died George Hill set down his experiences in 50 closely typed pages: 'This is my account of leading a life, for a time, that was totally contrary to my basic nature. What really surprises me, however, is just how much can be brought to the surface by careful and sustained memory-dredging and, even more so, the considerable amount of information held on "instant recall".

Hill made reference to the Chindit shoulder flash: a seated golden *Chinthé* (the fabulous lion) facing right towards a golden pagoda, on a dark blue circular field. It was worn on the right shoulder. Hill wrote: 'Wingate intended the flash as an honour, which was to be worn by an ex-Chindit for the rest of his service life, no matter with whom or where that was to be.'

Former RAF Officer John Knowles has warm words for his Chindit comrades:

'As far as I'm concerned, the British soldier is the best in the world. He has the ideal combination of guts, determination, intelligence and resourcefulness. With great adaptability he could, and did, somehow manage to make himself comfortable ... even in Hell.

'There is a timeless quality to the comradeship. I found comradeship within the Column was deeper and more rewarding than that on a fighter squadron – perhaps because we were totally reliant on each other for our lives. We suffered unbelievable physical hardship. Our Column was on the move constantly for 105 days, except for a couple of days at Aberdeen. No-one who has not gone through what we went through for some 800 miles can have the faintest idea of what it was like ... Something entered our souls that made it possible to bear the burden. This continues to

set us just a little bit apart from everyone else, including other soldiers in other campaigns. Like the ordained members of some strange priesthood, we are once and forever Chindits.'

Yet the waste of war can kindle an anger undiminished with time. During 1967 John Knowles was on a Canadian Government mission to New Zealand. He was invited to dinner by Bernard Fergusson, former 16 Brigade Commander and then Governor-General. Fergusson confirmed that Knowles' close friend, Flight Lieutenant Gillies DFM, had not survived Burma. Gillies was Knowles' opposite number in 21 Column. When they came across a huge complex of Japanese supply dumps, Gillies flew out to India and, flying a Hurricane, personally led a raid on one of the most important targets in North Burma. His Hurricane and a second aircraft, flown by Squadron Leader Roy Lane, were retained at Aberdeen. John Knowles:

'Gilly won the Military Cross for his role in destroying the supply dumps, but he never got to wear it. Both Gilly and Lane were lost flying those clapped-out Hurricanes. Lane was found by the Japanese and used for bayonet practice. To the best of my knowledge, Gilly never turned up at all. One of the last things he said to me was that, if ever he were forced down in enemy territory, the first thing he would do would be to brew up a mug of tea. I hope he had the chance. I was outraged as Gilly was a close friend. Roy Lane was one of three brothers, all killed in the war. We lost two first-class men who didn't deserve the couple of old crates they were given. Some rotten bastard of a Supply Officer saw the chance to offload them.'

Many former Chindits – especially, perhaps, those from city backgrounds with no previous experience of working with animals – remember the mules with great affection. Most men never lost their fear of being kicked, but everyone admired the way in which the mules continued until they dropped.

Today, it is possible to gain some impression of the world of the Chindit, his equipment, weapons and mules. 'Living History' enthusiasts Viv and John Marshall team up with 'Chindit Bill' Smith to portray the Chindit fighting soldier and the animals at military shows. Smith's father, Reg, was a York and Lancaster Chindit. Bill has a full range of Chindit equipment (including some items of his father's uniform) and Viv and John have two mules.

According to Bill Smith – a great admirer of mules – an ammunition mule's load would amount to around 440 pounds: two ammunition boxes (260 pounds), a

Living history: 'Chindit Bill' Smith's father, Reg, was with the 2nd York and Lancaster in Burma. Dressed as a 65 Column NCO, Bill sits in the partially reconstructed fuselage of a WACO CG-4A glider, under restoration at the Assault Glider Trust, RAF Shawbury. (Bill Smith)

box of 20 No. 231 fuses (68 pounds), two tarpaulins (24 pounds), harness and saddlery (70 pounds), and two nosebags with feed for one day (20 pounds). The strength of a mule can be gauged by comparing this load with the 560 pounds capacity of a WWII Jeep. Special forces have not forgotten the mule. They are still in use in the 21st Century, with US forces fighting the Taliban in the Afghan mountains.

Wingate's personality looms large over this story. This complex man left a legacy of mixed emotions. Harold Pettinger was with a REME detachment at Sylhet when the news broke that Wingate's plane had crashed:

'My little workshop at Sylhet made a small brass plate commemorating his loss and the deaths of those accompanying him. This was taken to the crash site. Later, it was replaced by a memorial, but the original plate was recovered and can now be seen in the Imperial War Museum's Special Forces section. Wingate may have been a genius but he was also impossible. He turned to my Sergeant and said: "My Jeep ... I want a total guarantee from you that it will never break down!" He was very difficult to deal with.'

Wingate committed the occasional faux pas when talking to ORs. Sergeant Major Bob Hobbs, an Operation *Longcloth* veteran, remembers Wingate's poor start when he arrived to give a talk: 'He asked everyone to hand in their cigarettes, adding, "You won't need them where you are going" – hardly a popular move!'

Links with Special Force were difficult to break. While at Sylhet Harold Pettinger was given a New Testament by Chris Perowne, Chaplain to Special Force and the brother of Brigadier Lance Perowne, Commander of 23 Brigade. In 1948 Pettinger was standing on a platform at Newcastle upon Tyne station when he bumped into Lance Perowne, complete with monocle. He introduced himself and Perowne saw his opportunity:

'He said: "You're in the TA – you'd better join my HQ!" At that time I was working for Otis as Newcastle Branch Manager. Perowne's offer suited me and I joined 151 TA Brigade, based in Newcastle and part of 50th Division. I went on to complete 22 years' service in the TA.'

There is rich irony in the fact that Wingate's detractors have ensured his continued prominence. As Sir Robert Thompson observed in *Make for the Hills*: 'It has made him such a controversial figure that his reputation will last forever.'

The *Official History of the War Against Japan* ignored all favourable appraisals of Wingate and Special Force. Instead, it presented a catalogue of faults and inadequacies. In his attempt to set the record straight, Rooney observed:

> In the final paragraph of the assessment came the most disgraceful and unprofessional statement: 'Just as timing played so great a part in his rise to prominence, so the moment of his death may perhaps have been equally propitious for him'. When the *Official History* virtually says it was just as well an officer was killed, it cannot claim to be a fair or balanced assessment.[2]

Admirers in what soon became the State of Israel mourned the loss of 'The Friend'. In a letter to Alice Hay, Wingate's mother-in-law, Israeli Prime Minister David Ben Gurion wrote:

> I have no doubt that great deeds were in store for this unique personality, had he not been cut off before his time. If he had been privileged to see the resuscitation of the State of Israel, I am certain that he would have led the Israeli Defence Forces in the War of Independence. I believe that this was his intimately cherished dream.'

Wingate had a way of making an impression that could last a lifetime. Alice Hay wrote that Emmanuel Yalan, a former Haganah Intelligence Officer, understood Wingate better than anyone beyond his own family circle.[3] Yalan wrote of Wingate:

> When a man has faith in God – the Governor of the world – lives in the presence of this Almighty Power and, moreover, is confident that he himself is, in some way, a messenger of that Power, he is naturally never lonely. These convictions permeated and formed his personality. Every meeting with him was an event. His approach to everyday matters was never routine. He believed that man has to fulfil his destiny and that towards that aim he must strive.[4]

Alice Hay wrote:

> It is repeatedly affirmed that it is as the leader of the Chindits in Burma that, in time to come, he will be best remembered. I disagree. What he was able to do (in Palestine) is of more significance and historical

importance than anything else he achieved in his short life.[5]

She wrote that Wingate proved to the Jews, 'over and over again, that they had all the qualities needed for success on the field of battle. It banished forever from their hearts and minds the spirit of the ghetto engendered by centuries of persecution.'

Perhaps echoes of Wingate's legacy continue to influence events in the Middle East. The Israeli Defence Forces have weathered many challenges, none greater than in 1973, but no-one can argue that the Israeli Army and Air Force lack confidence on the field of battle. Israeli military commanders, including Moshe Dayan, learned much from Wingate.

Many men (and not just his detractors) saw a callous streak in Wingate's nature. Alice Hay denied this, claiming Wingate had deep feelings for his men, although 'often disguised in an exaggerated soldierly manner.' After Wingate's death she remembered Matron McGeary telling the family that he was about to leave her hospital, after visiting Chindit casualties, when he turned and asked whether he had seen everyone. Matron McGeary told him that one man, named Heppinstall, was dying. He had been unconscious for days and there was no point in seeing him. Wingate disagreed:

> Orde bent over him and in a commanding voice he called: 'Heppinstall!' There was no response. Then he repeated, 'Heppinstall!', and, to the amazement of the little group gathered around the bed, the soldier's eyelids fluttered. Once more Orde called his name. The eyes opened; he looked at his leader and, trying to bring his arm to the salute, he said: 'Oh! Sir! I didn't know it was you!' 'Heppinstall', said Orde, 'you are to get well quickly, because I need you.' 'Yes, Sir', replied the sick man, 'I shall be there.' His recovery dated from that hour.[6]

Wingate had a sense of humour. Alice Hay offered an example very much in character. He once told his mother-in-law that Michael Calvert was the best soldier he knew, adding with a grin, 'Except me, of course.'[7]

There can be no denying the immense loyalty displayed by the Chindits towards Wingate. Perhaps the most important factor here was that Wingate was so very 'different' and, by association, those who served under him became 'different'. In this context, the name Special Force was something of a master stroke. The Chindits were special and at the conclusion of the operations, this was recognised by everyone without an axe to grind. In 1982 the Chindits Old Comrades' Association prepared its 'Appreciation' of Wingate, in response to decades of criticism. This outpouring of warmth for an Army Commander was without precedent.

In his introduction to this document, a compilation of comments from many former Chindits, Brigadier Walter Scott, DSO, MC, stressed the difficulty of those who had served under Wingate in accepting 'a number of incorrect, adverse and contemptuous statements made in the *Official History*'.

The 'Appreciation' is a blend of fulsome praise for Wingate and disdain for his critics. The comments made by Private J. Allmont, a member of a 2nd Leicesters Recce Platoon, convey the essence of the document:

'As an ex-Regular soldier of little education, who left school and enlisted as a drummer boy at 16, I feel unfitted to enter the lists as an advocate and champion of General Wingate and of those gallant comrades of mine who laid down their lives in Burma, fighting for the ideals that General Wingate personified.

'As a Chindit, I have long resented the treatment of General Wingate's personality and the denigration of his men's efforts … I feel that a great leader has been treated unjustly and the sacrifices and achievements of my colleagues have been belittled.'

Many years before, Brigadier Derek Tulloch, Special Force Chief of Staff, saved documents concerning Wingate's service in Burma, fearing that his critics might destroy them. Tulloch knew what was coming. He was to spend much of the rest of his life defending Wingate's reputation, at considerable personal cost.[8]

Fred Holliday, of the King's 82 Column, offers a view of other Chindit commanders:

'Calvert was a very unusual character. To be frank, he didn't care a toss about anything. He was bordering on the bloodthirsty. His personality was so different from that of Lentaigne and Masters. Calvert had a strong partnership with Wingate. The men of 77 Brigade worshipped Michael Calvert. When Lentaigne was chosen to succeed Wingate, they just couldn't believe it. We all expected Calvert to take over. Masters was given 111 Brigade. He was a capable man but I am not sure he was good enough to emulate Calvert. Then there was Stilwell. The less said about him the better! He hated the "Limeys" and the Limeys hated him. When we came under his command, everything went from bad to worse.'

Bill Smyly:

'Lentaigne and Masters were handed a poisoned chalice, which neither Wingate nor Calvert would have accepted without protest.'

Smyly contrasts the warm, highly successful Anglo-American relationship surrounding Operation *Thursday* while Wingate was alive with the bitter tensions under Stilwell's command:

'To us, Cochran's Air Commando were heroes and stars. We loathed Stilwell, not the Yanks. Stilwell was the wrong man in the wrong place and, typically, when he saw the price of his orders in Chindit casualty lists, he refused to believe them.'

The true character of Anglo-American relations is described by Air Commando Mustang pilot Olin B. Carter, who has the greatest respect for the Chindits:

'I was extremely impressed with them. They were a whole different breed – warriors, real fighters. I wouldn't have wanted to tangle with them. There were also the wonderful Gurkhas … they were tremendous warriors and great thieves when camped close to us.'

Carter attended every annual reunion of the Air Commando Association until 2007. At that point, he was the last of the original Mustang pilots present:

A participant in both Wingate operations: Bill Smyly pictured with his wife, Diana, during a trip to New York. (Bill Smyly)

'Looking back, it is amazing just how much time we had in the air before we flew in Burma. I always considered myself a fairly junior guy, yet I had 1,000 hours of fighter time before flying with Cochran's Air Commando.'

Carter almost achieved an ambition before leaving the Far East theatre. He and a group of friends had arranged with RAF pilots to exchange mounts. Carter had always wanted to fly a Spitfire:

'Well, the day came and four Spitfires appeared overhead, led by a Belgian pilot. One by one they went into a low level pass and roll. The last aircraft lost flying speed and stalled in, killing the pilot. That was the end of that. I never flew a Spitfire!'

Was the 1944 Chindit operation a success? Dick Hilder, with 14 Brigade's HQ Column, takes a straightforward view:

'At the military level, the Chindits disrupted three Japanese Divisions and took some of the weight off Imphal and Kohima. We dispelled the notion that the Japanese were invincible in the jungle. Until then, our soldiers really thought the Japanese were superhuman. I remember talking to people who felt that way.'

Former Chindit Platoon Commander Larry Gaines adds:

'Was it worthwhile? Some commentators think not. The real issue, however, is Japanese perceptions at the time. Contemporary documents clearly show that Operation Thursday had a significant impact on their thinking.'

Cameronian Norman Campbell talks of his pride:

'Very few people would have volunteered, knowing the physical and mental privations which had to be endured and overcome. Yet, having done it, I'm glad I had the strength to cope. The Chindits have every right to be proud of their achievements, somewhat limited though they may have been. We marched nearly 1,000 miles in five months, carrying a burden that no troops had carried continuously in any previous war, nor over such inhospitable terrain, in such a dreadful climate. At that time we didn't know enough to judge whether or not it had been a success. Certainly, we killed a lot of Japanese and destroyed a great deal of equipment. Most importantly, we disrupted the Japanese efforts to reinforce their thrusts and their push against Stilwell's Chinese.

'It was an unusual kind of warfare, invented by one man and, perhaps, to an excessive extent run by one man. His demise opened up an enormous void. Wingate should have had a Deputy virtually living with him. That Deputy should have been fully informed and as well known to the troops as Wingate himself. It is said that no-one is irreplaceable but Wingate, in these circumstances, was just that.'

Bill Smyly considers the 1944 Chindit campaign in phases:

'The fly-in was the first in history and remains unique in its jungle setting. White City was a highly successful "Block" and Mogaung is a reminder of the price paid when Generals and Commands squabble. Then there is Blackpool. If White City was the operation when all things went unexpectedly right, Blackpool was the reverse and illustrates the risks of war.

'The first expedition was important as it was our return to Burma after the catastrophic defeat of 1942. The second show cost a great deal more than the first. We were thrown out of Blackpool. Mogaung was a marvellously brave victory but won at an absurd cost in lives – quite unnecessary and not of our choosing. The action which justified the whole campaign was White City. This became the major killing ground for the Japanese soldiers sent to sort us out. It showed what Long Range Penetration could do and it owed its success to Mike Calvert. He was a man who made his own luck. He understood the system better than any other and he went out looking for trouble. White City was the Chindits' perfect operation. Mogaung was our bloodiest battle honour. Blackpool was our disaster.'

The official view at the time is set out in the *Report on Operations carried out by Special Force, October 1943 to September 1944*. This states that the first objective of Operation *Thursday* – to assist Stilwell's Chinese – was achieved by: the success of White City; the disruption of the supply and reinforcement of 18th Division; the drawing off of at least 10,000 men; the killing of over 5,000; the destruction of stores; the capture of Mogaung; the control over the Bhamo–Myitkyina road exercised by Morris Force; limitations imposed on the supply and reinforcement of Myitkyina; and the general confusion caused by the operation of Columns behind enemy lines.

Another objective was to harass communications supporting the Japanese attack on Imphal. Here, the report offers less definitive comment:

It is now known that 14 and 111 Brigades destroyed quantities of stores that were badly needed by the Japanese to supply the ill-fated Divisions which had crossed the Chindwin. The exact extent of the effect of these losses on the enemy cannot be judged, except in so far as it confirms that the operations of the Force achieved their object ... It requires but a moderate stretch of the imagination to assess some of the effects of an equivalent operation by the Japanese, had they in fact put down a Long Range Penetration force in the Brahmaputra Valley at a time when reinforcements were vital to both the Chindwin and North Burma fronts. It is by this standard that the success of the Special Force operation should be judged.

As to the cost, the *Report on Operations* states that the casualties over all six Brigades (that is, including 23 Brigade) totalled 297 officers and 3,627 ORs. 102 officers were killed in action or died of wounds. A further 171 were wounded and 24 were missing. A total of 888 ORs were killed in action or died of wounds. In addition, 2,255 ORs were wounded and 484 were missing. The six Brigades killed 5,381 Japanese and wounded 706, with an additional 86 listed as 'captured alive'. As might be expected, 77 Brigade suffered heavily, with 46 officers and 346 ORs killed in action or died of wounds, 84 officers and 1,156 ORs wounded and 11 officers and 168 ORs missing. This Brigade also inflicted the most casualties, killing 2,052 Japanese, wounding 69 and capturing 19. The Brigade's losses included Captain George Cairns VC, killed during the charge on Pagoda Hill. In May 1949 his widow received his Victoria Cross, the last to be awarded for valour in the Second World War.[9] These statistics, of course, concern battle casualties only and, therefore, tell only part of the story. There are also the more numerous casualties from disease.

It seems that Lord Louis Mountbatten, SEAC Supreme Commander, came to regard disease as a weapon of war. In a lecture on the campaign in South East Asia, presented at the Royal United Service Institution on Wednesday 9 October 1946 (published in the November edition of the Institution's journal), he made some remarkable comments on the subject of disease:

In 1943, for every man who was admitted to hospital with wounds, there had been 120 who were casualties from ... tropical diseases. By 1944, these 120 men had been reduced to 20, although hospital admissions still reached between 14,000 and 15,000 per week in peak periods.

By 1945 the rate had dropped to 10 men sick for every one battle casualty and, during the last six weeks of the war, these 10 had been reduced to six. The enemy had no medical advisory division and appears to have made no advances in medical research.

As our own troops became more and more immune from circumstances against which the Japanese had no remedy, I was determined to enlist disease as an additional weapon on our side and deliberately chose unhealthy areas in which to fight.

Operation *Thursday* would have been impossible without effective air supply and support. Here, the *Report on Operations* notes clear differences between RAF and USAAF practices. The RAF required detailed target indication in advance, to brief aircrews. In contrast, the USAAF was more flexible. American aircraft struck at targets indicated by R/T and smoke, as the situation demanded at the scene. The report described this as 'infinitely the more effective' in view of the difficulties of describing a jungle target by wireless and the need to take account of rapid developments on the ground.

The *Report on Operations* states that 3,648 supply sorties were scheduled from No. 1 Air Base in the February–August 1944 period and around two-thirds were successful. Just over half the unsuccessful sorties were aborted, the balance being cancelled. Of the 651 aborted sorties, weather was the cause in 406 cases; only 32 were due to failure to locate the drop zone. The aircraft delivered 5,438 tons 1,870 pounds (5,526 tonnes) of stores by parachute, free-drop and landing. The parachuted stores totalled 4,485 tons 1,756 pounds (4,558 tonnes).

Tonnages parachuted in increased dramatically in the second half of March, peaking at 391 tons 353 pounds in the week ending 26 March. Tonnages parachuted stayed high in April, May and the first half of June, then declined dramatically. In the six weeks ending 6 August, the highest weekly tonnage dropped by parachute totalled 50 tons (week ending 2 July). This decline reflects Monsoon weather, the redeployment of USAAF aircraft and, to some extent, expanded operations to evacuate the sick, wounded and exhausted.

Air supply began with 27 and 315 Troop Carrier Squadrons, USAAF, operating from No. 1 Air Base at Sylhet, dropping to 16 Brigade Columns marching in. For a 10–day period in March, during the fly-in of 77 and 111 Brigades, 27 and 315 squadrons were relieved by a detachment of 31 Squadron RAF, operating from No. 2 Air Base at Agartala, which took over support for 16 Brigade. With the initial fly-in over, 117 Squadron RAF served 77 Brigade, 27 Squadron USAAF 16 Brigade and 315 Squadron USAAF 111 Brigade.

Virtually all supply drops were made by night until 24 May, when Monsoon conditions required a switch to daylight operations for the rest of Operation *Thursday*. At the end of May, 27 and 315 Squadrons moved from Sylhet, leaving only a detachment for Special Force support.

In June, most sorties were flown by 117 Squadron, with additional flights by other RAF squadrons at Agartala. Due to lack of space at Sylhet, 14 and 23 Brigades were supported from Agartala. When 16 Brigade came out in May, the maintenance of 14 Brigade transferred gradually from No. 2 to No. 1 Air Base, with Agartala continuing to serve 23 Brigade. As the focus of operations turned north in May, it was decided to take advantage of better flying conditions in the Assam Valley, relative to Sylhet, by establishing a subsidiary support centre at Dinjan, designated No. 3 Air Base. This held 15 days' supplies for three Brigades. Supply drops from Dinjan began on 27 May, with sorties made by four aircraft from 315 Squadron.

Dinjan became more important as a supply base as weather at Sylhet continued to deteriorate in late May. This transfer accelerated as 117 Squadron was required by Third Tactical Air Force for other duties. There was a difficult period of transition. The QQ requests still came into Sylhet and had to be relayed to Dinjan, which became congested. It was a struggle for No.3 Air Base to satisfy the requirement of around 20 sorties daily. The last drop to a Special Force Brigade on operations was flown on 23 August.

According to the *Report on Operations*, the 1944 Chindit campaign resulted in the loss of 44 aircraft. The Japanese losses were put at 37 shot down, 78 destroyed on the ground, together with 20 'probables' and 54 'damaged'.

Turning to the evacuation of casualties, Medical HQ was established at Sylhet (No. 91 Indian General Hospital). In the Monsoon period most casualties were flown to Dakota strips at Warazup and Tingkawk. They were staged to Ledo and other strips by aircraft of the American Air Evacuation Unit. Casualties brought out by flying boat were admitted to hospital at Dibrugarh. Casualties leaving by rafts and boats from the north of Indawgyi Lake, along the Indaw Chaung to Kamaing, were then transported by American assault craft to Warazup. When it became safe to do so, the railway was also used to transport casualties.

The Sunderland flying boat sorties took place in two phases. According to the *Report on Operations*, the first flight was on 2 June, evacuating 31 casualties, with another sortie on each of the next two days, bringing out a further 76. On 5 June two sorties evacuated another 81. No sorties were flown on 6 June, but two were made on 7 June, bringing out 79. There was one sortie daily for the next three days, flying out 122. Over the period 2–10 June, the Sunderlands flew 10 sorties and evacuated 389 casualties.

There were no sorties involving Sunderlands from Indawgyi Lake over the period 11–30 June inclusive.

However, three more sorties were flown over 1–4 July, evacuating 120 from 'Dawlish' base. This brought the total flown out by Sunderlands to just over 500. The evacuation by boats began in mid-June.

———————

Wingate and his expeditions still generate heated argument over 65 years after his death. Bernard Fergusson's two books, *Beyond the Chindwin* (Operation *Longcloth*) and *The Wild Green Earth* (Operation *Thursday*), are evocative, powerful and intimate narratives, produced shortly after the events they describe. In the first, Fergusson wrote of Wingate: 'He seemed almost to rejoice in making enemies' but 'he was a military genius of a grandeur and stature seen not more than once or twice in a century'. In the second, Fergusson deals with arguments over Wingate's reputation: 'Some of those who now whisper that he was not all he was cracked up to be remind me of the mouse who has a swig of whisky and then says, "Now show me that bloody cat."'

Wingate's death brought tributes from many, including King George VI, Mountbatten and Wavell, but Wingate's many enemies now seized their opportunity. They included some who had been at GHQ, Delhi, when Wingate arrived, flushed with success at Quebec and determined to brush aside all opposition. Major-General Kirby, then Director of Staff Duties at GHQ, Delhi, was confronted with this whirlwind. Wingate tabled demands, refused to budge and relied on Wavell to overrule all objections. Kirby's opportunity came after the war, when preparing the *Official History of the War Against Japan*. Volume III dealt with Imphal, Kohima and the Chindits and was published in 1962. The subsequent row has reverberated ever since. As discussed earlier, there is a widespread view that the *Official History* is heavily biased against Wingate and the Chindits. Certainly, this was Tulloch's view. Tulloch exchanged some very bitter correspondence with Kirby in the first quarter of 1962. Six years earlier, in 1956, the publication of Slim's *Defeat into Victory* had already caused disquiet among Chindit veterans. They were shocked at its rather negative commentary on Wingate, the first expedition and the exploits of Special Force.[2]

In the immediate aftermath, Slim had been generous in his praise. By the mid-1950s, however, he wrote of *Longcloth*: 'It gave little tangible return for the losses it had suffered and the resources it had absorbed … if anything was learnt of air supply or jungle fighting, it was a costly schooling.'[10]

Turning to Operation *Thursday*, Slim also continued in a very different vein to 1944, causing discomfort among Special Force veterans who shared the widespread affection for him felt by all soldiers of the Far East theatre. Rooney suggests the change in tone is

Many remained in Burma: Les Stevens, of the Bedfordshire and Hertfordshire's 61 Column, reads an air-dropped copy of *Life* in the Burmese jungle. Stevens died of wounds. (John Riggs)

linked to Slim's decision to submit draft chapters of *Defeat into Victory* for comment by the anti-Wingate authors of the *Official History*.[2]

Even the place and manner of Wingate's burial (or, rather, burials) generated much controversy. Writing in the early 1960s, Wingate's mother-in-law, Alice Hay, described how her daughter had received a War Office telegram late on the night of 9 November 1950:

> This message said that, on the *following day*, the remains of General Wingate were to be reinterred in Arlington Cemetery, Virginia, USA. There was no time to arrange for any representative of the family to be present at the ceremony. Indeed, as we learned afterwards, neither Britain nor the British Army was represented. No British flag was seen that day when the remains of one of her most distinguished sons were laid in their last resting place.[11]

Within a few weeks *The Times* published a 'letter of protest' from Rachel Wingate, the eldest member of the family. This recalled the efforts of the original

burial party, led by Chris Perowne, the Chaplain to the Chindits. They trekked through Japanese-held territory to reach the crash site and bury the nine dead, including the American aircrew of five. Then, in 1947, Wingate's family read in the newspapers that a joint Anglo-American team intended to visit the original grave and recover remains for reburial in Imphal Military Cemetery. Rachel Wingate's letter commented:

> We had every reason to expect that the grave at Imphal, among their comrades in arms, would be their final resting place ... apart from the questionable decision to allow the Americans to transfer these remains to the United States, we do want to ask why, at no stage of these removals – which we now learn have been in hand over a year – did we ever hear from an official? The Imperial War Graves Commission, which has the position of trustee for the relatives in such matters, has been unable to offer any explanation for deliberately keeping the British relatives in the dark.[11]

The day after this letter appeared, *The Times* ran an article explaining that, under US law, the remains of all Americans who die abroad are repatriated. Under an Anglo-American agreement, such decisions rest with the country having the largest number of nationals buried in a common grave. This article then claimed that the War Office had no prior knowledge, a suggestion rejected by Wingate's family. According to Alice Hay, she called at the US War Department during a trip to Washington some years later and was assured that the War Office in London 'had been kept fully informed.'[11]

In a circular letter of December 1950, concerning the arrangements for Wingate's memorial at Charterhouse School, Derek Tulloch touched on the heated row over Arlington. He had received a reply to a letter to the President of the Imperial War Graves Commission. This pointed out that Anglo-American policy on such matters stemmed from a fundamental difference in approach. The Americans favoured repatriation and the British took the opposite view (reaffirmed in a public statement from the Imperial War Graves Commission in October 1945). The matter was settled in 1947 on the 'majority' principle. The Americans had respected this agreement, which also provided for action to be taken without prior consultation with the next of kin. Tulloch, however, went on to acknowledge that the way this particular case was handled was 'still far from satisfactory'. The phrase 'prior consultation' had been interpreted very differently. American next of kin were kept informed, whereas British families were simply not told before the event. Tulloch stressed that 'no blame of any kind can be laid on the American authorities.'

Wingate's unorthodox methods always attracted criticism. After the war the York and Lancaster's Battalion Commander, Philip Graves-Morris, DSO, MC, faced a court-martial for the flogging of two soldiers. One offender stole rations. The second was caught asleep on sentry duty. Each was sentenced to 28 days' field punishment – a meaningless sentence behind Japanese lines. Each was then given the option to accept 12 strokes with a bamboo cane. Both accepted this alternative and confirmed in writing. One man, however, talked to his family about the flogging on returning to Britain. Eventually, the story reached the press and an MP raised the matter in the House of Commons. The court-martial resulted.

Graves-Morris was acquitted, his plea of 'condona-tion' being accepted. The Court found that the floggings had been 'condoned' by Brigadier Brodie, who had received reports of the punishment. Officers giving evidence in Graves-Morris' favour included a Major who said he had attended a lecture by Wingate, who told them that Long Range Penetration was an unusual

type of warfare and that it would be their responsibility to maintain discipline at any cost. For serious offences, which might result in the loss of lives, they were empowered to flog offenders, turn them loose with their rations or, in exceptional cases, shoot them.

Later, it was held that Wingate had exceeded his powers, by introducing punishment contrary to the Army Act and King's Regulations. At the same time, the Chindit campaign was waged in what were described as conditions 'without parallel in military history', in 'indescribable discomfort'. The usual punishments were 'less exacting than the hardships suffered daily by all members of the Columns.' The system of summary pun-ishment was known throughout Special Force, generally accepted and only inflicted with the consent of the culprit.

Following his acquittal, Philip Graves-Morris' Army career progressed with various appointments, including periods as Military Attaché in Stockholm and Madrid. Brigadier Graves-Morris retired in 1959 and died in 1991, at the age of 84.

In the immediate post-war period the Chindits received little attention. In *The Wild Green Earth*, Bernard Fergusson wrote:

> For two long years we used to amuse ourselves dis-cussing the Victory March through London after the war and deciding which of us – and which mules – should represent the Force. In the end the question didn't arise, as the authorities ruled that the Force shouldn't be represented at all ... I fancy that we hadn't marched far enough to qualify.[12]

Things soon changed. Indeed, for some years the Chindits led the thousands of veterans marching past the Cenotaph every November, on Remembrance Sunday, with Major Neville Hogan as Right Marker: 'At that time, of course, we Chindits were 50–60 strong on parade.'

Michael Calvert, the embodiment of the Chindit fighting soldier, died in the Royal Star & Garter Home, Richmond, on 26 November 1998, at the age of 85.[13] Three years earlier, in August 1995, the celebrations marking the fiftieth anniversary of Victory over Japan and the end of the Second World War paid tribute to the men who had fought in the Far East. On Saturday 19 August 1995, Calvert was on parade, in his wheelchair, leading the contingent of the Chindits Old Comrades' Association.[14]

Captain Ronald Swann, RA, had the honour of car-rying the medals of Brigadier Michael Calvert, DSO and Bar, at a service of thanksgiving for his life at The

Return to White City: this photograph was taken in 1997. (Left to right) Ted Thompson, Jesse Dunn and Denis Arnold; Michael Calvert is seated. The Burmese woman was a young girl at the time of the White City battles. (Jesse Dunn)

Royal Hospital, Chelsea, on 6 May 1999. Orde Wingate's son gave the address. Major Bill Williams of the South Staffords, who had responded when Calvert shouted 'Charge!' on Pagoda Hill, gave an appreciation. He said: 'Uniquely, the Battalion Commanders of his Brigade united in recommending him for the VC, in recognition of his sustained courageous leadership that demanded the extraordinary achievement of his beloved 77 Brigade but, amazingly, nothing was added to the DSO awarded for the initial landing.'

The Chindits never lost their sense of gratitude to the Burmese who helped them survive, including the villagers of the remote hills and the men of the Burma Rifles. All took great risks to save lives. Bernard Fergusson and Michael Calvert made trips to Burma after the war, to contact old soldiers in their hill villages. Neville Hogan is among those who still contribute to the welfare of families in Burma. Bill Smyly also retains that link, ever mindful that he owes his life to them:

'I send a donation to the Burma Relief Association each year and my branch of the Burma Star Association sends something too. I believe it has been a bit of a lifeline in the hills. Britain owes these people, who were so loyal to us then and for whom peace, after the war, has been almost continual disaster.'

Philip Stibbe, with Bernard Fergusson's 5 Column during Operation *Longcloth*, was wounded at Hintha and hidden from the Japanese. Later, he discovered that his companion, Rifleman Maung Tun, nicknamed 'Moto', had endured torture and refused to disclose his whereabouts before being executed. According to Bill Smyly, Stibbe made contact with Maung Tun's family and arranged for an educational scholarship in his memory.

As might be expected, Chindit veterans have a broad spectrum of views on the Japanese. Feelings range from cold hatred to indifference and, in a minority of cases, a sense of *rapprochement* – occasionally expressed with great generosity of spirit. George MacDonald Fraser described an emotion felt by many Chindits: 'It is difficult for me to equate the Japanese of the forties with those neat, eager, apparently polite young men whom I see in airports and tourist centres … But old feelings persist and I prefer not to sit beside them. Nor will I buy a Japanese car.'[15]

In a letter home (Imperial War Museum, 80/49/1) on coming out of Burma, Captain Norman Durant MC described the enemy in the context of the times: 'They look like animals and behave like animals and they can be killed as unemotionally as swatting flies. And they need to be killed, not wounded, for as long as they breathe they're dangerous.'

Some hearts remain hardened to this day. Neville Hogan: 'I regard them as murdering swines. I hate the Japanese and have no wish to be involved in reconciliation.' Asked whether his strong Christian faith demanded forgiveness, he replied:

'Yes, I should forgive, but I saw the POWs. I saw the cut noses and tongues. They cut off the penises of two of my own men!'

Proud men: Jack Goldfinch of the Queen's, with a fellow Standard Bearer at the Burma Star Memorial, Margate. Jack helped to build this memorial in the 1980s. (the family of Jack Goldfinch)

Lancashire Fusilier Ian Niven was also blunt: 'I have no time for them. They committed terrible acts and were without conscience.' Niven added: 'When I think back, I feel I paid a visit to Hell.'

There are no words of reconciliation from Percy Stopher, who helped evacuate 23 Brigade's casualties. Years spent in the fierce sun of Egypt, India and Burma have taken their toll. Stopher's head is covered in skin grafts: 'I've had 103 of them. It's skin cancer.' Indeed, since 1989 Stopher has endured over 130 surgical procedures and, like everything else in life, they failed to break his spirit. When asked whether he was proud of his war service, he replied: 'No, I'm not proud, but I am satisfied with what I did. "Satisfied" is a better word.' On his feelings about the Japanese, Percy Stopher was succinct:

'What they did to our lads ... I could never forgive them. I have no time for them.'

John Simon, a former Bren gunner, also had little to say: 'I hated the Japanese. We heard a lot about them, but I don't know that I ever feared them.' *Longcloth* veteran Bob Hobbs made just one comment:

'We said the only good one was a dead one and we meant it. I don't feel any different today.'

Peter Heppell, a Chindit with the King's, commented:

'I had strong feelings about the Japanese at the time but these have been lost over the years. I visited the Army Museum in Chelsea and found the section on Burma. Standing behind me was a Japanese family, a mother and two children. They gave me a strange feeling, but there was no anger or antagonism in my mind.'

Some Chindit veterans left hatred behind. Jesse Dunn, of the South Staffords:

'The vast majority of Japanese alive today were not born in 1944. I am not particularly fond of the Japanese, but I have no hatred.'

Norman Campbell said much the same: 'I don't hate the Japanese. What would be the point? Hate is such an empty feeling.'

Florrie Goldfinch is the widow of Jack Goldfinch, of the Queen's. She said:

'Jack didn't talk about it very much, but you could sense his pride. He didn't want anything Japanese in the house, yet he wasn't the sort of man to be bitter. He was

too nice. Comradeship was very important to him. We still have his sweat-stained silk survival map.'

Bill Williams harbours no bitterness: 'It is important not to go on hating. I can now accept the Japanese.'

Ronald Swann, who was wounded at Blackpool, moved on:

'People today are not responsible for the past. One had to grow out of such things or spend the rest of one's life in a tormented world.'

Eric Sugden, a Bedfordshire and Hertfordshire Chindit, remembered that Michael Calvert, in an interview, expressed surprise that British troops – in the final phase of the campaign – shared their rations with half-starved Japanese prisoners:

'It didn't surprise me. When you are in that situation, you have plenty in common with anyone in a uniform. After all, those Japanese were just another bunch of poor blighters thousands of miles away from home.'

Bill Smyly echoes these views:

'If I met a Japanese veteran of Burma today, I think I would have feelings of comradeship. People get killed. Sometimes you kill, especially if it's "him or me". But now one would really like to meet up with people who shared very much the same problems and conditions. Perhaps that is what chivalry is about. That great warrior Mike Calvert would have agreed. He would have enjoyed meeting his opposite numbers in the Japanese Army. They would have recognised him as a Samurai.'

Occasionally, reconciliation can develop from a chance human contact. Bill Towill:

'A few years ago my wife and I decided to spend Christmas in Salzburg. On the last day I paid a visit to the castle on the hilltop, but Pamela stayed behind to finish the packing. When at the castle I spotted a Japanese with his two teenage daughters. Indeed, you could not help noticing them. The girls were so very full of life, enjoying not just each minute but, so it seemed, each second of their visit.

'The gentleman beckoned to me and I went to take the camera but he signalled me away. The girls then came up to me and stood, one either side, and hugged me as he took a picture. I have not the slightest idea why they did this, but it so broke me up that I had to turn away to hide my emotion. Previously, I had always hated the Japs, but this made me think again. It might

well be profoundly difficult for many who have suffered in their hands, but I think we have no option but to forgive them.'

Some men brought home physical reminders of the cruel war in Burma. Fred Holliday of the King's:

'I came home with a Japanese sword but my wife was horrified by it. Eventually, it was sold. As for my personal feelings, once I would never buy a Japanese car but, to be honest, feelings tend to dissipate over the years. Live and let live!'

John Knowles kept a memento of the Queen's battle at Milestone 20. He had picked up a Japanese map case, abandoned among the detritus of combat:

'It belonged to First Lieutenant Kootaroo Nakada of the Japanese Army Pay Corps. In 1972 I was in Tokyo on mission and tried to trace Nakada. I had in mind that I would buy him a drink, swap stories and return his map case, if I could find him.

'To my regret, I learned that he had succumbed to malaria while in Burma. The Japanese never made any effort to look after their own troops and it was sad that this poor guy had been left to die when I had been looked after so well by our people. I was treated royally during my several stays at the British Military Hospital in New Delhi.'

Knowles has no hatred for the Japanese:

'It is surely ridiculous to hate an entire race or nation. They are people, like you and me. Post-war, I have been friendly with a number of Japanese. As a UN Project Manager in Pakistan, I had a very competent Japanese consultant on my staff. He was a friendly chap with an excellent sense of humour. When I mentioned I had served in Burma, he said: "Ah! So that's why we lost!" '

What now of Burma? This country has been savaged by war and has been ruled by a despotic military regime since 1962. Aung San, a young nationalist used by the Japanese, later switched his allegiance to the Allies. He was assassinated in 1947. His daughter is Nobel Peace Prize laureate Aung San Suu Kyi, leader of the Burmese National League for Democracy, who has suffered many years of detention.[16]

Some men have had the chance to return to Burma but could not bring themselves to do so. Fred Holliday:

'I did think about it. I had intended to go back with my pal, Tom Pickering, who lost an eye in the fighting

around Mogaung. Tom was not in the best of health and his wife and children were against it. Tom's dead now. I might have been able to stomach the trip in Tom's company, although I had grave doubts.'

Some refuse to go back as a point of principle. Bill Williams: 'I would be reluctant to return to a country governed by a regime which has declared Britons persona non grata.'

Neville Hogan is a Karen. He and his wife, Glory, can never return:

'I am sad and angry. Opium fuels the Burmese economy. There has been no improvement for decades and it is difficult to see light in the darkness. Along the 300-mile border between Burma and Thailand, 125,000 Karens live in five large camps on the Thai side. I think of them with pride. These camps are clean and well run, but they were first established in the 1960s! On the other side of the border, 100,000 Karens are hunted by the 500,000-strong Burmese Army.'

Contact with the author Philip Chinnery sharpened Norman Campbell's recollections:

'The more I thought about Burma, the more I realised how lucky I had been. I am proud to have been a Cameronian and a Chindit. I walked out after 150 days. A total of 1,100 Cameronians – including reinforcements – took part and I was one of only 90 capable of walking properly at the end of it. I still have a clear mental picture of Blackpool Block. When I close my eyes I can see Namkwin Station and, at about 5 o'clock, the rail bridge blown during our first night at the Block.'

Other veterans think immediately of the railway whenever they think of Burma. Horace Howkins, of the South Staffords, returned to Burma in 2006, accompanied by his youngest daughter, Patricia: 'It did seem strange to be standing there again at White City. I could hardly recognise the site, but I had no problem recognising that railway!'

Frank Anderson of the King's returned to Burma in 2005, at the age of 92, in the company of his wife and one of his sons: 'It felt awful when we were back at Blackpool. There it was, including that railway line!'

Ronald Swann visited Burma in 2003, accompanied by his son, Ian. They returned the following year, determined to find the gun positions at Blackpool. This wasn't easy. The chaung had changed course and the area was much eroded: 'Nevertheless, we found my old Command Post, by a low hedge harbouring a tangle of rusty barbed wire.'

Jesse Dunn returned to Burma in 1997, for the first time since 1944:

'I found it to be a land of smiles. The people were full of laughter. I saw no evidence of difficult politics. I have made two more trips to Burma, visiting White City on each occasion.'

Peter Heppell and members of his family, including daughter Sally, stood together on Broadway clearing in March 2006. It was his third return to Burma. He had landed by assault glider on 5 March 1944, on his 24th birthday. He had returned 62 years and one day later. Sally wrote: 'He wanted to cross to the other side of the clearing. The going was more than hard. The sun was hot and the atmosphere humid. We were all tired and the ground was uneven. Churned and dried mud mingled with the burnt stubble of a kind of reed grown to provide roof thatch. The clearing was three-quarters of a mile across and, within minutes, we were soaked in perspiration and covered in ash. When finally we reached the other side we stepped into a small copse. Here were foxholes and dugouts, hardly changed in all those years. On a tall, proud teak tree that might well have been there in 1944, my brother nailed a brass plaque remembering the landings, Orde Wingate and the Chindits:

'We stood, our small group remembering so many. It was a very emotional moment. My father recited the Kohima Epitaph and our Burmese guides, instinctively knowing while not understanding a word, bowed their heads too and, as we stepped away, circled the plaque with a yellow ribbon of their own.'

The Chindit Colours were dedicated in Liverpool Cathedral on Sunday, 14 March 1948, by Dr Clifford Martin, Bishop of Liverpool. Music was provided by the band of The King's (Liverpool) and opened with the march 'Colonel Bogie on parade'.

At 15.15 on Thursday 27 February 1975, Captain Orde Jonathan Wingate attended a Service of Rededication at the burial marker over the grave (Section 12, No. 288) of his father and the eight others who died with him when their B.25 crashed. According to Thomas L. Sherlock, Historian at Arlington National Cemetery, 'Captain Wingate was the first person to place a floral tribute at the grave during that ceremony.'

Wingate's son was hosted by Lieutenant-Colonel Norman Dunkley, OBE, Deputy Head of British Defence Intelligence Liaison at the British Embassy in Washington D.C. He told the author:

Proud moment: H.R.H. The Prince of Wales, Patron, with Major Neville Hogan, MBE, Chairman of the Chindits Old Comrades'
Association, at Lichfield Cathedral on 19 June 2009, on the occasion of the laying-up of the Chindits' Standard.
(Stephen Evans Photography)

'I received a message from the Ambassador's office the day before the ceremony. I met with Captain Wingate, RA, who was very polite and unassuming. He was quiet and asked few questions. I drove him to Arlington. We were both in uniform. Wingate's son said very little, but he did express his thanks to me for escorting him to the ceremony.'

Orde Jonathan Wingate joined the Honourable Artillery Company after a Regular Army career in the Royal Artillery and rose through the ranks to become his Regiment's Commanding Officer and, later, Regimental Colonel. He died in 2000 at the age of 56 and is survived by his wife and two daughters.

H.R.H. Prince Philip unveiled the Chindit Memorial on The Victoria Embankment on 16 October 1990. H.R.H. The Prince of Wales, Patron of the Chindits Old Comrades' Association, attended the laying-up of the Chindits' Standard in Lichfield Cathedral on Friday 19 June 2009. Over 60 Chindit veterans attended, together with families and friends.

The Chindits Old Comrades' Association has declared that it will close only when its last member dies. The Friends of the Chindits organisation will continue to take forward the Chindit spirit, through fellowship among the families of former Chindits. In 2011, Alice Wingate, General Wingate's grand-daughter, became Patron of The Friends of the Chindits.

The Kohima Epitaph

When you go home
Tell them of us and say

For your tomorrow
We gave our today.

Notes

1. Stibbe, P. (1995), *Return via Rangoon*, 163–176
2. Rooney, D. (2000), *Wingate and the Chindits: Redressing the Balance*, 219–226
3. Hay, Alice Ivy (1963), *There Was a Man of Genius: Letters to my Grandson, Orde Jonathan Wingate*, 57
4. Ibid, 149
5. Ibid, 68–71
6. Ibid, 123–124
7. Ibid, 122
8. Rooney, D. (2000), 210–214
9. Fowler, W. (2009), *We Gave Our Today: Burma 1941–1945*, 106
10. Slim, Field Marshal Viscount (1999), *Defeat into Victory*, 162–163
11. Hay, Alice Ivy (1963), 130–133
12. Fergusson, B. (1946), *The Wild Green Earth*, 169
13. Fowler, W. (2009), 241
14. Rooney. D. (1997), *Mad Mike*, 1
15. Fraser, G. M. (1995), *Quartered Safe Out Here*, 125
16. Fowler, W. (2009), 239

POSTSCRIPT

WHEN THE Chindits' Colours were dedicated in Liverpool Cathedral, in March 1948, the Blessing declared:

> May the spirit of adventure and self-sacrifice be
> re-kindled and stay with us
> as we undertake the greatest adventure yet laid on
> the human race,
> to refashion a shattered world.

The surviving Chindits made their contribution to this second and greater task.

Peter Allnutt, 43 Column, 12th Nigeria Regiment

Peter Allnutt returned to England by air, having priority as a Colonial Administrator. Subsequently, he returned to Nigeria, but life then took a new direction. He joined The British Council and was posted to Latin America:

'Chindit service was tough. Some never got over it. It was very character-forming and, in most cases, it was a tremendous boost to self-confidence. I'm glad to have been part of a unique operation, devised by a man with unusual depth of vision.'

Frank Anderson, 81 Column, 1st King's (Liverpool)

Frank Anderson returned to the UK in 1946. He had married before he went overseas and he and his wife went on to have two sons. There are now four grandchildren. Frank returned to the plastering trade. His experiences as a Chindit made him confident in his own abilities:

'I realised that, money or not, other people were no different to me. I was the equal of any man. I always spoke my mind.'

Nevertheless, there are the scars of Chindit service:

'I found it difficult to sleep at night and had frequent nightmares. Much later in life I was diagnosed with Post-Traumatic Stress Syndrome. I now receive a war pension. Today, I can't forgive the Japanese. How can you forgive savages who tie people to trees and bayonet them?'

Denis Arnold, 29 Column, 7th Nigeria Regiment

Denis Arnold arrived back in May 1946. On disembarking at Southampton, a Customs official insisted he pay duty on some Black Label whisky:

'"Bugger you," I said. What a wonderful welcome!'

He was reunited with his wife, Evelyn, after an absence of three years. They had four children. He went on leave, finished his service career that September and returned to the cement industry. He found peace of a kind at APCM's plant at Kirton in Lindsey, Lincolnshire:

'I lived at a small hotel, the Angel at Brigg, and cycled the seven miles to the works. I came back to the UK as an Army officer. A few weeks later I found myself standing in a cement kiln, knocking out bricks with a sledgehammer. I was quite content with my lot.'

Malaria was never far away in the early years. Later, skin problems developed. In 1997 he returned to Burma with a party of former Chindits, including Mike Calvert. Denis Arnold lost his wife of 63 years in 2003.

Cyril Baldock, 54 Column, 45th Reconnaissance Regiment

Army life suited Cyril Baldock. He stayed in and obtained a Regular Commission in the Royal Armoured Corps:

'I joined the South Staffords in Germany during 1946. I had married while in India. We met when I was in the Parachute Regiment. Some girl soldiers were based in a nearby barracks and I suggested a hockey game. I spoke to the Sports Officer, who later became my wife. Kay and I have been married for 64 years.'

They have two children and two grandsons:

'I don't talk much about the war and Burma, although the oldest grandson is interested.'

Cyril Baldock left the Army in 1961, at the age of 40:

'My daughter was ill at that time and I didn't want another overseas posting. I was recruited by Tube Investments, stayed with that company for 20 years and retired at 60 as Head of the Forgings Division.'

Cyril Baldock died in 2010.

Charles J. Campbell, Engineer, C-47 'Assam Dragon'

Charles Campbell returned home in June 1945:

'I'd married before going overseas and my wife didn't want me to continue in the Air Force. I found work as a mechanic, studied with the American Institute of Banking and worked in banking for 10 years before switching to aeronautical engineering. I joined North American and, after a period, moved to their Missile Division. I stayed there for 30 years. Elizabeth and I have seven children. Life became very busy as the kids came along. I didn't go to Air Commando Association reunions, although I have always been a member.'

Campbell's pilot, 'Red' Austin, stayed in the Air Force after the war and retired as a full Colonel.

Norman Campbell, 90 Column, 1st Cameronians

Norman Campbell and his wife have two daughters and a son. In common with so many Chindits, he decided early on to say as little as possible about Burma. He disassociated himself from the past, although he did return from the Far East with two Japanese swords:

'My wife took a dislike to them. One evening an insurance man called. He showed interest in the swords and I gave them away to him.'

Norman joined the Burma Star Association in the 1980s, but resigned in protest when the British Royal Family was represented at Emperor Hirohito's funeral, in 1989:

'The Chindits made me a more disciplined person. I was demobbed in 1947 and approached my old boss, who was sympathetic. He encouraged me to go into sales. I became a van salesman, selling all kinds of bakery products. Several promotions followed and I took early retirement in 1985 as a member of senior management.'

Olin B. Carter, pilot, P.51 Mustang, 1st Air Commando, USAAF

Olin Carter left the USAAF after the war but was recalled in 1947, a couple of years before the Korean conflict. He became a munitions specialist and retired from the USAF in 1966. By that time he'd flown 39 different types:

'On retirement I "built" myself a new job. During my final year in the Air Force I was in charge of closing a base at Reno. When I retired I began developing the site for civil use. It became the venue for the National Championship Air Races — the world's premier air race. I joined the Board of Trustees for the races and was involved in this for 15 years. I was also Airport Director at Reno. I did some occasional contract flying but stopped that in 1980. Today, I am a Hangar Chief at Palm Springs Air Museum. Most Saturdays I am in charge of one of our three exhibition hangars.'

Olin Carter's first wife, Norma, died in a car accident after 40 years of marriage. Six years later, Carter met someone he had not seen for 50 years. He married Mary Lou but they later divorced. Today, he and his partner, Jeanne, live in Cathedral City, California.

Jesse Dunn, 80 Column, 1st South Staffords

Jesse Dunn's last weeks in India were spent in hospital in Poona. He arrived back in Britain just before Christmas 1944 and was admitted to Stourbridge Hospital:

'I was discharged on 28 February 1945. My elbow had been completely smashed. I made regular trips to Birmingham for medical examinations. I also attended a rehabilitation centre specialising in finding work for men who had been wounded. I began to recover more use of my left hand and succeeded in getting a job as a toolmaker.'

Jesse met his future wife, Elsie Preece, while in Stourbridge Hospital. They married in late 1946 and had two children. There are now four grandchildren and three great-grandchildren:

'I haven't said much about Burma, but my daughter does accompany me to Chindit reunions at Exeter and Walsall.'

Jesse Dunn had little difficulty adapting to life in the post-war world:

'It was a matter of making the best of things. I had plenty of movement in my left shoulder, had no problem driving and soon developed a technique for fastening my collar with one hand. The only effect, long term, is the occasional dream. In this dream, I am being called up again and I always find myself saying: "I've been once already!"'

Jesse Dunn's quiet dignity remained unshaken by the trials of life:

'I wouldn't have chosen the Chindit experience but I was there. Today, however, not many people know what a Chindit is. The experience didn't really change me but the wound did stop me riding motorbikes. Anyway, as far as I'm concerned, life is for living. I lost Elsie 25 years ago. Since then I have travelled the world.'

Jesse Dunn died in 2009.

Peter Fairmaner, Driver, Special Force Air Base

On arriving back in the UK, Peter Fairmaner returned to art school. He married and became a commercial artist and exhibition designer with the Electricity Board. This ended in 1966, when Peter lost his sight. Earlier, he had nursed his first wife until she died, leaving him with two young children. He married his second wife, June, in 1963:

'Peter was still having nightmares about the war when we were first married. He would never speak of his experiences. He had a very bad back and, eventually, I persuaded him to apply for a war pension. His application was rejected. The British Legion then fought his case and, after a long struggle, a pension was awarded. He also had recurrent bouts of malaria. Curiously, he always resented the fact that a 21st birthday present – promised to him while he was in the Far East – was never received. This unfinished business always rankled.'

Peter Fairmaner died in 2009.

George Fulton, Medical Orderly, 14 Brigade

George Fulton returned to Britain and put up with occasional bouts of malaria. In 1954 he and his wife, Jean, decided to make a new life for themselves in Canada. They now live in Pickering, Ontario:

'Before the war I did a lot of hopping from job to job. I came from a poor family and started work at 14. All four kids were working at that age, to boost the family's income. It seems incredible now, but all six of us lived in one room in a tenement attic. I needed a trade. I took advantage of a post-war government training scheme and became a painter and decorator. I returned to work for Aberdeen Town Council.

'My only son, young George, was born in September 1945. He lived until 1996, when we lost him to a brain tumour. Jean and I have two other children and seven grandchildren. Canada offered the chance of a better life and we have no regrets, although we still miss Aberdeen and return every year. Today, I have mixed feelings about Burma. On the positive side I remember the friendship, the warm comradeship. I met so many wonderful people.'

Larry Gaines, 66 Column, 6th Nigeria Regiment

Larry Gaines began a new phase in his life:

'I had no difficulty adjusting, having recovered quite well. I went back to the LSE in September 1946 and completed my economics degree, despite having to attend some lectures in candlelight during the grim winter of 1946–47.'

From 1949 to 1970 Larry Gaines worked for the Iraq Petroleum Company, primarily in the Lebanon and Iraq. In 1953, while in the Lebanon, Larry married Moira, also with IPC. Their daughters, Nicola and Diana, were born there. Always the keen traveller, Larry Gaines drove all the way to and from the Middle East three times. He retired from the company at 51 but continued to work in the oil industry until 1980, mainly in Algeria and the Democratic Republic of Congo. He retained his passion for travel when he finally stopped working. In late 1987 he went on a six-month world tour, bringing his total of countries visited to 62.

Alec Gibson, Cypher Officer, 3 Column, Operation *Longcloth*

Alec Gibson returned to the UK for the second time in late 1946 and married Kathleen the following year. There are two sons and six grandchildren. Alec left the Army and decided not to return to engineering draughtsmanship. As he had volunteered for the services, he was told he would have to re-start his five-year apprenticeship – at the age of 26! He changed direction and built a new career in local government finance.

Jack Goldfinch, 21 Column, 2nd Queen's

Jack Goldfinch was a fitter and worked on the railway after the war. He married and had three children, Eileen, Kathy and John. The front of his home, in Broadstairs, Kent, displays the Chindit badge with the familiar *Chinthé* device. In his later years he gave talks on his wartime service to several local schools. He felt very strongly about connecting with today's generation. Interviewed by a local newspaper at the time of the VJ fiftieth anniversary celebrations, in 1995, he commented: 'Many children don't know anything about the war or our experiences. It's sad.'

Jack and his second wife, Florrie, came together having been introduced at the Thanet Branch of the Burma Star Association. Jack died in 2008, aged 87. He had stayed in touch with his great friend, Sergeant Harry 'Smudger' Smith, who died in 2004.

Les Grainger, 1st South Staffords

Les Grainger was home for Christmas 1945 and left the Army:

'I had priority to go home, as I had volunteered in 1939. Returning to civilian life, I decided to rejoin the Leeds Permanent Building Society. I retired as a Securities Department Manager in 1981. I met Enid in 1953. I had planned a climbing holiday but it didn't work out and I went on a Moselle canoeing holiday instead. I met Enid on that trip. We married and had two children.'

Les Grainger died in 2009.

Peter Heppell, 82 Column, 1st King's (Liverpool)

Peter Heppell took a small sketchbook into Burma. It was still blank when he came out; he had found no inclination to draw. He did make some drawings later and this sketchbook is now in the RE Museum collection, Chatham, Kent.

He arrived back in Britain in late 1945 and was demobbed the following June. He returned to the London Agency where his father was Art Director:

'I became known as the "Art Director's son", so I left for another agency, but the owner did a lot of work for my father and a similar problem arose. I moved to Bowater Packaging, staying there from 1948 to 1985.'

Peter married in 1949 and he and his wife had two sons and a daughter. He lost his wife in 2001. Today, the Heppell family includes six grandchildren. Peter remained largely free of health problems, with only the one recurrence of malaria. He had no nightmares but did find it difficult to settle into civilian life. Getting used to the daily routine was the real problem:

'I was fortunate to have a very supportive family. My parents were very good to me. Father told them to let me be – not to ask questions. He was well meaning but they didn't ask ANY questions and I closed up. I joined the forces as an inexperienced youth and returned a mature man, with plenty of self-confidence. I am proud to have been a Chindit.

'I couldn't talk about it for a long time. I felt it was of no interest. I was in Burma for five months and saw only one road … and I crossed that on my stomach! Burma was so different to European warfare. It is amazing how quickly one adapts to living rough.'

Dick Hilder, HQ Column, 14 Brigade

Dick Hilder could have stayed in the Army after the war but he had other plans:

'I'd had my fill. I became an Essex farmer, married and raised a family.'

Malaria dogged Hilder for some years after the war:

'I used to get it twice a year until the 1960s. Later, I would get a bout of malaria and it would turn into a cold or flu.'

Service as a Chindit changed Hilder's life:

'At one point I became known as "Jungle Dick". I went a bit "jungly". My time as a Chindit sharpened me. The Chindits gave you confidence — a very strong feeling of self-reliance. I learnt to accept things. If something really lovely is destroyed, I don't mourn it but, instead, think: "Well, it's had its day." The Burmese jungle taught me that material things are just that ... things! So, I don't worry if I lose things. The sharpness of mind persists and my daughter once remarked on this. At one reunion she turned to me and said: "Dad, there is something about these old Chindits. They've all got their marbles." We turned into a lot of very sane old men. The Chindit experience left me with one thought: "You'll never have anything so bloody dreadful in your life again".

Bob Hobbs, 2 Column, Operation *Longcloth*

Bob Hobbs found it difficult to settle back to civilian life after the war:

'I had married Ann in 1942, before going overseas. When I got back, in late 1944, I treated her like a Private soldier.'

Ann died a few years after his return, leaving him with a young family to look after. He remarried in the late 1940s. Hobbs was a milkman for 20 years. He met Joy, his second wife, at a United Dairies Christmas party. Memories of Burma continued to trouble him:

'I don't believe in talking about bad times. It is gone and finished. I have never said anything about my war service to my family.'

Neville Hogan, 46 Column, 2nd King's Own

Neville Hogan recovered from his service with Special Force and rejoined his Battalion. At one point he was given the job of releasing internees held in a Japanese camp at Maymyo, Burma:

'There was no fighting. The Japanese were long gone by the time we relieved the camp. I met my future wife, Glory, in that camp. I ended up in Singapore and managed to worm my way into the signing ceremony marking the official Japanese surrender.

My next job was to join Colonel Buchanan, who was forming a new OTU at Maymyo. I met up with Colin Grant, an old schoolfriend and now a Sergeant in the Burma Intelligence Corps. He had an invitation to a Badminton party and asked me to come along, adding that I would have the chance to meet a lovely girl. The girl happened to be Glory. We were reunited ... it was pure coincidence. I pinched the Battalion motorbike and took her out for rides.'

The couple married on 30 April 1949, in Maymyo. Neville was extraordinarily lucky to be alive at that point. He had intended to marry Glory in the February but had been captured by rebels. The British had left Burma the year before:

'At that time I was in the 2nd Battalion, The Karen Rifles. We were in the central Burmese town of Meiktila in mid-February, when it was captured by one of five rival groups of Communist insurgents. I was among several officers jailed and later condemned to death. A friend, a Karen, got to hear of my capture and bribed the guards. I was sleeping on the floor of my bare cell when I was roused at 2 am. A voice said: "I've come for you." I replied: "How do I know you are not with the rebels?" He responded: "Here, take the gun!" We crept out of the prison and slipped down the road to a waiting truck. My rescuers drove like hell towards Mandalay. When we stopped I was told to wait for a convoy tomorrow — a Karen officer would pick me up and bring me to Mandalay and freedom.'

After their belated marriage, Neville Hogan and his young wife left Burma for England:

'I took that decision on the advice of several prominent men, including Bernard Fergusson and Mike Calvert. They told me I would be killed if I stayed. Apparently, from the insurgents' perspective, I had fought on the wrong side. There is also a traditional enmity between Burmese and Karens.'

The couple reached Britain in May 1950. He joined RCA, learned much about the cinema and eventually became Assistant Export Sales Manager. Other jobs followed. He spent 20 years with Sun Life of Canada and became a Senior Life Underwriter. He then went into local government.

Today, Neville Hogan and his wife devote much time to the Chindits Old Comrades' Association. Neville is the Chairman. Instincts honed during his sales career are now put to work raising funds for an Association with links across the world.

Neville Hogan received the MBE in January 2004 for services to the Chindits. He is also Chairman of the Burma Forces Welfare Association. This organisation helps 3,800 veterans who served the Crown pre-1948, together with 300 widows. He serves on the Council of the Royal Commonwealth Ex-Services League, helping veterans in 48 countries. He and his wife have been fund-raisers for the Gurkha Welfare Trust since 1969.

Fred Holliday, 82 Column, 1st King's (Liverpool)

Fred Holliday returned to Britain in October 1946 and was soon demobbed:

'I returned to Collins — now Harper-Collins — and stayed with them until 1954. I was then head-hunted by a printing and stationery company. I became Managing Director and stayed in that post until my retirement.'

Fred married in 1948. His wife, Megan, was a member of a Welsh choir giving ENSA concerts in the Far East:

'We met on board ship. It was a shipboard romance! Our daughter was born in 1949 and gave us two grandchildren. I got on with things and enjoyed my work. Looking back, I took to the Army like a duck to water. Perhaps that isn't surprising, as my father, grandfather and a brother had been Regular soldiers.'

Fred Holliday died in 2010.

Tony Howard, 21 Column, 2nd Queen's

Tony Howard was one of many former Chindits who found Civvy Street difficult:

'It was difficult to settle down. I had a lot of anger inside and was unhappy at home. I suppose I had lost all my friends. Rationing was tighter than ever and the terrible winter of 1947 brought on the "Fuel Crisis". I was back at the Telephone Exchange; even that virtually shut down that winter. I had enjoyed Army life and it was exciting compared to my new existence. I became increasingly browned off. I also had health problems. I had developed malaria and had had at least four spells in hospital in Ceylon and India. My last stay saw off the malaria but the disease weakened my system.'

Tony Howard married and he and his wife had a son and a daughter. There are now four grandchildren:

'I didn't talk about my experiences when I got home. In any event, everyone was more interested in the European war. My father had kept a diary of his entire war service and mentioned himself only twice — a reference to an injury during a football match and a one-word entry: "Gassed". I took my lead from him and never discussed Burma with my son.'

Howard's Signaller, George Hill, had a similar attitude. Demobbed in 1947, he soon joined the Chindits Old Comrades' Association, attended the first reunion in March 1948 and then lost contact:

'I decided I didn't want to be reminded of Burma. I preferred to put it behind me. For the next 41 years my memories of Burma lay virtually dormant.'

George Hill then decided to write it down.

Horace Howkins, 80 Column, 1st South Staffords

Horace Howkins recovered, regained A.1 fitness and expected to see more action:

'I went into the Airborne, ready to go into Siam (Thailand), but then the war finished. I was back in the UK in 1946 and demobbed the following year. I did five years altogether. I had no health problems and received a small pension for my wounds.'

Howkins worked as a bricklayer. He married in 1948; he and his wife have four daughters:

'Today I have no particular feelings about the Japanese, but I'm glad I wasn't captured. I have put the experience behind me. I'd been shot at and I'd been wounded. Then it was over and done with.'

Gordon Hughes, 22 Column, 2nd Queen's

Gordon Hughes built a new life in South Africa. For some years he gave the local VJ luncheon address. Later, due to his failing eyesight, daughter Barbara would read the address on his behalf. He died on 1 July 2008. Barbara read his last address – 'The family mourns' – a tribute to the parents of men who never returned. He referred to George Britnell, killed in action at Milestone 20 on the Banmauk–Indaw road. He remembered the letter from Britnell's mother: 'Can you possibly imagine the worry they must have felt for their remaining sons, hoping against hope that they would not suffer the same fate as George?'

His last speech mentioned the day he saw five men die of cerebral malaria. He also remembered his own Platoon Sergeant, Bert King, who 'grew weaker and weaker as the campaign progressed and although he managed, with difficulty, to last the campaign out, lost some 40 pounds and died of pneumonia on his return to India. I often wonder how his parents and young wife coped, after hearing he was safely out of Burma, only to die in India.' Now, over six decades later, Gordon Hughes himself is mourned.

John 'Jack' Hutchin, 80 Column, 1st South Staffords

Jack Hutchin arrived back in Britain in 1947, during one of the worst winters in living memory:

'I had regained A.1+ classification but was far from straight in my mind. I had been diagnosed with "Battle Anxiety", known as "Shellshock" in the Great War. I became deeply depressed but received no treatment. In fact, I paid for psychiatric help out of my own funds. Matters got worse. I found it difficult to sleep and swallowed lots of pills. Much later I was given a war pension, assessed at 20 per cent disability due to the wound, the malaria and Battle Anxiety.'

Hutchin told his old friend, Bryn Coulson, to claim a pension for his deafness:

'He did, but only very late in life. On examination, the doctors found that the head wound had totally destroyed his left eardrum.'

The Army hadn't quite finished with Jack Hutchin. In the Spring of 1947 he was with a small group return- ing Army offenders to their units in Germany. All had served time in the 'Glasshouse'. The 1st South Staffords was still in the Far East. The 2nd Battalion had fought in Europe and was now based around Hamburg:

'We collected this bunch of absolute bastards at Lichfield. I took the trouble to get them Easter leave and some repaid me by absconding.'

Hutchin's next job involved the dregs of humanity. He was detailed to escort war criminals to Nuremburg. Jack was demobbed in July 1947:

'I returned to the family home and began post- graduate studies in economics, statistics and industrial psychology. I joined the insurance company sponsoring my studies and eventually trained as a fire surveyor. I stayed with them for many years.

'I found it difficult to adjust after the war. I felt confused and remained very self-opinionated. On returning from Burma I felt important. I had been a Chindit, part of Special Force! Then I realised that it didn't really matter all that much. It was just like the Somme or Ypres – soon a part of history. I now had the rest of my life to live. I married Ann and we had two boys. I suffered from occasional flare-ups of malaria. The last occurred when my eldest son was just eight months old.

'Today, my service as a Chindit is a source of great pride. I have very warm feelings for the men I served with. I remember the comradeship and the single- minded purpose we shared.'

John Knowles, RAF Officer, 22 Column, 2nd Queen's

John Knowles regards himself as fortunate:

'I had a lucky war. I loved flying and enjoyed my relatively safe but utterly frustrating time in the Air Force, yet found my true calling in the Army. I sometimes think that, if I had to do it over again, that's where I would go.

'I was also lucky after the war. There was no way I was going back to Brooklyn! Becoming a Canadian citizen in 1945, while still overseas, is the luckiest thing I ever did. It led to a long career in Canadian public service. I became an Immigration Attaché and diplomat in Europe and a Trade Commissioner in Latin America, gained a BA and MA (Econ) on the way and, after retirement, found a second career with the United Nations.'

Since 1989 John and his wife, Linda Leblanc, have lived in Cyprus, where they pursue a lifelong interest in metaphysics, consciousness and the paranormal. In 1999 they founded a not-for-profit organisation for the study and dissemination of scientific information on the paranormal. In the same year, then aged 76, in good Chindit fashion, he and Linda trekked from Western Nepal through the High Himalayas into Tibet.

Walter Longstaff, RAF Officer, 65 Column, 2nd York and Lancaster

Walter Longstaff had the quality of acceptance common to many Chindits:

'I learned to accept things. Some things were good, like swapping a rifle for a lightweight carbine. Others were bad, including being anywhere but in the middle of the Column. In bivouac we had a habit of arranging ourselves in a circle, heads facing outwards – as the Romans did. Anyone approaching was clearly an enemy. Whenever I got lost I just wandered around, hoping to recognise something. I remember being attacked in night bivouac. It was just a lot of noise and confusion and we put in plenty of return fire. There were also lighter moments. I took a camera in. On one occasion I got a shot of the MO dealing with a boil on someone's backside. It seemed funny at the time.'

Longstaff returned to the Civil Service. He and his wife had a son and daughter. There are six grandchildren:

'Looking back, I think of the incredible spirit of the Chindits. There were many great characters, including the Padre who had been in Burma for some years. On one occasion a Burmese delegation visited us, wanting to pay their respects to the Padre and receive his blessing. That was quite impressive, all the more so as they had come such a long way to see him. Both Chindit operations were remarkable endeavours.'

Walter Longstaff died in 2011.

Ted McArdle, 82 Column, 1st King's (Liverpool)

When released from Japanese captivity, Ted McArdle sent a telegram to his mother. She had been notified long before that her son was 'missing, presumed killed':

'My mother was overcome. She ran around the streets, shouting to the neighbours that I was alive.'

McArdle struggled to adjust. Physically he was fit enough to take a job in the building trade. This was a stop-gap, to become acclimatised to the world of work. Mentally, things were very different:

'I had problems with my nerves and I saw plenty of doctors about that. Even now I can get very wound up. I often think about my days as a prisoner. I never lost my faith and I didn't suffer, in comparison with many, but my experiences turned me against the Japanese, even the present generation. It wasn't so much the beatings but, rather, the way they seemed to enjoy humiliating us. I remember those sick men, forced to hold a heavy barrel over their heads.'

In Rangoon Gaol he spent a lot of time thinking about food:

'I used to dream of fish and chips and corned beef sandwiches, but I really developed a taste for rice. I still enjoy it today.'

Ted married and found work at Dunlop, Vernon Pools and, later, Liverpool Telephone Exchange. He lost his wife in the mid-1990s. They had two daughters. He had five grandchildren and a great-granddaughter. Ted rarely discussed his experiences:

'I tend to find most people are not that interested. They always ask the same question: "What did they do to you?" I receive a war pension. I've been well treated and have no complaints. My friend Matty also survived captivity. I made contact with him after the war but, subsequently, we lost touch.'

Ted McArdle died in 2009.

Ted Meese, 17 Column, 2nd Leicesters

Back in Britain in 1946, Ted Meese was demobbed in May the following year. He returned to bricklaying and completed his seven-year apprenticeship. He spent 57½ years in the trade. He married Margaret in 1950 and they had a son and two daughters. The Meese family home was free of Japanese gadgets for many years; the few now present are tolerated grudgingly. Ted Meese:

'Chindit service made me feel very grown up. I was just 17½ when I went into the Army.'

Ray Newport, RAF Driver and 'Kicker'

Ray 'Lofty' Newport returned to the UK and East Kent in early 1946. Before he went overseas he had a girlfriend who lived locally:

'I told her I'd never write and that life was for living, not waiting. Anyway, I met her again the first Sunday after *returning home. That was it! I courted her for exactly 12 months. We married in 1947.'*

As the years passed Newport carried on as the butcher in Littlebourne, a village just east of Canterbury. Occasionally, when drifting in and out of sleep, his mind returned to the Far East:

'I saw the native packers at Air Base. Everyone knew they stole the cigarettes. They used them as currency. I relived the impact on my senses when first arriving in Calcutta. The filth was just incredible – I'd never seen anything like it. I also saw the golden glow of the roof of Rangoon's main pagoda. It was on the pagoda's steps that I met a young and very beautiful Burmese girl. Many decades later, walking along Littlebourne village street, I suddenly saw her coming towards me. I recognised her instantly. She did the same and put out her arms to embrace me. She has family connections in Kent and has visited twice. What are the chances of meeting again in that way?'

Ian Niven, 20 Column, 1st Lancashire Fusiliers

Ian Niven was still very ill when he arrived home in August 1946. He went straight to hospital:

'My treatment began at the Liverpool Tropical Diseases Hospital, then on to Manchester and Chester. I spent the entire 12 months to my demob in hospital and still had problems when I finally got out, including two bouts of malaria. It was like having bad flu for a week. The worst problem was my inability to keep food down. Whenever I ate a meal, it went straight through me like a baby. My bowel problems were never cured but I learned to cope. Even today, however, any shock or the slightest taint to food will send me straight to the toilet.

'I was offered a pension of a few shillings a week. I think it was in 1950 that people like me – especially the Far East lot – were offered the sum of £100 in final settlement, in exchange for that small pension. I took the money. At the time it was a godsend. I should not have accepted. I should have continued to fight for my pension. Much later, a pal of mine from 50 Column told me I still had pension rights. I was assessed and awarded a 40 per cent disability pension, despite the fact that I was in better condition than when I came out of Burma.'

Ian Niven had met Olive, his future wife, before he went overseas:

'We were very young and had known each other for only six weeks before I went abroad. She was a wonderful girl. We kept in contact throughout the war.'

The couple had two children, Olivia and Ian. Later, however, they divorced. Today, Ian has four grandchildren and four great-grandchildren. He kept quiet about Burma:

'I'd make the occasional remark but no-one in the family ever really asked me. I'd always thought it hadn't played on my mind but, looking back, I feel it changed me completely. My wife said I returned a different person. I certainly tried to recapture the lost years. I always went out with the lads on a Friday night. I managed to get hold of a car and drove around at 70 mph, trying to be 18 again. We didn't talk about the war but we all felt we had lost our youth. On occasion, the local policeman pulled us up. I would get a good telling off but never got booked. I sensed that he understood.

'I worked my socks off but couldn't find a decent job. On the railway my wage would have been just £3.50, whereas the average weekly wage was £5. There was no way I could go back to that! I tried everything. I had a market stall at one point, worked on Saturdays as a doorstep salesman and spent my Sundays on a coal round. I sold coal on credit and got 2/6 in the Pound commission.'

In 1949 Ian had success with his 'umpteenth' job application. He started with the Purchasing Department of wire manufacturers Richard Johnson & Nephew.

Ian Niven joined Manchester City Supporters' Club at the first opportunity. His abiding passion was MCFC and playing football. In 1970 Ian fought his way on to MCFC's Board. He was appointed Stadium Director – the Maine Road ground needed much attention:

'Malcolm Allison, Joe Mercer's No. 1, complained that the local youngsters predominantly wore red. We changed that by starting a City Junior Blues – with support from Malcolm and the players, together with City volunteers. We extended our hospitality to the Moss Side area. Youngsters from all ethnic backgrounds joined us.'

When news came of a plan to relocate the recreation ground, with its two football pitches, Ian Niven persuaded the Board to buy the land, with the establishment of an Academy in mind. Victorious in a Boardroom battle, Niven had his opportunity to open up new horizons for the youngsters of Moss Side.

'I received an MBE but it was really due to legions of volunteers dedicated to City and to youth. Virtually every club in the country now runs a similar movement. What spurred me on was loyalty to City and the young experience of being a cussed, bloody-minded Chindit.'

Ian is now a President of City and a Companion of the British Institute of Innkeeping. Brigadier Calvert once made a surprise visit to Niven's pub. Told that a man called Calvert was downstairs and asking for him he replied that he didn't know a Calvert. He changed his mind when told the Brigadier was waiting for him! Calvert then sent him a note. It began: 'To Ian Niven, who had the misfortune to serve under my command in Burma and, therefore, is lucky to be alive!'

John Pearson, RAF Signals Officer, 111 Brigade

John Pearson returned to England and was demobbed, having spent six months with the occupation forces in Japan. He then had a stroke of luck:

'It was suggested that instead of being an engineer in an engineering company, I would be better off being an engineer in a broader context. I found work at Tate & Lyle, in London's Silvertown, and stayed in Docklands for the next 15 years. I then went to Glasgow and helped establish sugar cane grinding equipment at locations around the world. I married in 1951. My wife and I have three children. There are now eight grandchildren.'

John Pearson died in 2010.

Major Harold Pettinger, MC

Harold Pettinger reached Liverpool on board the *Empress of Britain*. He had spent four years overseas:

'The occasion was marred when Customs officials tried to charge duty on souvenirs. I remember a heated row over someone's oriental carpet. I got to London on VE night. I wasn't in the mood for celebrating. I just wanted to get home. I rang my father and he nearly had a heart attack. He had no idea I was in the country! Fortunately, he knew a man who had a car and petrol and he drove me home through the night. Very soon I was back in my old bedroom.'

Harold Pettinger left the Army, joined Otis and married in 1946:

'My wife and I have three sons and a daughter. There are now nine grandchildren. I saw one of my grandsons, Joseph, pass out from the Royal Naval College, Dartmouth, in the Summer of 2009.'

Harold spent 40 years with Otis:

'I started making the tea and ended as a Board Member. How hard would that be today?'

Looking back, he is acutely aware that the leg injury which prevented him going into Burma in 1944 may well have saved his life.

John 'Jack' Redding, 2nd King's Own

Jack Redding returned to the UK in March 1946, having spent four years and four months overseas. He arrived at a London station and caught the suburban train to Hither Green, a short walk from home. His wife, Em, had tied a large banner to the front of the house: 'Welcome home, Jack!'

The early post-war years were far from easy and a young family helped to stabilise things. Jack worked as a track welder with British Rail for nearly 40 years. He spent five months in Burma helping to blow up railways and devoted the rest of his working life to repairing them. He specialised in the busy railway junctions linking London Bridge, Waterloo and Charing Cross.

Nothing much was said about Burma, other than the occasional aside – usually a reference to the same handful of 'stories' within the family. Looking back, the author can recognise certain traits which seem to relate to his father's Chindit service. Sometimes during dinner Jack had the habit of mashing everything together. He took pleasure in hearing rain on a car or shed roof. The author now appreciates that his delight had nothing to do with the sound of the rain but, rather, the fact that there was a roof over his head. Jack was a family man and lived by a simple maxim: 'the children come first.'

Jack Redding died in 2005.

John Riggs, 16 Column, 1st Bedfordshire and Hertfordshire

In contrast to most, John Riggs became increasingly concerned as the repatriation of those with long service overseas accelerated:

'I worried about going home. I hadn't seen my parents for 10 years! I'd spent the past four-and-a-half years with the Battalion. I joined them at the age of 19 and they were my life. I nearly opted to stay, but felt I should go.

'Later, I found out about my parents' war. My father, a Master Mariner, ended up in a bamboo cage in Shanghai. He had been working for British Intelligence and had been betrayed. Fortunately, the Foreign Office managed to get him out, together with my mother and teenaged sister, on the diplomatic exchange after six months. He went to SOE Headquarters in London to write his report.'

Riggs Senior then joined the Royal Naval Reserve and continued to serve. His son arrived at Greenock on 6 January 1945, in Arctic conditions:

'There was three inches of ice on the ship's deck! Typically, we were ordered off at 3 am on a Sunday morning and herded onto a train. We found a Sunday newspaper and a Mars Bar on every seat, thanks to the WVS. There were caustic comments throughout the train when we read the front page story, announcing the arrival of the first leave party from Europe after six months away. We had been overseas for five years!'

John Riggs had a month's leave:

'As a former Chindit I was given double ration books. I left the Army in May 1946. At that time I suffered a few relapses of malaria. The return to a cold climate could cause malaria to flare up.'

Before the war John had worked briefly for a firm of accountants. He had been accepted to join the Far East staff of the Hong Kong & Shanghai Bank when war intervened. This long-delayed career move was now about to be realised. John also married:

'My wife was no stranger to the Far East. In fact, she had been fortunate to escape from Singapore when it fell to the Japanese. I had a medical for the overseas posting and the bank's doctor told me I couldn't work in the Far East as I had had malaria. I explained that everyone had had malaria, including all the Bank staff interned by the Japanese. The doctor could not be swayed. I left the bank and rejoined the accountants. I qualified as a chartered accountant and then got a job with a firm in the Far East.

'I worked in Hong Kong, Japan and Singapore from 1954 to 1970. At first I said I wouldn't go to Japan. It wasn't a matter of my feelings alone. My wife's father had been left in Singapore, but escaped to Sumatra in

a small boat and eventually reached Ceylon. He was near to retirement from the Army, but died shortly afterwards. Nevertheless, we were eventually persuaded to go to Japan. We set off as a family, with a very young daughter and plenty of apprehension. We arrived in Yokohama in 1958, two years after the occupation ended. We were surprised and had a pleasant stay in Japan. We got on very well with the Japanese. I had expected to find it difficult, but I didn't.

'Most of my Japanese staff were in their sixties or very young. The whole of the middle age range — the thirties and forties - were missing. My Japanese contemporaries had become war casualties. The local business community and media never mentioned WWII, except for the occasional comment about the "Pacific Conflict", as if it were none of their concern. It was strange to see the Mayor of Yokohama alongside the British Consul-General at the Commonwealth War Cemetery on Armistice Day.'

John Simon, 16 Brigade HQ Column

John Simon returned to Britain in November 1945, having been away for over three years. He had someone to come home to:

'I was demobbed in February 1946 and received a £60 gratuity. My wife and I were trying to set up home at that time. We put aside the money for use when we had our own accommodation. I went back to F.H. Low, on a wage of £5 a week. I told them I wanted to start immediately after my repatriation leave. I joined the accounts staff and stayed there until 1948, when an opportunity came up to move to the firm's offices in Argentina. My first son, John, was just 12 months old when we moved to Buenos Aires. My second son, Nicolas, was born in 1957.'

Bill Smyly, Animal Transport Officer with 5 Column (Operation *Longcloth*) and 22 Column, 2nd Queen's, and 3rd/9th Gurkhas (Operation *Thursday*)

Bill Smyly was with the 3rd/6th Gurkhas in Siam when the war ended. He had planned to study Chinese at London's School of Oriental and African Studies. In the event he was tempted to go to Cambridge but found it the wrong choice for Chinese:

'Cambridge was a place where, for many years, retired missionaries chose to settle and the study of Classical

Chinese became a rather exclusive, very academic pursuit, having almost nothing to do with China. I passed my first exam but was advised not to take the Tripos. I switched to a pass degree in English Literature and joined the Daily Mail. *I was accepted simultaneously by the* Daily Mail *and the Chinese Department at the School of Oriental and African Studies. The Foreign Editor of the* Mail *agreed to hold the job for a year while I studied Chinese. I had hopes of becoming a foreign correspondent, possibly with a posting east. Instead, I ended up on a gossip column called "Tanfield's Diary". After that I joined the* South China Morning Post, *taught at the Diocesan Boys' School, the Chinese University of Hong Kong and served with The British Council in Thailand, Saudi Arabia, China and Hong Kong. There was also a period in England, when I joined the Education Department in Bedford Prison.'*

When at the Diocesan Boys' School, Bill Smyly met Diana Chan of the Diocesan Girls' School:

'We have a daughter, Eleanor, now a tattooist with a better degree than mine! She has a 1st Class Honours in Applied Art, is a guest artist at a number of studios and travels England and the world.'

Percy Stopher, Medical Orderly, 23 Brigade

During Percy Stopher's voyage home, a thief stole his kit, including the presents he had bought in Bombay. They included silks for the young lady who was to become his wife:

'We left our ship at Liverpool and spent 26 hours on a train. We arrived at Colchester at 8 o'clock in the morning, having had nothing to eat or drink. We then received a huge meal – everything you could put on a plate. We were told to stay in barracks overnight but we went out and had a good booze-up. We then went on leave. I remember walking the 10 minutes from the station to the family home in Walthamstow. I had two bags. My kitbag alone weighed one hundredweight and a half. A young couple passed me – they were probably only 18 – and they offered to help carry my kit. They insisted. The boy then tried to pick up my kitbag and promptly fell arse over head!

'I didn't let my experiences affect me one bit. I kept it all in my head. People asked me questions. I just said I didn't want to talk about it. I told them: "It's happened and I just want to forget it." I didn't want to talk about it because I knew they wouldn't understand.'

On the day of his return he remembers standing at the door of the family home, thinking that the neighbouring off-licence was convenient for the celebration. Stopher then visited his young lady, living at Chingford:

'I knocked on the door and, as I walked in, our eyes met. It was wonderful. We had a kiss and a cuddle, then went out for a walk. I was married to Bet for 58 years.'

Percy's family were greengrocers:

'I soon returned to the business, which had been looked after by my father during my years away. It took a long time to get back on my feet.'

Percy Stopher died in 2010.

Ronald Swann, U Troop, 160th Jungle Field Regiment, RA

Ronald Swann's eyesight was a matter of continuing concern. He had lost one eye and the other was damaged. He flew from Ledo to Calcutta on 5 July 1944, and, later, to Secunderabad and Poona. He suffered a severe bout of malaria while in hospital in Poona. On reaching the UK in October 1944 he was admitted to Alder Hey Hospital, Liverpool. He came under the care of the eye specialist Maurice Barton, at the Leicester Royal Infirmary:

'He saw me every month for two years – even after I was discharged from the Army – and then every three months. I was not, however, in a sorry state! I've played cricket since the war and I've knocked up a century and one or two fifties.'

Ronald Swann was demobbed in April 1946. He had married Roma on 17 February 1945, and he and his wife were among the vast crowds outside Buckingham Palace when the Royal Family and Sir Winston Churchill came to the balcony on VE Day.

The early post-war years were challenging, especially the trauma of learning to drive again. Ronald became soaked with sweat in his anxiety and concentration, all too conscious of his war injuries. There were also occasional, distressing nightmares. The Chindits and Burma were subjects never discussed within the family. Ronald's battlefield instincts stayed with him. He had a tendency to jump at sudden noise and 'hit the deck' on numerous occasions as a result of low-flying jets. On one occasion he was fishing close to a granite quarry in the Leicester area, unaware that blasting sometimes took place. It did on that day and he 'took cover', with a shower of chippings falling around him.

Ronald Swann had not heard the last of Dr Scheie, the brilliant American eye surgeon who had treated him in the Far East. Decades after the war he heard that Scheie had become President of the American Burma Star Association:

'I wrote to them and received a most gracious reply from Dr Scheie, then an internationally famous ophthalmologist. It was Scheie who had introduced the then standard surgical procedure for glaucoma. When I mentioned Scheie to my present ophthalmologist, he said: "Good heavens! We still use that operation now." He then exclaimed: "The old man himself!" Scheie is now deceased. There is a major Ophthalmology Department dedicated to him at one of the major universities in America.'

A third shrapnel fragment still resided in Ronald Swann's left temple. It was a small, greyish-looking irregular object, which appeared to be just below the skin but, in fact, was significantly deeper. Swann said he was the only British officer who, when using a prismatic compass to his right eye, got a bearing degrees off line:

'I did consider getting the shrapnel removed but never got round to it.'

Ronald Swann died in 2011.

Dick Stuckey, 43 Column, 12th Nigeria Regiment

Dick Stuckey returned to Britain in early 1946, having decided on a career as a professional soldier:

'I toyed with the idea of life in the colonies, perhaps South Africa. I married in 1945, however, and the Army offered solid prospects. I returned to India and my first daughter soon arrived. It became clear that career advancement depended on attending Staff College at Camberley. I did so in 1952. A fellow pupil became Chief of the General Staff. I stayed in the Army until 1970.'

Lieutenant Colonel Stuckey commanded the 1st Battalion, The Staffordshire Regiment in the UK and in Kenya. This is now the 3rd Battalion, Mercian Regiment (Staffords):

'Life in the Army is based entirely on loyalty: to the Sovereign, to the Regiment and to each other. I left as a full Colonel. I had prospects of further promotion but

retired early, at 49, with plans to become a farmer. This did not go well and, after some years, I established a period property restoration business. This was enjoyable and successful, but would have proved more lucrative had we held on to some of those properties!'

Eric Sugden, 61 Column, 1st Bedfordshire and Hertfordshire

Eric Sugden and his wife, Beryl, had two daughters. He lost his wife in 2000. Eric now lives in the Surrey house bought by his father in the late 1940s:

'I didn't find it difficult to settle down. Later, I realised that those of us who were not commissioned often found it easier to make their way in Civvy Street. Perhaps this had something to do with lower expectations? Anyway, I worked hard and became professionally qualified.'

Andrew Sutherland, 60 Column, 60th Regiment, RA

Andrew Sutherland returned to the UK by a series of staging flights, mostly by Liberators converted to troop carriers. He lived in Sussex until 1967, when he and his wife, two sons and a daughter settled in Canada – firstly in Alberta and then Vancouver Island. He wrote a lively account of his wartime experiences, entitled 'The last few hundred feet'.

Bill Towill, 3rd/9th Gurkhas

Bill Towill knew how much he could have lost in Burma:

'On my last leave before going in I had asked Pamela to marry me and she had accepted. We went to Boseck, the jewellers, and I bought a string of pearls and an engagement ring. Her parents were happy but asserted that, at 17, she was too young to get engaged and, furthermore, I was going into action and might not return. However, if I did return, we could have an engagement party at her 18th birthday.

'I did get back safely and was greatly looking forward to the party but, alas, come the day I was sent out by the Colonel on some special duty. So I missed the party, which was attended by some of my comrades — one of whom put the ring on her finger. At the party they ate the part of the cake labelled "Bill" but the remainder was very carefully parcelled up and passed to my comrades,

to take back to me. Some days later I received a letter from Pamela asking whether I had enjoyed the cake. The dreadful truth then emerged. My friends had eaten all of it on the way back to the Battalion!'

Bill and Pamela have two daughters:

'Now we are both frail, I much more so than Pamela, who is six years my junior. I never thought much or spoke about the war years until I joined the local branch of the Burma Star Association about 10 years ago. I now look back with pride at having given some service to my country.'

Ted Treadwell, 71 Column, 2nd Leicesters

Ted Treadwell returned to Britain 1945 and was soon laid low with a fresh bout of malaria. His Colonel told him he could not go on leave, as he was too ill:

'My mates thought otherwise. They told the Colonel they could "cure" me. They wrapped me from head to foot in blankets and an overcoat, to sweat it out. I was fine the next day and away I went, on leave.'

Ted Treadwell married in 1937. When he parted with his family, he said goodbye to his wife, a three-year-old daughter and a son, Ted, just three days old. When he returned in February 1945 his daughter was eight and his son was five. He was demobbed in 1946 and became a bus conductor:

'It was the worst job I ever had and I'd had enough after 18 months. I went into road resurfacing. I was a foreman within three months and spent 44 years with my next firm. My son is still in the business. When I first came home my children didn't know me. When I got into bed one night, just after I got back, I heard my son say: "There's a man in bed with mum!" In the beginning I didn't feel right in myself. When I first came home I drank heavily. I never really talked about what happened, even to my family. I don't like speaking about it. This is the first time I have talked about it.'

Ted Treadwell died in 2011.

Tom Turvey, 71 Column, 2nd Leicesters

Tom Turvey also found that bouts of malaria developed into heavy colds and flu during the winter months:

'That apart, I settled back to Civvy Street, although there were occasions when I wondered whether I did the right thing leaving the Army.'

Tom married his first wife in 1940. On his return the couple divorced. He married his second wife, Wyn, in 1952. He lost her in the late 1990s. Today, he has strong views about the Chindits:

'Speaking personally, I'm too old to be proud as such, but being a Chindit was special. It was an achievement. We lost a lot of good men but we would never have taken Burma back without the Chindits. Without us, perhaps the Japanese would have got into India and history might have been different.'

Jim Unsworth, 46 Column, 2nd King's Own

Jim Unsworth arrived back in Britain in March 1946, having spent much of the voyage home in the ship's hospital, trying to overcome malaria. He was demobbed in June:

'It took me some time to rebuild my fitness. I returned to work as a gardener but the malaria kept recurring. I remember going to the chemists to get my malaria tablets. You could buy them over the counter at that time. Plenty of others had the same problem.'

Jim had married Lilian at the outbreak of war. Shortly after his arrival in India, the Quartermaster informed Jim that he was the father of twins, a boy and a girl:

'Later, we were to have another son. There were five grandchildren but one, tragically, was killed by a hit-and-run driver.'

Unsworth remained a gardener. His brother-in-law helped him secure a good job, working for a Yorkshireman with a three-acre garden and greenhouses:

'This included two kitchen gardens, filled with veg every year. This harvest was one of the perks of the job and I sold the produce to a greengrocer in Lytham St. Annes. I retired with a pension after 25 years. It all worked out well.'

As the years passed the malaria disappeared but other problems arose:

'I blame my arthritis on being wet all the time in Burma. My memory of Chindit service is sharp, especially our three-man attack on that Japanese dump. I can recall every detail. I dream about my time in Burma. These dreams are not unpleasant but they are very vivid. It is just like looking at a film.

'It took me quite some time to settle into married life. I had two good mates at work and they helped a lot. I had difficult memories about the way the Japanese treated Burmese villagers. I want nothing to do with the Japanese. On one occasion I met Burmese families running from a village taken by the Japanese. One said that a party of Japs had just cut off a young woman's breasts. They were evil. I spent six years in the Army and four were spent in India. I was proud to be a Chindit and I remain proud. My son is interested and I have passed my medals and photographs to him.'

Tony Wailes, 60 Column, 60th Field Regiment, RA

Tony Wailes returned to the UK in April 1946 and joined Turner & Newall the following year. During the early 1950s he took advantage of a post-graduate scheme and went to the United States to continue his studies at Syracuse University. He met his future wife at Syracuse. They married in 1954 and had two children. During 1955 the couple went out to what was then Southern Rhodesia, settling in Salisbury. They returned to the UK in 1965 but went back to Africa 15 years later and lived in Zambia until 1983. Tony finally retired from Turner & Newall in 1986. At that point he was Group Development Director:

'My experiences in Burma didn't change me as such, other than better preparing me for post-war life in Africa. As for the Japanese, it is not done to say anything derogatory. All I can add is that I have had nothing to do with them since 1944.'

There is a curious postscript to Tony Wailes' involvement with the Chindits. His sister, Sylvia, married Jack Brothers. In retirement, during the 1970s, they moved to Haywards Heath. At one point they were in need of a gardener and advertised in the local newspaper. The successful applicant was none other than Brigadier Michael Calvert, then living in sheltered accommodation in the area. Sylvia recalls:

'"The Brigadier", as he was known to us, knew very little about plants but was happy to do the rough work in the garden. I suspect he really did it for the company. He and Jack, who had been in the Navy, got on well together. We would sit in the kitchen for coffee. The Brigadier would then hold forth about his service in Burma. There were occasions when I wondered why I was paying him to lecture me on jungle warfare but, nevertheless, our relationship stood the test of time and he worked in the garden for around 10 years. He became a family friend.'

Tony Wailes knew Calvert as the renowned former Commander of 77 Brigade and Wingate's most successful exponent of Chindit fighting:

'I met him at Jack and Sylvia's and we were soon on a "Tony and Mike" basis. Calvert eventually persuaded me to join the Chindits Old Comrades' Association.'

Bill Williams, 80 Column, 1st South Staffords

Bill Williams returned to the UK in January 1945 after five years overseas:

'I had been engaged when I went abroad and I married within a fortnight of my return. We went on to have three sons. Today, I have five grandchildren and five great-grandchildren.'

Bill Williams was demobbed in 1946 and, under the employment law of the time, he could then return to his previous job:

'I invested in the company and went on to own it. We made doorlocks and window furniture and fittings. The owner was in his seventies by the war's end and had not sorted out a successor. He gave me the opportunity to buy shares and become a Director. Eventually, he became ill. With no children, he left a sizeable block of shares to me and I built the company up to the point where it employed several hundred workers.'

COLUMN COMPOSITION

COLUMN COMPOSITION varied from Brigade to Brigade and according to the wishes of individual Column Commanders. 84 Column Chindit Fred Gerrard drew up a 'typical' composition:

	Officers	Other Ranks
Headquarters		
Column Commander		
2 i/c		
Adjutant		
Admin. Off.		
Staff and interpreters	4	9
Signals		
3–22 wireless sets		9
RAF Section		
Special RAF wireless set	1	3
Medical Section	1	2
Padre	1	1
Reconnaissance Platoon		
3 British and 1 Burma Rifles Sections (variable)	2	42
Commando Platoon		
3 Sections Royal Engineers		
1 Pioneer Section (infantry)	2	45
Rifle Company		
Admin. Section		
4 x Platoons (each having four Sections of 10 men)		
4 x PIAT Sections		
4 x 2 in. mortar Sections		
4 x Lifebuoy flamethrower Sections	6	200
Support Platoon		
2 x 3 in. mortars		
2 x Vickers machine guns	1	15
Transport Platoon		
12 x riding ponies		
58 mules (2 large mules for RAF wireless)		
2 x bullocks (mobile food/baggage carriers)		
Muleteers, farrier and saddler	1	77

Source: F.E. Gerrard, *Wingate's Chindits*, unpublished MS, October 2000

AMERICAN K-RATIONS

FOOD DROPPED to Chindit columns consisted, in the main, of American K-rations. All ranks, from the Column Commander down, were issued with, and were responsible for, their own rations. Each had three packs daily for up to five days, depending on availability. K-ration packets were a little smaller than a video cassette. The inner cover was heavily waxed and would burn long enough to boil a mess tin of water or start a cooking fire with wet sticks. Former Chindit Fred Gerrard noted the contents of his meals.

Morning
Small tin, spam-type meat
2 pkts, 4 finger biscuits
4 cigarettes
1 pkt, book matches
Chewing gum
1 pkt, powdered coffee
1 pkt, 'Refresher' sweets
2 cubes, sugar

Midday
Small tin, processed cheese
2 pkts, 4 finger biscuits
4 cigarettes
1 pkt, book matches
Chewing gum
1 pkt, powdered lemonade
1 compressed fruit bar
2 cubes, sugar

Evening
Small tin, pork Loaf
2 pkts, 4 finger biscuits
4 cigarettes
1 pkt, book matches
Chewing gum
1 pkt, powdered coffee
1 chocolate bar
2 cubes, sugar

The prototype American K-ration was developed for paratroopers early in the Second World War by the Subsistence Research Laboratory. The final version offered 2,830 calories daily. The test of K-rations in jungle conditions consisted of a three-day march, averaging only 11 miles daily, across flat or gently rolling terrain in Panama (using cleared roads). The test Platoon was very lightly loaded. At the end of three days, they were weighed, no abnormal weight loss was noted and the K-ration was pronounced a success. The K-ration gave 800–1,200 calories less than required daily by men operating in the Burmese jungle.

Source: F.E. Gerrard, *Wingate's Chindits*, unpublished MS, October 2000

GLOSSARY AND ACRONYMS

Aberdeen	jungle Stronghold, 27 miles north-west of Indaw
ADC	aide-de-camp
Air strike	air attack on troop concentrations, positions and other targets
ALO	Air Liaison Officer
Amatol	an explosive – a mixture of TNT and ammonium nitrate
Atabrin	a malaria suppressant (precursor to Mepacrine)
ATO	Animal Transport Officer, responsible for the Column's mules and ponies
AWOL	Absent Without Leave
B.25	American 'Mitchell' twin-engined medium bomber
Bangalore Torpedo	an explosive device, in the form of a long metal pole (or length of bamboo) packed with explosive, to blow gaps in barbed wire defences
Banzai attack	mass attack with no concern for casualties
Basha	hut, typically constructed of bamboo
Battle Group	Fighting unit of a Chindit column, without soft skin elements
BEF	British Expeditionary Force
Benzedrine	an amphetamine
Betty	twin-engined Japanese medium bomber
Block	Heavily fortified jungle base, positioned astride road/rail communications and preventing the enemy moving supplies and reinforcements
BNA	Burma National Army – fighting alongside the Japanese (sometimes known as the 'Burma Traitor Army')
Bofors	40mm anti-aircraft gun
BORs	British Other Ranks
Bren	British light machine gun with a 28-round magazine
Bren carrier	Small tracked vehicle
Broadway	jungle stronghold, 35 miles east-north-east of Indaw
Bully	tinned corned beef
Bunds	embankments enclosing paddy fields
Burgoo	biscuit mixed as a porridge, often cooked with chopped pork or other K-ration foods
Burrifs	The Burma Rifles
C-47	Douglas C-47, twin-engined military transport aircraft, otherwise known as the Dakota
Cab rank	aircraft 'queuing' over an air strike target
CAI	Chinese Army in India; General Stilwell's command
Carbine	American-made light semi-automatic weapon, with a 15-round magazine
Cerebral malaria	affecting the brain and central nervous system, often leading to deep coma and death
Chagul	canvas portable water carrier
Chaung	river or stream
Chinthé	the fabulous lion guarding Burmese pagodas
Chowringhee	landing ground, 35 miles east of Indaw
Clip	a cartridge clip
C/O	Commanding Officer (2i/c: Second in Command)
Column	Chindit fighting unit of 400–450 men and 60 or more animals (mules, ponies, bullocks and, occasionally, elephants). Each Column consisted of an over-strength Rifle Company, Recce Platoon (including Burma Rifles), Commando Platoon (Royal Engineers), Support Platoon and special units (e.g. Animal Transport Officer and Muleteers, Royal Signals, RAF Officer, Medical Officer, etc)
Column Snake	jungle marching formation (single file)
Commando Platoon	four Sections (Engineers and Infantry/Pioneers) – a unit of Sappers skilled in the use of explosives
Controlled feeding	dietary management, commencing with a light liquid or semi-liquid diet, for men in a starved condition and unable to take solid food

CP	Command Post
Curtiss C-46 Commando	twin-engined American military transport aircraft, slightly faster and larger than the C-47
Dah	Burmese jungle knife, similar to a machete
Dakota	RAF name for the C-47 twin-engined transport aircraft
Dannert Wire	barbed wire, or razor wire, in coils which can be extended, concertina-like, along a defended perimeter. Typically, it was used in conjunction with plain barbed wire and steel pickets
DAS	Direct Air Support
DC3	Civil airliner, from which the C-47 military transport was developed
DCM	Distinguished Conduct Medal
Debray	silencing a mule by crushing the vocal chords
DFC	Distinguished Flying Cross
DFM	Distinguished Flying Medal
Discharger Cup	device for firing a grenade from a rifle
Dispersal	tactic adopted when ambushed (or to otherwise evade the enemy). It involved breaking into small parties, usually with the aim of re-forming at a pre-arranged rendezvous
Dispersal Group	small party proceeding independently, following dispersal of a Column or larger formation
DSO	Distinguished Service Order
Dual Tow	a single C-47 towing two WACO gliders (one on a short tow; one on a long tow)
Dubbin	a waterproofing mixture of tallow and oil
DZ	drop zone
ENSA	Entertainments National Service Association
FDS	Field Dressing Station
Floater	a force acting aggressively, beyond a Block or Stronghold perimeter, to contribute to its defence and kill as many Japanese as possible
Free drop	a free-fall drop of fodder or other supplies (without statichute)
Galahad	Codename for Merrill's Marauders
Ghee	Clarified butter
Guncotton	an explosive, based on cellulose nitrate
Havildar	Sergeant
H.E.	High Explosive
H.F.	High Frequency
Hudson	an American-built, twin-engined medium bomber/reconnaissance aircraft
JEWTS	Jungle Exercises Without Trees
K-rations	US emergency rations, provided in individual packaged meal form, produced by Kelloggs
Kukri	a knife with a curved blade – the weapon of the Gurkhas
L.1	Vultee L.1 Vigilant light aircraft
L.5	Stinson L.5A Sentinel light aircraft
Lee Enfield	.303 rifle, the standard British infantry weapon
Lifebuoy	flamethrower
Longcloth, Operation	Wingate's Brigade-strength expedition into North Burma in 1943
LRP	Long Range Penetration – a concept for penetrating and then fighting behind enemy lines, using specially trained, lightly equipped troops supplied by air
M&B	May & Baker Ltd (now Sanofi-Aventis), the producers of a range of products effective against cocci infections – the forerunners of antibiotics
MC	Military Cross
Mepacrine	Mepacrine dihydrochloride – a malaria suppressant, one of the first synthetic substitutes for quinine
Merrill's Marauders	a Chindit-trained American Brigade under General Stilwell's command
Mitchell	B.25 twin-engined medium bomber
MM	Military Medal
MMG	Medium Machine Gun, such as the British Vickers
MO	Medical Officer
Mosaic	aerial photographic overlay of a gridded area, facilitating air/ground cooperation
Mustang	P.51, single-engined fighter
NAAFI	Navy, Army and Air Force Institutes – the organisation providing the British Military's canteens and shops
Naik	Corporal
Napalm	petrol gelled with aluminium soaps
NCO	Non-Commissioned Officer
Nisei	American-born Japanese
Norseman	Noorduyn UC-64 utility aircraft

Nullah	stream
O/C	Officer Commanding
OCTU	Officer Cadet Training Unit
ORs	Other Ranks
OTU	Officer Training Unit (RAF: Operational Training Unit)
Paddy	paddy fields, for rice cultivation
Panic Map	silk map of North Burma, issued to all Chindits
Panji	sharpened bamboo stick, set upright in the ground and covered with leaves (the tip could be smeared with faeces, to promote infection). Panji sticks were widely used by the Viet-Cong in the Vietnam War
Pannier	container, carried by mules
PIAT	Projector, Infantry, Anti-Tank – a weapon firing a projectile with a shaped charge
Piccadilly	jungle clearing not used during Operation *Thursday*, due to its obstruction by logs
POW	Prisoner of War
QK	Wireless confirmation of pending air drop
QQ	Wireless request for air drop
RA	Royal Artillery
RAF Officer	Royal Air Force Air Liaison Officer, attached to a Chindit column
RAFVR	Royal Air Force Volunteer Reserve
RAMC	Royal Army Medical Corps
RASC	Royal Army Service Corps
RAP	Regimental Aid Post
RCAF	Royal Canadian Air Force
RE	Royal Engineers
Recce Platoon	Reconnaissance Platoon, including a Burrif officer and a Burrif Section, with the role of scouting ahead, looking for water, drop sites and the enemy
REME	Royal Electrical and Mechanical Engineers
Reserved Occupation	an occupation from which an individual will not be called up for war service
Rifle Company	three or four Rifle Platoons, each of four Rifle Sections (each having two NCOs and eight Privates); four PIAT Sections; four 2 in. mortar Sections; and four Lifebuoy flamethrower Sections
Sausage	personal kit and weapons, tied into two groundsheets, forming a 'sausage' for river crossings
Scheme	a training exercise, usually on a large-scale
SEAC	South East Asia Command
Slashers	men at the head of a Chindit Column, cutting a way through the undergrowth
Snatch	technique for retrieving gliders by C-47 aircraft equipped with a fuselage-mounted hook, based on the in-flight 'pick-up' of a tow cable suspended between two tall poles
Soft Skin	elements of a Column not usually involved in fighting (e.g medical personnel, animal transport personnel, Signallers)
Statichute	parachute opened automatically by a static line – used for both supply drops and paratroop drops
Sten	British sub-machine gun, notoriously prone to jamming and accidental discharge
Stop	a block on a track or road, to protect a bivouac, prevent interference with a river/road or railway crossing, or to restrict enemy movements of supplies and personnel
Stronghold	jungle fortress, heavily defended and strongly garrisoned, acting as a base for mobile Columns
Support Platoon	3 in. mortars and Vickers machine-guns
TA	Territorial Army
Thursday, Operation	Wingate's large-scale incursion into Japanese-occupied North Burma in 1944, involving five Brigades (four inserted by air, using jungle airstrips)
Time Pencil	a time fuse connected to a detonator or short length of safety fuse. The timer is started by crushing the copper section of the pencil-like tube, breaking a vial of cupric chloride, which then slowly eats through the wire holding back the striker. 'No. 10 Delay Switches' had delays ranging from 10 minutes (Black) to 24 hours (Blue)
Tommy Gun	Thompson sub-machine gun
Type 22	H.F. wireless equipment (the RAF Detachment wireless was the 1082/1083 set)
USAAF	United States Army Air Force
VC	Victoria Cross
Very Pistol	hand-held pistol used to fire flares
VJ Day	Victory over Japan – 15 August 1945
VHF	Very High Frequency
Vickers	British belt-fed medium machine gun
WACO	CG-4A glider
Webbing	equipment straps
Zero	radial-engined, single seat Japanese fighter with extreme manoeuvrability

AWARDS

Victoria Cross
Lt George Cairns, attached South Staffords (posthumous)
Maj Frank Gerald Blaker, MC, attached 9th Gurkha Rifles (posthumous)
Rfn Tul Bahadur Pun, 6th Gurkha Rifles
Capt Michael Allmand, attached 6th Gurkha Rifles (posthumous)

CBE
1944
Maj-Gen W.D.A. Lentaigne, DSO, 4th Gurkha Rifles
Brig L.E.C.M. Perowne, Comd Inf Bde

OBE
1944
Lt-Col R. Chalkley, GM, Royal Army Ordnance
Lt-Col J.S. Pope, Royal Artillery
Col H.T. Alexander, Cameronians
Lt-Col H.J. Lord (General List)

MBE
1943
Capt H.J. Lord, HQ/organisation of air supplies
Maj G.M. Anderson, King's (Liverpool)
Maj R.B.G. Bromhead, 4 Column Commander
Capt N. Whitehead, 8 Column, Comd Burma Rifles
1944
Lt-Col E.F. Kyte, Royal Engineers
Maj P. Hothersall, Royal Engineers
Maj J.W. Robinson, Royal Engineers
Capt M.M. Campbell, RAMC
Maj J.S. McCrae, M.B., RAMC
Maj J.J. Elbert, RAMC
Maj K.I. Barlow, RAVC
Capt R. McCrea, RAVC
Maj F.B. Ledlie, RIASC
Capt A.A. Tuck, King's (Liverpool)
Maj R.H.R. Stainton, King's (Liverpool)
Capt L Lazum Tang, Burma Rifles
Lt J.G. Crowne, Nigeria
Maj K. Richmond, Royal Artillery
Maj R.D. Cheetham, RASC
Capt (QM) R. Abbott, Border
Lt-Col A.H. Knight, Gloucestershire

DSO
1943
2nd Bar to DSO
Brig O.C. Wingate, DSO, Brigade Commander

DSO
Capt Aung Thin, Burma Rifles
Lt-Col L.G. Wheeler, Burma Rifles
Maj J.M. Calvert, 3 Column Commander
Maj B.E. Fergusson, 5 Column Commander
1944
Bar to DSO
Brig J.R. Morris, DSO, 9th Gurkha Rifles
Brig J.M. Calvert, DSO, fly-in to Broadway

DSO
Maj T.D. Ross, Black Watch
Lt-Col G.G. Green, Black Watch

Lt-Col C.J. Wilkinson, Leicesters
Lt-Col J.N. Daniels, Leicesters
Maj L.G. Lockett, MC, Leicesters
Capt J.E.D. Wilcox, South Staffords
Lt-Col R. Degg, South Staffords
Maj D.G.C. Whyte, RAMC
Lt-Col J. Masters, 4th Gurkha Rifles
Lt-Col H.A. Skone, 6th Gurkha Rifles
Lt-Col N.F.B. Shaw, 6th Gurkha Rifles
Brig J.R. Morris, 9th Gurkha Rifles
Brig D.C.C. Tulloch, MC, Royal Artillery
Lt-Col W.P. Scott, MC, King's (Liverpool)
W/Cdr R.G.K. Thompson, MC, RAF
Col F.D. Rome, Royal Fusiliers
Lt-Col T.J. Barrow, Beds and Herts
Lt-Col P.H. Graves-Morris, MC, York and Lancs
Lt-Col T.V. Close, Queen's
Lt-Col C.P. Vaughan, Nigeria

IOM
1943
Jem Manbahadur Gurung, 3/2 Gurkha Rifles
1944
Jem Lalbir Guring, 6th Gurkha Rifles
Jem Riki Rami Ale, 6th Gurkha Rifles
Sub Tika Bahadur Khattri, 9th Gurkha Rifles

IDSM
1943
Sub Kum Sing Gurung, 2nd Gurkha Rifles
Sub Tikajit Pun, 2nd Gurkha Rifles
Hav Dhurbu Singh Thapa, 2nd Gurkha Rifles
Hav Ran Sing Gurung, 2nd Gurkha Rifles
L/Nk Arkar Bahadur Gurung, 2nd Gurkha Rifles
L/Nk Milbahadur Thapa, 2nd Gurkha Rifles
L/Nk Sherbahadur Ale, 2nd Gurkha Rifles
Rfn Ramkrishna Limbu, 2nd Gurkha Rifles
1944
Hav Top Bahadur Rana, 6th Gurkha Rifles
Nk Patti Thapa, 6th Gurkha Rifles
Nk Chaman Sing Thapa, 6th Gurkha Rifles
Nk Moti Lal Thapa, 6th Gurkha Rifles
Hav Tilak Bahadur Khattri, 9th Gurkha Rifles
Hav Chakra Bahadur Mall, 9th Gurkha Rifles
Rfn Narbahadur Khattri, 9th Gurkha Rifles
Hav Chakra Bahadur Mall, 9th Gurkha Rifles

MC
1943
Capt D.C. Herring, Burma Rifles
Capt W.B.E. Petersen, Burma Rifles
Capt P.C. Buchanan, Burma Rifles
Capt. G.P. Carne, Burma Rifles
Lt J.C. Bruce, Burma Rifles
Capt J.C. Fraser, Burma Rifles
Capt W.D. Griffiths, Burma Rifles
Lt Saw Chit Kyin, Burma Rifles
RSM W. Livingstone, King's (Liverpool)
Maj K.D. Gilkes, King's (Liverpool)
Lt G.H. Borrow, King's (Liverpool)
Lt D.C. Menzies, King's (Liverpool)
Maj W.P. Scott, King's (Liverpool)
Capt J.S. Pickering, King's (Liverpool)
Lt R.S. Clarke, 2nd Gurkha Rifles
2nd Lt H.D. James, 2nd Gurkha Rifles
Lt J.G. Lockett, Seaforth Highlanders
1944
Bar to MC

Maj J.C. Bruce, MC, Burma Rifles
Maj E.M.D. Vanderspar, MC, Leicesters
Capt C.V.E. Gordon, MC, Royal Engineers

MC
Maj G.H. Astell, Burma Rifles
Lt W.D. Hardless, Burma Rifles
Sub La Raw, Burma Rifles
Sub Khawma, Burma Rifles
Sub Kara Nand Surma, Burma Rifles
Sub Agu Di, Burma Rifles
Jem Lian Nawn, Burma Rifles
Jem John Hla Shein, Burma Rifles
Jem Bu Gyan, Burma Rifles
Sub Saw Min Maung, Burma Rifles
Sub La Bang La, Burma Rifles
Lt G.B. Down, Burma Rifles
2nd Lt Saw Lader, Burma Rifles
Capt F.B. Newbould, Burma Rifles
Jem Godwiller, Burma Rifles
Capt D.M.E. McGillycuddy, 4th Gurkha Rifles
Maj D.S. McCutcheon, 4th Gurkha Rifles
Lt B.S. Burns, 6th Gurkha Rifles
Jem Digbahadur Gurung, 6th Gurkha Rifles
Jem Bhagtbir Gurung, 6th Gurkha Rifles
Jem Digbadur Gurung, 6th Gurkha Rifles
Capt G.W.F. Smith, 6th Gurkha Rifles
Maj J.M. Ritchie, 6th Gurkha Rifles
Lt C.K. Rooke, 6th Gurkha Rifles
Lt-Col P.G. Cane, 9th Gurkha Rifles
Capt M.E. Busk, 9th Gurkha Rifles
Sub Indra Bahadur Khattri, 9th Gurkha Rifles
Sub Karna Bahadur Khattri, 9th Gurkha Rifles
Jem Yembahadur Sahi, 9th Gurkha Rifles
Jem Kesh Bahadur Khattri, 9th Gurkha Rifles
Sub Yem Bahadur Khattri, 9th Gurkha Rifles
Lt J.W. Passmore, 9th Gurkha Rifles
Lt D.L.G. Scholey, South Staffords
Maj E.L. Butler, South Staffords
Capt A.S. Railton, South Staffords
Lt N. Durrant, South Staffords
Capt H.P.N. Benson, South Staffords
Maj F. Hilton, South Staffords
Lt F. Halliwell, South Staffords
Capt J.S. Ross, Beds and Herts
Lt J.C. Salazar, Beds and Herts
Capt L.J. Stevens, Beds and Herts
Lt A.D. Pond, Beds and Herts
Lt J. Devlin, Beds and Herts
Capt T.C. Thorne, RAMC
Capt J.S.I. Chesshire, RAMC
Capt R.A.B. Kinloch, RAMC
Capt O.P. Llewellyn, RAMC
Capt T.A. Taylor MB, RAMC
Maj D.M. Scott, Border
Lt E. Brain, Border
Lt H.C. Marshall, Border
Lt R.D. Stevenson, Border
Sqn Ldr R.J. Jennings, RAF
F/Lt J. Gillies, DFM, RAF
F/Lt G. Allan, RAF
F/Lt B.J.V. Young, RAF
Lt E.R. Macaulay, Nigeria
Maj G.M.K. Hall, Nigeria
Lt D.E. Arnold, Nigeria
Maj C.C.A. Carfrae, Nigeria
Lt-Col B.J. Brennan, Cameronians

Reverend (Captain) T. Hawthorn, Cameronians
Lt P.B. Chambers, Cameronians
Capt W.A. Anderson, Black Watch
Lt G.F. Anderson, Black Watch
Capt H.W. Swannell, Black Watch
Lt F.H. Luxa, York and Lancs
Capt W.A. Johnston, York and Lancs
Lt G.S. Pearce, York and Lancs
Capt A.B. Whitehead, King's (Liverpool)
Lt T.A. Riley, King's (Liverpool)
Lt A.B.B. Woodburn, King's (Liverpool)
Lt S.J. Smith, Leicesters
Maj E.C. Booth, Leicesters
Maj J.C. Harrington, Lancs Fusiliers
Capt W.G.O. Butler, Lancs Fusiliers
Maj E.F.O. Stuart, Lancs Fusiliers
Maj J.C. White, Reconnaissance
Lt J.H. Virgo, Reconnaissance
Maj A.S. Gurling, RIASC
Lt A.S. Binnie, DWR
Capt G.V. Faulkner, IMS/IAMC
Capt W.M. Park, Royal Signals
Lt J.C. Finlay, Queen's
Capt T.L. Wilson-Jerrim, Warwickshire
Lt J.G.A. Lucas, Oxford and Bucks
Maj W. Nimmo, Argyll & Sutherland
Maj P. Cox, Royal Artillery

DCM
1943
CSM R.S. Blain, King's (Liverpool)
CSM R.M. Cheevers, King's (Liverpool)
Cpl P. Dorans, Black Watch
Sgt F.E. Pester, Royal Engineers
1944
Sgt J. Perry, South Staffords
L/Cpl J. Young, South Staffords
Sgt W. Bolton, King's Own
Pte J. Levene, King's (Liverpool)
Sgt A. Hough, Beds and Herts
CSM W. Cargill, Black Watch
Sgt J. Donald, Cameronians
Sgt J.T. Chandler, Leicesters
Sgt Alhassan Geiri, Nigeria

MM
1943
CSM T. Thomson, King's (Liverpool)
Sgt J. Thornborrow, King's (Liverpool)
Cpl H.H. Day, King's (Liverpool)
Pte C.N. Guest, King's (Liverpool)
CSM J. Cairns, King's (Liverpool)
1944
Bar to MM
Tpr M.J. Flynn, MM, Reconnaissance
Sgt G. Smith, MM, Essex

MM
Hav Shib Jang Gurung, 4th Gurkha Rifles
Nk Tum Bahadur Gurung, 4th Gurkha Rifles
Rfn Purna Bahadur, 4th Gurkha Rifles
Hav Tilbir Gurung, 6th Gurkha Rifles
Rfn Bhairabahadur Thapa, 6th Gurkha Rifles
Hav Bal Bahadur Pun, 6th Gurkha Rifles
Hav Bhimlal Gurung, 6th Gurkha Rifles
L/Hav Pahalsing Thapa, 6th Gurkha Rifles
Nk Tikaram Thapa, 6th Gurkha Rifles
L/Nk Thamansing Thapa, 6th Gurkha Rifles
L/Nk Tula Ram Gurung, 6th Gurkha Rifles
Rfn Chhiring Lama, 6th Gurkha Rifles
Hav Kul Bahadur Gurung, 6th Gurkha Rifles
Nk Chandra Prasad Rana, 6th Gurkha Rifles
Rfn Bahadur Thapa, 6th Gurkha Rifles
L/Nk Tek Bahadur Khattri, 9th Gurkha Rifles
L/Nk Lal Bahadur Gharti, 9th Gurkha Rifles
Rfn Gupta Bahadur Khandka, 9th Gurkha Rifles
Hav Tirth Bahadur Thapa, 9th Gurkha Rifles
Nk Khalbahadur Khattri, 9th Gurkha Rifles
Rfn Dilli Bahadur, 9th Gurkha Rifles
Sgt C.C. Perkins, Nigeria
Sgt Abdullai Banana, Nigeria
Cpl Adamu Gafasa, Nigeria
Cpl Ibrahim Mansu, Nigeria
Cpl Audu Tuberi, Nigeria
Pte Mailafu Shangev, Nigeria
Pte Umoru Malanawa, Nigeria

CSM A. Kitt, Nigeria
Sgt Umoru Numan, Nigeria
Cpl Adamu Bauchi, Nigeria
Sgt H. Cropper, Lancs Fusiliers
Sgt W.H. Haynes, Lancs Fusiliers
Sgt K.E. Crute, Lancs Fusiliers
Sgt J.J. Gibson, Lancs Fusiliers
Sgt B. Lowton, Lancs Fusiliers
L/Cpl W. Wedgewood, Lancs Fusiliers
Sgt H. Bottomley, Lancs Fusiliers
Sgt W. Bartlam, South Staffords
Sgt W. Clift, South Staffords
L/Sgt J.C. Jenkins, South Staffords
Cpl G.A. Ferrand, South Staffords
Pte W. Muggleton, South Staffords
Pte A.B. Bristow, South Staffords
Pte S.J.C. Danks, South Staffords
L/Cpl V.J. Higgins, South Staffords
CSM S. Robson, King's Own
Sgt F.W. Pratt, King's Own
L/Sgt L. Mahon, King's Own
L/Cpl A. Halsall, King's Own
Pte D. Brown, King's Own
C/Sgt R. Fox, King's Own
Cpl W.J. Conkey, Border
L/Sgt L. Rogerson, Border
Pte J.M. Bailey, Border
Cpl S. Henshaw, Border
Pte W. Ironside, Border
Sgt R.A. Ross, Leicesters
Sgt H. Eden, Leicesters
Sgt H.R. Cowie, Leicesters
Cpl F. Fox, Leicesters
Sgt S.D. McFall, King's (Liverpool)
Sgt J.J. McQuillam, King's (Liverpool)
Sgt W.H. Boon, King's (Liverpool)
Cpl H.W. Smith, King's (Liverpool)
Sgt C. McCluskey, Black Watch
L/Cpl D. McLellan, Black Watch
Pte J. Welsh, Black Watch
Gnr W.S. Sawyer, Royal Artillery
Bdr L.J. Summers, Royal Artillery
Gnr L.E. Turner, Royal Artillery
Gnr T. Condon, Royal Artillery
Sgt H. Dodd, Royal Signals
Sig J.H. Charleston, Royal Signals
Sig A.E. Ward, Royal Signals
Sgt H. Steen, York and Lancs
Cpl S. Priestley, York and Lancs
L/Cpl T.Y. Brown, York and Lancs
Pte J. Munt, RAMC
Sgt R.L.M. Waters, RAMC
Cpl J.F. Evans, Beds and Herts
Pte R. Boyd, Beds and Herts
Sgt R.C. Newton, Reconnaissance
Tpr M.J. Flynn, Reconnaissance
Pte T.B. Bramble, Queens
Gnr G.W. Parchment, Cameronians
Pte S. Cottle, Essex
Sgt A.N. Fraser, RAF

BGM
1943
L/Nk Tun Lwin, Burma Rifles
Rfn Hpau Wai La, Burma Rifles
Jem Lian Nawn, Burma Rifles
1944
Nk Lazang Tu, Burma Rifles
Nk Kya Lin, Burma Rifles
Hav Hla Maung, Burma Rifles
Sub La Bang La, Burma Rifles
Hav Sauk Kunga, Burma Rifles
Rfn Lal Bahadur Gurung, Burma Rifles

BEM
1943
Sgt P.R. Chivers, Royal Engineers
Cpl R.W. Pike, King's (Liverpool)
Sgt R.A. Rothwell, King's (Liverpool)
1944
Pte R. French, Beds and Herts
Sig H.E. Froom, Beds and Herts
L/Sgt J.C. Grummit, Beds and Herts
Sgt T. Collins, Border
Pte D. Irving, Border
L/Sgt S. Oliver, Royal Engineers
Cpl C.A. Ralph, Royal Signals

Sgt J.R. Roberts, RAMC
Sgt G.D. Barley, King's Own
S/Sgt W.L. Mearns, RASC

Certificates of Gallantry
1944
Sgt T. Temple, Cameronians
Sgt W.W. Trott, Reconnaissance
Sgt J.A. Chaplin, King's (Liverpool)
Sgt P.O. O'Connor, Lancs Fusiliers
Sgt C.W.J. Hart, York and Lancs
Cpl G. Fletcher, King's Own
Cpl L. Shepherd, Cameronians
Cpl L.E. Muggleton, Leicesters
L/Sgt T. Pickering, King's Own
Cpl G. Evans, Royal Signals
Cpl A.M. Yuille, Royal Signals
L/Cpl F.C. Brown, Reconnaissance
L/Cpl R. Williams, King's Own
L/Cpl J.A. Holden, South Staffords
Cpl J. Worsley, Lancs Fusiliers
L/Cpl F.C. Brown, Reconnaissance
L/Cpl J.E. Kirke, Royal Signals
Pte R. Tucker, Border
Pte C.T.J. Dunford, Border
Cpl H.M. Jones, Royal Signals
Pte A. Tomlinson, DWR
Pte T. Jones, Leicesters
Pte A. Reid, King's Own
Pte A.H. Spark, York and Lancs
Pte D.W. Thompson, King's Own
Pte J. Cramp, King's Own
Gnr W.H.C. Wales, Royal Artillery
Spr R. Thebold, Royal Engineers
Spr W.J. Terry, Royal Engineers
Jem Chhabi Lal Thapa, 6th Gurkha Rifles
Hav U Byit Tu, Burma Rifles
Hav Bahadur Gurung, 4th Gurkha Rifles
Hav Dila Sing Gurung, 4th Gurkha Rifles
Nk Sher Bahadur Thapa, 6th Gurkha Rifles
Nk Moti Ram Thapa, 6th Gurkha Rifles
Nk Balbir Pun, 6th Gurkha Rifles
L/Nk Rabi Lal Thapa, 6th Gurkha Rifles
L/Nk Gyan Bahadur Karki, 9th Gurkha Rifles
L/Nk Aitbur Pana, 4th Gurkha Rifles
Rfn Damar Bahadur Gurung, 4th Gurkha Rifles
Rfn Jagat Bahadur Khattri, 9th Gurkha Rifles
Rfn Jit Bahadur Thapa, 4th Gurkha Rifles
Sgt Shaibu Godabawa, Nigeria
Sgt Garaba Gombe, Nigeria
Cpl Buba Biu, Nigeria
Cpl Jemo Maidoba, Nigeria
Pte Yando Audu, Nigeria
Pte Baba Bruce, WAAMC

AMERICAN AWARDS
1944
Silver Star
Brig J.M. Calvert, DSO, Royal Engineers
Lt J.E.D. Wilcox, South Staffords
Jem Riki Ramjale, 6th Gurkha Rifles
L/Nk Balbir, 6th Gurkha Rifles

Soldiers' Medal
Maj K.I. Barlow, RAVC

Awards to Allied Personnel
1944
DSO
Brig-Gen W.D. Old, Troop Carrier Comd
Col P.J. Cochran, 1st Air Commando

OBE
Col Li Hung, Chinese Army

MC
Maj Pang Hak Lup, Chinese Army
Capt Su, Chinese Army

MM
S/Sgt R.S. Eudy, 1st Air Commando

(The author would welcome any advice concerning amendments/additions to this list).

BIBLIOGRAPHY

Allen, L. *Burma, the Longest War, 1941–45* (J.M. Dent & Sons Ltd, 1986)

Baty, J.A. *Surgeon in the Jungle War* (William Kimber, 1979)

Bidwell, S. *The Chindit War: The Campaign in Burma, 1944* (Book Club Associates/Hodder and Stoughton Limited, 1979)

Carfrae, C. *Chindit Column* (William Kimber, 1985)

Calvert, M. *Prisoners of Hope* (Corgi, 1973)

Calvert, M. *Fighting Mad* (Airlife Publishing Ltd, 1996)

Calvert, M. *Chindits, Long Range Penetration* (Pan/Ballantine, 1974)

Chinnery, P.D. *March or Die* (Airlife Publishing Ltd, 2002)

Cross, J.P. *Jungle Warfare* (Guild Publishing, 1989)

Edwards, E. *Kohima: The Furthest Battle* (The History Press, 2009)

Fergusson, B. *Beyond the Chindwin,* (Fontana, 1971)

Fergusson, B. *The Wild Green Earth* (Collins, 1946)

Fowler, W. *We Gave Our Today, Burma 1941–1945* (Weidenfield & Nicolson, 2009)

Hay, A.I. *There was a Man of Genius: Letters to my Grandson, Orde Jonathan Wingate* (The Garden City Press Limited, 1963)

Hill, J. *Slim's Burma Boys* (Spellmount Limited, 2007)

Jeffrey, W.F. *Sunbeams like Swords* (Hodder and Stoughton, 1950)

Larson, G.A. *Aerial Assault into Burma* (Xlibris Corporation, 2008)

MacHorton, I. *Safer than a Known Way* (Odhams, 1958)

Masters, J. *The Road Past Mandalay* (Michael Joseph Ltd, 1961)

Nesbit, R.C. *The Battle for Burma* (Pen & Sword Books Ltd, 2009)

O'Brien, T. *Out of the Blue* (Arrow Books Limited, 1988)

Rhodes James, R. *Chindit* (Sphere Books Ltd, 1981)

Rooney, D. *Wingate and the Chindits: Redressing the Balance* (Cassell Military Paperbacks, 2000)

Rooney, D. *Mad Mike* (Leo Cooper, 1997)

Sharpe, P. *To Be a Chindit* (The Book Guild Ltd, 1995)

Slim, Field Marshal Viscount, *Defeat into Victory* (Pan Books, 1999)

Stibbe, P. *Return via Rangoon* (Pen & Sword, 1995)

Thompson, Sir Robert *Make for the Hills* (Leo Cooper Ltd, 1989)

Towill, B. *A Chindit's Chronicle* (published privately, 2000)

Wilcox, W.A. *Chindit Column 76* (Longmans, Green & Co., Ltd, 1945)

INDEX